THE
WRITER'S
CRAFT

THE
WRITER'S
CRAFT

Edited by John Hersey

Alfred A. Knopf   New York

First Edition

987654321

Library of Congress Cataloging in Publication Data

Hersey, John Richard, 1914-   comp.
  The writer's craft.

  Bibliography: p.
  1. Authorship. I. Title.
PN151.H45 1974   808'.02   73-12283
ISBN 0-394-48762-1
ISBN 0-394-31799-8 (textbook)

Book design by Juli Hopfl
Cover design by Lawrence Daniel & Friends

ACKNOWLEDGMENTS

W. H. Auden, "Writing" from *The Dyer's Hand* by W. H. Auden. Copyright © 1962 by W. H. Auden. Reprinted by permission of Random House, Inc. First two lines of "The Choice" from *Collected Poems* by William Butler Yeats. Copyright 1933 by Macmillan Publishing Co., Inc.; renewed 1961 by Bertha Georgie Yeats. Reprinted by permission of Macmillan Publishing Co., Inc., W. B. Yeats, and Macmillan Company of Canada.

Saul Bellow, Interview with Saul Bellow by Gordon Lloyd Harper from *WRITERS AT WORK: The Paris Review Interviews*, Third Series. Copyright © 1967 by The Paris Review Inc. All rights reserved. Reprinted by permission of The Viking Press, Inc.

Elizabeth Bowen, "Notes on Writing a Novel" from *Collected Impressions* by Elizabeth Bowen. Published 1950 by Alfred A. Knopf, Inc. Reprinted by permission of the publisher and Curtis Brown Ltd.

William Burroughs, Interview with William Burroughs by Conrad Knickerbocker from *WRITERS AT WORK: The Paris Review Interviews*, Third Series. Copyright © 1967 by The Paris Review Inc. All rights reserved. Reprinted by permission of The Viking Press, Inc.

Joseph Conrad, *Preface to The Nigger of the "Narcissus"* by Joseph Conrad. Reprinted by permission of J. M. Dent & Sons, Ltd., and the Trustees of the Joseph Conrad Estate.

E. E. Cummings, from *I: Six Non-Lectures* by E. E. Cummings. Copyright 1953 by E. E. Cummings. Reprinted by permission of Harvard University Press. Poems by E. E. Cummings are reprinted by permission of Harcourt Brace Jovanovich, Inc. and are from his volume *Complete Poems 1913–1962*, copyright, 1923, 1925, 1931, 1935, 1951, 1953, 1959 by E. E. Cummings; copyright 1963, by Marion Morehouse Cummings.

Ralph Ellison, "A Completion of Personality": A Talk with Ralph Ellison from *Twentieth Century Views of Ralph Ellison*, edited by John Hersey. © 1973. Reprinted by permission of Prentice-Hall, Inc.

William Faulkner, from *Faulkner at West Point*, edited by Joseph L. Fant III and Robert Ashley. Copyright © 1964 by Random House, Inc. Reprinted by permission of the publisher.

Gustave Flaubert, "Letters to Louise Colet" from *The Selected Letters of Gustave Flaubert*, translated and edited by Francis Steegmuller. Copyright 1953 by Francis Steegmuller. Reprinted by permission of Farrar, Straus & Giroux, Inc.

E. M. Forster, from *Aspects of the Novel* by E. M. Forster. Copyright 1927 by Harcourt Brace Jovanovich, Inc.; Copyright 1955 by E. M. Forster. Reprinted by permission of Harcourt Brace Jovanovich, Inc. and Edward Arnold, Ltd.

JOHN FOWLES, "Notes on an Unfinished Novel" from *Harper's Magazine* (July 1968). © 1968 by J. R. Fowles Limited. Reprinted by permission.

MAXIM GORKY, "Reminiscences of Leo Nikolaevich Tolstoy" from *Reminiscences of Tolstoy, Chekhov and Andreev* by Maxim Gorky, translated by Mansfield, Koteliansky and Woolf. Reprinted by permission of the Hogarth Press.

GÜNTER GRASS, "On Writers as Court Jesters" from *Speak Out! Speeches, Open Letters, Commentaries* by Günter Grass, translated by Ralph Manheim. © 1968 by Hermann Luchterhand Verlag GmbH.; © 1969 by Harcourt Brace Jovanovich, Inc. Reprinted by permission of Harcourt Brace Jovanovich, Inc.

A. E. HOUSMAN, from *The Name and Nature of Poetry* by A. E. Housman. Reprinted by permission of Cambridge University Press.

HENRY JAMES, from *The Art of Fiction and Other Essays* by Henry James. Reprinted by permission of Alexander R. James, Literary Executor to the Estate of Henry James.

RUDYARD KIPLING, excerpts from "Working-Tools" from *Something of Myself for My Friends Known and Unknown* by Rudyard Kipling. Copyright 1937 by Rudyard Kipling. Reprinted by permission of Doubleday and Company, Inc., Mrs. George Bambridge, and Macmillan Company of Canada.

PERCY LUBBOCK, from *The Craft of Fiction* by Percy Lubbock. All rights reserved. Reprinted by permission of the Executors of the Estate of Percy Lubbock, Jonathan Cape, Ltd., and The Viking Press, Inc.

NORMAN MAILER, "Fourth Advertisement for Myself: The Last Draft of *The Deer Park*" from *Advertisements for Myself* by Norman Mailer. Copyright © 1959 by Norman Mailer. Reprinted by permission of G. P. Putnam's Sons.

THOMAS MANN, from *The Story of a Novel: The Genesis of Doctor Faustus* by Thomas Mann, translated by Richard and Clara Winston. Copyright © 1961 by Alfred A. Knopf, Inc. Reprinted by permission of the publisher.

FLANNERY O'CONNOR, "The Nature and Aim of Fiction" from *Mystery and Manners* by Flannery O'Connor, selected and edited by Sally and Robert Fitzgerald. Copyright © 1957, 1961, 1963, 1964, 1966, 1967, 1969 by the Estate of Mary Flannery O'Connor; copyright © 1962 by Flannery O'Connor; copyright © 1961 by Farrar, Straus and Cudahy. Reprinted by permission of Farrar, Straus & Giroux, Inc.

GEORGE ORWELL, "Politics and the English Language" from *Shooting an Elephant and Other Essays* by George Orwell. Reprinted by permission of Harcourt Brace Jovanovich, Inc., Mrs. Sonia Brownell Orwell, and Secker & Warburg.

BORIS PASTERNAK, from *Safe Conduct* by Boris Pasternak. Reprinted by permission of Elek Books, Ltd.

ALAIN ROBBE-GRILLET, "On Several Obsolete Notions," from *For a New Novel: Essays on Fiction* by Alain Robbe-Grillet. Copyright © 1965 by Grove Press, Inc. Reprinted by permission of Grove Press, Inc.

JEAN-PAUL SARTRE, from *The Words* by Jean-Paul Sartre, translated from the French by Bernard Frechtman. English translation copyright © 1964 by George Braziller, Inc. Reprinted by permission of George Braziller, Inc.

ALEXANDER SOLZHENITSYN, *The Nobel Lecture* by Alexander Solzhenitsyn, translated from the Russian by F. D. Reeve. Copyright © 1972 by the Nobel Foundation. Reprinted by permission of Farrar, Straus & Giroux, Inc.

GERTRUDE STEIN, from *Lectures in America* by Gertrude Stein. Copyright 1935, renewed 1963 by Alice B. Toklas. Reprinted by permission of Random House, Inc.

LEO TOLSTOY, from *What Is Art? 1898* and *Essays on Art 1861–1905* by Leo Tolstoy, translated by Louise and Aylmer Maude. Reprinted by permission of Oxford University Press.

THOMAS WOLFE, from *The Story of a Novel* by Thomas Wolfe. Copyright 1935 by The Saturday Review Company, Inc. Reprinted by permission of Charles Scribner's Sons. The selections in this book are those used by Norman Cousins, then editor of *The Saturday Review*, in *Writing for Love or Money* (New York: Books for Libraries, 1949), but they have been re-edited to conform to the original, and omissions have been indicated by ellipses.

VIRGINIA WOOLF, from *A Writer's Diary* by Virginia Woolf. Copyright 1953, 1954 by Leonard Woolf. Reprinted by permission of Harcourt Brace Jovanovich, Inc., the Author's Literary Estate, and The Hogarth Press.

From the definition of the word "Craft" from *The Shorter Oxford English Dictionary*, 3rd edition. Reprinted by permission of The Clarendon Press, Oxford.

CONTENTS

INTRODUCTION   3

PART ONE
The Aim of Art   13

Joseph Conrad
Preface to THE NIGGER OF THE "NARCISSUS"   14

Henry James
From THE ART OF FICTION   18

Leo Tolstoy
From WHAT IS ART?   25

William Faulkner
From FAULKNER AT WEST POINT
Edited by Joseph L. Fant III and Robert Ashley   31

Flannery O'Connor
THE NATURE AND AIM OF FICTION   46

PART TWO
The Whole Intricate Question of Method   57

Percy Lubbock
From THE CRAFT OF FICTION   58

E. M. Forster
From ASPECTS OF THE NOVEL   65

Elizabeth Bowen
NOTES ON WRITING A NOVEL   81

Alain Robbe-Grillet
ON SEVERAL OBSOLETE NOTIONS   93

PART THREE
Words Have to Do Everything   107

Gertrude Stein
From POETRY AND GRAMMAR   108

George Orwell
POLITICS AND THE ENGLISH LANGUAGE   123

PART FOUR
Writing and Survival   135

Günter Grass
ON WRITERS AS COURT JESTERS   136

Alexander Solzhenitsyn
NOBEL LECTURE   141

PART FIVE
The Writing Process   155

Samuel Taylor Coleridge
PREFATORY NOTE TO "KUBLA KHAN"   156

Edgar Allan Poe
THE PHILOSOPHY OF COMPOSITION   158

A. E. Housman
From THE NAME AND NATURE OF POETRY   168

Rudyard Kipling
From WORKING-TOOLS   175

PART SIX
The Writer's Life   179

Maxim Gorky
REMINISCENCES OF LEO NIKOLAEVICH TOLSTOY   180

Jean-Paul Sartre
From THE WORDS   189

E. E. Cummings
From I: SIX NON-LECTURES   206

Boris Pasternak
From SAFE CONDUCT   227

Anthony Trollope
From AN AUTOBIOGRAPHY   239

W. H. Auden
From THE DYER'S HAND   255

Ralph Ellison
"A COMPLETION OF PERSONALITY"
Interviewer: John Hersey   267

Saul Bellow
A PARIS REVIEW INTERVIEW
Interviewer: Gordon Lloyd Harper   283

William Burroughs
A PARIS REVIEW INTERVIEW
Interviewer: Conrad Knickerbocker   299

PART SEVEN
The Writing Itself   **321**

Gustave Flaubert
LETTERS TO LOUISE COLET   322

Norman Mailer
The Last Draft of THE DEER PARK   343

Thomas Mann
From THE STORY OF A NOVEL   362

Virginia Woolf
From A WRITER'S DIARY   374

Thomas Wolfe
From THE STORY OF A NOVEL   400

John Fowles
NOTES ON AN UNFINISHED NOVEL   411

SELECTED BIBLIOGRAPHY   423

THE
WRITER'S
CRAFT

INTRODUCTION

———

What a copious word the "craft" of our title is!

Deep in the center of the oldest meaning of this word is a sense of vigor; its cousin is the contemporary German and Scandinavian word, *Kraft*, for strength. Pasternak's phrase for the secret of art is "a ray of energy." The final test of a work of art is not whether it has beauty, but whether it has power. This power seeks no throne or ideology; it strongly speaks, as Faulkner says, to "the human heart in the struggle of its dilemma." It is to be found equally in Tolstoy, the yang, and Dostoevski, the yin. It has the resonance of what E. M. Forster calls "prophecy." It is not easy to say just what it is, but we surely feel it when it is there.

For our purposes the central meaning of the word is that of a trade requiring certain skills. What makes the writer's craft tantalizing is that in order for a writer to achieve in his work the level of art (a word which in its early development was itself almost interchangeable with "craft"), he must manifest something more than skillful workmanship. A good part of this mysterious something is contained in the meanings, both obsolete and modern, of "craft." Here are some of them:

There is embedded in the word a sense of gifts that can be put to work—the specific talent for the specific trade.

One of the original meanings of "craft" was power of an intellectual sort; another was the learning of the schools—and here one is reminded of Henry James' assertion: "The deepest quality of a work of art will always be the quality of the mind of the producer. . . . No good novel will ever proceed from a superficial mind."

Among the archaic meanings that may still be called up by the word "craft" are ability in planning and ingenuity in constructing—the underpinnings of form.

Now obsolete is the meaning of magic, of occult art; it is surprising how many writers speak of, and count on, something like magic to induce the altered state of consciousness that imaginative writing of a high order requires.

There is also the meaning of vocation, of calling—a life to which one must wholeheartedly give himself over.

There is the meaning of the company of practitioners, the guild; a serious writer must firmly place himself in this company, must decide exactly where he wants to stand in relation to the literary tradition he has inherited.

"Craft" is also thought to have a kinship with "crave"; the quality of yearning, of demanding, is strong in strong writers—yearning for a better world (Tolstoy), for money (not only in a Trollope, but in a pure artist like James, too), for sex (Balzac and Gide, Mailer and Updike), for power (especially in a sense most eloquently developed by Solzhenitsyn).

And finally—most important for the search this book will entail—the word speaks, with fascinating contradictions, to qualities of temperament. "Craft" 's original meaning of strength, as it is still preserved in other languages, has connotations of virtue and of daring, but as the English word has evolved it now seems that some of the elements of strength, of craft, may be less honorable. The chief modern meaning of "craft" is art or skill of a bad kind, that which overreaches, which is tricky, guileful, cunning, deceitful. (One of the dark wonders of the English language is the large number of words that have moved over the centuries from affirmative to negative meanings; it is a long trip within a single word from virtue to fraud.) "Every original genius," W. H. Auden writes, "be he an artist or a scientist, has something a bit shady about him, like a gambler or a medium." In trying to tell the truth, the literary artist must dare to lie, to make things up. "Everything one invents is true," writes Flaubert, having come in astonishment upon a real-life picnic which he had described in every detail in something he had written long before. If it were not for our great writers' courage and cunning in invention, there could never be such a strength-giving end result as poetic truth, that whole truth which is so much larger than the sum of the "facts" before our very eyes.*

This book is an attempt to put together all these aspects of the writer's craft. It makes its appeal through the insights of the members of the guild. It is a collection of writings by writers on writing.

I assume that it is not possible in formal classes to "teach" or to "learn" to write imaginative literature, not anyway beyond a primitive level of competence, but I believe that if a student has the needed gifts it may be possible to help him, or for him to help himself, to set them free. One desirable step in this freeing process may be for the young writer to come to understand, both through his own tentative experience of the craft and by learning about the experience of others in it, what it means to live by

---

*We have by no means exhausted this capable word, "craft." It has, of course, a sense I particularly love, that of a vessel for water or air carriage—the single word standing for the original phrase, "vessels of small craft": boats, lighters, coastwise trading bottoms, vessels of small seaman's art, or perhaps of small power; the Coast Guard still flies "small craft warnings" on windy days. "Craft" also has these senses: a magical spell; a device or artifice, a crafty act; a branch of learning; a science; skills of the hunt, or of certain sports. There is one other strange transition besides from good to bad: "the gentle craft," originally shoemaking, is now angling. And an especially beautiful sense, to my mind, is that of the gear used for fishing, especially for whaling.

and for writing. Thus writing may move for him beyond the naive stage of self-expression and be seen and felt, or at least tasted, as the central activity of a way of life. The student can begin to sense what attitudes writers take toward their work, how they go about it, what they think they are doing when they write, the obscure sources of the materials of their art, their methods of shaping and revising, their crises of confidence, their artistic goals and beliefs, their rituals, their pains and disappointments, their rewards; and he may be able to integrate these discoveries into his own ways of making and being.

If he can manage this, then there is nothing more for him to do but to write and to read, to read and to write. Only the masters, finally, can teach him; only he himself, by doing, by trial and error, can learn, can find his own unique voice in words. In the meantime he will have found out how to read in two ways at once—for pleasure in the work itself, and also constantly watching the author's hand, trying to see how the master's effects, large and small, have been crafted. He will gradually discover that there are two simultaneous acts in the writing, too—but we will come to that.

It is time to say that this book has a kind of plot, or at least that in the arrangement of its selections it attempts to follow an unfolding inner logic of the craft.

In the beginning there is the urge to create. Every person feels he has a book inside him; few are called to be writers. The psychological components of the call, when it comes, are complex, manifold. They range from the simple primitive wish to tell a child a tale to make him wily and wise, or to share with the clan what the eyes have seen and the ears have heard; through something deeply sexual and instinctual, analogous in eerie ways to a woman's drive to give birth; through wanting to be seen and recognized by more than a mirror; through a desire (usually misplaced) for money; all the way to a will to triumph over the one unbeatable enemy:

> So long as men can breathe, or eyes can see,
> So long lives this . . .

Whatever the mix of these motives, the called writer, if he be serious, very early knows he can satisfy them in only one way—by writing, or at least trying to write, something that has a special quality, to which we give the name of art. This, then, is our starting point: what some great writers have meant by the art for which they have striven.

We deal here—and mostly throughout the anthology—with the storyteller's craft, the craft of fiction. This choice is grounded on a supposition that the most basic and constant motive in the writer's call is the urge to hand along to another person a story, a vision, a mood, or, as Tolstoy insists, a set of powerful feelings. This is the basic work of fiction, though it could be argued that it is equally the work of drama, history, biography, serious journalism, and—though the discourse is of a different order—poetry; it is the task of all writing that "aspires, however humbly, to the condition of art."

I suppose I have to confront the absurd notion that fiction is dead, or at least dying. People have been doing this sort of handing-on for a very long time—Forster writes, his little twisted smile showing, "Neanderthal man listened to stories, if we may judge by the shape of his skull"—and they will go on doing it for a long time, too. Fiction that tells no story was never alive, and for various reasons we've been having a lot of that kind lately. One of the reasons has been good: original minds have been struggling to find new forms. But some of the reasons have been less good—laziness, tin ears, boozy or dopey narcissism, and too much publishing. We have also had to bear with the ill effects (mainly in the form of overkill) of the fight to break down the codes of prudery, a fight in which love of the buck has unfortunately been involved, even in the back of the minds of some of our most gifted writers. Fiction has undeniably been under a strain because reality itself has had a terrible fictive quality in recent years, and the creative temperament has been so often alienated. But it is precisely here, surely, that the larger tasks of fiction lie; Solzhenitsyn gives us a glimpse of them in his Nobel lecture.

As to the even more absurd suggestion that printed communication as a whole is dead or dying, I will not be the first to remind that Marshall McLuhan, the pop-culture hero of those who hold this view, has made his case to the world by printing it. But there is a stronger argument as to why the predictions of his followers are not likely to be borne out. Most of the processes of electronic communication ask of the human mind only that it be a passive receptor, or at best a channel. Lineal communication—writing and reading, even story-telling around the fire—entails a joint venture in creativity. The writer encodes his vision in printed symbols or spoken words; what is written or pronounced does not come to life until the reader or hearer actively puts *his* vision to work and in the light of *his* experience and imagination remakes the images that have been offered him. The art of the word—and there will be one as long as the human species has a tongue—can never be merely received. This art is made, and made again, and made again by every mind that takes it in.

Next we come to technique—the sum of the means by which art, or let us say formal quality in writing, may possibly be achieved. This is the usual subject of courses in creative writing. I believe this to be a wrong emphasis. It goes without saying that technique—the culture's given forms and conventions, the tried ways of beguiling—must at some point and in some way be learned by the called writer. He should know something about point of view, distancing, plotting, and so on. The first assumption about anyone who wants to make art by using words is that that person will love what he plans to use. The writer must love words—their shapes, their sounds, their shimmering meanings. Alas for some of us, the writer must eventually care about how words are spelled; misspell a word and you maim it, unless your name is Ring Lardner. The writer has to care about fine distinctions; it must be important to him that no matter where Sartre, to say nothing of irresponsible lexicographers, may have led us, "nauseous" and "nauseated" mean different things. If we lose distinctions, we lose not only art, we lose everything; we are led down the path along which non-linear communications inevitably take us—to minds crackling with colors and lights and vibrations while throats sound nothing but the one grunt that is left to us of vocabulary.

But conscious technique is not at the very heart of the craft. If the testimony assembled in this book has any focal meaning, this must be it. Say the word "craftsman," and you may think primarily of a workman who has put his mind first and last to mastering technical skills. But say such names as Melville, Dreiser, and Faulkner; Sterne, Blake, and Joyce; Stendhal, Balzac, and Camus; Gogol, Dostoevski, and Pasternak, and you draw on another, older, more massive meaning of the word "craft."

Our foremost concern in this anthology is not with what happens during the act of writing—our theme is a larger one, of the craft as a whole—and I have included only four pieces about the writing process, three by poets and one by a minor prose writer, which merely suggest the diversity and richness of the guesswork about creativity. But in trying to find the center of gravity, as it were, of the writing craft, perhaps we do need to consider some aspects of the actual moments of composition.

The testimony of most writers about the process of creation is vague. There seems to have been some staring going on; we gather there were strong feelings involved, ranging from ecstasy to despair; God knows there was a lot of work. When a writer becomes positive about what has happened, we grow suspicious; we can't help cocking an eyebrow at such a cool account of the writing of a poem as Poe's in "The Philosophy of Composition." That kind of analysis is cortical; whereas a large part of creation seems to come from the dark womb of the mind.

This is not to say that the intellect is uninvolved in the process of composition, or that James was wrong in insisting that it be of a high order. It is rather to say that there seem to be two collaborating, or perhaps contending, forces of the mind involved, only one of which calls on the organizing part of the intellect. There seems to have been a dim struggle, in the act of writing, between elements of the unconscious (or subconscious, or preconscious) mind, on the one hand, and the conscious mind, on the other—between what might be called a supplier and a censor.

Writers have long had names for the supplier—the Muse, inspiration, Coleridge's dream, Kipling's Daemon, Bellow's "inner prompter or commentator," to mention a few that crop up in this book. The supplier offers up both images and affects in rich and chaotic bounty. The richness and the chaos, indeed, are keys to the merits and faults that the supplier brings to the writing process. On the plus side, the supplier has access to an area of primary feelings, to a deep reservoir where memory and emotion lie close to one another, where old things are kept—Faulkner speaks of a "lumber room" in the subconscious. Though habitually imprisoned, the supplier is exuberant, canny, perhaps partly instinctual. He is radical, and he acts on his own, in ways the censor of the conscious mind neither understands nor can control. And so, on the minus side, he brings to the writing transaction a potential for excess, the euphoria of "automatic" writing, sounds of frenzy, of feeling gone haywire, of mawkish romanticism, and even of what the world calls madness.

The censor, nearer the surface of the mind, is therefore needed to select, filter, and give form; it may be that in "The Philosophy of Composition" Poe was writing only about the censor's part in the writing of "The Raven." He is the arbiter of taste, the enemy of chaos; but he is also an interrupter, an inhibitor—he is Coleridge's man from Porlock who deprived us of the rest of "Kubla Khan." He may be brilliant, he certainly is complex. In fact Auden personifies his own ideal self-critical force, which tells the poet what he may and may not let stand, as a sort of review council, a censorate: "A sensitive only child, a practical housewife, a logician, a monk, an irreverent buffoon, and even, perhaps, hated by all the others and returning their dislike, a brutal, foul-mouthed drill sergeant who considers all poetry rubbish." To every writer his own committee, and good luck. In his police function, the censor is conservative, repressive. It may be that one of several reasons why the Russian novelists have been so preeminent is that they have always had to contend with an external censorate, reposed in the state; this may have partly displaced, or paralyzed (with outrage), or discharged, the inner censors and therefore have given those novelists relatively free access to the inner prompter, the rich deep-brain source of primary feelings. In the West, on the other hand, the puritanical and ascetic aspects of the Jewish and Christian cultures have apparently encrusted the psyches of writers, so that the flow upward from the deeper regions is relatively inhibited.

I have mentioned the altered state of consciousness that any act of imaginative writing seems to require. During most of our waking lives the conscious mind, the intellect—alias the censor—is in more or less full command. In the throes of writing, when it is really going well, the writer seems to surrender himself to a state something like that of daydreaming, or even something like that of real dreaming, but apparently not exactly either one. He gives himself over, it seems, to some kind of struggle between the supplier and the censor. The supplier is aroused, almost dangerously active; the censor, who has serious formal work to do, is hard put to it to keep the supplier in hand. Flaubert speaks more than once of this condition; sometimes he has to step to the window to shake himself out of it, for fear of losing control of himself altogether.

Do not look to writers for reliable testimony on how to induce this invaluable state of consciousness, or, for that matter, on a more important question, either—a question which may lead us to the innermost courtyard of the maze.

On one side, the censor is amenable to training, acculturation, encouragement. This is his shaping side, his function as the imposer of form. This part of him accepts schooling in technique. On his other side, however, in his police function, the censor may be refractory, cruel, and arbitrary. It is not easy to get him to change his cop ways. As to the supplier, there is no hope of coaching him. He broods in his dark places and moves at his own whim. The taught side of the censor can affirm or deny him but cannot stir him.

The question, then, is this: How curb the censor's police function without also shackling his shaping function? Or to put the question the other way around, and more significantly: How set free the supplier without letting him run amuck?

That is the question. It goes without saying that a writer must strive for the sorts of technical mastery that are fundamental to other crafts, such as boatbuilding or masonry. But technical skill does not give a writer ready access to the deep areas of primary feelings. That access is what matters most. For the censor speaks with the culture's voice, and the supplier speaks with the writer's true, idiosyncratic, and singular voice.

It is the latter voice that counts in the making of the art of the word. The power of this craft, when it appears, is finally an expression of a certain unique configuration of energies in tension with each other. We read with our eyes, but we sense this power aurally. We speak of voice, of resonance. When we come on this power, Forster says, "great chords begin to sound behind us."

Does this power, when it makes itself heard, have any meaning? Is it good for anything? Or do its mere pitch, tone, and volume contain its entire message?

Ever since the nineteen thirties and forties we in the West have approached very gingerly the question whether literary art can be a matter of consequence. A number of diverse influences have come together to make us cautious in talking about the *effects* of art—the flatness of Socialist realism, which proclaimed literature as agitprop; the emphasis in Freudian psychology on duality and ambiguity, opening us to shocking deceptions, such as that good means bad, war means peace; the insistence of the New Criticism on close analysis of texts—a long-needed examination which gave us immensely valuable new insights but which seemed in the end to be over-fascinated by nuances in pitch, tone, and volume; the commercialization of American culture; and disasters of history—the Soviet trials, Hitler's massacre of the Jews, the Vietnam war, to give but three examples—so degrading as to have made us wonder whether humanity deserved art at all.

It seems to me that it is time to listen again to the insights of the makers. We must try to hear what Faulkner meant when he said, "I would like to think that my behavior is better for having read *Don Quixote*." I shall try to be exact here. Forster has given us a useful distinction, as between the preacher and the prophet. Novelists who are the former he dismisses. As to the latter, he stresses not the predictive faculty we usually attribute to prophets, but rather their resonant, timeless tone of voice. I do not think Faulkner was speaking of a socially useful morality he learned from Cervantes, or which *Don Quixote* roused in him. I believe that after reading Cervantes he kept hearing the sonorous, echoing tones of a seer, and that this distant thunder set him thinking, as he was prone to do anyway, of his relationship as an artist to the issue of an honorable survival for mankind.

Alexander Solzhenitsyn, whose art, coming from a crucible of unthinkable suffering, is in itself a kind of triumph of survival, believes that art can "help the modern world." Who but the artist, he asks in his Nobel Lecture, can open our eyes to distant truths? "Who will make clear for mankind what is really oppressive and unbearable, and what, for being so near, rubs us raw—and thus direct our anger against what is in fact terrible and not merely near at hand? Who is capable of extending such an understanding across the boundaries of his own personal experience? Who has the skill to make a narrow, obstinate human being aware of others' far-off grief and joy, to make him understand dimensions and delusions he himself has never lived through?"

Art praises and nourishes life, art hates death. This is what we mean when we say we recognize power in a work of art: The life forces in us are encouraged. We want to work, we feel a surge of sex, we can weep again, we are suddenly famished, our sufferings too are more acute, yet we seem to know better how to give and take. That art can have devastating effects in the real world is all too vividly borne out in the totalitarian states, which do not care for it. Some revisionist critics have been arguing lately that all art is reactionary, that all art is conceived for the purpose of keeping things the way they are. This is false doctrine. True art is neither revolutionary nor reactionary. This does not mean that it is neutral. No. It is rebellious in any setting. It will not accept lies, which are the essence of violence of whatever kind or color. Precisely because of art's foundation in temperament, it rejects systems altogether. This is why art says preacher no, prophet yes. Art enrages the ideologue because it attacks the lie in his ideology; he is too obsessed to notice that it also attacks the lie in his enemy's ideology.

At the very end of his lecture Solzhenitsyn quotes a Russian proverb: *One word of truth outweighs the world.*

And so we come to the climax of our story. the writer's life, and his work. We see it all resolved at last. All that has been theoretical, schematic, tentative, comes to trembling life; through Gorky's eyes we see the master Tolstoy holding a few playing cards in his strong hands not as pieces of cardboard but as if they were living birds. We have this glimpse of temperament in action. Standing farther back, we see a child's relationship to the world of words. We see the parents' touch on the young artist's forehead. We see the way in which the person chooses the craft—or does the craft choose the person? We sense a constant, undeviating energy, a force related to, perhaps part of, sexuality. We begin to understand how much work is involved, begin to perceive indeed that the life and the work are coterminous. The two are one, the work and the life of a writer. . . .

At last his book is done, and the writer gradually comes through to the other side of an inevitable post-partum depression—"the revulsion of feeling before the accomplished task," as Conrad puts it; then he looks back in relative calm at the struggle of writing and its completion. Sometimes he has an urge to share with us what his experiences in the writing were like. His recollection is as valuable, and perhaps also as suspect, as any autobiographical writing is. If he is still close to the work—in the case of Flaubert's letters to Louise Colet he is in the very midst of it—his fresh testimony may give some thrilling (and, when it comes to the work involved, chilling) insights into detailed aspects of the craft; if he is farther from it, as Thomas Mann is in writing about the writing of *Dr. Faustus*, he may have been able to filter out some larger hypotheses that at least need to be thought about, such as Mann's on a possible relationship between ill health and creative power.

In the writer's account of his life and of his writing we get some important hints about the working out of temperament in the craft of writing. We watch the blind months of preparation. We are aware of torrents of memory. The gradual placing of brick on brick. And patience, patience . . . verification, setting things straight, revising, polishing. But all these glimpses only give us hints, and the hints are elusive, at that. We are led, as all the way through this anthology we have been led, toward a conclusion that is neither comforting nor a surprise: that there is no set of rules for the making of literary art. But we are also led to an overwhelming sense of the range of the art of the word, its complexity and multiplicity, its challenge—temperament played upon by intellect in quest of the whole truth.

So the plot of this collection gradually unfolds. It is a strange and mysterious story, which like that of a fine novel does not end with the end of the book. And as with a novel that works, its story suggests far more than it contains: It points out there to *all* of the writer's craft.

Any anthology reflects personal choices, and the choices in this one, which might be replaced several times over by other choices from the very great wealth of material on the craft, need only a few words of comment.

For one thing, I have ruled out novelists' notebooks of raw materials for use in their novels. The reason for the exclusion, of course, is that to make sense these notebooks need the entire finished novels as context. On this account we do not, for instance, sample the Dostoevski notebooks for his novels, which have only recently been published in English and which give moving and instructive insights into the painstaking craft of that novelist; nor do we have Gide's notebooks for *The Counterfeiters*—particularly interesting to writers, since the novel is about the writing of a novel (entitled, like Gide's, *The Counterfeiters*) by an imagined novelist who keeps a notebook about the writing of his novel. . . . But I must not begin a catalogue of all that is not here; those things are for the called writer to come upon himself, in due time and in joy.

All the pieces that *are* here, save one, are by imaginative writers of substance. The exception is the chapter from the critic Percy Lubbock's *The Craft of Fiction*. I justify its inclusion partly on the ground that Lubbock's book was really a distillation of the opinions of a master craftsman of fiction, Henry James, and partly on the ground that it is probably the most concise argument that is to be found anywhere on a central problem of imaginative writing, point of view.

Not all the selections are complete; every omission, however, is clearly marked by an ellipsis.

And finally perhaps I should add that the relatively small number of pieces by living writers is also a matter of deliberate choice, one that underlines a point made earlier in this preface—that every serious new writer must firmly place himself in relation to the literary tradition that has been given him. The writer's craft, immensely supple though it is, and capable of change, nevertheless cannot be invented in a vacuum; like any other, it is handed on. Perhaps more than any other, because it is the craft of life. Our own year, our fashion, our time is only one flutter of the wing in the long flight of the word.

PART ONE

The Aim of Art

First, the writer's goals. "All I mean by art," Flannery O'Connor writes, easing the novice's mind a bit on the matter of reach, "is writing something that is valuable in itself and that works in itself." Every writer aims in his own way—"however humbly"—at art. The five pieces in this first section speak to this aim from different directions and in differing tones of voice. The pieces are not arranged in the order in which they were written. The first, a Conrad preface, is a credo, written by a man who has just realized that his fate is to *be* an artist. The second is part of a notable essay on fiction by Henry James, the most conscious—and probably also the most self-conscious—craftsman in our culture. This is followed by the surprisingly congruent thoughts on the art of writing of two men quite unlike James in method, two huge ramshackle natural storytellers who seem to stride heedless through the gardens of technique: Tolstoy and Faulkner. And finally Miss O'Connor, a younger spirit, but one closely in touch with the spirit of Conrad, of Flaubert, and of other artists of the past, talks to students in an easy yet cautionary tone of voice about her sense of what fiction can be.

Joseph Conrad

(1857–1924)

The Nigger of the "Narcissus" *was the novel through which Conrad gave him-self, once and for all, to the writing craft. It was his third book. The first,* Almayer's Folly, *had been written while he was still a merchant mariner, on ships and in ports, over five years; the second,* An Outcast of the Islands, *extended some of the characters of the first. These two works won quiet praise from a few critics, but in 1896 Conrad, soon to be forty, was still unsure of his fate. Then, out of the memories of a voyage he had made twelve years earlier on the sailing ship* Narcissus *from Bombay to Dunkirk, around the Cape of Good Hope, and out of the vast blue depths of his gifts, burst the suddenly realized power of one of literature's greatest masterpieces of life at sea. Later he recalled: "After writing the last words of that book, in the revulsion of feeling before the accomplished task, I understood that I had done with the sea, and that henceforth I had to be a writer."*

With the final installment of the novel in The New Review, *in December, 1897, Conrad included this preface, this credo of a writing man. This was not written with the mature and self-conscious hindsight of later years; this is the passionate declaration of a man who has just seen, in the writing of one book, what he must do as well as he can for the rest of his life.*

Preface to
THE NIGGER OF THE "NARCISSUS"

A work that aspires, however humbly, to the condition of art should carry its justification in every line. And art itself may be defined as a single-minded attempt to render the highest kind of justice to the visible universe, by bringing to light the truth, manifold and one, underlying its every aspect. It is an attempt to find in its forms, in its colors, in its light, in its shadows, in the aspects of matter and in the facts of life, what of each is fundamental, what is enduring and essential—their one illuminating and convincing quality—the very truth of their existence. The artist, then, like the thinker or the scientist, seeks the truth and makes his appeal. Impressed by the aspect of the world the thinker plunges into ideas, the scientist into facts—whence, presently, emerging they make their appeal to those quali-ties of our being that fit us best for the hazardous enterprise of living. They speak authoritatively to our common sense, to our intelligence, to our desire of peace or to our desire of unrest; not seldom to our prejudices, sometimes to our fears, often to our egoism——but always to our credulity. And their words are heard with reverence, for their concern is with weighty matters: with the cultivation of our minds and the proper care of our bodies, with the attainment of our ambitions, with the perfection of the means and the glorification of our precious aims.

It is otherwise with the artist.

Confronted by the same enigmatical spectacle the artist descends within himself, and in that lonely region of stress and strife, if he be deserving and fortunate, he finds the terms of his appeal. His appeal is made to our less obvious capacities: to that part of our nature which, because of the warlike conditions of existence, is necessarily kept out of sight within the more resisting and hard qualities—like the vulnerable body within a steel armor. His appeal is less loud, more profound, less distinct, more stirring —and sooner forgotten. Yet its effect endures forever. The changing wisdom of successive generations discards ideas, questions facts, demolishes theories. But the artist appeals to that part of our being which is not dependent on wisdom: to that in us which is a gift and not an acquisition—and, therefore, more permanently enduring. He speaks to our capacity for delight and wonder, to the sense of mystery surrounding our lives; to our sense of pity, and beauty, and pain; to the latent feeling of fellowship with all creation—to the subtle but invincible conviction of solidarity that knits together the loneliness of innumerable hearts, to the solidarity in dreams, in joy, in sorrow, in aspirations, in illusions, in hope, in fear, which binds men to each other, which binds together all humanity—the dead to the living and the living to the unborn.

It is only some such train of thought, or rather of feeling, that can in a measure explain the aim of the attempt, made in the tale which follows, to present an unrestful episode in the obscure lives of a few individuals out of all the disregarded multitude of the bewildered, the simple, and the voiceless. For, if any part of truth dwells in the belief confessed above, it becomes evident that there is not a place of splendor or a dark corner of the earth that does not deserve if only a passing glance of wonder and pity. The motive, then, may be held to justify the matter of the work; but this preface, which is simply an avowal of endeavor, cannot end here—for the avowal is not yet complete.

Fiction—if it at all aspires to be art—appeals to temperament. And in truth it must be, like painting, like music, like all art, the appeal of one temperament to all the other innumerable temperaments whose subtle and resistless power endows passing events with their true meaning, and creates the moral, the emotional atmosphere of the place and time. Such an appeal, to be effective, must be an impression conveyed through the senses; and, in fact, it cannot be made in any other way, because temperament, whether individual or collective, is not amenable to persuasion. All art, therefore, appeals primarily to the senses, and the artistic aim when expressing itself in written words must also make its appeal through the senses, if its high desire is to reach the secret spring of responsive emotions. It must strenuously aspire to the plasticity of sculpture, to the color of painting, and to the magic suggestiveness of music—which is the art of arts. And it is only through complete, unswerving devotion to the perfect blending of form and substance; it is only through an unremitting, never-discouraged care for the shape and ring of sentences that an approach can be made to plasticity, to color, and that the light of magic suggestiveness may be brought to play for an evanescent instant over the commonplace surface of words: of the old, old words, worn thin, defaced by ages of careless usage.

The sincere endeavor to accomplish that creative task, to go as far on that road as his strength will carry him, to go undeterred by faltering, weariness, or reproach, is the only valid justification for the worker in prose. And if his conscience is clear, his answer to those who in the fullness of a wisdom which looks for immediate profit, demand specifically to be edified, consoled, amused; who demand to be promptly improved, or encouraged, or frightened, or shocked, or charmed, must run thus:—My task which I am trying to achieve is, by the power of the written word, to make you hear, to make you feel—it is, before all, to make you *see*. That—and no more, and it is everything. If I succeed, you shall find there, according to your deserts, encouragement, consolation, fear, charm, all you demand—and, perhaps, also that glimpse of truth for which you have forgotten to ask.

To snatch, in a moment of courage, from the remorseless rush of time a passing phase of life, is only the beginning of the task. The task approached in tenderness and faith is to hold up unquestioningly, without choice and without fear, the rescued fragment before all eyes in the light of a sincere mood. It is to show its vibration, its color, its form; and through its movement, its form, and its color, reveal the substance of its truth—disclose its inspiring secret: the stress and passion within the core of each convincing moment. In a single-minded attempt of that kind, if one be deserving and fortunate, one may perchance attain to such clearness of sincerity that at last the presented vision of regret or pity, of terror or mirth, shall awaken in the hearts of the beholders that feeling of unavoidable solidarity; of the solidarity in mysterious origin, in toil, in joy, in hope, in uncertain fate, which binds men to each other and all mankind to the visible world.

It is evident that he who, rightly or wrongly, holds by the convictions expressed above cannot be faithful to any one of the temporary formulas of his craft. The enduring part of them—the truth which each only imperfectly veils—should abide with him as the most precious of his possessions, but they all—Realism, Romanticism, Naturalism, even the unofficial Sentimentalism (which, like the poor, is exceedingly difficult to get rid of)—all these gods must, after a short period of fellowship, abandon him—even on the very threshold of the temple—to the stammerings of his conscience and to the outspoken consciousness of the difficulties of his work. In that uneasy solitude the supreme cry of Art for Art itself loses the exciting ring of its apparent immorality. It sounds far off. It has ceased to be a cry, and is heard only as a whisper, often incomprehensible, but at times and faintly encouraging.

Sometimes, stretched at ease in the shade of a roadside tree, we watch the motions of a laborer in a distant field, and after a time, begin to wonder languidly as to what the fellow may be at. We watch the movements of his body, the waving of his arms; we see him bend down, stand up, hesitate, begin again. It may add to the charm of an idle hour to be told the purpose of his exertions. If we know he is trying to lift a stone, to dig a ditch, to uproot a stump, we look with a more real interest at his efforts; we are disposed to condone the jar of his agitation upon the restfulness of the landscape; and even, if in a brotherly frame of mind, we may bring ourselves to forgive his failure. We understand his object, and, after all, the fellow has tried, and perhaps he had not the strength—and perhaps he had not the knowledge. We forgive, go on our way—and forget.

And so it is with the workman of art. Art is long and life is short, and success is very far off. And thus, doubtful of strength to travel so far, we talk a little about the aim—the aim of art, which, like life itself, is inspiring, difficult—obscured by mists. It is not in the clear logic of a triumphant conclusion; it is not in the unveiling of one of those heartless secrets which are called the Laws of Nature. It is not less great, but only more difficult.

To arrest, for the space of a breath, the hands busy about the work of the earth, and compel men entranced by the sight of distant goals to glance for a moment at the surrounding vision of form and color, of sunshine and shadows; to make them pause for a look, for a sigh, for a smile—such is the aim, difficult and evanescent, and reserved only for a very few to achieve. But sometimes, by the deserving and the fortunate, even that task is accomplished. And when it is accomplished—behold!—all the truth of life is there: a moment of vision, a sigh, a smile—and the return to an eternal rest.

Henry James

(1843–1916)

In the spring of 1884 a Victorian novelist named Walter Besant, who had written eighteen novels in that many years, delivered a lecture at the Royal Institution in London on "Fiction As One of the Fine Arts." Besant argued that novel-writing was one of the arts, along with poetry, painting, and music, and that its elements should be taught to students of writing, just as harmony is taught in music, and perspective in painting. Henry James was then forty-one years old, and he had so far written, among other novels, The Europeans, Daisy Miller, *and* Washington Square. *He took fiction-writing seriously indeed as an art. When he read Besant's lecture, he was put off by some of what Besant had said, particularly by his assertion that a novel should have a "conscious moral purpose." James wrote for* Longman's Magazine *an answering essay, in which he defined the novel in a phrase that was just as challenging to the novice as Conrad's warning that a written work of art must justify itself in every line. A novel, James wrote, is "a personal, a direct impression of life." In his essay James seemed to be trying to imagine himself as one of the teachers Besant had proposed, and he spoke in it both to his fellow novelists as putative fellow teachers and to young writers just entering the craft. Having cautioned along the way that gifts are needed—"that no good novel will ever proceed from a superficial mind"—he concluded with an eloquent charge to the young writer, his imaginary student, to remember that "all life belongs to you. . . . Try and catch the color of life itself."*

FROM
THE ART OF FICTION

.   .   .

The only obligation to which in advance we may hold a novel, without incurring the accusation of being arbitrary, is that it be interesting. That general responsibility rests upon it, but it is the only one I can think of. The ways in which it is at liberty to accomplish this result (of interesting us) strike me as innumerable, and such as can only suffer from being marked out or fenced in by prescription. They are as various as the temperament of man, and they are successful in proportion as they reveal a particular mind, different from others. A novel is in its broadest definition a personal, a direct impression of life: that, to begin with, constitutes its value, which is greater or less according to the intensity of the impression. But there will be no intensity at all, and therefore no value, unless there is freedom to feel and say. The tracing of a line to be followed, of a tone to be taken, of a form to be filled out, is a limitation of that freedom and a suppression of the very thing that we are most curious about. The form, it seems to me, is to be appreciated after the fact: then the author's choice has been made, his standard has been indicated; then we can follow lines and directions and compare tones and resemblances. Then in a word we can enjoy one of the most charming of pleasures, we can estimate quality, we can apply the test of execution. The execution belongs to the author alone; it is what is most personal to him, and we measure him by that. The advantage, the luxury, as well as the torment and responsibility of the novelist, is that there is no limit to what he may attempt as an executant— no limit to his possible experiments, efforts, discoveries, successes. Here it is especially that he works, step by step, like his brother of the brush, of whom we may always say that he has painted his picture in a manner best known to himself. His manner is his secret, not necessarily a jealous one. He cannot disclose it as a general thing if he would; he would be at a loss to teach it to others. I say this with a due recollection of having insisted on the community of method of the artist who paints a picture and the artist who writes a novel. The painter *is* able to teach the rudiments of his practice, and it is possible, from the study of good work (granted the aptitude), both to learn how to paint and to learn how to write. Yet it remains true, without injury to the *rapprochement*, that the literary artist would be obliged to say to his pupil much more than the other, "Ah, well, you must do it as you can!" It is a question of degree, a matter of delicacy. If there are exact sciences, there are also exact arts, and the grammar of painting is so much more definite that it makes the difference. . . .

The characters, the situation, which strike one as real will be those that touch and interest one most, but the measure of reality is very difficult to fix. The reality of Don Quixote or of Mr. Micawber is a very delicate shade; it is a reality so coloured by the author's vision that, vivid as it may be, one would hesitate to propose it as a model: one would expose one's self to some very embarrassing questions on the part of a pupil. It goes without saying that you will not write a good novel unless you possess the sense of reality; but it will be difficult to give you a recipe for calling that sense into being. Humanity is immense, and reality has a myriad forms; the most one can affirm is that some of the flowers of fiction have the odour of it, and others have not; as for telling you in advance how your nosegay should be composed, that is another affair. It is equally excellent and inconclusive to say that one must write from experience; to our suppositious aspirant such a declaration might savour of mockery. What kind of experience is intended, and where does it begin and end? Experience is never limited, and it is never complete; it is an immense sensibility, a kind of huge spider-web of the finest silken threads suspended in the chamber of consciousness, and catching every air-borne particle in its tissue. It is the very atmosphere of the mind; and when the mind is imaginative—much more when it happens to be that of a man of genius—it takes to itself the faintest hints of life, it converts the very pulses of the air into revelations.

The young lady living in a village has only to be a damsel upon whom nothing is lost to make it quite unfair (as it seems to me) to declare to her that she shall have nothing to say about the military. Greater miracles have been seen than that, imagination assisting, she should speak the truth about some of these gentlemen. I remember an English novelist, a woman of genius, telling me that she was much commended for the impression she had managed to give in one of her tales of the nature and way of life of the French Protestant youth. She had been asked where she learned so much about this recondite being, she had been congratulated on her peculiar opportunities. These opportunities consisted in her having once, in Paris, as she ascended a staircase, passed an open door where, in the household of a *pasteur*, some of the young Protestants were seated at table round a finished meal. The glimpse made a picture; it lasted only a moment, but that moment was experience. She had got her direct personal impression, and she turned out her type. She knew what youth was, and what Protestantism; she also had the advantage of having seen what it was to be French, so that she converted these ideas into a concrete image and produced a reality. Above all, however, she was blessed with the faculty which when you give it an inch takes an ell, and which for the artist is a much greater source of strength than any accident of residence or of place in the social scale. The power to guess the unseen from the seen, to trace the implication of things, to judge the whole piece by the pattern, the condition of feeling life in general so completely that you are well on your way to knowing any particular corner of it—this cluster of gifts may almost be said to constitute experience, and they occur in country and in town, and in the most differing stages of education. If experience consists of impressions, it may be said that impressions *are* experience, just as (have we not seen it?) they are the very air we breathe. Therefore, if I should certainly say to a novice, "Write from experience and experience only," I should feel that this was rather a tantalizing monition if I were not careful immediately to add, "Try to be one of the people on whom nothing is lost!"

I am far from intending by this to minimize the importance of exactness —of truth of detail. One can speak best from one's own taste, and I may therefore venture to say that the air of reality (solidity of specification) seems to me to be the supreme virtue of a novel—the merit on which all its other merits . . . helplessly and submissively depend. If it be not there they are all as nothing, and if these be there, they owe their effect to the success with which the author has produced the illusion of life. The cultivation of this success, the study of this exquisite process, form, to my taste, the beginning and the end of the art of the novelist. They are his inspiration, his despair, his reward, his torment, his delight. It is here in very truth that he competes with life; it is here that he competes with his brother the painter in *his* attempt to render the look of things, the look that conveys their meaning, to catch the colour, the relief, the expression, the surface, the substance of the human spectacle. It is in regard to this that Mr. Besant is well inspired when he bids him take notes. He cannot possibly take too many, he cannot possibly take enough. All life solicits him, and to "render" the simplest surface, to produce the most momentary illusion, is a very complicated business. His case would be easier, and the rule would be more exact, if Mr. Besant had been able to tell him what notes to take. But this, I fear, he can never learn in any manual; it is the business of his life. He has to take a great many in order to select a few, he has to work them up as he can, and even the guides and philosophers who might have most to say to him must leave him alone when it comes to the application of precepts, as we leave the painter in communion with his palette. That his characters "must be clear in outline," as Mr. Besant says—he feels that down to his boots; but how he shall make them so is a secret between his good angel and himself. It would be absurdly simple if he could be taught that a great deal of "description" would make them so, or that on the contrary the absence of description and the cultivation of dialogue, or the absence of dialogue and the multiplication of "incident," would rescue him from his difficulties. Nothing, for instance, is more possible than that he be of a turn of mind for which this odd, literal opposition of description and dialogue, incident and description, has little meaning and light. People often talk of these things as if they had a kind of internecine distinctness, instead of melting into each other at every breath, and being intimately associated parts of one general effort of expression. I cannot imagine composition existing in a series of blocks, nor conceive, in any novel worth discussing at all, of a passage of description that is not in its intention narrative, a passage of dialogue that is not in its intention descriptive, a touch of truth of any sort that does not partake of the nature of incident, or an incident that derives its interest from any other source than the general and only source of the success of a work of art—that of being illustrative. A novel is a living thing, all one and continuous, like any other organism, and in proportion as it lives will it be found, I think, that in each of the parts there is something of each of the other parts. The critic who over the close texture of a finished work shall pretend to trace a geography of items will mark some frontiers as artificial, I fear, as any that have been known to history. There is an old-fashioned distinction between the novel of character and the novel of incident which must have cost many a smile to the intending fabulist who was keen about his work. It appears to me as little to the point as the equally celebrated distinction between the novel and the romance—to answer as little to any reality. There are bad novels and good novels, as there are bad pictures and good pictures; but that is the only distinction in which I see any meaning, and I can as little imagine speaking of a novel of character as I can imagine speaking of a picture of character. When one says picture one says of character, when one says novel one says of incident, and the terms may be transposed at will. What is character but the determination of incident? What is incident but the illustration of character? What is either a picture or a novel that is *not* of character? What else do we seek in it and find in it? It is an incident for a woman to stand up with her hand resting on a table and look out at you in a certain way; or if it be not an incident I think it will be hard to say what it is. At the same time it is an expression of character. If you say you don't see it (character in *that—allons donc!*), this is exactly what the artist who has reasons of his own for thinking he *does* see it undertakes to show you. When a young man makes up his mind that he has not faith enough after all to enter the church as he intended, that is an incident, though you may not hurry to the end of the chapter to see whether perhaps he doesn't change once more. I do not say that these are extraordinary or startling incidents. I do not pretend to estimate the degree of interest proceeding from them, for this will depend upon the skill of the painter. It sounds almost puerile to say that some incidents are intrinsically much more important than others, and I need not take this precaution after having professed my sympathy for the major ones in remarking that the only classification of the novel that I can understand is into that which has life and that which has it not. . . .

Nothing, of course, will ever take the place of the good old fashion of "liking" a work of art or not liking it: the most improved criticism will not abolish that primitive, that ultimate test. I mention this to guard myself from the accusation of intimating that the idea, the subject, of a novel or a picture, does not matter. It matters, to my sense, in the highest degree, and if I might put up a prayer it would be that artists should select none but the richest. Some, as I have already hastened to admit, are much more remunerative than others, and it would be a world happily arranged in which persons intending to treat them should be exempt from confusions and mistakes. This fortunate condition will arrive only, I fear, on the same day that critics become purged from error. Meanwhile, I repeat, we do not judge the artist with fairness unless we say to him,

Oh, I grant you your starting-point, because if I did not I should seem to prescribe to you, and heaven forbid I should take that responsibility. If I pretend to tell you what you must not take, you will call upon me to tell you then what you must take; in which case I shall be prettily caught. Moreover, it isn't till I have accepted your data that I can begin to measure you. I have the standard, the pitch; I have no right to tamper with your flute and then criticize your music. Of course I may not care for your idea at all; I may think it silly, or stale, or unclean; in which case I wash my hands of you altogether. I may content myself with believing that you will not have succeeded in being interesting, but I shall, of course, not attempt to demonstrate it, and you will be as indifferent to me as I am to you. I needn't remind you that there are all sorts of tastes: who can know it better? Some people, for excellent reasons, don't like to read about carpenters; others, for reasons even better, don't like to read about courtesans. Many object to Americans. Others (I believe they are mainly editors and publishers) won't look at Italians. Some readers don't like quiet subjects; others don't like bustling ones. Some enjoy a complete illusion, others the consciousness of large concessions. They choose their novels accordingly, and if they don't care about your idea they won't, *a fortiori*, care about your treatment.

So that it comes back very quickly, as I have said, to the liking: in spite of M. Zola, who reasons less powerfully than he represents, and who will not reconcile himself to this absoluteness of taste, thinking that there are certain things that people ought to like, and that they can be made to like. I am quite at a loss to imagine anything (at any rate in this matter of fiction) that people *ought* to like or to dislike. Selection will be sure to take care of itself, for it has a constant motive behind it. That motive is simply experience. As people feel life, so they will feel the art that is most closely related to it. This closeness of relation is what we should never forget in talking of the effort of the novel. Many people speak of it as a factitious, artificial form, a product of ingenuity, the business of which is to alter and arrange the things that surround us, to translate them into conventional, traditional moulds. This, however, is a view of the matter which carries us but a very short way, condemns the art to an eternal repetition of a few familiar *clichés*, cuts short its development, and leads us straight up to a dead wall. Catching the very note and trick, the strange irregular rhythm of life, that is the attempt whose strenuous force keeps Fiction upon her feet. In proportion as in what she offers us we see life *without* rearrangement do we feel that we are touching the truth; in proportion as we see it *with* rearrangement do we feel that we are being put off with a substitute, a compromise and convention. It is not uncommon to hear an extraordinary assurance of remark in regard to this matter of rearranging, which is often spoken of as if it were the last word of art. . . . Art is essentially selection, but it is a selection whose main care is to be typical, to be inclusive. For many people art means rose-coloured window-panes, and selection means picking a bouquet for Mrs. Grundy. They will tell you glibly that artistic considerations have nothing to do with the disagreeable, with the ugly; they will rattle off shallow commonplaces about the province of art and the limits of art till you are moved to some wonder in return as to the province and the limits of ignorance. It appears to me that no one can ever have made a seriously artistic attempt without becoming conscious of an immense increase—a kind of revelation—of freedom. One perceives in that case—by the light of a heavenly ray—that the province of art is all life, all feeling, all observation, all vision. . . . It is all experience. That is a sufficient answer to those who maintain that it must not touch the sad things of life, who stick into its divine unconscious bosom little prohibitory inscriptions on the end of sticks, such as we see in public gardens—"It is forbidden to walk on the grass; it is forbidden to touch the flowers; it is not allowed to introduce dogs or to remain after dark; it is requested to keep to the right." The young aspirant in the line of fiction whom we continue to imagine will do nothing without taste, for in that case his freedom would be of little use to him; but the first advantage of his taste will be to reveal to him the absurdity of the little sticks and tickets. If he have taste, I must add, of course he will have ingenuity, and my disrespectful reference to that quality just now was not meant to imply that it is useless in fiction. But it is only a secondary aid; the first is a capacity for receiving straight impressions. . . .

The deepest quality of a work of art will always be the quality of the mind of the producer. In proportion as that intelligence is fine will the novel, the picture, the statue partake of the substance of beauty and truth. To be constituted of such elements is, to my vision, to have purpose enough. No good novel will ever proceed from a superficial mind; that seems to me an axiom which, for the artist in fiction, will cover all needful moral ground: if the youthful aspirant take it to heart it will illuminate for him many of the mysteries of "purpose." There are many other useful things that might be said to him, but I have come to the end of my article, and can only touch them as I pass. . . . I should remind him first of the magnificence of the form that is open to him, which offers to sight so few restrictions and such innumerable opportunities. The other arts, in comparison, appear confined and hampered; the various conditions under which they are exercised are so rigid and definite. But the only condition that I can think of attaching to the composition of the novel is, as I have already said, that it be sincere. This freedom is a splendid privilege, and the first lesson of the young novelist is to learn to be worthy of it.

Enjoy it as it deserves [I should say to him]; take possession of it, explore it to its utmost extent, publish it, rejoice in it. All life belongs to you, and do not listen either to those who would shut you up into corners of it and tell you that it is only here and there that art inhabits, or to those who would persuade you that this heavenly messenger wings her way outside of life altogether, breathing a superfine air, and turning away her head from the truth of things. There is no impression of life, no manner of seeing it and feeling it, to which the plan of the novelist may not offer a place; you have only to remember that talents so dissimilar as those of Alexandre Dumas and Jane Austen, Charles Dickens and Gustave Flaubert have worked in this field with equal glory. Do not think too much about optimism and pessimism; try and catch the colour of life itself. In France to-day we see a prodigious effort (that of Emile Zola, to whose solid and serious work no explorer of the capacity of the novel can allude without respect), we see an extraordinary effort vitiated by a spirit of pessimism on a narrow basis. M. Zola is magnificent, but he strikes an English reader as ignorant; he has an air of working in the dark; if he had as much light as energy, his results would be of the highest value. As for the aberrations of a shallow optimism, the ground (of English fiction especially) is strewn with their brittle particles as with broken glass. If you must indulge in conclusions, let them have the taste of a wide knowledge. Remember that your first duty is to be as complete as possible—to make as perfect a work. Be generous and delicate and pursue the prize.

Leo Tolstoy

(1828–1910)

By the time he wrote his book on the nature of art, Tolstoy, in his late sixties, was probably the most famous and revered man on earth. Not only was he the author of two massive novels whose pages seemed drenched in sunlight; the renown, besides, of the new religion he had evolved—a purely ethical faith which urged non-violent resistance to all forms of violence, whether governmental or personal, physical or spiritual—had reached not merely Europe and America but China and India as well. (We have seen its influence in later years in the lives, for example, of Gandhi and Martin Luther King.) Tolstoy's book on art came from this period after his conversion; it was published in 1896—a year before The Nigger of the "Narcissus," *the preface of which reflected some of its views. The standards Tolstoy set for art were colored by his religious beliefs and led him to deny the value of some of his own earlier work. But his basic theory of the function of art and his tests of its quality, which are somewhat stiffly set forth in the following excerpts from the book, can and do stand alone. The final passage, in which Tolstoy quotes the painter Bryulóv, speaks to the mystery of the "infinitely minute degrees"—of pitch, of tone, of timing, of intensity, of truth —that separate art from all that is not art.*

FROM
WHAT IS ART?

In order to define art correctly it is necessary first of all to consider it as a means to pleasure, and to consider it as one of the conditions of human life. Viewing it in this way we cannot fail to observe that art is one of the means of intercourse between man and man.

Every work of art causes the receiver to enter into a certain kind of relationship both with him who produced or is producing the art, and with all those who, simultaneously, previously, or subsequently, receive the same artistic impression.

Speech transmitting the thoughts and experiences of men serves as a means of union among them, and art serves a similar purpose. The peculiarity of this latter means of intercourse, distinguishing it from intercourse by means of words, consists in this, that whereas by words a man transmits his thoughts to another, by art he transmits his feelings.

The activity of art is based on the fact that a man receiving through his sense of hearing or sight another man's expression of feeling, is capable of experiencing the emotion which moved the man who expressed it. To take the simplest example: one man laughs, and another who hears becomes merry, or a man weeps, and another who hears feels sorrow. A man is excited or irritated, and another man seeing him is brought to a similar state of mind. By his movements or by the sounds of his voice a man expresses courage and determination or sadness and calmness, and this state of mind passes on to others. A man suffers, manifesting his suffering by groans and spasms, and this suffering transmits itself to other people; a man expresses his feelings of admiration, devotion, fear, respect, or love, to certain objects, persons, or phenomena, and others are infected by the same feelings of admiration, devotion, fear, respect, or love, to the same objects, persons, or phenomena.

And it is on this capacity of man to receive another man's expression of feeling and to experience those feelings himself, that the activity of art is based.

If a man infects another or others directly, immediately, by his appearance or by the sounds he gives vent to at the very time he experiences the feeling; if he causes another man to yawn when he himself cannot help yawning, or to laugh or cry when he himself is obliged to laugh or cry, or to suffer when he himself is suffering—that does not amount to art.

Art begins when one person with the object of joining another or others to himself in one and the same feeling, expresses that feeling by certain external indications. To take the simplest example: a boy having experienced, let us say, fear on encountering a wolf, relates that encounter, and in order to evoke in others the feeling he has experienced, describes himself, his condition before the encounter, the surroundings, the wood, his own lightheartedness, and then the wolf's appearance, its movements, the distance between himself and the wolf, and so forth. All this, if only the boy when telling the story again experiences the feelings he had lived through, and infects the hearers and compels them to feel what he had experienced —is art. Even if the boy had not seen a wolf but had frequently been afraid of one, and if wishing to evoke in others the fear he had felt, he invented an encounter with a wolf and recounted it so as to make his hearers share the feelings he experienced when he feared the wolf, that also would be art. And just in the same way it is art if a man, having experienced either the fear of suffering or the attraction of enjoyment (whether in reality or in imagination), expresses these feelings on canvas or in marble so that others are infected by them. And it is also art if a man feels, or imagines to himself, feelings of delight, gladness, sorrow, despair, courage, or despondency, and the transition from one to another of these feelings, and expresses them by sounds so that the hearers are infected by them and experience them as they were experienced by the composer.

The feelings with which the artist infects others may be most various— very strong or very weak, very important or very insignificant, very bad or very good: feelings of love of one's country, self-devotion and submission to fate or to God expressed in a drama, raptures of lovers described in a novel, feelings of voluptuousness expressed in a picture, courage expressed in a triumphal march, merriment evoked by a dance, humour evoked by a funny story, the feeling of quietness transmitted by an evening landscape or by a lullaby, or the feeling of admiration evoked by a beautiful arabesque—it is all art.

If only the spectators or auditors are infected by the feelings which the author has felt, it is art.

To evoke in oneself a feeling one has once experienced and having evoked it in oneself then by means of movements, lines, colours, sounds, or forms expressed in words, so to transmit that feeling that others experience the same feeling—this is the activity of art.

Art is a human activity consisting in this, that one man consciously by means of certain external signs, hands on to others feelings he has lived through, and that others are infected by these feelings and also experience them. . . .

The chief peculiarity of this feeling is that the recipient of a truly artistic impression is so united to the artist that he feels as if the work were his own and not some one else's—as if what it expresses were just what he had long been wishing to express. A real work of art destroys in the consciousness of the recipient the separation between himself and the artist, and not that alone, but also between himself and all whose minds receive this work of art. In this freeing of our personality from its separation and isolation, in this uniting of it with others, lies the chief characteristic and the great attractive force of art.

If a man is infected by the author's condition of soul, if he feels this emotion and this union with others, then the object which has effected this is art; but if there be no such infection, if there be not this union with the author and with others who are moved by the same work—then it is not art. And not only is infection a sure sign of art, but the degree of infectiousness is also the sole measure of excellence in art.

The stronger the infection the better is the art, as art, speaking of it now apart from its subject-matter—that is, not considering the value of the feelings it transmits.

And the degree of the infectiousness of art depends on three conditions:—

(1) On the greater or lesser individuality of the feeling transmitted; (2) on the greater or lesser clearness with which the feeling is transmitted; (3) on the sincerity of the artist, that is, on the greater or lesser force with which the artist himself feels the emotion he transmits.

The more individual the feeling transmitted the more strongly does it act on the recipient; the more individual the state of soul into which he is transferred the more pleasure does the recipient obtain and therefore the more readily and strongly does he join in it.

Clearness of expression assists infection because the recipient who mingles in consciousness with the author is the better satisfied the more clearly that feeling is transmitted which, as it seems to him, he has long known and felt and for which he has only now found expression.

But most of all is the degree of infectiousness of art increased by the degree of sincerity in the artist. As soon as the spectator, hearer, or reader, feels that the artist is infected by his own production and writes, sings, or plays, for himself, and not merely to act on others, this mental condition of the artist infects the recipient; and, on the contrary, as soon as the spectator, reader, or hearer, feels that the author is not writing, singing, or playing, for his own satisfaction—does not himself feel what he wishes to express, but is doing it for him, the recipient—resistance immediately springs up, and the most individual and the newest feelings and the cleverest technique not only fail to produce any infection but actually repel.

I have mentioned three conditions of contagion in art, but they may all be summed up into one, the last, sincerity; that is, that the artist should be impelled by an inner need to express his feeling. That condition includes the first; for if the artist is sincere he will express the feeling as he experienced it. And as each man is different from every one else, his feeling will be individual for every one else; and the more individual it is—the more the artist has drawn it from the depths of his nature—the more sympathetic and sincere will it be. And this same sincerity will impel the artist to find clear expression for the feeling which he wishes to transmit.

Therefore this third condition—sincerity—is the most important of the three. It is always complied with in peasant art, and this explains why such art always acts so powerfully; but it is a condition almost entirely absent from our upper-class art, which is continually produced by artists actuated by personal aims of covetousness or vanity.

Such are the three conditions which divide art from its counterfeits, and which also decide the quality of every work of art considered apart from its subject-matter.

The absence of any one of these conditions excludes a work from the category of art and relegates it to that of art's counterfeits. If the work does not transmit the artist's peculiarity of feeling and is therefore not individual, if it is unintelligibly expressed, or if it has not proceeded from the author's inner need for expression—it is not a work of art. If all these conditions are present even in the smallest degree, then the work even if a weak one is yet a work of art.

The presence in various degrees of these three conditions: individuality, clearness, and sincerity, decides the merit of a work of art as art, apart from subject-matter. All works of art take order of merit according to the degree in which they fulfil the first, the second, and the third, of these conditions. In one the individuality of the feeling transmitted may predominate; in another, clearness of expression; in a third, sincerity; while a fourth may have sincerity and individuality but be deficient in clearness;

a fifth, individuality and clearness, but less sincerity; and so forth, in all possible degrees and combinations.

Thus is art divided from what is not art, and thus is the quality of art, as art, decided, independently of its subject matter, that is to say, apart from whether the feelings it transmits are good or bad.

But how are we to define good and bad art with reference to its content or subject-matter? . . .

Art like speech is a means of communication and therefore of progress, that is, of the movement of humanity forward towards perfection. Speech renders accessible to men of the latest generations all the knowledge discovered by the experience and reflection both of preceding generations and of the best and foremost men of their own times; art renders accessible to men of the latest generations all the feelings experienced by their predecessors and also those felt by their best and foremost contemporaries. And as the evolution of knowledge proceeds by truer and more necessary knowledge dislodging and replacing what was mistaken and unnecessary, so the evolution of feeling proceeds by means of art—feelings less kind and less necessary for the well-being of mankind being replaced by others kinder and more needful for that end. That is the purpose of art. And speaking now of the feelings which are its subject-matter, the more art fulfils that purpose the better the art, and the less it fulfils it the worse the art. . . .

I have elsewhere quoted the profound remark of the Russian artist Bryulóv on art, but I cannot here refrain from repeating it, because nothing better illustrates what can, and what cannot, be taught in the schools. Once when correcting a pupil's study, Bryulóv just touched it in a few places and the poor dead study immediately became animated. "Why, you only touched it a *wee bit,* and it is quite another thing!" said one of the pupils. "Art begins where the *wee bit* begins," replied Bryulóv, indicating by these words just what is most characteristic of art. The remark is true of all the arts, but its justice is particularly noticeable in the performance of music. That musical execution should be artistic, should be art, that is, should carry infection, three chief conditions must be observed. There are many others needed for musical perfection: the transition from one sound to another must be interrupted or continuous; the sound must increase or diminish steadily; it must be blended with one and not with another sound; the sound must have this or that timbre, and much besides,—but take the three chief conditions: the pitch, the time, and the strength of the sound. Musical execution is only then art, only then infects, when the sound is neither higher nor lower than it should be, that is, when exactly the infinitely small centre of the required note is taken; when that note is continued exactly as long as is needed; and when the strength of the sound is neither more nor less than is required. The slightest deviation of pitch in either direction, the slightest increase or decrease in time, or the slightest strengthening or weakening of the sound beyond what is needed, destroys the perfection and consequently the infectiousness of the work. So that the feeling of infection by the art of music, which seems so simple and so easily obtained, is a thing we receive only when the performer finds those infinitely minute degrees which are necessary to perfection in music. It is the same in all arts: a wee bit lighter, a wee bit darker, a wee bit higher, lower, to the right or the left—in painting; a wee bit weaker or stronger in intonation, a wee bit sooner or later—in dramatic art; a wee bit omitted, over-emphasized, or exaggerated—in poetry, and there is no contagion. Infection is only obtained when an artist finds those infinitely minute degrees of which a work of art consists, and only to the extent to which he finds them. And it is quite impossible to teach people by external means to find these minute degrees: they can only be found when a man yields to his feeling. No instruction can make a dancer catch just the time of the music, or a singer or a fiddler take exactly the infinitely minute centre of his note, or a sketcher draw of all possible lines the only right one, or a poet find the only right arrangement of the only suitable words. All this is found only by feeling. And therefore schools may teach what is necessary in order to produce something resembling art, but not art itself.

The teaching of the schools stops where the *wee bit* begins—consequently where art begins.

William Faulkner

(1897–1962)

One of William Faulkner's last public appearances was a reading from The
Reivers *that he gave in Thayer Hall at West Point to the corps of cadets on
April 19, 1962. After his reading, and again the next morning with two sections
of a course called* The Evolution of American Ideals as Reflected in American
Literature, *Faulkner answered questions; these questions (some of them slightly
condensed) and Faulkner's answers (untouched) were later published in a small
book from which the following pages come. No other American writer of his
time had created an imaginary world of such integrity and richness as that of
his Yoknapatawpha County. He was now an elder statesman of American
letters; he had won the Nobel Prize twelve years before. In his answers to the
cadets' questions, however, he must surely have been drawing on his memories
of the two decades and more before honors first reached him, memories of the
long lonely time when, in the face of reviewers' telling him over and over again
that he was massacring the language, that his characters were moral cripples,
that he lived in a lost past, he simply went on doing what he could not help
doing—creating and giving us the peopled land in his mind. Against the background of this irrepressible fertility one becomes aware of the resonance of his
thoughts about writing, so casually and charmingly spun out here, and of their
harmony with Tolstoy's idea of art as the means of passing feeling from one
man's heart to another's.*

FROM

FAULKNER AT WEST POINT
Edited by Joseph L. Fant III and Robert Ashley

QUESTION: Sir, in your address upon receiving the Nobel Prize you said it
was the writer's "privilege to help man endure by lifting his heart. . . ."
How do you believe that you have fulfilled this task in your work?

ANSWER: It's possible that I haven't. I think that that is the writer's dedication. It's his privilege, his dedication too, to uplift man's heart by
showing man the record of the experiences of the human heart, the
travail of man within his environment, with his fellows, with himself,
in such moving terms that the lessons of honesty and courage are evident and obvious. I think that that's the reason, possibly, the poet, the
writer, writes. Whether he's successful or not is something else. Probably the only reason the poet ever writes another poem is that the one

he just finished didn't quite serve that purpose—wasn't good enough—so he'll write another one.

QUESTION: Sir, I'd like to know, out of all the works you've written in your time of writing, which one do you personally consider to be your best, and what leads you to this decision?

ANSWER: That goes back to the answer I just gave. I think that no writer is ever quite satisfied with the work he has done, which is why he writes another one. If he ever wrote one which suited him completely, nothing remains but to cut the throat and quit. And in my own case, the one that is closest to me would be the one that failed the most, that gave me the most trouble. So no writer can judge what he thinks is the best. It's like the mother with the child who is an idiot or born crippled—that that child has a place in the heart which the hale, strong child never has. That may be true of any writer, that the one that's closest to him is the one he worked the hardest at—the failure which was the most painful failure. So I'd have to answer that question in the—which is the one that cost me the most anguish and that I still don't like the most, which is one called *The Sound and the Fury.* . . .

QUESTION: Sir, in your novel *Absalom, Absalom!*, what is your purpose in relating Colonel Sutpen's story through Quentin Compson—to reveal the character of Quentin, to portray merely Sutpen, or to just portray the South?

ANSWER: The primary job that any writer faces is to tell you a story, a story out of human experience—I mean by that, universal mutual experience, the anguishes and troubles and griefs of the human heart, which is universal, without regard to race or time or condition. He wants to tell you something which has seemed to him so true, so moving, either comic or tragic, that it's worth repeating. He's using his own poor means, which is the clumsy method of speech, of writing, to tell you that story. And that's why he invents involved style, or he invents the different techniques—he's simply trying to tell you a story which is familiar to everyone in some very moving way, a way so moving and so true that anyone would say, "Why yes—that's so. That happens to me, can happen to anybody." I think that no writer's got time to be drawing a picture of a region, or preaching anything—if he's trying to preach you a sermon, then he's really not a writer, he's a propagandist, which is another horse. But the writer is simply trying to tell a story of the human heart in conflict with itself, or with others, or with environment in a moving way. Does that answer?

QUESTION: Sir, what is your opinion of the value of modern literature, of the writing about woman's suffrage and confusion of roles as present in modern literature?

ANSWER: I look on them as the tools, the material of the trade; that is, they are the conditions which the writer can use in order to portray the human heart in some simple struggle with itself, with others, or with its environment. The sociological qualities are only, in my opinion, coincidental to the story—the story is still the story of the human being, the human heart struggling. To be braver than it is afraid it might be, to be more honest, to be more compassionate, to be nearer the figure that we mean when we say God than it thinks it might be. This integration, segregation, or the sociological conditions are simply tools which the writer uses in order to show the human heart in the struggle of that dilemma—in the battle which is any story. It's the—the individual meets a crisis, does he lick it or does it lick him? That's all any story comes to.

QUESTION: Sir, once again in your Nobel Prize speech, you stated, "Our tragedy today is a general and universal physical fear so long sustained by now that we can even bear it. There are no longer problems of the spirit. There is only the question: 'When will I be blown up?'" And I wonder, sir, do you feel that our generation today, the generation we're living in right now, is getting out of this feeling of "When will I be blown up?" less than we were, say, in 1950, when you gave this speech? Do you feel our literature is showing this?

ANSWER: I think that the young people have really never believed in that statement, that that was the condition of—a universal condition which is supported more by the older people, that the young people who have felt the same toward the beauty and passion of being alive that I felt when I was twenty-one years old, still feel it. But when I was twenty-one years old, we didn't have that general pessimistic, middle-aged feeling of "When shall I be blown up?" which seems to be in the world today. I don't think it's going to stop anybody from being poets; it's just too bad you've got to carry that load. And that didn't refer to the young people— the young people don't care what the old folks think.

QUESTION: Sir, based on what you just said, do you consider that the present world situation is likely to infuse a new spirit of nationalism into American literature?

ANSWER: If a spirit of nationalism gets into literature, it stops being literature. Let me elaborate that. I mean that the problems which the poet writes about which are worth writing about, or composing the music, or painting the pictures are the problems of the human heart which have nothing to do with what race you belong to, what color you are—they're the anguishes, the passions, of love, of hope, of the capacity, the doom of the fragile web of flesh and bone and mostly water, of which we are in articulation, must suffer, stuck together by a little electricity and a world of mostly coincidence, that we can endure it all. Yet there's something in us that makes the individual say, "My anguish is beautiful, it's meaningful," so he writes the poem, he composes the music, he paints the picture not to prove anything, not to defy his fate nor his circumstance, but simply because there is something that is so true and so moving in breathing that he has got to put it down, got to make a record of it. You might say that what drives every poet and writer—he knows that in a short time, three score and ten years, he must pass through the last and final oblivion into nothing, that he is at least going to leave on that wall the scrawl "Kilroy was here." His belief is that his own passions are important, and we must all agree with him. If our own passions, our own problems are not important, then there is no reason to be here. What do we get out of being here?

QUESTION: Sir, I would like to know who your favorite author is.

ANSWER: Well, that's a question that really don't make much sense to a writer because the writer is not concerned with who wrote, but what he wrote. To me, anyway, the character, the book is the thing, and who wrote it is not important; and the people that I know and love are Don Quixote, and Sarah Gamp and some of Conrad's people, a lot of Dickens' people, Balzac's people, but not Balzac especially, because I think some of Balzac's writing is bad writing. Some of Conrad's writing is bad writing, but some of Conrad's people that he created are marvelous and endured. So I think that—true of any writer—that he looks on the book and not who wrote it, not who made it.

QUESTION: Sir, in many of your works you deal with perversion and corruption in men. How do you feel this uplifts your readers, exemplified in courage and honor?

ANSWER: Well, the easy answer is, it may show them what I don't think they should do, which is easy and glib and meaningless. I think that the reason is that one must show man; the writer, the painter, the musician wants to show man not in his—not when he's dressed up for Sunday, but in all his phases, his conditions; then the very fact that to see man in his base attitudes, his base conditions, and still show that he goes on, he continues, he has outlived the dinosaur, he will outlive the atom bomb, and I'm convinced in time he will even outlive the wheel. He still has partaken of immortality, that the aberrations are part of his history, are part of himself, maybe. But within all that is the same thing that makes him want to endure, that makes him believe that war should be eradicated, that injustice should not exist, that little children shouldn't suffer.

QUESTION: Sir, you say that all works of literature arise from a passion and an agony of the heart. Let's say that you start your life on a river with passion and beauty and agony and, as you go through your life, you are trying to find some goal. What is the path that you find easiest—to withdraw from the river and watch it course by, or to succumb to it, stay with it? Should you withdraw from your emotions or stay with your emotions?

ANSWER: I would say by all means to stay with it, to be a part of it. To never be afraid of dirt or filth, or baseness or cowardice, but try always to be better than that, to be braver, to be compassionate, but not to be afraid of it, not to avoid it. I think that the worst perversion of all is to retire to the ivory tower. Get down in the market place and stay there. Certainly, if you want to be a painter or a writer, maybe if you want to be a philosopher, a mathematician, you can get off in a tower, but if you want to be a painter, or a writer, or a poet, you can't be afraid or ashamed—ashamed of your own behavior, not of other people's.

QUESTION: Sir, at the present time, you seem to have great optimism for the human race, but in some of your earlier writings during the period around the 1920's, this optimism was not too prevalent. Was there any period of life that changed your attitude toward the human race?

ANSWER: No, I wouldn't think so. I would say that this part of the human race which is going steadily on toward a continuation, toward that sort of immortality, are pretty dull folks. The ones that kick up and misbehave and are comic or tragic to me are interesting. But they are not the sum total of the human race. No one lives long enough in three score and ten years to be the human race; he just entered it for a little while—he was a tenant.

QUESTION: Sir, in the light of the answers you gave to some previous questions, that you believe it's the right and duty of an author to show a character in all its phases in any way that is feasible, what is your stand on present-day censorship?

ANSWER: Well, there should be no such thing as censorship. If the mind has got to be protected by the law from what will harm it, then it can't be very much of a mind to begin with. The first part of your question, can I have that again, please, sir?

QUESTION: You stated, sir, that you thought it was the right and duty of an author to tell the story of the human heart and its problems. I wonder if you do this and if you do it as *you* see it. You may not see it as others do.

ANSWER: I didn't say it was the right and duty. I think primarily the writer, the artist, works because it's fun. He hadn't found anything that is that much pleasure. He is simply telling a story in the most moving and dramatic way that he can think to do it. He's not following any right nor any duty to improve you; he simply has seen something in the magic and passion of breathing which seems so funny or so tragic that he wants to tell you. And he is trying to tell you in the most moving and economical way he can, so that you will be moved, will laugh or cry, as he did. It's no special right and duty—when he gets involved with right and duty, he's on the verge of becoming a propagandist, and he stops being an artist then. He's doing something simply because he likes it, it's his cup of tea. He'd rather do that than anything else he knows.

QUESTION: Sir, just where did you get the basis for your characterization of the Snopes and Sartoris families?

ANSWER: That's a difficult question to answer. The writer has three sources: one is observation; one is experience, which includes reading;

the other is imagination, and the Lord only knows where that comes from. It's like having three tanks on a collector—you open the collector valve, you don't know exactly how much comes from any one tank, so no one can say just where anything comes from, whether he imagined it, whether he saw it or read it or heard it, but you can count on one thing, that the reason they call it fiction is it *is* fiction—that any writer is a congenital liar incapable of telling the truth, and so even he can never say how much he embroidered, imagined anything because he simply could not take any fact he saw and let it alone. He's convinced he can do much better than God could, so he's going to improve it—change it.

QUESTION: Sir, it's been said that literature today tends toward atheism. What's your opinion of this?

ANSWER: I don't think so. I think that the literature of today is too much like the literature of all times, which has been the struggle, the history, the record of the struggle of the human heart. What it's struggling toward, a condition, an esoteric condition like atheism or Puritanism or integration or segregation, is not important—it's the battle the heart goes through in trying to be better than it is, to be less cowardly than it is afraid it might be.

QUESTION: Sir, you're described, I believe, as a naturalistic writer. In America, we've progressed quite a ways in naturalism. What work, if you care not to speak about authors, would you describe as furthering naturalism most in America?

ANSWER: To begin with, I don't know what naturalism means. Can you be a little more specific?

QUESTION: I would say, sir, that we've come a long way since before the 1900's. One of the books that I had in mind was *Sister Carrie* by Theodore Dreiser. And also, works by Sinclair Lewis, I believe, would be described as naturalistic, or naturalistic as opposed to romantic.

ANSWER: Yes, I see what you mean. I still think that the job which the writer is doing is to tell you a moving story of the human heart in conflict. I would say that Dreiser used the best material he had, the best method, the best skill he had, which wasn't very much. He was a bad writer. But he had a tremendous drive to tell you of the conflict of the human spirit. And that's what I meant by saying that I didn't know what a naturalist writer was. That to me, the writer is simply trying to use the best method he possibly can find to tell you a true and moving and familiar old, old story of the human heart in conflict with itself for the old, old human verities and truth, which are love, hope, fear, compassion, greed, lust. He uses naturalism, romanticism as the tools to his hand just as the carpenter uses the hammer or the saw which fits his hand best to trim the board, but he's simply trying to tell you the same story of the human heart in conflict with itself for the eternal verities which haven't changed too much since man first found how to record them.

. . .

QUESTION: Sir, last night you stated that the basic goal of an author was to portray the conflict of the human heart. Now, just what do you feel to-day is the chief trouble with which people are concerned, or should be, and how much has this changed since, let's say in particular, the time of the Depression?

ANSWER: I don't think it has changed at all basically. Only the ephemeral symptoms alter—they are not too important. But basically the drives of the heart are the same. It's the verities, for the verities have been the same ever since Socrates, which are courage and pride and honor—compassion. It's man's knowledge that at bottom he is not very brave, that he is not very compassionate, but he wants to be—his conscience—call it what you will, call it God, but he wants to be better than he is afraid that he might be—that he might fail, yet he still tries. I think that is shown in the people that portray incredible courage in battle; that man is fighting too, yet something—we don't know what it is—drove him to do what he himself didn't believe he could; that people show pity—they are the verities which all the writing is about. The temporary conditional things of the time are not too important. At this time, in my country, the South, there is a problem of segregation and integration—racial trouble. But they are not really important in the long view of man's record. At other times, unemployment; at other times, women's rights—they were important ephemerally at the moment, but not important as measured against the passions and hopes of man's heart.

QUESTION: Sir, I am interested in this hope of man. Hemingway in his early work, especially I'm thinking of his "Snows of Kilimanjaro," pictures man as someone who is disillusioned, who has no real hope, no life to him. Yet in his later work—I'm thinking of *The Old Man and the Sea*—he pictures man as someone with life, with faith, with hope, and with resolution. It seems strange to me that he would kill himself after he seems to have regained a faith in man. I was wondering if you know any possible reason why, after he seems to have regained his faith, he would then decide to take his life.

ANSWER: The only reason I would undertake to guess would be that every writer wishes to reduce the sum of all experience, of all the passion and beauty of being alive, into something that will last after him. If he's the first-rate poet, he tries to do it in a quatrain. If he's not a first-rate poet, then he tries to do it in ten pages—he's a short-story writer. If he can't be a short-story writer, then he resorts to eighty thousand words and becomes a third-stage novelist. But he is trying to reduce the passion and beauty that he saw of being alive into something concrete that can be held in the hand, and he fails, and he tries again. I would say that there was a certain point that Ernest reached where he said, "I can't do it, no man can do it, and there's nothing remains worth staying alive for." Or he could have been sick and in pain, and I think that that had something to do with it because he had spent a lot of time in the hospital. The last time I saw him he was a sick man. But I prefer to believe that he had reached that point that the writer must reach—Shakespeare reached it in *The Tempest*—he said, "I don't know the answer either," and wrote *The Tempest* and broke the pencil. But he didn't commit suicide. Hemingway broke the pencil and shot himself. . . .

QUESTION: Sir, when you feel moved by something so that you want to write about it and make a story out of it, do you write immediately and spontaneously and completely write out the whole story, or is it a gradual process? I'm interested in how you go about writing.

ANSWER: There's no rule for that in my case. I'm very disorderly. I never did make notes nor set myself a stint of work. I write while the idea is hot, and the only rule I have is to stop while it's still hot—never to write myself out—to leave something to be anxious to get at tomorrow. Since I have no order, I know nothing about plots. The stories with me begin with an anecdote or a sentence or an expression, and I'll start from there and sometimes I write the thing backwards—I myself don't know exactly where any story is going. I write—I'm dealing simply with people who suddenly have got up and have gotten into motion—men and women who are moving, who are involved in the universal dilemmas of the human heart. Then when I have got a lot of it down, the policeman has got to come in and say, "Now look here, you've got to give this some sort of unity and coherence and emphasis," the old grammatical rules—and then the hard work begins. But it's a pleasure—it's just like you get pleasure out of a hard, fast tennis game—with me, only at some moment the policeman has got to compel the unity and coherence and emphasis to make it a readable story.

QUESTION: Sir, do you ever feel tempted to get your characters out of trouble? Once their characteristics have gotten them into some sort of trouble, do you feel tempted to help them out?

ANSWER: I don't have time—by that time, I'm running along behind them with a pencil trying to put down what they say and do.

QUESTION: Sir, thinking of a definition that Tolstoy once had of literature —that good literature was something which taught a good lesson, bad literature was something which taught a bad lesson, and that great literature was something that taught a good lesson that was applicable to all mankind, what is your idea of such a definition?

ANSWER: I agree with him absolutely. Only I do think that the writer has not got time to say, "Now, I'm going to teach you a lesson." The writer is saying, "I'm going to tell you a story that is funny or tragic." The lesson is coincidental, even accidental, but all the good books do fall into those categories—he's quite right, I agree with him. But he himself didn't set down to write a book to teach anyone a lesson, I think. He was simply writing about people involved in the passion and hope of the human dilemma.

QUESTION: Sir, in answer to one of the questions last night—I believe it was, "How your portraying more or less perverted characters would help uplift the human heart"—you said that if nothing else it would show that it would be a good idea not to be like these people. I wonder if you ever do portray people who are more or less perverted with the idea of presenting them as unfavorable, or do you just present them just as they are—just as a story about them in the struggle of their heart. Do you ever try to present them as either unfavorable or favorable?

ANSWER: Not really. The first thing that a writer has is compassion for all his characters—any other writer's characters. He himself does not feel that he has the power to judge, and these characters, these evils are there. In the story he's telling, it seems to him necessary and good and the best way to tell his story to use this. He doesn't advocate it, he's not condemning it, it's there, and in his clumsy way the first thing he must do is to love all mankind, even when he hates individual ones. Some of the characters I've created, I hate very much, but it's not for me to judge them, to condemn them; they are there, they are part of the scene that we all live in. We can't abolish evil by refusing to mention these people. . . .

QUESTION: Sir, recently in the newspapers and national magazines, there have been several articles about government aid to the artist. I was wondering how do you feel about this?

ANSWER: Why, I would think that the artist ought to get whatever help he can get from any source. All he really needs is a little whiskey and a little tobacco and a little fun. And it don't do him any harm to have to do a little hard work for it, too, but I don't think that a little help is going to ruin the good artist. I don't think that the good artist has got to come from the gutter, either. So whatever he can get from his government, let him take it.

QUESTION: Sir, then you don't feel that government aid might lead to, say, control of the artist?

ANSWER: Not to the good one. The good one, nobody can control him because he can't control himself. The second-rate one might be turned into a machine, a propagandist, but the first-rate one can't be—nobody can control him, not even himself.

QUESTION: You spoke just now, sir, of first- and second-rate artists. Now how, exactly, would you separate first- and second-rate authors? Would it be by the trueness or the accuracy of the story which they are telling or just by their style—which one, or both?

ANSWER: It would, in my opinion, be absolutely by the trueness that they are telling, and I don't mean the sticking to fact because facts and truth don't really have much to do with each other. It's to stick to the fundamental truth of man's struggle within the human dilemma. He can be a bad writer, he can—I mean by that he could be a bad punctuator or grammarian—but he's still a first-rate writer if the people that he's portraying follow the universal patterns of man's behavior inside the human condition.

QUESTION: Quite a few of the writers back in about 1900—when they would write a story such as about the meat packers in Chicago—would try to tell the story of individuals, but with a thought in mind that they saw an evil in society which should be corrected. Do you think, sir, that a writer has an obligation to try to point out through his stories an evil that he sees in a society or should he just tell a story of individuals and not try to make any generalization about society?

ANSWER: Let him stick to his story. If he feels that evil enough, he can't keep it out of the story. He don't have to make an effort to bring it in to show anyone. Let him stick to his story dealing with men and women in the human dilemma. If he feels that social evil enough, it will be there. That was the case of Sherwood Anderson and Sandburg and Dreiser and the other people writing in Chicago about that time—they were not propagandists on social evils. They couldn't keep the evil, the awareness of it, out, because it moved them as people. That was a part of their own dilemma. . . .

9:30 A.M.–10:25 A.M., April 20, 1962

QUESTION: Could you tell us, Mr. Faulkner, exactly what qualities Don Quixote has that make him one of your favorite characters?

ANSWER: It's admiration and pity and amusement—that's what I get from him—and the reason is that he is a man trying to do the best he can in this ramshackle universe he's compelled to live in. He has ideals which are by our—the pharisaical standards are nonsensical. But by my standards they are not nonsensical. His method of trying to put them into practice is tragic and comic. I can see myself in Don Quixote by reading a page or two now and then, and I would like to think that my behavior is better for having read *Don Quixote*.

QUESTION: Mr. Faulkner, there have been several comments recently concerning your style. I am thinking specifically of your sentence structure, in which you seem to have run-on sentences consisting possibly of twenty-six or twenty-seven lines, and also of your vague pronoun references. By vague pronoun reference I am thinking of the first five or six pages of *Intruder in the Dust*. When you speak of a "he" and do not refer to the subject of this "he," I wonder if you have any special purpose in doing this, or is this just the result of the thoughts in your mind as you are trying to express your thoughts?

ANSWER: The germ of it was a special purpose—not at all to be obscure. I think that any artist, musician, writer, painter would like to take all of the experience which he has seen, observed, felt and reduce that to one single color or tone or word, which is impossible. In fact, he would like to reduce all human experience onto the head of the pin as the man engraved the Lord's Prayer on the head of a pin once. He can't do that, but he is still going to try. And the obscurity, the prolixity which you find in writers is simply that desire to put all that experience into one word. Then he has got to add another word, another word becomes a sentence, but he's still trying to get it into one unstopping whole—a paragraph or a page—before he finds a place to put a full stop. The style—I think the story the writer is trying to tell invents, compels its style. That no writer has got the time to be obscure for the sake of obscurity. It's because at that moment he couldn't think of any better way to tell the story he was trying to tell.

QUESTION: Sir, do you believe that the events in an author's life have any significant effect upon his writing?

ANSWER: I think that every experience of the author affects his writing. That he is amoral or thief, he will rob and steal from any and every source; he will use everything; everything is grist to his mill from the telephone book up or down, and naturally all his own experience is stored away. He has a sort of a lumber room in his subconscious that all this goes into, and none of it is ever lost. Some day he may need some experience that he experienced or saw, observed or read about, and so he digs it out and uses it. I don't think he gets off to suffer experience just to use it. But everything that happens to him he remembers. And it will be grist to his mill.

QUESTION: Sir, I just finished reading *As I Lay Dying*. You stated last night that there are three things that a person, a writer, may draw upon in order to get his ideas for a story. One was imagination, another was experience, and the third was observation. I would like to know where you got the idea for *As I Lay Dying*.

ANSWER: They are people that I have known all my life in the country I was born in. The actions, the separate actions, I may have seen, remembered. It was the imagination probably that tied the whole thing together into a story. It's difficult to say just what part of any story comes specifically from imagination, what part from experience, what part from observation. It's like having—as I said last night—three tanks with a collector valve. And you don't know just how much comes from which tank. All you know is a stream of water runs from the valve when you open it, drawn from the three tanks—observation, experience, imagination.

QUESTION: Sir, I would like to know if at present you have any ideas concerning what you are going to write in the future. Do you have any feelings that you feel you would like to put down on paper sometime in the future or that you are working on right now?

ANSWER: No, a disorderly writer like me is incapable of making plans and plots. He writes simply about people, and the story begins with a phrase, an anecdote, or a gesture, and it goes from there and he tries to stop it as soon as he can. If he can stop it in ten pages, he does. If it needs a hundred pages, it demands a hundred pages. But it's not done with any plan or schedule of work tomorrow. I am simply writing about people, man in his comic or tragic human condition, in motion, to tell a story—give it some order and unity and coherence—that to me seems tragic or funny.

QUESTION: Sir, I would like to know if you could tell us where and when you first learned to give these stories of yours this unity and coherence and meaning. Was there some definite time of your life in which this was taught to you or you learned it?

ANSWER: I learned it by what seems to me necessity. I was the oldest of four brothers, and we had certain chores—milking and feeding and things like that to do at home—and I found pretty soon that if I told stories the others did the work. That was when I begun to dabble in fiction. And I could get boys from the neighborhood in when there was a lot of work to be done, get that done too—I sort of contracted out, you see.

QUESTION: Do you think an American author, Mr. Faulkner, has to have another job besides writing?

ANSWER: Yes, I do. I think any author should because, if you are not careful, you'll begin to think of the work you do in terms of how much you can make. And everybody likes a little money for tobacco and whiskey and a little fun occasionally besides something to eat. And it's best to have a job so that the writer can remain an amateur all the time; never let the writing get involved with earning the daily bread. So I think that any writer should have another job, unless he is rich. . . .

QUESTION: Sir, when you are actually putting something on paper, do you let yourself flow out freely until you, say, feel temporarily empty, or do you have to force yourself to write for an extended period of time?

ANSWER: I have, myself, one simple rule, which is to write it only when it is hot, and always stop before it cools off so I will have something to go back to; never to write myself out. But there is somewhere, whether you realize it or not, there is the policeman that insists on some order, some unity in the work. But I would say to never force yourself to write anything. Once you do that you begin to think, "Well, I might as well force myself to write something and make a little money out of it." And then you are sunk—you are gone, you have stopped being a writer. You must be an amateur writer always. You must do it because it's fun, just like you play a hard set of tennis because it's fun, not for profit—because it's your cup of tea. . . .

QUESTION: Sir, last night you made a statement that you yourself write to tell a story, primarily. And you write it the best way possible and as vividly and as descriptively as possible. Do you believe that most authors are bound by this rule or that they do have some motive such as teaching a lesson or, to put it tritely, that they have a phrase, "The moral of the story is . . ."?

ANSWER: I am inclined to believe that we all write for the same reason. There can be a writer who has been so harried and so outraged by a social condition that he can't keep that social condition out of his story. But he is primarily telling a story of man struggling in the human condition—not a sociological condition but the condition of the heart's dilemma. I don't believe that he realizes until after that he has preached a sermon too. I think that he was primarily telling a story. . . .

QUESTION: Sir, I would like to know exactly what it was that inspired you to become a writer.

ANSWER: Well, I probably was born with the liking for inventing stories. I took it up in 1920. I lived in New Orleans, I was working for a bootlegger. He had a launch that I would take down the Pontchartrain into the Gulf to an island where the rum, the green rum, would be brought up from Cuba and buried, and we would dig it up and bring it back to New Orleans, and he would make scotch or gin or whatever he wanted. He had the bottles labeled and everything. And I would get a hundred dollars a trip for that, and I didn't need much money, so I would get along until I ran out of money again. And I met Sherwood Anderson by chance, and we took to each other from the first. I'd meet him in the afternoon, we would walk and he would talk and I would listen. In the evening we would go somewhere to a speakeasy and drink, and he would talk and I would listen. The next morning he would say, "Well I have to work in the morning," so I wouldn't see him until the next afternoon. And I thought if that's the sort of life writers lead, that's the life for me. So I wrote a book and, as soon as I started, I found out it was fun. And I hadn't seen him and Mrs. Anderson for some time until I met her on the street, and she said, "Are you mad at us?" and I said, "No, ma'am, I'm writing a book," and she said, "Good Lord!" I saw her again, still having fun writing the book, and she said, "Do you want Sherwood to see your book when you finish it?" and I said, "Well, I hadn't thought about it." She said, "Well, he will make a trade with you; if he don't have to read that book, he will tell his publisher to take it." I said, "Done!" So I finished the book and he told Liveright to take it and Liveright took it. And that was how I became a writer—that was the mechanics of it. . . .

INSTRUCTOR: Would you recommend any specific works for these aspiring soldiers to read, sir, or would you recommend a particular sequence of your works that might help them in an approach to your novels?

ANSWER: To my notion, literature is such a pleasant thing, having kept it amateur, that I wouldn't advise anyone to read or write either as a job or duty. But I would say that, read everything. It don't matter what it is. Trash, the best, the worst, read everything. And if anyone does want to be a writer, he certainly must learn his craft, and the best way to learn it is from the people who can do it well. But I would read for pleasure and I would write for pleasure—not for money, not as a duty.

QUESTION: Sir, could you tell us something about your grandfather? I understand that he was an interesting man and may have had some influence on your writing.

ANSWER: Yes, he was. He came into Mississippi on foot when he was fourteen years old. Ran away from home in Virginia looking for a distant relation—found him. At the moment his uncle was in jail for having shot a man. He—well, the story is that he saw a young girl in a yard that he passed and said, "When I get big I am going to marry her." And he did. That is, all this is the sort of thing that any hack writer might invent, you see, as a character. But later he got into politics. He went to the Mexican War as a friend of Jefferson Davis. In 1860 he organized, raised, and paid most of the expenses for the Second Mississippi Infantry and came to Virginia as its colonel. He commanded, as senior colonel, the brigade with Jackson until Lee arrived and took command before First Manassas. He went back after the—in the election of officers the next year at Opequon Creek—he was a martinet, and his men elected his lieutenant colonel to command the regiment, and my grandfather got mad and went back to Mississippi, and got bored after a while and raised a company of partisan cavalry that was finally brigaded into Forrest, and he finished the war there as a cavalryman. And later got in politics and made some money. He built a railroad there—the first railroad in the country. He made the grand tour in Europe, and then he took to writing books, and I may have inherited the ink stain from him. He was killed in a duel before I was born. . . .

QUESTION: Sir, in your book *The Sound and the Fury*, in the first part things are seen through the eyes of the idiot Benjy. Why did you do this?

ANSWER: That was that same hope that I tried to express that the artist feels to condense all experiences onto the head of the pin. That began as the story of a funeral. It's first—the first thing I thought of was the picture of the muddy seat of that little girl's drawers climbing the pear tree to look in the parlor window to see what in the world the grown people were doing that the children couldn't see, and I decided that the most effective way to tell that would be through the eyes of the idiot child who didn't even know, couldn't understand what was going on. And that went on for a while, and I thought it was going to be a ten-page short story. The first thing I knew I had about a hundred pages. I finished, and I still hadn't told that story. So I chose another one of the children, let him try. That went for a hundred pages, and I still hadn't told that story. So I picked out the other one, the one that was the nearest to what we call sane to see if maybe he could unravel the thing. He talked for a hundred pages, he hadn't told it, then I let Faulkner try it for a hundred pages. And when I got done, it still wasn't finished, and so twenty years later I wrote an appendix to it, tried to tell that story. That's all I was doing on the first page, was trying to tell what to me seemed a beautiful and tragic story of that doomed little girl climbing the pear tree to see the funeral. . . .

QUESTION: Why did you have so much trouble trying to end *The Sound and the Fury*? If an author has something in his heart that he has to get down on paper, why is it such a struggle to bring it about?

ANSWER: He wants to make it on paper as startling, as comic, anyway as moving, as true, as important as it seems in the imagination. And in the process of getting it into cold words on the paper, something escapes from it. It's still not as good as when he dreamed it. Which is the reason that when he finishes that to the best of his ability, he writes, tries again —he writes another one. He is still trying to capture that dream, that image of man, either victorious or defeated, in some splendid, beautiful gesture inside the dilemma of the human heart.

QUESTION: Sir, I was wondering if you read much of the criticism that is written about your own work.

ANSWER: Don't read any of it. I'd rather read my fiction at firsthand, I think.

QUESTION: Sir, have you ever desired to be anything besides a writer?

ANSWER: Why sure, I'd like to be a brave, courageous soldier; I have thought of all sorts of things I'd like to be. I'd like to be a beautiful woman. I'd like to be a millionaire.

Flannery O'Connor

(1925–1964)

Flannery O'Connor's first story was published when she was barely twenty-one. Paul Engle, who taught her in the Writer's Workshop at Iowa University, wrote about her at that age: "The will to be a writer was adamant; nothing could resist it, not even her own sensibility about her own work. Cut, alter, try it again . . ."* And so she did, and did, and did, through a series of novels and stories that are among the most concrete, vivid, odd, and disturbing fictions in American literature. When she died in 1964, at thirty-nine, of lupus, against which she had wrestled for fourteen years, she left dozens of texts of lectures she had given, with the barest notations on them as to where they had been read and usually none as to when. A number of these were published in Mystery *and* Manners, *edited by the poet Robert Fitzgerald and his wife Sally, with whom Miss O'Connor had lived in Connecticut for a time; Fitzgerald was Miss O'Connor's literary executor. To the severe, though often funny and piercingly illuminating speech that follows here, Flannery O'Connor brought the great authority of her unwillingness to be hasty or shoddy in her own struggle for art. "No one," she wrote Paul Engle about what turned out to be the five-year labor of writing* Wise Blood, *"will understand my need to work this novel out in my own way better than you, although you may feel that I should work faster. I work all the time, but I cannot work fast. No one can convince me I shouldn't rewrite as much as I do."*

THE NATURE AND AIM OF FICTION

I understand that this is a course called "How the Writer Writes," and that each week you are exposed to a different writer who holds forth on the subject. The only parallel I can think of to this is having the zoo come to you, one animal at a time; and I suspect that what you hear one week from the giraffe is contradicted the next week by the baboon.

My own problem in thinking what I should say to you tonight has been how to interpret such a title as "How the Writer Writes." In the first place, there is no such thing as THE writer, and I think that if you don't know that now, you should by the time such a course as this is over. In fact, I predict that it is the one thing you can be absolutely certain of learning.

But there is a widespread curiosity about writers and how they work,

**Letter to Robert Giroux, July 13, 1971.*

and when a writer talks on this subject, there are always misconceptions and mental rubble for him to clear away before he can even begin to see what he wants to talk about. I am not, of course, as innocent as I look. I know well enough that very few people who are supposedly interested in writing are interested in writing well. They are interested in publishing something, and if possible in making a "killing." They are interested in being a writer, not in writing. They are interested in seeing their names at the top of something printed, it matters not what. And they seem to feel that this can be accomplished by learning certain things about working habits and about markets and about what subjects are currently acceptable.

If this is what you are interested in, I am not going to be of much use to you. I feel that the external habits of the writer will be guided by his common sense or his lack of it and by his personal circumstances; and that these will seldom be alike in two cases. What interests the serious writer is not external habits but what Maritain calls, "the habit of art"; and he explains that "habit" in this sense means a certain quality or virtue of the mind. The scientist has the habit of science; the artist, the habit of art.

Now I'd better stop here and explain how I'm using the word *art*. Art is a word that immediately scares people off, as being a little too grand. But all I mean by art is writing something that is valuable in itself and that works in itself. The basis of art is truth, both in matter and in mode. The person who aims after art in his work aims after truth, in an imaginative sense, no more and no less. St. Thomas said that the artist is concerned with the good of that which is made; and that will have to be the basis of my few words on the subject of fiction.

Now you'll see that this kind of approach eliminates many things from the discussion. It eliminates any concern with the motivation of the writer except as this finds its place inside the work. It also eliminates any concern with the reader in his market sense. It also eliminates that tedious controversy that always rages between people who declare that they write to express themselves and those who declare that they write to fill their pocketbooks, if possible.

In this connection I always think of Henry James. I know of no writer who was hotter after the dollar than James was, or who was more of a conscientious artist. It is true, I think, that these are times when the financial rewards for sorry writing are much greater than those for good writing. There are certain cases in which, if you can only learn to write poorly enough, you can make a great deal of money. But it is not true that if you write well, you won't get published at all. It is true that if you want to write well and live well at the same time, you'd better arrange to inherit money or marry a stockbroker or a rich woman who can operate a typewriter. In any case, whether you write to make money or to express your soul or to insure civil rights or to irritate your grandmother will be a matter for you and your analyst, and the point of departure for this discussion will be the good of the written work.

The kind of written work I'm going to talk about is story-writing, because that's the only kind I know anything about. I'll call any length of fiction a story, whether it be a novel or a shorter piece, and I'll call anything a story in which specific characters and events influence each other to form a meaningful narrative. I find that most people know what a story is until they sit down to write one. Then they find themselves writing a sketch with an essay woven through it, or an essay with a sketch woven through it, or an editorial with a character in it, or a case history with a moral, or some other mongrel thing. When they realize that they aren't writing stories, they decide that the remedy for this is to learn something that they refer to as the "technique of the short story" or "the technique of the novel." Technique in the minds of many is something rigid, something like a formula that you impose on the material; but in the best stories it is something organic, something that grows out of the material, and this being the case, it is different for every story of any account that has ever been written.

I think we have to begin thinking about stories at a much more fundamental level, so I want to talk about one quality of fiction which I think is its least common denominator—the fact that it is concrete—and about a few of the qualities that follow from this. We will be concerned in this with the reader in his fundamental human sense, because the nature of fiction is in large measure determined by the nature of our perceptive apparatus. The beginning of human knowledge is through the senses, and the fiction writer begins where human perception begins. He appeals through the senses, and you cannot appeal to the senses with abstractions. It is a good deal easier for most people to state an abstract idea than to describe and thus re-create some object that they actually see. But the world of the fiction writer is full of matter, and this is what the beginning fiction writers are very loath to create. They are concerned primarily with unfleshed ideas and emotions. They are apt to be reformers and to want to write because they are possessed not by a story but by the bare bones of some abstract notion. They are conscious of problems, not of people, of questions and issues, not of the texture of existence, of case histories and of everything that has a sociological smack, instead of with all those concrete details of life that make actual the mystery of our position on earth.

The Manicheans separated spirit and matter. To them all material things were evil. They sought pure spirit and tried to approach the infinite directly without any mediation of matter. This is also pretty much the modern spirit, and for the sensibility infected with it, fiction is hard if not impossible to write because fiction is so very much an incarnational art.

One of the most common and saddest spectacles is that of a person of really fine sensibility and acute psychological perception trying to write fiction by using these qualities alone. This type of writer will put down one intensely emotional or keenly perceptive sentence after the other, and the result will be complete dullness. The fact is that the materials of the fiction writer are the humblest. Fiction is about everything human and we are made out of dust, and if you scorn getting yourself dusty then you shouldn't try to write fiction. It's not a grand enough job for you.

Now when the fiction writer finally gets this idea through his head and into his habits, he begins to realize what a job of heavy labor the writing of fiction is. A lady who writes, and whom I admire very much, wrote me that she had learned from Flaubert that it takes at least three activated sensuous strokes to make an object real; and she believes that this is connected with our having five senses. If you're deprived of any of them, you're in a bad way, but if you're deprived of more than two at once, you almost aren't present.

All the sentences in *Madame Bovary* could be examined with wonder, but there is one in particular that always stops me in admiration. Flaubert has just shown us Emma at the piano with Charles watching her. He says, "She struck the notes with aplomb and ran from top to bottom of the keyboard without a break. Thus shaken up, the old instrument, whose strings buzzed, could be heard at the other end of the village when the window was open, and often the bailiff's clerk, passing along the highroad, bareheaded and in list slippers, stopped to listen, his sheet of paper in his hand."

The more you look at a sentence like that, the more you can learn from it. At one end of it, we are with Emma and this very solid instrument "whose strings buzzed," and at the other end of it we are across the village with this very concrete clerk in his list slippers. With regard to what happens to Emma in the rest of the novel, we may think that it makes no difference that the instrument has buzzing strings or that the clerk wears list slippers and has a piece of paper in his hand, but Flaubert had to create a believable village to put Emma in. It's always necessary to remember that the fiction writer is much less *immediately* concerned with grand ideas and bristling emotions than he is with putting list slippers on clerks.

Now of course this is something that some people learn only to abuse. This is one reason that strict naturalism is a dead end in fiction. In a strictly naturalistic work the detail is there because it is natural to life, not because it is natural to the work. In a work of art we can be extremely literal, without being in the least naturalistic. Art is selective, and its truthfulness is the truthfulness of the essential that creates movement.

The novel works by a slower accumulation of detail than the short story does. The short story requires more drastic procedures than the novel because more has to be accomplished in less space. The details have to carry more immediate weight. In good fiction, certain of the details will tend to accumulate meaning from the story itself, and when this happens, they become symbolic in their action.

Now the word *symbol* scares a good many people off, just as the word *art* does. They seem to feel that a symbol is some mysterious thing put in arbitrarily by the writer to frighten the common reader—sort of a literary Masonic grip that is only for the initiated. They seem to think that it is a way of saying something that you aren't actually saying, and so if they can be got to read a reputedly symbolic work at all, they approach it as if it were a problem in algebra. Find x. And when they do find or think they find this abstraction, x, then they go off with an elaborate sense of satisfaction and the notion that they have "understood" the story. Many students confuse the *process* of understanding a thing with understanding it.

I think that for the fiction writer himself, symbols are something he uses simply as a matter of course. You might say that these are details that, while having their essential place in the literal level of the story, operate in depth as well as on the surface, increasing the story in every direction.

I think the way to read a book is always to see what happens, but in a good novel, more always happens than we are able to take in at once, more happens than meets the eye. The mind is led on by what it sees into the greater depths that the book's symbols naturally suggest. This is what is meant when critics say that a novel operates on several levels. The truer the symbol, the deeper it leads you, the more meaning it opens up. To take an example from my own book, *Wise Blood*, the hero's rat-colored automobile is his pulpit and his coffin as well as something he thinks of as a means of escape. He is mistaken in thinking that it is a means of escape, of course, and does not really escape his predicament until the car is destroyed by the patrolman. The car is a kind of death-in-life symbol, as his blindness is a life-in-death symbol. The fact that these meanings are there makes the book significant. The reader may not see them but they have their effect on him nonetheless. This is the way the modern novelist sinks, or hides, his theme.

The kind of vision the fiction writer needs to have, or to develop, in order to increase the meaning of his story is called anagogical vision, and that is the kind of vision that is able to see different levels of reality in one image or one situation. The medieval commentators on Scripture found three kinds of meaning in the literal level of the sacred text: one they called allegorical, in which one fact pointed to another; one they called tropological, or moral, which had to do with what should be done; and one they called anagogical, which had to do with the Divine life and our participation in it. Although this was a method applied to biblical exegesis, it was also an attitude toward all of creation, and a way of reading nature which included most possibilities, and I think it is this enlarged view of the human scene that the fiction writer has to cultivate if he is ever going to write stories that have any chance of becoming a permanent part of our literature. It seems to be a paradox that the larger and more complex the personal view, the easier it is to compress it into fiction.

People have a habit of saying, "What is the theme of your story?" and they expect you to give them a statement: "The theme of my story is the economic pressure of the machine on the middle class"—or some such absurdity. And when they've got a statement like that, they go off happy and feel it is no longer necessary to read the story.

Some people have the notion that you read the story and then climb out of it into the meaning, but for the fiction writer himself the whole story is the meaning, because it is an experience, not an abstraction.

Now the second common characteristic of fiction follows from this, and it is that fiction is presented in such a way that the reader has the sense that it is unfolding around him. This doesn't mean he has to identify himself with the character or feel compassion for the character or anything like that. It just means that fiction has to be largely presented rather than reported. Another way to say it is that though fiction is a narrative art, it relies heavily on the element of drama.

The story is not as extreme a form of drama as the play, but if you know anything about the history of the novel, you know that the novel as an art form has developed in the direction of dramatic unity.

The major difference between the novel as written in the eighteenth century and the novel as we usually find it today is the disappearance from it of the author. Fielding, for example, was everywhere in his own work, calling the reader's attention to this point and that, directing him to give his special attention here or there, clarifying this and that incident for him so that he couldn't possibly miss the point. The Victorian novelists did this, too. They were always coming in, explaining and psychologizing about their characters. But along about the time of Henry James, the author began to tell his story in a different way. He began to let it come through the minds and eyes of the characters themselves, and he sat behind the scenes, apparently disinterested. By the time we get to James Joyce, the author is nowhere to be found in the book. The reader is on his own, floundering around in the thoughts of various unsavory characters. He finds himself in the middle of a world apparently without comment.

But it is from the kind of world the writer creates, from the kind of character and detail he invests it with, that a reader can find the intellectual meaning of a book. Once this is found, however, it cannot be drained off and used as a substitute for the book. As the late John Peale Bishop said: "You can't say Cézanne painted apples and a tablecloth and have said what Cézanne painted." The novelist makes his statements by selection, and if he is any good, he selects every word for a reason, every detail for a reason, every incident for a reason, and arranges them in a certain time-sequence for a reason. He demonstrates something that cannot possibly be demonstrated any other way than with a whole novel.

Art forms evolve until they reach their ultimate perfection, or until they reach some state of petrifaction, or until some new element is grafted on and a new art form made. But however the past of fiction has been or however the future will be, the present state of the case is that a piece of fiction must be very much a self-contained dramatic unit.

This means that it must carry its meaning inside it. It means that any abstractly expressed compassion or piety or morality in a piece of fiction is only a statement added to it. It means that you can't make an inadequate dramatic action complete by putting a statement of meaning on the end of it or in the middle of it or at the beginning of it. It means that when you write fiction you are speaking *with* character and action, not *about* character and action. The writer's moral sense must coincide with his dramatic sense.

It's said that when Henry James received a manuscript that he didn't like, he would return it with the comment, "You have chosen a good subject and are treating it in a straightforward manner." This usually pleased the person getting the manuscript back, but it was the worst thing that James could think of to say, for he knew, better than anybody else, that the straightforward manner is seldom equal to the complications of the good subject. There may never be anything new to say, but there is always a new way to say it, and since, in art, the way of saying a thing becomes a part of what is said, every work of art is unique and requires fresh attention.

It's always wrong of course to say that you can't do this or you can't do that in fiction. You can do anything you can get away with, but nobody has ever gotten away with much.

I believe that it takes a rather different type of disposition to write novels than to write short stories, granted that both require fundamentally fictional talents. I have a friend who writes both, and she says that when she stops a novel to work on short stories, she feels as if she has just left a dark wood to be set upon by wolves. The novel is a more diffused form and more suited to those who like to linger along the way; it also requires a more massive energy. For those of us who want to get the agony over in a hurry, the novel is a burden and a pain. But no matter which fictional form you are using, you are writing a story, and in a story something has to happen. A perception is not a story, and no amount of sensitivity can make a story-writer out of you if you just plain don't have a gift for telling a story.

But there's a certain grain of stupidity that the writer of fiction can hardly do without, and this is the quality of having to stare, of not getting the point at once. The longer you look at one object, the more of the world you see in it; and it's well to remember that the serious fiction writer always writes about the whole world, no matter how limited his particular scene. For him, the bomb that was dropped on Hiroshima affects life on the Oconee River, and there's not anything he can do about it.

People are always complaining that the modern novelist has no hope and that the picture he paints of the world is unbearable. The only answer to this is that people without hope do not write novels. Writing a novel is a terrible experience, during which the hair often falls out and the teeth decay. I'm always highly irritated by people who imply that writing fiction is an escape from reality. It is a plunge into reality and it's very shocking to the system. If the novelist is not sustained by a hope of money, then he must be sustained by a hope of salvation, or he simply won't survive the ordeal.

People without hope not only don't write novels, but what is more to the point, they don't read them. They don't take long looks at anything, because they lack the courage. The way to despair is to refuse to have any kind of experience, and the novel, of course, is a way to have experience. The lady who only read books that improved her mind was taking a safe course —and a hopeless one. She'll never know whether her mind is improved or not, but should she ever, by some mistake, read a great novel, she'll know mighty well that something is happening to her.

A good many people have the notion that nothing happens in modern fiction and that nothing is supposed to happen, that it is the style now to write a story in which nothing happens. Actually, I think more happens in modern fiction—with less furor on the surface—than has ever happened in fiction before. A good example of this is a story by Caroline Gordon called "Summer Dust." It's in a collection of her stories called *The Forest of the South*, which is a book that repays study.

"Summer Dust" is divided into four short sections, which don't at first appear to have any relation between them and which are minus any narrative connection. Reading the story is at first rather like standing a foot away from an impressionistic painting, then gradually moving back until it comes into focus. When you reach the right distance, you suddenly see that a world has been created—and a world in action—and that a complete story has been told, by a wonderful kind of understatement. It has been told more by showing what happens around the story than by touching directly on the story itself.

You may say that this requires such an intelligent and sophisticated reader that it is not worth writing, but I'm rather inclined to think that it is more a false sophistication that prevents people from understanding this kind of story than anything else. Without being naturalistic in the least, a story like "Summer Dust" is actually much closer in form to life than a story that follows a narrative sequence of events.

The type of mind that can understand good fiction is not necessarily the educated mind, but it is at all times the kind of mind that is willing to have its sense of mystery deepened by contact with reality, and its sense of reality deepened by contact with mystery. Fiction should be both canny and uncanny. In a good deal of popular criticism, there is the notion operating that all fiction has to be about the Average Man, and has to depict average ordinary everyday life, that every fiction writer must produce what used to be called "a slice of life." But if life, in that sense, satisfied us, there would be no sense in producing literature at all.

Conrad said that his aim as a fiction writer was to render the highest possible justice to the visible universe. That sounds very grand, but it is really very humble. It means that he subjected himself at all times to the limitations that reality imposed, but that reality for him was not simply coextensive with the visible. He was interested in rendering justice to the visible universe because it suggested an invisible one, and he explained his own intentions as a novelist in this way:

> . . . and if the [artist's] conscience is clear, his answer to those who in the full-ness of a wisdom which looks for immediate profit, demand specifically to be edified, consoled, amused; who demand to be promptly improved, or encouraged, or frightened, or shocked or charmed, must run thus: My task which I am trying to achieve is, by the power of the written word, to make you hear, to make you feel—it is, before all, to make you *see*. That—and no more, and it is everything. If I succeed, you shall find there, according to your deserts, encouragement, consolation, fear, charm, all you demand—and, perhaps, also that glimpse of truth for which you have forgotten to ask.

You may think from all I say that the reason I write is to make the reader see what I see, and that writing fiction is primarily a missionary activity. Let me straighten this out.

Last spring I talked here, and one of the girls asked me, "Miss O'Connor, why do you write?" and I said, "Because I'm good at it," and at once I felt a considerable disapproval in the atmosphere. I felt that this was not thought by the majority to be a high-minded answer; but it was the only answer I could give. I had not been asked why I write the way I do, but why I write at all; and to that question there is only one legitimate answer.

There is no excuse for anyone to write fiction for public consumption unless he has been called to do so by the presence of a gift. It is the nature of fiction not to be good for much unless it is good in itself.

A gift of any kind is a considerable responsibility. It is a mystery in itself, something gratuitous and wholly undeserved, something whose real uses will probably always be hidden from us. Usually the artist has to suffer certain deprivations in order to use his gift with integrity. Art is a virtue of the practical intellect, and the practice of any virtue demands a certain asceticism and a very definite leaving-behind of the niggardly part of the ego. The writer has to judge himself with a stranger's eye and a stranger's severity. The prophet in him has to see the freak. No art is sunk in the self, but rather, in art the self becomes self-forgetful in order to meet the demands of the thing seen and the thing being made.

I think it is usually some form of self-inflation that destroys the free use of a gift. This may be the pride of the reformer or the theorist, or it may only be that simple-minded self-appreciation which uses its own sincerity as a standard of truth. If you have read the very vocal writers from San Francisco, you may have got the impression that the first thing you must do in order to be an artist is to loose yourself from the bonds of reason, and thereafter, anything that rolls off the top of your head will be of great value. Anyone's unrestrained feelings are considered worth listening to because they are unrestrained and because they are feelings.

St. Thomas called art "reason in making." This is a very cold and very beautiful definition, and if it is unpopular today, this is because reason has lost ground among us. As grace and nature have been separated, so imagination and reason have been separated, and this always means an end to art. The artist uses his reason to discover an answering reason in everything he sees. For him, to be reasonable is to find, in the object, in the situation, in the sequence, the spirit which makes it itself. This is not an easy or simple thing to do. It is to intrude upon the timeless, and that is only done by the violence of a single-minded respect for the truth.

It follows from all this that there is no technique that can be discovered and applied to make it possible for one to write. If you go to a school where there are classes in writing, these classes should not be to teach you how to write, but to teach you the limits and possibilities of words and the respect due them. One thing that is always with the writer—no matter how long he has written or how good he is—is the continuing process of learning how to write. As soon as the writer "learns to write," as soon as he knows what he is going to find, and discovers a way to say what he knew all along, or worse still, a way to say nothing, he is finished. If a writer is any good, what he makes will have its source in a realm much larger than that which his conscious mind can encompass and will always be a greater surprise to him than it can ever be to his reader.

I don't know which is worse—to have a bad teacher or no teacher at all. In any case, I believe the teacher's work should be largely negative. He can't put the gift into you, but if he finds it there, he can try to keep it from going in an obviously wrong direction. We can learn how not to write, but this is a discipline that does not simply concern writing itself but concerns the whole intellectual life. A mind cleared of false emotion and false sentiment and egocentricity is going to have at least those roadblocks removed from its path. If you don't think cheaply, then there at least won't be the quality of cheapness in your writing, even though you may not be able to write well. The teacher can try to weed out what is positively bad, and this should be the aim of the whole college. Any discipline can help your writing: logic, mathematics, theology, and of course and particularly drawing. Anything that helps you to see, anything that makes you look. The writer should never be ashamed of staring. There is nothing that doesn't require his attention.

We hear a great deal of lamentation these days about writers having all taken themselves to the colleges and universities where they live decorously instead of going out and getting firsthand information about life. The fact is that anybody who has survived his childhood has enough information about life to last him the rest of his days. If you can't make something out of a little experience, you probably won't be able to make it out of a lot. The writer's business is to contemplate experience, not to be merged in it.

Everywhere I go I'm asked if I think the universities stifle writers. My opinion is that they don't stifle enough of them. There's many a best-seller that could have been prevented by a good teacher. The idea of being a writer attracts a good many shiftless people, those who are merely burdened with poetic feelings or afflicted with sensibility. . . .

Now in every writing class you find people who care nothing about writing, because they think they are already writers by virtue of some experience they've had. It is a fact that if, either by nature or training, these people can learn to write badly enough, they can make a great deal of money, and in a way it seems a shame to deny them this opportunity; but then, unless the college is a trade school, it still has its responsibility to truth, and I believe myself that these people should be stifled with all deliberate speed.

Presuming that the people left have some degree of talent, the question is what can be done for them in a writing class. I believe the teacher's work is largely negative, that it is largely a matter of saying "This doesn't work because . . ." or "This does work because . . ." The *because* is very important. The teacher can help you understand the nature of your medium, and he can guide you in your reading. I don't believe in classes where students criticize each other's manuscripts. Such criticism is generally composed in equal parts of ignorance, flattery, and spite. It's the blind leading the blind, and it can be dangerous. A teacher who tries to impose a way of writing on you can be dangerous too. Fortunately, most teachers I've known were too lazy to do this. In any case, you should beware of those who appear overenergetic.

In the last twenty years the colleges have been emphasizing creative writing to such an extent that you almost feel that any idiot with a nickel's worth of talent can emerge from a writing class able to write a competent story. In fact, so many people can now write competent stories that the short story as a medium is in danger of dying of competence. We want competence, but competence by itself is deadly. What is needed is the vision to go with it, and you do not get this from a writing class.

PART TWO

The Whole Intricate Question of Method

Sooner or later, and usually sooner than late, and often too soon, the novice begins to think about workmanship—about what E. M. Forster once called, in a quiet joke, the sounds we so often hear a novelist make, especially toward the end of his story, of "hammering and screwing." If only the writer's craft *were* the carpenter's, and the novel were a good solid chest of drawers! The apprentice could easily learn to fit and glue a tenon into a mortise with precision; he could soon learn the secrets of giving high finish with varnish. But art in fiction is more elusive than art in cabinetmaking; as we have seen, it is a matter of the *wee bit*, it is a matter of temperament, it is a matter of manner. How can we learn the tricks of the trade from a Faulkner who confesses that he runs along behind his characters with pencil in hand, trying to keep up with what they are saying and doing? The following section on method cannot, alas, serve as a manual of conscious technical means for the achievement of art. Each of the four authors in this section has extremely valuable things to tell us. Any writer can learn much from any one of them. The trouble is, they contradict each other. Each flies off in his own idiosyncratic direction. We are left with an exhilarating but baffling sense of diversity of means, a sense that there *are* right ways of doing things, but that for each writer those right ways are special ways, which he must somehow discover for himself.

Percy Lubbock

(1879–1965)

Conrad has set the writer's aim. "My task which I am trying to achieve is, by the power of the written word, to make you hear, to make you feel—it is, before all, to make you see. *That—and no more, and it is everything." Above all, to* see. *But at once questions of craft arise. See what from where? Is the storyteller to be in the reader's field of vision? Does the reader look over the author's shoulder at the play of action? Does he look into the minstrel's face? Through whose eyes does the reader really see—his own, the author's, a character's?*

These are questions Percy Lubbock takes up in The Craft of Fiction. *Published in 1921, the book was a landmark: a critic had devoted a whole volume to fiction as an art. Lubbock was the editor of the letters of Henry James and of the last few volumes of the New York edition of James's novels; he was a Jamesian, an admirer of conscious artistic control. His method in the book is to use a series of novels to exemplify various ways of working out "the relation in which the narrator stands to the story."* War and Peace, Madame Bovary, Vanity Fair, Maupassant's stories, Henry Esmond, The Ambassadors, The Wings of the Dove, The Awkward Age, *the novels of Balzac,* Anna Karenina—*one by one we see the different means great novelists have used to make picture and drama visible in readers' eyes. This passage is the summary chapter.*

FROM
THE CRAFT OF FICTION

The whole intricate question of method, in the craft of fiction, I take to be governed by the question of the point of view—the question of the relation in which the narrator stands to the story. He tells it as *he* sees it, in the first place; the reader faces the story-teller and listens, and the story may be told so vivaciously that the presence of the minstrel is forgotten, and the scene becomes visible, peopled with the characters of the tale. It may be so, it very often is so for a time. But it is not so always, and the story-teller himself grows conscious of a misgiving. If the spell is weakened at any moment, the listener is recalled from the scene to the mere author before him, and the story rests only upon the author's direct assertion. Is it not possible, then, to introduce another point of view, to set up a fresh narrator to bear the brunt of the reader's scrutiny? If the story-teller is *in* the story himself, the author is dramatized; his assertions gain in weight, for they are backed by the presence of the narrator in the pictured scene. It is advantage scored; the author has shifted his responsibility, and it now falls where the reader can see and measure it; the arbitrary quality which may at any time be detected in the author's voice is disguised in the voice of his spokesman. Nothing is now imported into the story from without; it is self-contained, it has no associations with anyone beyond its circle.

Such is the first step towards dramatization, and in very many a story it may be enough. The spokesman is there, in recognizable relation with his matter; no question of his authority can arise. But now a difficulty may be started by the nature of the tale that he tells. If he has nothing to do but to relate what he has seen, what anyone might have seen in his position, his account will serve very well; there is no need for more. Let him unfold his chronicle as it appears in his memory. But if he is himself the subject of his story, if the story involves a searching exploration of his own consciousness, an account in his own words, after the fact, is not by any means the best imaginable. Far better it would be to see him while his mind is actually at work in the agitation, whatever it may be, which is to make the book. The matter would then be objective and visible to the reader, instead of reaching him in the form of a report at second hand. But how to manage this without falling back upon the author and *his* report, which has already been tried and for good reasons, as it seemed, abandoned? It is managed by a kind of repetition of the same stroke, a further shift of the point of view. The spectator, the listener, the reader, is now himself to be placed at the angle of vision; not an account or a report, more or less convincing, is to be offered him, but a direct sight of the matter itself, while it is passing. Nobody expounds or explains; the story is enacted by its look and behaviour at particular moments. By the first stroke the narrator was brought into the book and set before the reader; but the action appeared only in his narrative. Now the action is there, proceeding while the pages are turned; the narrator is forestalled, he is watched while the story is in the making. Such is the progress of the writer of fiction towards drama; such is his method of evading the drawbacks of a mere reporter and assuming the advantages, as far as possible, of a dramatist. How far he may choose to push the process in his book— that is a matter to be decided by the subject; it entirely depends upon the kind of effect that the theme demands. It may respond to all the dramatization it can get, it may give all that it has to give for less. The subject dictates the method.

And now let the process be reversed, let us start with the purely dramatic subject, the story that will tell itself in perfect rightness, unaided, to the eye of the reader. This story never deviates from a strictly scenic form; one occasion or episode follows another, with no interruption for any reflective summary of events. Necessarily it must be so, for it is only while the episode is proceeding that no question of a narrator can arise; when the scene closes the play ceases till the opening of the next. To glance upon the story from a height and to give a general impression of its course —this is at once to remove the point of view from the reader and to set up a new one somewhere else; the method is no longer consistent, no longer purely dramatic. And the dramatic story is not only scenic, it is also limited to so much as the ear can hear and the eye see. In rigid drama of this kind there is naturally no admission of the reader into the private mind of any of the characters; their thoughts and motives are transmuted into action. A subject wrought to this pitch of objectivity is no doubt given weight and compactness and authority in the highest degree; it is like a piece of modelling, standing in clear space, casting its shadow. It is the most finished form that fiction can take.

But evidently it is not a form to which fiction can aspire in general. It implies many sacrifices, and these will easily seem to be more than the subject can usefully make. It is out of the question, of course, wherever the main burden of the story lies within some particular consciousness, in the study of a soul, the growth of a character, the changing history of a temperament; there the subject would be needlessly crossed and strangled by dramatization pushed to its limit. It is out of the question, again, wherever the story is too big, too comprehensive, too widely ranging, to be treated scenically, with no opportunity for general and panoramic survey; it has been discovered, indeed, that even a story of this kind *may* fall into a long succession of definite scenes, under some hands, but it has also appeared that in doing so it incurs unnecessary disabilities, and will likely suffer. These stories, therefore, which will not naturally accommodate themselves to the reader's point of view, and the reader's alone, we regard as rather pictorial than dramatic—meaning that they call for some narrator, somebody who *knows*, to contemplate the facts and create an impression of them. Whether it is the omniscient author or a man in the book, he must gather up his experience, compose a vision of it as it exists in his mind, and lay *that* before the reader. It is the reflection of an experience; and though there may be all imaginable diversity of treatment within the limits of the reflection, such is its essential character. In a pictorial book the principle of the structure involves a point of view which is not the reader's.

It is open to the pictorial book, however, to use a method in its picture-making that is really no other than the method of drama. It is somebody's experience, we say, that is to be reported, the general effect that many things have left upon a certain mind; it is a fusion of innumerable elements, the deposit of a lapse of time. The straightforward way to render it would be for the narrator—the author or his selected creature—to view the past retrospectively and discourse upon it, to recall and mediate and summarize. That is picture-making in its natural form, using its own method. But exactly as in drama the subject is distributed among the characters and enacted by them, so in picture the effect may be entrusted to the elements, the reactions of the moment, and *performed* by these. The mind of the narrator becomes the stage, his voice is no longer heard. His voice *is* heard so long as there is narrative of any sort, whether he is speaking in person or is reported obliquely; his voice is heard, because in either case the language and the intonation are his, the direct expression of his experience. In the drama of his mind there is no personal voice, for there is no narrator; the point of view becomes the reader's once more. The shapes of thought in the man's mind tell their own story. And that is the art of picture-making when it uses the dramatic method.

But it cannot always do so. Constantly it must be necessary to offer the reader a summary of facts, an impression of a train of events, that can only be given as somebody's narration. Suppose it were required to render the general effect of a certain year in a man's life, a year that has filled his mind with a swarm of many memories. Looking into his consciousness after the year has gone, we might find much there that would indicate the nature of the year's events without any word on his part; the flickers and flashes of thought from moment to moment might indeed tell us much. But we shall need an account from him too, no doubt; too much has happened in a year to be wholly acted, as I call it, in the movement of the man's thought. He must narrate—he must make, that is to say, a picture of the events as he sees them, glancing back. Now if he speaks in the first person there can, of course, be no uncertainty in the point of view; he has his fixed position, he cannot leave it. His description will represent the face that the facts in their sequence turned towards *him*; the field of vision is defined with perfect distinctness, and his story cannot stray outside it. The reader, then, may be said to watch a reflection of the facts in a mirror of which the edge is nowhere in doubt; it is rounded by the bounds of the narrator's own personal experience.

This limitation may have a convenience and a value in the story, it may contribute to the effect. But it need not be forfeited, it is clear, if the first person is changed to the third. The author may use the man's field of vision and keep as faithfully within it as though the man were speaking for himself. In that case he retains this advantage and adds to it another, one that is likely to be very much greater. For now, while the point of view is still fixed in space, still assigned to the man in the book, it is free in *time*; there no longer stretches, between the narrator and the events of which he speaks, a certain tract of time, across which the past must appear in a more or less distant perspective. All the variety obtainable by a shifting relation to the story in time is thus in the author's hand; the safe serenity of a far retrospect, the promising or threatening urgency of the present, every gradation between the two, can be drawn into the whole effect of the book, and all of it without any change of the seeing eye. It is a liberty that may help the story indefinitely, raising this matter into strong relief, throwing that other back into vaguer shade.

And next, still keeping mainly and ostensibly to the same point of view, the author has the chance of using a much greater latitude than he need appear to use. The seeing eye is with somebody in the book, but its vision is reinforced; the picture contains more, becomes richer and fuller, because it is the author's as well as his creature's, both at once. Nobody notices, but in fact there are now two brains behind that eye; and one of them is the author's, who adopts and shares the *position* of his creature, and at the same time supplements his wit. If you analyse the picture that is now presented, you find that it is not all the work of the personage whose vision the author has adopted. There are touches in it that go beyond any sensation of his, and indicate that someone else is looking over his shoulder —seeing things from the same angle, but seeing more, bringing another mind to bear upon the scene. It is an easy and natural extension of the personage's power of observation. The impression of the scene may be deepened as much as need be; it is not confined to the scope of one mind, and yet there is no blurring of the focus by a double point of view. And thus what I have called the sound of the narrator's voice (it is impossible to avoid this mixture of metaphors) is less insistent in oblique narration, even while it seems to be following the very same argument that it would in direct, because another voice is speedily mixed and blended with it.

So this is another resource upon which the author may draw according to his need; sometimes it will be indispensable, and generally, I suppose, it will be useful. It means that he keeps a certain hold upon the narrator *as an object*; the sentient character in the story, round whom it is grouped, is not utterly subjective, completely given over to the business of seeing and feeling on behalf of the reader. It is a considerable point; for it helps to meet one of the great difficulties in the story which is carefully aligned towards a single consciousness and consistently so viewed. In that story the man or woman who acts as the vessel of sensation is always in danger of seeming a light, uncertain weight compared with the other people in the book—simply because the other people are objective images, plainly outlined, while the seer in the midst is precluded from that advantage, and must see without being directly seen. He, who doubtless ought to bulk in the story more massively than anyone, tends to remain the least recognizable of the company, and even to dissolve in a kind of impalpable blur. By his method (which I am supposing to have been adopted in full strictness) the author is of course forbidden to look this central figure in the face, to describe and discuss him; the light cannot be turned upon him immediately. And very often we see the method becoming an embarrassment to the author in consequence, and the devices by which he tries to mitigate it, and to secure some reflected sight of the seer, may even be tiresomely obvious. But the resource of which I speak is of a finer sort.

It gives to the author the power of imperceptibly edging away from the seer, leaving his consciousness, ceasing to use his eyes—though still without substituting the eyes of another. To revert for a moment to the story told in the first person, it is plain that in that case the narrator has no such liberty; his own consciousness must always lie open; the part that he plays in the story can never appear in the same terms, on the same plane, as that of the other people. Though he is not visible in the story to the reader, as the others are, he is at every moment *nearer* than they, in his capacity of the seeing eye, the channel of vision; nor can he put off his function, he must continue steadily to see and to report. But when the author is reporting *him* there is a margin of freedom. The author has not so completely identified himself, as narrator, with his hero that he can give him no objective weight whatever. If necessary he can allow him something of the value of a detached and phenomenal personage, like the rest of the company in the story, and that without violating the principle of his method. He cannot make his hero actually visible—there the method is uncompromising; he cannot step forward, leaving the man's point of view, and picture him from without. But he can place the man at the same distance from the reader as the other people, he can almost lend him the same effect, he can make of him a dramatic actor upon the scene.

And how? Merely by closing (when it suits him) the open consciousness of the seer—which he can do without any look of awkwardness or violence, since it conflicts in no way with the rule of the method. That rule only required that the author, having decided to share the point of view of his character, should not proceed to set up another of his own; it did not debar him from allowing his hero's act of vision to lapse, his function as the sentient creature in the story to be intermitted. The hero (I call him so for convenience—he may, of course, be quite a subordinate onlooker in the story) can at any moment become impenetrable, a human being whose thought is sealed from us; and it may seem a small matter, but in fact it has the result that he drops into the plane of the people whom he has hitherto been seeing and judging. Hitherto subjective, communicative in solitude, he has been in a category apart from them; but now he may mingle with the rest, engage in talk with them, and his presence and his talk are no more to the fore than theirs. As soon as some description or discussion of them is required, then, of course, the seer must resume his part and unseal his mind; but meanwhile, though the reader gets no direct view of him, still he is there in the dialogue with the rest, his speech (like theirs) issues from a hidden mind and has the same dramatic value. It is enough, very likely, to harden our image of him, to give precision to his form, to save him from dissipation into that luminous blur of which I spoke just now. For the author it is a resource to be welcomed on that account, and not on that account alone.

For besides the greater definition that the seer acquires, thus detached from us at times and relegated to the plane of his companions, there is much benefit for the subject of the story. In the tale that is quite openly and nakedly somebody's narrative there is this inherent weakness, that a scene of true drama is impossible. In true drama nobody *reports* the scene; it *appears*, it is constituted by the aspect of the occasion and the talk and the conduct of the people. When one of the people who took part in it sets out to report the scene, there is at once a mixture and a confusion of effects; for his own contribution to the scene has a different quality from the rest, cannot have the same crispness and freshness, cannot strike in with a new or unexpected note. This weakness may be well disguised, and like everything else in the whole craft it may become a positive and right effect in a particular story, for a particular purpose; it is always there, however, and it means that the full and unmixed effect of drama is denied to the story that is rigidly told from the point of view of one of the actors. But when that point of view is held in the manner I have described, when it is open to the author to withdraw from it silently and to leave the actor to play his part, true drama—or something so like it that it passes for true drama—is always possible; all the figures of the scene are together in it, one no nearer than another. Nothing is wanting save only that direct, unequivocal sight of the hero which the method does indeed absolutely forbid.

Finally there is the old, immemorial, unguarded, unsuspicious way of telling a story, where the author entertains the reader, the minstrel draws his audience round him, the listeners rely upon his word. The voice is then confessedly and alone the author's; he imposes no limitation upon his freedom to tell what he pleases and to regard his matter from a point of view that is solely his own. And if there is anyone who can proceed in this fashion without appearing to lose the least of the advantages of a more cautious style, for him the minstrel's licence is proper and appropriate; there is no more to be said. But we have yet to discover him; and it is not very presumptuous in a critic, as things are, to declare that a story will never yield its best to a writer who takes the easiest way with it. He curtails his privileges and chooses a narrower method, and immediately the story responds; its better condition is too notable to be forgotten, when once it has caught the attention of a reader. The advantages that it gains are not nameless, indefinable graces, pleasing to a critic but impossible to fix in words; they are solid, we can describe and recount them. And I can only conclude that if the novel is still as full of energy as it seems to be, and is not a form of imaginative art that, having seen the best of its day, is preparing to give place to some other, the novelist will not be willing to miss the inexhaustible opportunity that lies in its treatment. The easy way is no way at all; the only way is that by which the most is made of the story to be told, and the most was never made of any story except by a choice and disciplined method.

E. M. Forster

(1879–1970)

It was ironic that Percy Lubbock's book appeared in the same year as James Joyce's Ulysses. *The one pointed, with delicacy, to the finest molds on the shelf; the other shattered them all. Three years later another novel was published, a far less explosive one than Joyce's but a fine book all the same, E. M. Forster's* A Passage to India. *Forster's novel, while tightly controlled in some ways, had also a strange, disturbing, effective looseness about it; within well-built walls, an eerie largeness; room for echoes, whispers, overtones—and prophecy. Three years later still Forster published his reflections on the craft that had gone into* Howard's End *and his other novels, as well as into* A Passage to India. *At one point in this book he acknowledges Percy Lubbock's earlier work. "Those who follow him," Forster writes, "will lay a sure foundation for the aesthetics of fiction." With a modesty which is something of a trap for the unwary reader, he says he cannot promise such a foundation, for his is a "ramshackly survey"; he is less interested in formulas than in "the power of the writer to bounce the reader into accepting what he says." There is more to a novel than point of view, which is only one of its several "aspects." The excerpts from Forster's book that follow are somewhat lean; the book itself is crowded with rich examples from many novels. These selections may at least lead some readers to the original.*

FROM
ASPECTS OF THE NOVEL

The Story

We shall all agree that the fundamental aspect of the novel is its story-telling aspect, but we shall voice our assent in different tones, and it is on the precise tone of voice we employ now that our subsequent conclusions will depend.

Let us listen to three voices. If you ask one type of man, "What does a novel do?" he will reply placidly: "Well—I don't know—it seems a funny sort of question to ask—a novel's a novel—well, I don't know—I suppose it kind of tells a story, so to speak." He is quite good-tempered and vague, and probably driving a motor-bus at the same time and paying no more attention to literature than it merits. Another man, whom I visualize as on a golf-course, will be aggressive and brisk. He will reply: "What does a novel do? Why, tell a story of course, and I've no use for it if it didn't. I like a story. Very bad taste on my part, no doubt, but I like a story. You can take your art, you can take your literature, you can take your music, but give me a good story. And I like a story to be a story, mind, and my wife's the same." And a third man he says in a sort of drooping regretful voice, "Yes—oh, dear, yes—the novel tells a story." I respect and admire the first speaker. I detest and fear the second. And the third is myself. Yes—oh, dear, yes—the novel tells a story. That is the fundamental aspect without which it could not exist. That is the highest factor common to all novels, and I wish that it was not so, that it could be something different—melody, or perception of the truth, not this low atavistic form.

For the more we look at the story (the story that is a story, mind), the more we disentangle it from the finer growths that it supports, the less shall we find to admire. It runs like a backbone—or may I say a tapeworm, for its beginning and end are arbitrary. It is immensely old—goes back to neolithic times, perhaps to paleolithic. Neanderthal man listened to stories, if one may judge by the shape of his skull. The primitive audience was an audience of shock-heads, gaping round the campfire, fatigued with contending against the mammoth or the woolly rhinoceros, and only kept awake by suspense. What would happen next? The novelist droned on, and as soon as the audience guessed what happened next, they either fell asleep or killed him. We can estimate the dangers incurred when we think of the career of Scheherazade in somewhat later times. Scheherazade avoided her fate because she knew how to wield the weapon of suspense—the only literary tool that has any effect upon tyrants and savages. Great novelist though she was—exquisite in her descriptions, tolerant in her judgments, ingenious in her incidents, advanced in her morality, vivid in her delineations of character, expert in her knowledge of three Oriental capitals—it was yet on none of these gifts that she relied when trying to save her life from her intolerable husband. They were but incidental. She only survived because she managed to keep the king wondering what would happen next. Each time she saw the sun rising she stopped in the middle of a sentence, and left him gaping. "At this moment Scheherazade saw the morning appearing and, discreet, was silent." This uninteresting little phrase is the backbone of the *One Thousand and One Nights*, the tapeworm by which they are tied together and the life of a most accomplished princess was preserved.

We are all like Scheherazade's husband, in that we want to know what happens next. That is universal and that is why the backbone of a novel has to be a story. Some of us want to know nothing else—there is nothing in us but primeval curiosity, and consequently our other literary judgments are ludicrous. And now the story can be defined. It is a narrative of events arranged in their time sequence—dinner coming after breakfast, Tuesday after Monday, decay after death, and so on. *Qua* story, it can only have one merit: that of making the audience want to know what happens next. And conversely it can only have one fault: that of making the audience not want to know what happens next. These are the only two criticisms that can be made on the story that is a story. It is the lowest and simplest of literary organisms. Yet it is the highest factor common to all the very complicated organisms known as novels.

When we isolate the story like this from the nobler aspects through which it moves, and hold it out on the forceps—wriggling and interminable, the naked worm of time—it presents an appearance that is both unlovely and dull. But we have much to learn from it. Let us begin by considering it in connection with daily life.

Daily life is also full of the time-sense. We think one event occurs after or before another, the thought is often in our minds, and much of our talk and action proceeds on the assumption. Much of our talk and action, but not all; there seems something else in life besides time, something which may conveniently be called "value," something which is measured not by minutes or hours, but by intensity, so that when we look at our past it does not stretch back evenly but piles up into a few notable pinnacles, and when we look at the future it seems sometimes a wall, sometimes a cloud, sometimes a sun, but never a chronological chart. Neither memory nor anticipation is much interested in Father Time, and all dreamers, artists and lovers are partially delivered from his tyranny; he can kill them, but he cannot secure their attention, and at the very moment of doom, when the clock collected in the tower its strength and struck, they may be looking the other way. So daily life, whatever it may be really, is practically composed of two lives—the life in time and the life by values—and our conduct reveals a double allegiance. "I only saw her for five minutes, but it was worth it." There you have both allegiances in a single sentence. And what the story does is to narrate the life in time. And what the entire novel does—if it is a good novel—is to include the life by values as well; using devices hereafter to be examined. It, also, pays a double allegiance. But in it, in the novel, the allegiance to time is imperative: no novel could be written without it. Whereas in daily life the allegiance may not be necessary: we do not know, and the experience of certain mystics suggests, indeed, that it is not necessary, and that we are quite mistaken in supposing that Monday is followed by Tuesday, or death by decay. It is always possible for you or me in daily life to deny that time exists and act accordingly even if we become unintelligible and are sent by our fellow citizens to what they choose to call a lunatic asylum. But it is never possible for a novelist to deny time inside the fabric of his novel: he must cling however lightly to the thread of his story, he must touch the interminable tapeworm, otherwise he becomes unintelligible, which, in his case, is a blunder. . . .

People

Having discussed the story—that simple and fundamental aspect of the novel—we can turn to a more interesting topic: the actors. We need not ask what happened next, but to whom did it happen; the novelist will be appealing to our intelligence and imagination, not merely to our curiosity. A new emphasis enters his voice: emphasis upon value. . . .

Since the novelist is himself a human being, there is an affinity between him and his subject-matter which is absent in many other forms of art. The historian is also linked, though, as we shall see, less intimately. The painter and sculptor need not be linked: that is to say they need not represent human beings unless they wish, no more need the poet, while the musician cannot represent them even if he wishes, without the help of a programme. The novelist, unlike many of his colleagues, makes up a number of word-masses roughly describing himself (roughly: niceties shall come later), gives them names and sex, assigns them plausible gestures, and causes them to speak by the use of inverted commas, and perhaps to behave consistently. These word-masses are his characters. They do not come thus coldly to his mind, they may be created in delirious excitement; still, their nature is conditioned by what he guesses about other people, and about himself, and is further modified by the other aspects of his work. This last point—the relation of characters to the other aspects of the novel—will form the subject of a future inquiry. At present we are occupied with their relation to actual life. What is the difference between people in a novel and people like the novelist or like you, or like me, or Queen Victoria?

There is bound to be a difference. If a character in a novel is exactly like Queen Victoria—not rather like but exactly like—then it actually is Queen Victoria, and the novel, or all of it that the character touches, becomes a memoir. A memoir is history, it is based on evidence. A novel is based on evidence $+$ or $-$ x, the unknown quantity being the temperament of the novelist, and the unknown quantity always modifies the effect of the evidence, and sometimes transforms it entirely.

The historian deals with actions, and with the characters of men only so far as he can deduce them from their actions. He is quite as much concerned with character as the novelist, but he can only know of its existence when it shows on the surface. If Queen Victoria had not said, "We are not amused," her neighbours at table would not have known she was not amused, and her ennui could never have been announced to the public. She might have frowned, so that they would have deduced her state from that—looks and gestures are also historical evidence. But if she remained impassive—what would anyone know? The hidden life is, by definition, hidden. The hidden life that appears in external signs is hidden no longer, has entered the realm of action. And it is the function of the novelist to reveal the hidden life at its source: to tell us more about Queen Victoria than could be known, and thus to produce a character who is not the Queen Victoria of history.

The interesting and sensitive French critic who writes under the name of Alain has some helpful if slightly fantastic remarks on this point. He gets a little out of his depth, but not as much as I feel myself out of mine, and perhaps together we may move toward the shore. Alain examines in turn the various forms of aesthetic activity, and coming in time to the novel (*le roman*) he asserts that each human being has two sides, appropriate to history and fiction. All that is observable in a man—that is to say his actions and such of his spiritual existence as can be deduced from his actions—falls into the domain of history. But his romanceful or romantic side (*sa partie romanesque ou romantique*) includes "the pure passions, that is to say the dreams, joys, sorrows and self-communings which politeness or shame prevent him from mentioning"; and to express this side of human nature is one of the chief functions of the novel. "What is fictitious in a novel is not so much the story as the method by which thought develops into action, a method which never occurs in daily life. . . . History, with its emphasis on external causes, is dominated by the notion of fatality, whereas there is no fatality in the novel; there, everything is founded on human nature, and the dominating feeling is of an existence where everything is intentional, even passions and crimes, even misery."[1]

This is perhaps a roundabout way of saying what every British schoolboy knew, that the historian records whereas the novelist must create. Still, it is a profitable roundabout, for it brings out the fundamental difference between people in daily life and people in books. In daily life we never understand each other, neither complete clairvoyance nor complete confessional exists. We know each other approximately, by external signs, and these serve well enough as a basis for society and even for intimacy. But people in a novel can be understood completely by the reader, if the novelist wishes; their inner as well as their outer life can be exposed. And this is why they often seem more definite than characters in history, or even our own friends; we have been told all about them that can be told; even if they are imperfect or unreal they do not contain any secrets, whereas our friends do and must, mutual secrecy being one of the conditions of life upon this globe. . . .

We may divide characters into flat and round. Flat characters were called "humorous" in the seventeenth century, and are sometimes called types, and sometimes caricatures. In their purest form, they are constructed round a single idea or quality: when there is more than one factor in them, we get the beginning of the curve towards the round. The really flat character can be expressed in one sentence such as "I never will desert Mr. Micawber." There is Mrs. Micawber—she says she won't desert Mr. Micawber, she doesn't, and there she is. . . .

One great advantage of flat characters is that they are easily recognized whenever they come in—recognized by the reader's emotional eye, not by the visual eye, which merely notes the recurrence of a proper name. In Russian novels, where they so seldom occur, they would be a decided help.

---

[1]*Paraphrased from* Système des Beaux Arts, *pp. 314-315. I am indebted to M. André Maurois for introducing me to this stimulating essay.*

It is a convenience for an author when he can strike with his full force at once, and flat characters are very useful to him, since they never need reintroducing, never run away, have not to be watched for development, and provide their own atmosphere—little luminous disks of a pre-arranged size, pushed hither and thither like counters across the void or between the stars; most satisfactory.

A second advantage is that they are easily remembered by the reader afterwards. They remain in his mind as unalterable for the reason that they were not changed by circumstances; they moved through circumstances, which gives them in retrospect a comforting quality, and preserves them when the book that produced them may decay. . . .

As for the round characters proper, they have already been defined by implication and no more need be said. All I need do is to give some examples of people in books who seem to me round so that the definition can be tested afterwards:

All the principal characters in *War and Peace,* all the Dostoevsky characters, and some of the Proust—for example, the old family servant, the Duchess of Guermantes, M. de Charlus, and Saint Loup; Madame Bovary—who, like Moll Flanders, has her book to herself, and can expand and secrete unchecked; some people in Thackeray—for instance, Becky and Beatrix; some in Fielding—Parson Adams, Tom Jones; and some in Charlotte Brontë, most particularly Lucy Snowe. (And many more—this is not a catalogue.) The test of a round character is whether it is capable of surprising in a convincing way. If it never surprises, it is flat. If it does not convince, it is a flat pretending to be round. It has the incalculability of life about it—life within the pages of a book. And by using it sometimes alone, more often in combination with the other kind, the novelist achieves his task of acclimatization and harmonizes the human race with the other aspects of his work. . . .

"The whole intricate question of method, in the craft of fiction," says Mr. Percy Lubbock, "I take to be governed by the question of the *point of view*—the question of the relation in which the narrator stands to the story." And his book *The Craft of Fiction* examines various points of view with genius and insight. The novelist, he says, can either describe the characters from outside, as an impartial or partial onlooker; or he can assume omniscience and describe them from within; or he can place himself in the position of one of them and affect to be in the dark as to the motives of the rest; or there are certain intermediate attitudes.

Those who follow him will lay a sure foundation for the aesthetics of fiction—a foundation which I cannot for a moment promise. This is a ramshackly survey and for me the "whole intricate question of method" resolves itself not into formulae but into the power of the writer to bounce the reader into accepting what he says—a power which Mr. Lubbock admits and admires, but locates at the edge of the problem instead of at the centre. I should put it plumb in the centre. Look how Dickens bounces us in *Bleak House.* Chapter I of *Bleak House* is omniscient. Dickens takes us into the Court of Chancery and rapidly explains all the people there. In Chapter II he is partially omniscient. We still use his eyes, but for some unexplained reason they begin to grow weak: he can explain Sir Leicester Dedlock to us, part of Lady Dedlock but not all, and nothing of Mr. Tulkinghorn. In Chapter III he is even more reprehensible: he goes straight across into the dramatic method and inhabits a young lady, Esther Summerson. "I have a great deal of difficulty in beginning to write my portion of these pages, for I know I am not clever," pipes up Esther, and continues in this strain with consistency and competence, so long as she is allowed to hold the pen. At any moment the author of her being may snatch it from her, and run about taking notes himself, leaving her seated goodness knows where, and employed we do not care how. Logically, *Bleak House* is all to pieces, but Dickens bounces us, so that we do not mind the shiftings of the view-point.

Critics are more apt to object than readers. Zealous for the novel's eminence, they are a little too apt to look out for problems that shall be peculiar to it, and differentiate it from the drama; they feel it ought to have its own technical troubles before it can be accepted as an independent art; and since the problem of a point of view certainly is peculiar to the novel they have rather overstressed it. I do not myself think it is so important as a proper mixture of characters—a problem which the dramatist is up against also. And the novelist must bounce us; that is imperative.

Let us glance at two other examples of a shifting view-point.

The eminent French writer, André Gide, has published a novel called *Les Faux Monnayeurs*[2]—for all its modernity, this novel of Gide's has one aspect in common with *Bleak House:* it is all to pieces logically. Sometimes the author is omniscient: he explains everything, he stands back, *"il juge ses personnages"*; at other times his omniscience is partial; yet again he is dramatic, and causes the story to be told through the diary of one of the characters. There is the same absence of view-point, but whereas in Dickens it was instinctive, in Gide it is sophisticated; he expatiates too much about the jolts. The novelist who betrays too much interest in his own method can never be more than interesting; he has given up the creation of character and summoned us to help analyse his own mind, and a heavy drop in the emotional thermometer results. *Les Faux Monnayeurs* is among the more interesting of recent works: not among the vital: and greatly as we shall have to admire it as a fabric we cannot praise it unrestrictedly now.

For our second example we must again glance at *War and Peace.* Here

---

[2]*Translated by Dorothy Bussy as* The Counterfeiters, *Knopf.*

the result is vital: we are bounced up and down Russia—omniscient, semi-omniscient, dramatized here or there as the moment dictates—and at the end we have accepted it all. Mr. Lubbock does not, it is true: great as he finds the book, he would find it greater if it had a view-point; he feels Tolstoy has not pulled his full weight. I feel that the rules of the game of writing are not like this. A novelist can shift his view-point if it comes off, and it came off with Dickens and Tolstoy. Indeed this power to expand and contract perception (of which the shifting view-point is a symptom), this right to intermittent knowledge:—I find it one of the great advantages of the novel-form, and it has a parallel in our perception of life. We are stupider at some times than others; we can enter into people's minds occasionally but not always, because our own minds get tired; and this intermittence lends in the long run variety and colour to the experiences we receive. A quantity of novelists, English novelists especially, have behaved like this to the people in their books: played fast and loose with them, and I cannot see why they should be censured. . . .

The Plot

Let us define a plot. We have defined a story as a narrative of events arranged in their time-sequence. A plot is also a narrative of events, the emphasis falling on causality. "The king died and then the queen died" is a story. "The king died, and then the queen died of grief" is a plot. The time-sequence is preserved, but the sense of causality overshadows it. Or again: "The queen died, no one knew why, until it was discovered that it was through grief at the death of the king." This is a plot with a mystery in it, a form capable of high development. It suspends the time-sequence, it moves as far away from the story as its limitations will allow. Consider the death of the queen. If it is in a story we say "and then?" If it is in a plot we ask "why?" That is the fundamental difference between these two aspects of the novel. A plot cannot be told to a gaping audience of cave-men or to a tyrannical sultan or to their modern descendant the movie-public. They can only be kept awake by "and then—and then——" They can only supply curiosity. But a plot demands intelligence and memory also. . . .

Intelligence first. The intelligent novel-reader, unlike the inquisitive one who just runs his eye over a new fact, mentally picks it up. He sees it from two points of view: isolated, and related to the other facts that he has read on previous pages. Probably he does not understand it, but he does not expect to do so yet awhile. The facts in a highly organized novel (like *The Egoist*) are often of the nature of cross-correspondences and the ideal spectator cannot expect to view them properly until he is sitting up on a hill at the end. This element of surprise or mystery—the detective element as it is sometimes rather emptily called—is of great importance in a plot. It occurs through a suspension of the time-sequence; a mystery is a pocket in time, and it occurs crudely as in "Why did the queen die?" and more subtly in half-explained gestures and words, the true meaning of which only dawns pages ahead. Mystery is essential to a plot, and cannot be appreciated without intelligence. To the curious it is just another "and then——" To appreciate a mystery, part of the mind must be left behind, brooding, while the other part goes marching on.

That brings us to our second qualification: memory.

Memory and intelligence are closely connected, for unless we remember we cannot understand. If by the time the queen dies we have forgotten the existence of the king we shall never make out what killed her. The plot-maker expects us to remember, we expect him to leave no loose ends. Every action or word ought to count; it ought to be economical and spare; even when complicated it should be organic and free from dead-matter. It may be difficult or easy, it may and should contain mysteries, but it ought not to mislead. And over it, as it unfolds, will hover the memory of the reader (that dull glow of the mind of which intelligence is the bright advancing edge) and will constantly rearrange and reconsider, seeing new clues, new chains of cause and effect, and the final sense (if the plot has been a fine one) will not be of clues or chains, but of something aesthetically compact, something which might have been shown by the novelist straight away, only if he had shown it straight away it would never have become beautiful. We come up against beauty here—for the first time in our inquiry: beauty at which a novelist should never aim, though he fails if he does not achieve it. I will conduct beauty to her proper place later on. Meanwhile please accept her as part of a completed plot. She looks a little surprised at being there, but beauty ought to look a little surprised: it is the emotion that best suits her face, as Botticelli knew when he painted her risen from the waves, between the winds and the flowers. The beauty who does not look surprised, who accepts her position as her due—she reminds us too much of a prima donna. . . .

In the losing battle that the plot fights with the characters, it often takes a cowardly revenge. Nearly all novels are feeble at the end. This is because the plot requires to be wound up. Why is this necessary? Why is there not a convention which allows a novelist to stop as soon as he feels muddled or bored? Alas, he has to round things off, and usually the characters go dead while he is at work, and our final impression of them is through deadness. . . .

Most novels do fail here—there is this disastrous standstill while logic takes over the command from flesh and blood. If it was not for death and marriage I do not know how the average novelist would conclude. Death and marriage are almost his only connection between his characters and his plot, and the reader is more ready to meet him here, and take a bookish view of them, provided they occur later on in the book: the writer, poor fellow, must be allowed to finish up somehow, he has his living to get like anyone else, so no wonder that nothing is heard but hammering and screwing. . . .

Fantasy

The idea running through these lectures is by now plain enough: that there are in the novel two forces: human beings and a bundle of various things not human beings, and that it is the novelist's business to adjust these two forces and conciliate their claims. That is plain enough, but does it run through the novel too? Perhaps our subject, namely the books we have read, has stolen away from us while we theorize, like a shadow from an ascending bird. The bird is all right—it climbs, it is consistent and eminent. The shadow is all right—it has flickered across roads and gardens. But the two things resemble one another less and less, they do not touch as they did when the bird rested its toes on the ground. . . .

There is more in the novel than time or people or logic or any of their derivatives, more even than Fate. And by "more" I do not mean something that excludes these aspects nor something that includes them, embraces them. I mean something that cuts across them like a bar of light, that is intimately connected with them at one place and patiently illumines all their problems, and at another place shoots over or through them as if they did not exist. We shall give that bar of light two names, fantasy and prophecy.

Our easiest approach to a definition of any aspect of fiction is always by considering the sort of demand it makes on the reader. Curiosity for the story, human feelings and a sense of value for the characters, intelligence and memory for the plot. What does fantasy ask of us? It asks us to pay something extra. It compels us to an adjustment that is different to an adjustment required by a work of art, to an additional adjustment. The other novelists say "Here is something that might occur in your lives," the fantasist says "Here's something that could not occur. I must ask you first to accept my book as a whole, and secondly to accept certain things in my book." Many readers can grant the first request, but refuse the second. "One knows a book isn't real," they say, "still one does expect it to be natural, and this angel or midget or ghost or silly delay about the child's birth—no, it is too much." They either retract their original concession and stop reading, or if they do go on it is with complete coldness, and they watch the gambols of the author without realizing how much they may mean to him.

No doubt the above approach is not critically sound. We all know that a work of art is an entity, etc., etc.; it has its own laws which are not those of daily life, anything that suits it is true, so why should any question arise about the angel, etc., except whether it is suitable to its book? Why place an angel on a different basis from a stockbroker? Once in the realm of the fictitious, what difference is there between an apparition and a mortgage? I see the soundness of this argument, but my heart refuses to assent. The general tone of novels is so literal that when the fantastic is introduced it produces a special effect: some readers are thrilled, others choked off: it demands an additional adjustment because of the oddness of its method or subject matter—like a sideshow in an exhibition where you have to pay sixpence as well as the original entrance fee. Some readers pay with delight, it is only for the sideshows that they entered the exhibition, and it is only to them I can now speak. Others refuse with indignation, and these have our sincere regards, for to dislike the fantastic in literature is not to dislike literature. It does not even imply poverty of imagination, only a disinclination to meet certain demands that are made on it. . . .

Let us now distinguish between fantasy and prophecy.

They are alike in having gods, and unlike in the gods they have. There is in both the sense of mythology which differentiates them from other aspects of our subject. An invocation is again possible, therefore on behalf of fantasy let us now invoke all beings who inhabit the lower air, the shallow water, and the smaller hills, all Fauns and Dryads and slips of the memory, all verbal coincidences, Pans and puns, all that is medieval this side of the grave. When we come to prophecy, we shall utter no invocation, but it will have been to whatever transcends our abilities, even when it is human passion that transcends them, to the deities of India, Greece, Scandinavia and Judaea, to all that is medieval beyond the grave and to Lucifer son of the morning. By their mythologies we shall distinguish these two sorts of novels.

A number of rather small gods then should haunt us today—I would call them fairies if the word were not consecrated to imbecility. (Do you believe in fairies? No, not under any circumstances.) The stuff of daily life will be tugged and strained in various directions, the earth will be given little tilts mischievous or pensive, spotlights will fall on objects that have no reason to anticipate or welcome them, and tragedy herself, though not excluded, will have a fortuitous air as if a word would disarm her. The power of fantasy penetrates into every corner of the universe, but not into the forces that govern it—the stars that are the brain of heaven, the army of unalterable law, remain untouched—and novels of this type have an improvised air, which is the secret of their force and charm. They may contain solid character-drawing, penetrating and bitter criticism of conduct and civilization; yet our simile of the beam of light must remain, and if one god must be invoked specially, let us call upon Hermes—messenger, thief, and conductor of souls to a not-too-terrible hereafter.

You will expect me now to say that a fantastic book asks us to accept the supernatural. I will say it, but reluctantly, because any statement as to their subject-matter brings these novels into the claws of critical apparatus, from which it is important that they should be saved. It is truer of them than of most books that we can only know what is in them by reading them, and their appeal is specially personal—they are sideshows inside the main show. So I would rather hedge as much as possible, and say that they ask us to accept either the supernatural or its absence. . . .

Well, that must serve as our definition of fantasy. It implies the supernatural, but need not express it. Often it does express it, and were that type of classification helpful, we could make a list of the devices which writers of a fantastic turn have used—such as the introduction of a god, ghost, angel, monkey, monster, midget, witch into ordinary life; or the introduction of ordinary men into no man's land, the future, the past, the interior of the earth, the fourth dimension; or divings into and dividings of personality; or finally the device of parody or adaptation. These devices need never grow stale; they will occur naturally to writers of a certain temperament, and be put to fresh use; but the fact that their number is strictly limited is of interest; and suggests that the beam of light can only be manipulated in certain ways.

Prophecy

With prophecy in the narrow sense of foretelling the future we have no concern, and we have not much concern with it as an appeal for righteousness. What will interest us today—what we must respond to, for interest now becomes an inappropriate word—is an accent in the novelist's voice, an accent for which the flutes and saxophones of fantasy may have prepared us. His theme is the universe, or something universal, but he is not necessarily going to "say" anything about the universe; he proposes to sing, and the strangeness of song arising in the halls of fiction is bound to give us a shock. How will song combine with the furniture of common sense? we shall ask ourselves, and shall have to answer "not too well": the singer does not always have room for his gestures, the tables and chairs get broken, and the novel through which bardic influence has passed often has a wrecked air, like a drawing-room after an earthquake or a children's party. Readers of D. H. Lawrence will understand what I mean.

Prophecy—in our sense—is a tone of voice. It may imply any of the faiths that have haunted humanity—Christianity, Buddhism, dualism, Satanism, or the mere raising of human love and hatred to such a power that their normal receptacles no longer contain them: but what particular view of the universe is recommended—with that we are not directly concerned. It is the implication that signifies and will filter into the turns of the novelist's phrase, and in this lecture, which promises to be so vague and grandiose, we may come nearer than elsewhere to the minutiae of style. We shall have to attend to the novelist's state of mind and to the actual words he uses; we shall neglect as far as we can the problems of common sense. As far as we can: for all novels contain tables and chairs, and most readers of fiction look for them first. Before we condemn him for affectation and distortion we must realize his view-point. He is not looking at the tables and chairs at all, and that is why they are out of focus. We only see what he does not focus—not what he does—and in our blindness we laugh at him.

I have said that each aspect of the novel demands a different quality in the reader. Well, the prophetic aspect demands two qualities: humility and the suspension of the sense of humour. Humility is a quality for which I have only a limited admiration. In many phases of life it is a great mistake and degenerates into defensiveness or hypocrisy. But humility is in place just now. Without its help we shall not hear the voice of the prophet, and our eyes will behold a figure of fun instead of his glory. And the sense of humour—that is out of place: that estimable adjunct of the educated man must be laid aside. Like the schoolchildren in the Bible, one cannot help laughing at a prophet—his bald head is so absurd— but one can discount the laughter and realize that it has no critical value and is merely food for bears. . . .

Though I believe this lecture is on a genuine aspect of the novel, not a fake aspect, I can only think of four writers to illustrate it—Dostoevsky, Melville, D. H. Lawrence and Emily Brontë. . . .

We have indeed to lay aside the single vision which we bring to most of literature and life and have been trying to use through most of our inquiry, and take up a different set of tools. Is this right? Another prophet, Blake, had no doubt that it was right.

> May God us keep
> From single vision and Newton's sleep,

he cried and he has painted that same Newton with a pair of compasses in his hand, describing a miserable mathematical triangle, and turning his back upon the gorgeous and immeasurable water growths of *Moby Dick*. Few will agree with Blake. Fewer will agree with Blake's Newton. Most of us will be eclectics to this side or that according to our temperament. The human mind is not a dignified organ, and I do not see how we can exercise it sincerely except through eclecticism. And the only advice I would offer my fellow eclectics is: "Do not be proud of your inconsistency. It is a pity, it is a pity that we should be equipped like this. It is a pity that Man cannot be at the same time impressive and truthful." . . .

Pattern and Rhythm

Now we must consider something which springs mainly out of the plot, and to which the characters and any other element present also contribute. For this new aspect there appears to be no literary word— indeed the more the arts develop the more they depend on each other for definition. We will borrow from painting first and call it the pattern. Later we will borrow from music and call it rhythm. . . .

Pattern is an aesthetic aspect of the novel, and . . . though it may be nourished by anything in the novel—any character, scene, word—it draws most of its nourishment from the plot. We noted, when discussing the plot, that it added to itself the quality of beauty; beauty a little surprised at her own arrival: that upon its neat carpentry there could be seen, by those who cared to see, the figure of the Muse; that Logic, at the moment of finishing its own house, laid the foundation of a new one. Here, here is the point where the aspect called pattern is most closely in touch with its material; here is our starting point. It springs mainly from the plot, accompanies it like a light in the clouds, and remains visible after it has departed. Beauty is sometimes the shape of the book, the book as a whole, the unity. . . .

Rhythm is sometimes quite easy. Beethoven's Fifth Symphony, for instance, starts with the rhythm "diddidy dum," which we can all hear and tap to. But the symphony as a whole has also a rhythm—due mainly to the relation between its movements—which some people can hear but no one can tap to. This second sort of rhythm is difficult, and whether it is substantially the same as the first sort only a musician could tell us. What a literary man wants to say though is that the first kind of rhythm, the diddidy dum, can be found in certain novels and may give them beauty. And the other rhythm, the difficult one—the rhythm of the Fifth Symphony as a whole—I cannot quote you any parallels for that in fiction, yet it may be present. . . .

Is there any effect in novels comparable to the effect of the Fifth Symphony as a whole, where, when the orchestra stops, we hear something that has never actually been played? The opening movement, the andante, and the trio-scherzo-trio-finale that composes the third block, all enter the mind at once, and extend one another into a common entity. This common entity, this new thing, is the symphony as a whole, and it has been achieved mainly (though not entirely) by the relation between the three big blocks of sound which the orchestra has been playing. I am calling this relation "rhythmic." If the correct musical term is something else, that does not matter; what we have now to ask ourselves is whether there is any analogy to it in fiction.

I cannot find any analogy. Yet there may be one; in music fiction is likely to find its nearest parallel.

The position of the drama is different. The drama may look towards the pictorial arts, it may allow Aristotle to discipline it, for it is not so deeply committed to the claims of human beings. Human beings have their great chance in the novel. They say to the novelist: "Recreate us if you like, but we must come in," and the novelist's problem, as we have seen all along, is to give them a good run and to achieve something else at the same time. Whither shall he turn? not indeed for help but for analogy. Music, though it does not employ human beings, though it is governed by intricate laws, nevertheless does offer in its final expression a type of beauty which fiction might achieve in its own way. Expansion. That is the idea the novelist must cling to. Not completion. Not rounding off but opening out. When the symphony is over we feel that the notes and tunes composing it have been liberated, they have found in the rhythm of the whole their individual freedom. Cannot the novel be like that? Is not there something of it in *War and Peace?*—the book with which we began and in which we must end. Such an untidy book. Yet, as we read it, do not great chords begin to sound behind us, and when we have finished does not every item—even the catalogue of strategies—lead a larger existence than was possible at the time?

Conclusion

Will the creative process itself alter? Will the mirror get a new coat of quicksilver? In other words, can human nature change? Let us consider this possibility for a moment—we are entitled to that much relaxation.

It is amusing to listen to elderly people on this subject. Sometimes a man says in confident tones: "Human nature's the same in all ages. The primitive cave-man lies deep in us all. Civilization—pooh! a mere veneer. You can't alter facts." He speaks like this when he is feeling prosperous and fat. When he is feeling depressed and is worried by the young, or is being sentimental about them on the ground that they will succeed in life when he has failed, then he will take the opposite view and say mysteriously, "Human nature is not the same. I have seen fundamental changes in my own time. You must face facts." And he goes on like this day after day, alternately facing facts and refusing to alter them.

All I will do is to state a possibility. If human nature does alter it will be because individuals manage to look at themselves in a new way. Here and there people—a very few people, but a few novelists are among them—are trying to do this. Every institution and vested interest is against such a search: organized religion, the state, the family in its economic aspect, have nothing to gain, and it is only when outward prohibitions weaken that it can proceed: history conditions it to that extent. Perhaps the searchers will fail, perhaps it is impossible for the instrument of contemplation to contemplate itself, perhaps if it is possible it means the end of imaginative literature—which if I understand him rightly is the view of that acute inquirer, Mr. I. A. Richards. Anyhow—that way lies movement and even combustion for the novel, for if the novelist sees himself differently he will see his characters differently and a new system of lighting will result.

I do not know on the verge of which philosophy or what rival philosophies the above remarks are wavering, but as I look back at my own scraps of knowledge and into my own heart, I see these two movements of the human mind: the great tedious onrush known as history, and a shy crablike sideways movement. Both movements have been neglected in these lectures: history because it only carries people on, it is just a train full of passengers; and the crablike movement because it is too slow and cautious to be visible over our tiny period of two hundred years. So we laid it down as an axiom when we started that human nature is unchangeable, and that it produces in rapid succession prose fictions, which fictions, when they contain 50,000 words or more, are called novels. If we had the power or license to take a wider view, and survey all human and prehuman activity, we might not conclude like this; the crablike movement, the shiftings of the passengers, might be visible, and the phrase "the development of the novel" might cease to be a pseudo-scholarly tag or a technical triviality, and become important, because it implied the development of humanity.

Elizabeth Bowen

(1899–1973)

Broad matters of method that Lubbock and Forster have considered in the round Elizabeth Bowen now disassembles, one by one, to examine each in all its parts and movements—with her sharp idiosyncratic eye. These "notes," as Miss Bowen calls them, are thoughts about technique by a writer who, through a series of novels and stories—including The Death of the Heart, The Heat of the Day, Ivy Gripped the Steps—*laid claim to artistic kinship with Forster, and also with Jane Austen and George Eliot, and with Virginia Woolf, who was her friend. Born in Ireland, she lived much of her writing life in the intellectual worlds of London and Oxford. Her work is impressionistic, but it has a concreteness and tautness which give the reader a sense not so much of dreaming about life as of remembering it from a distance. A tall, sturdy, handsome woman, Irish in her pungency and candor, English in her courage, Miss Bowen had a slight stutter which gave great power to her spoken utterances; indeed, the remarkable passage on dialogue in these notes seems to describe her own forceful economy, both in speaking and writing: ". . . more to be said than can come through."*

NOTES ON WRITING A NOVEL

Plot—Essential.   The Pre-Essential.

Plot might seem to be a matter of choice. It is not. The particular plot is something the novelist is driven to. It is what is left after the whittling-away of alternatives. The novelist is confronted, at a moment (or at what appears to the moment: actually its extension may be indefinite) by the impossibility of saying what is to be said in any other way.

He is forced towards his plot. By what? By the "what is to be said." What is "what is to be said?" A mass of subjective matter that has accumulated —impressions received, feelings about experience, distorted results of ordinary observation, and something else—x. This matter is *extra* matter. It is superfluous to the non-writing life of the writer. It is luggage left in the hall between two journeys, as opposed to the perpetual furniture of rooms. It is destined to be elsewhere. It cannot move till its destination is known. Plot is the knowing of destination.

Plot is diction. Action of language, language of action.

Plot is story. It is also "a story" in the nursery sense = lie. The novel lies, in saying that something happened that did not. It must, therefore, contain uncontradictable truth, to warrant the original lie.

Story involves action. Action towards an end not to be foreseen (by the reader) but also towards an end which, having *been* reached, must be seen to have been from the start inevitable.

Action by whom? The Characters (see CHARACTERS). Action in view of what, and because of what? The "what is to be said."

What about the idea that the function of action is to *express* the characters? This is wrong. The characters are there to provide the action. Each character is created, and must only be so created, as to give his or her action (or rather, contributory part in the novel's action) verisimilitude.

What about the idea that plot should be ingenious, complicated—a display of ingenuity remarkable enough to command attention? If more than such a display, what? Tension, or mystification towards tension, are good for emphasis. For their own sakes, bad.

Plot must further the novel towards its object. What object? The non-poetic statement of a poetic truth.

Have not all poetic truths been already stated? The essence of a poetic truth is that no statement of it can be final.

Plot, story, is in itself un-poetic. At best it can only be not anti-poetic. It cannot claim a single poetic license. It must be reasoned—onward from the moment when its non-otherness, its only-possibleness has become apparent. Novelist must always have one foot, sheer circumstantiality, to stand on, whatever the other foot may be doing. (N.B.—Much to be learnt from story-telling to children. Much to be learnt from the detective story—especially non-irrelevance. [See RELEVANCE.])

Flaubert's "*Il faut intéresser.*" Stress on manner of telling: keep in mind, "I will a tale *unfold.*" Interest of watching silk handkerchief drawn from a conjuror's watch.

Plot must not cease to move forward. (See ADVANCE.) The *actual* speed of the movement must be even. *Apparent* variations in speed are good, necessary, but there must be no actual variations in speed. To obtain those apparent variations is part of the illusion-task of the novel. Variations in texture can be made to give the effect of variations in speed. Why are *apparent* variations in speed necessary? (a) For emphasis. (b) For non-resistance, or "give," to the nervous time-variations of the reader. Why is *actual* evenness, non-variation, of speed necessary? For the sake of internal evenness for its own sake. Perfection of evenness = perfection of control. The evenness of the speed should be the evenness inseparable from tautness. The tautness of the taut string is equal (or even) all along and at any part of the string's length.

Characters

Are the characters, then, to be constructed to formula—the formula pre-decided by the plot? Are they to be drawn, cut out, jointed, wired, in order to be manipulated for the plot?

No. There is no question as to whether this would be right or wrong. It would be impossible. One cannot "make" characters, only marionettes. The manipulated movement of the marionette is not the "action" necessary for plot. Characterless action is not action at all, in the plot sense. It is the indivisibility of the act from the actor, and the inevitability of *that* act on the part of *that* actor, that gives action verisimilitude. Without that, action is without force or reason. Forceless, reasonless action disrupts plot. The term "creation of character" (or characters) is misleading. Characters pre-exist. They are *found*. They reveal themselves slowly to the novelist's perception—as might fellow-travellers seated opposite one in a very dimly-lit railway carriage.

The novelist's perceptions of his characters take place *in the course of the actual writing of the novel*. To an extent, the novelist is in the same position as his reader. But his perceptions should be always just in advance.

The ideal way of presenting character is to invite perception.

In what do the characters pre-exist? I should say, in the mass of matter (see Plot) that had accumulated before the inception of the novel.

(N.B.—The unanswerability of the question, from an outsider: "Are the characters in your novel invented, or are they from real life?" Obviously, neither is true. The outsider's notion of "real life" and the novelist's are hopelessly apart.)

How, then, is the pre-existing character—with its own inner spring of action, its contrarieties—to be made to play a preassigned rôle? In relation to character, or characters, once these have been contemplated, *plot* must at once seem over-rigid, arbitrary.

What about the statement (in relation to Plot) that "each character is created in order, and only in order, that he or she may supply the required action?" To begin with, strike out "created." Better, the character is *recognized* (by the novelist) by the signs he or she gives of unique capacity to act in a certain way, which "certain way" fulfils a need of the plot.

The character is there (in the novel) for the sake of the action he or she is to contribute to the plot. Yes. But also, he or she exists *outside* the action being contributed to the plot.

Without that existence of the character outside the (necessarily limited) action, the action itself would be invalid.

Action is the simplification (for story purposes) of complexity. For each one act, there are an x number of rejected alternatives. It is the palpable presence of the alternatives that gives action interest. Therefore, in each of the characters, while he or she is acting, the play and pull of alternatives must be felt. It is in being seen to be capable of alternatives that the character becomes, for the reader, valid.

Roughly, the action of a character should be unpredictable before it has been shown, inevitable when it has been shown. In the first half of a novel, the unpredictability should be the more striking. In the second half, the inevitability should be the more striking.

(Most exceptions to this are, however, masterpiece-novels. In *War and*

Peace, *L'Education Sentimentale* and *La Recherche du Temps Perdu*, unpredictability dominates up to the end.)

The character's prominence in the novel (pre-decided by the plot) decides the character's range—of alternatives. The novelist must allot (to the point of rationing) psychological space. The "hero," "heroine" and "villain" (if any) are, by agreement, allowed most range. They are entitled, for the portrayal of their alternatives, to time and space. Placing the characters in receding order of their importance to the plot, the number of their alternatives may be seen to diminish. What E. M. Forster has called the "flat" character has no alternatives at all.

The ideal novel is without "flat" characters.

Characters must *materialize*—i.e., must have a palpable physical reality. They must be not only see-able (visualizable); they must be to be felt. Power to give physical reality is probably a matter of the extent and nature of the novelist's physical sensibility, or susceptibility. In the main, English novelists are weak in this, as compared to French and Russians. Why?

Hopelessness of categoric "description." Why? Because this is static. Physical personality belongs to action: cannot be separated from it. Pictures must be in movement. Eyes, hands, stature, etc., must appear, and only appear, *in play*. Reaction to physical personality is part of action—love, or sexual passages, only more marked application of this general rule.

(Conrad an example of strong, non-sexual use of physical personality.)

The materialization (in the above sense) of the character for the novelist must be instantaneous. It happens. No effort of will—and obviously no effort of intellect—can induce it. The novelist can *use* a character that has not yet materialized. But the unmaterialized character represents an enemy pocket in an area that has been otherwise cleared. This cannot go on for long. It produces a halt in plot.

When the materialization *has* happened, the chapters written before it happened will almost certainly have to be recast. From the plot point of view, they will be found invalid.

Also, it is essential that for the reader the materialization of the character should begin early. I say begin, because for the *reader* it may, without harm, be gradual.

Is it from this failure, or tendency to fail, in materialization that the English novelist depends so much on engaging emotional sympathy for his characters?

Ruling sympathy out, a novel must contain at least one *magnetic* character. At least one character capable of keying the reader up, as though he (the reader) were in the presence of someone he is in love with. This is not a rule of salesmanship but a pre-essential of *interest*. The character must do to the reader what he has done to the novelist—magnetize towards himself perceptions, sense-impressions, desires.

The unfortunate case is, where the character has, obviously, acted magnetically upon the author, but fails to do so upon the reader.

There must be combustion. Plot depends for its movement on internal combustion.

Physically, characters are almost always copies, or composite copies. Traits, gestures, etc., are searched for in, and assembled from, the novelist's memory. Or, a picture, a photograph or the cinema screen may be drawn on. Nothing physical can be *invented*. (Invented physique stigmatizes the inferior novel.) Proust (in last volume) speaks of this assemblage of traits. Though much may be lifted from a specific person in "real life," no person in "real life" could supply everything (physical) necessary for the character in the novel. No such person could have just that exact degree of physical intensity required for the character.

Greatness of characters is the measure of the unconscious greatness of the novelist's vision. They are "true" in so far as he is occupied with poetic truth. Their degrees in realness show the degrees of his concentration.

Scene—Is a derivative of Plot. Gives actuality to Plot.

Nothing can happen nowhere. The locale of the happening always colours the happening, and often, to a degree, shapes it.

Plot having pre-decided what is to happen, scene, scenes, must be so found, so chosen, as to give the happening the desired force.

Scene, being physical, is, like the physical traits of the characters, generally a copy, or a composite copy. It, too, is assembled—out of memories which, in the first place, may have had no rational connection with one another. Again, pictures, photographs, the screen are sources of supply. Also dreams.

Almost anything drawn from "real life"—house, town, room, park, landscape—will almost certainly be found to require *some* distortion for the purposes of the plot. Remote memories, already distorted by the imagination, are most useful for the purposes of scene. Unfamiliar or once-seen places yield more than do familiar often-seen places.

Wholly invented scene is as unsatisfactory (thin) as wholly invented physique for a character.

Scene, much more than character, is inside the novelist's conscious power. More than any other constituent of the novel, it makes him conscious *of* his power.

This can be dangerous. The weak novelist is always, compensatorily, scene-minded. (Jane Austen's economy of scene-painting, and her abstentions from it in what might be expected contexts, could in itself be proof of her mastery of the novel.)

Scene is only justified in the novel where it can be shown, or at least felt, to act upon action or character. In fact, where it has dramatic use.

Where not intended for dramatic use, scene is a sheer slower-down. Its staticness is a dead weight. It cannot make part of the plot's movement by being shown *in play*. (Thunderstorms, the sea, landscape flying past car or railway-carriage windows are not scene but *happenings*.)

The deadeningness of straight and prolonged "description" is as apparent with regard to scene as it is with regard to character. Scene must be evoked. For its details relevance (see RELEVANCE) is essential. Scene must, like the characters, not fail to materialize. In this it follows the same law—instantaneous for the novelist, gradual for the reader.

In "setting a scene" the novelist directs, or attempts to direct, the reader's visual imagination. He must allow for the fact that the reader's memories will not correspond with his own. Or, at least, not at all far along the way.

Dialogue—Must (1) Further Plot. (2) Express Character.

Should not on any account be a vehicle for ideas for their own sake. Ideas only permissible where they provide a key to the character who expresses them.

Dialogue requires more art than does any other constituent of the novel. Art in the *celare artem* sense. Art in the trickery, self-justifying distortion sense. Why? Because dialogue must appear realistic without being so. Actual realism—the lifting, as it were, of passages from a stenographer's take-down of a "real life" conversation—would be disruptive. Of what? Of the illusion of the novel. In "real life" everything is diluted; in the novel everything is condensed.

What are the realistic qualities to be imitated (or faked) in novel dialogue?—Spontaneity. Artless or hit-or-miss arrival at words used. Ambiguity (speaker not sure, himself, what he means). Effect of choking (as in engine): more to be said than can come through. Irrelevance. Allusiveness. Erraticness: unpredictable course. Repercussion.

What must novel dialogue, behind mask of these faked realistic qualities, really be and do? It must be pointed, intentional, relevant. It must crystallize situation. It must express character. It must advance plot.

During dialogue, the characters confront one another. The confrontation is in itself an occasion. Each one of these occasions, throughout the novel, is unique. Since the last confrontation, something has changed, advanced. What is being said is the effect of something that has happened; at the same time, what is being said *is in itself something happening*, which will, in turn, leave its effect.

Dialogue is the ideal means of showing what is between the characters. It crystallizes relationships. It *should*, ideally, so be effective as to make analysis or explanation of the relationships between the characters unnecessary.

Short of a small range of physical acts—a fight, murder, love-making—dialogue is the most vigorous and visible inter-action of which characters in a novel are capable. Speech is what the characters *do to each other*.

Dialogue provides means for the psychological materialization of the characters. It should short-circuit description of mental traits. Every sentence in dialogue should be descriptive of the character who is speaking. Idiom, tempo, and shape of each spoken sentence should be calculated by novelist, towards this descriptive end.

Dialogue is the first case of the novelist's need for notation from real life. Remarks or turns of phrase indicatory of class, age, degree of intellectual pretension, *idées reçues*, nature and strength of governing fantasy, sexual temperament, persecution-sense or acumen (fortuitous arrival at general or poetic truth) should be collected. (N.B.—Proust, example of this semi-conscious notation and putting to use of it.)

All the above, from *class* to *acumen*, may already have been established, with regard to each character, by a direct statement by the novelist to the reader. It is still, however, the business of dialogue to show these factors, or qualities, in play.

There must be present in dialogue—*i.e.*, in each sentence spoken by each character—*either* (a) calculation, or (b) involuntary self-revelation.

Each piece of dialogue *must* be "something happening." Dialogue *may* justify its presence by being "illustrative"—but this secondary use of it must be watched closely, challenged. Illustrativeness can be stretched too far. Like straight description, it then becomes static, a dead weight—halting the movement of the plot. The "amusing" for its *own* sake, should above all be censored. So should infatuation with any idiom.

The functional use of dialogue for the plot must be the first thing in the novelist's mind. Where functional usefulness cannot be established, dialogue must be left out.

What is this functional use? That of a bridge.

Dialogue is the thin bridge which must, from time to time, carry the entire weight of the novel. Two things to be kept in mind—(a) the bridge is there to permit *advance*, (b) the bridge must be strong enough for the weight.

Failure in any one piece of dialogue is a loss, at once to the continuity and the comprehensibility of the novel.

Characters should, on the whole, be under rather than over-articulate. What they *intend* to say should be more evident, more striking (because of its greater inner importance to the plot) than what they arrive at *saying*.

Angle

The question of *angle* comes up twice over in the novel.

Angle has two senses—(a) visual; (b) moral.

(a) *Visual Angle.*—This has been much discussed—particularly, I think, by Henry James. Where is the camera-eye to be located? (1) In the breast or brow of *one* of the characters? This is, of course, simplifying and integrating. But it imposes on the novel the limitations of the "I"—whether the first person is explicitly used or not. Also, with regard to any matter that the specific character does not (cannot) know, it involves the novelist in long cumbrous passages of cogitation, speculation and guesses. *E.g.*—of any character other than the specific (or virtual) "I" it must always be "he appeared to feel," "he could be seen to see," rather than "he felt," "he saw." (2) In the breast or brow of a succession of characters? This is better. It *must*, if used, involve very careful, considered division of the characters, by the novelist, in the *seeing* and the *seen*. Certain characters gain in importance and magnetism by being only *seen*: this makes them more romantic, fatal-seeming, sinister. In fact, no character in which these qualities are, for the plot, essential should be allowed to enter the *seeing* class. (3) In the breast or brow of omniscient story-teller (the novelist)? This, though appearing naïve, would appear best. The novelist should retain right of entry, at will, into any of the characters: their memories, sensations and thought-processes should remain his, to requisition for appropriate use. What conditions "appropriateness"? The demands of the plot. Even so, the novelist must not lose sight of point made above—the gain in necessary effect, for some characters, of their remaining *seen*—their remaining closed, apparently, even to the omniscience of the novelist.

The cinema, with its actual camera-work, is interesting study for the novelist. In a good film, the camera's movement, angle and distance have all worked towards one thing—the fullest possible realization of the director's idea, the completest possible surrounding of the subject. Any trick is justified if it adds a statement. With both film and novel, plot is the pre-imperative. The novelist's relation to the novel is that of the director's relation to the film. The cinema, cinema-going, has no doubt built up in novelists a great authoritarianism. This seems to me good.

(b) *Moral Angle.*—This too often means, pre-assumptions—social, political, sexual, national, aesthetic, and so on. These may all exist, sunk at different depths, in the same novelist. Their existence cannot fail to be palpable; and their nature determines, more than anything else, the sympatheticness or antipatheticness of a given novel to a given circle of readers.

Pre-assumptions are bad. They limit the novel to a given circle of readers. They cause the novel to act immorally *on* that given circle. (The lady asking the librarian for a "nice" novel to take home is, virtually, asking for a novel whose pre-assumptions will be identical with her own.) Outside the given circle, a novel's pre-assumptions must invalidate it for all other readers. The increasingly bad smell of most pre-assumptions probably accounts for the growing prestige of the detective story: the detective story works on the single, and universally acceptable, pre-assumption that an act of violence is anti-social, and that the doer, in the name of injured society, must be traced.

Great novelists write without pre-assumption. They write from outside their own nationality, class or sex.

To write thus should be the ambition of any novelist who wishes to state poetic truth.

Does this mean he must have no angle, no moral view-point? No, surely.

Without these, he would be (a) incapable of maintaining the *conviction* necessary for the novel; (b) incapable of *lighting* the characters, who to be seen at all must necessarily be seen in a moral light.

From what source, then, must the conviction come? and from *what* morality is to come the light to be cast on the characters?

The conviction must come from certainty of the validity of the truth the novel is to present. The "moral light" has not, actually, a moral source; it is moral (morally powerful) according to the strength of its power of revelation. Revelation of what? The virtuousness or non-virtuousness of the action of the character. What is virtue in action? Truth in action. Truth by what ruling, in relation to what? Truth by the ruling of, and in relation to, the inherent poetic truth that the novel states.

The presence, and action, of the poetic truth is the motive (or motor) morality of the novel.

The direction of the action of the poetic truth provides—in fact, *is*— the moral angle of the novel. If he remains with that truth in view, the novelist has no option as to his angle.

The action, or continuous line of action, of a character is "bad" in so far as it runs counter to, resists, or attempts to deny, the action of the poetic truth. It is predisposition towards such action that constitutes "badness" in a character.

"Good" action, or "goodness" in the character, from predisposition to-wards such action, is movement along with, expressive of and contributory to, the action of the poetic truth.

If the novelist's moral angle is (a) decided by recognition of the poetic truth, and (b) maintained by the necessity of stating the truth by show-ing the truth's action, it will be, as it should be, impersonal. It will be, and (from the "interest" point of view) will be able to stand being, pure of pre-assumptions—national, social, sexual, etc.

N.B.—"Humour" is the weak point in the front against pre-assumptions. Almost all English humour shows social (sometimes, now, backed by political) pre-assumptions. (Extreme cases—that the lower, or employed, classes are quaint or funny—that aristocrats, served by butlers, are absurd. National pre-assumptions show in treatment of foreigners.)

Advance

It has been said that the plot must advance; that the underlying (or inner) speed of the advance must be even. How is this arrived at?

(1) Obviously, first, by the succession, the succeedingness, of events or happenings. It is to be remembered that *everything* put on record at all— an image, a word spoken, an interior movement of thought or feeling on the part of a character—is an event or happening. These proceed out of one another, give birth to one another, in a continuity that must be (a) obvious, (b) unbroken.

(2) Every happening cannot be described, stated. The reader must be made to feel that what has not been described or stated has, none the less, happened. How? By the showing of subsequent events or happenings whose source *could* only have been in what has not actually been stated. Tuesday is Tuesday by virtue of being the day following Monday. The stated Tuesday must be shown as a derivative of the unstated Monday.

(3) For the sake of emphasis, time must be falsified. But the novelist's consciousness of the subjective, arbitrary and emotional nature of the falsification should be evident to the reader. Against this falsification—in fact, increasing the force of its effect by contrast—a clock should be heard always impassively ticking away at the same speed. The passage of time, and its demarcation, should be a factor in plot. The either concentration or even or uneven spacing-out of events along time is important.

The statement "Ten years had passed," or the statement "It was now the next day"—each of these is an event.

(4) Characters most of all promote, by showing, the advance of the plot. How? By the advances, from act to act, in their action. By their showing (by emotional or physical changes) the effects both of action and of the passage of time. The diminution of the character's alternatives shows (because it is the work of) advance—by the end of a novel the character's alternatives, many at the beginning, have been reduced to almost none. In the novel, everything that happens happens either *to* or *because* of one of the characters. By the end of the novel, the character has, like the silkworm at work on the cocoon, spun itself out. Completed action is marked by the exhaustion (from one point of view) of the character. Throughout the novel, each character is expending potentiality. This expense of potentiality must be felt.

(5) Scene promotes, or contributes to, advance by its freshness. Generically, it is fresh, striking, from being unlike the scene before. It is the new "here and now." Once a scene ceases to offer freshness, it is a point-blank enemy to advance. Frequent change of scene *not* being an imperative of the novel—in fact, many novels by choice, and by wise choice, limiting themselves severely in this matter—how is there to continue to be freshness? By means of ever-differing presentation. Differing because of what? Season of year, time of day, effects of a happening (*e.g.*, with house, rise or fall in family fortunes, an arrival, a departure, a death), beholding character's mood. At the first presentation, the *scene* has freshness; afterwards, the freshness must be in the *presentation*. The same scene can, by means of a series of presentations, each having freshness, be made to ripen, mature, to actually advance. The *static* properties in scene can be good for advance when so stressed as to show advance by contrast—advance on the part of the characters. Striking "unchangingness" gives useful emphasis to change. Change should not be a factor, at once, in *both* scene and character; either unchanged character should see, or be seen against, changed scene, or changed character should see, or be seen, against un-

changed scene. *Two* changes obviously cancel each other out, and would cancel each other's contribution to the advance of plot.

Relevance

Relevance—the question of it—is the headache of novel-writing.

As has been said, the model for relevance is the well-constructed detective story: nothing is "in" that does not tell. But the detective story is, or would appear to be, simplified by having *fact* as its kernel. The detective story makes towards concrete truth; the novel makes towards abstract truth.

With the detective story, the question "relevant to *what?*" can be answered by the intelligence. With the novel, the same question must constantly, and in every context, be referred to the intuition. The intelligence, in a subsequent check over, may detect, but cannot itself put right, blunders, lapses or false starts on the part of the intuition.

In the notes on Plot, Character, Scene and Dialogue, everything has come to turn, by the end, on relevance. It is seen that all other relevances are subsidiary to the relevance of the plot—*i.e.*, the relevance to itself that the plot demands. It is as contributory, in fact relevant, to plot that character, scene and dialogue are examined. To be perfectly contributory, these three must be perfectly relevant. If character, scene or dialogue has been weakened by anything irrelevant *to itself*, it can only be imperfectly relevant—which must mean, to a degree disruptive—to the plot.

The main hope for character (for each character) is that it should be magnetic—*i.e.*, that it should *attract* its parts. This living propensity of the character to assemble itself, to integrate itself, to make itself in order to *be* itself will not, obviously, be resisted by the novelist. The magnetic, or magnetizing, character can be trusted as to what is relevant *to itself*. The trouble comes when what is relevant to the character is found to be not relevant to the plot. At this point, the novelist must adjudicate. It is possible that the character may be right; it is possible that there may be some flaw in the novelist's sense of what is relevant to the plot.

Again, the character may, in fact must, decide one half of the question of relevance in dialogue. The character attracts to itself the right, in fact the only possible, idiom, tempo and phraseology for *that* particular character in speech. In so far as dialogue is *illustrative*, the character's, or characters', pull on it must not be resisted.

But in so far as dialogue must be "something happening"—part of action, a means of advancing plot—the other half of the question of dialogue-relevance comes up. Here, the pull from the characters may conflict with the pull from the plot. Here again the novelist must adjudicate. The recasting and recasting of dialogue that is so often necessary is, probably, the search for ideal compromise.

Relevance in scene is more straightforward. Chiefly, the novelist must control his infatuation with his own visual power. *No* non-contributory image, must be the rule. Contributory to what? To the mood of the 'now,' the mood that either projects or reflects action. It is a good main rule that objects—chairs, trees, glasses, mountains, cushions—introduced into the novel should be stage-properties, necessary for "business." It will be also recalled that the well-set stage shows many objects *not* actually necessary for "business," but that these have a right to place by being descriptive—explanatory. In a play, the absence of the narrating voice makes it necessary to establish the class, period and general psychology of the characters by means of objects that can be seen. In the novel, such putting of objects to a descriptive (explanatory) use is excellent—alternative to the narrator's voice.

In scene, then, relevance demands either usefulness for action or else explanatory power in what is shown. There is no doubt that with some writers (Balzac, sometimes Arnold Bennett) categoricalness, in the presentation of scene, is effective. The aim is, usually, to suggest, by multiplication and exactitude of detail, either a scene's material oppressiveness or its intrinsic authority. But in general, for the purposes of most novelists, the number of objects genuinely necessary for explanation will be found to be very small.

Irrelevance, in any part, is a cloud and a drag on, a weakener of, the novel. It dilutes meaning. Relevance crystallizes meaning.

The novelist's—any writer's—object is, to whittle down his meaning to the exactest and finest possible point. What, of course, is fatal is when he does not know what he does mean: he has no point to sharpen.

Much irrelevance is introduced into novels by the writer's vague hope that at least some of this *may* turn out to be relevant, after all. A good deal of what might be called provisional writing goes to the first drafts of first chapters of most novels. At a point in the novel's progress, relevance becomes clearer. The provisional chapters are then recast.

The most striking fault in work by young or beginning novelists submitted for criticism, is irrelevance—due either to infatuation or indecision. To direct such an author's attention to the imperative of relevance is certainly the most useful—and possibly the only—help that can be given.

Alain Robbe-Grillet

(1922–   )

After the second World War there emerged in France a "new wave" of novel-
ists. They were a disparate group—Alain Robbe-Grillet, Nathalie Sarraute,
Samuel Beckett, Michel Butor, and several others—who had in common their
revolt not only against fictional standards inherited from the nineteenth century
but also against more recent novel forms, of existentialism and of the absurd.
Their quite various works were given collective names: the new novel, the anti-
novel. Robbe-Grillet became the spokesman for the wing of the group that in-
vented what it called chosisme—*"thingism." The novelist was to serve solely as*
eye. He was to bring to objects, for the first time in literature, their full weight,
their visible texture, the life in their colors, in sum their active quality; *and so*
their motive force in the lives of fictional characters, who would also only be
*seen. Robbe-Grillet's novels—*The Erasers, Jealousy, In the Labyrinth, The
Voyeur, *and others—though often baffling, often scaffolded with contrivance,*
are nevertheless always concrete, vivid, shimmering with visual sensation; and
they sometimes attain an intensity like that of the mystery novel. In this essay,
which appeared in 1957, by which time the new wave had well crested, Robbe-
Grillet rejects, or at least shakes to their roots, all the assumptions taken as a
matter of course by the previous writers in this section.

ON SEVERAL OBSOLETE NOTIONS

Traditional criticism has its vocabulary. Though it noisily abstains from
offering systematic judgments on literature (claiming, on the contrary, to
enjoy this or that work freely, according to such "natural" criteria as good
sense, the heart, etc.), one merely needs to read its analyses with a little
attention to discover a network of key words, betraying nothing less than
a system.

But we are so accustomed to discussions of "character," "atmosphere,"
"form," and "content," of "message" and "narrative ability" and "true
novelists" that it requires an effort to free ourselves from this spider web
and realize that it represents an idea about the novel (a ready-made idea,
which everyone admits without argument, hence a dead idea), and not at
all that so-called "nature" of the novel in which we are supposed to
believe.

Even more dangerous, perhaps, are the terms commonly employed to
describe the books which escape these accepted rules. The word "avant-
garde," for example, despite its note of impartiality, generally serves to
dismiss—as though by a shrug of the shoulders—any work that risks giv-

ing a bad conscience to the literature of mass consumption. Once a writer renounces the well-known formulas and attempts to create his own way of writing, he finds himself stuck with the label "avant-garde."

In principle, this means no more than that he is somewhat ahead of his times, and that this way of writing will be used tomorrow by the body of his colleagues. But in fact, the reader, warned by a wink, immediately thinks of some hirsute young men who smirkingly set off their firecrackers under the Academy's armchairs for the sole purpose of making a commotion or shocking the bourgeoisie. "They want to saw off the branch we're sitting on," writes the serious Henri Clouard, quite without malice.

The branch in question is actually dead of natural causes, by the simple action of time; it is not our fault if it is now rotting. And if all those who cling to it so desperately would glance up just once toward the top of the tree, they would discover that new, green, vigorous, hardy branches have grown out long since. *Ulysses* and *The Castle* are already over thirty. *The Sound and the Fury* was translated into French over twenty years ago. Many others have followed. In order not to see them, our good critics have, each time, pronounced one or another of their magic words: "avant-garde," "laboratory," "anti-novel" . . . in other words: "Let's close our eyes and go back to the sane values of the French tradition."

Character

How much we've heard about the "character"! Moreover, I fear we haven't heard the last. Fifty years of disease, the death notice signed many times over by the most serious essayists, yet nothing has yet managed to knock it off the pedestal on which the nineteenth century had placed it. It is a mummy now, but one still enthroned with the same—phony—majesty, among the values revered by traditional criticism. In fact, that is how this criticism recognizes the "true" novelist: "he creates characters". . . .

In order to justify the cogency of this point of view, the customary reasoning is employed: Balzac has given us Père Goriot, Dostoevski has created the Karamazovs, hence writing novels can no longer be anything but that: adding some modern figures to the portrait gallery constituted by our literary history.

A character—everyone knows what the word means. It is not a banal *he*, anonymous and transparent, the simple subject of the action expressed by the verb. A character must have a proper name, two if possible: a surname and a given name. He must have parents, a heredity. He must have a profession. If he has possessions as well, so much the better. Finally, he must possess a "character," a face which reflects it, a past which has molded that face and that character. His character dictates his actions, makes him react to each event in a determined fashion. His character permits the reader to judge him, to love him, to hate him. It is thanks to his character that he will one day bequeath his name to a human type, which was waiting, it would seem, for the consecration of this baptism.

For the character must be unique and at the same time must rise to the level of a category. He must have enough individuality to remain irreplaceable, and enough generality to become universal. One may, for variety's sake, to give oneself some impression of freedom, choose a hero who seems to transgress one of these rules: a foundling, a vagrant, a madman, a man whose uncertain character harbors here and there some small surprise. . . . One must not exaggerate, however, in this direction: that is the road to perdition, which leads straight to the modern novel.

None of the great contemporary works, in fact, corresponds on this point to the norms of criticism. How many readers recall the narrator's name in *Nausea* or in *The Stranger*? Are these human types? Would it not be, on the contrary, the worst absurdity to regard these books as character studies? And does the *Journey to the End of the Night* describe a character? Does anyone suppose, moreover, that it is an accident these three novels are written in the first person? Beckett changes his hero's name and shape in the course of the same narrative. Faulkner purposely gives the same name to two different persons. As for the K of *The Castle*, he is content with an initial, he possesses nothing, has no family, no face; he is probably not even a land surveyor at all.

The examples can be multiplied. As a matter of fact, the creators of characters, in the traditional sense, no longer manage to offer us anything more than puppets in which they themselves have ceased to believe. The novel of characters belongs entirely to the past, it describes a period: that which marked the apogee of the individual.

Perhaps this is not an advance, but it is evident that the present period is rather one of administrative numbers. The world's destiny has ceased, for us, to be identified with the rise or fall of certain men, of certain families. The world itself is no longer our private property, hereditary and convertible into cash, a prey which it is not so much a matter of knowing as of conquering. To have a name was doubtless very important in the days of Balzac's bourgeoisie. A character was important—all the more important for being the weapon in a hand-to-hand struggle, the hope of a success, the exercise of a domination. It was something to have a face in a universe where personality represented both the means and the end of all exploration.

Our world, today, is less sure of itself, more modest perhaps, since it has renounced the omnipotence of the person, but more ambitious too, since it looks beyond. The exclusive cult of the "human" has given way to a larger consciousness, one that is less anthropocentric. The novel seems to stagger, having lost what was once its best prop, the hero. If it does not manage to right itself, it is because its life was linked to that of a society now past. If it does manage, on the contrary, a new course lies open to it, with the promise of new discoveries.

Story

A novel, for most readers—and critics—is primarily a "story." A true novelist is one who knows how to "tell a story." The felicity of "telling," which sustains him from one end of his work to the other, is identified with his vocation as a writer. To invent thrilling, moving, dramatic vicissitudes constitutes both his delight and his justification.

Hence to criticize a novel often comes down to reporting its anecdote, more or less briefly, depending on whether one has six columns or two to fill, with more or less emphasis on the essential passages: the climaxes and denouements of the plot. The judgment made on the book will consist chiefly in an appreciation of this plot, of its gradual development, its equilibrium, the expectations or surprises it affords the panting reader. A loophole in the narrative, a clumsily introduced episode, a lag in interest will be the major defects of the book; vivacity and spontaneity its highest virtues.

The writing itself will never be in question. The novelist will merely be praised for expressing himself in correct language, in an agreeable, striking, evocative manner. . . . Thus the style will be no more than a means, a manner; the basis of the novel, its *raison d'être*, what is inside it, is simply the story it tells.

Yet from serious people (those who admit that literature need not be a mere diversion) to the enthusiasts of the worst sentimental, detective, or exotic junk, everyone is in the habit of demanding a particular quality from the anecdote. It is not enough that it be entertaining, or extraordinary, or enthralling; to have its measure of human truth, it must also succeed in convincing the reader that the adventures he is hearing about have really happened to real characters, and that the novelist is confining himself to reporting, to transmitting events of which he has been the witness. A tacit convention is established between the reader and the author: the latter will pretend to believe in what he is telling, the former will forget that everything is invented and will pretend to be dealing with a document, a biography, a real-life story. To tell a story well is therefore to make what one writes resemble the prefabricated schemas people are used to, in other words, their ready-made idea of reality.

Thus, whatever the unexpected nature of the situations, the accidents, the fortuitous reactions, the narrative must flow without jolts, as though of its own accord, with that irrepressible *élan* which immediately wins our adherence. The least hesitation, the slightest oddity (two contradictory elements, for example, or two that do not exactly match), and unexpectedly the current of the novel ceases to sustain the reader, who suddenly wonders if he is not being "told a story" and who threatens to return to authentic testimonies, about which at least he will not have to ask himself questions as to the verisimilitude of things. Even more than to divert, the issue here is to reassure him.

Lastly, if he wants the illusion to be complete, the novelist is always supposed to know more than he says; the notion of a "slice of life" shows the extent of the knowledge he is supposed to have about what happened before and after. In the very interior of the duration he describes, he must give the impression of offering only the essentials, but of being able, if the reader insisted, to tell much more. The substance of the novel, in the image of reality, must appear inexhaustible.

Lifelike, spontaneous, limitless, the story must, in a word, be natural. Unfortunately, even while admitting that there is still something "natural" in the relations of man and the world, it turns out that writing, like any form of art, is on the contrary an intervention. What constitutes the novelist's strength is precisely that he invents, that he invents quite freely, without a model. The remarkable thing about modern fiction is that it asserts this characteristic quite deliberately, to such a degree that invention and imagination become, at the limit, the very subject of the book.

And no doubt such a development constitutes only one of the aspects of the general change in the relations man sustains with the world in which he lives. The narrative, as our academic critics conceive it—and many readers after them—represents an order. This order, which we may in effect qualify as natural, is linked to an entire rationalistic and organizing system, whose flowering corresponds to the assumption of power by the middle class. In that first half of the nineteenth century which saw the apogee—with *The Human Comedy*—of a narrative form which understandably remains for many a kind of paradise lost of the novel, certain important certainties were in circulation: in particular the confidence in a logic of things that was just and universal.

All the technical elements of the narrative—systematic use of the past tense and the third person, unconditional adoption of chronological development, linear plots, regular trajectory of the passions, impulse of each episode toward a conclusion, etc.—everything tended to impose the image of a stable, coherent, continuous, unequivocal, entirely decipherable universe. Since the intelligibility of the world was not even questioned, to tell a story did not raise a problem. The style of the novel could be innocent.

But then, with Flaubert, everything begins to vacillate. A hundred years later, the whole system is no more than a memory; and it is to that memory, to that dead system, that some seek with all their might to keep the novel fettered. Yet here, too, it is enough to read the great novels of the beginning of our century to realize that, while the disintegration of the plot has become insistently clearer in the course of the last few years, the plot itself had long since ceased to constitute the armature of the narrative. The demands of the anecdote are doubtless less constraining for Proust than for Flaubert, for Faulkner than for Proust, for Beckett than for Faulkner. . . . Henceforth, the issue is elsewhere. To tell a story has become strictly impossible.

Yet it is wrong to claim that nothing happens any longer in modern novels. Just as we must not assume man's absence on the pretext that the traditional character has disappeared, we must not identify the search for new narrative structures with an attempt to suppress any event, any passion, any adventure. The books of Proust and Faulkner are, in fact, crammed with stories; but in the former, they dissolve in order to be recomposed to the advantage of a mental architecture of time; whereas, in the latter, the development of themes and their many associations overwhelms all chronology to the point of seeming to bury again, to drown in the course of the novel what the narrative has just revealed. Even in Beckett, there is no lack of events, but these are constantly in the process of contesting themselves, jeopardizing themselves, destroying themselves, so that the same sentence may contain an observation and its immediate negation. In short, it is not the anecdote that is lacking, it is only its character of certainty, its tranquillity, its innocence.

And if I may cite my own works after these illustrious precursors, I should like to point out that *The Erasers* and *The Voyeur* both contain a plot, an "action" quite readily detectable, rich moreover in elements generally regarded as dramatic. If they at first seem without action to certain readers, is this not simply because the movement of the style is more important to them than that of passions and crimes? But I can readily imagine that in a few decades—sooner, perhaps—when this kind of writing, assimilated, becoming academic, will pass unnoticed in its turn, and when the young novelists, of course, will be doing something else, the criticism of the day, finding once again that nothing happens in their books, will reproach them for their lack of imagination and point to our novels as an example: "Look," they will say, "look how, back in the fifties, people knew how to invent stories!"

Commitment

Since telling a story to divert is "a waste of time," and telling a story to win belief has become suspect, the novelist thinks he sees another course of action: telling a story to teach. Tired of being told with condescension by "serious" people: "I don't read novels any more, I'm too old for it, it's all right for women (who have nothing to do), I prefer reality . . ." and other inanities, the novelist will fall back on didactic literature. Here at least he hopes to regain the advantage: reality is too disturbing, too ambiguous, for everyone to learn a lesson from it. When it is a question of proving something (whether showing the misery of man without God, explaining the feminine heart, or awakening class consciousness), the invented story may regain its rights: it will be so much more convincing!

Unfortunately, it no longer convinces anyone; the moment the "novelistic" is suspect, it risks, on the contrary, casting discredit on psychology, socialist morality, religion. The man interested in these disciplines will read essays, and risk less. Once again, literature is rejected into the category of the frivolous. The thesis-novel has rapidly become a genre despised more than any other. . . . Yet only a few years ago, we saw it reborn on the Left in new clothes: "commitment," "engagement"; and in the East too, with more naive colors, as "socialist realism."

Of course, the idea of a possible conjunction between an artistic renewal and a politico-economic revolution is one of those which come most naturally to mind. This idea, initially seductive from the emotional viewpoint, also seems to find support in the most obvious logic. Yet the problems raised by such a union are serious and difficult, urgent but perhaps insoluble.

At the start, the relation seems simple enough. On the one hand, the artistic forms which have succeeded one another in the history of nations seem to us to be linked to this or that type of society, to the preponderance of this or that class, to the exercise of an oppression or to the flowering of a liberty. In France, for example, in the realm of literature, it is not gratuitous to see a close relation between Racinian tragedy and the success of a court aristocracy, between the Balzacian novel and the triumph of the bourgeoisie, etc.

Since, further, it is readily admitted, even by our conservatives, that the great contemporary artists, writers or painters, generally belong (or have belonged in the period of their most important works) to the parties of the Left, we indulge ourselves by constructing this idyllic schema: Art and Revolution advancing hand in hand, struggling for the same cause, passing through the same ordeals, facing the same dangers, gradually achieving the same conquests, acceding finally to the same apotheosis.

Unfortunately, once we turn to the realm of practice, things do not turn out so well. The least we can say, today, is that the *données* of the problem are not so simple. Everyone knows the farces and the dramas which for fifty years have troubled—which trouble still—the various attempts to effect the wonderful marriage that was believed to be one of both love and reason. How could we forget the successive submissions and withdrawals, the echoing quarrels, the excommunications, the imprisonments, the suicides? How could we help seeing what painting has become, to cite only one example, in the nations where the Revolution has triumphed? How keep from smiling before the accusations of "decadence," of "gratuitousness," of "formalism" applied at random by the most zealous of the revolutionaries to everything that counts for us in contemporary art? How avoid fearing to find ourselves caught one day in the same net?

It is too easy—let us say so at once—to accuse bad leaders, bureaucratic routine, Stalin's lack of culture, the stupidity of the French Communist Party. We know from experience that it is just as delicate a matter to plead the cause of art to any politician, within any leftist group. Let us admit quite frankly: the Socialist Revolution is suspicious of Revolutionary Art and, moreover, there is no reason to believe that it is wrong to be so.

Indeed, from the viewpoint of the Revolution, everything must directly contribute to the final goal: the liberation of the proletariat. . . . Everything, including literature, painting, etc. But for the artist, on the contrary, and despite his firmest political convictions—even despite his good will as a militant revolutionary—art cannot be reduced to the status of a means in the service of a cause which transcends it, even if this cause were the most deserving, the most exalting; the artist puts nothing above his work, and he soon comes to realize that he can create only *for nothing*; the least external directive paralyzes him, the least concern for didacticism, or even for signification, is an insupportable constraint; whatever his attachment to his party or to generous ideas, the moment of creation can only bring him back to the problems of his art, and to them alone.

Yet, even at the moment when art and society, after comparable flowerings, seem to be experiencing parallel crises, it remains obvious that the problems each raises cannot be solved in the same manner. Later on, no doubt, sociologists will discover in the solutions new similarities. But for us, in any case, we must acknowledge honestly, clearly, that the struggle is not the same one, and that, today as always, there is a direct antagonism between the two points of view. Either art is nothing; and in that case, painting, literature, sculpture, music can be enrolled in the service of the revolutionary cause; they will then no longer be anything but instruments, comparable to motorized armies, to mechanized tools, to agricultural tractors; only their direct and immediate effectiveness will count.

Or else art will continue to exist as art; and in that case, for the artist at least, it will remain *the most important thing in the world*. Vis-à-vis political action, it will then always appear somewhat backward, useless, even frankly reactionary. Yet we know that in the history of peoples, art alone, this supposedly gratuitous art, will find its place, perhaps at the side of the trade unions and the barricades.

Meanwhile, that generous but utopian way of talking about a novel, a painting, or a statue, as if they might count for as much in everyday action as a strike, a mutiny, or the cry of a victim denouncing his executioners, is a disservice, ultimately, to both Art and Revolution. Too many such confusions have been perpetrated, in recent years, in the name of socialist realism. The total artistic indigence of the works which insist on its tenets is certainly not the effect of chance: the very notion of a work created *for* the expression of a social, political, economic, or moral content constitutes a lie.

Hence we must now, once and for all, stop taking seriously the accusations of gratuitousness, stop fearing "art for art's sake" as the worst of evils; we must challenge this terrorist apparatus brandished under our noses as soon as we speak of anything besides the class struggle or the anticolonialist war.

Yet not everything was condemnable a priori in that Soviet theory of "socialist realism." In literature, for example, was there not also a reaction against an accumulation of false philosophy which had finally invaded everything, from poetry to the novel? Opposing metaphysical allegories, struggling against abstract "higher worlds" which they imply, as well as against verbal delirium without an object or a vague sentimentalism of the passions, socialist realism could have a healthy influence.

Here the deceptive ideologies and the myths no longer have any currency. Literature simply reveals the situation of man and of the universe with which he is at grips. Along with the earthly "values" of bourgeois society disappear the magical, religious, or philosophical recourses to any spiritual transcendence of our visible world. The themes of despair or absurdity, now fashionable, are denounced as alibis that are too easy. Thus Ilya Ehrenburg did not hesitate to write immediately after the war: "Anxiety is a bourgeois vice. As for us, we are rebuilding."

There was every reason to hope, given such principles, that man and things would be cleansed of their systematic *romanticism*, to adopt the term so dear to Lukacs, and that at last they could be merely *what they are*. Reality would no longer be constantly situated elsewhere, but *here and now*, without ambiguity. The world would no longer find its justification in a hidden meaning, whatever it might be, its existence would no longer reside anywhere but in its concrete, solid, material presence; beyond what we see (what we perceive by our senses) there would henceforth be nothing.

Now let us consider the result. What does socialist realism offer us? Obviously, this time, the good are the good and the wicked the wicked. But precisely, the insistence that this be obvious has nothing to do with what we observe in the world. What progress is made if, in order to escape the doubling of appearances and essences, we fall into a Manicheism of good and evil?

Worse still: when, in less naive narratives, we find ourselves reading about believable men, in a complex world endowed with a sensuous existence, we soon realize in spite of everything that these men have been constructed with a view to an interpretation. Moreover, their authors do not hide it: their primary concern is to illustrate, with the utmost precision, certain historical, economic, social, political behavior.

Yet from the viewpoint of literature, economic truths, Marxist theories of surplus value and usurpation are also abstract "higher worlds." Leftist novels are to have a reality only in relation to these functional explanations of the visible world—explanations prepared in advance, tested, acknowledged—it is difficult to see what their power of discovery or invention can be; and above all, this would be only one more way of denying the world its most certain quality: the simple fact that it is there. An explanation, whatever it may be, can only be *in excess*, confronted with the presence of things. A theory of their social function, if it has governed their description, can only confuse their outline, falsify them in exactly the same way as the old psychological and moral theories, or the symbolism of metaphysical allegories.

Which explains, ultimately, why socialist realism has no need of any experiment in novelistic form, why it so mistrusts any innovation in the technique of the arts, why what suits it best, as we see every day, is the most "bourgeois" expression.

But for some time, an uneasiness has been growing in Russia and in the Peoples' Republics. The leaders are coming to understand that they have taken the wrong path, and that despite appearances, the so-called "laboratory" experiments with the structure and language of the novel, even if they interest only specialists at first, are perhaps not so futile as the party of the Revolution affects to believe.

Then what remains of commitment? Sartre, who had seen the danger of this moralizing literature, advocated a *moral* literature, which claimed only to awaken political awareness by stating the problems of our society, but which would escape the spirit of propaganda by returning the reader to his liberty. Experience has shown that this too was a utopia: once there appears the concern to signify something (something external to art), literature begins to retreat, to disappear.

Let us, then, restore to the notion of commitment the only meaning it can have for us. Instead of being of a political nature, commitment is, for the writer, the full awareness of the present problems of his own language, the conviction of their extreme importance, the desire to solve them *from within*. Here, for him, is the only chance of remaining an artist and, doubtless too, by means of an obscure and remote consequence, of some day serving something—perhaps even the Revolution.

Form and Content

One thing must trouble the partisans of socialist realism, and that is the precise resemblance of their arguments, their vocabulary, their values to those of the most hardened bourgeois critics. For example, in the matter of separating the "form" of a novel from its "contents," that is, of contrasting the *style* (choice of words and their arrangement, use of grammatical tenses and persons, structure of the narrative, etc.) with the anecdote it serves to report (events, actions of the characters, their motivations, morality implied or revealed).

Only the doctrine differs, between the academic literature of the West and that of the nations of the East. Moreover, it does not differ as much as either side claims. The story told remains in any case (according to their common optic) the important thing; a good novelist remains the one who invents splendid stories or who tells them best; thus the "great" novel, in either case, is merely one whose signification transcends its anecdote, transcends it in the direction of a profound human truth, a morality, or a metaphysic.

Hence it is natural that the accusation of "formalism" should be one of the most serious in the mouths of our critics on both sides. Here again, in spite of all they say, the word reveals a systematic decision about the novel; and here again, for all its "natural" look, the system conceals the worst abstractions—if not the worst absurdities. Further, we can discern in it a certain contempt for literature, implicit but flagrant, which is as surprising coming from its official champions—the defenders of art and tradition—as from those who have made of mass culture their favorite warhorse.

What, precisely, do they mean by formalism? Clearly enough, what is meant is an excessively marked concern for form—and, in the specific instance, for the technique of the novel—at the expense of the story and of its meaning, its signification. That leaky old boat—the academic opposition of form and content—has not yet been entirely scuttled.

In fact, quite the contrary, it seems that this stock notion has broken out more virulently than ever. If we encounter the reproach of formalism under the pens of the worst enemies reconciled on this point (enthusiasts of belles-lettres and the minions of Zhdanov), it is obviously not the result of a fortuitous encounter; they are in agreement on at least one essential point: to deny art its principal condition of existence, freedom. On one hand they choose to see literature only as one more instrument in the service of the Socialist Revolution, on the other, they require it to express that vague humanism which has survived the heyday of a society now on the wane, of which they are the last defenders.

In both cases, the point is to reduce the novel to a signification external to it, to make the novel a means of achieving some value which transcends it, some spiritual or terrestrial "beyond," future Happiness or eternal Truth. Whereas if art is something, it is *everything*, which means that it must be self-sufficient, and that there is nothing *beyond*.

There is a famous Russian cartoon in which a hippopotamus, in the bush, points out a zebra to another hippopotamus: "You see," he says, "now that's formalism." The existence of a work of art, its weight, are not at the mercy of interpretative grids which may or may not coincide with its contours. The work of art, like the world, is a living form: it *is*, it has no need of justification. The zebra is real, to deny it would not be reasonable, though its stripes are doubtless meaningless. The same is true of a symphony, a painting, a novel: it is in their form that their reality resides.

But—and this is where our socialist realists must beware—it is also in their form that their meaning resides, their "profound signification," that is, their content. There are not, for a writer, two possible ways to write the same book. When he thinks of a future novel, it is always a *way of writing* which first of all occupies his mind, and demands his hand. He has in mind certain rhythms of sentences, certain architectures, a vocabulary, certain grammatical constructions, exactly as a painter has in mind certain lines and colors. What will happen in the book comes afterward, as though secreted by the style itself. And, once the work is concluded, what will strike the reader is again this form so many affect to despise, a form whose meaning he often cannot define in any exact way, but which for him will constitute the writer's individual world.

We can make the experiment with any important work of our literature. Take *The Stranger*, for instance. It suffices to change the tense of its verbs, to replace that first person in the perfect tense (whose quite uncustomary use extends throughout the narrative) by the usual third person in the past tense, for Camus' universe to disappear at once, and all the interest of his book with it; as it suffices to change the arrangement of the words, in *Madame Bovary*, for there to be nothing left of Flaubert.

Whence the embarrassment we feel in the "committed" novels which claim to be revolutionary because they treat the condition of the workers and the problems of socialism. Their literary form, which generally dates from before 1848, makes them the most backward of bourgeois novels: their real signification, which is quite evident upon reading, the values they enjoin, are identical to those of our capitalist nineteenth century, with its humanitarian ideals, its morality, its mixture of rationalism and spirituality.

Thus it is the style, the *écriture*, and it alone which is "responsible," to adopt a word so often abused by those who accuse us of betraying our mission as writers. To speak of the content of a novel as something independent of its form comes down to striking the genre as a whole from the realm of art. For the work of art contains nothing, in the strict sense of the term (that is, as a box can hold—or be empty of—some object of an alien nature). Art is not a more or less brilliantly colored envelope intended to embellish the author's "message," a gilt paper around a package of cookies, a whitewash on a wall, a sauce that makes the fish go down easier. Art endures no servitude of this kind, nor any other pre-established function. It is based on no truth that exists before it; and one may say that it expresses nothing but itself. It creates its own equilibrium and its own meaning. It stands all by itself, like the zebra; or else it falls.

We thus see the absurdity of that favorite expression of our traditional criticism: "X has something to say and says it well." Might we not advance on the contrary that the genuine writer has nothing to say? He has only a way of speaking. He must create a world, but starting from nothing, from the dust. . . .

It is then the reproach of "gratuitousness" which is lodged against us, on the pretext that we assert our nondependence. Art for art's sake does not have a good press: it suggests a game, imposture, dilettantism. But the *necessity* a work of art acknowledges has nothing to do with utility. It is an internal necessity, which obviously appears as gratuitousness when the system of references is fixed *from without*: from the viewpoint of the Revolution, for example, as we have said, the highest art may seem a secondary, even absurd enterprise.

Here is where the difficulty—one is tempted to say the impossibility—of creation resides: the work must seem necessary, but necessary *for nothing*; its architecture is without use; its strength is untried. If such obvious points appear today as paradoxes in connection with the novel, whereas everyone readily admits them in the case of music, this is only because of what we must call the *alienation* of literature in the modern world. This alienation, which the writers themselves generally suffer without even realizing it, is maintained by the quasi-totality of our critics, beginning with those of the extreme Left who claim, in all other realms, to be combating the alienated condition of man. And we see that the situation is still worse in the socialist countries, where the liberation of the workers is, it is said, a *fait accompli*.

Like every alienation, this one effects, of course, a general inversion of values as well as of vocabulary, so that it becomes quite difficult to react against it, and so that one hesitates to use words in their normal acceptation. Such is the case for the term "formalism." Taken in its pejorative sense, it should actually apply—as Nathalie Sarraute has pointed out—only to the novelists overly concerned with their "content" who, to make themselves more clearly understood, abjure any exploration of style likely to displease or surprise: those who, precisely, adopt a form—a mold—which has given its proofs, but which has lost all force, all life. They are formalists because they have accepted a ready-made, sclerotic form which is no more than a formula, and because they cling to this fleshless carcass.

The public in its turn readily associates a concern for form with coldness. But this is no longer true from the moment form is invention and not formula. And coldness, like formalism, is entirely on the side of respect for dead rules. As for all the great novelists of the last hundred years or so, we know from their journals, their correspondence, that the constant focus of their work, the thing that constituted their passion, their most spontaneous requirement, their life, in fact, was precisely this form, by which their work has survived.

PART THREE

Words Have to Do Everything

In an interview on his return to his native England after many years' residence in the United States, W. H. Auden, asked some questions about the role of the politically committed writer, said at one point, "As a poet—not as a citizen—there is only one political duty, and that is to defend one's language from corruption. And that is particularly serious now. It is being so quickly corrupted. When it's corrupted people lose faith in what they hear, and this leads to violence."* There now follow two pieces about language in the writing craft—is it to be refreshed or further corrupted? Language is all a writer has at his command to use. It is to literature what oil and pigments are to the painter's art, what the instrument is to the musician's. Yet it is more, really, than those counterparts, for it is not, as they are, inert until touched by the artist's hand. Language has a life of its own quite beyond the writer's reach—on people's tongues. One of these two pieces argues that the writer should examine language so closely and freshly as to set himself free from all the accepted conventions; the other insists that well-tried conventions give language meaning, and that sloppiness in thinking about language, and in using its conventions, has dangers both for the writing craft and— because of the influential power of the craft—for humankind.

New York Times, 19 October 1971.

Gertrude Stein

(1874–1946)

For almost the entire first half of the twentieth century, Gertrude Stein's home in Paris, at 27 rue de Fleurus, was a cultural incubator. There, over the decades, came many young men and women, some known, mostly so far unknown, to talk and especially to listen to the large, plainly dressed woman with close-cropped hair who talked, laughed loud, swore, sang, and talked and talked—and, in her way, endlessly taught. Sherwood Anderson, Ernest Hemingway, Matisse, Cézanne, Picasso, Gris, Ezra Pound, Ford Maddox Ford, André Gide, and many others came under her spell. As a writer she has been called a cubist; she played incessant games with words, her sentences spun and spiraled with deliberate repetitions and onrushing rhythms. The Autobiography of Alice B. Toklas *(1933), cleanly, simply, and intelligibly written, pretends to be about Gertrude Stein's secretary and companion of many years but is really her own life story. Her literary production, in the end, was less important than her literary influence; she was a stylistic mentor to both Anderson and Hemingway. The following lecture was one she gave on a tour of the United States which she made the year after the* Autobiography *was published.*

FROM
POETRY AND GRAMMAR

What is poetry and if you know what poetry is what is prose.

There is no use in telling more than you know, no not even if you do not know it.

But do you do you know what prose is and do you know what poetry is.

I have said that the words in plays written in poetry are more lively than the same words written by the same poet in other kinds of poetry. It undoubtedly was true of Shakespeare, is it inevitably true of everybody. That is one thing to think about. I said that the words in a play written in prose are not as lively words as the words written in other prose by the same writer. This is true of Goldsmith and I imagine it is true of almost any writer.

There again there is something to know.

One of the things that is a very interesting thing to know is how you are feeling inside you to the words that are coming out to be outside of you.

Do you always have the same kind of feeling in relation to the sounds as the words come out of you or do you not. All this has so much to do with grammar and with poetry and with prose.

Words have to do everything in poetry and prose and some writers write more in articles and prepositions and some say you should write in nouns, and of course one has to think of everything.

A noun is a name of anything, why after a thing is named write about it. A name is adequate or it is not. If it is adequate then why go on calling it, if it is not then calling it by its name does no good.

People if you like to believe it can be made by their names. Call anybody Paul and they get to be a Paul call anybody Alice and they get to be an Alice perhaps yes perhaps no, there is something in that, but generally speaking, things once they are named the name does not go on doing anything to them and so why write in nouns. Nouns are the name of anything and just naming names is alright when you want to call a roll but is it any good for anything else. To be sure in many places in Europe as in America they do like to call rolls.

As I say a noun is a name of a thing, and therefore slowly if you feel what is inside that thing you do not call it by the name by which it is known. Everybody knows that by the way they do when they are in love and a writer should always have that intensity of emotion about whatever is the object about which he writes. And therefore and I say it again more and more one does not use nouns.

Now what other things are there beside nouns, there are a lot of other things beside nouns.

When you are at school and learn grammar grammar is very exciting. I really do not know that anything has ever been more exciting than diagraming sentences. I suppose other things may be more exciting to others when they are at school but to me undoubtedly when I was at school the really completely exciting thing was diagraming sentences and that has been to me ever since the one thing that has been completely exciting and completely completing. I like the feeling the everlasting feeling of sentences as they diagram themselves.

In that way one is completely possessing something and incidentally one's self. Now in that diagraming of the sentences of course there are articles and prepositions and as I say there are nouns but nouns as I say even by definition are completely not interesting, the same thing is true of adjectives. Adjectives are not really and truly interesting. In a way anybody can know always has known that, because after all adjectives effect nouns and as nouns are not really interesting the thing that effects a not too interesting thing is of necessity not interesting. In a way as I say anybody knows that because of course the first thing that anybody takes out of anybody's writing are the adjectives. You see of yourself how true it is that which I have just said.

Beside the nouns and the adjectives there are verbs and adverbs. Verbs and adverbs are more interesting. In the first place they have one very nice quality and that is that they can be so mistaken. It is wonderful the number of mistakes a verb can make and that is equally true of its adverb.

Nouns and adjectives never can make mistakes can never be mistaken but verbs can be so endlessly, both as to what they do and how they agree or disagree with whatever they do. The same is true of adverbs.

In that way any one can see that verbs and adverbs are more interesting than nouns and adjectives.

Beside being able to be mistaken and to make mistakes verbs can change to look like themselves or to look like something else, they are, so to speak on the move and adverbs move with them and each of them find themselves not at all annoying but very often very much mistaken. That is the reason any one can like what verbs can do. Then comes the thing that can of all things be most mistaken and they are prepositions. Prepositions can live one long life being really being nothing but absolutely nothing but mistaken and that makes them irritating if you feel that way about mistakes but certainly something that you can be continuously using and everlastingly enjoying. I like prepositions the best of all, and pretty soon we will go more completely into that.

Then there are articles. Articles are interesting just as nouns and adjectives are not. And why are they interesting just as nouns and adjectives are not. They are interesting because they do what a noun might do if a noun was not so unfortunately so completely unfortunately the name of something. Articles please, a and an and the please as the name that follows cannot please. They the names that is the nouns cannot please, because after all you know well after all that is what Shakespeare meant when he talked about a rose by any other name.

I hope now no one can have any illusion about a noun or about the adjective that goes with the noun.

But an article an article remains as a delicate and a varied something and any one who wants to write with articles and knows how to use them will always have the pleasure that using something that is varied and alive can give. That is what articles are.

Beside that there are conjunctions, and a conjunction is not varied but it has a force that need not make any one feel that they are dull. Conjunctions have made themselves live by their work. They work and as they work they live and even when they do not work and in these days they do not always live by work still nevertheless they do live.

So you see why I like to write with prepositions and conjunctions and articles and verbs and adverbs but not with nouns and adjectives. If you read my writing you will you do see what I mean.

Of course then there are pronouns. Pronouns are not as bad as nouns because in the first place practically they cannot have adjectives go with them. That already makes them better than nouns.

Then beside not being able to have adjectives go with them, they of course are not really the name of anything. They represent some one but they are not its or his name. In not being his or its or her name they already have a greater possibility of being something than if they were as a noun is the name of anything. Now actual given names of people are more lively than nouns which are the name of anything and I suppose that this is because after all the name is only given to that person when they are born, there is at least the element of choice even the element of change and anybody can be pretty well able to do what they like, they may be born Walter and become Hub, in such a way they are not like a noun. A noun has been the name of something for such a very long time. . . .

There are some punctuations that are interesting and there are some punctuations that are not. Let us begin with the punctuations that are not. Of these the one but the first and the most the completely most uninteresting is the question mark. The question mark is alright when it is all alone when it is used as a brand on cattle or when it could be used in decoration but connected with writing it is completely entirely completely uninteresting. It is evident that if you ask a question you ask a question but anybody who can read at all knows when a question is a question as it is written in writing. Therefore I ask you therefore wherefore should one use it the question mark. Beside it does not in its form go with ordinary printing and so it pleases neither the eye nor the ear and it is therefore like a noun, just an unnecessary name of something. A question is a question, anybody can know that a question is a question and so why add to it the question mark when it is already there when the question is already there in the writing. Therefore I never could bring myself to use a question mark, I always found it positively revolting, and now very few do use it. Exclamation marks have the same difficulty and also quotation marks, they are unnecessary, they are ugly, they spoil the line of the writing or the printing and anyway what is the use, if you do not know that a question is a question what is the use of its being a question. The same thing is true of an exclamation. And the same thing is true of a quotation. When I first began writing I found it simply impossible to use question marks and quotation marks and exclamation points and now anybody sees it that way. Perhaps some day they will see it some other way but now at any rate anybody can and does see it that way.

So there are the uninteresting things in punctuation uninteresting in a way that is perfectly obvious, and so we do not have to go any farther into that. There are besides dashes and dots, and these might be interesting spaces might be interesting. They might if one felt that way about them. . . .

So now to come to the real question of punctuation, periods, commas, colons, semi-colons and capitals and small letters.

I have had a long and complicated life with all these.

Let us begin with these I use the least first and these are colons and semi-colons, one might add to these commas.

When I first began writing, I felt that writing should go on, I still do feel that it should go on but when I first began writing I was completely possessed by the necessity that writing should go on and if writing should

go on what had colons and semi-colons to do with it, what had commas
to do with it, what had periods to do with it what had small letters and
capitals to do with it to do with writing going on which was at that time
the most profound need I had in connection with writing. What had
colons and semi-colons to do with it what had commas to do with it what
had periods to do with it.

What had periods to do with it. Inevitably no matter how completely
I had to have writing go on, physically one had to again and again stop
sometime and if one had to again and again stop some time then periods
had to exist. Beside I had always liked the look of periods and I liked what
they did. Stopping sometime did not really keep one from going on, it
was nothing that interfered, it was only something that happened, and
as it happened as a perfectly natural happening, I did believe in periods
and I used them. I really never stopped using them.

Beside that periods might later come to have a life of their own to commence breaking up things in arbitrary ways, that has happened lately
with me. . . . They could begin to act as they thought best and one might
interrupt one's writing with them that is not really interrupt one's writing with them but one could come to stop arbitrarily stop at times in one's
writing and so they could be used and you could use them. Periods could
come to exist in this way and they could come in this way to have a life of
their own. They did not serve you in any servile way as commas and
colons and semi-colons do. Yes you do feel what I mean.

Periods have a life of their own a necessity of their own a feeling of their
own a time of their own. And that feeling that life that necessity that time
can express itself in an infinite variety that is the reason that I have
always remained true to periods so much so that as I say recently I have
felt that one could need them more than one had ever needed them.

You can see what an entirely different thing a period is from a comma,
a colon or a semi-colon.

There are two different ways of thinking about colons and semi-colons
you can think of them as commas and as such they are purely servile or
you can think of them as periods and then using them can make you feel
adventurous. I can see that one might feel about them as periods but I
myself never have. . . . I think however lively they are or disguised they
are they are definitely more comma than period and so really I cannot
regret not having used them. They are more powerful more imposing
more pretentious than a comma but they are a comma all the same. They
really have within them deeply within them fundamentally within them
the comma nature. And now what does a comma do and what has it to
do and why do I feel as I do about them.

What does a comma do.

I have refused them so often and left them out so much and did without them so continually that I have come finally to be indifferent to them.
I do not now care whether you put them in or not but for a long time I

felt very definitely about them and would have nothing to do with them.

As I say commas are servile and they have no life of their own, and their use is not a use, it is a way of replacing one's own interest and I do decidedly like to like my own interest my own interest in what I am doing. A comma by helping you along holding your coat for you and putting on your shoes keeps you from living your life as actively as you should lead it and to me for many years and I still do feel that way about it only now I do not pay as much attention to them, the use of them was positively degrading. Let me tell you what I feel and what I mean and what I felt and what I meant.

When I was writing those long sentences of The Making of Americans, verbs active present verbs with long dependent adverbial clauses became a passion with me. I have told you that I recognize verbs and adverbs aided by prepositions and conjunctions with pronouns as possessing the whole of the active life of writing.

Complications make eventually for simplicity and therefore I have always liked dependent adverbial clauses. I have liked dependent adverbial clauses because of their variety of dependence and independence. You can see how loving the intensity of complication of these things that commas would be degrading. Why if you want the pleasure of concentrating on the final simplicity of excessive complication would you want any artificial aid to bring about that simplicity. Do you see now why I feel about the comma as I did and as I do.

Think about anything you really like to do and you will see what I mean.

When it gets really difficult you want to disentangle rather than to cut the knot, at least so anybody feels who is working with any thread, so anybody feels who is working with any tool so anybody feels who is writing any sentence or reading it after it has been written. And what does a comma do, a comma does nothing but make easy a thing that if you like it enough is easy enough without the comma. A long complicated sentence should force itself upon you, make you know yourself knowing it and the comma, well at the most a comma is a poor period that it lets you stop and take a breath but if you want to take a breath you ought to know yourself that you want to take a breath. It is not like stopping altogether which is what a period does stopping altogether has something to do with going on, but taking a breath well you are always taking a breath and why emphasize one breath rather than another breath. Anwyay that is the way I felt about it and I felt that about it very very strongly. And so I almost never used a comma. The longer, the more complicated the sentence the greater the number of the same kinds of words I had following one after another, the more the very many more I had of them the more I felt the passionate need of their taking care of themselves by themselves and not helping them, and thereby enfeebling them by putting in a comma. . . .

Another part of punctuation is capital letters and small letters. Anybody can really do as they please about that and in English printing one may say that they always have.

If you read older books you will see that they do pretty well what they please with capitals and small letters and I have always felt that one does do pretty well what one pleases with capitals and small letters. Sometimes one feels that Italians should be with a capital and sometimes with a small letter, one can feel like that about almost anything. I myself do not feel like that about proper names, I rather like to look at them with a capital on them but I can perfectly understand that a great many do not feel that way about it. In short in prose capitals and small letters have really nothing to do with the inner life of sentences and paragraphs as the other punctuation marks have as I have just been saying. . . .

Sentences and paragraphs. Sentences are not emotional but paragraphs are. I can say that as often as I like and it always remains as it is, something that is.

I said I found this out first in listening to Basket my dog drinking. And anybody listening to any dog's drinking will see what I mean.

When I wrote The Making of Americans I tried to break down this essential combination by making enormously long sentences that would be as long as the longest paragraph and so to see if there was really and truly this essential difference between paragraphs and sentences, if one went far enough with this thing with making the sentences long enough to be as long as any paragraph and so producing in them the balance of a paragraph not a balance of a sentence, because of course the balance of a paragraph is not the same balance as the balance of a sentence.

It is only necessary to read anything in order to know that. I say if I succeeded in making my sentences so long that they held within themselves the balance of both both sentences and paragraphs, what was the result.

I did in some sentences in The Making of Americans succeed in doing this thing in creating a balance that was neither the balance of a sentence nor the balance of a paragraph and in doing so I felt dimly that I had done something that was not leading to anything because after all you should not lose two things in order to have one thing because in doing so you make writing just that much less varied.

That is one thing about what I did. There is also another thing and that was a very important thing, in doing this in achieving something that had neither the balance of a sentence nor the balance of a paragraph but a balance a new balance that had to do with a sense of movement of time included in a given space which as I have already said is a definitely American thing.

An American can fill up a space in having his movement of time by adding unexpectedly anything and yet getting within the included space everything he had intended getting.

A young french boy he is a red-haired descendant of the niece of Madame Recamier went to America for two weeks most unexpectedly and I said to him what did you notice most over there. Well he said at first they were not as different from us frenchmen as I expected them to be and then I did see that they were that they were different. And what, said I, well he said, when a train was going by at a terrific pace and we waved a hat the engine driver could make a bell quite carelessly go ting ting ting, the way anybody playing at a thing could do, it was not if you know what I mean professional he said. Perhaps you do see the connection with that and my sentences that had no longer the balance of sentences because they were not the parts of a paragraph nor were they a paragraph but they had made in so far as they had come to be so long and with the balance of their own that they had they had become something that was a whole thing and in so being they had a balance which was the balance of a space completely not filled but created by something moving as moving is not as moving should be. As I said Henry James in his later writing had had a dim feeling that this was what he knew he should do.

And so though as I say there must always be sentences and paragraphs the question can really be asked must there always be sentences and paragraphs is it not possible to achieve in itself and not by sentences and paragraphs the combination that sentences are not emotional and paragraphs are. . . .

In spite of my intending to write about grammar and poetry I am still writing about grammar and prose, but and of course it may or may not be true if you find out essentially what prose is and essentially what poetry is may you not have an exciting thing happening as I had it happen with sentences and paragraphs.

After all the natural way to count is not that one and one make two but to go on counting by one and one as chinamen do as anybody does as Spaniards do as my little aunts did. One and one and one and one and one. That is the natural way to go on counting.

Now what has this to do with poetry. It has a lot to do with poetry.

Everything has a lot to do with poetry everything has a lot to do with prose.

And has prose anything to do with poetry and has poetry anything to do with prose.

And what have nouns to do with poetry and periods and capital letters. The other punctuation marks we never have to mention again. People may do as they like with them but we never have to mention them. But nouns still have to be mentioned because in coming to avoid nouns a great deal happens and has happened. It was one of the things that happened in a book I called Tender Buttons.

In The Making of Americans a long a very long prose book made up of sentences and paragraphs and the new thing that was something neither the sentence or the paragraph each one alone or in combination had ever done, I said I had gotten rid of nouns and adjectives as much as possible by the method of living in adverbs in verbs in pronouns, in adverbial clauses written or implied and in conjunctions.

But and after I had gone as far as I could in these long sentences and paragraphs that had come to do something else I then began very short things and in doing very short things I resolutely realized nouns and decided not to get around them but to meet them, to handle in short to refuse them by using them and in that way my real acquaintance with poetry was begun.

I will try to tell a little more clearly and in more detail just what happened and why it was if it was like natural counting, that is counting by one one one one one.

Nouns as you all know are the names of anything and as the names of anything of course one has had to use them. And what have they done. And what has any one done with them. That is something to know. It is as you may say as I may say a great deal to know.

Nouns are the name of anything and anything is named, that is what Adam and Eve did and if you like it is what anybody does, but do they go on just using the name until perhaps they do not know what the name is or if they do know what the name is they do not care about what the name is. This may happen of course it may. And what has poetry got to do with this and what has prose and if everything like a noun which is a name of anything is to be avoided what takes place. And what has that to do with poetry. A great deal I think and all this too has to do with other things with short and long lines and rhymes.

But first what is poetry and what is prose. I wonder if I can tell you.

We do know a little now what prose is. Prose is the balance the emotional balance that makes the reality of paragraphs and the unemotional balance that makes the reality of sentences and having realized completely realized that sentences are not emotional while paragraphs are, prose can be the essential balance that is made inside something that combines the sentence and the paragraph. . . .

Now if that is what prose is and that undoubtedly is what prose is you can see that prose real prose really great written prose is bound to be made up more of verbs adverbs prepositions prepositional clauses and conjunctions than nouns. The vocabulary in prose of course is important if you like vocabulary is always important, in fact one of the things that you can find out and that I experimented with a great deal in How to Write vocabulary in itself and by itself can be interesting and can make sense. Anybody can know that by thinking of words. It is extraordinary how it is impossible that a vocabulary does not make sense. But that is natural indeed inevitable because a vocabulary is that by definition, and so because this is so the vocabulary in respect to prose is less important than the parts of speech, and the internal balance and the movement within a given space.

So then we understand we do know what prose is.

But what is poetry.

Is it more or is it less difficult to know what poetry is. I have sometimes thought it more difficult to know what poetry is but now that I do know what poetry is and if I do know what poetry is then it is not more difficult to know what it is than to know what prose is.

What is poetry.

Poetry has to do with vocabulary just as prose has not.

So you see prose and poetry are not at all alike. They are completely different.

Poetry is I say essentially a vocabulary just as prose is essentially not.

And what is the vocabulary of which poetry absolutely is. It is a vocabulary entirely based on the noun as prose is essentially and determinately and vigorously not based on the noun.

Poetry is concerned with using with abusing, with losing with wanting, with denying with avoiding with adoring with replacing the noun. It is doing that always doing that, doing that and doing nothing but that. Poetry is doing nothing but using losing refusing and pleasing and betraying and caressing nouns. That is what poetry does, that is what poetry has to do no matter what kind of poetry it is. And there are a great many kinds of poetry.

When I said.

A rose is a rose is a rose is a rose.

And then later made that into a ring I made poetry and what did I do I caressed completely caressed and addressed a noun.

Now let us think of poetry any poetry all poetry and let us see if this is not so. Of course it is so anybody can know that.

I have said that a noun is a name of anything by definition that is what it is and a name of anything is not interesting because once you know its name the enjoyment of naming it is over and therefore in writing prose names that is nouns are completely uninteresting. But and that is a thing to be remembered you can love a name and if you love a name then saying that name any number of times only makes you love it more, more violently more persistently more tormentedly. Anybody knows how anybody calls out the name of anybody one loves. And so that is poetry really loving the name of anything and that is not prose. Yes any of you can know that.

Poetry like prose has lived through a good deal. Anybody or anything lives through a good deal. Sometimes it included everything and sometimes it includes only itself and there can be any amount of less and more at any time of its existence.

Of course when poetry really began it practically included everything it included narrative and feelings and excitements and nouns so many nouns and all emotions. It included narrative but now it does not include narrative.

I often wonder how I am ever to come to know all that I am to know about narrative. Narrative is a problem to me. I worry about it a good deal these days and I will not write or lecture about it yet, because I am still too worried about it worried about knowing what it is and how it is and where it is and how it is and how it will be what it is. However as I say now and at this time I do not I will not go into that. Suffice it to say that for the purpose of poetry it has now for a long time not had anything to do with being there.

Perhaps it is a mistake perhaps not that it is no longer there.

I myself think that something else is going to happen about narrative and I work at it a great deal at this time not work but bother about it. Bother is perhaps the better word for what I am doing just now about narrative. But anyway to go back to poetry.

Poetry did then in beginning include everything and it was natural that it should because then everything including what was happening could be made real to anyone by just naming what was happening in other words by doing what poetry always must do by living in nouns.

Nouns are the name of anything. Think of all that early poetry, think of Homer, think of Chaucer, think of the Bible and you will see what I mean you will really realize that they were drunk with nouns, to name to know how to name earth sea and sky and all that was in them was enough to make them live and love in names, and that is what poetry is it is a state of knowing and feeling a name. I know that now but I have only come to that knowledge by long writing.

So then as I say that is what poetry was and slowly as everybody knew the names of everything poetry had less and less to do with everything. Poetry did not change, poetry never changed, from the beginning until now and always in the future poetry will concern itself with the names of things. The names may be repeated in different ways and very soon I will go into that matter but now and always poetry is created by naming names the names of something the names of somebody the names of anything. Nouns are the names of things and so nouns are the basis of poetry.

Before we go any further there is another matter. Why are the lines of poetry short, so much shorter than prose, why do they rhyme, why in order to complete themselves do they have to end with what they began, why are all these things the things that are in the essence of poetry even when the poetry was long even when now the poetry has changed its form.

Once more the answer is the same and that is that such a way to express oneself is the natural way when one expresses oneself in loving the name of anything. Think what you do when you do do that when you love the name of anything really love its name. Inevitably you express yourself in that way, in the way poetry expresses itself that is in short lines in repeating what you began in order to do it again. Think of how you talk to anything whose name is new to you a lover a baby or a dog or a new land or any part of it. Do you not inevitably repeat what you call out and is that calling out not of necessity in short lines. Think about it and you will see what I mean by what you feel.

So as I say poetry is essentially the discovery, the love, the passion for the name of anything.

Now to come back to how I know what I know about poetry.

I was writing The Making of Americans, I was completely obsessed by the inner life of everything including generations of everybody's living and I was writing prose, prose that had to do with the balancing the inner balancing of everything. I have already told you all about that.

And then, something happened and I began to discover the names of things, that is not discover the names but discover the things the things to see the things to look at and in so doing I had of course to name them not to give them new names but to see that I could find out how to know that they were there by their names or by replacing their names. And how was I to do so. They had their names and naturally I called them by the names they had and in doing so having begun looking at them I called them by their names with passion and that made poetry, I did not mean it to make poetry but it did. . . .

I discovered everything then and its name, discovered it and its name. I had always known it and its name but all the same I did discover it.

I remember very well when I was a little girl and I and my brother found as children will the love poems of their very very much older brother. This older brother had just written one and it said that he had often sat and looked at any little square of grass and it had been just a square of grass as grass is, but now he was in love and so the little square of grass was all filled with birds and bees and butterflies, the difference was what love was. The poem was funny we and he knew the poem was funny but he was right, being in love made him make poetry, and poetry made him feel the things and their names, and so I repeat nouns are poetry.

So then in Tender Buttons I was making poetry but and it seriously troubled me, dimly I knew that nouns made poetry but in prose I no longer needed the help of nouns and in poetry did I need the help of nouns. Was there not a way of naming things that would not invent names, but mean names without naming them.

I had always been very impressed from the time that I was very young by having had it told me and then afterwards feeling it myself that Shakespeare in the forest of Arden had created a forest without mentioning the things that make a forest. You feel it all but he does not name its names.

Now that was a thing that I too felt in me the need of making it be a thing that could be named without using its name. After all one had known its name anything's name for so long, and so the name was not new but the thing being alive was always new.

What was there to do.

I commenced trying to do something in Tender Buttons about this thing. I went on and on trying to do this thing. I remember in writing An Acquaintance With Description looking at anything until something that was not the name of that thing but was in a way that actual thing would come to be written.

Naturally, and one may say that is what made Walt Whitman naturally that made the change in the form of poetry, that we who had known the names so long did not get a thrill from just knowing them. We that is any human being living has inevitably to feel the thing anything being existing, but the name of that thing of that anything is no longer anything to thrill any one except children. So as everybody has to be a poet, what was there to do. This that I have just described, the creating it without naming it, was what broke the rigid form of the noun the simple noun poetry which now was broken.

Of course you all do know that when I speak of naming anything, I include emotions as well as things.

So then there we were and what were we to do about it. Go on, of course go on what else does anybody do, so I did, I went on.

Of course you might say why not invent new names new languages but that cannot be done. It takes a tremendous amount of inner necessity to invent even one word, one can invent imitating movements and emotions in sounds, and in the poetical language of some languages you have that, the german language as a language suffers from this what the words mean sound too much like what they do, and children do these things by one sort or another of invention but this has really nothing to do with language. Language as a real thing is not imitation either of sounds or colors or emotions it is an intellectual recreation and there is no possible doubt about it and it is going to go on being that as long as humanity is anything. So every one must stay with the language their language that has come to be spoken and written and which has in it all the history of its intellectual recreation. . . .

So then poetry up to the present time has been a poetry of nouns a poetry of naming something of really naming that thing passionately completely passionately naming that thing by its name.

Slowly and particularly during the nineteenth centry the English nineteenth century everybody had come to know too well very much too well the name anything had when you called it by its name.

That is something that inevitably happened. And what else could they do. They had to go on doing what they did, that is calling anything by its name passionately but if as I say they really knew its name too well could they call it its name simply in that way. Slowly they could not.

And then Walt Whitman came. He wanted really wanted to express the thing and not call it by its name. He worked very hard at that, and he called it Leaves of Grass because he wanted it to be as little a well known name to be called upon passionately as possible. I do not at all know whether Whitman knew that he wanted to do this but there is no doubt at all but that is what he did want to do.

You have the complete other end of this thing in a poet like Longfellow, I cite him because a commonplace poet shows you more readily and clearly just what the basis of poetry is than a better one. And Longfellow knew all about calling out names, he on the whole did it without passion but he did it very well.

Of course in the history of poetry there have been many who have also tried to name the thing without naming its names, but this is not a history of poets it is a telling what I know about poetry.

And so knowing all this about poetry I struggled more and more with this thing. . . . I struggled with the ridding myself of nouns, I knew nouns must go in poetry as they had gone in prose if anything that is everything was to go on meaning something.

And so I went on with this exceeding struggle of knowing really knowing what a thing was really knowing it knowing anything I was seeing anything I was feeling so that its name could be something, by its name coming to be a thing in itself as it was but would not be anything just and only as a name.

I wonder if you do see what I mean.

What I mean by what I have just said is this. I had to feel anything and everything that for me was existing so intensely that I could put it down in writing as a thing in itself without at all necessarily using its name. The name of a thing might be something in itself if it could come to be real enough but just as a name it was not enough something. At any rate that is the way I felt and still do feel about it.

And so I went through a very long struggle and in this struggle I began to be troubled about narrative a narrative of anything that was or might be happening.

The newspapers tell us about it but they tell it to us as nouns tell it to us that is they name it, and in naming it, it as a telling of it is no longer anything. That is what a newspaper is by definition just as a noun is a name by definition.

And so I was slowly beginning to know something about what poetry was. And here was the question if in poetry one could lose the noun as I had really and truly lost it in prose would there be any difference between poetry and prose. As this thing came once more to be a doubt inside me I began to work very hard at poetry. . . .

I decided that if one definitely completely replaced the noun by the thing in itself, it was eventually to be poetry and not prose which would have to deal with everything that was not movement in space. There could no longer be form to decide anything, narrative that is not newspaper narrative but real narrative must of necessity be told by any one having come to the realization that the noun must be replaced not by inner balance but by the thing in itself and that will eventually lead to everything. I am working at this thing and what will it do this I do not know but I hope that I will know. In the Four In America I have gone on beginning but I am sure that there is in this what there is that it is necessary to do if one is to do anything or everything. Do you see what I mean. Well anyway that is the way that I do now feel about it, and this is all that I do know, and I do believe in knowing all I do know, about prose and poetry. The rest will come considerably later.

George Orwell

(1903–1950)

The author of Animal Farm *and* 1984 *had a different kind of influence on litera-*
ture from Gertrude Stein's, and an extraordinary one it was, for he was able to
help any who would read him to look at, through, and beyond the violently
contending ideologies of the twentieth century, and to consider the real mean-
ing, rather than any propagandized version of the meaning, of human freedom.
He had two selves. For the first three decades of his life he was Eric Blair—son
of a British Sub-Deputy Opium Agent, First Grade, in India; Etonian; policeman
in Burma. Then, for only seventeen years, until his premature death in 1950 at
forty-seven years of age, he turned face about and became George Orwell—an
incognito explorer in the lower depths of society, an emigrant from privilege, a
writer in search of raw truth. It is Orwell's insistence on seeing things as they
are, not as they are commonly thought to be, nor as one might wish they were,
nor yet as centers of power may insist that they are, that shines through all of
his writing—including the essay that follows.

POLITICS AND THE ENGLISH LANGUAGE

Most people who bother with the matter at all would admit that the English language is in a bad way, but it is generally assumed that we cannot
by conscious action do anything about it. Our civilization is decadent and
our language—so the argument runs—must inevitably share in the general
collapse. It follows that any struggle against the abuse of language is a
sentimental archaism, like preferring candles to electric light or hansom
cabs to aeroplanes. Underneath this lies the half-conscious belief that
language is a natural growth and not an instrument which we shape for
our own purposes.

Now, it is clear that the decline of a language must ultimately have
political and economic causes: it is not due simply to the bad influence of
this or that individual writer. But an effect can become a cause, reinforcing
the original cause and producing the same effect in an intensified form,
and so on indefinitely. A man may take to drink because he feels himself
to be a failure, and then fail all the more completely because he drinks.
It is rather the same thing that is happening to the English language. It
becomes ugly and inaccurate because our thoughts are foolish, but the
slovenliness of our language makes it easier for us to have foolish
thoughts. The point is that the process is reversible. Modern English,
especially written English, is full of bad habits which spread by imitation
and which can be avoided if one is willing to take the necessary trouble.

If one gets rid of these habits one can think more clearly, and to think clearly is a necessary first step towards political regeneration: so that the fight against bad English is not frivolous and is not the exclusive concern of professional writers. I will come back to this presently, and I hope that by that time the meaning of what I have said here will have become clearer. Meanwhile, here are five specimens of the English language as it is now habitually written.

These five passages have not been picked out because they are especially bad—I could have quoted far worse if I had chosen—but because they illustrate various of the mental vices from which we now suffer. They are a little below the average, but are fairly representative samples. I number them so that I can refer back to them when necessary:

"(1) I am not, indeed, sure whether it is not true to say that the Milton who once seemed not unlike a seventeenth-century Shelley had not become, out of an experience ever more bitter in each year, more alien [*sic*] to the founder of that Jesuit sect which nothing could induce him to tolerate."

Professor Harold Laski
(Essay in *Freedom of Expression*)

"(2) Above all, we cannot play ducks and drakes with a native battery of idioms which prescribes such egregious collocations of vocables as the Basic *put up with* for *tolerate* or *put at a loss* for *bewilder*."

Professor Lancelot Hogben
(*Interglossa*)

"(3) On the one side we have the free personality: by definition it is not neurotic, for it has neither conflict nor dream. Its desires, such as they are, are transparent, for they are just what institutional approval keeps in the forefront of consciousness; another institutional pattern would alter their number and intensity; there is little in them that is natural, irreducible, or culturally dangerous. But *on the other side*, the social bond itself is nothing but the mutual reflection of these self-secure integrities. Recall the definition of love. Is not this the very picture of a small academic? Where is there a place in this hall of mirrors for either personality or fraternity?"

Essay on psychology in *Politics* (New York)

"(4) All the 'best people' from the gentlemen's clubs, and all the frantic fascist captains, united in common hatred of Socialism and bestial horror of the rising tide of the mass revolutionary movement, have turned to acts of provocation, to foul incendiarism, to medieval legends of poisoned wells, to legalize their own destruction of proletarian organizations, and rouse the agitated petty-bourgeoisie to chauvinistic fervour on behalf of the fight against the revolutionary way out of the crisis."

Communist pamphlet

"(5) If a new spirit *is* to be infused into this old country, there is one thorny and contentious reform which must be tackled, and that is the humanization and galvanization of the B.B.C. Timidity here will bespeak canker and atrophy of the soul. The heart of Britain may be sound and of strong beat, for instance, but the British lion's roar at present is like that of Bottom in Shakespeare's *Midsummer Night's Dream*—as gentle as any sucking dove. A virile new Britain cannot continue indefinitely to be traduced in the eyes or rather ears, of the world by the effete languors of Langham Place, brazenly masquerading as 'standard English'. When the Voice of Britain is heard at nine o'clock, better far and infinitely less ludicrous to hear aitches honestly dropped than the present priggish, inflated, inhibited, school-ma'amish arch braying of blameless bashful mewing maidens!"

Letter in Tribune

Each of these passages has faults of its own, but, quite apart from avoidable ugliness, two qualities are common to all of them. The first is staleness of imagery: the other is lack of precision. The writer either has a meaning and cannot express it, or he inadvertently says something else, or he is almost indifferent as to whether his words mean anything or not. This mixture of vagueness and sheer incompetence is the most marked characteristic of modern English prose, and especially of any kind of political writing. As soon as certain topics are raised, the concrete melts into the abstract and no one seems able to think of turns of speech that are not hackneyed: prose consists less and less of *words* chosen for the sake of their meaning, and more and more of *phrases* tacked together like the sections of a prefabricated hen-house. I list below, with notes and examples, various of the tricks by means of which the work of prose-construction is habitually dodged:

Dying Metaphors. A newly invented metaphor assists thought by evoking a visual image, while on the other hand a metaphor which is technically "dead" (e.g. *iron resolution*) has in effect reverted to being an ordinary word and can generally be used without loss of vividness. But in between these two classes there is a huge dump of worn-out metaphors which have lost all evocative power and are merely used because they save people the trouble of inventing phrases for themselves. Examples are: *Ring the changes on, take up the cudgels for, toe the line, ride roughshod over, stand shoulder to shoulder with, play into the hands of, no axe to grind, grist to the mill, fishing in troubled waters, on the order of the day, Achilles' heel, swan song, hotbed.* Many of these are used without knowledge of their meaning (what is a "rift", for instance?), and incompatible metaphors are frequently mixed, a sure sign that the writer is not interested in what he is saying. Some metaphors now current have been twisted out of their original meaning without those who use them even being aware of the fact. For example, *toe the line* is sometimes written *tow the line.* Another example is *the hammer and the anvil,* now always used with the implication that the anvil gets the worst of it. In real life it is always the anvil that breaks the hammer, never the other way about: a writer who stopped to think what he was saying would be aware of this, and would avoid perverting the original phrase.

Operators or *verbal false limbs.* These save the trouble of picking out appropriate verbs and nouns, and at the same time pad each sentence with extra syllables which give it an appearance of symmetry. Characteristic phrases are: *render inoperative, militate against, make contact with, be subjected to, give rise to, give grounds for, have the effect of, play a leading part (role) in, make itself felt, take effect, exhibit a tendency to, serve the purpose of, etc., etc.* The keynote is the elimination of simple verbs. Instead of being a single word, such as *break, stop, spoil, mend, kill,* a verb becomes a *phrase,* made up of a noun or adjective tacked on to some general-purposes verb such as *prove, serve, form, play, render.* In addition, the passive voice is wherever possible used in preference to the active, and noun constructions are used instead of gerunds (*by examination of* instead of *by examining*). The range of verbs is further cut down by means of the *-ize* and *de-* formations, and the banal statements are given an appearance of profundity by means of the *not un-* formation. Simple conjunctions and prepositions are replaced by such phrases as *with respect to, having regard to, the fact that, by dint of, in view of, in the interests of, on the hypothesis that;* and the ends of sentences are saved from anticlimax by such resounding commonplaces as *greatly to be desired, cannot be left out of account, a development to be expected in the near future, deserving of serious consideration, brought to a satisfactory conclusion,* and so on and so forth.

Pretentious diction. Words like *phenomenon, element, individual* (as noun), *objective, categorical, effective, virtual, basic, primary, promote, constitute, exhibit, exploit, utilize, eliminate, liquidate,* are used to dress up simple statement and give an air of scientific impartiality to biased judgments. Adjectives like *epoch-making, epic, historic, unforgettable, triumphant, age-old, inevitable, inexorable, veritable,* are used to dignify the sordid processes of international politics, while writing that aims at glorifying war usually takes on an archaic colour, its characteristic words being: *realm, throne, chariot, mailed fist, trident, sword, shield, buckler, banner, jackboot, clarion.* Foreign words and expressions such as *cul de sac, ancien régime, deus ex machina, mutatis mutandis, status quo, gleichschaltung, weltanschauung,* are used to give an air of culture and elegance. Except for the useful abbreviations *i.e., e.g.,* and *etc.,* there is no real need for any of the hundreds of foreign phrases now current in English. Bad writers, and especially scientific, political and sociological writers, are nearly always haunted by the notion that Latin or Greek words are grander than Saxon ones, and unnecessary words like *expedite, ameliorate, predict, extraneous, deracinated, clandestine, subaqueous* and hundreds of others constantly gain ground from their Anglo-Saxon opposite numbers.[1] The jargon peculiar to Marxist writing (*hyena, hangman, cannibal, petty*

---

[1] *An interesting illustration of this is the way in which the English flower names which were in use till very recently are being ousted by Greek ones,* snapdragon *becoming* antirrhinum, forget-me-not *becoming* myosotis, *etc. It is hard to see any practical reason for this change of fashion: it is probably due to an instinctive turning-away from the more homely word and a vague feeling that the Greek word is scientific.*

bourgeois, these gentry, lacquey, flunkey, mad dog, White Guard, etc.) consists largely of words and phrases translated from Russian, German or French; but the normal way of coining a new word is to use a Latin or Greek root with the appropriate affix and, where necessary, the -ize formation. It is often easier to make up words of this kind (*deregionalize, impermissible, extramarital, non-fragmentatory* and so forth) than to think up the English words that will cover one's meaning. The result, in general, is an increase in slovenliness and vagueness.

Meaningless words. In certain kinds of writing, particularly in art criticism and literary criticism, it is normal to come across long passages which are almost completely lacking in meaning.[2] Words like *romantic, plastic, values, human, dead, sentimental, natural, vitality,* as used in art criticism, are strictly meaningless, in the sense that they not only do not point to any discoverable object, but are hardly ever expected to do so by the reader. When one critic writes, "The outstanding feature of Mr. X's work is its living quality", while another writes, "The immediately striking thing about Mr. X's work is its peculiar deadness", the reader accepts this as a simple difference of opinion. If words like *black* and *white* were involved, instead of the jargon words *dead* and *living,* he would see at once that language was being used in an improper way. Many political words are similarly abused. The word *Fascism* has now no meaning except in so far as it signifies "something not desirable". The words *democracy, socialism, freedom, patriotic, realistic, justice,* have each of them several different meanings which cannot be reconciled with one another. In the case of a word like *democracy,* not only is there no agreed definition, but the attempt to make one is resisted from all sides. It is almost universally felt that when we call a country democratic we are praising it: consequently the defenders of every kind of régime claim that it is a democracy, and fear that they might have to stop using the word if it were tied down to any one meaning. Words of this kind are often used in a consciously dishonest way. That is, the person who uses them has his own private definition, but allows his hearer to think he means something quite different. Statements like *Marshal Pétain was a true patriot, The Soviet Press is the freest in the world, The Catholic Church is opposed to persecution,* are almost always made with intent to deceive. Other words used in variable meanings, in most cases more or less dishonestly, are: *class, totalitarian, science, progressive, reactionary, bourgeois, equality.*

Now that I have made this catalogue of swindles and perversions, let me give another example of the kind of writing that they lead to. This time it

---

[2]*Example:* "*Comfort's catholicity of perception and image, strangely Whitmanesque in range, almost the exact opposite in aesthetic compulsion, continues to evoke that trembling atmospheric accumulative hinting at a cruel, an inexorably serene timelessness . . . Wrey Gardiner scores by aiming at simple bull's-eyes with precision. Only they are not so simple, and through this contented sadness runs more than the surface bitter-sweet of resignation.*" (Poetry Quarterly.)

must of its nature be an imaginary one. I am going to translate a passage of good English into modern English of the worst sort. Here is a well-known verse from *Ecclesiastes*:

> "I returned and saw under the sun, that the race it not to the swift, nor the battle to the strong, neither yet bread to the wise, nor yet riches to men of understanding, nor yet favour to men of skill; but time and chance happeneth to them all."

Here it is in modern English:

> "Objective considerations of contemporary phenomena compels the conclusion that success or failure in competitive activities exhibits no tendency to be commensurate with innate capacity, but that a considerable element of the unpredictable must invariably be taken into account."

This is a parody, but not a very gross one. Exhibit (3), above, for instance, contains several patches of the same kind of English. It will be seen that I have not made a full translation. The beginning and ending of the sentence follow the original meaning fairly closely, but in the middle the concrete illustrations—race, battle, bread—dissolve into the vague phrase "success or failure in competitive activities". This had to be so, because no modern writer of the kind I am discussing—no one capable of using phrases like "objective consideration of contemporary phenomena" —would ever tabulate his thoughts in that precise and detailed way. The whole tendency of modern prose is away from concreteness. Now analyse these two sentences a little more closely. The first contains forty-nine words but only sixty syllables, and all its words are those of everyday life. The second contains thirty-eight words of ninety syllables: eighteen of its words are from Latin roots, and one from Greek. The first sentence contains six vivid images, and only one phrase ("time and chance") that could be called vague. The second contains not a single fresh, arresting phrase, and in spite of its ninety syllables it gives only a shortened version of the meaning contained in the first. Yet without a doubt it is the second kind of sentence that is gaining ground in modern English. I do not want to exaggerate. This kind of writing is not yet universal, and outcrops of simplicity will occur here and there in the worst-written page. Still, if you or I were told to write a few lines on the uncertainty of human fortunes, we should probably come much nearer to my imaginary sentence than to the one from *Ecclesiastes*.

As I have tried to show, modern writing at its worst does not consist in picking out words for the sake of their meaning and inventing images in order to make the meaning clearer. It consists in gumming together long strips of words which have already been set in order by someone else, and making the results presentable by sheer humbug. The attraction of this way of writing is that it is easy. It is easier—even quicker, once you have the habit—to say *In my opinion it is a not unjustifiable assumption that* than to say *I think*. If you use ready-made phrases, you not only don't have to hunt about for words; you also don't have to bother with the rhythms of your sentences, since these phrases are generally so arranged as to be more or less euphonious. When you are composing in a hurry—when you are dictating to a stenographer, for instance, or making a public speech—it is natural to fall into a pretentious, Latinized style. Tags like *a consideration which we should do well to bear in mind* or *a conclusion to which all of us would readily assent* will save many a sentence from coming down with a bump. By using stale metaphors, similes and idioms, you save much mental effort, at the cost of leaving your meaning vague, not only for your reader but for yourself. This is the significance of mixed metaphors. The sole aim of a metaphor is to call up a visual image. When these images clash—as in *The Fascist octopus has sung its swan song, the jackboot is thrown into the melting pot*—it can be taken as certain that the writer is not seeing a mental image of the objects he is naming; in other words he is not really thinking. Look again at the examples I gave at the beginning of this essay. Professor Laski (1) uses five negatives in fifty-three words. One of these is superfluous, making nonsense of the whole passage, and in addition there is the slip *alien* for akin, making further nonsense, and several avoidable pieces of clumsiness which increase the general vagueness. Professor Hogben (2) plays ducks and drakes with a battery which is able to write prescriptions, and, while disapproving of the everyday phrase *put up with*, is unwilling to look *egregious* up in the dictionary and see what it means. (3), if one takes an uncharitable attitude towards it, is simply meaningless: probably one could work out its intended meaning by reading the whole of the article in which it occurs. In (4), the writer knows more or less what he wants to say, but an accumulation of stale phrases chokes him like tea leaves blocking a sink. In (5), words and meaning have almost parted company. People who write in this manner usually have a general emotional meaning—they dislike one thing and want to express solidarity with another—but they are not interested in the detail of what they are saying. A scrupulous writer, in every sentence that he writes, will ask himself at least four questions, thus: What am I trying to say? What words will express it? What image or idiom will make it clearer? Is this image fresh enough to have an effect? And he will probably ask himself two more: Could I put it more shortly? Have I said anything that is avoidably ugly? But you are not obliged to go to all this trouble. You can shirk it by simply throwing your mind open and letting the ready-made phrases come crowding in. They will construct your sentences for you—even think your thoughts for you, to a certain extent—and at need they will perform the important service of partially concealing your meaning even from yourself. It is at this point that the special connection between politics and the debasement of language becomes clear.

In our time it is broadly true that political writing is bad writing. Where it is not true, it will generally be found that the writer is some kind of rebel, expressing his private opinions and not a "party line". Orthodoxy, of whatever colour, seems to demand a lifeless, imitative style. The political dialects to be found in pamphlets, leading articles, manifestos, White Papers and the speeches of under-secretaries do, of course, vary from party to party, but they are all alike in that one almost never finds in them a fresh, vivid, home-made turn of speech. When one watches some tired hack on the platform mechanically repeating the familiar phrases— *bestial atrocities, iron heel, bloodstained tyranny, free peoples of the world, stand shoulder to shoulder*—one often has a curious feeling that one is not watching a live human being but some kind of dummy: a feeling which suddenly becomes stronger at moments when the light catches the speaker's spectacles and turns them into blank discs which seem to have no eyes behind them. And this is not altogether fanciful. A speaker who uses that kind of phraseology has gone some distance towards turning himself into a machine. The appropriate noises are coming out of his larynx, but his brain is not involved as it would be if he were choosing his words for himself. If the speech he is making is one that he is accustomed to make over and over again, he may be almost unconscious of what he is saying, as one is when one utters the responses in church. And this reduced state of consciousness, if not indispensable, is at any rate favourable to political conformity.

In our time, political speech and writing are largely the defence of the indefensible. Things like the continuance of British rule in India, the Russian purges and deportations, the dropping of the atom bombs on Japan, can indeed be defended, but only by arguments which are too brutal for most people to face, and which do not square with the professed aims of political parties. Thus political language has to consist largely of euphemism, question-begging and sheer cloudy vagueness. Defenceless villages are bombarded from the air, the inhabitants driven out into the countryside, the cattle machine-gunned, the huts set on fire with incendiary bullets: this is called *pacification*. Millions of peasants are robbed of their farms and sent trudging along the roads with no more than they can carry: this is called *transfer of population* or *rectification of frontiers*. People are imprisoned for years without trial, or shot in the back of the neck or sent to die of scurvy in Arctic lumber camps: this is called *elimination of unreliable elements*. Such phraseology is needed if one wants to name things without calling up mental pictures of them. Consider for instance some comfortable English professor defending Russian totalitarianism. He cannot say outright, "I believe in killing off your opponents when you can get good results by doing so". Probably, therefore, he will say something like this:

"While freely conceding that the Soviet régime exhibits certain features which the humanitarian may be inclined to deplore, we must, I think, agree that a certain curtailment of the right to political opposition is an unavoidable concomitant of transitional periods, and that the rigours which the Russian people have been called upon to undergo have been amply justified in the sphere of concrete achievement."

The inflated style is itself a kind of euphemism. A mass of Latin words falls upon the facts like soft snow, blurring the outlines and covering up all the details. The great enemy of clear language is insincerity. When there is a gap between one's real and one's declared aims, one turns as it were instinctively to long words and exhausted idioms, like a cuttlefish squirting out ink. In our age there is no such thing as "keeping out of politics". All issues are political issues, and politics itself is a mass of lies, evasions, folly, hatred and schizophrenia. When the general atmosphere is bad, language must suffer. I should expect to find—this is a guess which I have not sufficient knowledge to verify—that the German, Russian and Italian languages have all deteriorated in the last ten or fifteen years, as a result of dictatorship.

But if thought corrupts language, language can also corrupt thought. A bad usage can spread by tradition and imitation, even among people who should and do know better. The debased language that I have been discussing is in some ways very convenient. Phrases like *a not unjustifiable assumption, leaves much to be desired, would serve no good purpose, a consideration which we should do well to bear in mind*, are a continuous temptation, a packet of aspirins always at one's elbow. Look back through this essay, and for certain you will find that I have again and again committed the very faults I am protesting against. By this morning's post I have received a pamphlet dealing with conditions in Germany. The author tells me that he "felt impelled" to write it. I open it at random, and here is almost the first sentence that I see: "(The Allies) have an opportunity not only of achieving a radical transformation of Germany's social and political structure in such a way as to avoid a nationalistic reaction in Germany itself, but at the same time of laying the foundations of a co-operative and unified Europe." You see, he "feels impelled" to write—feels, presumably, that he has something new to say—and yet his words, like cavalry horses answering the bugle, group themselves automatically into the familiar dreary pattern. This invasion of one's mind by ready-made phrases (*lay the foundations, achieve a radical transformation*) can only be prevented if one is constantly on guard against them, and every such phrase anaesthetizes a portion of one's brain.

I said earlier that the decadence of our language is probably curable. Those who deny this would argue, if they produced an argument at all, that language merely reflects existing social conditions, and that we cannot influence its development by any direct tinkering with words and constructions. So far as the general tone or spirit of a language goes, this may be true, but it is not true in detail. Silly words and expressions have often disappeared, not through any evolutionary process but owing to the conscious action of a minority. Two recent examples were *explore every avenue* and *leave no stone unturned*, which were killed by the jeers of a few journalists. There is a long list of flyblown metaphors which could similarly be got rid of if enough people would interest themselves in the job; and it should also be possible to laugh the *not un-* formation out of existence,[3] to reduce the amount of Latin and Greek in the average sentence, to drive out foreign phrases and strayed scientific words, and, in general, to make pretentiousness unfashionable. But all these are minor points. The defence of the English language implies more than this, and perhaps it is best to start by saying what it does *not* imply.

To begin with it has nothing to do with archaism, with the salvaging of obsolete words and turns of speech, or with the setting up of a "standard English" which must never be departed from. On the contrary, it is especially concerned with the scrapping of every word or idiom which has outworn its usefulness. It has nothing to do with correct grammar and syntax, which are of no importance so long as one makes one's meaning clear, or with the avoidance of Americanisms, or with having what is called a "good prose style". On the other hand it is not concerned with fake simplicity and the attempt to make written English colloquial. Nor does it even imply in every case preferring the Saxon word to the Latin one, though it does imply using the fewest and shortest words that will cover one's meaning. What is above all needed is to let the meaning choose the word, and not the other way about. In prose, the worst thing one can do with words is to surrender to them. When you think of a concrete object, you think wordlessly, and then, if you want to describe the thing you have been visualizing you probably hunt about till you find the exact words that seem to fit it. When you think of something abstract you are more inclined to use words from the start, and unless you make a conscious effort to prevent it, the existing dialect will come rushing in and do the job for you, at the expense of blurring or even changing your meaning. Probably it is better to put off using words as long as possible and get one's meaning as clear as one can through pictures or sensations. Afterwards one can choose—not simply *accept*—the phrases that will best cover the meaning, and then switch round and decide what impression one's words are likely to make on another person. This last effort of the mind cuts out all stale or mixed images, all prefabricated phrases, needless repetitions, and humbug and vagueness generally. But one can often be in doubt about the effect of a word or a phrase, and one needs rules that one can rely on when instinct fails. I think the following rules will cover most cases:

(i) Never use a metaphor, simile or other figure of speech which you are used to seeing in print.

(ii) Never use a long word where a short one will do.

(iii) If it is possible to cut a word out, always cut it out.

---

[3]*One can cure oneself of the* not un- *formation by memorizing this sentence:* A not unblack dog was chasing a not unsmall rabbit across a not ungreen field.

(iv) Never use the passive where you can use the active.
 (v) Never use a foreign phrase, a scientific word or a jargon word if you can think of an everyday English equivalent.
(vi) Break any of these rules sooner than say anything outright barbarous.

These rules sound elementary, and so they are, but they demand a deep change of attitude in anyone who has grown used to writing in the style now fashionable. One could keep all of them and still write bad English, but one could not write the kind of stuff that I quoted in those five specimens at the beginning of this article.

I have not here been considering the literary use of language, but merely language as an instrument for expressing and not for concealing or preventing thought. Stuart Chase and others have come near to claiming that all abstract words are meaningless, and have used this as a pretext for advocating a kind of political quietism. Since you don't know what Fascism is, how can you struggle against Fascism? One need not swallow such absurdities as this, but one ought to recognize that the present political chaos is connected with the decay of language, and that one can probably bring about some improvement by starting at the verbal end. If you simplify your English, you are freed from the worst follies of orthodoxy. You cannot speak any of the necessary dialects, and when you make a stupid remark its stupidity will be obvious, even to yourself. Political language—and with variations this is true of all political parties, from Conservatives to Anarchists—is designed to make lies sound truthful and murder respectable, and to give an appearance of solidity to pure wind. One cannot change this all in a moment, but one can at least change one's own habits, and from time to time one can even, if one jeers loudly enough, send some worn-out and useless phrase—some *jackboot, Achilles' heel, hotbed, melting pot, acid test, veritable inferno* or other lump of verbal refuse—into the dustbin where it belongs.

PART FOUR
Writing and Survival

All of George Orwell's writings ran counter to the assumption,
honored for a long time in the West, that literature and politics,
art and morality, are, and should be, strangers to each other.
In Europe and America in recent years it has been fashionable
to claim for art a total aesthetic autonomy, a freedom from
any consideration whatsoever of consequence. One of its tasks
indeed has seemed to be to expose the sham in traditional
moralities, without thought for renewal and replacement. Art
has sometimes seemed to be a diving search for the sea-floor
of the id. Orwell could not accept art on those terms. With his
burning skepticism and anger he pushed art and morality
together again, no matter how uncomfortably. At the height of
the era of totalitarian states, in each of which an effort had
been made to put all writing at the service of the reigning
power, Orwell reopened, for all creative artists to face, the
question of artistic responsibility. In this section are two essays
which take two views—one post-Nazi German, one post-Stalin
Russian; one sardonic, one in fearful earnest—of this
responsibility.

Günter Grass

(1927–   )

Not long after the Second World War, two German writers who had met as prisoners of war founded a literary magazine, Der Ruf, *to publish what came to be called Rubble Literature, writings that expressed the bitterness of the young "betrayed generation." (One of the leading spokesmen of that generation was Heinrich Böll, the 1972 Nobel Prize winner.) After sixteen issues the American occupation authorities, who disapproved of the magazine's politics, shut it down. In 1947 a number of writers tried to start another, to be called* Der Skorpion, *but this time the Americans refused permission to publish in advance, and so the writers agreed to meet annually and read manuscripts to each other; the circle came to be known as Group 47, which in some years awarded a prize to a newcomer it considered specially gifted. In 1958 the group's prize was awarded to Günter Grass for a chapter of his first novel,* The Tin Drum. *Grass's work epitomized the effort of the Group 47 writers to distance themselves from the literal bitterness of Rubble Literature; to achieve detachment; to deal with their past by coming at it indirectly, through a visionary, dreamlike, and often grotesque literature. Grass's reputation rests mainly on his two novels,* The Tin Drum *and* Dog Years. *In the 1960s he began to be active in politics; he wrote speeches for Willy Brandt, then mayor of West Berlin, and later began making political speaking tours himself across West Germany.*

ON WRITERS AS COURT JESTERS

They seldom meet, and then as strangers: I am referring to our overtired politicians and our uncertain writers with their quickly formulated demands that always cry out for immediate fulfillment. Where is the calendar that would permit the mighty of our day to hold court, to seek utopian advice, or to cleanse themselves from the compromises of everyday life by listening to expositions of preposterous utopias? True, there has been the already legendary Kennedy era; and to this day an overworked Willy Brandt listens with close attention when writers tot up his past errors or darkly prophesy future defeats. Both examples are meager; at the very most they prove that there are no courts and hence no advisers to princes, or court jesters. But let's assume for the fun of it that there is such a thing as a literary court jester, who would like to be an adviser at court or in some foreign ministry; and let's assume at the same time that there is no such thing, that the literary court jester is only the invention of a serious and slow-working writer who, merely because he has given his mayor a few bits of advice that were not taken, fears in social gatherings to be mistaken for a court jester. If then we assume both that he exists and that he does not, then he exists as a fiction, hence in reality. But the question is: Is the literary court jester worth talking about?

When I consider the fools of Shakespeare and Velázquez, or let us say the dwarfish power components of the baroque age—for there is a connection between fools and power, although seldom between writers and power—I wish the literary court jester existed; and as we shall see, I know a number of writers who are well fitted for this political service. Except that they are far too touchy. Just as a "housekeeper" dislikes to be called a "cleaning woman," they object to being called fools. "Fool" is not enough. They just want to be known to the Bureau of Internal Revenue as "writers"; nor do they wish to be ennobled by the title of "poet." This self-chosen middle—or middle-class—position enables them to turn up their noses at the disreputable, asocial element, the fools and poets. Whenever society demands fools and poets—and society knows what it needs and likes—whenever, in Germany, for example, a writer of verse or a storyteller is addressed by an old lady or a young man as a "poet," the writer of verse or storyteller—including the present speaker—hastens to make it clear that he wishes to be known as a writer. This modesty, this humility, is underlined by short, embarrassed sentences: "I practice my trade like any shoemaker," or "I work seven hours a day with language, just as other self-respecting citizens lay bricks for seven hours a day." Or differing only in tone of voice and Eastern or Western ideology: "I take my place in socialist society" or "I stand foursquare behind the pluralistic society and pay my taxes as a citizen among citizens."

Probably this well-bred attitude, this gesture of self-belittlement, is in part a reaction to the genius cult of the nineteenth century, which in Germany continued to produce its pungent-smelling houseplants down to the period of expressionism. Who wants to be a Stefan George running around with fiery-eyed disciples? Who wants to disregard his doctor's advice and live the concentrated life of a Rimbaud, without life insurance? Who does not shy away from the prospect of climbing the steps of Olympus every morning, who does not shun the gymnastics to which Gerhart Hauptmann still subjected himself or the tour de force that even Thomas Mann—if only by way of irony—performed as long as he lived?

Today we have adapted ourselves to modern life. You won't find a Rilke doing handstands in front of the mirror; Narcissus has discovered sociology. There is no genius, and to be a fool is inadmissible because a fool is genius in reverse. So there he sits, the domesticated writer, deathly afraid of Muses and laurel wreaths. His fears are legion. The already mentioned fear of being called a poet. The fear of being misunderstood. The fear of not being taken seriously. The fear of entertaining, that is, of giving enjoyment: the fear, invented in Germany but since then thriving in other countries, of producing something Lucullan. For although a writer is intent to the point of fear and trembling on being a part of society, he still wants very much to mold this society according to his fiction but chronically distrusts fiction as something smacking of the poet and fool; from the *"Nouveau Roman"* to "socialist realism," writers, sustained by choruses of lettered teenagers, are earnestly striving to offer more than mere fiction. The writer who does not wish to be a poet distrusts his own artifices. And clowns who disavow their circus are not very funny.

Is a horse whiter because we call it white? And is a writer who says he is "committed" a white horse? We are all familiar with the writer who, far removed from the poet and the fool, but not satisfied with the naked designation of his trade, appends an adjective calling himself and encouraging others to call him a "committed" writer, which always—forgive me—reminds me of titles such as "court pastry cook" or "Catholic bicycle rider." From the start, before even inserting his paper into the typewriter, the committed writer writes not novels, poems or comedies, but "committed literature." When a body of literature is thus plainly stamped, the obvious implication is that all other literature is "uncommitted." Everything else, which takes in a good deal, is disparaged as art for art's sake. Insincere applause from the Right calls forth insincere applause from the Left, and fear of applause from the wrong camp calls forth anemic hopes of applause from the right camp. Such complex and anguished working conditions engender manifestos, and the sweat of anguish is replaced by professions of faith. When, for instance, Peter Weiss, who after all did write *The Shadow of the Coachman's Body*, suddenly discovers that he is a "humanist writer," when a writer and poet versed in all the secrets of language fails to recognize that even in Stalin's day this adjective had already become an empty expletive, the farce of the committed humanist writer becomes truly theatrical. It would be better if he were the fool he is.

You will observe that I confine myself, in utter provincialism, to German affairs, to the smog in which I myself am at home. However, I trust that the United States of America has committed and humanist writers and poets as well as those others who are so readily defamed, and possibly also literary fools; because it is here in this country that this topic was proposed to me: Special adviser or court jester.

The "or" means no doubt that a court jester can never be a special adviser and that a special adviser must under no circumstances regard himself as a court jester, but rather perhaps as a committed writer. He is the great sage; to him financial reform is no Chinese puzzle; and it is he, hovering high above the strife of parties and factions, who in every instance pronounces the final word of counsel. After centuries of hostility the fictitious antitheses are reconciled. Mind and power walk hand in hand. Something like this: After many sleepless nights the Chancellor summons the writer Heinrich Böll to his bungalow. At first the committed writer listens in silence to the Chancellor's troubles. Then, when the Chancellor sinks back into his chair, the writer delivers himself of succinct, irresistible counsel. Relieved of his cares, the Chancellor springs from his chair eager to embrace the committed writer; but the writer takes an attitude of aloofness, he does not wish to become a court jester. He admonishes the Chancellor to convert writer's word into Chancellor's deed. The next day an amazed world learns that Chancellor Erhard has resolved to demobilize the army, to recognize the German Democratic Republic and the Oder-Neisse line, and to expropriate all capitalists.

Encouraged by this feat, the humanist author Peter Weiss journeys from Sweden to the recently recognized German Democratic Republic and leaves his card at the office of Walter Ulbricht, Chairman of the Council of State. Like Erhard at a loss for good advice, Ulbricht receives the humanist writer at once. Advice is given, embrace rejected, word converted into deed; and next day an amazed world learns that the Chairman of the Council of State has countermanded the order to fire on those attempting to cross the borders of his state in either direction and transformed the political sections of all prisons and penitentiaries into people's kindergartens. Thus counseled, the Chairman of the Council of State apologizes to Wolf Biermann, the poet and ballad singer, and asks him to sing away his—Ulbricht's—Stalinist past with bright and mordant rhymes.

Of course, court jesters, should there be any, cannot hope to compete with such accomplishments. Have I exaggerated? Of course I have exaggerated. But when I think of the wishes, often stated in an undertone, of committed and humanist writers, I don't think I have exaggerated so very much. And in my weaker moments I find it easy to see myself acting in just such a well-intentioned, or rather, committed and humanist manner: After losing the parliamentary elections the opposition candidate for the Chancellorship sends, in his perplexity, for the writer here addressing you, who listens, gives advice, and does not allow himself to be embraced; and the next day an amazed world learns that the Social Democrats have discarded the Godesberg Program and replaced it with a sharp, sparkling and once again revolutionary manifesto encouraging the workers to discard hats for caps. No, no revolution breaks out, because for all its sharpness this manifesto is so much to the point that neither capital nor Church can resist its arguments. Without a blow the government is handed over to the Social Democrats, et cetera. The United States of America, I should think, offers similar possibilities. Why, for example, shouldn't the President call on Allen Ginsberg, say, for advice?

These short-winded utopias remain—utopias. Reality speaks a different language. We have no special advisers or court jesters. All I see—and here I am including myself—is bewildered writers and poets who doubt the value of their own trade and avail themselves fully, partially or not at all of their infinitesimal possibilities of playing a part in the events of our time—not with advice but with action. It is meaningless to generalize about "the writer" and his position in society; writers are highly diversified individuals, shaken in varying degree by ambition, neuroses and marital crises. Court jester or special adviser—both are disembodied little men—five, six lines and a circle—such as the members of a discussion panel draw in their notebooks when they get bored. Nevertheless, they have given rise to a cult that, especially in Germany, is assuming an almost religious character. Students, young trade-unionists, young Protestants, high school boys and Boy Scouts, dueling and nondueling fraternities— all these and more never weary of organizing discussions revolving around questions like: "Ought a writer to be committed?" or "Is the writer the conscience of the nation?" Even men with critical minds and a genuine love of literature persist in calling upon writers to deliver protests, declarations and professions of faith. I don't mean that anyone asks them to take a partisan attitude toward political parties, to come out for or against the Social Democrats, for example; no, the idea is that speaking as writers, as a kind of shamefaced elite, they should protest, condemn war, praise peace and display noble sentiments. Yet anyone who knows anything about writers is well aware that even if they band together at congresses they remain eccentric individuals. True, I know a good many who cling with touching devotion to their revolutionary heirlooms, who make use of Communism, that burgundy-colored plush sofa with its well-worn springs, for afternoon reveries. But even these conservative "progressives" are split into one-man factions, each of which reads Marx in his own way. Others in turn are briefly mobilized by their daily glance at the paper and wax indignant at the breakfast table: "Something ought to be done, something ought to be done!" When helplessness lacks wit, it begins to snivel. And yet there is a great deal to do, more than can be expressed in manifestos and protests. But there are also a great many writers, known and unknown, who, far from presuming to be the "conscience of the nation," occasionally bolt from their desks and busy themselves with the trivia of democracy. Which implies a readiness to compromise. Something we must get through our heads is this: a poem knows no compromise, but men live by compromise. The individual who can stand up under this contradiction and act is a fool and will change the world.

Alexander Solzhenitsyn

(1918–   )

Born just as the First World War had ended, Alexander Solzhenitsyn served his country bravely as an artillery officer in the second; he was twice decorated. In February, 1945, during the battle for Königsberg, his divisional commander stripped him of his badges of rank and valor, and of his revolver, and arrested him: he had been writing letters to a friend criticizing "the whiskered one"— Stalin. Counterintelligence agents picked him up, interrogated and beat him, and put him in Lubyanka Prison in Moscow, where one of Stalin's notorious troika courts sentenced him, without a hearing, to eight years in prison and perpetual exile. First he was assigned to laying parquet floors in an apartment house for secret-police officials; then, when authorities learned of his education in mathematics and physics, he served as a prisoner-mathematician for four years in Mavrino, a prison research institute in the Moscow suburbs—the setting, eventually, for The First Circle. His refusal to cooperate with Mavrino authorities—"I could not make moral compromises"—earned him a transfer to a forced labor camp in Kazakhstan (One Day in the Life of Ivan Denisovich); while there he was crudely operated on for cancer. When he had served out his sentence, still in exile, he began to write, but the cancer recurred; this time he was successfully treated with modern equipment in a hospital in Tashkent (Cancer Ward). In 1957 he was politically rehabilitated. One Day was published in 1962, but thereafter none of his works was approved for publication in his own country. In 1970 he was awarded the Nobel Prize; he was not allowed by the Soviet government to go to Stockholm to receive it, but he wrote and sent this acceptance speech. In it he sounds the theme of the artist's moral responsibility— and of art's potential power—which he had once succinctly expressed in The First Circle: "And a great writer—forgive me, perhaps I shouldn't say this, I'll lower my voice—a great writer is, so to speak, a second government. That's why no regime anywhere has ever loved its great writers, only its minor ones."

NOBEL LECTURE

1

As the savage, who in bewilderment has picked up a strange sea-leaving, a thing hidden in the sand, or an incomprehensible something fallen out of the sky—something intricately curved, sometimes shimmering dully, sometimes shining in a bright ray of light—turns it this way and that, turns it looking for a way to use it, for some ordinary use to which he can put it, without suspecting an extraordinary one . . .

So we, holding Art in our hands, self-confidently consider ourselves its owners, brashly give it aim, renovate it, re-form it, make manifestoes of it, sell it for cash, play up to the powerful with it, and turn it around at times for entertainment, even in vaudeville songs and in nightclubs, and at times—using stopper or stick, whichever comes first—for transitory political or limited social needs. But Art is not profaned by our attempts, does not because of them lose touch with its source. Each time and by each use it yields us a part of its mysterious inner light.

But will we comprehend *all* that light? Who will dare say that he has DEFINED art? That he has tabulated all its facets? Perhaps someone in ages past did understand and named them for us, but we could not hold still; we listened; we were scornful; we discarded them at once, always in a hurry to replace even the best with anything new! And when the old truth is told us again, we do not remember that we once possessed it.

One kind of artist imagines himself the creator of an independent spiritual world and shoulders the act of creating that world and the people in it, assuming total responsibility for it—but he collapses, for no mortal genius is able to hold up under such a load. Just as man, who once declared himself the center of existence, has not been able to create a stable spiritual system. When failure overwhelms him, he blames it on the age-old discord of the world, on the complexity of the fragmented and torn modern soul, or on the public's lack of understanding.

Another artist acknowledges a higher power above him and joyfully works as a common apprentice under God's heaven, although his responsibility for all that he writes down or depicts, and for those who understand him, is all the greater. On the other hand, he did not create the world, it is not given direction by him, it is a world about whose foundations he has no doubt. The task of the artist is to sense more keenly than others the harmony of the world, the beauty and the outrage of what man has done to it, and poignantly to let people know. In failure as well as in the lower depths—in poverty, in prison, in illness—the consciousness of a stable harmony will never leave him.

All the irrationality of art, however, its blinding sudden turns, its unpredictable discoveries, its profound impact on people, are too magical to be exhausted by the artist's view of the world, by his overall design, or by the work of his unworthy hands.

Archaeologists have uncovered no early stages of human existence so primitive that they were without art. Even before the dawn of civilization we had received this gift from Hands we were not quick enough to discern. And we were not quick enough to ask: WHAT is this gift FOR? What are we to do with it?

All who predict that art is disintegrating, that it has outgrown its forms, and that it is dying are wrong and will be wrong. We will die, but art will remain. Will we, before we go under, ever understand all its facets and all its ends?

Not everything has a name. Some things lead us into a realm beyond words. Art warms even an icy and depressed heart, opening it to lofty spiritual experience. By means of art we are sometimes sent—dimly, briefly—revelations unattainable by reason.

Like that little mirror in the fairy tales—look into it, and you will see not yourself but, for a moment, that which passeth understanding, a realm to which no man can ride or fly. And for which the soul begins to ache . . .

2

Dostoevsky once enigmatically let drop the phrase: "Beauty will save the world." What does this mean? For a long time I thought it merely a phrase. Was such a thing possible? When in our bloodthirsty history did beauty ever save anyone from anything? Ennobled, elevated, yes; but whom has it saved?

There is, however, something special in the essence of beauty, a special quality in art: the conviction carried by a genuine work of art is absolute and subdues even a resistant heart. A political speech, hasty newspaper comment, a social program, a philosophical system can, as far as appearances are concerned, be built smoothly and consistently on an error or a lie; and what is concealed and distorted will not be immediately clear. But then to counteract it comes a contradictory speech, commentary, program, or differently constructed philosophy—and again everything seems smooth and graceful, and again hangs together. That is why they inspire trust—and distrust.

There is no point asserting and reasserting what the heart cannot believe.

A work of art contains its verification in itself: artificial, strained concepts do not withstand the test of being turned into images; they fall to pieces, turn out to be sickly and pale, convince no one. Works which draw on truth and present it to us in live and concentrated form grip us, compellingly involve us, and no one ever, not even ages hence, will come forth to refute them.

Perhaps then the old trinity of Truth, Goodness, and Beauty is not simply the dressed-up, worn-out formula we thought it in our presumptuous, materialistic youth? If the crowns of these three trees meet, as scholars have asserted, and if the too obvious, too straight sprouts of Truth and Goodness have been knocked down, cut off, not let grow, perhaps the whimsical, unpredictable, unexpected branches of Beauty will work their way through, rise up TO THAT VERY PLACE, and thus complete the work of all three?

Then what Dostoevsky wrote—"Beauty will save the world"—is not a slip of the tongue but a prophecy. After all, *he* had the gift of seeing much, a man wondrously filled with light.

And in that case could not art and literature, in fact, help the modern world?

What little I have managed to learn about this over the years I will try to set forth here today.

3

To reach this chair from which the Nobel Lecture is delivered—a chair by no means offered to every writer and offered only once in a lifetime— I have mounted not three or four temporary steps but hundreds or even thousands, fixed, steep, covered with ice, out of the dark and the cold where I was fated to survive, but others, perhaps more talented, stronger than I, perished. I myself met but few of them in the Gulag Archipelago,[1] a multitude of scattered island fragments. Indeed, under the millstone of surveillance and mistrust, I did not talk to just any man; of some I only heard; and of others I only guessed. Those with a name in literature who vanished into that abyss are, at least, known; but how many were unrecognized, never once publicly mentioned? And so very few, almost no one ever managed to return. A whole national literature is there, buried without a coffin, without even underwear, naked, a number tagged on its toe. Not for a moment did Russian literature cease, yet from outside it seemed a wasteland. Where a harmonious forest could have grown, there were left, after all the cutting, two or three trees accidentally overlooked.

And today how am I, accompanied by the shades of the fallen, my head bowed to let pass forward to this platform others worthy long before me, today how am I to guess and to express what *they* would have wished to say?

This obligation has long lain on us, and we have understood it. In Vladimir Solovyov's words:

> But even chained, we must ourselves complete
> That circle which the gods have preordained.

In agonizing moments in camp, in columns of prisoners at night, in the freezing darkness through which the little chains of lanterns shone, there often rose in our throats something we wanted to shout out to the whole world, if only the world could have heard one of us. Then it seemed very clear what our lucky messenger would say and how immediately and positively the whole world would respond. Our field of vision was filled with physical objects and spiritual forces, and in that clearly focused world nothing seemed to outbalance them. Such ideas came not from books and were not borrowed for the sake of harmony or coherence; they were formulated in prison cells and around forest campfires, in conversations with persons now dead, were hardened by *that* life, developed *out*

---

[1]*Gulag is the state prison-camp administration.*

of there.

When the outside pressures were reduced, my outlook and our outlook widened, and gradually, although through a tiny crack, that "whole world" outside came in sight and was recognized. Startlingly for us, the "whole world" turned out to be not at all what we had hoped: it was a world leading "not up there" but exclaiming at the sight of a dismal swamp, "What an enchanting meadow!" or at a set of prisoner's concrete stocks, "What an exquisite necklace!"—a world in which, while flowing tears rolled down the cheeks of some, others danced to the carefree tunes of a musical.

How did this come about? Why did such an abyss open? Were we unfeeling, or was the world? Or was it because of a difference in language? Why are people not capable of grasping each other's every clear and distinct speech? Words die away and flow off like water—leaving no taste, no color, no smell. Not a trace.

Insofar as I understand it, the structure, import, and tone of speech possible for me—of my speech here today—have changed with the years.

It now scarcely resembles the speech which I first conceived on those freezing nights in prison camp.

4

For ages, such has been man's nature that his view of the world (when not induced by hypnosis), his motivation and scale of values, his actions and his intentions have been determined by his own personal and group experiences of life. As the Russian proverb puts it, "Don't trust your brother, trust your own bad eye." This is the soundest basis for understanding one's environment and one's behavior in it. During the long eras when our world was obscurely and bewilderingly fragmented, before a unified communications system had transformed it and it had turned into a single, convulsively beating lump, men were unerringly guided by practical experience in their own local area, then in their own community, in their own society, and finally in their own national territory. The possibility then existed for an individual to see with his own eyes and to accept a common scale of values—what was considered average, what improbable; what was cruel, what beyond all bounds of evil; what was honesty, what deceit. Even though widely scattered peoples lived differently and their scales of social values might be strikingly dissimilar, like their systems of weights and measures, these differences surprised none but the occasional tourist, were written up as heathen wonders, and in no way threatened the rest of not yet united mankind.

In recent decades, however, mankind has imperceptibly, suddenly, become one, united in a way which offers both hope and danger, for shock and infection in one part are almost instantaneously transmitted to others, which often have no immunity. Mankind has become one, but not in the way the community or even the nation used to be stably united, not through accumulated practical experience, not through its own, good-naturedly so-called bad *eye*, not even through its own well-understood, native tongue, but, leaping over all barriers, through the international press and radio. A wave of events washes over us and, in a moment, half the world hears the splash, but the standards for measuring these things and for evaluating them, according to the laws of those parts of the world about which we know nothing, are not and cannot be broadcast through the ether or reduced to newsprint. These standards have too long and too specifically been accepted by and incorporated in too special a way into the lives of various lands and societies to be communicated in thin air. In various parts of the world, men apply to events a scale of values achieved by their own long suffering, and they uncompromisingly, self-reliantly judge only by their own scale, and by no one else's.

If there are not a multitude of such scales in the world, nevertheless there are at least several: a scale for local events, a scale for things far away; for old societies, and for new; for the prosperous, and for the disadvantaged. The points and markings on the scale glaringly do not coincide; they confuse us, hurt our eyes, and so, to avoid pain, we brush aside all scales not our own, as if they were follies or delusions, and confidently judge the whole world according to our own domestic values. Therefore, what seems to us more important, more painful, and more unendurable is really not what is more important, more painful, and more unendurable but merely that which is closer to home. Everything distant which, for all its moans and muffled cries, its ruined lives and, even, millions of victims, does not threaten to come rolling up to our threshold today we consider, in general, endurable and of tolerable dimensions.

On one side, persecuted no less than under the old Romans, hundreds of thousands of mute Christians give up their lives for their belief in God. On the other side of the world, a madman (and probably he is not the only one) roars across the ocean in order to FREE us from religion with a blow of steel at the Pontiff! Using his own personal scale, he has decided things for everyone.

What on one scale seems, from far off, to be enviable and prosperous freedom, on another, close up, is felt to be irritating coercion calling for the overturning of buses. What in one country seems a dream of improbable prosperity in another arouses indignation as savage exploitation calling for an immediate strike. Scales of values differ even for natural calamities: a flood with two hundred thousand victims matters less than a local traffic accident. Scales differ for personal insults: at times, merely a sardonic smile or a dismissive gesture is humiliating, whereas, at others, cruel beatings are regarded as a bad joke. Scales differ for punishments and for wrongdoing. On one scale, a month's arrest, or exile to the country, or "solitary confinement" on white bread and milk rocks the imagination and fills the newspaper columns with outrage. On another, both accepted and excused are prison terms of twenty-five years, solitary confinement in cells with ice-covered walls and prisoners stripped to their underclothing, insane asylums for healthy men, and border shootings of countless foolish people who, for some reason, keep trying to escape. The heart is especially at ease with regard to that exotic land about which nothing is known, from which no events ever reach us except the belated and trivial conjectures of a few correspondents.

For such ambivalence, for such thickheaded lack of understanding of someone else's far-off grief, however, mankind is not at fault: that is how man is made. But for mankind as a whole, squeezed into one lump, such mutual lack of understanding carries the threat of imminent and violent destruction. Given six, four, or even two scales of values, there cannot be one world, one single humanity: the difference in rhythms, in oscillations, will tear mankind asunder. We will not survive together on one Earth, just as a man with two hearts is not meant for this world.

5

Who will coordinate these scales of values, and how? Who will give mankind one single system for reading its instruments, both for wrongdoing and for doing good, for the intolerable and the tolerable as they are distinguished from each other today? Who will make clear for mankind what is really oppressive and unbearable and what, for being so near, rubs us raw—and thus direct our anger against what is in fact terrible and not merely near at hand? Who is capable of extending such an understanding across the boundaries of his own personal experience? Who has the skill to make a narrow, obstinate human being aware of others' far-off grief and joy, to make him understand dimensions and delusions he himself has never lived through? Propaganda, coercion, and scientific proofs are all powerless. But, happily, in our world there is a way. It is art, and it is literature.

There is a miracle which they can work: they can overcome man's unfortunate trait of learning only through his own experience, unaffected by that of others. From man to man, compensating for his brief time on earth, art communicates whole the burden of another's long life experience with all its hardships, colors, and vitality, re-creating in the flesh what another has experienced, and allowing it to be acquired as one's own.

More important, much more important: countries and whole continents belatedly repeat each other's mistakes, sometimes after centuries when, it would seem, everything should be so clear! No: what some nations have gone through, thought through, and rejected, suddenly seems to be the latest word in other nations. Here too the only substitute for what we ourselves have not experienced is art and literature. They have the marvelous capacity of transmitting from one nation to another—despite differences in language, customs, and social structure—practical experience, the harsh national experience of many decades never tasted by the other nation. Sometimes this may save a whole nation from what is a dangerous or mistaken or plainly disastrous path, thus lessening the twists and turns of human history.

Today, from this Nobel lecture platform, I should like to emphasize this great, beneficent attribute of art.

Literature transmits condensed and irrefutable human experience in still another priceless way: from generation to generation. It thus becomes the living memory of a nation. What has faded into history it thus keeps warm and preserves in a form that defies distortion and falsehood. Thus literature, together with language, preserves and protects a nation's soul.

(It has become fashionable in recent times to talk of the leveling of nations, and of various peoples disappearing into the melting pot of contemporary civilization. I disagree with this, but that is another matter; all that should be said here is that the disappearance of whole nations would impoverish us no less than if all people were to become identical, with the same character and the same face. Nations are the wealth of humanity, its generalized personalities. The least among them has its own special colors, and harbors within itself a special aspect of God's design.)

But woe to the nation whose literature is cut off by the interposition of force. That is not simply a violation of "freedom of the press"; it is stopping up the nation's heart, carving out the nation's memory. The nation loses its memory; it loses its spiritual unity—and, despite their supposedly common language, fellow countrymen suddenly cease understanding each other. Speechless generations are born and die, having recounted nothing of themselves either to their own times or to their descendants. That such masters as Akhmatova and Zamyatin were buried behind four walls for their whole lives and condemned even to the grave to create in silence, without hearing one reverberation of what they wrote, is not only their own personal misfortune but a tragedy for the whole nation—and, too, a real threat to all nationalities.

In certain cases, it is a danger for all mankind as well: when HISTORY as a whole ceases to be understood because of that silence.

6

At various times in various places people have argued hotly, angrily, and elegantly about whether art and the artist should have a life of their own or whether they should always keep in mind their duty to society and serve it, even though in an unbiased way. For me there is no problem here, but I will not again go into this argument. One of the most brilliant speeches on this subject was Albert Camus's Nobel lecture, the conclusions of which I happily support. Indeed, for decades Russian literature has leaned in that direction—not spending too much time in self-admiration, not flitting about too frivolously—and I am not ashamed to continue in that tradition as best I can. From way back, ingrained in Russian literature has been the notion that a writer can do much among his own people—and that he must.

We will not trample on the artist's RIGHT to express exclusively personal experiences and observations, ignoring everything that happens in the rest of the world. We will not DEMAND anything of the artist, but we will be permitted to reproach him, to make requests, to appeal to him and to coax him. After all, he himself only partially develops his talent, the greater portion of which is breathed into him, ready-made, at birth and, along with it, responsibility for his free will. Even granting that the artist DOES NOT OWE anybody anything, it is painful to see how, retreating into a world of his own creation or into the vast spaces of subjective fancies, he CAN deliver the real world into the hands of self-seeking, insignificant, or even insane people.

Our twentieth century has turned out to be more cruel than those preceding it, and all that is terrible in it did not come to an end with the first half. The same old caveman feelings—greed, envy, violence, and mutual hate, which along the way assumed respectable pseudonyms like class struggle, racial struggle, mass struggle, labor-union struggle—are tearing our world to pieces. The caveman refusal to accept compromise has been turned into a theoretical principle and is considered to be a virtue of orthodoxy. It demands millions of victims in endless civil wars; it packs our hearts with the notion that there are no fixed universal human concepts called good and justice, that they are fluid, changing, and that therefore one must always do what will benefit one's party. Any and every professional group, as soon as it finds a convenient moment TO RIP OFF A PIECE, unearned or not, extra or not, immediately rips it off, let all of society come crashing down if it will. As seen from outside, the mass of waste in Western society is approaching the limit beyond which the system will become metastable and must collapse. Violence, less and less restricted by the framework of age-old legality, brazenly and victoriously strides throughout the world, unconcerned that its futility has been demonstrated and exposed by history many times. It is not simply naked force that triumphs but its trumpeted justification: the whole world overflows with the brazen conviction that force can do everything and justice nothing. Dostoevsky's DEMONS,[2] a provincial nightmare of the last century, one would have thought, are, before our very eyes, crawling over the whole world into countries where they were unimaginable, and by the hijacking of planes, by seizing HOSTAGES, by the bomb explosions, and by the fires of recent years signal their determination to shake civilization apart and to annihilate it! And they may very well succeed. Young people, being at an age when they have no experience except sexual, when they have as yet no years of personal suffering and personal wisdom behind them, en-

[2] A reference to the novel known as The Possessed and The Devils, but which in Russian is literally The Demons.

thusiastically repeat our discredited Russian lessons of the nineteenth century and think that they are discovering something new. They take as a splendid example the Chinese Red Guard's degradation of people into nonentities. A superficial lack of understanding of the timeless essence of humanity, a naïve smugness on the part of their inexperienced hearts—We'll kick out *those* fierce, greedy oppressors, those governors, and the rest (we!), we'll then lay down our grenades and machine guns, and become just and compassionate. Oh, of course! Of those who have lived their lives and have come to understand, who could refute the young, many DO NOT DARE argue against them; on the contrary, they flatter them in order not to seem "conservative," again a Russian phenomenon of the nineteenth century, something which Dostoevsky called SLAVERY TO HALF-COCKED PROGRESSIVE IDEAS.

The spirit of Munich has by no means retreated into the past; it was not a brief episode. I even venture to say that the spirit of Munich is dominant in the twentieth century. The intimidated civilized world has found nothing to oppose the onslaught of a suddenly resurgent fang-baring barbarism, except concessions and smiles. The spirit of Munich is a disease of the will of prosperous people; it is the daily state of those who have given themselves over to a craving for prosperity in every way, to material well-being as the chief goal of life on earth. Such people—and there are many of them in the world today—choose passivity and retreat, anything if only the life to which they are accustomed might go on, anything so as not to have to cross over to rough terrain today, because tomorrow, see, everything will be all right. (But it never will! The reckoning for cowardice will only be more cruel. Courage and the power to overcome will be ours only when we dare to make sacrifices.)

We are also threatened by the catastrophe that the physically squeezed, constrained world is not allowed to become one spiritually; molecules of knowledge and compassion are not allowed to move across from one half of the world to the other. This is a grave danger: THE STOPPAGE OF INFORMATION between the parts of the planet. Contemporary science knows that such stoppage is the way of entropy, of universal destruction. Stoppage of information makes international signatures and treaties unreal: within the zone of STUNNED SILENCE any treaty can easily be reinterpreted at will or, more simply, covered up, as if it had never existed (Orwell understood this beautifully). Within the zone of stunned silence lives—seemingly not Earth's inhabitants at all—a Martian expeditionary force, knowing nothing whatever about the rest of the Earth and ready to trample it flat in the holy conviction that they are "liberating" it.

A quarter of a century ago, with the great hopes of mankind, the United Nations was born. Alas, in the immoral world it, too, became immoral. It is not a United Nations but a United Governments, in which those freely elected and those imposed by force and those which seized power by arms are all on a par. Through the mercenary bias of the majority, the UN

jealously worries about the freedom of some peoples and pays no attention to the freedom of others. By an officious vote it rejected the review of
PRIVATE COMPLAINTS—the groans, shouts, and pleadings of individual, common PLAIN PEOPLE—insects too small for such a great organization. The UN
never tried to make BINDING on governments, a CONDITION of their member-
ship, the Declaration of Human Rights, the outstanding document of its
twenty-five years—and thus the UN betrayed the common people to the
will of governments they had not chosen.

One might think that the shape of the modern world is entirely in the
hands of scientists, that they determine mankind's technological steps.
One might think that what will happen to the world depends not on
politicians but specifically on the international cooperation of scientists.
Especially because the example of individuals shows how much could be
accomplished by moving together. But no; scientists have made no clear
effort to become an important, independently active force of mankind.
Whole congresses at a time, they back away from the suffering of others;
it is more comfortable to stay within the bounds of science. That same
spirit of Munich has spread its debilitating wings over them.

In this cruel, dynamic, explosive world on the edge of its ten destruc-
tions, what is the place and role of the writer? We send off no rockets, do
not even push the lowliest handcart, are scorned by those who respect
only material power. Would it not be natural for us, too, to retreat, to lose
our faith in the steadfastness of good, in the indivisibility of truth, and
merely to let the world have our bitter observations, as of a bystander,
about how hopelessly corrupted mankind is, how petty men have become,
and how difficult it is for lonely, sensitive, beautiful souls today?

We do not have even this way out. Once pledged to the WORD, there is
no getting away from it: a writer is no sideline judge of his fellow countrymen and contemporaries; he is equally guilty of all the evil done in his
country or by his people. If his country's tanks spill blood on the streets of
some alien capital, the brown stains are splashed forever on the writer's
face. If, some fatal night, his trusting friend is choked to death while
sleeping, the bruises from the rope are on the writer's hands. If his young
fellow citizens in their easygoing way declare the superiority of debauch-
ery over frugal labor, abandon themselves to drugs or seize HOSTAGES,
the stink of it mixes with the writer's breathing.

Will we have the impudence to announce that we are not responsible
for the sores of the world today?

7

I am, however, encouraged by a keen sense of WORLD LITERATURE as the
one great heart that beats for the cares and misfortunes of our world, even
though each corner sees and experiences them in a different way.

In past times, also, besides age-old national literatures there existed a concept of world literature as the link between the summits of national literatures and as the aggregate of reciprocal literary influences. But there was a time lag: readers and writers came to know foreign writers only belatedly, sometimes centuries later, so that mutual influences were delayed and the network of national literary high points was visible not to contemporaries but to later generations.

Today, between writers of one country and the readers and writers of another, there is an almost instantaneous reciprocity, as I myself know. My books, unpublished, alas, in my own country, despite hasty and often bad translations have quickly found a responsive world readership. Critical analysis of them has been undertaken by such leading Western writers as Heinrich Böll. During all these recent years, when both my work and my freedom did not collapse, when against the laws of gravity they held on seemingly in thin air, seemingly ON NOTHING, on the invisible, mute surface tension of sympathetic people, with warm gratitude I learned, to my complete surprise, of the support of the world's writing fraternity. On my fiftieth birthday I was astounded to receive greetings from well-known European writers. No pressure put on me now passed unnoticed. During the dangerous weeks when I was being expelled from the Writers' Union, THE PROTECTIVE WALL put forward by prominent writers of the world saved me from worse persecution, and Norwegian writers and artists hospitably prepared shelter for me in the event that I was exiled from my country. Finally, my being nominated for a Nobel Prize was originated not in the land where I live and write but by François Mauriac and his colleagues. Afterward, national writers' organizations expressed unanimous support for me.

As I have understood it and experienced it myself, world literature is no longer an abstraction or a generalized concept invented by literary critics, but a common body and common spirit, a living, heartfelt unity reflecting the growing spiritual unity of mankind. State borders still turn crimson, heated red-hot by electric fences and machine-gun fire; some ministries of internal affairs still suppose that literature is "an internal affair" of the countries under their jurisdiction; and newspaper headlines still herald, "They have no right to interfere in our internal affairs!" Meanwhile, no such thing as INTERNAL AFFAIRS remains on our crowded Earth. Mankind's salvation lies exclusively in everyone's making everything his business, in the people of the East being anything but indifferent to what is thought in the West, and in the people of the West being anything but indifferent to what happens in the East. Literature, one of the most sensitive and responsive tools of human existence, has been the first to pick up, adopt, and assimilate this sense of the growing unity of mankind. I therefore confidently turn to the world literature of the present, to hundreds of friends whom I have not met face to face and perhaps never will see.

My friends! Let us try to be helpful, if we are worth anything. In our own countries, torn by differences among parties, movements, castes, and groups, who for ages past has been not the dividing but the uniting force? This, essentially, is the position of writers, spokesmen of a national language, of the chief tie binding the nation, the very soil which the people inhabit, and, in fortunate circumstances, the nation's spirit too.

I think that world literature has the power in these frightening times to help mankind see itself accurately despite what is advocated by partisans and by parties. In has the power to transmit the condensed experience of one region to another, so that different scales of values are combined, and so that one people accurately and concisely knows the true history of another with a power of recognition and acute awareness as if it had lived through that history itself—and could thus be spared repeating old mistakes. At the same time, perhaps we ourselves may succeed in developing our own WORLD-WIDE VIEW, like any man, with the center of the eye seeing what is nearby but the periphery of vision taking in what is happening in the rest of the world. We will make correlations and maintain world-wide standards.

Who, if not writers, are to condemn their own unsuccessful governments (in some states this is the easiest way to make a living; everyone who is not too lazy does it) as well as society itself, whether for its cowardly humiliation or for its self-satisfied weakness, or the lightheaded escapades of the young, or the youthful pirates brandishing knives?

We will be told: What can literature do against the pitiless onslaught of naked violence? Let us not forget that violence does not and cannot flourish by itself; it is inevitably intertwined with LYING. Between them there is the closest, the most profound and natural bond: nothing screens violence except lies, and the only way lies can hold out is by violence. Whoever has once announced violence as his METHOD must inexorably choose lying as his PRINCIPLE. At birth, violence behaves openly and even proudly. But as soon as it becomes stronger and firmly established, it senses the thinning of the air around it and cannot go on without befogging itself in lies, coating itself with lying's sugary oratory. It does not always or necessarily go straight for the gullet; usually it demands of its victims only allegiance to the lie, only complicity in the lie.

The simple act of an ordinary courageous man is not to take part, not to support lies! Let *that* come into the world and even reign over it, but not through me. Writers and artists can do more: they can VANQUISH LIES! In the struggle against lies, art has always won and always will. Conspicuously, incontestably for everyone. Lies can stand up against much in the world, but not against art.

Once lies have been dispelled, the repulsive nakedness of violence will be exposed—and hollow violence will collapse.

That, my friends, is why I think we can help the world in its red-hot hour: not by the nay-saying of having no armaments, not by abandoning oneself to the carefree life, but by going into battle!

In Russian, proverbs about TRUTH are favorites. They persistently express the considerable, bitter, grim experience of the people, often astonishingly:

ONE WORD OF TRUTH OUTWEIGHS THE WORLD.

On such a seemingly fantastic violation of the law of the conservation of mass and energy are based both my own activities and my appeal to the writers of the whole world.

PART FIVE

The Writing Process

Writers seem to be leery of guessing about the inner processes of creativity. They are delighted to talk about how hard they have worked; we will see later in this collection that they have striking and charming and sometimes insightful memories of their triumphs over difficulties. They are not afraid to speak of the agonies and joys of creation. But it is hard, perhaps they feel it is dangerous, for them to search inside themselves for the wellsprings of art. Some writers openly confess that they are superstitious about these unseen sources; even such a grindingly rational craftsman as Thomas Mann speaks of standing in a "magic circle" as he writes. Some authors tell of surrounding themselves with petty desktop rituals to keep the magic from being disturbed. The section that follows has recourse to three poets and one tale teller for testimony on the inner process. The purpose of this section is not to try to answer any of the many questions surrounding artistic gestation and birth; it is simply to give the mystery its insistent place in the larger context of the writer's craft. So long as the writer writes, the mystery stands at his shoulder.

Samuel Taylor Coleridge

(1772–1834)

Coleridge tells us that as a child he was a dreamer, a tenant of far realms of imagination. Throughout his life he was acutely sensitized to everything he saw, and especially to the images in his extraordinarily wide reading, and his mind, which he characterized as "energic"—forever in motion—played uncontrolled over all that was in it and reshaped its myriad chaotic impressions into shimmering fragments of poetry, philosophy, and literary criticism. "Christabel," the "Ancient Mariner," "Kubla Khan," "Love," "Youth and Age," and others of his poems have in them an unearthly music. This short piece is his famous account of the writing of "Kubla Khan"—not nearly enough, it goes without saying, to explain the real making of the poem. In another notation on the poem, Coleridge identified the "anodyne" that gave birth to the dream and the poem: "This fragment with a good deal more, not recoverable, composed in a sort of Reverie brought on by two grains of Opium, taken to check a dysentery, at a Farm House between Porlock and Linton, a quarter of a mile from Culbone Church, in the fall of the year 1797."

PREFATORY NOTE TO "KUBLA KHAN"

The following fragment is here published at the request of a poet of great and deserved celebrity, and, as far as the Author's own opinions are concerned, rather as a psychological curiosity, than on the ground of any supposed *poetic* merits.

In the summer of the year 1797, the Author, then in ill health, had retired to a lonely farm-house between Porlock and Linton, on the Exmoor confines of Somerset and Devonshire. In consequence of a slight indisposition, an anodyne had been prescribed, from the effects of which he fell asleep in his chair at the moment that he was reading the following sentence, or words of the same substance, in "Purchas's Pilgrimage": "Here the Khan Kubla commanded a palace to be built, and a stately garden thereunto. And thus ten miles of fertile ground were inclosed with a wall." The Author continued for about three hours in a profound sleep, at least of the external senses, during which time he has the most vivid confidence, that he could not have composed less than from two to three hundred lines; if that indeed can be called composition in which all the images rose up before him as *things*, with a parallel production of the correspondent expressions, without any sensation or consciousness of effort. On awaking he appeared to himself to have a distinct recollection of the whole, and taking his pen, ink, and paper, instantly and eagerly wrote

down the lines that are here preserved. At this moment he was unfortunately called out by a person on business from Porlock, and detained by
him above an hour, and on his return to his room, found, to his no small
surprise and mortification, that though he still retained some vague and
dim recollection of the general purport of the vision, yet, with the exception of some eight or ten scattered lines and images, all the rest had passed
away like the images on the surface of a stream into which a stone has
been cast, but alas! without the after restoration of the latter!

> Then all the charm
> Is broken—all that phantom-world so fair
> Vanishes, and a thousand circlets spread,
> And each mis-shape the other. Stay awhile,
> Poor youth! who scarcely dar'st lift up thine eyes—
> The stream will soon renew its smoothness, soon
> The visions will return! And lo, he stays,
> And soon the fragments dim of lovely forms
> Come trembling back, unite, and now once more
> The pool becomes a mirror.

Yet from the still surviving recollections in his mind, the Author has
frequently purposed to finish for himself what had been originally, as it
were, given to him Σάμερον ἅδιον ἄσω: but the tomorrow is yet to come.

Edgar Allan Poe

(1809–1849)

Poe, like his master Coleridge, had a never-resting imagination, yet Poe's testimony on the writing of "The Raven" gives us quite a different picture from that of Coleridge's drugged dream. There were two Poes: One of them, himself deeply divided, was a haunted idealist, obliging in repose, caustic and arrogant when stirred, by turns a hard worker and a hard drinker, now a pale admirer of pale women of a disembodied perfection, now a haggard wakening refugee from unspeakable visions of crime. The other Poe, all of a piece, was a cool logician, a systematic thinker, an observer with a camera eye for concrete details, a detective-story writer, a numberer, cryptographer, problem-solver—one who prided himself on his ability to dissect, sort, and arrange. It is not hard to say which Poe wrote the essay that follows; he considered it "my best specimen of analysis." A question, however remains: May the other Poe actually have written the poem?

THE PHILOSOPHY OF COMPOSITION

Charles Dickens, in a note now lying before me, alluding to an examination I once made of the mechanism of *Barnaby Rudge*, says—"By the way, are you aware that Godwin wrote his *Caleb Williams* backwards? He first involved his hero in a web of difficulties, forming the second volume, and then, for the first, cast about him for some mode of accounting for what had been done."

I cannot think this the *precise* mode of procedure on the part of Godwin —and indeed what he himself acknowledges is not altogether in accordance with Mr. Dickens' idea—but the author of *Caleb Williams* was too good an artist not to perceive the advantage derivable from at least a somewhat similar process. Nothing is more clear than that every plot, worth the name, must be elaborated to its *dénouement* before anything be attempted with the pen. It is only with the *dénouement* constantly in view that we can give a plot its indispensable air of consequence, or causation, by making the incidents, and especially the tone at all points, tend to the development of the intention.

There is a radical error, I think, in the usual mode of constructing a story. Either history affords a thesis—or one is suggested by an incident of the day —or, at best, the author sets himself to work in the combination of striking events to form merely the basis of his narrative—designing, generally, to fill in with description, dialogue, or autorial comment, whatever crevices of fact, or action, may, from page to page, render themselves apparent.

I prefer commencing with the consideration of an *effect*. Keeping originality *always* in view—for he is false to himself who ventures to dispense with so obvious and so easily attainable a source of interest—I say to myself, in the first place, "Of the innumerable effects, or impressions, of which the heart, the intellect, or (more generally) the soul is susceptible, what one shall I, on the present occasion, select?" Having chosen a novel, first, and secondly a vivid effect, I consider whether it can be best wrought by incident or tone—whether by ordinary incidents and peculiar tone, or the converse, or by peculiarity both of incident and tone—afterward looking about me (or rather within) for such combinations of event, or tone, as shall best aid me in the construction of the effect.

I have often thought how interesting a magazine paper might be written by any author who would—that is to say, who could—detail, step by step, the processes by which any one of his compositions attained its ultimate point of completion. Why such a paper has never been given to the world, I am much at a loss to say—but, perhaps, the autorial vanity has had more to do with the omission than any one other cause. Most writers— poets in especial—prefer having it understood that they compose by a species of fine frenzy—an ecstatic intuition—and would positively shudder at letting the public take a peep behind the scenes, at the elaborate and vacillating crudities of thought—at the true purposes seized only at the last moment—at the innumerable glimpses of idea that arrived not at the maturity of full view at the fully-matured fancies discarded in despair as unmanageable—at the cautious deletions and rejections—at the painful erasures and interpolations—in a word, at the wheels and pinions—the tackle for scene-shifting—the step-ladders, the demon-traps—the cock's feathers, the red paint and the black patches, which, in ninety-nine cases out of a hundred, constitute the properties of the literary *histrio*.

I am aware, on the other hand, that the case is by no means common, in which an author is at all in condition to retrace the steps by which his conclusions have been attained. In general, suggestions, having arisen pell-mell, are pursued and forgotten in a similar manner.

For my own part, I have neither sympathy with the repugnance alluded to, nor, at any time, the least difficulty in recalling to mind the progressive steps of any of my compositions, and, since the interest of an analysis or reconstruction, such as I have considered a *desideratum*, is quite independent of any real or fancied interest in the thing analysed, it will not be regarded as a breach of decorum on my part to show the *modus operandi* by which some one of my own works was put together. I select "The Raven" as most generally known. It is my design to render it manifest that no one point in its composition is referable either to accident or intuition— that the work proceeded step by step, to its completion, with the precision and rigid consequence of a mathematical problem.

Let us dismiss, as irrelevant to the poem, *per se*, the circumstance—or say the necessity—which, in the first place, gave rise to the intention of composing a poem that should suit at once the popular and the critical taste.

We commence, then, with this intention.

The initial consideration was that of extent. If any literary work is too long to be read at one sitting, we must be content to dispense with the immensely important effect derivable from unity of impression—for, if two sittings be required, the affairs of the world interfere, and everything like totality is at once destroyed. But since, *ceteris paribus*, no poet can afford to dispense with *anything* that may advance his design, it but remains to be seen whether there is, in extent, any advantage to counterbalance the loss of unity which attends it. Here I say no, at once. What we term a long poem is, in fact, merely a succession of brief ones—that is to say, of brief poetical effects. It is needless to demonstrate that a poem is such only inasmuch as it intensely excites, by elevating the soul; and all intense excitements are, through a psychal necessity, brief. For this reason, at least, one-half of the "Paradise Lost" is essentially prose—a succession of poetical excitements interspersed, *inevitably*, with corresponding depressions—the whole being deprived, through the extremeness of its length, of the vastly important artistic element, totality, or unity of effect.

It appears evident, then, that there is a distinct limit, as regards length, to all works of literary art—the limit of a single sitting—and that, although in certain classes of prose composition, such as *Robinson Crusoe* (demanding no unity), this limit may be advantageously overpassed, it can never properly be overpassed in a poem. Within this limit the extent of a poem may be made to bear mathematical relation to its merit—in other words, to the excitement or elevation—again, in other words, to the degree of the true poetical effect which it is capable of inducing; for it is clear that the brevity must be in direct ratio of the intensity of the intended effect—this, with one proviso—that a certain degree of duration is absolutely requisite for the production of any effect at all.

Holding in view these considerations, as well as that degree of excitement which I deemed not above the popular, while not below the critical taste, I reached at once what I conceived the proper *length* for my intended poem—a length of about one hundred lines. It is, in fact, a hundred and eight.

My next thought concerned the choice of an impression, or effect, to be conveyed: and here I may as well observe that, throughout the construction, I kept steadily in view the design of rendering the work *universally* appreciable. I should be carried too far out of my immediate topic were I to demonstrate a point upon which I have repeatedly insisted, and which, with the poetical, stands not in the slightest need of demonstration—the point, I mean, that Beauty is the sole legitimate province of the poem. A few words, however, in elucidation of my real meaning, which some of my friends have evinced a disposition to misrepresent. That pleasure which is at once the most intense, the most elevating, and the most pure is, I believe, found in the contemplation of the beautiful. When, indeed, men speak of Beauty, they mean, precisely, not a quality, as is supposed, but an effect—they refer, in short, just to that intense and pure elevation of *soul—not* of intellect, or of heart—upon which I have commented, and which is experienced in consequence of contemplating the "beautiful." Now I designate Beauty as the province of the poem, merely because it is an obvious rule of Art that effects should be made to spring from direct causes—that objects should be attained through means best adapted for their attainment—no one as yet having been weak enough to deny that the peculiar elevation alluded to is *most readily* attained in the poem. Now the object Truth, or the satisfaction of the intellect, and the object Passion, or the excitement of the heart, are, although attainable to a certain extent in poetry, far more readily attainable in prose. Truth, in fact, demands a precision, and Passion, a *homeliness* (the truly passionate will comprehend me), which are absolutely antagonistic to that Beauty which, I maintain, is the excitement, or pleasurable elevation of the soul. It by no means follows, from anything here said, that passion, or even truth, may not be introduced, and even profitably introduced, into a poem for they may serve in elucidation, or aid the general effect, as do discords in music, by contrast—but the true artist will always contrive, first, to tone them into proper subservience to the predominant aim, and, secondly, to enveil them, as far as possible, in that Beauty which is the atmosphere and the essence of the poem.

Regarding, then, Beauty as my province, my next question referred to the *tone* of its highest manifestation—and all experience has shown that this tone is one of *sadness*. Beauty of whatever kind, in its supreme development, invariably excites the sensitive soul to tears. Melancholy is thus the most legitimate of all the poetical tones.

The length, the province, and the tone, being thus determined, I betook myself to ordinary induction, with the view of obtaining some artistic piquancy which might serve me as a key-note in the construction of the poem—some pivot upon which the whole structure might turn. In carefully thinking over all the usual artistic effects—or more properly *points*, in the theatrical sense—I did not fail to perceive immediately that no one had been so universally employed as that of the *refrain*. The universality of its employment sufficed to assure me of its intrinsic value, and spared me the necessity of submitting it to analysis. I considered it, however, with regard to its susceptibility of improvement, and soon saw it to be in a primitive condition. As commonly used, the *refrain*, or burden, not only is limited to lyric verse, but depends for its impression upon the force of monotone—both in sound and thought. The pleasure is deduced solely from the sense of identity—of repetition. I resolved to diversify, and so heighten the effect, by adhering in general to the monotone of sound, while

I continually varied that of thought: that is to say, I determined to produce continuously novel effects, by the variation of *the application* of the *refrain* itself remaining, for the most part, unvaried.

These points being settled, I next bethought me of the *nature* of my *refrain*. Since its application was to be repeatedly varied it was clear that the *refrain* itself must be brief, for there would have been an insurmountable difficulty in frequent variations of application in any sentence of length. In proportion to the brevity of the sentence would, of course, be the facility of the variation. This led me at once to a single word as the best *refrain*.

The question now arose as to the character of the word. Having made up my mind to a *refrain*, the division of the poem into stanzas was of course a corollary, the *refrain* forming the close to each stanza. That such a close, to have force, must be sonorous and susceptible of protracted emphasis, admitted no doubt, and these considerations inevitably led me to the long *o* as the most sonorous vowel in connection with *r* as the most producible consonant.

The sound of the *refrain* being thus determined, it became necessary to select a word embodying this sound, and at the same time in the fullest possible keeping with that melancholy which I had pre-determined as the tone of the poem. In such a search it would have been absolutely impossible to overlook the word "Nevermore." In fact it was the very first which presented itself.

The next *desideratum* was a pretext for the continuous use of the one word "Nevermore." In observing the difficulty which I had at once found in inventing a sufficiently plausible reason for its continuous repetition, I did not fail to perceive that this difficulty arose solely from the pre-assumption that the word was to be so continuously or monotonously spoken by a *human* being—I did not fail to perceive, in short, that the difficulty lay in the reconciliation of this monotony with the exercise of reason on the part of the creature repeating the word. Here, then, immediately arose the idea of a *non*-reasoning creature capable of speech, and infinitely more in keeping with the intended tone.

I had now gone so far as the conception of a Raven, the bird of ill omen, monotonously repeating the one word "Nevermore" at the conclusion of each stanza in a poem of melancholy tone, and in length about one hundred lines. Now, never losing sight of the object—*supremeness* or perfection at all points, I asked myself—"Of all melancholy topics what, according to the *universal* understanding of mankind, is the *most* melancholy?" Death, was the obvious reply. "And when," I said, "is this most melancholy of topics most poetical?" From what I have already explained at some length the answer here also is obvious—"When it most closely allies itself to *Beauty*: the death then of a beautiful woman is unquestionably the most poetical topic in the world, and equally is it beyond doubt that the lips best suited for such topic are those of a bereaved lover."

I had now to combine the two ideas of a lover lamenting his deceased mistress and a Raven continuously repeating the word "Nevermore." I had to combine these, bearing in mind my design of varying at every turn the *application* of the word repeated, but the only intelligible mode of such combination is that of imagining the Raven employing the word in answer to the queries of the lover. And here it was that I saw at once the opportunity afforded for the effect on which I had been depending, that is to say, the effect of the *variation of application*. I saw that I could make the first query propounded by the lover—the first query to which the Raven should reply "Nevermore"—that I could make this first query a commonplace one, the second less so, the third still less, and so on, until at length the lover, startled from his original *nonchalance* by the melancholy character of the word itself, by its frequent repetition, and by a consideration of the ominous reputation of the fowl that uttered it, is at length excited to superstition, and wildly propounds queries of a far different character—queries whose solution he has passionately at heart—propounds them half in superstition and half in that species of despair which delights in self-torture—propounds them not altogether because he believes in the prophetic or demoniac character of the bird (which reason assures him is merely repeating a lesson learned by rote), but because he experiences a frenzied pleasure in so modelling his questions as to receive from the *expected* "Nevermore" the most delicious because the most intolerable of sorrows. Perceiving the opportunity thus afforded me—or, more strictly, thus forced upon me in the progress of the construction—I first established in mind the climax, or concluding query—that query to which "Nevermore" should be in the last place an answer—that query in reply to which this word "Nevermore" should involve the utmost conceivable amount of sorrow and despair.

Here then the poem may be said to have had its beginning—at the end where all works of art should begin—for it was here at this point of my preconsiderations that I first put pen to paper in the composition of the stanza:

> "Prophet!" said I, "thing of evil! prophet still if bird or devil!
> By that Heaven that bends above us—by that God we both adore,
> Tell this soul with sorrow laden, if, within the distant Aidenn,
> It shall clasp a sainted maiden whom the angels name Lenore—
> Clasp a rare and radiant maiden whom the angels name Lenore."
> Quoth the Raven—"Nevermore."

I composed this stanza, at this point, first that, by establishing the climax, I might the better vary and graduate, as regards seriousness and importance, the preceding queries of the lover, and secondly, that I might definitely settle the rhythm, the metre, and the length and general arrangement of the stanza, as well as graduate the stanzas which were to precede, so that none of them might surpass this in rhythmical effect. Had I been able in the subsequent composition to construct more vigorous stanzas I should without scruple have purposely enfeebled them so as not to interfere with the climacteric effect.

And here I may as well say a few words of the versification. My first object (as usual) was originality. The extent to which this has been neglected in versification is one of the most unaccountable things in the world. Admitting that there is little possibility of variety in mere *rhythm*, it is still clear that the possible varieties of metre and stanza are absolutely infinite, and yet, *for centuries, no man, in verse, has ever done, or ever seemed to think of doing, an original thing*. The fact is that originality (unless in minds of very unusual force) is by no means a matter, as some suppose, of impulse or intuition. In general, to be found, it must be elaborately sought, and although a positive merit of the highest class, demands in its attainment less of invention than negation.

Of course I pretend to no originality in either the rhythm or metre of the "Raven." The former is trochaic—the latter is octametre acatalectic, alternating with heptametre catalectic repeated in the *refrain* of the fifth verse, and terminating with tetrametre catalectic. Less pedantically—the feet employed throughout (trochees) consist of a long syllable followed by a short; the first line of the stanza consists of eight of these feet, the second of seven and a half (in effect two-thirds), the third of eight, the fourth of seven and a half, the fifth the same, the sixth three and a half. Now, each of these lines taken individually has been employed before, and what originality the "Raven" has, is in their *combination into stanzas;* nothing even remotely approaching this combination has ever been attempted. The effect of this originality of combination is aided by other unusual and some altogether novel effects arising from an extension of the application of the principles of rhyme and alliteration.

The next point to be considered was the mode of bringing together the lover and the Raven—and the first branch of this consideration was the *locale.* For this the most natural suggestion might seem to be a forest, or the fields—but it has always appeared to me that a close *circumscription of space* is absolutely necessary to the effect of insulated incident—it has the force of a frame to a picture. It has an indisputable moral power in keeping concentrated the attention, and, of course, must not be confounded with mere unity of place.

I determined, then, to place the lover in his chamber—in a chamber rendered sacred to him by memories of her who had frequented it. The room is represented as richly furnished—this in mere pursuance of the ideas I have already explained on the subject of Beauty, as the sole true poetical thesis.

The *locale* being thus determined, I had now to introduce the bird—and the thought of introducing him through the window was inevitable. The idea of making the lover suppose, in the first instance, that the flapping of the wings of the bird against the shutter, is a "tapping" at the door, originated in a wish to increase, by prolonging, the reader's curiosity, and in a desire to admit the incidental effect arising from the lover's throwing open the door, finding all dark, and thence adopting the half-fancy that it was the spirit of his mistress that knocked.

I made the night tempestuous, first to account for the Raven's seeking admission, and secondly, for the effect of contrast with the (physical) serenity within the chamber.

I made the bird alight on the bust of Pallas, also for the effect of contrast between the marble and the plumage—it being understood that the bust was absolutely *suggested* by the bird—the bust of *Pallas* being chosen, first, as most in keeping with the scholarship of the lover, and secondly, for the sonorousness of the word, Pallas, itself.

About the middle of the poem, also, I have availed myself of the force of contrast, with a view of deepening the ultimate impression. For example, an air of the fantastic—approaching as nearly to the ludicrous as was admissible—is given to the Raven's entrance. He comes in "with many a flirt and flutter."

> Not the *least obeisance made he*—not a moment stopped or stayed he,
> But *with mien of lord or lady*, perched above my chamber door.

In the two stanzas which follow, the design is more obviously carried out:—

> Then this ebony bird, beguiling my sad fancy into smiling
> By the *grave and stern decorum of the countenance it wore*,
> "Though thy *crest be shorn and shaven*, thou," I said, "art sure no craven,
> Ghastly grim and ancient Raven wandering from the Nightly shore—
> Tell me what thy lordly name is on the Night's Plutonian shore?"
>   Quoth the Raven—"Nevermore."
>
> Much I marvelled *this ungainly fowl* to hear discourse so plainly,
> Though its answer little meaning—little relevancy bore;
> For we cannot help agreeing that no living human being
> *Ever yet was blessed with seeing bird above his chamber door*—
> Bird or beast upon the sculptured bust above his chamber door,
>   With such name as "Nevermore."

The effect of the *dénouement* being thus provided for, I immediately drop the fantastic for a tone of the most profound seriousness—this tone commencing in the stanza directly following the one last quoted, with the line,

> But the Raven, sitting lonely on that placid bust, spoke only, etc.

From this epoch the lover no longer jests—no longer sees anything even of the fantastic in the Raven's demeanour. He speaks of his as a "grim, ungainly, ghastly, gaunt, and ominous bird of yore," and feels the "fiery eyes" burning into his "bosom's core." This revolution of thought, or fancy, on the lover's part, is intended to induce a similar one on the part of the reader—to bring the mind into a proper frame for the *dénouement*—which is now brought about as rapidly and as *directly* as possible.

With the *dénouement* proper—with the Raven's reply, "Nevermore," to the lover's final demand if he shall meet his mistress in another world—the poem, in its obvious phase, that of a simple narrative, may be said to have its completion. So far, everything is within the limits of the accountable—of the real. A raven, having learned by rote the single word "Nevermore," and having escaped from the custody of its owner, is driven at midnight through the violence of a storm to seek admission at a window from which a light still gleams—the chamber window of a student, occupied half in poring over a volume, half in dreaming of a beloved mistress deceased. The casement being thrown open at the fluttering of the bird's wings, the bird itself perches on the most convenient seat out of the immediate reach of the student, who amused by the incident and the oddity of the visitor's demeanour, demands of it, in jest and without looking for reply, its name. The raven addressed, answers with its customary word, "Nevermore"—a word which finds immediate echo in the melancholy heart of the student, who, giving utterance aloud to certain thoughts suggested by the occasion, is again startled by the fowl's repetition of "Nevermore." The student now guesses the state of the case, but is impelled, as I have before explained, by the human thirst for self-torture, and in part by superstition, to propound such queries to the bird as will bring him, the lover, the most of the luxury of sorrow, through the anticipated answer, "Nevermore." With the indulgence, to the extreme, of this self-torture, the narration, in what I have termed its first or obvious phase, has a natural termination, and so far there has been no overstepping of the limits of the real.

But in subjects so handled, however skillfully, or with however vivid an array of incident, there is always a certain hardness or nakedness which repels the artistical eye. Two things are invariably required—first, some amount of complexity, or more properly, adaptation; and, secondly, some amount of suggestiveness—some under-current, however indefinite, of meaning. It is this latter, in especial, which imparts to a work of art so much of that *richness* (to borrow from colloquy a forcible term), which we are too fond of confounding with *the ideal*. It is the *excess* of the suggested meaning—it is the rendering this the upper instead of the under-current of the theme—which turns into prose (and that of the very flattest kind), the so-called poetry of the so-called transcendentalists.

Holding these opinions, I added the two concluding stanzas of the poem —their suggestiveness being thus made to pervade all the narrative which has preceded them. The under-current of meaning is rendered first apparent in the line—

> "Take thy beak from out *my heart*, and take thy form from off my door!"
> Quoth the Raven "Nevermore!"

It will be observed that the words, "from out my heart," involve the first metaphorical expression in the poem. They, with the answer, "Nevermore," dispose the mind to seek a moral in all that has been previously narrated. The reader begins now to regard the Raven as emblematical—but it is not until the very last line of the very last stanza that the intention of making him emblematical of *Mournful and never ending Remembrance* is permitted distinctly to be seen:

> And the Raven, never flitting, still is sitting, still is sitting,
> On the pallid bust of Pallas just above my chamber door;
> And his eyes have all the seeming of a demon that is dreaming,
> And the lamplight o'er him streaming throws his shadow on the floor;
> And my soul *from out that shadow* that lies floating on the floor
>   Shall be lifted—nevermore.

A. E. Housman

(1859–1936)

"Not only is it difficult to know the truth about anything," A. E. Housman writes in a part of the following essay omitted here, "but to tell the truth when one knows it, to find words which will not obscure or pervert it, is in my experience an exhausting effort." Housman, after a bitterly unhappy homosexual experience as a student at Oxford, failed his examinations, the "Greats" in classics, and was sent down without a degree. The rest of his long life was an unswerving manifold repayment for the agony of that year, his twenty-first. With something like a monk's serene devotion Housman drove himself to become one of the world's foremost classical scholars and, as "A. E.," a poet of simple controlled forms and controlled strong feelings. His definition of the function of poetry, also from this essay, is strikingly reminiscent of Tolstoy's definition of the function of art as a whole: "And I think that to transfer emotion—not to transmit thought but to set up in the reader's sense a vibration corresponding to what was felt by the writer—is the peculiar function of poetry." We can only guess whether Housman's account of how he composed a poem was really the truth for him, or any more or less the truth about the inner process of writing than Coleridge's confession or Poe's boast.

FROM
THE NAME AND NATURE OF POETRY

Poetry is not the thing said but a way of saying it. Can it then be isolated and studied by itself? for the combination of language with its intellectual content, its meaning, is as close a union as can well be imagined. Is there such a thing as pure unmingled poetry, poetry independent of meaning?

Even when poetry has a meaning, as it usually has, it may be inadvisable to draw it out. "Poetry gives most pleasure" and Coleridge "when only generally and not perfectly understood"; the perfect understanding will sometimes almost extinguish pleasure. The Haunted Palace is one of Poe's best poems so long as we are content to swim in the sensations it evokes and only vaguely to apprehend the allegory. We are roused to discomfort, at least I am, when we begin to perceive how exact in detail the allegory is; when it dawns upon us that the fair palace door is Roderick Usher's mouth, the pearl and ruby his teeth and lips, the yellow banners his hair, the ramparts plumed and pallid his forehead, and when we are reduced to hoping, for it is no more than a hope, that the wingèd odours have no connexion with hair-oil.

Meaning is of the intellect, poetry is not. If it were, the eighteenth century would have been able to write it better. As matters actually stand, who are the English poets of that age in whom pre-eminently one can hear and recognize the true poetic accent emerging clearly from the contemporary dialect? These four: Collins, Christopher Smart, Cowper, and Blake. And what other characteristic had these four in common? They were mad. Remember Plato: "He who without the Muses' madness in his soul comes knocking at the door of poesy and thinks that art will make him anything fit to be called a poet, finds that the poetry which he indites in his sober senses is beaten hollow by the poetry of madmen."

That the intellect is not the fount of poetry, that it may actually hinder its production, and that it cannot even be trusted to recognize poetry when produced, is best seen in the case of Smart. Neither the prize founded in this University by the Rev. Thomas Seaton nor the successive contemplation of five several attributes of the Supreme Being could incite him to good poetry while he was sane. The only poem by which he is remembered, a poem which came to its own in the kinder climate of the nineteenth century and has inspired one of the best poems of the twentieth, was written, if not, as tradition says, in actual confinement, at any rate very soon after release; and when the eighteenth century, the age of sanity and intelligence, collected his poetical works, it excluded this piece as "bearing melancholy proofs of the recent estrangement of his mind."

Collins and Cowper, though they saw the inside of madhouses, are not supposed to have written any of their poetry there; and Blake was never mad enough to be locked up. But elements of their nature were more or less insurgent against the centralised tyranny of the intellect, and their brains were not thrones on which the great usurper could sit secure. And so it strangely came to pass that in the eighteenth century, the age of prose and of unsound or unsatisfying poetry, there sprang up one well of the purest inspiration. For me the most poetical of all poets is Blake. I find his lyrical note as beautiful as Shakespeare's and more beautiful than anyone else's; and I call him more poetical than Shakespeare, even though Shakespeare has so much more poetry, because poetry in him preponderates more than in Shakespeare over everything else, and instead of being confounded in a great river can be drunk pure from a slender channel of its own. Shakespeare is rich in thought, and his meaning has power of itself to move us, even if the poetry were not there: Blake's meaning is often unimportant or virtually non-existent, so that we can listen with all our hearing to his celestial tune.

Even Shakespeare, who had so much to say, would sometimes pour out his loveliest poetry in saying nothing.

> Take O take those lips away
>   That so sweetly were forsworn,
> And those eyes, the break of day,
>   Lights that do mislead the morn;

> But my kisses bring again,
>   bring again,
> Seals of love, but seal'd in vain,
>   seal'd in vain.

That is nonsense; but it is ravishing poetry. When Shakespeare fills such poetry with thought, and thought which is worthy of it, as in *Fear no more the heat o' the sun* or *O mistress mine, where art thou roaming?* those songs, the very summits of lyrical achievement, are indeed greater and more moving poems, but I hardly know how to call them more poetical.

Now Blake again and again, as Shakespeare now and then, gives us poetry neat, or adulterated with so little meaning that nothing except poetic emotion is perceived and matters.

> Hear the voice of the Bard,
>   Who present, past, and future sees;
> Whose ears have heard
> The Holy Word
>   That walk'd among the ancient trees,
>
> Calling the lapsèd soul
>   And weeping in the evening dew;
> That might control
> The starry pole,
>   And fallen, fallen light renew.
>
> 'O Earth, O Earth, return!
>   Arise from out the dewy grass;
> Night is worn,
> And the morn
>   Rises from the slumberous mass.
>
> 'Turn away no more;
>   Why wilt thou turn away?
> The starry floor,
> The watery shore
>   Is giv'n thee till the break of day.'

That mysterious grandeur would be less grand if it were less mysterious; if the embryo ideas which are all that it contains should endue form and outline, and suggestion condense itself into thought.

> Memory, hither come
>   And tune your merry notes;
> And while upon the wind
>   Your music floats
>
> I'll pore upon the stream
> Where sighing lovers dream,
> And fish for fancies as they pass
> Within the watery glass.

That answers to nothing real; memory's merry notes and the rest are empty phrases, not things to be imagined; the stanza does but entangle the reader in a net of thoughtless delight. The verses which I am now going to read probably possessed for Blake a meaning, and his students think that they have found it; but the meaning is a poor foolish disappointing thing in comparison with the verses themselves.

My Spectre around me night and day
Like a wild beast guards my way;
My Emanation far within
Weeps incessantly for my sin.

A fathomless and boundless deep,
There we wander, there we weep;
On the hungry craving wind
My Spectre follows thee behind.

He scents thy footsteps in the snow
Wheresoever thou dost go:
Through the wintry hail and rain
When wilt thou return again?

Dost thou not in pride and scorn
Fill with tempests all my morn,
And with jealousies and fears
Fill my pleasant nights with tears?

Seven of my sweet loves thy knife
Has bereavèd of their life.
Their marble tombs I built with tears
And with cold and shuddering fears.

Seven more loves weep night and day
Round the tombs where my loves lay,
And seven more loves attend each night
Around my couch with torches bright.

And seven more loves in my bed
Crown with wine my mournful head,
Pitying and forgiving all
Thy transgressions great and small.

When wilt thou return and view
My loves, and them to life renew?
When wilt thou return and live?
When wilt thou pity as I forgive?

I am not equal to framing definite ideas which would match that magnificent versification and correspond to the strong tremor of unreasonable excitement which those words set up in some region deeper than the mind.

Lastly take this stanza, addressed "to the Accuser who is the God of this World."

> Tho' thou are worship'd by the names divine
>   Of Jesus and Jehovah, thou are still
> The Son of Morn in weary Night's decline,
>   The lost traveller's dream under the hill.

It purports to be theology: what theological sense, if any, it may have, I cannot imagine and feel no wish to learn: it is pure and self-existent poetry, which leaves no room in me for anything besides.

In most poets, as I said, poetry is less often found thus disengaged from its usual concomitants, from certain things with which it naturally unites itself and seems to blend indistinguishably. For instance:

> Sorrow, that is not sorrow, but delight;
> And miserable love, that is not pain
> To hear of, for the glory that redounds
> Therefrom to human kind, and what we are.

The feeling with which those lines are read is composite, for one constituent is supplied by the depth and penetrating truth of the thought. Again:

> Though love repine and reason chafe,
>   There came a voice without reply,—
> " 'Tis man's perdition to be safe,
>   When for the truth he ought to die."

Much of the emotion kindled by that verse can be referred to the nobility of the sentiment. But in these six simple words of Milton—

> Nymphs and shepherds, dance no more—

what is it that can draw tears, as I know it can, to the eyes of more readers than one? What in the world is there to cry about? Why have the mere words the physical effect of pathos when the sense of the passage is blithe and gay? I can only say, because they are poetry, and find their way to something in man which is obscure and latent, something older than the present organisation of his nature, like the patches of fen which still linger here and there in the drained lands of Cambridgeshire.

Poetry indeed seems to me more physical than intellectual. A year or two ago, in common with others, I received from America a request that I would define poetry. I replied that I could no more define poetry than a terrier can define a rat, but that I thought we both recognized the object by the symptoms which it provokes in us. One of these symptoms was described in connexion with another object by Eliphaz the Temanite: "A spirit passed before my face: the hair of my flesh stood up." Experience has taught me, when I am shaving of a morning, to keep watch over my thoughts, because, if a line of poetry strays into my memory, my skin bristles so that the razor ceases to act. This particular symptom is accompanied by a shiver down the spine; there is another which consists in a constriction of the throat and a precipitation of water to the eyes; and there is a third which I can only describe by borrowing a phrase from one of Keats's last letters, where he says, speaking of Fanny Brawne, "everything that reminds me of her goes through me like a spear." The seat of this sensation is the pit of the stomach.

My opinions on poetry are necessarily tinged, perhaps I should say tainted, by the circumstance that I have come into contact with it on two sides. We were saying a while ago that poetry is a very wide term, and inconveniently comprehensive: so comprehensive is it that it embraces two books, fortunately not large ones, of my own. I know how this stuff came into existence; and though I have no right to assume that any other poetry came into existence in the same way, yet I find reason to believe that some poetry, and quite good poetry, did. Wordsworth for instance says that poetry is the spontaneous overflow of powerful feelings, and Burns has left us this confession. "I have two or three times in my life composed from the wish rather than the impulse, but I never succeeded to any purpose." In short I think that the production of poetry, in its first stage, is less an active than a passive and involuntary process; and if I were obliged, not to define poetry, but to name the class of things to which it belongs, I should call it a secretion; whether a natural secretion, like turpentine in the fir, or a morbid secretion, like the pearl in the oyster. I think that my own case, though I may not deal with the material so cleverly as the oyster does, is the latter; because I have seldom written poetry unless I was rather out of health, and the experience, though pleasurable, was generally agitating and exhausting. If only that you may know what to avoid, I will give some account of the process.

Having drunk a pint of beer at luncheon—beer is a sedative to the brain, and my afternoons are the least intellectual portion of my life—I would go out for a walk of two or three hours. As I went along, thinking of nothing in particular, only looking at things around me and following the progress of the seasons, there would flow into my mind, with sudden and unaccountable emotion, sometimes a line or two of verse, sometimes a whole stanza at once, accompanied, not preceded, by a vague notion of the poem which they were destined to form part of. Then there would usually be a lull of an hour or so, then perhaps the spring would bubble up again. I say bubble up, because, so far as I could make out, the source of the suggestions thus proffered to the brain was an abyss which I have already had occasion to mention, the pit of the stomach. When I got home I wrote them down, leaving gaps, and hoping that further inspiration might be forthcoming another day. Sometimes it was, if I took my walks in a receptive and expectant frame of mind; but sometimes the poem had to be taken in hand and completed by the brain, which was apt to be a matter of trouble and anxiety, involving trial and disappointment, and sometimes ending in failure. I happen to remember distinctly the genesis of the piece which stands last in my first volume. Two of the stanzas, I do not say which, came into my head, just as they are printed, while I was crossing the corner of Hampstead Heath between the Spaniard's Inn and the footpath to Temple Fortune. A third stanza came with a little coaxing after tea. One more was needed, but it did not come: I had to turn to and compose it myself, and that was a laborious business. I wrote it thirteen times, and it was more than a twelvemonth before I got it right.

Rudyard Kipling

(1865–1936)

The Anglo-Indian imperialism for which Rudyard Kipling was a spokesman is now a ghost in history, and his work is out of fashion. But there is a hot energy in it which attracted and influenced a number of writers of the mid-twentieth century, among them Orwell. Because of his Plain Tales *Kipling was famous in England by the time he was twenty-four years old; he won the Nobel Prize when he was only forty-two. His* Something of Myself *tells of his writing life. Its last chapter, called "Working-Tools," has some shrewd observations on the craft— for example, on the way cutting can increase a story's power: "A tale from which pieces have been raked out is like a fire that has been poked. One does not know that the operation has been performed, but everyone feels the effect." The point of the chapter, however, is urged through its title, and it has to do with Kipling's sense that some kind of magic was involved in his writing—a sense of being possessed, or at least guided, by an external force, a muse, what Kipling called his Daemon. The writer is only a kind of agent; his Daemon lurks in his pen and is mysteriously influenced by the rest of the working-tools on his desk.*

FROM
WORKING-TOOLS

Let us now consider the Personal Daemon of Aristotle and others, of whom it has been truthfully written, though not published:

> This is the doom of the Makers—their Daemon lives in their pen.
> If he be absent or sleeping, they are even as other men.
> But if he be utterly present, and they swerve not from his behest,
> The word that he gives shall continue, whether in earnest or jest.

Most men, and some most unlikely, keep him under an alias which varies with their literary or scientific attainments. Mine came to me early when I sat bewildered among other notions, and said: "Take this and no other." I obeyed, and was rewarded. It was a tale in the little Christmas Magazine *Quartette* which we four wrote together, and it was called 'The Phantom Rickshaw.' Some of it was weak, much was bad and out of key; but it was my first serious attempt to think in another man's skin.

After that I learned to lean upon him and recognise the sign of his approach. If ever I held back, Ananias fashion, anything of myself (even though I had to throw it out afterwards) I paid for it by missing what I *then* knew the tale lacked. As an instance, many years later I wrote about a mediaeval artist, a monastery, and the premature discovery of the microscope. ("The Eye of Allah.") Again and again it went dead under my hand,

and for the life of me I could not see why. I put it away and waited. Then said my Daemon—and I was meditating something else at the time—"Treat it as an illuminated manuscript." I had ridden off on hard black-and-white decoration, instead of pumicing the whole thing ivory-smooth, and loading it with thick colour and gilt. Again, in a South African, post–Boer War tale called "The Captive," which was built up round the phrase "a first-class dress parade for Armageddon," I could not get my lighting into key with the tone of the monologue. The background insisted too much. My Daemon said at last: "Paint the background first once for all, as hard as a public-house sign, and leave it alone." This done, the rest fell into place with the American accent and outlook of the teller.

My Daemon was with me in the *Jungle Books*, *Kim*, and both Puck books, and good care I took to walk delicately, lest he should withdraw. I know that he did not, because when those books were finished they said so themselves with, almost, the water-hammer click of a tap turned off. One of the clauses in our contract was that I should never follow up "a success," for by this sin fell Napoleon and a few others. *Note here*. When your Daemon is in charge, do not try to think consciously. Drift, wait, and obey. . . .

And with what tools did I work in my own mould-loft? I had always been choice, not to say coquettish in this respect. In Lahore for my *Plain Tales* I used a slim, octagonal-sided, agate penholder with a Waverley nib. It was a gift, and when in an evil hour it snapped I was much disturbed. Then followed a procession of impersonal hirelings each with a Waverley, and next a silver penholder with a quill-like curve, which promised well but did not perform. In Villiers Street I got me an outsize office pewter ink-pot, on which I would gouge the names of the tales and books I wrote out of it. But the housemaids of married life polished those titles away till it grew as faded as a palimpsest.

I then abandoned hand-dipped Waverleys—a nib I never changed—and for years wallowed in the pin-pointed "stylo" and its successor the "fountain" which for me meant geyser-pens. In later years I clung to a slim, smooth, black treasure (Jael was her office name) which I picked up in Jerusalem. I tried pump-pens with glass insides, but they were of "intolerable entrails."

For my ink I demanded the blackest, and had I been in my Father's house, as once I was, would have kept an ink-boy to grind me Indian-ink. All "blue-blacks" were an abomination to my Daemon, and I never found a bottled vermilion fit to rubricate initials when one hung in the wind waiting.

My writing-blocks were built for me to an unchanged pattern of large, off-white, blue sheets, of which I was most wasteful. All this old-maiderie did not prevent me when abroad from buying and using blocks, and tackle, in any country.

With a lead pencil I ceased to express—probably because I had to use a pencil in reporting. I took very few notes except of names, dates, and addresses. If a thing didn't stay in my memory, I argued it was hardly worth writing out. But each man has his own method. I rudely drew what I wanted to remember.

Like most men who ply one trade in one place for any while, I always kept certain gadgets on my work-table, which was ten feet long from North to South and badly congested. One was a long, lacquer, canoe-shaped pen-tray full of brushes and dead "fountains"; a wooden box held clips and bands; another, a tin one, pins; yet another, a bottle-slider, kept all manner of unneeded essentials from emery-paper to small screw-drivers; a paper-weight, said to have been Warren Hastings'; a tiny, weighted fur-seal and a leather crocodile sat on some of the papers; an inky foot-rule and a Father of Penwipers which a much-loved housemaid of ours presented yearly, made up the main-guard of these little fetishes.

My treatment of books, which I looked upon as tools of my trade, was popularly regarded as barbarian. Yet I economised on my multitudinous pen-knives, and it did no harm to my fore-finger. There were books which I respected because they were put in locked cases. The others, all the house over, took their chances.

Left and right of the table were two big globes, on one of which a great airman had once outlined in white paint those air-routes to the East and Australia which were well in use before my death.

PART SIX

The Writer's Life

And so we come to the crux of the craft: what it is that gives some writings their power. I have hypothesized that this power, where it shows itself, is the product of a certain unique combination of temperament and intellect. Like any other guess about the origins of good writing, this one has to be approached in a gingerly way. We will do so here, coming at it from several directions. First, we will see Gorky's picture—itself a thing of power—of Tolstoy as an old man. Then we will watch a child, the young Sartre, making his connection with writing. Then, in E. E. Cummings' charming account of his development to the point of self-recognition as a poet, we see the powerful influence of parents and of the parents' world in the making of a writer. Boris Pasternak tells of an emotional crisis which, through its shock and apparent release of deep energies, announced to Pasternak his calling as a poet and novelist. We listen as an old pro, Anthony Trollope, tells us, sparing no candor, what it is like to stay two or three novels ahead of his publisher year after year. And finally, through notes in one case and interviews in the others, we hear about writing and the writer's life from four contemporary authors—W. H. Auden, Ralph Ellison, Saul Bellow, and William Burroughs.

Maxim Gorky

(1868–1936)

Leo Tolstoy was already in his seventies and convalescing from an illness by the Black Sea when Maxim Gorky, then a young man in his mid-thirties, made the older author's acquaintance. The contrasts between the two writers could hardly have been greater. Gorky was the grandson of a dyer and the son of a failed upholsterer; he had had to begin to earn his own way at the age of nine; while working in railway workships in Tiflis he had published his first story in a local paper; and when he was twenty-nine had won fame throughout Russia with a collection of stories about social outcasts. Tolstoy was the son of a count and of a rich princess; his mother had died when he was three, his father when he was nine, and he had been brought up by elderly upper-class women relatives and educated by French tutors in an antiquated foreign culture; his young years had been spent in high society, in trying to manage his family's feudal estate, Yasnaya Polyana, and as a gentleman-soldier in the Caucasus; and finally when he had turned to his craft he had writeen about the Russian elite. Gorky's recollections of "the sorcerer," as he called Tolstoy, were set down some years after Tolstoy's death. They have nothing to say directly about the great man's craft, but they give an incomparable picture, glimpse by fragmentary glimpse, of the temperament that had underpinned the art and the power of War and Peace *and* Anna Karenina.

REMINISCENCES OF LEO NIKOLÆVICH TOLSTOY

He has wonderful hands—not beautiful, but knotted with swollen veins, and yet full of a singular expressiveness and the power of creativeness. Probably Leonardo da Vinci had hands like that. With such hands one can do anything. Sometimes, when talking, he will move his fingers, gradually close them into a fist, and then, suddenly opening them, utter a good, full-weight word. He is like a god, not a Sabaoth or Olympian, but the kind of Russian god who "sits on a maple throne under a golden lime tree," not very majestic, but perhaps more cunning than all the other gods.

He treats Sulerzhitski with the tenderness of a woman. For Chekhov his love is paternal—in this love is the feeling of the pride of a creator—Suler rouses in him just tenderness, a perpetual interest and rapture which never seem to weary the sorcerer. Perhaps there is something a little ridiculous in this feeling, like the love of an old maid for a parrot, a pug-dog, or a tom-cat. Suler is a fascinatingly wild bird from some strange unknown land. A hundred men like him could change the face, as well as the soul, of a provincial town. Its face they would smash and its soul they would fill with a passion for riotous, brilliant, headstrong wildness. One loves Suler easily and gaily, and when I see how carelessly women accept him, they surprise and anger me. Yet under this carelessness is hidden, perhaps, caution. Suler is not reliable. What will he do to-morrow? He may throw a bomb or he may join a troupe of public-house minstrels. He has energy enough for three lifetimes, and fire of life—so much that he seems to sweat sparks like over-heated iron. . . .

"Romanticism comes from the fear of looking straight into the eyes of truth," he said yesterday with regard to Balmont's poems. Suler disagreed with him and, lisping with excitement, read very feelingly some more poems.

"These, Liovushka, are not poems; they are charlatanism, rubbish, as people said in the Middle Ages, a nonsensical stringing together of words. Poetry is art-less; when Fet wrote:

> I know not myself what I will sing,
> But only my song is ripening,

he expressed a genuine, real, people's sense of poetry. The peasant, too, doesn't know that he's a poet—oh, oi, ah, and aye—and there comes off a real song, straight from the soul, like a bird's. These new poets of yours are inventing. There are certain silly French things called *articles de Paris*—well, that's what your stringers of verses produce. Nekrasov's miserable verses, too, are invented from beginning to end."

"And Béranger?" Suler asked.

"Béranger—that's quite different. What's there in common between the French and us? They are sensualists; the life of the spirit is not as important to them as the flesh. To a Frenchman woman is everything. They are a worn-out, emasculated people. Doctors say that all consumptives are sensualists."

Suler began to argue with his peculiar directness, pouring out a random flood of words. Leo Nikolaevich looked at him and said with a broad smile:

"You are peevish to-day, like a girl who has reached the age when she should marry but has no lover.". . .

If he were a fish, he would certainly swim only in the ocean, never coming to the narrow seas, and particularly not to the flat waters of earthly rivers. Around him here there rest or dart hither and thither the little fishes: what he says does not interest them, is not necessary to them, and his silence does not frighten or move them. Yet his silence is impressive, like that of a real hermit driven out from this world. Though he speaks a great deal and as a duty upon certain subjects, his silence is felt to be still greater. Certain things one cannot tell to anyone. Surely he has some thoughts of which he is afraid. . . .

I read my story *The Bull* to him. He laughed much, and praised my knowledge of "the tricks of the language."

"But your treatment of words is not skilful; all your peasants speak cleverly. In actual life what they say is silly and incoherent, and at first you cannot make out what a peasant wants to say. That is done deliberately; under the silliness of their words is always concealed a desire to allow the other person to show what is in his mind. A good peasant will never show at once what is in his own mind: it is not profitable. He knows that people approach a stupid man frankly and directly, and that's the very thing he wants. You stand revealed before him and he at once sees all your weak points. He is suspicious, he is afraid to tell his inmost thoughts even to his wife. But with your peasants in every story everything is revealed: it's a universal counsel of wisdom. And they all speak in aphorisms; that's not true to life, either; aphorisms are not natural to the Russian language."

"What about sayings and proverbs?"

"That's a different thing. They are not of to-day's manufacture."

"But you yourself often speak in aphorisms."

"Never. There again you touch everything up; people as well as Nature —especially people. So did Lyeskov, an affected, finicking writer whom nobody reads now. Don't let anyone influence you, fear no one, and then you'll be all right."

In his diary which he gave me to read, I was struck by a strange aphorism: "God is my desire."

To-day, on returning him the book, I asked him what it meant.

"An unfinished thought," he said, glancing at the page and screwing up his eyes. "I must have wanted to say: 'God is my desire to know Him.' . . . No, not that. . . ." He began to laugh, and, rolling up the book into a tube, he put it into the big pocket of his blouse. With God he has very suspicious relations; they sometimes remind me of the relation of "two bears in one den.". . .

Of women he talks readily and much, like a French novelist, but always with the coarseness of a Russian peasant. Formerly it used to affect me unpleasantly. To-day in the Almond Park he asked Anton Chekhov:

"You whored a great deal when you were young?"

Anton Pavlovich, with a confused smile, and pulling at his little beard, muttered something inaudible, and Leo Nikolaevich, looking at the sea, confessed:

"I was an indefatigable. . . ."

He said this penitently, using at the end of the sentence a salty peasant word. And I noticed for the first time how simply he used the word, as though he knew no more fitting one to use. All those kinds of words, coming from his shaggy lips, sound simple and natural and lose their soldierly coarseness and filth. I remember my first meeting with him and his talk about *Varenka Oliessova* and *Twenty-six and One*. From the ordinary point of view what he said was a string of indecent words. I was perplexed by it and even offended. I thought that he considered me incapable of understanding any other kind of language. I understand now: it was silly to have felt offended.

He sat on the stone bench in the shade of the cypresses, looking very lean, small and grey, and yet resembling Sabaoth, who is a little tired and is amusing himself by trying to whistle in tune with a chaffinch. The bird sang in the darkness of the thick foliage: he peered up at it, screwing up his sharp little eyes, and, pursing his lips like a child, he whistled incompetently.

"What a furious little creature. It's in a rage. What bird is it?"

I told him about the chaffinch and its characteristic jealousy.

"All life long one song," he said, "and yet jealous. Man has a thousand songs in his heart and is yet blamed for jealousy; is it fair?" He spoke musingly, as though asking himself questions. "There are moments when a man says to a woman more than she ought to know about him. He speaks and forgets, but she remembers. Perhaps jealousy comes from the fear of degrading one's soul, of being humiliated and ridiculous? Not that a woman is dangerous who holds a man by his . . . but she who holds him by his soul. . . ."

When I pointed out the contradiction in this with his *Kreutzer Sonata*, the radiance of a sudden smile beamed through his beard, and he said: "I am not a chaffinch."

In the evening, while walking, he suddenly said: "Man survives earthquakes, epidemics, the horrors of disease, and all the agonies of the soul, but for all time his most tormenting tragedy has been, is, and will be—the tragedy of the bedroom."

Saying this, he smiled triumphantly: at times he has the broad, calm smile of a man who has overcome something extremely difficult or from whom some sharp, long-gnawing pain has lifted suddenly. Every thought burrows into his soul like a tick; he either tears it out at once or allows it to have its fill of his blood, and then, when full, it just drops off of itself. . . .

In the morning some "stundists" came to Tolstoy from Feodosia, and to-day all day long he spoke about peasants with rapture.

At lunch: "They came both so strong and fleshy; says one: 'Well, we've come uninvited,' and the other says: 'With God's help we shall leave unbeaten,'" and he broke out into childlike laughter, shaking all over.

After lunch, on the terrace:

"We shall soon cease completely to understand the language of the people. Now we say: 'The theory of progress,' 'the role of the individual in history,' 'the evolution of science'; and a peasant says: 'You can't hide an awl in a sack,' and all theories, histories, evolutions become pitiable and ridiculous, because they are incomprehensible and unnecessary to the people. But the peasant is stronger than we; he is more tenacious of life, and there may happen to us what happened to the tribe of Atzurs, of whom it was reported to a scholar: 'All the Atzurs have died out, but there is a parrot here who knows a few words of their language.' ". . .

He likes putting difficult and malicious questions:
What do you think of yourself?
Do you love your wife?
Do you think my son, Leo, has talent?
How do you like Sophie Andreevna?[1]
Once he asked: "Are you fond of me, Alexei Maximovich?"
This is the maliciousness of a "bogatyr"[2]: Vaska Buslaev played such pranks in his youth, mischievous fellow. He is experimenting, all the time testing something, as if he were going to fight. It is interesting, but not much to my liking. He is the devil, and I am still a babe, and he should leave me alone.

Perhaps peasant to him means merely—bad smell. He always feels it, and involuntarily has to talk of it.
Last night I told him of my battle with General Kornet's widow; he laughed until he cried, and he got a pain in his side and groaned and kept on crying out in a thin scream:
"With the shovel! On the bottom with the shovel, eh? Right on the bottom! Was it a broad shovel?"
Then, after a pause, he said seriously: "It was generous in you to strike her like that; any other man would have struck her on the head for that. Very generous! You understood that she wanted you?"
"I don't remember. I hardly think that I can have understood."
"Well now! But it's obvious. Of course she wanted you."
"I did not live for that then."
"Whatever you may live for, it's all the same. You are evidently not much of a lady's man. Anyone else in your place would have made his fortune out of the situation, would have become a landed proprietor and have ended by making one of a pair of drunkards."
After a silence: "You are funny—don't be offended—very funny. And it's very strange that you should still be good-natured when you might well be spiteful. . . . Yes, you might well be spiteful. . . . You're strong . . . that's good. . . ."

[1]*Tolstoy's wife.*
[2]*A hero in Russian legend, brave, but wild and self-willed like a child.*

And after another silence, he added thoughtfully: "Your mind I don't understand—it's a very tangled mind—but your heart is sensible . . . yes, a sensible heart."

NOTE.—When I lived in Kazan, I entered the service of General Kornet's wife as doorkeeper and gardener. She was a Frenchwoman, a general's widow, a young woman, fat, and with the tiny feet of a little girl. Her eyes were amazingly beautiful, restless and always greedily alert. Before her marriage she was, I think, a huckstress or a cook or, possibly, even a woman of the town. She would get drunk early in the morning and come out in the yard or garden dressed only in a chemise with an orange-coloured gown over it, in Tartar slippers made of red morocco, and on her head a mane of thick hair. Her hair, carelessly done, hung about her red cheeks and shoulders. A young witch! She used to walk about the garden, humming French songs and watching me work, and every now and then she would go to the kitchen window and call:

"Pauline, give me something."

"Something" always meant the same thing—a glass of wine with ice in it.

In the basement of her house there lived three young ladies, the Princesses D. G., whose mother was dead and whose father, a Commissariat-General, had gone off elsewhere. General Kornet's widow took a dislike to the girls and tried to get rid of them by doing every kind of offensive thing to them. She spoke Russian badly, but swore superbly, like an expert drayman. I very much disliked her attitude towards these harmless girls—they looked so sad, frightened, and defenceless. One afternoon, two of them were walking in the garden when suddenly the General's widow appeared, drunk as usual, and began to shout at them to drive them out of the garden. They began walking silently away, but the General's widow stood in the gateway, completely blocking it with her body like a cork, and started swearing at them and using Russian words like a regular drayman. I asked her to stop swearing and let the girls go out, but she shouted:

"You, I know you! You get through their window at night."

I was angry, and, taking her by the shoulders, pushed her away from the gate; but she broke away, and, facing me, quickly undid her dress, lifted up her chemise, and shouted:

"I'm nicer than those rats."

Then I lost my temper. I took her by the neck, turned her round, and struck her with my shovel below the back, so that she skipped out of the gate and ran across the yard, crying out three times in great surprise: "O! O! O!"

After that, I got my passport from her confidante, Pauline—also a drunken but very wily woman—took my bundle under my arm, and left the place; and the General's widow, standing at the window with a red shawl in her hand, shouted:

"I won't call the police—it's all right—listen—come back—don't be afraid.". . .

How strange that he is so fond of playing cards. He plays seriously, passionately. His hands become nervous when he takes the cards up, exactly as if he were holding live birds instead of inanimate pieces of cardboard. . . .

I read him some scenes from my play, *The Lower Depths*; he listened attentively, and then asked:

"Why do you write that?"

I explained as best I could.

"One always notices that you jump like a cock on to everything. And more—you always want to paint all the grooves and cracks over with your own paint. You remember that Andersen says: 'The gilt will come off and the pig-skin will remain'; just as our peasants say: 'Everything will pass away, the truth alone will remain.' You'd much better not put the plaster on, for you yourself will suffer for it later. Again, your language is very skilful, with all kinds of tricks—that's no good. You ought to write more simply; people speak simply, even incoherently, and that's good. A peasant doesn't ask: 'Why is a third more than a fourth, if four is always more than three,' as one learned young lady asked. No tricks, please."

He spoke irritably; clearly he disliked very much what I had read to him. And after a silence, looking over my head, he said gloomily:

"Your old man is not sympathetic, one does not believe in his goodness. The actor is all right, he's good. You know *Fruits of Enlightenment*? My cook there is rather like your actor. Writing plays is difficult. But your prostitute also came off well, they must be like that. Have you known many of them?"

"I used to."

"Yes, one can see that. Truth always shows itself. Most of what you say comes out of yourself, and therefore you have no characters, and all your people have the same face. I should think you don't understand women; they don't come off with you. One does not remember them. . . ."

At this moment A. L.'s wife came in and called us to come to tea, and he got up and went out very quickly, as if he were glad to end the conversation.

"What is the most terrible dream you have ever had?" Tolstoy asked me.

I rarely have dreams and remember them badly, but two have remained in my memory and probably will for the rest of my life.

I dreamt once that I saw the sky scrofulous, putrescent, greenish-yellow, and the stars in it were round, flat, without rays, without lustre, like scabs on the skin of a diseased person. And there glided across this putrescent sky slowly reddish forked lightning, rather like a snake, and when it touched a star the star swelled up into a ball and burst noiselessly, leaving behind it a darkish spot, like a little smoke; and then the spot vanished quickly in the bleared and liquid sky. Thus all the stars one after another burst and perished, and the sky, growing darker and more horrible, at last whirled upwards, bubbled, and, bursting into fragments, began to fall on my head in a kind of cold jelly, and in the spaces between the fragments there appeared a shiny blackness as though of iron. Leo Nikolaevich said: "Now that comes from a learned book; you must have read something on astronomy; hence the nightmare. And the other dream?"

The other dream: a snowy plain, smooth like a sheet of paper; no hillock, no tree, no bush anywhere, only—barely visible—a few rods poked out from under the snow. And across the snow of this dead desert from horizon to horizon there stretched a yellow strip of a hardly distinguishable road, and over the road there marched slowly a pair of grey felt topboots—empty.

He raised his shaggy, werewolf eyebrows, looked at me intently and thought for a while.

"That's terrible. Did you really dream that?—you didn't invent it? But there's something bookish in it also."

And suddenly he got angry, and said, irritably, sternly, rapping his knee with his finger: "But you're not a drinking man? It's unlikely that you ever drank much. And yet there's something drunken in these dreams. There was a German writer, Hoffmann, who dreamt that card tables ran about the street, and all that sort of thing, but then he was a drunkard—a 'calaholic,' as our literate coachmen say. Empty boots marching—that's really terrible. Even if you did invent it, it's good. Terrible."

Suddenly he gave a broad smile, so that even his cheek-bones beamed.

"And imagine this: suddenly, in the Tverskaya Street, there runs a card table with its curved legs, its boards clap, clap, raising a chalky dust, and you can even still see the numbers on the green cloth—excise clerks playing whist on it for three days and nights on end—the table could not bear it any longer and ran away."

He laughed, and then, probably noticing that I was a little hurt by his distrust of me:

"Are you hurt because I thought your dreams bookish? Don't be annoyed; sometimes, I know, one invents something without being aware of it, something which one cannot believe, which can't possibly be believed, and then one imagines that one dreamt it and did not invent it at all. There was a story which an old landowner told. He dreamt that he was walking in a wood and came out of it on to a steppe. On the steppe he saw two hills, which suddenly turned into a woman's breasts, and between them rose up a black face, which, instead of eyes, had two moons like white spots. The old man dreamt that he was standing between the woman's legs, in front of him a deep, dark ravine, which sucked him in. After the dream his hair began to grow grey and his hands to tremble, and he went abroad to Doctor Kneip to take a water cure. But, really, he must have seen something of the kind—he was a dissolute fellow."

He patted me on the shoulder.

"But you are neither a drunkard nor dissolute—how do you come to have such dreams?"

"I don't know."

"We know nothing about ourselves."

He sighed, screwed up his eyes, thought for a bit, and then added in a low voice. "We know nothing."

This evening, during our walk, he took my arm and said:

"The boots are marching—terrible, eh? Quite empty—tiop, tiop—and the snow scrunching. Yes, it's good; but you are very bookish, very. Don't be cross, but it's bad and will stand in your way."

I am scarcely more bookish than he, and at the time I thought him a cruel rationalist despite all his pleasant little phrases. . . .

Suler tells how he was once walking with Leo Nikolaevich in Tverskaya Street when Tolstoy noticed in the distance two soldiers of the Guards. The metal of their accoutrements shone in the sun; their spurs jingled; they kept step like one man; their faces, too, shone with the self-assurance of strength and youth.

Tolstoy began to grumble at them: "What pompous stupidity! Like animals trained by the whip. . . ."

But when the Guardsmen came abreast with him, he stopped, followed them caressingly with his eyes, and said enthusiastically: "How handsome! Old Romans, eh, Liovushka? Their strength and beauty! O Lord! How charming it is when man is handsome, how very charming!"

Jean-Paul Sartre

(1905–   )

The mind of Jean-Paul Sartre has negotiated every highway, byway, lane, and alley of the twentieth century. Sartre has written novels, short stories, and plays; he has been a phenomenological philosopher, founder of a school; he has been a literary critic and biographer, author of what amounted to a discovery of Jean Genet, and of an immense critical work on Flaubert; he has been a polemicist, a theoretician of practical politics, and even a streetcorner activist. Of all his diverse works, the one which comes closest to unifying at least the motive force of all the others, and to explaining the energy, restlessness, and depths of Sartre's curiosity, is this witty, self-mocking, charming book, The Words. The excerpts given here come from the second half of the book, called "Writing." The first part tells of young Jean-Paul's previous introduction to the world of words through reading. His father died soon after Jean-Paul was born, and the young boy grew up the pampered idol of his mother and of his crotchety maternal grandfather. "I began my life," Sartre writes, "as I shall no doubt end it: amidst books. In my grandfather's study there were books everywhere." Even before he could read he "revered those standing stones." First he was read to by his mother; then he sat on his cot with an open book pretending to read; then he taught himself to read from a book that had been read aloud to him so often he knew it by heart—and then: "I was allowed to browse in the library and I took man's wisdom by storm." The second part of the book tells how Sartre moved from the world of reading, of imagining, of acting, of making up stories in his head, finally to the labor of his life, writing. At last: "It's a habit, and besides, it's my profession. For a long time I took my pen for a sword; I now know we're powerless. No matter, I write. . . ."

FROM
THE WORDS

Charles Schweitzer had never taken himself for a writer, but the French language still filled him with wonder at the age of seventy because he had had a hard time learning it and it did not quite belong to him. He played with it, took pleasure in the words, loved to pronounce them, and his relentless diction did not spare a single syllable. When he had time, his pen would arrange them in bouquets. He was only too ready to shed luster on family and academic events by works written for the occasion: New Year wishes, birthday greetings, congratulations for wedding parties, speeches in verse for Saint Charlemagne's day, sketches, charades, verses in set rhymes, amiable trivialities; at conventions, he improvised quatrains in German and French.

At the beginning of the summer, the two women and I would leave for Arcachon before my grandfather finished his courses. He would write to us three times a week, two pages for Louise, a post-script for Anne Marie and a whole letter in verse for me. In order to make me fully aware of my good fortune, my mother learned and taught me the rules of prosody. Someone taught me to scribble out a versified reply. I was urged to finish it, I was helped. When the two women sent off the letter, they laughed till the tears came at the thought of the recipient's astonishment. I received by return mail a poem to my glory; I replied with a poem. The habit was formed; the grandfather and his grandson were united by a new bond. They spoke to each other, like the Indians, like the Montmartre pimps, in a language from which women were barred. I was given a rhyming dictionary. I became a versifier. I wrote madrigals for Vévé, a blond little girl who never left her couch and who died a few years later. The little girl didn't care a damn about them: she was an angel. But the admiration of a large public consoled me for this indifference. I have dug up a few of these poems. All children have genius, except Minou Drouet, said Cocteau in 1955. In 1912, they all had it, except me. I wrote in imitation, for the sake of the ceremony, in order to act like a grown-up; above all, I wrote because I was Charles Schweitzer's grandson. I was given La Fontaine's *Fables*. I didn't care for them: the author was too casual. I decided to rewrite them in alexandrines. The undertaking was too much for me, and I had an impression that it made the others smile. That was my last poetical experience. But I had got a start. I shifted from verse to prose and had not the slightest difficulty reinventing, in writing, the exciting adventures that I read in *Cri-Cri*. It was high time: I was going to discover the inanity of my dreams. In the course of my fantastic gallops, it was reality that I was seeking. When my mother would ask me, without taking her eyes from her score: "Poulou, what are you doing?", I would sometimes break my vow of silence and answer: "I'm playing moving-pictures." Indeed, I was trying to pluck the pictures from my head and *realize* them outside of me, between real pieces of furniture and real walls as bright and visible as those that flashed on the screens. But all in vain. I could no longer be blind to my double imposture: I was pretending to be an actor, pretending to be a hero.

Hardly did I begin to write than I laid down my pen to rejoice. The imposture was the same, but I have said that I regarded words as the quintessence of things. Nothing disturbed me more than to see my scrawls little by little change their will-o'-the-wisp gleam for the dull consistency of matter: it was the realization of the imaginary. Caught in the trap of naming, a lion, a captain of the Second Empire, or a Bedouin would be brought into the dining room; they remained captive there forever, embodied in signs. I thought I had anchored my dreams in the world by the scratchings of a steel nib. I asked for and was given a notebook and a bottle of purple ink. I inscribed on the cover: "Novel Notebook." The first story I completed was entitled *For a Butterfly*. A scientist, his daughter, and an athletic young explorer sailed up the Amazon in search of a precious butterfly. The argument, the characters, the particulars of the adventures, and even the title were borrowed from a story in pictures that had appeared in the preceding quarter. This cold-blooded plagiarism freed me from my remaining misgivings; everything was necessarily true since I invented nothing. I did not aspire to be published, but I had contrived to be printed in advance, and I did not pen a line that was not guaranteed by my model. Did I take myself for an imitator? No, but for an original author. I retouched, I livened things up. For example, I was careful to change the names of the characters. This slight tampering entitled me to blend memory and imagination. New sentences, already written, took shape in my head with the implacable sureness ascribed to inspiration. I transcribed them. They took on, beneath my eyes, the density of things. If, as is commonly believed, the inspired author is other than himself in the depths of his soul, I experienced inspiration between the ages of seven and eight.

I was never completely taken in by this "automatic writing." But I also enjoyed the game for its own sake. Being an only child, I could play it by myself. Now and then I would stop writing. I would pretend to hesitate, I would pucker my brow, assume a moonstruck expression, so as to feel I was a *writer*. I loved plagiarism, out of pretentiousness, be it added, and I deliberately carried it to an extreme, as will be seen presently.

Boussenard and Jules Verne did not miss an opportunity to be educational. At the most critical moments, they would break off the story to go into a description of a poisonous plant, of a native dwelling. As reader, I skipped these didactic passages; as author, I padded my novels with them. I meant to teach my contemporaries everything that I didn't know: the customs of the Fuegians, the flora of Africa, the climate of the desert. The collector of butterflies and his daughter, who had been separated by a stroke of fate and were then aboard the same ship without knowing it and victims of the same shipwreck, clung to the same life-buoy, raised their heads, and cried out: "Daisy!", "Papa!" Alas, a shark was on the prowl for fresh meat; it drew near; its belly shone in the waves. Would the unfortunate pair escape death? I went to get volume "Pr-Z" of the Big Larousse, carried it painfully to my desk, opened it to the right page, and, starting a new paragraph, copied out, word for word: "Sharks are common in the South Atlantic. These big sea-fish, which are very voracious, are sometimes forty feet long and weigh as much as eight tons . . ." I would take my time transcribing the article. I felt charmingly boring, as distinguished as Boussenard, and, not yet knowing how I was going to save my heroes, I would stew slowly in an exquisite trance.

This new activity was destined in every way to be an additional imitation. My mother was lavish with encouragement. She would bring visitors into the dining-room so that they could surprise the young creator at his school-desk. I pretended to be too absorbed to be aware of my admirers' presence. They would withdraw on tiptoe, whispering that I was too cute for words, that it was too-too charming. My uncle Emile gave me a little typewriter, which I didn't use. Mme. Picard bought me a globe so that I would make no mistakes in laying out my globetrotters' itinerary. Anne Marie copied out my second novel, *The Banana-seller*, on glossy paper. It was shown about. "At least," she would say, "he behaves himself, he doesn't make any noise." Fortunately, the consecration was put off by my grandfather's displeasure.

Karl had never approved of what he called my "unwholesome reading-matter." When my mother informed him that I had begun to write, he was at first delighted, expecting, I suppose, an account of our family life with pungent observations and adorably naïve remarks. He took my notebook, leafed through it, scowled, and left the dining-room, furious at finding a repetition of the "nonsense" of my favorite gazettes. Eventually, he ignored my writings. My mother was mortified and tried several times to trick him into reading *The Banana-seller*. She would wait until he had put on his slippers and settled down in his armchair. While he rested silently, staring grimly ahead, with his hands in his lap, she would pick up my manuscript, leaf through it casually, and then, as if suddenly taken with it, would start laughing to herself. Finally, as if irresistibly carried away, she would hand it to my grandfather: "Do read it, Papa! It's *too* funny for words." But he would thrust the notebook aside, or, if he did glance at it, it was to point out, irritably, my spelling mistakes. In the course of time my mother was intimidated. Not daring to congratulate me and afraid of hurting me, she stopped reading my work so as not to have to talk to me about it.

Ignored and barely tolerated, my literary activities became semi-clandestine. Nevertheless, I continued them diligently, during recreation periods, on Thursdays and Sundays, during vacation, and, when I had the luck to be sick, in bed. I remember happy convalescences and a black, red-edged notebook which I would take up and lay down like a tapestry. I "played movies" less often; my novels took the place of everything. In short, I wrote for my own pleasure.

My plots grew complicated. I introduced the most varied episodes, I indiscriminately poured everything I read, good or bad, into these catch-alls. The stories suffered as a result. Nevertheless, I gained thereby, for I had to join things up, which meant inventing, and I consequently did less plagiarizing. In addition, I split myself in two. The year before, when I "played movies," I played my own role, I threw myself body and soul into the imaginary, and I thought more than once that I would be completely swallowed up in it. As author, the hero was still myself; I projected my epic dreams upon him. All the same, there were two of us: he did not have my name, and I referred to him only in the third person. Instead of endowing him with my gestures, I fashioned for him, by means of words, a body that I made an effort to see. This sudden "distancing" might have frightened me; it charmed me. I was delighted to be *him* without his quite being me. He was my doll, I could bend him to my whims, could pierce his side with a lance and then nurse and cure him the way my mother nursed and cured me. My favorite authors, who did have a certain sense of shame, stopped short of the sublime. Even in Zévaco, no valiant knight ever slew more than twenty knaves at a time. I wanted to change the adventure novel radically. I threw verisimilitude overboard. I multiplied enemies and dangers tenfold. In order to save his fiancée and future father-in-law, the young explorer in *For a Butterfly* fought the sharks for three days and three nights; in the end, the sea was red. The same character, wounded, escaped from a ranch that was besieged by Apaches, crossed the desert with his guts in his hands, and refused to let himself be sewn up before he spoke to the general. A little later, under the name of Goetz von Berlichingen, the same character routed an army. One against all: that was my rule. Let the source of this grim and grandiose reverie be sought in the bourgeois, puritan individualism of my environment.

As a hero, I fought against tyranny. As a demiurge, I became a tyrant myself. I experienced all the temptations of power. I was harmless, I became wicked. What prevented me from plucking Daisy's eyes out? Scared to death, I answered: nothing. And pluck them out I did, as I would have plucked off the wings of a fly. I wrote, with beating heart: "Daisy ran her hand over her eyes. She had become blind," and I sat there stunned, with my pen in the air. I had produced an event in the realm of the absolute that compromised me delightfully. I was not really sadistic: my perverse joy would immediately change into panic, I would annul all my decrees, I would cross them out over and over until they were indecipherable. The girl would regain her sight, or rather she had never lost it. But the memory of my caprices tormented me for a long time: I seriously worried myself.

The written word also worried me. At times, weary of mild massacres for children, I would let myself daydream; I would discover, in a state of anguish, ghastly possibilities, a monstrous universe that was only the underside of my omnipotence; I would say to myself: anything can happen! and that meant: I can imagine anything. Tremulously, always on the point of tearing up the page, I would relate supernatural atrocities. If my mother happened to read over my shoulder, she would utter a cry of glory and alarm: "What an imagination!" She would suck her lips, wanting to speak, and, finding nothing to say, would suddenly rush off. Her retreat heightened my anguish. But the imagination was not involved. I did not invent those horrors; I found them, like everything else, in my memory.

In that period, the western world was choking to death: that is what was called "the sweetness of living." For want of visible enemies, the bourgeoisie took pleasure in being scared of its own shadow. It exchanged its boredom for a directed anxiety. People spoke of spiritism, of ectoplasm. At 2 Rue le Goff, opposite our house, there were sessions of table turning. They took place on the fourth floor, "in the magician's apartment," as my grandmother put it. She would sometimes call us, and we would arrive in time to see pairs of hands on a pedestal table, but someone would come to the window and draw the curtains. Louise claimed that children of my age, accompanied by their mothers, visited the magician every day. "And," she said, "I see him. There's a laying on of hands." My grandfather would shake his head. Although he condemned those practices, he dared not make fun of them. My mother was afraid of them. My grandmother, for once, seemed more intrigued than sceptical. Finally they would all agree: "The main thing is not to get involved in it. It drives you crazy!" Fantastic stories were all the rage. High-minded newspapers dished out two or three a week to that dechristianized public which was nostalgic for the beauties of faith. The narrator would relate, in all objectivity, a disturbing fact. He would give positivism a chance. However strange the event might be, it had to entail a rational explanation. The author would seek this explanation, find it, and present it fairly. But at once he would cunningly make us realize how inadequate and slight it was. Nothing more: the account would end with a question. But that was enough; the Other World was there, all the more formidable in that it was not named.

When I opened *Le Matin*, I would be frozen with fear. One story in particular struck me. I still remember the title of it: "Wind in the Trees." One summer evening, a sick woman, alone on the first floor of a country house, is tossing about in bed. A chestnut tree pushes its branches into the room through the open window. On the ground floor, several persons are sitting and talking. They are watching darkness settle on the garden. Suddenly someone points to the chestnut tree: "Look at that! Can it be windy?" They are surprised. They go out on the porch. Not a breath of air. Yet the leaves are shaking. At that moment, a cry! The sick woman's husband rushes upstairs and finds his young wife sitting up in bed. She points to the tree and falls over dead. The tree is as quiet as ever. What did she see? A lunatic has escaped from the asylum. It must have been he, hidden in the tree, who showed his grinning face. It's he, it *must* be he, for the reason that no other explanation can be satisfactory. And yet . . . How is it that no one saw him go up or down? How is it that the dogs didn't bark? How could he have been arrested, six hours later, sixty miles from the estate? Questions without an answer. The writer starts a new paragraph and concludes casually: "According to the people of the village, it was Death that shook the branches of the chestnut tree." I threw the paper aside, stamped my foot, and cried aloud: "No! No!" My heart was bursting in my chest. One day, in a train going to Limoges, I thought I would faint as I turned the pages of the Hachette Almanac. I had come upon a drawing that was enough to make one's hair stand on end: a quay beneath the moon; a long gnarled claw came out of the water, took hold of a drunkard, and dragged him to the bottom. The picture illustrated a text that I read eagerly and that ended—or almost—with the following words: "Was it the hallucination of an alcoholic? Had Hell opened up?" I was afraid of the water, afraid of crabs and trees. Afraid of books in particular. I cursed the fiends who filled their stories with such atrocious figures. Yet I imitated them.

Of course, an occasion was necessary. For example, nightfall. The dining-room would be bathed in shadow. I would push my little desk against the window. The anguish would start creeping up again. The docility of my heroes, who were unfailingly sublime, unappreciated and rehabilitated, would reveal their unsubstantiality. Then *it* would come, a dizzying, invisible being that fascinated me. In order to be seen, it had to be described. I quickly finished off the adventure I was working on, took my characters to an entirely different part of the globe, generally subterranean or underseas, and hastily exposed them to new dangers: as improvised geologists or deep-sea divers, they would pick up the Being's trail, follow it, and suddenly encounter it. What flowed from my pen at that point—an octopus with eyes of flame, a twenty-ton crustacean, a giant spider that talked—was I myself, a child monster; it was my boredom with life, my fear of death, my dullness and my perversity. I did not recognize myself. No sooner was the foul creature born than it rose up against me, against my brave speleologists. I feared for their lives. My heart would race away; I would forget my hand; penning the words, I would think I was reading them. Very often things ended there; I wouldn't deliver the men up to the Beast, but I didn't get them out of trouble either. In short, it was enough that I had put them in contact. I would get up and go to the kitchen or the library. The next day, I would leave a page or two blank and launch my characters on a new venture. Strange "novels," always unfinished, always begun over or, if you like, continued under other titles, odds and ends of gloomy tales and cheery adventures, of fantastic events and encyclopedia articles. I have lost them and I sometimes think it's a pity. If it had occurred to me to lock them up, they would reveal to me my entire childhood.

I was beginning to find myself. I was almost nothing, at most an activity without content, but that was all that was needed. I was escaping from play-acting. I was not yet working, but I had already stopped playing. The liar was finding his truth in the elaboration of his lies. I was born of writing. Before that, there was only a play of mirrors. With my first novel I knew that a child had got into the hall of mirrors. By writing I was existing, I was escaping from the grown-ups, but I existed only in order to write, and if I said "I," that meant "I who write." In any case, I knew joy. The public child was making private appointments with himself.

It was too good to last. I would have remained sincere if I had stuck to my clandestine existence. But I was yanked away from it. I was reaching the age when bourgeois children were supposed to show the first signs of their vocation. We had been informed long before that my Schweitzer cousins, in Guérigny, would be engineers, like their father. There was not another minute to lose. Mme. Picard wanted to be the first to discover the sign I bore on my brow. "The child will be a writer," she said with conviction. Louise, much annoyed, responded with her curt little smile. Blanche Picard turned to her and repeated sternly: "He'll be a writer! He's meant to be a writer." My mother knew that Charles was not very encouraging. She was afraid of complications and looked at me closely. "You think so, Blanche? You think so?" But in the evening, as I jumped up and down on my bed, in my nightshirt, she hugged my shoulders hard and said with a smile: "My little man will be a writer!" My grandfather was informed very cautiously. An outburst was feared. He merely nodded, and the following Thursday I heard him say confidentially to M. Simonnot that in the evening of life no one could witness the budding of a talent without being thrilled. He continued to pay no attention to my scribbling, but when his German pupils came to dine at the house, he would place his hand on my skull and repeat, separating the syllables so as not to miss an opportunity to teach them French locutions by the direct method: "He has the bump of literature."

He didn't believe a word of what he said, but what of it? The harm was done. Had he been dead set against me, he might only have made matters worse. I might have stuck to my guns obstinately. Karl proclaimed my vocation in order to be able to divert me from it. He was the opposite of a cynic, but he was growing old; his enthusiasms tired him. I am sure that deep down, in a cold desert zone which he seldom visited, *he* knew what to think about me, the family, and himself. One day, as I lay reading between his feet, during one of the endless silences he imposed on us, he was suddenly struck by an idea that made him forget my presence. He looked at my mother reproachfully: "And what if he got it into his head to live by his pen?" My grandfather appreciated Verlaine, of whom he had a volume of selected poems. But he thought he had seen him enter a bar in 1894 "as drunk as a pig." That encounter had thoroughly confirmed his contempt for professional writers; they were mere miracle-mongers who asked for a gold-piece to show you the moon and ended by showing you their behind for five francs. My mother looked frightened but didn't answer. She knew that Charles had other plans for me. In most of the lycées, the teachers of German were Alsatians who had chosen France and who had been given their posts in reward for their patriotism. Caught between two nations, between two languages, their studies had been somewhat irregular, and there were gaps in their culture. That made them suffer. They also complained that they were left out of things in the academic community because of their colleagues' hostility. I would be their avenger; I would avenge my grandfather. Grandson of an Alsatian, I was at the same time a Frenchman of France. Karl would help me acquire universal knowledge. I would take the royal road: in my person, martyred Alsace would enter the Ecole Normale Supérieure, would pass the teaching examination with flying colors, and would become that prince, a teacher of letters. One evening he announced that he wanted to talk to me man to man. The women withdrew. He sat me down on his lap and spoke to me very seriously. I would be a writer, that was understood, I knew him well enough not to fear that he would oppose my wishes. But I had to know exactly what I was in for: literature did not fill a man's belly. Did I know that famous writers had died of hunger? That others had sold themselves in order to eat? If I wanted to remain independent, I would do well to choose a second profession. Teaching gave a man leisure. Scholarly interests went hand in hand with those of men of letters. I would move back and forth from one priestly function to the other. I would live in close contact with the great writers. At one and the same time, I would reveal their works to my pupils and draw upon them for inspiration. I would beguile my provincial solitude by composing poems, by translating Horace into blank verse. I would write short literary articles for the local papers, a brilliant essay on the teaching of Greek for the *Pedagogic Review*, another on the psychology of adolescents. Upon my death, unpublished works would be found among my papers, a meditation on the sea, a one-act comedy, a few sensitive and scholarly pages on the monuments of Aurillac, enough to fill a thin volume that would be edited by former pupils.

For some time now, my grandfather's raptures over my virtues left me cold. I still pretended to listen to the voice that trembled with love when it called me a "gift from heaven," but I stopped hearing it. Why did I listen to it that day, when it lied to me most deliberately? As a result of what misunderstanding did I make it say the opposite of what it claimed to be teaching me? The fact is that it had changed: it had dried and hardened, and I took it for that of the absent father who had begotten me. Charles had two faces: when he played grandfather, I regarded him as a buffoon of my own kind and did not respect him. But when he spoke to M. Simonnot or to his sons, when he made the women wait on him at table, by pointing, without a word, at the oil and vinegar cruets or the bread-basket, I admired his authority. I was particularly impressed by the play of his forefinger: he would be careful not to point, but would move it vaguely in the air, half bent, so that the designation remained imprecise and the two servants had to guess at his orders. At times, in exasperation, my grandmother would make a mistake and hand him the fruit-bowl when he asked for wine. I would lay the blame on my grandmother. I deferred to these royal desires that wished to be anticipated more than to be satisfied. If Charles had flung his arms wide open and cried out from afar: "Here comes the new Hugo, here's a budding Shakespeare!", I would now be an industrial draughtsman or a teacher of literature. He was careful not to. For the first time, I was dealing with the patriarch. He seemed forbidding and all the more venerable in that he had forgotten to adore me. He was Moses dictating the new law. My law. He had mentioned my vocation only in order to point out its disadvantages. I concluded that he took it for granted. Had he predicted that my pages would be drenched with tears or that I would roll on the rug, my bourgeois restraint would have been shocked. He convinced me of my vocation by giving me to understand that such showy disorders were not in store for me: in order to discuss Aurillac or pedagogy, there was no need, alas, of fever or tumult. Others would heave the immortal sobs of the twentieth century. I resigned myself to never being thunder or lightning; I would shine in literature by virtue of my domestic qualities, my amiability, my steadiness. The craft of writing appeared to me as an adult activity, so ponderously serious, so trifling, and, at bottom, so lacking in interest that I didn't doubt for a moment that it was in store for me. I said to myself both "that's all it is" and "I'm gifted." Like all dreamers, I confused disenchantment with truth.

Karl had turned me inside out like a rabbit skin. I had thought I was going to write only in order to set down my dreams, whereas, if I were to believe him, I dreamed only in order to exercise my pen. My anguish and imaginary passions were only the ruses of my talent; their sole function was to send me back to my desk every day and provide me with narrative themes suitable to my age while I awaited the great dictations of experience and maturity. I lost my fabulous illusions. "Ah!" my grandfather would say, "it's not enough to have eyes. You must learn to use them. Do you know what Flaubert did when de Maupassant was a little boy? He sat him down in front of a tree and gave him two hours to describe it." I therefore learned to see. As a predestined singer of the glories of Aurillac, I would gaze with melancholy at those other monuments: the blotter, the piano, the clock which would also be immortalized—why not—by my future lucubrations. I observed. It was a dismal and disappointing game: I had to stand in front of the stamped velvet armchair and inspect it. What was there to say about it? Well, that it was covered wih fuzzy green material, that it had two arms, four legs, a back surmounted by two little wooden pine-cones. That was all for the moment, but I would come back to it, I would do better next time, I would end by knowing it inside out.

Later, I would describe it; my readers would say: "How well observed it is, how accurately! It's exactly right! That's the kind of thing one doesn't invent!" Depicting real objects with real words that were penned with a real pen, I'd be hanged if I didn't become real myself! In short, I knew once and for all what to answer the ticket-collectors who asked me for my ticket.

One can well imagine that I appreciated my good fortune! The trouble was that I didn't enjoy it. My appointment had been confirmed, I had very kindly been given a future, and I openly declared it was delightful, but I secretly loathed it. Had I asked for that clerk's job? Associating with great men had convinced me that one could not be a writer without becoming illustrious. But when I compared the glory that had befallen me with the few scanty booklets I would leave behind, I felt I had been fooled. Could I really believe that my grand-nephews would re-read me and be enthusiastic about so slight an output, about subjects that bored me in advance? I sometimes told myself that I would be saved from oblivion by my "style," that enigmatic virtue which my grandfather denied Stendhal and recognized in Renan. But those meaningless words did not succeed in reassuring me.

Above all, I had to renounce my own self. Two months earlier I had been a swashbuckler, an athlete. That was over! I was being called upon to choose between Corneille and Pardaillan. I dismissed Pardaillan, whom I really and truly loved; out of humility, I decided in favor of Corneille. I had seen heroes running and fighting in the Luxembourg. Staggered by their beauty, I had realized that I belonged to the lesser breed. I had to proclaim the fact, to sheathe my sword, to go back to the common herd, to resume relations with the great writers, those little squirts who didn't intimidate me. They had been rickety children; at least I resembled them in that. They had become sickly adults, rheumy old men; I would resemble them in that. A nobleman had had Voltaire beaten, and I perhaps would be horsewhipped by a captain, a former park bully.

I felt gifted out of resignation. In Charles Schweitzer's study, amidst worn, torn, battered books, talent was what was valued least of all. Similarly, under the Old Regime, many a younger son who was doomed by birth to the priesthood would have sold his soul to command a battalion. The dismal pomp of fame was long epitomized for me by the following scene: on a long table covered with a white cloth were pitchers of orangeade and bottles of sparkling wine; I took a glass; men in evening clothes who surrounded me—there were a good fifteen of them—drank a toast to my health; I could sense behind us the bare, dusty vastness of a hired hall. It's obvious that I expected nothing more from life than that it revive for me, late in life, the annual party of the Modern Language Institute.

Thus, in the course of discussions that were repeated over and over, my destiny was being shaped at number one Rue le Goff, in a fifth-floor apartment, below Goethe and Schiller, above Molière, Racine, and La Fontaine, on a par with Heinrich Heine and Victor Hugo. Karl and I would send the women away; we would hug each other tightly; we would continue at close range that deaf men's dialogue, each word of which left its mark on me. By deft little strokes Charles convinced me that I wasn't a genius. Indeed I wasn't, I knew it, I didn't give a damn. Heroism, absent and impossible, was the sole object of my passion, heroism, the blazing flame of the poor in spirit. My inner poverty and the feeling of being gratuitous did not allow me to renounce it entirely. I no longer dared be enraptured by my future gesture, but at bottom I was terrorized. Someone must have been mistaken about the child or the vocation. Since I was lost, I accepted, in obedience to Karl, the studious career of a writer. In short, he drove me into literature by the care he took to divert me from it, to such an extent that even now I sometimes wonder, when I am in a bad mood, whether I have not consumed so many days and nights, covered so many pages with ink, thrown on the market so many books that nobody wanted, solely in the mad hope of pleasing my grandfather. That would be a farce. At the age of more than fifty, I would find myself engaged, in order to carry out the will of a man long dead, in an undertaking which he would not have failed to repudiate.

The fact is that I resemble Swann when he has gotten over his love: "To think," he sighs, "that I messed up my life for a woman who wasn't my type!" At times, I'm secretly a skunk; it's a matter of elementary hygiene. Now, the skunk is always right, but up to a certain point. It's true that I'm not a gifted writer. I've been told so, I've been called labored. So I am; my books reek of sweat and effort; I grant that they stink in the nostrils of our aristocrats. I've often written them against myself, which means against everybody,[1] with an intentness of mind that has ended by becoming high blood pressure. My commandments were sewn into my skin; if I go a day without writing, the scar burns me; if I write too easily, it also burns me. This simple-minded exigency still acts upon me by its rigidity, its clumsiness. It resembles the solemn, prehistoric crabs that the ocean throws up on the beaches of Long Island. Like them, it is a survival of a bygone era. For a long time, I envied the concierges of the Rue Lacépède sitting astride their chairs when summer evenings brought them out on the sidewalk. Their innocent eyes saw without being commissioned to look.

But the fact is this: apart from a few old men who dip their pens in eau de Cologne and little dandies who write like butchers, all writers have to

---

[1] *Be self-indulgent, and those who are also self-indulgent will like you. Tear your neighbor to pieces, and the other neighbors will laugh. But if you beat your soul, all souls will cry out.*

sweat. That's due to the nature of the Word: one speaks in one's own language, one writes in a foreign language. I conclude from this that we're all alike in our profession: we're all galley-slaves, we're all tattooed. Besides, the reader has realized that I loathe my childhood and whatever has survived of it. I wouldn't listen to my grandfather's voice, that recorded voice which wakes me with a start and drives me to my table, if it were not my own, if, between the ages of eight and ten, I had not arrogantly assumed responsibility for the supposedly imperative mandate that I had received in all humility.

> "I quite realize that I am only a machine which makes books."
> (Chateaubriand)

I almost gave up. In the last analysis, all that I saw in the gift to which Karl paid lip-service, deeming it unwise to deny it entirely, was a matter of chance that was unable to legitimize that other matter of chance, myself. My mother had a beautiful voice; *therefore* she sang. She nevertheless didn't travel without a ticket. I had the bump of literature; therefore I would write, I would work that vein all my life. Well and good. But Art lost—at least for me—its sacred powers. I would remain a vagabond—with a little more security, that was all. In order for me to feel necessary, someone would have had to express a need for me. My family had been feeding me that illusion for some time; they had told me again and again that I was a gift of heaven, that I had been eagerly awaited, that I was indispensable to my grandfather, to my mother. I no longer believed it, but I did continue to feel that one is born superfluous unless one is brought into the world with the special purpose of fulfilling an expectation. My pride and forlornness were such at the time that I wished I were dead or that I were needed by the whole world.

I had stopped writing. Mme. Picard's declarations had given such importance to the soliloquies of my pen that I no longer dared to continue them. When I wanted to go back to my novel, to save at least the young couple that I had left in the middle of the Sahara Desert with neither provisions nor helmets, I suffered the horrors of impotence. No sooner was I seated than my head filled with fog. I chewed at my nails and frowned: I had lost my innocence. I got up and prowled about the apartment with the soul of an incendiary. Unfortunately, I never set fire to it. Docile by virtue of circumstances, by taste, by custom, I came to rebellion later only because I had carried submission to an extreme. I was given a "homework notebook" with a cloth cover and red edges. No external sign distinguished it from my "novel notebook." As soon as I looked at it, my school work and my personal obligations merged; I identified the author with the pupil, the pupil with the future teacher. The act of writing and the teaching of grammar came to one and the same thing. My pen, which had been socialized, dropped from my hand, and several months went by without my picking it up. My grandfather smiled in his beard whenever I dragged my sullenness into his study. He no doubt thought to himself that his policy was bearing its first fruits.

It failed because I had an epic mind. Thrown back among the commoners, with my sword broken, I often had the following anxiety dream: I was in the Luxembourg, near the pond, facing the Senate Building. I had to protect a blond little girl from an unknown danger; she resembled Vévé, who had died a year earlier. The girl looked up at me calmly and confidently with her serious eyes. Often she was holding a hoop. It was I who was frightened: I was afraid of abandoning her to invisible forces. But how I loved her, with how mournful a love! I still love her. I have looked for her, lost her, found her again, held her in my arms, lost her again: she is the Epic. At the age of eight, just as I was about to resign myself, I pulled myself together; in order to save that dead little girl, I launched out upon a simple and mad operation that shifted the course of my life: I palmed off on the writer the sacred powers of the hero.

At the source of this was a discovery, or rather a reminiscence, for I had had a foreboding of it two years earlier: great writers are akin to knights-errant in that both elicit passionate signs of gratitude. In the case of Pardaillan, no further proof was needed: the back of his hand was furrowed with the tears of fair orphans. But if I was to believe the encyclopedia and the obituaries that I read in the newspapers, the writer was not less favored: if only he lived long enough, he invariably ended by receiving a letter from an unknown person who *thanked him.* From then on, thanks kept pouring in; they piled up on his desk, cluttered his home; foreigners crossed the seas to pay tribute to him; his fellow-countrymen took up a collection after his death to erect a monument to him; in his native town and sometimes in the capital of his country, streets were named after him. In themselves, these gratifications did not interest me; they reminded me too much of the family play-acting. There was, however, a certain drawing that staggered me: the famous novelist Dickens is going to land in New York in a few hours; the ship on which he is sailing can be seen in the distance; the crowd is gathered on the pier to welcome him; it opens all its mouths and waves a thousand caps; it is so dense that children are suffocating; yet it is lonely, an orphan and a widow, depopulated by the mere absence of the man for whom it is waiting. I murmured: "There's someone missing here. It's Dickens!", and my eyes filled with tears. However, I brushed aside the effects and went straight to their cause: in order to be so wildly acclaimed, I thought to myself, men of letters must face the greatest dangers and render the most distinguished service to mankind. Once in my life I had witnessed a similar burst of enthusiasm: hats went flying, men and women cried "bravo," "hurray"; it was a July 14th; the Algerian riflemen were parading by. This memory finally convinced me: despite their physical defects, their primness, their seeming femininity, writers risked their lives as free lances in mysterious combats; their military courage was applauded even more than their talent. "So it's true," I said to myself, "they're *needed!*" In Paris, in New York, in Moscow, they are awaited, with anguish or ecstasy, before they have published their first book, before they have begun to write, even before they are born.

But then . . . what about me? Me, whose mission it was to write? Well, they were waiting for me. I transformed Corneille into Pardaillan: he retained his bandy legs, narrow chest, and dismal face, but I took away his avarice and love of lucre; I deliberately blended the art of writing and generosity. After that, it was the easiest thing in the world to change myself into Corneille and to confer upon myself the mandate of protecting the race. My new imposture was preparing me for an odd future. For the moment, I had everything to gain by it. I had been born with disadvantages, and have spoken of my efforts to be born over: entreaties of innocence in jeopardy had called me forth a thousand times. But it was all in fun: fake knight that I was, I performed fake exploits, the hollowness of which finally disgusted me. But my dreams were now being given back to me and were becoming real. For my vocation *was* real; I could have no doubt about it, since the high priest vouched for it. I, the imaginary child, was becoming a true paladin whose exploits would be real books. I was being summoned! People were awaiting my work, the first volume of which, despite my zeal, would not come out before 1935. Around 1930, people would start losing patience: "He's certainly taking his time! He's been living off the fat of the land for twenty-five years! Are we going to die without reading him?" I would answer with my 1913 voice: "Say! Let me have time to work!" But nicely. I could see that they needed my help— only God knew why—and that this need had begotten me, me, the only means of satisfying it. I strove to catch a glimpse, deep inside me, of that universal expectation, my gushing spring and my reason for living. I would sometimes feel I was about to succeed, and then, after a moment, I would drop the whole business. In any case, those false illuminations were enough for me. I looked out, reassured: perhaps I was already being missed in certain places. But no, it was too soon. I was the bright object of a desire that was still unborn, and I gladly consented to remain incognito for a while. At times, my grandmother would take me with her to her circulating library, and it would amuse me to see tall, pensive, unsatisfied ladies gliding from wall to wall in search of the author who would satisfy them: he was not to be found, since he was I, that youngster who was standing under their very noses and whom they didn't even look at. . . .

[The conclusion of the book:]

I have changed. I shall speak later on about the acids that corroded the distorting transparencies which enveloped me; I shall tell when and how I served my apprenticeship to violence and discovered my ugliness—which for a long time was my negative principle, the quicklime in which the wonderful child was dissolved; I shall also explain the reason why I came to think systematically against myself, to the extent of measuring the obvious truth of an idea by the displeasure it caused me. The retrospective illusion has been smashed to bits; martyrdom, salvation, and immortality are falling to pieces; the edifice is going to rack and ruin; I collared the Holy Ghost in the cellar and threw him out; atheism is a cruel and long-range affair: I think I've carried it through. I see clearly, I've lost my illusions, I know what my real jobs are, I surely deserve a prize for good citizenship. For the last ten years or so I've been a man who's been waking up, cured of a long, bitter-sweet madness, and who can't get over the fact, a man who can't think of his old ways without laughing and who doesn't know what to do with himself. I've again become the traveler without a ticket that I was at the age of seven: the ticket-collector has entered my compartment; he looks at me, less severely than in the past; in fact, all he wants is to go away, to let me finish the trip in peace; he'll be satisfied with a valid excuse, any excuse. Unfortunately I can't think of any; and besides, I don't even feel like trying to find one. We remain there looking at each other. Feeling uncomfortable, until the train gets to Dijon where I know very well that no one is waiting for me.

I've given up the office but not the frock: I still write. What else can I do?

Nulla dies sine linea.

It's a habit, and besides, it's my profession. For a long time, I took my pen for a sword; I now know we're powerless. No matter. I write and will keep writing books; they're needed; all the same, they do serve some purpose. Culture doesn't save anything or anyone, it doesn't justify. But it's a product of man: he projects himself into it, he recognizes himself in it; that critical mirror alone offers him his image. Moreover, that old, crumbling structure, my imposture, is also my character: one gets rid of a neurosis, one doesn't get cured of one's self. Though they are worn out, blurred, humiliated, thrust aside, ignored, all of the child's traits are still to be found in the quinquagenarian. Most of the time they lie low, they bide their time; at the first moment of inattention, they rise up and emerge, disguised; I claim sincerely to be writing only for my time, but my present notoriety annoys me; it's not glory, since I'm alive, and yet that's enough to belie my old dreams; could it be that I still harbor them secretly? I have, I think, adapted them: since I've lost the chance of dying unknown, I sometimes flatter myself that I'm being misunderstood in my lifetime. Griselda's not dead. Pardaillan still inhabits me. So does Strogoff. I'm answerable only to them, who are answerable only to God, and I don't believe in God. So try to figure it out. As for me, I can't, and I sometimes wonder whether I'm not playing winner loses and not trying hard to stamp out my one-time hopes so that everything will be restored to me a hundredfold. In that case, I would be Philoctetes; that magnificent and stinking cripple gave everything away unconditionally, including his bow; but we can be sure that he's secretly waiting for his reward.

Let's drop that. Mamie would say:

"Gently, mortals, be discreet."

What I like about my madness is that it has protected me from the very beginning against the charms of the "élite": never have I thought that I was the happy possessor of a "talent"; my sole concern has been to save myself—nothing in my hands, nothing up my sleeve—by work and faith. As a result, my pure choice did not raise me above anyone. Without equipment, without tools, I set all of me to work in order to save all of me. If I relegate impossible Salvation to the proproom, what remains? A whole man, composed of all men and as good as all of them and no better than any.

E. E. Cummings

(1894–1962)

In the academic year 1952–53, Edward Estlin Cummings held the Charles Eliot Norton Professorship at Harvard—an honorific chair which is offered each year to a distinguished writer, composer, or critic. Cummings used the Norton lectureship as an occasion to answer the question, "Who am I"? He was, he said, two parts of a self "united by a certain wholly mysterious moment which signifies self-discovery": first, "the son of my parents and whatever is happening to him," and second, "my writing." The excerpts that follow are from the first three lectures and encompass that son and that happening; they lead up to the self-discovery. As a writer, Cummings is on the printed page to be found. He was first seen as an innovator, a convention-breaker, one who played intricate games with form and with the myriad tracks of meaning print could make on white paper. Later he came to be seen as an arch-individualist, dead set against any sort of collective loss of the person. Later—since over and over again he affirmed love, springtime, beauty, and the inviolate individual—he came to be regarded by harder heads of a ruinous century as a backward-looking transcendentalist and even a sentimentalist. But, whatever critics might say, there he still was on the printed page—fresh, astringent, lyrical, a strong and happy swimmer making his stubborn way upstream. In the foreword of a book of poems, Is 5, he wrote about his theory of technique: "I can express it in fifteen words, by quoting The Eternal Question and Immortal Answer of burlesk, viz. 'Would you hit a woman with a child?—No, I'd hit her with a brick.' Like the burlesk comedian, I am abnormally fond of that precision which creates movement."

FROM
I: SIX NON-LECTURES

1

Inspecting my autobiographical problem at close range, I see that it comprises two problems; united by a certain wholly mysterious moment which signifies selfdiscovery. Until this mysterious moment, I am only incidentally a writer: primarily I am the son of my parents and whatever is happening to him. After this moment, the question "who am I?" is answered by what I write—in other words, I become my writing; and my autobiography becomes the exploration of my stance as a writer. Two questions now make their appearance. The first—what constitutes this writing of mine?—can be readily answered: my writing consists of a pair of miscalled novels; a brace of plays, one in prose, the other in blank

verse; nine books of poems; an indeterminate number of essays; an un-
titled volume of satire; and a ballet scenario. The second question—where,
in all this material, do I find my stance as a writer most clearly expressed?
—can be answered almost as readily: I find it expressed most clearly in the
later miscalled novel, the two plays, perhaps twenty poems, and half a
dozen of the essays. Very well; I shall build the second part of my
autobiography around this prose and this poetry, allowing (wherever possible) the prose and the poetry to speak for themselves. But the first part
of my autobiography presents a problem of another order entirely. To
solve that problem, I must create a longlost personage—my parents' son—
and his vanished world. How can I do this? I don't know; and because I
don't know, I shall make the attempt. . . .

By way of describing my father, let me quote a letter and tell you a
story. The letter was written by me to my good friend Paul Rosenfeld;
who used it in an essay which graced the fifth number of that ambiguously
entitled periodical The Harvard Wake:

> I wot not how to answer your query about my father. He was a New Hampshire
> man, 6 foot 2, a crack shot & a famous fly-fisherman & a firstrate sailor (his
> sloop was named The Actress) & a woodsman who could find his way through
> forests primeval without a compass & a canoeist who'd stillpaddle you up to a
> deer without ruffling the surface of a pond & an ornithologist & taxidermist &
> (when he gave up hunting) an expert photographer (the best I've ever seen) &
> an actor who portrayed Julius Caesar in Sanders Theatre & a painter (both in
> oils & watercolours) & a better carpenter than any professional & an architect
> who designed his own houses before building them & (when he liked) a plumber
> who just for the fun of it installed all his own waterworks & (while at Harvard)
> a teacher with small use for professors—by whom (Royce, Lanman, Taussig, etc.)
> we were literally surrounded (but not defeated)—& later (at Doctor Hale's so-
> called South Congregational really Unitarian church) a preacher who announced,
> during the last war, that the Gott Mit Uns boys were in error since the only
> thing which mattered was for man to be on God's side (& one beautiful Sunday
> in Spring remarked from the pulpit that he couldn't understand why anyone
> had come to hear him on such a day) & horribly shocked his pewholders by
> crying "the Kingdom of Heaven is no spiritual roofgarden: it's inside you" &
> my father had the first telephone in Cambridge & (long before any Model T
> Ford) he piloted an Orient Buckboard with Friction Drive produced by the Wal-
> tham watch company & my father sent me to a certain public school because its
> principal was a gentle immense coalblack negress & when he became a diplomat
> (for World Peace) he gave me & my friends a tremendous party up in a tree at
> Sceaux Robinson & my father was a servant of the people who fought Boston's
> biggest & crookedest politician fiercely all day & a few evenings later sat down
> with him cheerfully at the Rotary Club & my father's voice was so mag-
> nificent that he was called on to impersonate God speaking from Beacon Hill
> (he was heard all over the common) & my father gave me Plato's metaphor of
> the cave with my mother's milk.

This, I feel, is an accurate sketch of Edward Cummings, Harvard '83—
except as regards his neighbourliness. He certainly had "small use for

professors" in general; but with the particular professors around him his relations were nearly always amicable and in certain cases affectionate. The neighbour whom my father unquestionably preferred was William James; and it's odd that I should have forgotten to mention so true a friend and so great a human being. Not only is it odd: it's ungrateful— since I may be said to owe my existence to professor James, who introduced my father to my mother.

Now for the story.

Thirty-five years ago, a soiled envelope with a French stamp on it arrived at 104 Irving Street, Cambridge. The envelope contained a carefully phrased scrawl; stating (among other things) that I was interned in a certain concentration camp, with a fine friend named Brown whom I'd met on the boat going to France—he, like myself, having volunteered as an ambulance driver with Messers Norton (not Charles Eliot) and Harjes. Immediately my father—than whom no father on this earth ever loved or ever will love his son more profoundly—cabled his friend Norton; but Mr. Norton hadn't even missed us, and consequently could do less than nothing. Next, through a mere but loyal acquaintance, my father set the American army on our trail; forcefully stipulating that my friend and I must be rescued together. Many days passed. Suddenly the telephone rang—top brass demanding Reverend Edward Cummings. "Hello" my father said. "This is Major Soandso" an angry voice sputtered. "That friend of your son is no damned good. May even be a spy. Unpatriotic anyhow. He deserves what's coming to him. Do you understand?" "I understand" said my deeply patriotic father. "We won't touch Brown" the sputter continued "so it's your son or nothing. And I guarantee that your son alone will be out of that hellhole in five days—what do you say about that?" "I say" replied my father "don't bother." And he hung up.

Incidentally, the major bothered; and as a result, my friend Slater Brown is also alive.

Let me only add that while my father was speaking with the American army, my mother was standing beside him; for these two wonderful human beings, my father and my mother, loved each other more than themselves—

> if there are any heavens my mother will(all by herself)have
> one.   It will not be a pansy heaven nor
> a fragile heaven of lilies-of-the-valley but
> it will be a heaven of blackred roses
>
> my father will be(deep like a rose
> tall like a rose)

standing near my

swaying over her
(silent)
with eyes which are really petals and see

nothing with the face of a poet really which
is a flower and not a face with
hands
which whisper
This is my beloved my

                              (suddenly in sunlight

he will bow,

& the whole garden will bow)

—as for me, I was welcomed as no son of any king and queen was ever welcomed. Here was my joyous fate and my supreme fortune. If somehow a suggestion of this illimitable blessing should come to you from me, my existence here and now would be justified: otherwise, anything I may say to you will have not the slightest significance. For as surely as each November has its April, mysteries only are significant; and one mystery-of-mysteries creates them all:

        nothing false and possible is love
        (who's imagined,therefore limitless)
        love's to giving as to keeping's give;
        as yes is to if,love is to yes

I shall not attempt a description of my mother. But let me try to give you a few glimpses of the most amazing person I've ever met. She came of highly respectable Roxbury stock: so highly respectable (indeed) that one of her distinguished forbears; the Reverend Pitt Clarke, withdrew his grown son by the ear from what we should consider a painfully decorous dance. Nor did Clarke respectability stop there. When my mother's father, who was in business with his father-in-law, affixed (on one occasion) the latter's name to a cheque, that worthy not only sent his son-in-law to the Charles Street jail but obliterated his name from the family archives. My mother told me that all during her childhood she supposed that her father had been hanged. She also assured me that she grew up a shy—or (as we now say) neurotic—girl; who had to be plucked from under sofas whenever friends came to call; and this statement I found almost unbelievable, though she could no more have told a lie than flown over the housetop. For never have I encountered anyone more joyous, anyone healthier in body and mind, anyone so quite incapable of remembering a wrong, or anyone so completely and humanly and unaffectedly generous. Whereas my father had created his Unitarianism (his own father being a Christian of the hellfire variety) she had inherited hers; it was an integral part of herself, she expressed it as she breathed and as she smiled. The two indispensable factors in life, my mother always maintained, were "health and a sense of humor." And although her health eventually failed her, she kept her sense of humor to the beginning.

It isn't often you meet a true heroine. I have the honour to be a true heroine's son. My father and mother were coming up from Cambridge to New Hampshire, one day, in their newly purchased automobile—an aircooled Franklin, with an ash frame. As they neared the Ossippees, snow fell. My mother was driving; and, left to herself, would never have paused for such a trifle as snow. But as the snow increased, my father made her stop while he got out and wiped the windshield. Then he got in; and she drove on. Some minutes later, a locomotive cut the car in half, killing my father instantly. When two brakemen jumped from the halted train, they saw a woman standing—dazed but erect—beside a mangled machine; with blood "spouting" (as the older said to me) out of her head. One of her hands (the younger added) kept feeling of her dress, as if trying to discover why it was wet. These men took my sixty-six year old mother by the arms and tried to lead her toward a nearby farmhouse; but she threw them off, strode straight to my father's body, and directed a group of scared spectators to cover him. When this had been done (and only then) she let them lead her away.

A day later, my sister and I entered a small darkened room in a country hospital. She was still alive—why, the headdoctor couldn't imagine. She wanted only one thing: to join the person she loved most. He was very near her, but she could not quite reach him. We spoke, and she recognized our voices. Gradually her own voice began to understand what its death would mean to these living children of hers; and very gradually a miracle happened. She decided to live. "There's something wrong with my head" she kept telling us faintly; and she didn't mean the fracture of her skull. As days and nights passed, we accidentally discovered that this ghastly wound had been sewn up by candlelight when all the town lights went out at once. But the headdoctor had no intention of losing his patient —"move her?" he cried "impossible! It would kill her just to sit up" and several centuries wandered away before we found a method of overruling him. When the ambulance arrived, ready to transfer my mother to a big Boston hospital, she was sitting up (fully dressed and smiling) by the entrance-door. She admired the ambulance, conversed cheerfully with its chauffeur, and refused to lie down because by so doing she'd miss the scenery en route. We shot through towns and tore through cities. "I like going fast" she told us; beaming. At last came the goal. After an interminable time in an operatingroom—where (we learned later) she insisted on watching in a handmirror whatever was happening, while a great brainsurgeon removed a piece of bone and carefully cleansed the wound—up came my mother in a wheelchair; very erect, and waving triumphantly a small bottle in which (at her urgent request) he'd placed the dirt and grime and splinters of whose existence his predecessor had been blissfully unaware. "You see?" she cried to us, smiling "I was right!"

And, though the wound had later to be reopened, she came out of that hospital in record time; recovered completely at home in a few months—attending, now and then, a nearby meeting of The Society of Friends—then boarded a train alone for New York, and began working as a volunteer for the Travellers' Aid in the Grand Central Station. "I'm tough!" was her dauntless comment when we tried to express our amazement and our joy.

2

For the benefit of those of you who can't imagine what the word "home" implies, or what a home could possibly have been like, I should explain that the idea of home is the idea of privacy. But again—what is privacy? You probably never heard of it. Even supposing that (from time to time) walls exist around you, those walls are no longer walls; they are merest pseudosolidities, perpetually penetrated by the perfectly predatory collective organs of sight and sound. Any apparent somewhere which you may inhabit is always at the mercy of a ruthless and omnivorous everywhere. The notion of a house, as one single definite particular and unique place to come into, from the anywhereish and everywhereish world outside—that notion must strike you as fantastic. You have been brought up to believe that a house, or a universe, or a you, or any other object, is only seemingly solid: really (and you are realists, whom nobody and nothing can deceive) each seeming solidity is a collection of large holes—and, in the case of a house, the larger the holes the better; since the principal function of a modern house is to admit whatever might otherwise remain outside. You haven't the least or feeblest conception of being here, and now, and alone, and yourself. Why (you ask) should anyone want to be here, when (simply by pressing a button) anyone can be in fifty places at once? How could anyone want to be now, when anyone can go whening all over creation at the twist of a knob? What could induce anyone to desire aloneness, when billions of soi-disant dollars are mercifully squandered by a good and great government lest anyone anywhere should ever for a single instant be alone? As for being yourself—why on earth should you be yourself; when instead of being yourself you can be a hundred, or a thousand, or a hundred thousand thousand, other people? The very thought of being oneself in an epoch of interchangeable selves must appear supremely ridiculous.

Fine and dandy: but, so far as I am concerned, poetry and every other art was and is and forever will be strictly and distinctly a question of individuality. If poetry were anything—like dropping an atombomb—which anyone did, anyone could become a poet merely by doing the necessary anything; whatever that anything might or might not entail. But (as it happens) poetry is being, not doing. If you wish to follow, even at a distance, the poet's calling (and here, as always, I speak from my own totally biased and entirely personal point of view) you've got to come out of the measurable doing universe into the immeasurable house of being. I am quite aware that, wherever our socalled civilization has slithered, there's every reward and no punishment for unbeing. But if poetry is your goal, you've got to forget all about punishments and all about rewards and all about selfstyled obligations and duties and responsibilities etcetera ad infinitum and remember one thing only: that it's you—nobody else—who determine your destiny and decide your fate. Nobody else can be alive for you; nor can you be alive for anybody else. Toms can be Dicks and Dicks can be Harrys, but none of them can ever be you. There's the artist's responsibility; and the most awful responsibility on earth. If you can take it, take it—and be. If you can't, cheer up and go about other people's business; and do (or undo) till you drop.

My own home faced the Cambridge world as a finely and solidly constructed mansion, preceded by a large oval lawn and ringed with an imposing white-pine hedge. Just in front of the house itself stood two huge appletrees; and faithfully, every spring, these giants lifted their worlds of fragrance toward the room where I breathed and dreamed. Under one window of this room flourished (in early summer) a garden of magnificent roses: the gift of my parents' dear friend "stubby" Child—who (I learned later) baptized me and who (I still later discovered) was the Child of English And Scottish Ballads. As a baby, I sported a white sweater; on which my mother had embroidered a red H, for Harvard.

Our nearest neighbour, dwelling (at a decent distance) behind us, was Roland Thaxter; primarily the father of my loveliest playmate and ultimately the professor of cryptogamic botany. To our right, on Irving Street, occurred professors James and Royce and Warren; to our left, on Scott Street, transpired professor of economics Taussig. Somewhat back of the Taussig house happened professor Lanman—"known and loved throughout India" as my mother would say, with a pensive smile. She had been slightly astonished by an incident which embellished her official introduction to Mr and Mrs Lanman: the celebrated Sanscrit scholar having, it seems, seized his would-be interlocutor's hand, yanked her aside, and violently whispered "do you see anything peculiar about my wife?"—then (without giving my mother time to reply) "she has new shoes on" professor Lanman hissed "and they hurt her!" I myself experienced astonishment when first witnessing a spectacle which frequently thereafter repeated itself at professor Royce's gate. He came rolling peacefully forth, attained the sidewalk, and was about to turn right and wander up Irving, when Mrs Royce shot out of the house with a piercing cry "Josie! Josie!" waving something stringlike in her dexter fist. Mr Royce politely paused, allowing his spouse to catch up with him; he then shut both eyes, while she snapped around his collar a narrow necktie possessing a permanent bow; his eyes thereupon opened, he bowed, she smiled, he advanced, she retired, and the scene was over. As for professor Taussig, he had a cocker spaniel named Hamlet; and the Taussig family always put Hamlet out when they played their pianola—no doubt the first law of economics—but Hamlet's hearing was excellent, and he yodelled heartrendingly as long as the Hungarian Rhapsody persisted. Genial professor Warren's beautiful wife (whose own beautiful name was Salomé Machado) sometimes came to call on my maternal grandmother; and Salomé always brought her guitar. I remember sitting spellbound on our upstairs porch among apple-blossoms, one heavenly spring afternoon, adoring the quick slim fingers of Salomé Machado's exquisite left hand—and I further remember how, as Salomé sang and played, a scarlet tanager alighted in the blossoms; and listened, and disappeared.

One of the many wonderful things about a home is that it can be as lively as you please without ever becoming public. The big Cambridge house was in this respect, as in all other respects, a true home. Although I could be entirely alone when I wished, a varied social life awaited me whenever aloneness palled. A father and mother—later, a sister—two successive grandmothers and an aunt (all three of whom sang, or played the piano, or did both, extremely well) and one uncle, plus three or four hearty and jovial servants, were at my almost unlimited disposal. The servants—and this strikes me as a more than important point—very naturally enjoyed serving: for they were not ignobly irresponsible impersons, they were not shamelessly overpaid and mercilessly manipulated anonymities, they were not pampered and impotent particles of a greedy and joyless collective obscenity. In brief: they were not slaves. Actually, these good and faithful servants (of whom I speak) were precisely everything which no slave can ever be—they were alive; they were loved and loving human beings. From them, a perfect ignoramus could and did learn what any unworld will never begin to begin to so much as suspect: that slavery, and the only slavery, is service without love.

After myself and my father and mother, I loved most dearly my mother's brother George. He was by profession a lawyer, by inclination a bon vivant, and by nature a joyous human being. When this joyous human being wasn't toiling in his office, or hobnobbing with socalled swells at the Brookline country club, he always became my playfellow. No more innocently goodhearted soul ever kissed the world goodnight; but when it came to literature, bloodthirsty was nothing to him. And (speaking of bloodthirstiness) I here devoutly thank a beneficent Providence for allowing me to live my childhood and my boyhood and even my youth without ever once glimpsing that typical item of an era of at least penultimate confusion—the uncomic nonbook. No paltry supermen, no shadowy space-cadets, no trifling hyperjunglequeens and pantless pantherwomen insulted my virginal imagination. I read or was read, at an early age, the most immemorial myths, the wildest wild animal stories, lots of Scott and quantities of Dickens (including the immortal Pickwick Papers), Robinson Crusoe and The Swiss Family Robinson, Gulliver's Travels, Twenty Thousand Leagues Under The Sea, poetry galore, The Holy Bible, and The Arabian Nights. One city winter I floated through chivalry with Mallory and Froissart: the following country summer—we had by then acquired a farm—I dressed as a Red Indian, slept in a teepee, and almost punctured our best Jersey cow with a random arrow; in emulation of the rightful inhabitants of my wrongful native land.

A gruesome history of the Tower Of London had been conscientiously compiled by a prominent British prelate, endowed with what would now be termed sadistic trends; and suddenly this fearful opus burgeoned in our midst. Every night after dinner, if George were on deck, he would rub his hands and wink magnificently in my direction and call to my maiden aunt "Jane, let's have some ruddy gore!" whereupon Jane would protestingly join us in the parlour; and George would stealthily produce the opus; and she would blushfully read; and I would cling to the sofa in exquisite terror. We also read—for sheer relaxation—Lorna Doone (with whom I fell sublimely in love) and Treasure Island (as a result of which, the blind pirate Pew followed me upstairs for weeks; while for months, if not years, onelegged John Silver stood just behind me as my trembling fingers fumbled the electric light chain).

Out of Brookline's already mentioned country club, I readily conjured a gorgeous and dangerous play-world: somewhat resembling the three ring circus of the five Ringling brothers; and dedicated by dashing gentlemen to fair ladies and fine horses and other entrancing symbols of luxurious living. George had not been born into this fashionable cosmos, but he loved it so much that he learned to smoke cigars: and if he hadn't learned anything, the cosmos would certainly have welcomed him for his own abundant self's sake. His own abundant self wrote vers de société; which he recited at orgies or banquets—I was never sure which—but also, for my benefit, chez lui. And no sooner had George discovered my liking for verse than he presented me with an inestimable treasure entitled The Rhymester—opening which totally unostentatious masterpiece, I entered my third poetic period.

Poetic period number one had been nothing if not individualistic; as

two almost infantile couplets, combining fearless expression with keen
observation, amply testify. The first of these primeval authenticities
passionately exclaims

> O,the pretty birdie,O;
> with his little toe,toe,toe!

while the second mercilessly avers

> there was a little farder
> and he made his mudder harder

—but, alas! a moribund mental cloud soon obscured my vital psychic sky.
The one and only thing which mattered about any poem (so ran my second
poetic period's credo) was what the poem said; its socalled meaning. A
good poem was a poem which did good, and a bad poem was a poem which
didn't: Julia Ward Howe's Battle Hymn Of The Republic being a good
poem because it helped free the slaves. Armed with this ethical immutabil-
ity, I composed canticles of comfort on behalf of the griefstricken relatives of persons recently deceased; I implored healthy Christians to assist
poor-whites afflicted with The Curse Of The Worm (short for hookworm);
and I exhorted right-minded patriots to abstain from dangerous fireworks
on the 4th of July. Thus it will be seen that, by the year 1900, one growing
American boy had reached exactly that stage of "intellectual development" beyond which every ungrowing Marxist adult of today is strictly
forbidden, on pain of physical disappearance, ever to pass.

The Rhymester diverted my eager energies from what to how: from
substance to structure. I learned that there are all kinds of intriguing verse-
forms, chiefly French; and that each of these forms can and does exist
in and of itself, apart from the use to which you or I may not or may put
it. A rondel is a rondel, irrespective of any idea which it may be said to
embody; and whatever a ballade may be about, it is always a ballade—
never a villanelle or a rondeau. With this welcome revelation, the mental
cloud aforesaid ignominiously dissolved; and my psychic sky joyfully re-
appeared, more vital even than before.

One ever memorable day, our ex-substantialist (deep in structural
meditation) met head-on professor Royce; who was rolling peacefully
home from a lecture. "Estlin" his courteous and gentle voice hazarded "I
understand that you write poetry." I blushed. "Are you perhaps" he
inquired, regarding a particular leaf of a particular tree "acquainted with
the sonnets of Dante Gabriel Rossetti?" I blushed a different blush and
shook an ignorant head. "Have you a moment?" he shyly suggested, less
than half looking at me; and just perceptibly appended "I rather imagine
you might enjoy them." Shortly thereafter, sage and ignoramus were

sitting opposite each other in a diminutive study (marvellously smelling of tobacco and cluttered with student notebooks of a menacing bluish shade) —the ignoramus listening, enthralled; the sage intoning, lovingly and beautifully, his favorite poems. And very possibly (although I don't, as usual, know) that is the reason—or more likely the unreason—I've been writing sonnets ever since.

En route to a university whose name begins with H, our unhero attended four Cambridge schools: the first, private—where everybody was extraordinarily kind; and where (in addition to learning nothing) I burst into tears and nosebleeds—the other three, public; where I flourished like the wicked and learned what the wicked learn and where almost nobody cared about somebody else. Two figures emerge from this almost: a Miss Maria Baldwin and a Mr Cecil Derry. Miss Baldwin, the dark lady mentioned in my first nonlecture (and a lady if ever a lady existed) was blessed with a delicious voice, charming manners, and a deep understanding of children. Never did any demidivine dictator more gracefully and easily rule a more unruly and less graceful populace. Her very presence emanated an honour and a glory: the honour of spiritual freedom—no mere freedom from —and the glory of being, not (like most extant mortals) really undead, but actually alive. From her I marvellingly learned that the truest power is gentleness. Concerning Mr Derry, let me say only that he was (and for me will always remain) one of those blessing and blessed spirits who deserve the name of teacher: predicates who are utterly in love with their subject; and who, because they would gladly die for it, are living for it gladly. From him I learned (and am still learning) that gladness is next to godliness. He taught me Greek. This may be as apt a moment as any to state that in the world of my boyhood—long, long ago; before time was space and Oedipus was a complex and religion was the opiate of the people and pigeons had learned to play pingpong—social stratification not merely existed but luxuriated. All women were not, as now, ladies; a gentleman was a gentleman; and a mucker (as the professorial denizens of Irving and Scott streets knew full well: since their lofty fragment of Cambridge almost adjoined plebeian Somerville) was a mucker. Being myself a professor's (& later a clergyman's) son, I had every socalled reason to accept these conventional distinctions without cavil; yet for some unreason I didn't. The more implacably a virtuous Cambridge drew me toward what might have been her bosom, the more sure I felt that soi-disant respectability comprised nearly everything which I couldn't respect, and the more eagerly I explored sinful Somerville. But while sinful Somerville certainly possessed a bosom (in fact, bosoms) she also possessed fists which hit below the belt and arms which threw snowballs containing small rocks. Little by little and bruise by teacup, my doubly disillusioned spirit made an awe-inspiring discovery; which (on more than several occasions) has prevented me from wholly misunderstanding socalled humanity: the discovery, namely, that

all groups, gangs, and collectivities—no matter how apparently disparate—
are fundamentally alike; and that what makes any world go round is not
the trivial difference between a Somerville and a Cambridge, but the
immeasurable difference between either of them and individuality. Whether
this discovery is valid for you, I can't pretend to say: but I can and do
say, without pretending, that it's true for me—inasmuch as I've found (and
am still finding) authentic individuals in the most varied environments
conceivable. Nor will anything ever persuade me that, by turning Somerville into Cambridge or Cambridge into Somerville or both into neither,
anybody can make an even slightly better world. Better worlds (I suggest)
are born, not made; and their birthdays are the birthdays of individuals.
Let us pray always for individuals; never for worlds. "He who would do
good to another" cries the poet and painter William Blake "must do it in
Minute Particulars"—and probably many of you are familiar with this
greatly pitying line. But I'll wager that not three of you could quote me
the line which follows it

General Good is the plea of the scoundrel, hypocrite, & flatterer

for that deeply terrible line spells the doom of all unworlds; whatever their
slogans and their strategies, whoever their heroes or their villains.

Only a butterfly's glide from my home began a mythical domain of
semiwilderness; separating cerebral Cambridge and orchidaceous Somerville. Deep in this magical realm of Between stood a palace, containing
Harvard University's far-famed Charles Eliot Norton: and lowly folk,
who were neither professors nor professors' children, had nicknamed
the district Norton's Woods. Here, as a very little child, I first encountered
that mystery who is Nature; here my enormous smallness entered Her
illimitable being; and here someone actually infinite or impossibly alive—
someone who might almost (but not quite) have been myself—wonderingly
wandered the mortally immortal complexities of Her beyond imagining
imagination

> O sweet spontaneous
> earth how often have
> the
> doting
>
>   fingers of
> prurient philosophers pinched
> and
> poked
>
> thee
> ,has the naughty thumb
> of science prodded
> thy

                                    beauty   .how
                        often have religions taken
                        thee upon their scraggy knees
                        squeezing and

                        buffeting thee that thou mightest conceive
                        gods
                                (but
                        true

                        to the incomparable
                        couch of death thy
                        rhythmic
                        lover

                                thou answerest

                        them only with

                                spring)

—later, this beyond imagining imagination revealed a not believably moun-
taining ocean, at Lynn; and, in New Hampshire, oceaning miraculously
mountains. But the wonder of my first meeting with Herself is with me now;
and also with me is the coming (obedient to Her each resurrection) of a
roguish and resistless More Than Someone: Whom my deepest selves unfailingly recognized, though His disguise protected him from all the world

                        in Just-
                        spring   when the world is mud-
                        luscious the little
                        lame balloonman

                        whistles   far   and wee

                        and eddyandbill come
                        running from marbles and
                        piracies and it's
                        spring

                        when the world is puddle-wonderful

                        the queer
                        old balloonman whistles
                        far   and   wee
                        and bettyandisbel come dancing

                        from hop-scotch and jump-rope and

                        it's
                        spring
                        and
                                the

                        goat-footed

            balloonMan   whistles
            far
            and
            wee

this Turbulent Individual Incognito must have rendered his disciple even
less law-abiding than usual; for I vividly remember being chased (with two
charming little girls) out of the tallest and thickest of several palatial
lilac bushes: our pursuer being a frantic scarecrow-demon masquerading
as my good friend Bernard Magrath, professor Charles Eliot Norton's
gifted coachman. But why not? Then it was spring; and in spring anything may happen.

Absolutely anything.

3

As it was my miraculous fortune to have a true father and a true mother,
and a home which the truth of their love made joyous, so—in reaching outward from this love and this joy—I was marvellously lucky to touch and
seize a rising and striving world; a reckless world, filled with the curiosity
of life herself; a vivid and violent world welcoming every challenge; a
world worth hating and adoring and fighting and forgiving: in brief, a
world which was a world. This inwardly immortal world of my adolescence
recoils to its very roots whenever, nowadays, I see people who've been
endowed with legs crawling on their chins after quote security unquote.
"Security?" I marvel to myself "what is that? Something negative, undead, suspicious and suspecting; an avarice and an avoidance; a self-sur-
rendering meanness of withdrawal; a numerable complacency and an
innumerable cowardice. Who would be 'secure'? Every and any slave. No
free spirit ever dreamed of 'security'—or, if he did, he laughed; and lived
to shame his dream. No whole sinless sinful sleeping waking breathing
human creature ever was (or could be) bought by, and sold for, 'security.'
How monstrous and how feeble seems some unworld which would rather
have its too than eat its cake!"

                Jehova buried,Satan dead,
                do fearers worship Much and Quick;
                badness not being felt as bad,
                itself thinks goodness what is meek;
                obey says toc,submit says tic,
                Eternity's a Five Year Plan:
                if Joy with Pain shall hang in hock
                who dares to call himself a man?

For the benefit of any heretical members of my audience who do not regard manhood as a barbarous myth propagated by sinister powers envisaging the subjugation of womankind, let me (at this point) cheerfully risk a pair of perhaps not boring anecdotes.

Back in the days of dog-eat-dog—my first anecdote begins—there lived a playboy; whose father could easily have owned the original supersky-scraper-de-luxe: a selfstyled Cathedral Of Commerce, endowed with every impetus to relaxation; not excluding ultraelevators which (on the laudable assumption that even machinery occasionally makes mistakes) were regularly tested. Testing an ultraelevator meant that its car was brought clean up, deprived of safety devices, and dropped. As the car hurtled downward, a column of air confined by the elevator shaft became more and more compressed; until (assuming that nothing untoward happened) it broke the car's fall completely—or so I was told by somebody who should know. At any rate, young Mr X was in the habit not only of attending these salubrious ceremonies, but of entering each about-to-be-dropped car, and of dropping with it as far and as long as the laws of a preEinsteinian universe permitted. Eventually, of course, somebody who shouldn't know telephoned a newspaper; which sent a reporter: who (after scarcely believing his senses) asked the transcender of Adam point-blank why he fell so often. Our playful protagonist shrugged his well-tailored shoulders—"for fun" he said simply; adding (in a strictly confidential undertone) "and it's wonderful for a hangover."

Here, I feel, we have the male American stance of my adolescence; or (if you prefer) the adolescent American male stance of what some wit once nicknamed a "lost generation": whereof—let me hastily append—the present speaker considers himself no worthy specimen. My point, however, isn't that many of us were even slightly heroic; and is that few of us declined a gamble. I don't think we enjoyed courting disaster. I do feel we liked being born.

And now let me give you my second anecdote: which concerns (appropriately enough) not a single human being whose name I forget, but a millionary mishmash termed The Public.

Rather recently—in New York City—an old college chum, whom I hadn't beheld for decades, appeared out of nowhere to tell me he was through with civilization. It seems that ever since Harvard he'd been making (despite all sorts of panics and panaceas) big money as an advertising writer; and this remarkable feat unutterably depressed him. After profound meditation, he concluded that America, and the world which she increasingly dominated, couldn't really be as bad as she and it looked through an advertising writer's eyes; and he promptly determined to seek another view—a larger view; in fact, the largest view obtainable.

Bent on obtaining this largest obtainable view of America and America's world, my logical expal wangled an appointment with a subsubeditor of a magazine (if magazine it may be called) possessing the largest circulation on earth: a periodical whose each emanation appears simultaneously in almost every existing human language. Our intrepid explorer then straightened his tie, took six deep breaths, cleared his throat, swam right up, presented his credentials, and was politely requested to sit down. He sat down. "Now listen" the subsubeditor suggested "if you're thinking of working with us, you'd better know The Three Rules." "And what" my friend cheerfully inquired "are The Three Rules?" "The Three Rules" explained his mentor "are: first, eight to eighty; second, anybody can do it; and third, makes you feel better." "I don't quite understand" my friend confessed. "Perfectly simple" his interlocutor assured him. "Our first Rule means that every article we publish must appeal to anybody, man woman or child, between the ages of eight and eighty years—is that clear?" My friend said it was indeed clear. "Second" his enlightener continued "every article we publish must convince any reader of the article that he or she could do whatever was done by the person about whom the article was written. Suppose (for instance) you were writing about Lindbergh, who had just flown the Atlantic ocean for the first time in history, with nothing but unlimited nerve and a couple of chicken (or ham was it?) sandwiches— do you follow me?" "I'm ahead of you" my friend murmured. "Remembering Rule number two" the subsub went on "you'd impress upon your readers' minds, over and over again, the fact that (after all) there wouldn't have been anything extraordinary about Lindbergh if he hadn't been just a human being like every single one of them. See?" "I see" said my friend grimly. "Third" the subsub intoned "we'll imagine you're describing a record-breaking Chinese flood—millions of poor unfortunate men and women and little children and helpless babies drowning and drowned; millions more perishing of slow starvation: suffering inconceivable, untold agonies, and so forth—well, any reader of this article must feel definitely and distinctly better, when she or he finishes the article, than when he or she began it." "Sounds a trifle difficult" my friend hazarded. "Don't be silly" the oracle admonished. "All you've got to do, when you're through with your horrors, is to close by saying: but (thanks to an all-merciful Providence) we Americans, with our high standard of living and our Christian ideals, will never be subjected to such inhuman conditions; as long as the Stars and Stripes triumphantly float over one nation indivisible, with liberty and justice for all—get me?" "I get you" said my disillusioned friend. "Good bye."

So ends the second anecdote. You may believe it or not, as you wish. As far as I'm concerned, it's the unbelievable—but also unquestionable— selfportrait of a one hundred and one percent pseudoworld: in which truth has become televisionary, in which goodness means not hurting people, and in which beauty is shoppe. Just (or unjust) how any species of authentic individualism could stem from such a collective quagmire, I don't—as always—know; but here are four lines of a poem which didn't:

(While you and i have lips and voices which
are for kissing and to sing with
who cares if some oneeyed son of a bitch
invents an instrument to measure Spring with?

As regards my own self-finding, I have to thank first of all that institution whose initial I flaunted unknowingly during my very earliest days. Officially, Harvard presented me with a smattering of languages and sciences; with a glimpse of Homer, a more than glimpse of Aeschylus Sophocles Euripides and Aristophanes, and a deep glance at Dante and Shakespeare. Unofficially, she gave me my first taste of independence: and the truest friends any man will ever enjoy. The taste of independence came during my senior year, when I was so lucky as to receive a room by myself in the Yard—for living in the Yard was then an honour, not a compulsion; and this honour very properly reserved itself for seniors, who might conceivably appreciate it. Hitherto I had ostensibly lived at home; which meant that intimate contacts with the surrounding world were somewhat periculous. Now I could roam that surrounding world sans peur, if not sans reproche: and I lost no time in doing so. A town called Boston, thus observed, impressed my unsophisticated spirit as the mecca of all human endeavors—and be it added that, in this remote era, Boston had her points. Well do I recall how our far from hero (backed by the most physically imposing of his acquaintances) dared a stifling dump near Howard Street, denominated Mother Shannon's; and how we stopped short, to avoid treading on several spreadeagled sailors; and how my backer, with irreproachable nonchalance, exchanged a brace of dollar bills for two tumblers of something even viler than honest Jack Delaney served during soi-disant prohibition; and finally how, having merely sampled our nonbeverages, we successfully attained Scollay Square—to be greeted by the dispassionate drone of a pintsize pimp, conspicuously stationed on the populous sidewalk under a blaze of movie bulbs and openly advertising two kinds of love for twenty-five cents each. Moreover that distant Boston comprised such authentic incarnations of genius as Bernhardt, whose each intonation propitiated demons and angels; Pavlova, who danced a ditty called Nix On The Glowworm into the most absolute piece of aristocracy since Ming; and a lady of parts (around whose waist any man's hand immediately dreamed it could go three times) named Polaire. Those were the days (and nights) of The Turkey Trot and The Bunny Hug; of Everybody's Doing It, Alexander's Ragtime Band, Has Anybody Here Seen Kelly, There's A Little Bit Of Bad In Every Good Little Girl, On The Banks Of The Saskatchewan, and Here Comes My Daddy Now (O Pop, O Pop, O Pop, O Pop). Nothing could exceed the artistry of Washington Street bartenders, who positively enjoyed constructing impeccable Pousse-Cafés in the midst of Ward Eights and Hop Toads; nor could anything approach the courtesy of Woodcock waiters, who never obeyed any ring but your own and always knocked twice before entering. I am further indebted to Boston town for making me acquainted (and in no uncertain manner) with the sinister splendors of censorship. One evening, The Old Howard would be As Is; the next, you guessed you were embracing a funeral. When Miss Gertrude Hoffman brought her lissome self and her willowy girls to Boston, they and she were violently immersed in wrist-and-ankle-length underwear. A local tobacconist drew jail for selling a box of cigars adorned with the usual gauzily apparelled but unmistakably symbolic females— and vainly did an outraged lawyer object that his client was happily married. Meanwhile, watching-and-warding Mr Sumner's matchless collection of indecent items constituted a favorite topic of conversation with high and low alike. But if the predations of puritanism astonished me nearly forty years ago, I was recently more than amazed to learn that you cannot now show a woman's entire breast in any American moviehouse unless she isn't (to coin a plagiarism) white. Verily, democracy unquote is a strange disease: nor (I submit) can any human being help sympathizing, in his or her heart of hearts, with the bad bald poet who sings

              come(all you mischief-
           hatchers hatch
       mischief)all you

           guilty
              scamper(you bastards throw dynamite)
              let knowings magic
           with bright credos each divisible fool

           (life imitate gossip fear unlife
       mean
        -ness,and
           to succeed in not
              dying)

           Is will still occur;birds disappear
           becomingly:a thunderbolt compose poems
       not because harm symmetry
           earthquakes starfish(but
              because nobody
              can sell the Moon to The)moon

Let us now consider friendship.

Through Harvard, I met Scofield Thayer; and at Harvard, Sibley Watson—two men who subsequently transformed a dogooding periodical called The Dial into a firstrate magazine of the fine arts; and together fought the eternal fight of selfhood against mobism, the immortal battle of beauty against ugliness. It would not even slightly surprise me to learn that most of you have remained, till now, quite unaware of the existence of these literally heroic individuals and of their actually unparalleled achievement. Never have I seen courage and courtesy, taste and intelligence, prodigious patience and incredible generosity, quite so jealously mistrusted or so basely misprized or so savagely detested as by The Dial's detractors. Even today, more than twenty years after this true and noble adventure's culmination, the adventurers' chastisement continues—through such a conspiracy of silence on the part of America's intellectual gangsters as would be ludicrous if it were not abominable; nor will that chastisement begin to diminish while general good outflanks minute particulars and spiritual treachery is the order of the unday.

At Harvard (moreover) I met Stewart Mitchell, who soon became editor-in-chief of our university's only serious undergraduate magazine—The Monthly—and was subsequently managing editor of The Dial; John Dos Passos, through whose devoted efforts a dangerous compilation known as Eight Harvard Poets appeared; and S Foster Damon, who opened my eyes and ears not merely to Domenico Theotocopuli and William Blake, but to all ultra (at that moment) modern music and poetry and painting. Nor can or do I forget Theodore Miller; who gladly brought me such treasures as the exquisite

> lugete, o Veneres Cupidinesque
> et quantumst hominum venustiorum

of Catullus; the sublime

> labuntur anni; nec pietas moram
> rugis et instanti senectae
> adferet, indomitaeque morti

of Horace; and Sappho's magically luminous invocation

> ποικιλόθρον', ἀθάνατ' 'Αφρόδιτα

but the token of whose most memorable kindness was a volume combining poems and letters by that glorious human being who confessed

> I am certain of nothing but of the holiness of the Heart's affections,
> and the truth of Imagination.

Whereupon—deep in those heights of psychic sky which had greeted my boyish escape from moralism—an unknown and unknowable bird began singing.

After Harvard, I thank (for selfdiscovery) a phenomenon and a miracle. The phenomenon was a telemicroscopic chimera, born of the satanic rape of matter by mind; a phallic female phantasm, clothed in thunderous anonymity and adorned with colossally floating spiderwebs of traffic; a stark irresistibly stupendous newness, mercifully harboring among its pitilessly premeditated spontaneities immemorial races and nations

by god i want above fourteenth

fifth's deep purring biceps,the mystic screetch
of Broadway,the trivial stink of rich

frail firm asinine life
            (i pant

for what's below. The singer. Wall. i want
the perpendicular lips the insane teeth
the vertical grin

                        give me the Square in spring,
the little barbarous Greenwich perfumed fake

and most, the futile fooling labyrinth
where noisy colours stroll . . . . and the Baboon

sniggering insipidities while. i sit, sipping
singular anisettes as. One opaque
big girl jiggles thickly hips to the kanoun

but Hassan chuckles seeing the Greeks breathe)

in New York I also breathed: and as if for the first time.

The truly first of first times was (however) still to come. It arrived with a socalled war. Being neither warrior nor conscientiousobjector, saint nor hero, I embarked for France as an ambulancedriver. And as my earliest taste of independence had been excelled by the banquet which I later sampled among Manhattan's skyscrapers, so was that banquet surpassed by the freedom which I now tasted:

Paris;this April sunset completely utters
utters serenely silently a cathedral

before whose upward lean magnificent face
the streets turn young with rain,

two realms, elsewhere innately hostile, here cordially coexisted—each (by its very distinctness) intensifying the other—nor could I possibly have imagined either a loveliness so fearlessly of the moment or so nobly beautiful a timelessness. Three thousand oceanic miles away and some terrestrial years before, a son of New England had observed those realms bitterly struggling for dominion: then, as a guest of verticality, our impuritan had attended the overwhelming triumph of the temporal realm. Now, I participated in an actual marriage of material with immaterial things; I celebrated an immediate reconciling of spirit and flesh, forever and now, heaven and earth. Paris was for me precisely and complexly this homogeneous duality: this accepting transcendence; this living and dying more than death or life. Whereas—by the very act of becoming its improbably gigantic self—New York had reduced mankind to a tribe of pygmies, Paris (in each shape and gesture and avenue and cranny of her being) was continuously expressing the humanness of humanity. Everywhere I sensed a miraculous presence, not of mere children and women and men, but of living human beings; and the fact that I could scarcely understand their language seemed irrelevant, since the truth of our momentarily mutual aliveness created an imperishable communion. While (at the hating touch of some madness called La Guerre) a once rising and striving world toppled into withering hideously smithereens, love rose in my heart like a sun and beauty blossomed in my life like a star. Now, finally and first, I was myself: a temporal citizen of eternity; one with all human beings born and unborn.

Thus through an alma mater whose scholastic bounty appeared the smallest of her blessings—and by way of those even more munificent institutions of learning, New York and Paris—our ignoramus reaches his supreme indebtedness. Last but most, I thank for my self-finding certain beautiful givers of illimitable gladness

> whose any mystery makes every man's
> flesh put space on;and his mind take off time

Boris Pasternak

(1890–1960)

Boris Pasternak, like Alexander Solzhenitsyn after him, won the Nobel Prize and, like Solzhenitsyn after him, decided not to go to Stockholm to receive it "because of the significance given to this award in the society to which I belong." Pasternak's autobiographical work, Safe Conduct, *had appeared much earlier—when he was forty-one, more than a quarter of a century before the novel that made him famous in the West,* Doctor Zhivago, *was published in Italy. In* Safe Conduct *Pasternak tells that Scriabin was his first hero, music was his first love. Next he turned to philosophy. The passage quoted here is his story of being jarred awake, by an episode of unfulfilled love, to his destiny. The crisis came when he was twenty-two, while he was studying philosophy at the University of Marburg, and it revealed to him that he must thenceforth be a servant of art. For many years he worked as a poet. There is evidence, though, that he began writing his masterwork not long after* Safe Conduct *came out. In the late thirties a playwright friend of his, A. N. Afinogenov, wrote in his diary about Pasternak's view of that work: "For him the main thing is art, and nothing but art. That is why he doesn't care to go into town but chooses to live here the whole time, going for walks by himself or reading Macaulay's* History of England, *sitting by the window and looking out at the starry night, sorting out his thoughts, or else, finally, writing his novel. But all of this is inside art and for the sake of art. He is not even interested in the end-product. The main thing is the work at it, the enthusiasm for it. . . ."*

FROM
SAFE CONDUCT

I took a room on the outskirts of the town. It was in one of the last houses out on the Giessen road, at a point where the chestnuts lining the road dressed, shoulder to shoulder, and the whole column of them suddenly veered to the right. After which, with one more glance back at the frowning knoll with its miniature, old-world town, the high-road plunged into the forest.

Outside my window was a rickety little balcony which overhung the next-door garden, where stood an obsolete Marburg tram-car, taken off its wheels and transformed into a henhouse. . . .

About this time the V——e sisters visited Marburg. Their parents were very affluent. In Moscow, as far back as my high-school years I had been the friend of the elder of the two girls and had given her occasional lessons, I am not quite sure of what—the most likely thing is that the family paid me anyway and I delivered dissertations on the most unenvisaged subjects.

But in the spring of 1908 it so happened that we both of us completed our school careers together and simultaneously with my own swotting I undertook to tutor her. Most of my register-cards included gaps, where I had light-heartedly omitted to work at the right time, when this or that section of a subject was being studied in class. I had not sufficient nights now at my disposal to make all this up. Yet I did somehow succeed in snatching the time, regardless of the clock. More often than not day was already breaking when I would race round to V——a to work at subjects which were not always quite in step with my own, because the schedules of work in our respective schools naturally enough did not quite coincide, a twist which rather complicated the situation for me, though I was unaware of it. But as for my feelings for V——a, far from new as they were, of those I had been aware since I was fourteen.

V——a was lovely, she had great charm, and she had been exquisitely brought up, spoiled indeed, from early childhood, by an elderly French governess who was quite ignorant of her spirit. This governess was well aware, however, that the geometry which at screech of dawn I brought her pet was more that of Abelard than of Euclid, and, brightly making a great ado of her perspicacity, she never once left us alone to our lessons. For this interference I was secretly grateful to her. While she was present my precious emotions could remain immaculate. Not that I condemned either them or myself. I was eighteen years old. But whatever the situation, my mental make-up and upbringing had been such that I should never have dared let my feelings have free play.

All this took place in that season in which folk were busy pouring boiling water into crocks to knock up distemper and, left to themselves, gardens still cluttered with snow piled in from everywhere else were idly sunning themselves. To their very limits they swam with limpid, still waters, while, beyond their borders, out on the other side of the walls and fences, all along the horizons stood the gardeners, in serried ranks with the rooks and the belfries, all across the town exchanging loud observations—as many as two or three words a day. Full of lingering remnants of the night, the dank, shaggy grey heavens rubbed their muzzle against the open casement. For hours on end, hours and hours, they maintained silence, then, suddenly stirring into action, sent rolling into my room the tiny, round rumble of a wagon wheel, and so unexpectedly too that it might have been all part of a boisterous country game and that wagon had nothing better to do than leap from cobbles to casement, so that now it would not have to cart any more. Still more mysterious, however, was the vacancy of silence which burst bubbling as if from many springs into the deep rut that the clamorous wheel had cut.

Why all this should be imprinted on my mind in the form of a schoolroom blackboard not quite cleaned of its chalk, I do not know. Oh, if only we had been halted then, the blackboard washed till it gleamed damp and black, and instead of theorems about pyramids of equal dimensions, copperplate writing, all thicks and thins, had set out before our eyes what lay before us in the years to come, oh how aghast we would have been!

Whence that thought, and why did it come to me precisely at that point?

Because it was spring, spring with its blackness, at last winding up the tenantry of the cold half of the year, and all round me, facing upwards, like so many mirrors yet to be hung up, all over the land lay lakes and pools, eloquent of the fact that the madly capacious world had now been cleaned up, and the apartment was ready for a new letting. Because in that moment it was free for whoever wanted to embrace and experience all the life our world contains. Because I was in love with V—a.

There is however in the world what is known as a sublimer attitude towards woman. I am going to say a few words about this. There is a vast circle of phenomena which in adolescence can drive to suicide. There is a circle of errors of the youthful imagination—the distortions of childhood, the hunger-strikes of youth, a circle of *Kreutzer Sonatas* and of sonatas written against the *Kreutzer Sonatas*. I have been in that circle, and I spent a shamefully long time in it too. What exactly is it all?

It frets one away. It does nothing but harm. Yet man will never be free from it. Everything by which we make history will always go through it. Because these sonatas which constitute the ante-room to the only complete moral freedom are not written by the Tolstoys or the Wedekinds, but by Nature herself, using their hand. And her concept is only to be seen in full in their mutual contradictoriness.

Having based matter on mutual resistance and separated fact from illusion by a wall called *love*, Nature is as concerned about the solidity of that wall as she is about the wholeness of the world. Here is where the insanity and the diseased exaggerations of love begin. Here one can with all truth say that love cannot take a single step without making a mountain out of a molehill.

But, sorry, does not Nature then make real mountains? I am told this is her principal occupation. Or are those mere words? What of the history of species? Of the history of human names? After all, this is precisely where Nature prepares them—in dammed off sectors of living evolution, at those barriers where her exacerbated imagination lets itself go.

Would it not therefore be possible to say that we exaggerate in childhood and our imagination goes crazy *because* in this period of our lives Nature is turning us, as molehills, into mountains?

Holding the philosophic outlook by which only the *almost-impossible* is real, Nature has made the emotions of everything that lives extremely difficult. She has made them difficult in one way for the animal world, in quite another, for the vegetable. The way she has fashioned those difficulties for man reveals her high opinion of him. She has made our emotions difficult for us not by any automatically acting trickery, but by something which at a glance from her is endowed with absolute power. She has made those difficulties for us by the sensation of our own mole-hill insignificance, which attacks each of us in direct proportion to how far removed we are from the molehill stage. This was expressed brilliantly by Andersen in his *Ugly Duckling.*

Like the word *sex* itself, all the literature about the subject breathes an insufferable commonplaceness and this is its purpose. It is solely by rea-son of that hateful quality that it can be of any use to Nature, for her con-tact with us happens to be based on fear of the commonplace, and nothing that was not commonplace could possibly serve her as her means of supervision.

Whatever material our thought may produce about the subject, its *fate* is in her hands. And with the aid of instinct brought in by Nature out of the whole to be of assistance to us, she invariably makes such use of that material that all the efforts that teachers of the young may direct towards making naivety easy, ineluctably hamper it, and *that is how it should be.*

This is necessary so that our emotions should really have something to struggle against. If not this panic, then some other. And no matter at all what detestable thing, what nonsense, goes to the making of the barrier. The impulse by which the barrier is engendered is the purest in the whole universe. And that purity alone which has conquered such countless times through the centuries, would be enough by itself for all else to stand out as abysmal filth.

There is also art. This is not interested in man, but in the symbol of man. And, so it appears, the symbol of man is greater than man himself. It can however be engendered solely in motion. Though not any motion. Only in the passage from molehill to mountain.

What does an honest man do when he speaks *solely* the truth? While the truth was being uttered, life moved on, and the truth which was uttered had lagged behind, a deceptive truth. Is it really necessary for man to go on and on talking, everywhere and always?

But in art, you see, man is gagged. In art man himself becomes silent, and it is the symbol that speaks. And it seems that *solely* symbols can keep pace with the achievements of Nature.

The Russian verb *vratj*[1] means *to introduce something superfluous* rather than *to try to deceive.* It is in this sense that art 'lies'. Its symbols embrace life itself. They are not in search of an audience. The truths of art are not representational. They are however on the other hand capable of eternal development. It is *solely* art which through the centuries in its assertions about love has not found itself at the disposal of instinct, as yet another means of hampering emotion. As it leaps the barriers of new spiritual development a generation preserves its lyrical truth, rather than, as one might imagine from a very great distance, throwing it aside. It is as

---

[1]*Usually translated* to lie.

if it is indeed in the form of lyrical truth that humanity is gradually assembled by the generations.

All this is unusual. It is all breathtakingly difficult.

It is taste that teaches us moral ways, while taste itself is taught by strength.

The sisters had been spending the summer in Belgium. From a third party they learned that I was at Marburg. At this juncture they were called to join their family in Berlin, and on the way there they felt they should look me up.

They put up at the best hotel in our little town, in the oldest part of Marburg. The three days, every hour of which I spent with them, were as unlike my usual life as any festival is like a working day. Endlessly relating one thing and another to them, I soaked myself in their smiles and the indications they gave of really understanding whomever they happened to meet. I took them around with me and they were both of them to be seen with me at university lectures. And then came the day of their departure!

The evening before, as he prepared the table for supper, the waiter remarked to me: '*Das ist wohl Ihr Henkersmahl, nicht wahr?*' i.e., "Enjoy your last meal, tomorrow it's the gallows for you, is it not?"

When I entered the hotel that morning, I met the younger sister in the corridor. She gave me one look and then, realizing something, slipped back into her room without even bidding me good morning and locked herself in. I went on to the elder one's room, and there, terribly agitated, told her that things could not go on like that, she must decide my fate. Apart from my insistence, there was of course nothing new in all this. V——a rose quickly from her chair and, faced by my obvious agitation, which seemed about to fall on her, stumbled back, away from me. Then, suddenly, as she reached the wall, she remembered that there did exist a way of putting a stop to all that without any fuss and—she rejected me. A moment later came a thudding in the corridor outside. It was a trunk being dragged from the next room. It was followed at once by a knock at the door. Swiftly, I made myself presentable. It was time to go to the station. This was five minutes' walk away.

There, the ability to say good-bye left me entirely, I had scarcely realized that I had said good-bye to the younger, but not even begun to do so to the elder, when there along the platform loomed the fast train from Frankfurt and almost in the same movement had swiftly taken up its passengers and was starting out again. I raced along beside it and at the end of the platform—the train then going full tilt—leapt on to the footboard. The heavy door at the end of the coach had not yet been banged to. A furious conductor barred my way, at the same time supporting me with one arm round my shoulder, in case I was mad enough, shamed by his remonstrances, to commit suicide. My departing visitors now hurried out to the corridor end and to save me thrust into the conductor's hand the where-withal to pay my fare. And he relented. I went into the compartment with the sisters, and on we rushed, heading for Berlin. My fabulous fairy-tale holiday, so nearly truncated, was thus prolonged, increased tenfold by the furious speed with which we were rushing and a blissful headache from all I had gone through.

I had jumped on to the train footboard merely to bid her good-bye, but now again forgot to do this, only once more to remember it when it was already too late. For I had not really come to myself when the day was gone and evening had come, and the panting, reverberating roof of the Berlin terminus towered over us and pinned us to the ground. The sisters were to be met at the station. It was undesirable for me to be seen with them in the agitated state I was in. They convinced me that now we really had said good-bye. It was merely that I had not noticed it. And there I was, tight in the grip of the gaseous booming of the station, and sank in the crowd.

It was night, a wretched drizzle falling. I had absolutely nothing to do in Berlin. The next train back did not leave till early the next morning, and I might easily have spent the waiting time at the station. However, I could not remain in public. My features were convulsed and tears kept welling into my eyes. My craving for that one last farewell which would have laid waste to everything was still unassuaged. It was like a craving for a grand cadence such as might shake a great piece of music to the very roots and be strong enough to wrench it right out at last by the heave of that final harmony. But I had been refused that alleviation. And a sort of chromatic distress enclosed me.

It was night, a wretched drizzle falling. It was as smoky on the asphalt outside the station as on the platform, the iron-framed glazing of the sta-tion roof like a ball in a string net. The swishing of the wet streets was like soda-water bubbling. Everything was wrapped in the soft fermenta-tion of the rain. As this trip of mine was so utterly unforeseen, I was dressed just as I had run round to the girls' hotel, that is to say, *sans* overcoat, *sans* luggage, *sans* papers of identity. And though they were all polite enough to make the excuse of being full up, every hotel dismissed me the moment they set eyes on me. At last I did find a place where my unsubstantiality was no obstacle. It was an hotel of the lowest kind. Alone at last in my room, I sat myself down sideways on a chair standing by the window. Beside me was a small table. I lay my head on this.

Why do I indicate my posture with such detail? Because that is precisely how I spent the whole night. At rare intervals, as if somebody had touched me, I raised my head and did something to the wall, the broad expanse of which sloped away from me up to the dark ceiling. With unseeing stare I measured it from bottom up as with a rule. Then my sobs would begin again, and once more my face flopped on to my arms.

I have indicated the position of my body with such precision because this had been its position the previous morning on the footboard of that flying train, and it was stamped for ever with that memory. It was the posture of a man staggering back off something lofty which for long had held him and supported him, but in due course had let him go and now was sweeping noisily past him overhead, to vanish for ever round the corner.

At last I stood up. I examined the room and opened the window wide. Night had gone, the rain was but a misty dust. Impossible to affirm whether still falling, or stopped. I had paid my bill in advance. There was not a soul in the hall. I announced my departure to nobody.

What struck me here was merely something which had probably commenced early on, but had all this time been concealed by the closeness of it, and by the unseemliness of a grown man crying.

I was surrounded by objects which had all of them changed. Something never before experienced had crept into the substance of reality. Morning knew what I looked like and had come to me precisely in order to be present and *never* leave me. The mist cleared, promising a hot day. Little by little the city came to life. In every direction light wagons, bicycles, lorries and trains slipped past me. Above them, invisible Sultans, were strung out human schemes and aspirations. They steamed and moved with the conciseness of allegories which, even uninterpreted, were familiar. Birds, houses and dogs, trees and horses, tulips and human beings had become shorter and brisker than childhood had known them. The fresh laconic quality of life was revealed to me. It crossed the road, it took me by the hand, it led me along the sidewalk. Less than ever before did I deserve the brotherhood of that vast summertime sky. But this was for the moment not mentioned. For the time being I was forgiven everything. Some time in the future, somewhere or other, I was to earn the morning's confidence. And all about me was dizzily encouraging, like some law by which loans of *that* sort never put one in the red.

Having without any difficulty acquired a ticket, I took my place in the train. I did not have long to wait before it started. And there I was once again coasting from Berlin to Marburg, but this time, in distinction from the first, travelling by day, and not only to a life that was already shaped out, but a completely new man. I travelled comfortably too, on money taken from V. on loan. And as I went the contours of my room in Marburg floated before me.

Facing me, back to the engine, and smoking, were a man in *pince-nez* which constantly threatened to slip off his nose into the newspaper which he held close up to them, an official of the Department of Forestry, complete with hunting bag slung over one shoulder and a fowling-piece in the rack above. And another. And yet another. They cramped me no more than did my Marburg room, which I saw in thought. The nature of my silence quite hypnotized them. I broke it only at rare intervals, and then merely to confirm what power it had over them. For they understood it. That silence was travelling with me. On the road, I was its travelling-companion and wore its uniform, one they could recognize from their own experience. Otherwise, it goes without saying, they would never have rewarded me with that tacit sympathy for rather treating them courteously than having anything to do with them and rather posing without any pose to the compartment than occupying a seat in it. There was certainly more human-kindness and dog-sense in it than there was tobacco smoke or engine smoke. Ancient towns rushed up to meet us. And I kept seeing the whole layout of my room in Marburg. Now what exactly was the cause of that?

About two weeks before the two sisters had descended on me there had occurred a trifling event which for me at the time was of some importance. I read a paper to both seminars. And with some success, too. Both papers received approval.

I was then advised to develop my propositions in greater detail and offer them again at the end of the Summer Term. And I had agreed to do so, taking up the idea at once and beginning to work with redoubled enthusiasm.

It was however precisely by that fire of mine that an experienced observer would have been able to decide that I was never going to be a scholar. I *lived* the study of science more powerfully than the subject as such demands. There was what might be called a vegetative sort of ratiocination in me. Its characteristic was that any secondary idea would proliferate to excess in my reasoning till it began to demand food and attention for itself and when under its influence I turned to books, I did so not from disinterested interest in knowledge, but merely to find literary quotations to support that idea of mine. And although my work was being realized with the aid of logic, imagination, paper and ink, I principally loved it because as it developed on paper it became encrusted with an ever denser ornamentation of quotations and comparisons. And as through lack of time I would at any moment have to give up my quotation-extracting, instead of doing this I began quite simply depositing my authors at the necessary points where I proposed to straighten out my argument, so that in time my thesis became quite concrete, visible from beginning to end to the merest layman as soon as he entered the room. It straggled out across the room like a sort of tree fern, depositing leafy ramifications all over table, couch and window-sill. Any transposition of the books would have amounted to destruction of my whole line of argument, and a complete weekly clean-out of the room would have been equivalent to the destruction by fire of a manuscript of which there was no fair copy. My landlady was under the very strictest of injunctions not to touch a thing, and latterly my room had not once been done out. And when in my imagination, in the train coming home, I saw my room, it was really my philosophy and its probable fate that I was seeing.

When I got back I simply did not recognize Marburg. The mountain had grown. It was higher than before, and the town was thinner, darker.

My landlady opened the door to me. Eyeing me from head to foot, she requested me in such cases in future to inform either her or her daughter in good time. I explained that I could not possibly have told her in advance, it was utterly unexpectedly that I had found it so essential to go to Berlin without delay and without first coming back to my lodgings. She rewarded me with an even more sarcastic glance. My speedy reappearance, quite lightly dressed, as if returning from an evening stroll, but stating that I had been to the other side of Germany, did not at all fit in with her conception of life. To her it all seemed most unseemly eccentricity. Still shaking her head, she then handed me a letter and a postcard with the Marburg date-stamp. The letter was from a girl cousin of Petersburg, who happened to be in Frankfort. She was on her way to Switzerland, she said, and would be in Frankfort for three days. One-third of its space occupied by impersonal neat writing, the postcard bore a signature which I knew only too well from university announcements. It was that of Professor Cohen. The message was an invitation to dine with him the very next Sunday.

Between myself and my landlady there now took place in German a conversation which ran more or less as follows:

"What day is it today?"

"Saturday."

"I shall not need any tea. But, in case I forget to tell you later—I have to go to Frankfurt tomorrow, please wake me in time for the first train."

"But surely, if I am not mistaken, the Herr Privy Councillor . . ."

"That doesn't matter, I shall be back."

"But you cannot possibly be! The Herr Privy Councillor dines punctually at midday, and you . . ."

But I found something unseemly in such concern for my personal affairs. With an expressive glance at the old lady, I went to my room.

I sat down on my bed, at my wits' end, though for not more than a minute, after which, mastering an upsurge of importuning regret, I went down to the kitchen for a brush and dustpan. I locked my door, took off my jacket, rolled up my shirt-sleeves, and set to work to clean up that gnarled botanical exhibit of mine. Half an hour later my room looked as it had when I first saw it. Even the books I had assembled on my fundamental subject did not impinge on its orderliness. Them I tied into four neat parcels, so they would be handy when I happened to be going to the library, and with my foot I tucked them deep away under the bed.

At this moment, my landlady knocked. She had come, time-table in hand, to give me the exact hour of departure of tomorrow's train. When her eyes beheld the change which had taken place she stood transfixed. Then, with a flutter of petticoats, blouse and coiffure, as if there were some spherical sort of plumage which she had sprouted, she floated through the air towards me in a state of quivering excitement. Holding out her hand with wooden gesture, and an expression of triumph, she offered her congratulations on the completion of my thesis. I did not want to disappoint her a second time, so I left her to her noble illusion.

This over, I turned to my toilet. As I dried my face I went out on to the balcony. Evening was falling. Towelling away at my neck, I gazed into the distance, at the road which linked Ockerhausen and Marburg. I found it already impossible to recall what impressions that view had given me on my first evening there. It was the end. The very end. The end of philosophy, that is, the end of all thoughts about it. Like my travelling companions, philosophy would have to reconcile itself to the fact that every real shock is a passage to a new faith.

It is astonishing that I did not return to Russia there and then. The value of Marburg resided in its school of philosophy. I no longer needed that. But now suddenly Marburg proved to have another value.

There is a psychology of creativeness, of the problem of poetics. But of all art this is precisely the origin which is most immediately experienced, and one should not produce guess-work about it.

We cease to recognize reality. It appears to us in a totally new category, which seems to us as its own state, not ours. Apart from that state, everything in the world has been labelled. Only this is new and unlabelled. We try to give it a name. We get art.

The clearest, most memorable and important feature of art is how it arises, and in their telling of the most varied things, the finest works in the world in fact all tell us of their own birth. It was in this period I am now talking about that I first understood this, in all its broad implications.

Although my declaration of love to V——a and her rejection of me were acts not followed by anything which might have changed my position, they were nevertheless events which in their train brought surprises resembling happiness. I had been desperate, she had tried to console me, and that simple contact between her and myself was such a treasure that with a sudden wave of rejoicing it swept away the clear-cut gall of what I had heard, which was irrevocable. The circumstances of that day were all transformed into a whirl of high-speed movement. It was like an incessant racing into darkness and re-emerging without taking breath. In this way, without once considering what we were at, for the twentieth time that day we found ourselves in the wheel-room of a ship crowded with people, and whence the paddle-wheels of the galley of time were set in motion. It was that very same adult, grown-up world of which I had been so envious when in my childhood the schoolboy loved the schoolgirl and I jealously thought that V——a loved that world.

When I had got back to Marburg I found myself separated not from a young girl whom I had known for six years, but from a woman whom I had only seen for a few moments after her rejection of me. My shoulders and arms no longer belonged to me. As if not mine they kept begging me to let them get at the chains by which a man is fettered to the common cause. And as now I could not think even of her apart from fetters, I loved solely in fetters, loved solely as a prisoner, solely by that cold sweat with which beauty gets rid of its allegiance. Every thought about her at once linked me with that fraternally choral something that fills the world with a forest of movements established for all time by inspiration and all together is like a battle, like convict labour, like the hell and the high skill of the medieval world. Here I have in mind what children do not know and I shall call a sense of reality.

Early in this *Safe Conduct* I remarked that there are moments when love runs before the sun. What I had in mind was the evidential nature of the emotion, every morning meeting all its surroundings with the incontrovertibility of a report of something for the hundredth time repeated but a moment before. In comparison with this, even the rising of the sun assumed the character of mere town gossip which, however sensational, still demanded verification. In other words, what I had in view was the evidential nature of a form of energy which exceeded the evidential nature of light.

Were I now with my present knowledge, ability and with the time I have at my disposal to think of writing an aesthetic of the creative act, I would base my work on two concepts, the concept of energy and the concept of the symbol. I would show that, in distinction from science, which perceives Nature by means of a section of a column of light, art is interested in life by the projection of a ray of energy through it. I would take the concept *energy* in the same very broad sense in which theoretical physics takes it, the only difference being that here one would not be discussing the principle of energy but its voice or presence. Here I would explain that within the bounds of our consciousness energy is what we call emotion.

When we assume that in *Tristan, Romeo and Juliet* and other great works we have the depiction of powerful passion, this is an underestimation of their content. Their theme is vaster than that, however powerful this one too may be. Their theme is that of energy.

It is indeed from this theme that art is born. Art is more one-sided than people think. It cannot be arbitrarily directed in whatever direction one wills, like a telescope. Applied to a reality integrated by emotion, art is the recording of that integration. It is a direct, factual record of the integration. How can the factual be integrated? Detail gains in brilliance what it loses in independence of meaning. Any detail can be replaced by another. Any is precious. Any you care to choose is suitable as evidential deposition about the state which embraces the whole of a transferred reality.

When the symptoms of such a state are transferred to paper, the features of life become those of a creative work and these latter are more striking to us than the former. They are better studied. They have their recognized names. They are known as devices.

Art is realistic as activity, and as fact it is symbolical. It is realistic in that it has not merely conceived a metaphor, but found that metaphor in Nature and with reverence reproduced it. Just as the parts of integrated reality are devoid of meaning in themselves, so is the metaphysical sense too equally devoid of meaning in itself; it is a reference to the general spirit of all art.

Art is also symbolical by all the attractive force of its imagery. Its unique symbol is in the brilliance and the unimperative quality of its images peculiar to it. The mutual interchangeability of images is a symptom of a state in which the parts of reality are mutually indifferent. That indeed is just what art is—mutual interchangeability of images, a symbol of energy.

It is of course really only energy that requires a language of concrete proofs. The other aspects of perception are durable without pointers. They have a direct path to the visual analogies of light: to number, precise notion, idea. But energy, the factualness of energy, energy whose duration is limited to the instant of its manifestation, has no other form of expression but the shifting language of symbols. The direct speech of emotion is a double-speech, and there is nothing to take its place.[2]

[2]To avoid any misunderstanding, let me point out that I am not speaking of the material content and substance of art, but the sense of its manifestation, its place in life. Individual images by themselves are visual and built on analogy with light. The individual words of art, like all concepts, live by being perceived. But the irreducible, the quoted word of all art, consists in double-speech, it speaks of energy by symbols.

Anthony Trollope

(1815–1882)

In less than forty years Anthony Trollope wrote forty-seven novels and twenty-five other books besides. (His mother and brother and second wife were all novelists; his mother wrote fifty books, including the caustic Domestic Manners of the Americans.) *A contemporary of Dickens and Thackeray—respectively three and four years younger than they—he left us no work as copious as* David Copperfield *or* Great Expectations, *or as vivid as* Vanity Fair *or* Henry Esmond, *but his six Barsetshire novels and quite a few others, such as* Orley Farm, Can You Forgive Her?, Phineas Finn, *and* The Way We Live Now, *are remarkable books. His wonderfully candid and often funny* Autobiography, *published soon after he died, went far to ruin his then lofty reputation, because it showed the workaday and somewhat cynical way he had gone about his writing. For writers,* An Autobiography *is a joyous grabbag; above all, it gives off energy. Trollope worked full-time for the British postal system, for seven years in London, for eighteen in Ireland, then for eight more in England until his retirement at the age of fifty-two out of pique at being passed over for promotion; all his adult life he hunted foxes with ferocious, headlong recklessness; he traveled as a postal inspector to the West Indies, Egypt, the United States, Australia, New Zealand, and South Africa—enough life for a vigorous man. But besides, nearly every day of all those full years, he got up at five o'clock in the morning and wrote; he was always two or three books ahead of his publisher.*

FROM
AN AUTOBIOGRAPHY

As a boy, even as a child, I was thrown much upon myself. I have explained, when speaking of my school-days, how it came to pass that other boys would not play with me. I was therefore alone, and had to form my plays within myself. Play of some kind was necessary to me then, as it has always been. Study was not my bent, and I could not please myself by being all idle. Thus it came to pass that I was always going about with some castle in the air firmly built within my mind. Nor were these efforts in architecture spasmodic, or subject to constant change from day to day. For weeks, for months, if I remember rightly, from year to year, I would carry on the same tale, binding myself down to certain laws, to certain proportions, and proprieties, and unities. Nothing impossible was ever introduced, nor even anything which, from outward circumstances, would seem to be violently improbable. I myself was, of course, my own hero. Such is a necessity of castle-building. But I never became a king, or a duke—much less, when my height and personal appearance were fixed, could I be an Antinous, or six feet high. I never was a learned man, nor even a philosopher. But I was a very clever person, and beautiful young women used to be fond of me. And I strove to be kind of heart, and open of hand, and noble in thought, despising mean things; and altogether I was a very much better fellow than I have ever succeeded in being since. . . .

I hated the office. I hated my work. More than all I hated my idleness. I had often told myself since I left school that the only career in life within my reach was that of an author, and the only mode of authorship open to me that of a writer of novels. In the journal which I read and destroyed a few years since, I found the matter argued out before I had been in the Post-office two years. Parliament was out of the question. I had not means to go to the Bar. In official life, such as that to which I had been introduced, there did not seem to be any opening for real success. Pens and paper I could command. Poetry I did not believe to be within my grasp. The drama, too, which I would fain have chosen, I believed to be above me. For history, biography, or essay writing I had not sufficient erudition. But I thought it possible that I might write a novel. I had resolved very early that in that shape must the attempt be made. But the months and years ran on, and no attempt was made. And yet no day was passed without thoughts of attempting, and a mental acknowledgment of the disgrace of postponing it. What reader will not understand the agony of remorse produced by such a condition of mind? . . .

I found that the surveyor to whom I had been sent kept a pack of hounds, and therefore I bought a hunter. I do not think he liked it, but he could not well complain. He never rode to hounds himself, but I did; and then and thus began one of the great joys of my life. I have ever since been constant to the sport, having learned to love it with an affection which I cannot myself fathom or understand. Surely no man has labored at it as I have done, or hunted under such drawbacks as to distances, money, and natural disadvantages. I am very heavy, very blind, have been —in reference to hunting—a poor man, and am now an old man. I have often had to travel all night outside a mail-coach, in order that I might hunt the next day. Nor have I ever been in truth a good horseman. And I have passed the greater part of my hunting life under the discipline of the civil service. But it has been for more than thirty years a duty to me to ride to hounds; and I have performed that duty with a persistent energy. Nothing has ever been allowed to stand in the way of hunting, neither the writing of books, nor the work of the Post-office, nor other pleasures. . . .

The first effort was made after the following fashion. I was located at a little town called Drumsna, or, rather, village, in the County Leitrim, where the postmaster had come to some sorrow about his money; and my friend John Merivale was staying with me for a day or two. As we were taking a walk in that most uninteresting country, we turned up through a deserted gateway, along a weedy, grass-grown avenue, till we came to the modern ruins of a country-house. It was one of the most melancholy spots I ever visited. I will not describe it here, because I have done so in the first chapter of my first novel. We wandered about the place, suggesting to each other causes for the misery we saw there, and while I was still among the ruined walls and decayed beams I fabricated the plot of "The Macdermots of Ballycloran." As to the plot itself, I do not know that I ever made one so good—or, at any rate, one so susceptible of pathos. I am aware that I broke down in the telling, not having yet studied the art. Nevertheless, "The Macdermots" is a good novel, and worth reading by anyone who wishes to understand what Irish life was before the potato disease, the famine, and the Encumbered Estates Bill.

When my friend left me, I set to work and wrote the first chapter or two. Up to this time I had continued that practice of castle-building of which I have spoken, but now the castle I built was among the ruins of that old house. The book, however, hung with me. It was only now and then that I found either time or energy for a few pages. I commenced the book in September, 1843, and had only written a volume when I was married, in June, 1844. . . .

When I had been married a year my first novel was finished. In July, 1845, I took it with me to the north of England, and intrusted the manuscript to my mother, to do with it the best she could among the publishers in London. No one had read it but my wife; nor, as far as I am aware, has any other friend of mine ever read a word of my writing before it was printed. She, I think, has so read almost everything, to my very great advantage in matters of taste. I am sure I have never asked a friend to read a line; nor have I ever read a word of my own writing aloud, even to her. With one exception—which shall be mentioned as I come to it—I have never consulted a friend as to a plot, or spoken to any one of the work I have been doing. My first manuscript I gave up to my mother, agreeing with her that it would be as well that she should not look at it before she gave it to a publisher. I knew that she did not give me credit for the sort of cleverness necessary for such work. I could see in the faces and hear in the voices of those of my friends who were around me at the house in Cumberland—my mother, my sister, my brother-in-law, and, I think, my brother—that they had not expected me to come out as one of the family authors. There were three or four in the field before me, and it seemed to be almost absurd that another should wish to add himself to the number. My father had written much—those long ecclesiastical descriptions—quite unsuccessfully. My mother had become one of the popular authors of the day. My brother had commenced, and had been fairly well paid for his work. My sister, Mrs. Tilley, had also written a novel, which was at the time in manuscript—which was published afterwards without her name, and was called "Chollerton." I could perceive that this attempt of mine was felt to be an unfortunate aggravation of the disease.

My mother, however, did the best she could for me, and soon reported that Mr. Newby, of Mortimer Street, was to publish the book. It was to be printed at his expense, and he was to give me half the profits. Half the profits! Many a young author expects much from such an undertaking. I can with truth declare that I expected nothing. And I got nothing. Nor did I expect fame, or even acknowledgment. I was sure that the book would fail, and it did fail most absolutely. I never heard of a person reading it in those days. If there was any notice taken of it by any critic of the day, I did not see it. I never asked any questions about it, or wrote a single letter on the subject to the publisher. I have Mr. Newby's agreement with me, in duplicate, and one or two preliminary notes; but beyond that I did not have a word from Mr. Newby. I am sure that he did not wrong me in that he paid me nothing. It is probable that he did not sell fifty copies of the work; but of what he did sell he gave me no account.

I do not remember that I felt in any way disappointed or hurt. I am quite sure that no word of complaint passed my lips. I think I may say that after the publication I never said a word about the book, even to my wife. The fact that I had written and published it, and that I was writing another, did not in the least interfere with my life or with my determination to make the best I could of the Post-office. In Ireland, I think that no one knew that I had written a novel. But I went on writing. "The Macdermots" was published in 1847, and the "The Kellys and the O'Kellys" followed in 1848. I changed my publisher, but did not change my fortune. This second Irish story was sent into the world by Mr. Colburn, who had long been my mother's publisher, who reigned in Great Marlborough Street, and I believe created the business which is now carried on by Messrs. Hurst & Blackett. He had previously been in partnership with Mr. Bentley in New Burlington Street. I made the same agreement as before as to half profits, and with precisely the same results. The book was not only not read, but was never heard of—at any rate, in Ireland. And yet it is a good Irish story, much inferior to "The Macdermots" as to plot, but superior in the mode of telling. Again I held my tongue, and not only said nothing, but felt nothing. Any success would, I think, have carried me off my legs, but I was altogether prepared for failure. Though I thoroughly enjoyed the writing of these books, I did not imagine, when the time came for publishing them, that any one would condescend to read them.

But in reference to "The O'Kellys" there arose a circumstance which set my mind to work on a subject which has exercised it much ever since. I made my first acquaintance with criticism. A dear friend of mine, to whom the book had been sent—as have all my books—wrote me word to Ireland that he had been dining at some club with a man high in authority among the gods of the *Times* newspaper, and that this special god had almost promised that "The O'Kellys" should be noticed in that most influential of "organs." The information moved me very much; but it set me thinking whether the notice, should it ever appear, would not have been more valuable, at any rate, more honest, if it had been produced by other means; if, for instance, the writer of the notice had been instigated by the merits or demerits of the book instead of by the friendship of a friend. And I made up my mind then that, should I continue this trade of authorship, I would have no dealings with any critic on my own behalf. I would neither ask for nor deplore criticism, nor would I ever thank a critic for praise, or quarrel with him, even in my own heart, for censure. To this rule I have adhered with absolute strictness, and this rule I would recommend to all young authors. What can be got by touting among the critics is never worth the ignominy. The same may of course be said of all things acquired by ignominious means. But in this matter it is so easy to fall into the dirt. *Facilis descensus Averni.* There seems to be but little fault in suggesting to a friend that a few words in this or that journal would be of service. But any praise so obtained must be an injustice to the public, for whose instruction, and not for the sustentation of the author, such notices are intended. And from such mild suggestion the descent to crawling at the critic's feet, to the sending of presents, and at last to a mutual understanding between critics and criticised, is only too easy. Other evils follow, for the denouncing of which this is hardly the place; though I trust I may find such place before my work is finished. I took no notice of my friend's letter, but I was not the less careful in watching the *Times*. At last the review came—a real review in the *Times*. I learned it by heart, and can now give, if not the words, the exact purport. "Of, 'The Kellys and the O'Kellys' we may say what the master said to his footman, when the man complained of the constant supply of legs of mutton on the kitchen table. 'Well, John, legs of mutton are good substantial food;' and we may say also what John replied: 'Substantial, sir; yes, they are substantial, but a little coarse.'" That was the review, and even that did not sell the book!

From Mr. Colburn I did receive an account, showing that 375 copies of the book had been printed, that 140 had been sold—to those, I presume, who liked substantial food though it was coarse—and that he had incurred a loss of £63 10s. 1½d. The truth of the account I never for a moment doubted; nor did I doubt the wisdom of the advice given to me in the following letter, though I never thought of obeying it:

"GREAT MARLBOROUGH STREET,
November 11, 1848.

"MY DEAR SIR,—I am sorry to say that absence from town and other circumstances have prevented me from earlier inquiring into the results of the sale of 'The Kellys and the O'Kellys,' with which the greatest efforts have been used, but in vain. The sale has been, I regret to say, so small that the loss upon the publication is very considerable; and it appears clear to me that although, in consequence of the great number of novels that are published, the sale of each, with some few exceptions, must be small, yet it is evident that readers do not like novels on Irish subjects as well as on others. Thus you will perceive it is impossible for me to give any encouragement to you to proceed in novel-writing.

"As, however, I understand you have nearly finished the novel 'La Vendée,' perhaps you will favor me with a sight of it when convenient.

"I remain, etc., etc.,

H. Colburn."

This, though not strictly logical, was a rational letter, telling a plain truth plainly. I did not like the assurance that "the greatest efforts had been used," thinking that any efforts which might be made for the popularity of a book ought to have come from the author; but I took in good part Mr. Colburn's assurance that he could not encourage me in the career I had commenced. I would have bet twenty to one against my own success. But by continuing I could lose only pen and paper; and if the one chance in twenty did turn up in my favor, then how much might I win! . . .

In the course of the job I visited Salisbury, and while wandering there one midsummer evening round the purlieus of the cathedral I conceived the story of "The Warden"—from whence came that series of novels of which Barchester, with its bishops, deans, and archdeacon, was the central site. I may as well declare at once that no one at their commencement could have had less reason than myself to presume himself to be able to write about clergymen. I have been often asked in what period of my early life I had lived so long in a cathedral city as to have become intimate with the ways of a close. I never lived in any cathedral city, except London, never knew anything of any close, and at that time had enjoyed no peculiar intimacy with any clergyman. My archdeacon, who has been said to be life-like, and for whom I confess that I have all a parent's fond affection, was, I think, the simple result of an effort of my moral consciousness. It was such as that, in my opinion, that an archdeacon should be, or, at any rate, would be, with such advantages as an archdeacon might have; and lo! an archdeacon was produced, who has been declared by competent authorities to be a real archdeacon down to the very ground. And yet, as far as I can remember, I had not then even spoken to an archdeacon. . . .

The novel-reading world did not go mad about "The Warden"; but I soon felt that it had not failed as the others had failed. There were notices of it in the press, and I could discover that people around me knew that I had written a book. Mr. Longman was complimentary, and after a while informed me that there would be profits to divide. At the end of 1855 I received a check for £9 8s. 8d., which was the first money I had ever earned by literary work—that £20 which poor Mr. Colburn had been made to pay certainly never having been earned at all. At the end of 1856 I received another sum of £10 15s. 1d. The pecuniary success was not great. Indeed, as regarded remuneration for the time, stone-breaking would have done better. A thousand copies were printed, of which, after a lapse of five or six years, about three hundred had to be converted into another form, and sold as belonging to a cheap edition. In its original form "The Warden" never reached the essential honor of a second edition.

I have already said of the work that it failed altogether in the purport for which it was intended. But it has a merit of its own, a merit by my own perception of which I was enabled to see wherein lay whatever strength I did possess. The characters of the bishop, of the archdeacon, of the archdeacon's wife, and especially of the warden, are all well and clearly drawn. I had realized to myself a series of portraits, and had been able so to put them on the canvas that my readers should see that which I meant them to see. There is no gift which an author can have more useful to him than this. And the style of the English was good, though, from most unpardonable carelessness, the grammar was not unfrequently faulty. With such results I had no doubt but that I would at once begin another novel. . . .

It was while I was engaged on "Barchester Towers" that I adopted a system of writing which, for some years afterwards, I found to be very serviceable to me. My time was greatly occupied in travelling, and the nature of my travelling was now changed. I could not any longer do it on horseback. Railroads afforded me my means of conveyance, and I found that I passed in railway-carriages very many hours of my existence. Like others, I used to read—though Carlyle has since told me that a man when travelling should not read, but "sit still and label his thoughts." But if I intended to make a profitable business out of my writing, and, at the same time, to do my best for the Post-office, I must turn these hours to more account than I could do even by reading. I made for myself, therefore, a little tablet, and found after a few days' exercise that I could write as quickly in a railway-carriage as I could at my desk. I worked with a pencil, and what I wrote my wife copied afterwards. In this way was composed the greater part of "Barchester Towers" and of the novel which succeeded it, and much also of others subsequent to them. My only objection to the practice came from the appearance of literary ostentation, to which I felt myself to be subject when going to work before four or five fellow-passengers. But I got used to it, as I had done to the amazement of the west country farmers' wives when asking them after their letters. . . .

I received my £100, in advance, with profound delight. It was a positive and most welcome increase to my income, and might probably be regarded as a first real step on the road to substantial success. I am well aware that there are many who think that an author in his authorship should not regard money—nor a painter, or sculptor, or composer, in his art. I do not know that this unnatural self-sacrifice is supposed to extend itself further. A barrister, a clergyman, a doctor, an engineer, and even actors and architects, may without disgrace follow the bent of human nature, and endeavor to fill their bellies and clothe their backs, and also those of their wives and children, as comfortably as they can, by the exercise of their abilities and their crafts. They may be as rationally realistic as may the butchers and the bakers; but the artist and the author forget the high glories of their calling if they condescend to make a money return a first object. They who preach this doctrine will be much offended by my theory, and by this book of mine, if my theory and my book come beneath their notice. They require the practice of a so-called virtue which is contrary to nature, and which, in my eyes, would be no virtue if it were practised. They are like clergymen who preach sermons against the love of money, but who know that the love of money is so distinctive a characteristic of humanity that such sermons are mere platitudes, called for by customary but unintelligent piety. All material progress has come from man's desire to do the best he can for himself and those about him. . . .

I have, certainly, also had always before my eyes the charms of reputation. Over and above the money view of the question, I wished from the beginning to be something more than a clerk in the Post-office. To be known as somebody, to be Anthony Trollope, if it be no more, is to me much. The feeling is a very general one, and I think beneficent. It is that which has been called the "last infirmity of noble mind." The infirmity is so human that the man who lacks it is either above or below humanity. I own to the infirmity. But I confess that my first object in taking to literature as a profession was that which is common to the barrister when he goes to the bar, and to the baker when he sets up his oven. I wished to make an income on which I and those belonging to me might live in comfort.

If, indeed, a man writes his books badly, or paints his pictures badly, because he can make his money faster in that fashion than by doing them well, and at the same time proclaims them to be the best he can do, if, in fact, he sells shoddy for broadcloth, he is dishonest, as is any other fraudulent dealer. So may be the barrister who takes money that he does not earn, or the clergyman who is content to live on a sinecure. No doubt the artist or the author may have a difficulty which will not occur to the seller of cloth, in settling within himself what is good work and what is bad, when labor enough has been given, and when the task has been scamped. It is a danger as to which he is bound to be severe with himself—in which he ought to feel that his conscience should be set fairly in the balance against the natural bias of his interest. If he do not do so, sooner or later his dishonesty will be discovered, and will be estimated accordingly. But in this he is to be governed only by the plain rules of honesty which should govern us all. Having said so much, I shall not scruple as I go on to attribute to the pecuniary result of my labors all the importance which I felt them to have at the time. . . .

I had finished "The Three Clerks" just before I left England, and when in Florence was cudgelling my brain for a new plot. Being then with my brother, I asked him to sketch me a plot, and he drew out that of my next novel, called "Doctor Thorne." I mention this particularly, because it was the only occasion in which I have had recourse to some other source than my own brains for the thread of a story. How far I may unconsciously have adopted incidents from what I have read—either from history or from works of imagination—I do not know. It is beyond question that a man employed as I have been must do so. But when doing it I have not been aware that I have done it. I have never taken another man's work, and deliberately framed my work upon it. I am far from censuring this practice in others. Our greatest masters in works of imagination have obtained such aid for themselves. Shakespeare dug out of such quarries wherever he could find them. Ben Jonson, with heavier hand, built up his structures on his studies of the classics, not thinking it beneath him to give, without direct acknowledgment, whole pieces translated both from poets and historians. But in those days no such acknowledgment was usual. Plagiary existed, and was very common, but was not known as a sin. It is different now; and I think that an author, when he uses either the words or the plot of another, should own as much, demanding to be credited with no more of the work than he has himself produced. I may say also that I have never printed as my own a word that has been written by others.[1] It might probably have been better for my readers had I done so, as I am informed that "Doctor Thorne," the novel of which I am now speaking, has a larger sale than any other book of mine. . . .

As I journeyed across France to Marseilles, and made thence a terribly rough voyage to Alexandria, I wrote my allotted number of pages every day. On this occasion more than once I left my paper on the cabin table, rushing away to be sick in the privacy of my stateroom. It was February, and the weather was miserable; but still I did my work. *Labor omnia vincit improbus.* I do not say that to all men has been given physical strength sufficient for such exertion as this, but I do believe that real exertion will enable most men to work at almost any season. I had previously to this arranged a system of task-work for myself, which I would strongly recommend to those who feel as I have felt, that labor, when not made absolutely obligatory by the circumstances of the hour, should never be allowed to become spasmodic. There was no day on which it was my

[1] *I must make one exception to this declaration. The legal opinion as to heirlooms in "The Eustace Diamonds" was written for me by Charles Merewether, the present Member for Northampton. I am told that it has become the ruling authority on the subject.*

positive duty to write for the publishers, as it was my duty to write reports for the Post-office. I was free to be idle if I pleased. But as I had made up my mind to undertake this second profession, I found it to be expedient to bind myself by certain self-imposed laws. When I have commenced a new book, I have always prepared a diary, divided into weeks, and carried it on for the period which I have allowed myself for the completion of the work. In this I have entered, day by day, the number of pages I have written, so that if at any time I have slipped into idleness for a day or two, the record of that idleness has been there, staring me in the face, and demanding of me increased labor, so that the deficiency might be supplied. According to the circumstances of the time—whether my other business might be then heavy or light, or whether the book which I was writing was or was not wanted with speed—I have allotted myself so many pages a week. The average number has been about 40. It has been placed as low as 20, and has risen to 112. And as a page is an ambiguous term, my page has been made to contain 250 words; and as words, if not watched, will have a tendency to straggle, I have had every word counted as I went. In the bargains I have made with publishers I have—not, of course, with their knowledge, but in my own mind—undertaken always to supply them with so many words, and I have never put a book out of hand short of the number by a single word. I may also say that the excess has been very small. I have prided myself on completing my work exactly within the proposed dimensions. But I have prided myself especially in completing it within the proposed time—and I have always done so. There has ever been the record before me, and a week passed with an insufficient number of pages has been a blister to my eye, and a month so disgraced would have been a sorrow to my heart.

I have been told that such appliances are beneath the notice of a man of genius. I have never fancied myself to be a man of genius, but had I been so I think I might well have subjected myself to these trammels. Nothing, surely, is so potent as a law that may not be disobeyed. It has the force of the water-drop that hollows the stone. A small daily task, if it be really daily, will beat the labors of a spasmodic Hercules. It is the tortoise which always catches the hare. The hare has no chance. He loses more time in glorifying himself for a quick spurt than suffices for the tortoise to make half his journey.

I have known authors whose lives have always been troublesome and painful because their tasks have never been done in time. They have ever been as boys struggling to learn their lesson as they entered the school gates. Publishers have distrusted them, and they have failed to write their best, because they have seldom written at ease. I have done double their work—though burdened with another profession—and have done it almost without an effort. I have not once, through all my literary career, felt myself even in danger of being late with my task. I have known no anxiety as to "copy." The needed pages far ahead—very far ahead—have almost always been in the drawer beside me. And that little diary, with its dates and ruled spaces, its record that must be seen, its daily, weekly demand upon my industry, has done all that for me.

There are those who would be ashamed to subject themselves to such a taskmaster, and who think that the man who works with his imagination should allow himself to wait till—inspiration moves him. When I have heard such doctrine preached, I have hardly been able to repress my scorn. To me it would not be more absurd, if the shoemaker were to wait for inspiration, or the tallow-chandler for the divine moment of melting. If the man whose business it is to write has eaten too many good things, or has drunk too much, or smoked too many cigars—as men who write sometimes will do—then his condition may be unfavorable for work; but so will be the condition of a shoemaker who has been similarly imprudent. I have sometimes thought that the inspiration wanted has been the remedy which time will give to the evil results of such imprudence. *Mens sana in corpore sano.* The author wants that, as does every other workman—that and a habit of industry. I was once told that the surest aid to the writing of a book was a piece of cobbler's wax on my chair. I certainly believe in the cobbler's wax, much more than the inspiration.

It will be said, perhaps, that a man whose work has risen to no higher pitch than mine has attained has no right to speak of the strains and impulses to which real genius is exposed. I am ready to admit the great variations in brain power which are exhibited by the products of different men, and am not disposed to rank my own very high; but my own experience tells me that a man can always do the work for which his brain is fitted if he will give himself the habit of regarding his work as a normal condition of his life. I therefore venture to advise young men who look forward to authorship as the business of their lives, even when they propose that that authorship shall be of the highest class known, to avoid enthusiastic rushes with their pens, and to seat themselves at their desks day by day, as though they were lawyers' clerks; and so let them sit until the allotted task shall be accomplished. . . .

While I was in Egypt I finished "Doctor Thorne," and on the following day began "The Bertrams." . . .

It will, I think, be accorded to me by Essex men generally that I have ridden hard. The cause of my delight in the amusement I have never been able to analyze to my own satisfaction. In the first place, even now, I know very little about hunting—though I know very much of the accessories of the field. I am too blind to see hounds turning, and cannot therefore tell whether the fox has gone this way or that. Indeed, all the notice I take of hounds is not to ride over them. My eyes are so constituted that I can never see the nature of a fence. I either follow some one, or ride at it with the full conviction that I may be going into a horse-pond or a gravel-pit. I have jumped into both one and the other. I am very heavy, and have never ridden expensive horses. I am also now old for such work, being so stiff that I cannot get on to my horse without the aid of a block or a bank. But I ride still after the same fashion, with a boy's energy, determined to get ahead if it may possibly be done, hating the roads, despising young men who ride them, and with a feeling that life cannot, with all her riches, have given me anything better than when I have gone through a long run to the finish, keeping a place, not of glory, but of credit, among my juniors. . . .

Giving to the subject the best of my critical abilities, and judging of my own work as nearly as possible as I would that of another, I believe that the work which has been done quickest has been done the best. I have composed better stories—that is, have created better plots—than those of "The Small House at Allington" and "Can You Forgive Her?" and I have portrayed two or three better characters than are to be found in the pages of either of them; but taking these books all through, I do not think that I have ever done better work. Nor would these have been improved by any effort in the art of story-telling, had each of these been the isolated labor of a couple of years. How short is the time devoted to the manipulation of a plot can be known only to those who have written plays and novels—I may say also, how very little time the brain is able to devote to such wearing work. There are usually some hours of agonizing doubt, almost of despair—so, at least, it has been with me—or perhaps some days. And then, with nothing settled in my brain as to the final development of events, with no capability of settling anything, but with a most distinct conception of some character or characters, I have rushed at the work as a rider rushes at a fence which he does not see. Sometimes I have encountered what, in hunting language, we call a cropper. I had such a fall in two novels of mine, of which I have already spoken—"The Bertrams" and "Castle Richmond." I shall have to speak of other such troubles. But these failures have not arisen from over-hurried work. When my work has been quicker done—and it has sometimes been done very quickly—the rapidity has been achieved by hot pressure, not in the conception, but in the telling of the story. Instead of writing eight pages a day, I have written sixteen; instead of working five days a week, I have worked seven. I have trebled my usual average, and have done so in circumstances which have enabled me to give up all my thoughts for the time to the book I have been writing. This has generally been done at some quiet spot among the mountains—where there has been no society, no hunting, no whist, no ordinary household duties. And I am sure that the work so done has had in it the best truth and the highest spirit that I have been able to produce. At such times I have been able to imbue myself thoroughly with the characters I have had in hand. I have wandered alone among the rocks and woods, crying at their grief, laughing at their absurdities, and thoroughly enjoying their joy. I have been impregnated with my own creations till it has been my only excitement to sit with the pen in my hand, and drive my team before me at as quick a pace as I could make them travel. . . .

There is, perhaps, no career of life so charming as that of a successful man of letters. Those little unthought-of advantages which I just now named are in themselves attractive. If you like the town, live in the town, and do your work there; if you like the country, choose the country. It may be done on the top of a mountain or in the bottom of a pit. It is compatible with the rolling of the sea and the motion of a railway. The clergyman, the lawyer, the doctor, the Member of Parliament, the clerk in a public office, the tradesman, and even his assistant in the shop, must dress in accordance with certain fixed laws; but the author need sacrifice to no grace, hardly even to propriety. He is subject to no bonds such as those which bind other men. Who else is free from all shackle as to hours? The judge must sit at ten, and the attorney-general, who is making his £20,000 a year, must be there with his bag. The prime-minister must be in his place on that weary front bench shortly after prayers, and must sit there, either asleep or awake, even though —— or —— should be address-ing the House. During all that Sunday which he maintains should be a day of rest, the active clergyman toils like a galley-slave. The actor, when eight o'clock comes, is bound to his footlights. The civil-service clerk must sit there from ten till four—unless his office be fashionable, when twelve to six is just as heavy on him. The author may do his work at five in the morning, when he is fresh from his bed, or at three in the morning, before he goes there. And the author wants no capital, and encounters no risks. When once he is afloat, the publisher finds all that—and indeed, unless he be rash, finds it whether he be afloat or not. But it is in the consideration which he enjoys that the successful author finds his richest reward. He is, if not of equal rank, yet of equal standing with the highest; and if he be open to the amenities of society, may choose his own circles. He, without money, can enter doors which are closed against almost all but him and the wealthy. I have often heard it said that in this country the man of letters is not recognized. I believe the meaning of this to be that men of letters are not often invited to be knights and baronets. I do not think that they wish it—and if they had it they would, as a body, lose much more than they would gain. I do not at all desire to have letters put after my name, or to be called Sir Anthony, but if my friends Tom Hughes and Charles Reade became Sir Thomas and Sir Charles, I do not know how I might feel—or how my wife might feel— if we were left unbedecked. As it is, the man of letters who would be selected for titular honor, if such bestowal of honors were customary, receives from the general respect of those around him a much more pleasant recognition of his worth.

If this be so—if it be true that the career of the successful literary man be thus pleasant—it is not wonderful that many should attempt to win the prize. But how is a man to know whether or not he has within him the qualities necessary for such a career? He makes an attempt, and fails; repeats his attempt, and fails again! So many have succeeded at last who have failed more than once or twice! Who will tell him the truth as to himself? Who has power to find out that truth? The hard man sends him off without a scruple to that office-stool; the soft man assures him that there is much merit in his manuscript.

Oh, my young aspirant—if ever such a one should read these pages—be sure that no one can tell you! To do so it would be necessary not only to know what there is now within you, but also to foresee what time will produce there. This, however, I think may be said to you, without any doubt as to the wisdom of the counsel given, that if it be necessary for you to live by your work, do not begin by trusting to literature. Take the stool in the office, as recommended to you by the hard man; and then, in such leisure hours as may belong to you, let the praise which has come from the lips of that soft man induce you to persevere in your literary attempts. Should you fail, then your failure will not be fatal; and what better could you have done with the leisure hours had you not so failed? Such double toil, you will say, is severe. Yes; but if you want this thing, you must submit to severe toil. . . .

The career, when success has been achieved, is certainly very pleasant; but the agonies which are endured in the search for that success are often terrible. And the author's poverty is, I think, harder to be borne than any other poverty. The man, whether rightly or wrongly, feels that the world is using him with extreme injustice. The more absolutely he fails, the higher, it is probable, he will reckon his own merits; and the keener will be the sense of injury in that he, whose work is of so high a nature, cannot get bread, while they whose tasks are mean are lapped in luxury. "I, with my well-filled mind, with my clear intellect, with all my gifts, cannot earn a poor crown a day, while that fool, who simpers in a little room behind a shop, makes his thousands every year." The very charity, to which he too often is driven, is bitterer to him than to others. While he takes it he almost spurns the hand that gives it to him, and every fibre of his heart within him is bleeding with a sense of injury.

The career, when successful, is pleasant enough, certainly; but when unsuccessful, it is of all careers the most agonizing. . . .

It was my practice to be at my table every morning at 5.30; and it was also my practice to allow myself no mercy. An old groom, whose business it was to call me, and to whom I paid £5 a year extra for the duty, allowed himself no mercy. During all those years at Waltham Cross he was never once late with the coffee which it was his duty to bring me. I do not know that I ought not to feel that I owe more to him than to any one else for the success I have had. By beginning at that hour I could complete my literary work before I dressed for breakfast.

All those, I think, who have lived as literary men—working daily as literary laborers—will agree with me that three hours a day will produce as much as a man ought to write. But then he should so have trained himself that he shall be able to work continuously during those three hours—so have tutored his mind that it shall not be necessary for him to sit nibbling his pen, and gazing at the wall before him, till he shall have found the words with which he wants to express his ideas. It had at this time become my custom—and it still is my custom, though of late I have become a little lenient to myself—to write with my watch before me, and to require from myself 250 words every quarter of an hour. I have found that the 250 words have been forthcoming as regularly as my watch went. But my three hours were not devoted entirely to writing. I always began my task by reading the work of the day before, an operation which would take me half an hour, and which consisted chiefly in weighing with my ear the sound of the words and phrases. I would strongly recommend this practice to all tyros in writing. That their work should be read after it has been written is a matter of course; that it should be read twice, at least, before it goes to the printers, I take to be a matter of course. But by reading what he has last written, just before he recommences his task, the writer will catch the tone and spirit of what he is then saying, and will avoid the fault of seeming to be unlike himself. This division of time allowed me to produce over ten pages of an ordinary novel volume a day, and if kept up through ten months, would have given as its results three novels of three volumes each in the year—the precise amount which so greatly acerbated the publisher in Paternoster Row, and which must, at any rate, be felt to be quite as much as the novel-readers of the world can want from the hands of one man.

I have never written three novels in a year; but by following the plan above described I have written more than as much as three novels; and by adhering to it over a course of years I have been enabled to have always on hand—for some time back now—one or two, or even three, unpublished novels in my desk beside me. . . .

And so I end the record of my literary performances, which I think are more in amount than the works of any other living English author. If any English authors not living have written more—as may probably have been the case—I do not know who they are. I find that, taking the books which have appeared under our names, I have published much more than twice as much as Carlyle. I have also published considerably more than Voltaire, even including his letters. We are told that Varro, at the age of eighty, had written 480 volumes, and that he went on writing for eight years longer. I wish I knew what was the length of Varro's volumes; I comfort myself by reflecting that the amount of manuscript described as a book in Varro's time was not much. Varro, too, is dead, and Voltaire; whereas I am still living, and may add to the pile. . . .

It will not, I am sure, be thought that, in making my boast as to quantity, I have endeavored to lay claim to any literary excellence. That, in the writing of books, quantity without quality is a vice and a misfortune, has been too manifestly settled to leave a doubt on such a matter. But I do lay claim to whatever merit should be accorded to me for persevering diligence in my profession. And I make the claim, not with a view to my own glory, but for the benefit of those who may read these pages, and when young may intend to follow the same career. *Nulla dies sine linea.* Let that be their motto. And let their work be to them as is his common work to the common laborer. No gigantic efforts will then be necessary. He need tie no wet towels round his brow, nor sit for thirty hours at his desk without moving—as men have sat, or said that they have sat. More than nine tenths of my literary work has been done in the last twenty years, and during twelve of those years I followed another profession. I have never been a slave to this work, giving due time, if not more than due time, to the amusements I have loved. But I have been constant—and constancy in labor will conquer all difficulties. *Gutta cavat lapidem non vi, sed saepe cadendo.*

It may interest some if I state that during the last twenty years I have made by literature something near £70,000. As I have said before in these pages, I look upon the result as comfortable, but not splendid.

It will not, I trust, be supposed by any reader that I have intended in this so-called autobiography to give a record of my inner life. No man ever did so truly—and no man ever will. Rousseau probably attempted it, but who doubts but that Rousseau has confessed in much the thoughts and convictions rather than the facts of his life? If the rustle of a woman's petticoat has ever stirred my blood; if a cup of wine has been a joy to me; if I have thought tobacco at midnight in pleasant company to be one of the elements of an earthly paradise; if now and again I have somewhat recklessly fluttered a £5 note over a card table; of what matter is that to any reader? I have betrayed no woman. Wine has brought me to no sorrow. It has been the companionship of smoking that I have loved, rather than the habit. I have never desired to win money, and I have lost none. To enjoy the excitement of pleasure, but to be free from its vices and ill effects—to have the sweet, and leave the bitter untasted—that has been my study. The preachers tell us that this is impossible. It seems to me that hitherto I have succeeded fairly well. I will not say that I have never scorched a finger—but I carry no ugly wounds.

For what remains to me of life I trust for my happiness still chiefly to my work—hoping, that when the power of work be over with me, God may be pleased to take me from a world in which, according to my view, there can be no joy; secondly, to the love of those who love me; and then, to my books. That I can read, and be happy while I am reading, is a great blessing. . . .

W. H. Auden

(1907–   )

The first Auden, product of British boarding schools and of Oxford, was a poet of left-wing politics, whose poems and verse plays were published in his very young years. In the nineteen thirties he emigrated from the regions of his youth to America and Christianity. In the seventies, by then long having been an American citizen but never having been anything but British in voice and style, he went back to England to live—less to find still another ideological base, apparently, than for simple carnal comfort and safety. The body of his writing is much more diverse than even these major shifts suggest. He has been satirist, journalist, travel-writer, playwright, librettist, translator, and teacher, and he has invented and borrowed and modified scores of forms and voices and manners. Over much of his work has played a mordant, sybaritic, satirical wit; his lines have for the most part been airy, clean, and swift. Rock-hard under the cheery surface, however, his poems have always explored the troubles of a troubled time—the age of anxiety, as he called it. The observations that follow are from his book The Dyer's Hand.

FROM
THE DYER'S HAND

All those whose success in life depends neither upon a job which satisfies some specific and unchanging social need, like a farmer's, nor, like a surgeon's, upon some craft which he can be taught by others and improve by practice, but upon "inspiration," the lucky hazard of ideas, live by their wits, a phrase which carries a slightly pejorative meaning. Every "original" genius, be he an artist or a scientist, has something a bit shady about him, like a gambler or a medium.

Literary gatherings, cocktail parties and the like, are a social nightmare because writers have no "shop" to talk. Lawyers and doctors can entertain each other with stories about interesting cases, about experiences, that is to say, related to their professional interests but yet impersonal and outside themselves. Writers have no impersonal professional interests. The literary equivalent of talking shop would be writers reciting their own work at each other, an unpopular procedure for which only very young writers have the nerve.

No poet or novelist wishes he were the only one who ever lived, but most of them wish they were the only one alive, and quite a number fondly believe their wish has been granted.

In theory, the author of a good book should remain anonymous, for it is to his work, not to himself, that admiration is due. In practice, this seems to be impossible. However, the praise and public attention that writers sometimes receive does not seem to be as fatal to them as one might expect. Just as a good man forgets his deed the moment he has done it, a genuine writer forgets a work as soon as he has completed it and starts to think about the next one; if he thinks about his past work at all, he is more likely to remember its faults than its virtues. Fame often makes a writer vain, but seldom makes him proud.

Writers can be guilty of every kind of human conceit but one, the conceit of the social worker: "We are all here on earth to help others; what on earth the others are here for, I don't know."

When a successful author analyzes the reasons for his success, he generally underestimates the talent he was born with, and overestimates his skill in employing it.

Every writer would rather be rich than poor, but no genuine writer cares about popularity as such. He needs approval of his work by others in order to be reassured that the vision of life he believes he has had is a true vision and not a self-delusion, but he can only be reassured by those whose judgment he respects. It would only be necessary for a writer to secure universal popularity if imagination and intelligence were equally distributed among all men.

When some obvious booby tells me he has liked a poem of mine, I feel as if I had picked his pocket.

Writers, poets especially, have an odd relation to the public because their medium, language, is not, like the paint of the painter or the notes of the composer, reserved for their use but is the common property of the linguistic group to which they belong. Lots of people are willing to admit that they don't understand painting or music, but very few indeed who have been to school and learned to read advertisements will admit that they don't understand English. As Karl Kraus said: "The public doesn't understand German, and in Journalese I can't tell them so."

How happy the lot of the mathematician! He is judged solely by his peers, and the standard is so high that no colleague or rival can ever win a reputation he does not deserve. No cashier writes a letter to the press complaining about the incomprehensibility of Modern Mathematics and comparing it unfavorably with the good old days when mathematicians were content to paper irregularly shaped rooms and fill bathtubs without closing the waste pipe.

To say that a work is inspired means that, in the judgment of its author or his readers, it is better than they could reasonably hope it would be, and nothing else.

All works of art are commissioned in the sense that no artist can create one by a simple act of will but must wait until what he believes to be a good idea for a work "comes" to him. Among those works which are failures because their initial conceptions were false or inadequate, the number of self-commissioned works may well be greater than the number commissioned by patrons.

The degree of excitement which a writer feels during the process of composition is as much an indication of the value of the final result as the excitement felt by a worshiper is an indication of the value of his devotions, that is to say, very little indication.

The Oracle claimed to make prophecies and give good advice about the future; it never pretended to be giving poetry readings.

If poems could be created in a trance without the conscious participation of the poet, the writing of poetry would be so boring or even unpleasant an operation that only a substantial reward in money or social prestige could induce a man to be a poet. From the manuscript evidence, it now appears that Coleridge's account of the composition of "Kubla Khan" was a fib.

It is true that, when he is writing a poem, it seems to a poet as if there were two people involved, his conscious self and a Muse whom he has to woo or an Angel with whom he has to wrestle, but, as in an ordinary wooing or wrestling match, his role is as important as Hers. The Muse, like Beatrice in *Much Ado*, is a spirited girl who has as little use for an abject suitor as she has for a vulgar brute. She appreciates chivalry and good manners, but she despises those who will not stand up to her and takes a cruel delight in telling them nonsense and lies which the poor little things obediently write down as "inspired" truth.

> When I was writing the chorus in G minor, I suddenly dipped my pen into the medicine bottle instead of the ink; I made a blot, and when I dried it with sand (blotting paper had not been invented then) it took the form of a natural, which instantly gave me the idea of the effect which the change from G minor to G major would make, and to this blot all the effect—if any—is due.
> (Rossini to Louis Engel.)

Such an act of judgment, distinguishing between Chance and Providence, deserves, surely, to be called an inspiration.

To keep his errors down to a minimum, the internal Censor to whom a poet submits his work in progress should be a Censorate. It should include, for instance, a sensitive only child, a practical housewife, a logician, a monk, an irreverent buffoòn and even, perhaps, hated by all the others and returning their dislike, a brutal, foul-mouthed drill sergeant who considers all poetry rubbish.

In the course of many centuries a few laborsaving devices have been introduced into the mental kitchen—alcohol, coffee, tobacco, Benzedrine, etc.—but these are very crude, constantly breaking down, and liable to injure the cook. Literary composition in the twentieth century A.D. is pretty much what it was in the twentieth century B.C.: nearly everything has still to be done by hand.

Most people enjoy the sight of their own handwriting as they enjoy the smell of their own farts. Much as I loathe the typewriter, I must admit that it is a help in self-criticism. Typescript is so impersonal and hideous to look at that, if I type out a poem, I immediately see defects which I missed when I looked through it in manuscript. When it comes to a poem by somebody else, the severest test I know of is to write it out in longhand. The physical tedium of doing this ensures that the slightest defect will reveal itself; the hand is constantly looking for an excuse to stop.

Most artists are sincere and most art is bad, though some insincere (sincerely insincere) works can be quite good. (STRAVINSKY.) Sincerity is like sleep. Normally, one should assume that, of course, one will be sincere, and not give the question a second thought. Most writers, however, suffer occasionally from bouts of insincerity as men do from bouts of insomnia. The remedy in both cases is often quite simple: in the case of the latter, to change one's diet, in the case of the former, to change one's company.

The schoolmasters of literature frown on affectations of style as silly and unhealthy. Instead of frowning, they ought to laugh indulgently. Shakespeare makes fun of the Euphuists in *Love's Labour's Lost* and in *Hamlet*, but he owed them a great deal and he knew it. Nothing, on the face of it, could have been more futile than the attempt of Spencer, Harvey and others to be good little humanists and write English verse in classical meters, yet, but for their folly, many of Campion's most beautiful songs and the choruses in *Samson Agonistes* would never have been written. In literature, as in life, affectation, passionately adopted and loyally persevered in, is one of the chief forms of self-discipline by which mankind has raised itself by its own bootstraps.

A mannered style, that of Góngora or Henry James, for example, is like eccentric clothing: very few writers can carry it off, but one is enchanted by the rare exception who can.

When a reviewer describes a book as "sincere," one knows immediately that it is a) insincere (insincerely insincere) and b) badly written. Sincerity in the proper sense of the word, meaning authenticity, is, however, or ought to be, a writer's chief preoccupation. No writer can ever judge exactly how good or bad a work of his may be, but he can always know, not immediately perhaps, but certainly in a short while, whether something he has written is authentic—in his handwriting—or a forgery.

The most painful of all experiences to a poet is to find that a poem of his which he knows to be a forgery has pleased the public and got into the anthologies. For all he knows or cares, the poem may be quite good, but that is not the point; *he* should not have written it.

The work of a young writer—*Werther* is the classic example—is sometimes a therapeutic act. He finds himself obsessed by certain ways of feeling and thinking of which his instinct tells him he must be rid before he can discover his authentic interests and sympathies, and the only way by which he can be rid of them forever is by surrendering to them. Once he has done this, he has developed the necessary antibodies which will make him immune for the rest of his life. As a rule, the disease is some spiritual malaise of his generation. If so, he may, as Goethe did, find himself in an embarrassing situation. What he wrote in order to exorcise certain feelings is enthusiastically welcomed by his contemporaries because it expresses just what they feel but, unlike him, they are perfectly happy to feel in this way; for the moment they regard him as their spokesman. Time passes. Having gotten the poison out of his system, the writer turns to his true interests which are not, and never were, those of his early admirers, who now pursue him with cries of "Traitor!"

> *The intellect of man is forced to choose*
> *Perfection of the life or of the work.* (YEATS.)

This is untrue; perfection is possible in neither. All one can say is that a writer who, like all men, has his personal weaknesses and limitations, should be aware of them and try his best to keep them out of his work. For every writer, there are certain subjects which, because of defects in his character and his talent, he should never touch.

What makes it difficult for a poet not to tell lies is that, in poetry, all facts and all beliefs cease to be true or false and become interesting possibilities. The reader does not have to share the beliefs expressed in a poem in order to enjoy it. Knowing this, a poet is constantly tempted to make use of an idea or a belief, not because he believes it to be true, but because he sees it has interesting poetic possibilities. It may not, perhaps, be absolutely necessary that he *believe* it, but it is certainly necessary that his emotions be deeply involved, and this they can never be unless, as a man, he takes it more seriously than as a mere poetic convenience.

The integrity of a writer is more threatened by appeals to his social conscience, his political or religious convictions, than by appeals to his cupidity. It is morally less confusing to be goosed by a traveling salesman than by a bishop.

Some writers confuse authenticity, which they ought always to aim at, with originality, which they should never bother about. There is a certain kind of person who is so dominated by the desire to be loved for himself alone that he has constantly to test those around him by tiresome behavior; what he says and does must be admired, not because it is intrinsically admirable, but because it is *his* remark, *his* act. Does not this explain a good deal of avant-garde art?

Slavery is so intolerable a condition that the slave can hardly escape deluding himself into thinking that he is choosing to obey his master's commands when, in fact, he is obliged to. Most slaves of habit suffer from this delusion and so do some writers, enslaved by an all too "personal" style.

> "Let me think: was I the same when I got up this morning? . . . But if I'm not the same, the next question is 'Who in the world am I?' . . . I'm sure I'm not Ada . . . for her hair goes in such long ringlets and mine doesn't go in ringlets at all; and I'm sure I can't be Mabel, for I know all sorts of things, and she, oh! she knows such a very little! Besides *she's* she and *I'm* I and—oh dear, how puzzling it all is! I'll try if I know all the things I used to know. . . ." Her eyes filled with tears . . . : "I must be Mabel after all, and I shall have to go and live in that poky little house, and have next to no toys to play with, and oh!—ever so many lessons to learn! No, I've made up my mind about it: if I'm Mabel, I'll stay down here!"
>
> (*Alice in Wonderland.*)

> At the next peg the Queen turned again and this time she said: "Speak in French when you can't think of the English for a thing—turn your toes out as you walk—and remember who you are."
>
> (*Through the Looking-Glass.*)

Most writers, except the supreme masters who transcend all systems of classification, are either Alices or Mabels. For example:

Alice	*Mabel*
Montaigne	Pascal
Marvell	Donne
Burns	Shelley
Jane Austen	Dickens
Turgenev	Dostoievski
Valéry	Gide
Virginia Woolf	Joyce
E. M. Forster	Lawrence
Robert Graves	Yeats

"Orthodoxy," said a real Alice of a bishop, "is reticence."

Except when used as historical labels, the terms *classical* and *romantic* are misleading terms for two poetic parties, the Aristocratic and the Democratic, which have always existed and to one of which every writer belongs, though he may switch his party allegiance or, on some specific issue, refuse to obey his Party Whip.

The Aristocratic Principle as regards subject matter:

No subject matter shall be treated by poets which poetry cannot digest. It defends poetry against didacticism and journalism.

The Democratic Principle as regards subject matter:

No subject matter shall be excluded by poets which poetry is capable of digesting. It defends poetry against limited or stale conceptions of what is "poetic."

The Aristocratic Principle as regards treatment:

No irrelevant aspects of a given subject shall be expressed in a poem which treats it. It defends poetry against barbaric vagueness.

The Democratic Principle as regards treatment:

No relevant aspect of a given subject shall remain unexpressed in a poem which treats it. It defends poetry against decadent triviality.

Every work of a writer should be a first step, but this will be a false step unless, whether or not he realize it at the time, it is also a further step. When a writer is dead, one ought to be able to see that his various works, taken together make one consistent *oeuvre*.

It takes little talent to see clearly what lies under one's nose, a good deal of it to know in which direction to point that organ.

The greatest writer cannot see through a brick wall but, unlike the rest of us, he does not build one.

Only a minor talent can be a perfect gentleman; a major talent is always more than a bit of a cad. Hence the importance of minor writers—as teachers of good manners. Now and again, an exquisite minor work can make a master feel thoroughly ashamed of himself.

The poet is the father of his poem; its mother is a language: one could list poems as race horses are listed—*out of L by P.*

A poet has to woo, not only his own Muse but also Dame Philology, and, for the beginner, the latter is the more important. As a rule, the sign that a beginner has a genuine original talent is that he is more interested in playing with words than in saying something original; his attitude is that of the old lady, quoted by E. M. Forster—"How can I know what I think till I see what I say?" It is only later, when he has wooed and won Dame Philology, that he can give his entire devotion to his Muse.

Rhymes, meters, stanza forms, etc., are like servants. If the master is fair enough to win their affection and firm enough to command their respect, the result is an orderly happy household. If he is too tyrannical, they give notice; if he lacks authority, they become slovenly, impertinent, drunk and dishonest.

The poet who writes "free" verse is like Robinson Crusoe on his desert island: he must do all his cooking, laundry and darning for himself. In a few exceptional cases, this manly independence produces something original and impressive, but more often the result is squalor—dirty sheets on the unmade bed and empty bottles on the unswept floor.

There are some poets, Kipling for example, whose relation to language reminds one of a drill sergeant: the words are taught to wash behind their ears, stand properly at attention and execute complicated maneuvers, but at the cost of never being allowed to think for themselves. There are others, Swinburne, for example, who remind one more of Svengali: under their hypnotic suggestion, an extraordinary performance is put on, not by raw recruits, but by feeble-minded schoolchildren.

Due to the Curse of Babel, poetry is the most provincial of the arts, but today, when civilization is becoming monotonously the same all the world over, one feels inclined to regard this as a blessing rather than a curse: in poetry, as least, there cannot be an "International Style."

My language is the universal whore whom I have to make into a virgin. (KARL KRAUS.) It is both the glory and the shame of poetry that its medium is not its private property, that a poet cannot invent his words and that words are products, not of nature, but of a human society which uses them for a thousand different purposes. In modern societies where language is continually being debased and reduced to nonspeech, the poet is in constant danger of having his ear corrupted, a danger to which the painter and the composer, whose media are their private property, are not exposed. On the other hand he is more protected than they from another modern peril, that of solipsist subjectivity; however esoteric a poem may be, the fact that all its words have meanings which can be looked up in a dictionary makes it testify to the existence of other people.

Even the language of *Finnegans Wake* was not created by Joyce *ex nihilo;* a purely private verbal world is not possible.

The difference between verse and prose is self-evident, but it is a sheer waste of time to look for a definition of the difference between poetry and prose. Frost's definition of poetry as the untranslatable element in language looks plausible at first sight but, on closer examination, will not quite do. In the first place, even in the most rarefied poetry, there are some elements which are translatable. The sound of the words, their rhythmical relations, and all meanings and association of meanings which depend upon sound, like rhymes and puns, are, of course, untranslatable, but poetry is not, like music, pure sound. Any elements in a poem which are not based on verbal experience are, to some degree, translatable into another tongue, for example, images, similes and metaphors which are drawn from sensory experience. Moreover, because one characteristic that all men, whatever their culture, have in common is uniqueness—every man is a member of a class of one—the unique perspective on the world which every genuine poet has survives translation. If one takes a poem by Goethe and a poem by Hölderlin and makes literal prose cribs of them, every reader will recognize that the two poems were written by two different people. In the second place, if speech can never become music, neither can it ever become algebra. Even in the most "prosy" language, in informative and technical prose, there is a personal element because language is a personal creation. *Ne pas se pencher au dehors* has a different feeling tone from *Nichthinauslehnen.* A purely poetic language would be unlearnable, a purely prosaic not worth learning.

Valéry bases his definitions of poetry and prose on the difference between the gratuitous and the useful, play and work, and uses as an analogy the difference between dancing and walking. But this will not do either. A commuter may walk to his suburban station every morning, but at the same time he may enjoy the walk for its own sake; the fact that his walk is necessary does not exclude the possibility of its also being a form of play. Vice versa, a dance does not cease to be play if it is also believed to have a useful purpose like promoting a good harvest.

If French poets have been more prone than English to fall into the heresy of thinking that poetry ought to be as much like music as possible, one reason may be that, in traditional French verse, sound effects have always played a much more important role than they have in English verse. The English-speaking peoples have always felt that the difference between poetic speech and the conversational speech of everyday should be kept small, and, whenever English poets have felt that the gap between poetic and ordinary speech was growing too wide, there has been a stylistic revolution to bring them closer again. In English verse, even in Shake-

speare's grandest rhetorical passages, the ear is always aware of its relation to everyday speech. A good actor must—alas, today he too seldom
does—make the audience hear Shakespeare's lines as verse not prose, but if
he tries to make the verse sound like a different language, he will make
himself ridiculous.

But French poetry, both in the way it is written and the way it is recited,
has emphasized and gloried in the difference between itself and ordinary
speech; in French drama, verse and prose *are* different languages. Valéry
quotes a contemporary description of Rachel's powers of declamation; in
reciting she could and did use a range of two octaves, from F below Middle
C to F in alt; an actress who tried to do the same with Shakespeare as
Rachel did with Racine would be laughed off the stage.

One can read Shakespeare to oneself without even mentally *hearing*
the lines and be very moved; indeed, one may easily find a performance
disappointing because almost anyone with an understanding of English
verse can speak it better than the average actor and actress. But to read
Racine to oneself, even, I fancy, if one is a Frenchman, is like reading the
score of an opera when one can hardly play or sing; one can no more get
an adequate notion of *Phèdre* without having heard a great performance,
than one can of *Tristan und Isolde* if one has never heard a great Isolde
like Leider or Flagstad.

(Monsieur St. John Perse tells me that, when it comes to everyday
speech, it is French which is the more monotonous and English which has
the wider range of vocal inflection.)

I must confess that French classical tragedy strikes me as being opera
for the unmusical. When I read the *Hippolytus*, I can recognize, despite all
differences, a kinship between the world of Euripides and the world of
Shakespeare, but the world of Racine, like the world of opera, seems to be
another planet altogether. Euripides' Aphrodite is as concerned with fish
and fowl as she is with human beings; Racine's Venus is not only unconcerned with animals, she takes no interest in the Lower Orders. It is impossible to imagine any of Racine's characters sneezing or wanting to go
to the bathroom, for in his world there is neither weather nor nature. In
consequence, the passions by which his characters are consumed can only
exist, as it were, on stage, the creation of the magnificent speech and the
grand gestures of the actors and actresses who endow them with flesh and
blood. This is also the case in opera, but no speaking voice, however
magnificent, can hope to compete, in expressiveness through sound, with a
great singing voice backed by an orchestra.

*Whenever people talk to me about the weather, I always feel certain that
they mean something else.* (OSCAR WILDE.) The only kind of speech which
approximates to the symbolist's poetic ideal is polite tea table conversation, in which the meaning of the banalities uttered depends almost en-

tirely upon vocal inflections.

Owing to its superior power as a mnemonic, verse is superior to prose as a medium for didactic instruction. Those who condemn didacticism must disapprove *a fortiori* of didactic prose; in verse, as the Alka-Seltzer advertisements testify, the didactic message loses half its immodesty. Verse is also certainly the equal of prose as a medium for the lucid exposition of ideas; in skillful hands, the form of the verse can parallel and reinforce the steps of the logic. Indeed, contrary to what most people who have inherited the romantic conception of poetry believe, the danger of argument in verse—Pope's *Essay on Man* is an example—is that the verse may make the ideas *too* clear and distinct, more Cartesian than they really are.

On the other hand, verse is unsuited to controversy, to proving some truth or belief which is not universally accepted, because its formal nature cannot but convey a certain skepticism about its conclusions.

> Thirty days hath September,
> April, June and November

is valid because nobody doubts its truth. Were there, however, a party who passionately denied it, the lines would be powerless to convince him because, formally, it would make no difference if the lines ran:

> Thirty days hath September,
> August, May and December.

Poetry is not magic. In so far as poetry, or any other of the arts, can be said to have an ulterior purpose, it is, by telling the truth, to disenchant and disintoxicate.

"The unacknowledged legislators of the world" describes the secret police, not the poets.

Catharsis is properly effected, not by works of art, but by religious rites. It is also effected, usually improperly, by bullfights, professional football matches, bad movies, military bands and monster rallies at which ten thousand girl guides form themselves into a model of the national flag.

The condition of mankind is, and always has been, so miserable and depraved that, if anyone were to say to the poet: "For God's sake stop singing and do something useful like putting on the kettle or fetching bandages," what just reason could he give for refusing? But nobody says this. The self-appointed unqualified nurse says: "You are to sing the patient a song which will make him believe that I, and I alone, can cure him. If you can't or won't, I shall confiscate your passport and send you to the mines." And the poor patient in his delirium cries: "Please sing me a song which will give me sweet dreams instead of nightmares. If you succeed, I will give you a penthouse in New York or a ranch in Arizona."

Ralph Ellison

(1914–   )

In his writings Ralph Ellison has moved far outside the parish into which he was born; he has spoken not only for his race but for humanity. In 1965 Book Week conducted a poll of literary critics, and they adjudged Ellison's Invisible Man the most distinguished novel of the previous twenty years; the book has seemed to gain power with each decade that has passed. Over these years, while going on with his proper work, Ellison has also granted a number of interviews, each remarkable in its way, all more or less dominated by an argument Ellison himself did not really choose but which has been thrust upon him more than on any other first-rank novelist of our time, save perhaps Alexander Solzhenitsyn— namely, the polemic-versus-artistic argument, the discussion whether art should persuade or simply be. In the face of all sorts of political and social pressure, Ellison has managed to keep his eyes steadfastly on the far, wide, mountainous skyline of his craft. In this interview he turns away from that argument and tells some of what his eyes have seen along those ranges—tells of the deep familial and existential sources of his vision, of how his mind works through creative problems, of how his connections with his own and others' cultures have shaped his work, of his uses of dream and musical sound and unconscious pattern in the patient building of his massive fictions.

"A COMPLETION OF PERSONALITY"
Interviewer: John Hersey

HERSEY: You were talking about your mother last night, and as you talked I wondered how much she had been a force in moving you toward your calling as a writer, and even in supplying materials that you have drawn on.

ELLISON: She certainly had something to do with encouraging my interest in reading. She had no idea that I was going to become a writer, or if she did, she had more insight into me than I had into myself, because I thought I was going to be a musician. My mother always encouraged me to do *something*, and to be good at it—she insisted upon that.

It was my father who wanted me to be a writer. I didn't discover that until many years later—he died when I was three—until after I had written *Invisible Man* and talked with an older cousin, who told me that my father had used to say, "I'm raising this boy to be a poet." Of course he had given me the name [Ralph Waldo].

But my mother did feed my passion for reading. She brought home books and magazines. My concern with the Picassos and Stravinskys of this world started at an earlier age than usual because she brought home *Vanity Fair*. Here was a world so far from Oklahoma City, in any expected sense, yet it was shaping my sense of what was possible. And she understood that that was what was going on.

And what I did get from my mother was an understanding of people. I was very quick-tempered and impatient, and things began to happen when I reached adolescence—and she would just talk about how people acted, what motives were, and why things were sometimes done. I remember being so outraged by something one of her friends had said that I didn't want to see her or her husband anymore. At thirteen I went to work as the husband's office boy and this close friend of my father was so delighted with having me around that his childless wife was upset. Her reaction was to spread the word around that she suspected that I was actually her husband's child—Oh, boy! When the gossip reached me I was outraged—and not only over what it implied about my mother, but because of my love for my father. I had learned to walk at six months and had been his companion from that time until his death, and I was so far from accepting the reality of his death that I was still telling myself that any day he would reappear to take his place as the head of our family. Now I suspect that my fondness for my employer-friend and my vague awareness that he was, in fact, something of a father-figure added to my shock and outrage. At any rate, when I went to my mother about this matter she proceeded to calm me down.

"Well now," she said, "you should understand what's happening. You remember your daddy and you've been around and seen a few people and have some idea how they act. You've been working in drugstores and barbershops and at that office and since you've been around . . . and . . . as much as you have, you must know that she's crazy. So use your head. She doesn't have to be put in an institution, but you have to understand and accept the fact that she isn't responsible."

It was a rather shocking notion for me and I didn't want to surrender my anger, but I realized that my mother was right. What's more, I realized that very often I could save myself a lot of wear and tear with people if I just learned to understand them.

Beyond that, although she was religious, my mother had a great tolerance for the affairs of the world which had nothing to do with religion, and I think that that helped me to sort of balance things out, so to speak. The great emphasis in my school was upon classical music, but such great jazz musicians as Hot Lips Paige, Jimmy Rushing, and Lester Young were living in Oklahoma City, and through her allowing me to attend public dances and to maintain a certain friendship with some of them, even though she watched what I was doing, she made it possible to approach the life of the Negro community there with some sense of its wholeness instead of trying to distort it into some hoped-for religion-conceived perfection. As it turned out, the perfection, the artistic dedication which helped me as a writer, was not so much in the classical emphasis as within the jazz itself.

She also helped me to escape the limitations of trying to impose any in-group class distinctions upon the people of my community. We were very poor, but my father had been a small businessman who sold ice and coal to both whites and blacks, and since he and my mother were pioneers in a young state, my mother knew some of the city's leaders; they were my father's friends and remained as my mother's after his death. So she didn't strive to be part of the social leadership of the black community, that was left to the wives of professional men, to teachers and preachers. Her background and attitudes were such that all kinds of people came into the house, or we visited their homes. That was one of the enriching parts of my experience, because I knew people who went right back to the farm and plantation, along with those who had gone to college and medical school. Thus my sense of their stories and life-styles, and so on, was never very far from mind. My mother had grown up on a Georgia plantation herself, she was a farm girl; and then she left and went to live in Atlanta. It gave me a sense of a past which was far from narrow.

She liked to talk. She never allowed me to lose the vividness of my father, and she told me all kinds of things that he had done—that he had run away from his own father in South Carolina when he was quite young, and had become a professional soldier, and had been in Cuba and in the Philippines and in China. He was with our troops that fought against the Boxer Rebellion. Afterwards, he and his brother had operated a candy kitchen in Chattanooga. He had also operated a restaurant —always trying to get at something—and then had become a construction foreman; that was how they came west to Oklahoma.

There was also her overt and explicit concern with political conditions. There was never a time when I was not aware of what these were all about. When I was in college, my mother broke a segregated-housing ordinance in Oklahoma City, and they were throwing her in jail, and the NAACP would get her out, and they'd come back and throw her in jail again. This went on until my brother beat up one of the white inspectors, then she decided that it was about time to get out of that situation before he got himself shot. She had that kind of forthrightness, and I like to think that that was much more valuable than anything literary that she gave me.

HERSEY: The creative drive seems always to have been strong in you, ever since childhood. You said once that you couldn't remember a time when you hadn't wanted to make something—a one-tube radio, a crystal set, a toy; a little later you had an urge to compose music. Where do you think this drive came from?

ELLISON: I don't know where it comes from. Maybe it had something to do with my father's working as a construction foreman, building buildings. It certainly came from some of the boys that I grew up with, as a child. They were always *doing* things. I always admired the guys who could make things, who could draw. This was something that gave me a great deal of pleasure.

But maybe the desire to write goes back to a Christmas gift. One Christmas my mother gave me—I must have been five—a little roll-top desk and a chair, not a swivel chair but a little straight chair, oak, and a little toy typewriter. I had forgotten that. We were living in the parsonage of the old A.M.E. Church, Avery Chapel, which the leaders of the congregation turned over to my mother after the new minister turned out to have his own home. "Why don't you be the janitress of the church and live in the parsonage?" they said. And we did, and that's where I got the desk and the little typewriter. I was also given a chemistry set. Now this might have been unusual in such relatively uneducated families—I think my mother went to the eighth grade in school—but she felt that these were the kinds of things that her boys should have. She was also very explicit, as we grew older, about our economic condition. We knew why we could not have a bicycle, why we could not have this, that, or the other. She explained that we could not have such things because she didn't have the money, and we had to accept that fact. So what did we do? We learned to do other things. Instead of playing with store-bought toys, you made your own. You fished and hunted, you listened to music, you danced and you spent a great amount of time reading and dreaming over books.

When Mr. Mead, next door, taught me the fundamentals of playing an old brass alto horn, my mother bought me a pawn-shop cornet. She could afford that, and owning the instrument made it possible for me to acquire enough skill to get into the school band. So she did what she could, and in addition to encouraging my interest in reading she encouraged my interest in music, and so on.

But the desire to make something out of my imagination and to experiment was constant. In one story of mine there is an incident taken from life, where my brother and I took baby chickens and made little parachutes and got up on top of the chicken house and dropped them down. The lady next door told my mother, and we caught hell for that. We didn't kill the chickens, understand, we just floated them down. We did that, you see, because we had learned to take iron taps and tie strings to them and then attach the strings to pieces of cloth. When we threw these into the air we'd get a parachute effect and imagine that the taps were parachutists. We just took it a step further.

HERSEY: What would you say was the starting point for your new novel?

ELLISON: I guess it started with the idea of an old man being so outraged by his life that he goes poking around in the cellar to find a forgotten coffin, which he had bought years before to insure against his possible ruin. He discovers that he has lived so long that the coffin is full of termites, and that even the things he had stored in the coffin have fallen apart. Somehow, this said something to my imagination and got me started. You can see that it could go in *any* direction. But then it led to the other idea, which I wrote first, of a little boy being placed in a coffin, in a ritual of death and transcendence, celebrated by a Negro evangelist who was unsure whether he was simply exploiting the circus side-show shock set off by the sight of a child rising up out of a coffin, or had hit upon an inspired way of presenting the sacred drama of the Resurrection. In my mind all of this is tied up in some way with the significance of being a Negro in America and at the same time with the problem of our democratic faith as a whole. Anyway, as a product of the imagination it's like a big sponge, maybe, or a waterbed, with a lot of needles sticking in it at various points. You don't know what is being touched, where the needles are going to end up once you get them threaded and penetrated, but somehow I kept trying to tie those threads together and the needle points pressing home without letting whatever lies in the center leak out.

HERSEY: How soon after *Invisible Man* was published [1952] did you start working on the new novel?

ELLISON: I was pretty depleted by *Invisible Man*, so I didn't start on another book immediately. I played around with various ideas and spent some time trying to salvage material I had edited out of *Invisible Man*. It was in Rome, during 1956, that I began to think vaguely about this book and conceived the basic situation, which had to do with a political assassination; this was involved with the other patterns—the coffin business.

HERSEY: This was before the Kennedys and King were assassinated, of course.

ELLISON: Yes, this was before. Almost eight years before. One of the things which really chilled me—and slowed down the writing—was that eruption of assassinations, especially the first. Because, you see, much of the mood of this book was conceived as comic. Not that the assassination was treated comically, but there is humor involved, and that was rather chilling for me, because suddenly life was stepping in and imposing itself upon my fiction. Anyway, I managed to keep going with it, I guess because there was nothing else to do. I know that it led me to try to give the book a richer structuring, so that the tragic elements could contain the comic and the comic the tragic, without violating our national pieties—if there are any left. Americans have always been divided in their pieties, but today there is such a deliberate flaunting of the pieties and traditions—of others, anyway—that it's become rather difficult to distinguish what is admissible from that which is inadmissible. Even the flag and motherhood are under attack.

HERSEY: With such fast-moving reality so close at hand, how much in control of your fictional characters can you feel that you are?

ELLISON: Once a logic is set up for a character, once he begins to move, then that which is implicit within him tends to realize itself, and for you to discover the *form* of the fiction, you have to go where he takes you, you have to follow him. In the process you change your ideas. You remember, Dostoievski wrote about eight versions of a certain scene in *The Brothers Karamazov*, and in some instances the original incidents were retained but the characters who performed them were changed. I find that happens with me. I get to the point where something has to be done and discover that it isn't logical for the character who started out to do it, to do it; and suddenly another character pops up. In this book there is an instance wherein McIntyre has to interview the man who burns his Cadillac. This man is being held in the observation cell of a hospital because the authorities believe that a Negro who burns his own Cadillac has to be crazy. So for McIntyre to see the man there has to be an intermediary—so suddenly I found myself dealing with a new character, a Negro employed by the hospital, who gets McIntyre past the barriers and to the car-burner. This fellow wasn't foreseen; he simply appeared to help me get on with the form.

HERSEY: About motive—what gives you the psychic energy to take on a massive work and keep at it for a very long time?

ELLISON: I guess it is the writing itself. I am terribly stubborn, and once I get engaged in that kind of project, I just have to keep going until I finally make something out of it. I don't know what the something is going to be, but the process is one through which I make a good part of my own experience meaningful. I don't mean in any easy auto-biographical sense, but the matter of drawing actual experience, thought, and emotion together in a way that creates an artifact through which I can reach other people. Maybe that's vanity; I don't know. Still I believe that fiction does help create value, and I regard this as a very serious—I almost said "sacred"—function of the writer.

Psychic energy? I don't know, I think of myself as kind of lazy. And yet, I do find that working slowly, which is the only way I seem able to work—although I write fast much of the time—the problem is one of being able to receive from my work that sense of tension, that sense of high purpose being realized, that keeps me going. This is a crazy area that I don't understand—none of the Freudian explanations seem ade-quate.

HERSEY: As to the short range, you used a phrase last night that inter-ested me. You said you wanted to keep the early morning free "in case the night before had generated something that could be put to good use." What did you mean by that?

ELLISON: I never know quite what has gone on in my subconscious in the night, I dream vividly, and all kinds of things happen; by morning they have fallen below the threshold again. But I like to feel that whatever takes place becomes active in some way in what I do at the typewriter. In other words, I believe that a human being's life is of a whole, and that he lives the full twenty-four hours. And if he is a writer or an artist, what happens during the night feeds back, in some way, into what he does consciously during the day—that is, when he is doing that which is self-achieving, so to speak. Part of the pleasure of writing, as well as the pain, is involved in pouring into that thing which is being created all of what he cannot understand and cannot say and cannot deal with, or cannot even admit, in any other way. The artifact is a completion of personality.

HERSEY: Do you experience anything like daydreaming or dreaming when you are writing? Do you feel that the writing process may involve a somewhat altered state of consciousness in itself?

ELLISON: I think a writer learns to be as conscious about his craft as he can possibly be—not because this will make him absolutely lucid about what he does, but because it prepares the stage for structuring his daydreaming and allows him to draw upon the various irrational elements involved in writing. You know that when you begin to structure literary forms you are going to have to play variations on your themes, and you are going to have to make everything vivid, so that the reader can see and hear and feel and smell, and, if you're lucky, even taste. All that is on a conscious level and very, very important. But then, once you get going, strange things occur. There are things in *Invisible Man*, for instance, that I can't *imagine* my having consciously planned. They materialized as I worked consciously at other things. Take three of the speeches: the speech made at the eviction, the funeral address in Mount Morris Park, and the one that Barbee made in chapel. Now, I realized consciously, or I *discovered* as I wrote, that I was playing variations on what Otto Rank identified as the myth of the birth and death of the hero. So in the re-writing that conscious knowledge, that insight, made it possible to come back and add elements to the design which I had written myself into under the passion of telling a story.

What should also be said in this connection is that somewhere—it doesn't have to be right in the front of the mind, of the consciousness—writers, like other artists, are involved in a process of comparative culture. I looked at the copy of *The Lower Depths* on the table there this morning, and I remembered how much of Gorki I had read, and how I was always—not putting his characters into blackface, but finding equivalents for the experience he depicted; the equivalents for turns of phrase, for parables and proverbs, which existed within the various backgrounds which I knew. And I think that something of that goes on when a conscious writer goes about creating a fiction. It's part of his workshop, his possession of the culture of the form in which he works.

HERSEY: You once said that it took you a long time to learn how to adapt myth and ritual into your work. Faulkner speaks of a "lumber room of the unconscious," where old things are kept. How do you get at the sources of these things deep down in your mind?

ELLISON: I think I get at them through sheer work, converting incidents into patterns—and also by simply continuing at a thing when I don't seem to be getting anywhere. For instance, I wrote a scene in which Hickman is thinking about the difficulty of communicating with someone as constituting a "wall"; he thinks this as he is drifting off to sleep. Well, later in my work I suddenly realized that the damn wall had turned up again in another form. And that's when that voice in my unconscious finally said, "Hey, *this* is what you've been getting at." And looking back, I saw that I had worked up a little pattern of these walls. What the unconscious mind does is to put all manner of things into juxtaposition. The conscious mind has to provide the logical structure of narrative and incident through which these unconscious patterns can be allowed to radiate by throwing them into artful juxtaposition on the page.

HERSEY: Do you, as some writers do, have a sense of standing in a magic circle when you write?

ELLISON: To the extent that unexpected things occur, that characters say things, or see things which, for all my attempts to be conscious and to work out of what I call a conceptual outline, are suddenly just *there*. That *is* magical, because such things seem to emerge out of the empty air. And yet, you know that somehow the dreams, emotions, ironies, and hidden implications of your material often find ways of making themselves manifest. You work to make them reveal themselves.

HERSEY: Do you, when you are writing, sometimes find yourself so totally engaged by a character that you are carried away outside yourself by *his* feelings—are literally beside yourself?

ELLISON: I find myself carried away and emotionally moved, sometimes quite unexpectedly, and my tendency is to distrust it, feeling that perhaps I'm being sentimental, being caught in a situation which I am not adequately transforming into art. So I put it aside and wait awhile, maybe months, and then go back, and if it still works after I've examined it as well as I can, as objectively as I can, I then perhaps read it to Fanny, and if she doesn't indicate that it's slobbering sentimentality, in bad taste, or just poorly achieved—then I leave it in.

HERSEY: Would you say that, by and large, when you have had these surges of feeling the writing does hold up in the long run?

ELLISON: Sometimes it does, sometimes it doesn't. I won't be able to say about this book until it has been read by enough objective readers. I won't be able to judge until then because it has some crazy developments.

I found myself writing a scene in which Hickman and Wilhite, his deacon, go into a strange house in Washington, and find a bunch of people in the hallway who are very upset because the police won't tell them what has happened in the apartment of one of their neighbors. Then one of the women goes hysterical and pretty soon she's outraging the crowd by talking about the most personal matters as she addresses herself to a bewildered Wilhite and Hickman. Not only was I shocked to discover myself writing this unplanned scene, but I still have questions about how it functions. Yet, for all its wild, tragicomic emotion— there it is! Now when your material takes over like that you are really being pushed. Thus, when this woman started confessing, she forced *me* to think about Hickman's role as minister on a different level; I mean on the theological level; which was something I hadn't planned, since I wasn't writing an essay but a novel. Finally, Hickman came to my aid by recognizing that the woman had been unfolding a distorted and highly personalized dream-version of the immaculate birth. To me she sounded merely irrational and comic, but Hickman, being a minister, forced himself to look beneath her raving, even though she is without question a most unacceptable surrogate for the Virgin. After that, I was forced to realize that this crazy development was really tied in with the central situation of the novel: that of an old man searching throughout the years for a little boy who ran away. So I guess it sprang from that magic circle you referred to, from that amorphous level which lies somewhere between the emotions and the intellect, between the consciousness and the unconscious which supports our creative powers but which we cannot control.

HERSEY: I have wondered about the ways in which your musical experience has fed into your writing.

ELLISON: My sense of form, my basic sense of artistic form, is musical. As a boy I tried to write songs, marches, exercises in symphonic form, really before I received any training, and then I studied it. I listened constantly to music, trying to learn the processes of developing a theme, of expanding and contracting and turning it inside out, of making bridges, and working with techniques of musical continuity, and so on. I think that basically my instinctive approach to writing is through *sound*. A change of mood and mode comes to me in terms of sound. That's one part of it, in the sense of composing the architecture of a fiction.

On the other hand, one of the things I work for is to make a line of prose *sound* right, or for a bit of dialogue to fall on the page in the way I hear it, aurally, in my mind. The same goes for the sound and intonation of a character's voice. When I am writing of characters who speak in the Negro idiom, in the vernacular, it is still a real problem for me to make their accents fall in the proper place in the visual line.

HERSEY: Which comes first for you in writing, hearing or seeing?

ELLISON: I might conceive of a thing aurally, but to realize it you have got to make it vivid. The two things must operate together. What is the old phrase—"the planned dislocation of the senses"? That *is* the condition of fiction, I think. Here is where sound becomes sight and sight becomes sound, and where sign becomes symbol and symbol becomes sign; where fact and idea must not just be hanging there but must become a functioning part of the total design, involving itself in the reader as idea as well as drama. You do this by providing the reader with as much detail as is possible in terms of the visual *and* the aural, *and* the rhythmic—to allow him to involve himself, to attach himself, and then begin to collaborate in the creation of the fictional spell. Because you simply cannot put it all there on the page, you can only evoke it—or evoke what is already there, implicitly, in the reader's head: his sense of life.

HERSEY: You mentioned "making bridges" a minute ago. I remember that you once said that your anxiety about transitions greatly prolonged the writing of *Invisible Man*.

ELLISON: Yes, that has continued to be something of a problem. I try to tell myself that it is irrational, but it is what happens when you're making something, and you know that you are *making* something rather than simply relating an anecdote that actually happened. But at the same time you have to strike a balance between that which you can imply and that which you must make explicit, so that the reader can follow you. One source of this anxiety comes, I think, from my sense of the variations in American backgrounds—especially as imposed by the racial situation. I can't always be certain that what I write is going to be understood. Now, this doesn't mean that I am writing for whites, but that I realize that as an American writer I have a problem of communicating across our various social divisions, whether of race, class, education, region, or religion—and much of this holds true even within my own racial group. It's dangerous to take things for granted.

This reminds me of something that happened out at a northwestern university. A young white professor said to me, "Mr. Ellison, how does it feel to be able to go to places where most Negroes can't go?" Before I could think to be polite I answered, "What you mean is: 'How does it feel to be able to go places where most *white* men can't go?'" He was shocked and turned red, and I was embarrassed; nevertheless, it was a teaching situation so I told him the truth. I wanted him to understand that individuality is still operative beyond the racial structuring of American society. And that, conversely, there are many areas of black society that are closed to *me* while open to certain whites. Friendship and shared interests make the difference.

When you are writing fiction out of your individual sense of American life it's difficult to know what to take for granted. For instance, I don't know whether I can simply refer to an element of decor and communicate the social values it stands for, because so much depends upon the way a reader makes associations. I am more confident in such matters than I was when writing *Invisible Man*, but for such an allusion—say, to a certain type of chair or vase or painting—to function, the reader must not be allowed to limit his understanding of what is implied simply because the experience you are presenting is, in its immediate sense, that of blacks. So the writer must be aware that the reality of race conceals a complex of manners and culture. Because such matters influence the shaping of fictional form and govern, to a large extent, the writer's sense of proportion, and determine what he feels obligated to render as well as what he feels he can simply imply.

I had to learn, for instance, that in dramatic scenes, if you got the reader going along with your own rhythm; you could omit any number of explanations. You could leave great gaps, because in his sense of urgency the reader would say, "Hell, don't waste time telling me how many steps he walked to get there, I want to know what he *did* once he got there!" An ellipsis was possible and the reader would fill the gap.

Still, I have uncertainty about some of the things I'm doing, and especially when I'm using more than one main voice, and with a time scheme that is much more fragmented than in *Invisible Man*. There I was using a more tidy dramatic form. This novel is dramatic within its incidents, but it moves back and forth in time. In such a case I guess an act of faith is necessary, a faith that if what you are writing is of social and artistic importance and its diverse parts are presented vividly in the light of its overall conception, and if you *render* the story rather than just tell it, then the reader will go along. That's a lot of 'ifs,' but if you can involve him in the process his reading becomes a pleasurable act of discovery.

HERSEY: Do you have in mind an image of some actualized reader to whom you are communicating as you write?

ELLISON: There is no *specific* person there, but there is a sort of ideal reader, or informed persona, who has some immediate sense of the material that I'm working with. Beyond that there is my sense of the rhetorical levers within American society, and these attach to all kinds of experiences and values. I don't want to be a behaviorist here, but I'm referring to the systems of values, the beliefs and customs and sense of the past, and that hope for the future which have evolved through the history of the republic. These do provide a medium of communication.

For instance, the old underdog pattern. It turns up in many guises, and it allows the writer to communicate with the public over and beyond whatever the immediate issues of his fiction happen to be. That is, deep down we believe in the underdog, even though we give him hell; and this provides a rhetoric through which the writer can communicate with a reader beyond any questions of their disagreements over class values, race, or anything else. But the writer must be aware that that is what is there. On the other hand, I do not think he can manipulate his readers too directly; it must be an oblique process, if for no other reason than that to do it too directly throws you into propaganda, as against that brooding, questioning stance that is necessary for fiction.

HERSEY: How do literary influences make themselves felt concretely in your work? You have spoken often of Joyce, Eliot, Dostoievski, Hemingway, Stein, Malraux, and others as having influenced you early. How do the influences manifest themselves? How have you transformed them for your own ends?

ELLISON: It is best, of course, when they don't show themselves directly, but they are there in many ways. Joyce and Eliot, for instance, made me aware of the playful possibilities of language. You look at a page of *Finnegan's Wake* and see references to all sorts of American popular music, yet the context gives it an extension from the popular back to the classical and beyond. This is just something that Joyce teaches you that you can do, and you can abstract the process and apply it to a frame of reference which is American and historical, and it can refer to class, it can refer to the fractions and frictions of color, to popular and folk culture—it can do many things.

On the other hand, a writer makes himself present in your work through allowing you to focus upon certain aspects of experience. Malraux's concern with the individual caught up consciously in a historical situation, a revolutionary situation, provided insights which allowed me to understand certain possibilities in the fictional material around me. From him I learned that the condition of that type of individual is essentially the same, regardless of his culture or the political climate in which he finds his existence.

Or again, some writers—say, Dostoievski, or even Tolstoy—will make you very much aware of what is possible in depicting a society in which class lines are either fluid or have broken down without the cultural style and values on either extreme of society being dissipated. From such writers you learn to explore the rich fictional possibilities to be achieved in juxtaposing the peasant's consciousness with that of the aristocrat and the aristocrat's with the peasant's. This insight is useful when you are dealing with American society. For years, white people went through Grand Central Station having their luggage carried by Ph.D.s. They couldn't see the Ph.D.s because their race and class attitudes had trained them to see only the uniforms and the dark faces, but the Ph.D.s could see them and judged them on any number of levels. This makes for drama, and it is a drama which goes right to the core of the democratic faith. So you get your moral perception of the contradictions of American class and personality from such literature, even more, perhaps, than from psychiatry or sociology, because such novelists have always dealt with the drama of social living.

HERSEY: You once had some very interesting things to say about the similarities and differences of the stances of black and Jewish writers in this country. It seems clear that Russian novelists have had a special kind of access to the deeper resources we were talking about earlier, access to primary feelings. Do you think there are particular ways in which Negro writers have had a corresponding access to those deeper resources—different in kind or degree from that of the Jewish writer, or the white Protestant writer in America, say, or the Russian writer, or the English writer?

ELLISON: You will have to be very careful about that, because writers are individuals, each unique in his own way. But I would think that the access to primary feelings that the great Russian novelists had grew out of the nature of their society and the extreme disruption of hierarchal relationships which occurred during the nineteenth century. Then you had a great declassed aristocracy, with the Tsar still at the top, and an awakening peasantry at the bottom. On one hand, society was plunging headlong into chaos, and on the other there was a growing identification on the part of many declassed aristocrats with the peasantry, an identification across traditional hierarchal divisions which was sustained by the unifying force of Russian Greek Orthodox Christianity. The friction generated by these social unities and divisions in that chaotic scene made possible all kinds of intensities of emotion and aggravations of sensibility. The belief in the Tsar as a sacred "Little Father" remained a unifying force, but was no longer strong enough to rationalize and impose order upon the expression of primary emotions —class hate, greed, ambition and so on. Such disruption of the traditional ordering of society, as in our own country since 1954, made for an atmosphere of irrationality, and this created a situation of unrestrained expressiveness. Eyeballs were peeled, nerves were laid bare and private sensibilities were subjected to public laceration. In fact, life became so theatrical (not to say nightmarish) that even Dostoievski's smoking imagination was barely able to keep a step ahead of what was actually happening in the garrets and streets. Today, here in the U.S. we have something similar, but there's no point in my trying to explain Russian extremism, or the genius of the great nineteenth-century Russian novelists. Not even Dostoievski was able to do that.

Anyway, for all its expressiveness and chaos, the Negro American situation is something else, both in degree and source. Except for the brief period of Reconstruction, when we helped create the new constitutions of the southern states and attempted to restructure society so as to provide a more equal set of relationships between the classes and races, we were *below* the threshold of social hierarchy. Our social mobility was strictly, and violently, limited—and in a way that neither our Christianity nor belief in the principles of the Constitution could change. As the sociologists say, we were indeed disadvantaged, both by law and by custom. And yet, our actual position was ambiguous. For although we were outside the social compact, we were existentially right in the middle of the social drama. I mean that as servants we were right in the bedroom, so to speak. Thus we saw things, and we understood the difference between ideal assertions and crude realities. Much of the rhetorical and political energy of white society went toward proving to itself that we were not human and that we had no sense of the refinement of human values. But this in itself pressured you, motivated you, to make even finer distinctions, both as to personality and value. You *had* to, because your life depended upon it and your sense of your own humanity demanded that you do so. You had to identify those values which were human and preserving of your life and interests as against those which were inhuman and destructive. So we were thrown upon our own resources and sense of life. We were forced to define and act out our own idea of the heights and depths of the human condition. Because human beings cannot live in a situation where violence can be visited upon them without any concern for justice—and in many instances without possibility of redress—without developing a very intense sense of the precariousness of all human life, not to mention the frailty and arbitrariness of human institutions. So you were forced to be existential in your outlook, and this gives a poignancy and added value to little things and you discover the value of modes and attitudes that are rejected by the larger society. It also makes you terribly brutal and thick-skinned toward some values while ultra-sensitive to others.

Now this background provides the black writer with much to write about. As fictional material it rivals that of the nineteenth-century Russians. But to the extent that other American writers, writers of different backgrounds, understand this material, or can implicate it in their own experience, they, too, have a way into what is currently known as "the black experience"—which I prefer to call, "the *Negro* American experience"—because for it to be worthy of fictional treatment, worthy of art, it has to be meaningful to others who do not share in its immediacy. I'll add that since it is both my own and an irrevocable part of the basic experience of the U.S., I think that it is not only worthy but indispensable to any profoundly *American* depiction of reality.

To repeat myself, this society has structured itself so as to be unaware of what it owes in both the positive and negative sense to the condition of inhumanity that it has imposed upon a great mass of its citizens. The fact that many whites refuse to recognize this is responsible for much of the anger erupting among young blacks today. It makes them furious when whites respond to their complaints with, "Yes, but *I* had nothing to do with any of that," or who reply to their demands for equal opportunity in a racially rigged society with, "We're against a quota system because *we* made it on our individual merits"—because this not only sidesteps a pressing reality, but it is only partially true. Perhaps they *did* make it on their own, but if that's true the way was made easier because their parents did not have to contend with *my* parents, who were ruled out of the competition. They had their troubles too, but the relative benevolence of democracy shared by their parents, and now by them, was paid for by *somebody* other than themselves, and was being paid long before many of them arrived on these shores. *We* know that as the nation's unwilling scapegoat we paid for much of it. Nor is this knowledge a matter of saying, "Pay us off," or saying, in the words of the old joke, "Your granddaddy kicked my granddaddy a hundred years ago, so now I've come to collect the debt, bend over." That's not the point. The point is one of moral perception, the perception of the wholeness of American life and the cost of its successes and its failures. What makes for a great deal of black fury is the refusal of many Americans to understand that somebody paid for the nation's peace and prosperity in terms of blood and frustrated dreams; that somebody now denied his proper share helped convert the raw materials into the sophisticated gadgetry. I don't mean to imply that only the blacks did this; the poor southern whites, the Irish—and numbers of peoples did. They, too, underwent the crudities and inequities of democracy so that the high rhetoric could retain some resonance of possibility and truth.

HERSEY: How much is anger a motive force for novelists of all kinds? Does the artist start with anger more than with other emotions?

ELLISON: I don't think that he necessarily starts with anger. Indeed, anger can get in the way, as it does for a fighter. If the writer starts with anger, then if he is truly writing he immediately translates it through his craft into consciousness, and thus into understanding, into insight, perception. Perhaps, that's where the morality of fiction lies. You see a situation which outrages you, but as you write about the characters who embody that which outrages, your sense of craft and the moral role of your craft demands that you depict those characters in the breadth of their humanity. You try to give them the density of the human rather than the narrow intensity of the demonic. That means that you try to delineate them as men and women who possess feelings and ideals, no matter how much you reject their feelings and ideals. Anyway, I find this happening in my own work; it humanizes *me*. So the main motive is not to express raw anger, but to present—as sentimental as it might sound—the wonder of life, in the fullness of which all these outrageous things occur.

HERSEY: Have you felt some defiance of death as a writer—in the sense that what you are making may possibly circumvent death?

ELLISON: No, I dare not. *(He laughs)* No, you just write for your own time, while trying to write in terms of the density of experience, knowing perfectly well that life repeats itself. Even in this rapidly changing

United States it repeats itself. The mystery is that while repeating itself it always manages slightly to change its mask. To be able to grasp a little of that change within continuity and to communicate it across all these divisions of background and individual experience seems enough for me. If you're lucky, of course, if you splice into one of the deeper currents of life, then you have a chance of your work lasting a little bit longer.

Saul Bellow

(1915–   )

In Captain Stormfield's Visit to Heaven, Mark Twain pictures a paradise where happiness and justice are meted out to all; where, therefore, when it comes to establishing a pecking order of the immortals of literature, Shakespeare and Homer are given their high places, but the highest place of all is given to a humble tailor from a village in Tennessee who wrote poetry all his life and was thought to be a halfwit—the greatest artist of all time, unread and undiscovered. When the handful of American eminences of the twenties and thirties of this century—Fitzgerald, Hemingway, Dos Passos, Faulkner—had all disappeared, the ranking game, idiotic as Mark Twain had shown it to be, became irresistible. And Saul Bellow emerged as one of the prime contenders for the championship so hankered after, in the earlier days, by Hemingway. He was the first American Jewish writer to reach a wide audience. He reached it because, like Ellison, he wrote not for a parish but for humankind. His achievement, especially in The Adventures of Augie March, Herzog, *and* Mr. Sammler's Planet, *has been one rooted in vitality. Whereas many of the giants of the nineteenth century—a time we now regard as having been relatively livable—taught humanity salutary lessons of its misery and degradation, Saul Bellow, writing in a time that has seemed far more terrible, and while depicting characters in varying degrees impotent, pathetic, wretched, and comical, has managed to build themes of integrity, of dignity, and even of hope. Like all good writers he has written against the grain. And these themes have come to life because he is a conscious and intelligent craftsman. In this interview he defines the literary tradition within which he works, and talks some shop about that craftsmanship.*

A PARIS REVIEW INTERVIEW
Interviewer: Gordon Lloyd Harper

The interview "took place" over a period of several weeks. Beginning with some exploratory discussions during May of 1965, it was shelved during the summer, and actually accomplished during September and October. Two recording sessions were held, totaling about an hour and a half, but this was only a small part of the effort Mr. Bellow gave to this interview. A series of meetings, for over five weeks, was devoted to the most careful revision of the original material. Recognizing at the outset the effort he would make for such an interview, he had real reluctance about beginning it at all. Once his decision had been reached, however, he gave a remarkable amount of his time freely to the task—up to two hours a day, at least twice and often three times a week throughout the entire five-week period. It had become an opportunity, as he put it, to say some things which were important but which weren't being said.

Certain types of questions were ruled out in early discussions. Mr. Bellow was not interested in responding to criticisms of his work which he found trivial or stupid. He quoted the Jewish proverb that a fool can throw a stone into the water which ten wise men cannot recover. Nor did he wish to discuss what he considered his personal writing habits, whether he used a pen or typewriter, how hard he pressed on the page. For the artist to give such loving attention to his own shoelaces was dangerous, even immoral. Finally, there were certain questions that led into too "wide spaces" for this interview, subjects for fuller treatment on other occasions.

The two tapes were made in Bellow's University of Chicago office on the fifth floor of the Social Sciences Building. The office, though large, is fairly typical of those on the main quadrangles: much of it rather dark with one brightly lighted area, occupied by his desk, immediately before a set of three dormer windows; dark-green metal bookcases line the walls, casually used as storage for a miscellany of books, magazines, and correspondence. A set of *The Complete Works of Rudyard Kipling* ("it was given to me") shares space with examination copies of new novels and with a few of Bellow's own books, including recent French and Italian translations of *Herzog*. A table, a couple of typing stands, and various decrepit and mismatched chairs are scattered in apparently haphazard fashion throughout the room. A wall rack just inside the door holds his jaunty black felt hat and his walking cane. There is a general sense of disarray, with stacks of papers, books, and letters lying everywhere. When one comes to the door, Bellow is frequently at his typing stand, rapidly pounding out on a portable machine responses to some of the many letters he gets daily. Occasionally a secretary enters and proceeds to type away on some project at the far end of the room.

During the two sessions with the tape recorder, Bellow sat at his desk, between the eaves which project prominently into the room, backlighted by the dormer windows which let in the bright afternoon sun from the south. Four stories below lie Fifty-ninth Street and Chicago's Midway, their automobile and human noises continually penetrating the office. As the questions were asked, Bellow listened carefully and often developed an answer slowly, pausing frequently to think out the exact phrasing he sought. His answers were serious, but full of his special quality of humor. He took obvious pleasure in the amusing turns of thought with which he often concluded an answer. Throughout, he was at great pains to make his ideas transparent to the interviewer, asking repeatedly if this was clear or if he should say more on the subject. His concentration during these sessions was intense enough to be tiring, and both tapes were brought to a close with his confessing to some exhaustion.

Following each taping session, a typescript of his remarks was prepared. Bellow worked over these typed sheets extensively with pen and ink, taking as many as three separate meetings to do a complete revision. Then another typescript was made, and the process started over. This work was done when the interviewer could be present, and again the changes were frequently tested on him. Generally these sessions occurred at Bellow's office or at his apartment, overlooking the Outer Drive and Lake Michigan. Once, however, revisions were made while he and the interviewer sat on a Jackson Park bench on a fine October afternoon, and one typescript was worked on along with beer and hamburgers at a local bar.

Revisions were of various sorts. Frequently there were slight changes in meaning: "That's what I really meant to say." Other alterations tightened up his language or were in the nature of stylistic improvements. Any sections which he judged to be excursions from the main topic were deleted. Most regretted by the interviewer were prunings that eliminated certain samples of the characteristic Bellow wit: in a few places he came to feel he was simply "exhibiting" himself, and these were scratched out. On the other hand, whenever he could substitute for conventional literary diction an unexpected colloquial turn of phrase—which often proved humorous in context—he did so.

INTERVIEWER: Some critics have felt that your work falls within the tradition of American naturalism, possibly because of some things you've said about Dreiser. I was wondering if you saw yourself in a particular literary tradition?

BELLOW: Well, I think that the development of realism in the nineteenth century is still the major event of modern literature. Dreiser, a realist of course, had elements of genius. He was clumsy, cumbersome, and in some respects a poor thinker. But he was rich in a kind of feeling which has been ruled off the grounds by many contemporary writers—the kind of feeling that every human being intuitively recognizes as primary. Dreiser has more open access to primary feelings than any American writer of the twentieth century. It makes a good many people uncomfortable that his emotion has not found a more developed literary form. It's true his art may be too "natural." He sometimes conveys his understanding by masses of words, verbal approximations. He blunders, but generally in the direction of truth. The result is that we are moved in an unmediated way by his characters, as by life, and then we say that his novels are simply torn from the side of life, and therefore not novels. But we can't escape reading them. He somehow conveys, without much refinement, depths of feeling that we usually associate with Balzac or Shakespeare.

INTERVIEWER: This realism, then, is a particular kind of sensibility, rather than a technique?

BELLOW: Realism specializes in *apparently* unmediated experiences. What stirred Dreiser was simply the idea that you could bring unmediated feeling to the novel. He took it up naïvely without going to the trouble of mastering an art. We don't see this because he makes so many familiar "art" gestures, borrowed from the art fashions of his day, and even from the slick magazines, but he is really a natural, a primitive. I have great respect for his simplicities and I think they are worth more than much that has been praised as high art in the American novel.

INTERVIEWER: Could you give me an example of what you mean?

BELLOW: In a book like *Jennie Gerhardt* the delicacy with which Jennie allows Lester Kane to pursue his conventional life while she herself lives unrecognized with her illegitimate daughter, the depth of her understanding, and the depth of her sympathy and of her truthfulness impress me. She is not a sentimental figure. She has a natural sort of honor.

INTERVIEWER: Has recent American fiction pretty much followed this direction?

BELLOW: Well, among his heirs there are those who believe that clumsiness and truthfulness go together. But cumbersomeness does not necessarily imply a sincere heart. Most of the "Dreiserians" lack talent. On the other hand, people who put Dreiser down, adhering to a "high art" standard for the novel, miss the point.

INTERVIEWER: Aside from Dreiser, what other American writers do you find particularly of interest?

BELLOW: I like Hemingway, Faulkner, and Fitzgerald. I think of Hemingway as a man who developed a significant manner as an artist, a lifestyle which is important. For his generation, his language created a lifestyle, one which pathetic old gentlemen are still found clinging to. I don't think of Hemingway as a great novelist. I like Fitzgerald's novels better, but I often feel about Fitzgerald that he couldn't distinguish between innocence and social climbing. I am thinking of *The Great Gatsby*.

INTERVIEWER: If we go outside American literature, you've mentioned that you read the nineteenth-century Russian writers with a good deal of interest. Is there anything particular about them that attracts you?

BELLOW: Well, the Russians have an immediate charismatic appeal—excuse the Max Weberism. Their conventions allow them to express freely their feelings about nature and human beings. We have inherited a more restricted and imprisoning attitude toward the emotions. We have to work around puritanical and stoical restraints. We lack the Russian openness. Our path is narrower.

INTERVIEWER: In what other writers do you take special interest?

BELLOW: I have a special interest in Joyce; I have a special interest in Lawrence. I read certain poets over and over again. I can't say where they belong in my theoretical scheme; I only know that I have an attachment to them. Yeats is one such poet. Hart Crane is another. Hardy and Walter de la Mare. I don't know what these have in common—

probably nothing. I know that I am drawn repeatedly to these men.

INTERVIEWER: It's been said that one can't like *both* Lawrence and Joyce, that one has to choose between them. You don't feel this way?

BELLOW: No. Because I really don't take Lawrence's sexual theories very seriously. I take his art seriously, not his doctrine. But he himself warned us repeatedly not to trust the artist. He said trust the work itself. So I have little use for the Lawrence who wrote *The Plumed Serpent* and great admiration for the Lawrence who wrote *The Lost Girl*.

INTERVIEWER: Does Lawrence at all share the special feeling you find attractive in Dreiser?

BELLOW: A certain openness to experience, yes. And a willingness to trust one's instinct, to follow it freely—that Lawrence has.

INTERVIEWER: You mentioned before the interview that you would prefer not to talk about your early novels, that you feel you are a different person now from what you were then. I wonder if this is all you want to say, or if you can say something about how you have changed.

BELLOW: I think that when I wrote those early books I was timid. I still felt the incredible effrontery of announcing myself to the world (in part I mean the WASP world) as a writer and an artist. I had to touch a great many bases, demonstrate my abilities, pay my respects to formal requirements. In short, I was afraid to let myself go.

INTERVIEWER: When do you find a significant change occurring?

BELLOW: When I began to write *Augie March*. I took off many of these restraints. I think I took off too many, and went too far, but I was feeling the excitement of discovery. I had just increased my freedom, and like any emancipated plebeian I abused it at once.

INTERVIEWER: What were these restraints that you took off in *Augie March*?

BELLOW: My first two books are well made. I wrote the first quickly but took great pains with it. I labored with the second and tried to make it letter-perfect. In writing *The Victim* I accepted a Flaubertian standard. Not a bad standard, to be sure, but one which, in the end, I found repressive—repressive because of the circumstances of my life and because of my upbringing in Chicago as the son of immigrants. I could not, with such an instrument as I developed in the first two books, express a variety of things I knew intimately. Those books, though useful, did not give me a form in which I felt comfortable. A writer should be able to express himself easily, naturally, copiously in a form which frees his mind, his energies. Why should he hobble himself with formalities? With a borrowed sensibility? With the desire to be "correct"? Why should I force myself to write like an Englishman or a contributor to *The New Yorker*? I soon saw that it was simply not in me to be a mandarin. I should add that for a young man in my position there were social inhibitions, too. I had good reason to fear that I would be put down as a foreigner, an interloper. It was made clear to me when I studied literature in the university that as a Jew and the son of Russian Jews I would probably never have the right *feeling* for Anglo-Saxon traditions, for English words. I realized even in college that the people who told me this were not necessarily disinterested friends. But they had an effect on me, nevertheless. This was something from which I had to free myself. I fought free because I had to.

INTERVIEWER: Are these social inhibitors as powerful today as they were when you wrote *Dangling Man?*

BELLOW: I think I was lucky to have grown up in the Middle West, where such influences are less strong. If I'd grown up in the East and attended an Ivy League university, I might have been damaged more badly. Puritan and Protestant America carries less weight in Illinois than in Massachusetts. But I don't bother much with such things now.

INTERVIEWER: Did another change in your writing occur between *Augie March* and *Herzog?* You've mentioned writing *Augie March* with a great sense of freedom, but I take it that *Herzog* was a very difficult book to write.

BELLOW: It was. I had to tame and restrain the style I developed in *Augie March* in order to write *Henderson* and *Herzog.* I think both those books reflect that change in style. I wouldn't really know how to describe it. I don't care to trouble my mind to find an exact description for it, but it has something to do with a kind of readiness to record impressions arising from a source of which we know little. I suppose that all of us have a primitive prompter or commentator within, who from earliest years has been advising us, telling us what the real world is. There is such a commentator in me. I have to prepare the ground for him. From this source come words, phrases, syllables; sometimes only sounds, which I try to interpret, sometimes whole paragraphs, fully punctuated. When E. M. Forster said, "How do I know what I think until I see what I say?" he was perhaps referring to his own prompter. There is that observing instrument in us—in childhood at any rate. At the sight of a man's face, his shoes, the color of light, a woman's mouth or perhaps her ear, one receives a word, a phrase, at times nothing but a nonsense syllable from the primitive commentator.

INTERVIEWER: So this change in your writing—

BELLOW: —was an attempt to get nearer to that primitive commentator.

INTERVIEWER: How do you go about getting nearer to him, preparing the way for him?

BELLOW: When I say the commentator is primitive, I don't mean that he's crude; God knows he's often fastidious. But he won't talk until the situation's right. And if you prepare the ground for him with too many difficulties underfoot, he won't say anything. I must be terribly given to fraud and deceit because I sometimes have great difficulty preparing a suitable ground. This is why I've had so much trouble with my last two novels. I appealed directly to my prompter. The prompter, however, has to find the occasion perfect—that is to say, truthful, and necessary. If there is any superfluity or inner falsehood in the preparations, he is aware of it. I have to stop. Often I have to begin again, with the first word. I can't remember how many times I wrote *Herzog*. But at last I did find the acceptable ground for it.

INTERVIEWER: Do these preparations include your coming to some general conception of the work?

BELLOW: Well, I don't know exactly how it's done. I let it alone a good deal. I try to avoid common forms of strain and distortion. For a long time, perhaps from the middle of the nineteenth century, writers have not been satisfied to regard themselves simply as writers. They have required also a theoretical farmework. Most often they have been their own theoreticians, have created their own ground as artists, and have provided an exegesis for their own works. They have found it necessary to take a position, not merely to write novels. In bed last night I was reading a collection of articles by Stendhal. One of them amused me very much, touched me. Stendhal was saying how lucky writers were in the age of Louis XIV not to have anyone take them very seriously. Their obscurity was very valuable. Corneille had been dead for several days before anyone at court considered the fact important enough to mention. In the nineteenth century, says Stendhal, there would have been several public orations, Corneille's funeral covered by all the papers. There are great advantages in not being taken *too* seriously. Some writers are excessively serious about themselves. They accept the ideas of the "cultivated public." There is such a thing as overcapitalizing the A in artist. Certain writers and musicians understand this. Stravinsky says the composer should practice his trade exactly as a shoemaker does. Mozart and Haydn accepted commissions—wrote to order. In the nineteenth century, the artist loftily waited for Inspiration. Once you elevate yourself to the rank of a cultural institution, you're in for a lot of trouble.

Then there is a minor modern disorder—the disease of people who live by an image of themselves created by papers, television, Broadway, Sardi's, gossip, or the public need for celebrities. Even buffoons, prize fighters, and movie stars have caught the bug. I avoid these "images." I have a longing, not for downright obscurity—I'm too egotistical for that—but for peace, and freedom from meddling.

INTERVIEWER: In line with this, the enthusiastic response to *Herzog* must have affected your life considerably. Do you have any thoughts as to why this book became and remained the bestseller it did?

BELLOW: I don't like to agree with the going view that if you write a bestseller it's because you betrayed an important principle or sold your soul. I know that sophisticated opinion believes this. And although I don't take much stock in sophisticated opinion, I have examined my conscience. I've tried to find out whether I had unwittingly done wrong. But I haven't yet discovered the sin. I do think that a book like *Herzog,* which ought to have been an obscure book with a total sale of eight thousand, has such a reception because it appeals to the unconscious sympathies of many people. I know from the mail I've received that the book described a common predicament. *Herzog* appealed to Jewish readers, to those who have been divorced, to those who talk to themselves, to college graduates, readers of paperbacks, autodidacts, to those who yet hope to live awhile, etc.

INTERVIEWER: Do you feel there were deliberate attempts at lionizing by the literary tastemakers? I was thinking that the recent deaths of Faulkner and Hemingway have been seen as creating a vacuum in American letters, which we all know is abhorrent.

BELLOW: Well, I don't know whether I would say a vacuum. Perhaps a pigeonhole. I agree that there is a need to keep the pigeonholes filled and that people are uneasy when there are vacancies. Also the mass media demand material—grist—and literary journalists have to create a major-league atmosphere in literature. The writers don't offer to fill the pigeonholes. It's the critics who want figures in the Pantheon. But there are many people who assume that every writer must be bucking for the niche. Why should writers wish to be rated—seeded—like tennis players? Handicapped like racehorses? What an epitaph for a novelist: "He won all the polls"!

INTERVIEWER: How much are you conscious of the reader when you write? Is there an ideal audience that you write for?

BELLOW: I have in mind another human being who will understand me. I count on this. Not on perfect understanding, which is Cartesian, but on approximate understanding, which is Jewish. And on a meeting of sympathies, which is human. But I have no ideal reader in my head, no. Let me just say this, too. I seem to have the blind self-acceptance of the eccentric who can't conceive that his eccentricities are not clearly understood.

INTERVIEWER: So there isn't a great deal of calculation about rhetoric?

BELLOW: These are things that can't really be contrived. People who talk about contrivance must think that a novelist is a man capable of building a skyscraper to conceal a dead mouse. Skyscrapers are not raised simply to conceal mice.

INTERVIEWER: It's been said that contemporary fiction sees man as a victim. You gave this title to one of your early novels, yet there seems to be very strong opposition in your fiction to seeing man as simply determined or futile. Do you see any truth to this claim about contemporary fiction?

BELLOW: Oh, I think that realistic literature from the first has been a victim literature. Pit any ordinary individual—and realistic literature con-

cerns itself with ordinary individuals—against the external world, and
the external world will conquer him, of course. Everything that people
believed in the nineteenth century about determinism, about man's
place in nature, about the power of productive forces in society, made it
inevitable that the hero of the realistic novel should not be a hero but
a sufferer who is eventually overcome. So I was doing nothing very
original by writing another realistic novel about a common man and
calling it *The Victim*. I suppose I was discovering independently the
essence of much of modern realism. In my innocence, I put my finger
on it. Serious realism also contrasts the common man with aristocratic
greatness. He is overborne by fate, just as the great are in Shakespeare
or Sophocles. But this contrast, inherent in literary tradition, always
damages him. In the end the force of tradition carries realism into
parody, satire, mock-epic—Leopold Bloom.

INTERVIEWER: Haven't you yourself moved away from the suggestion of
plebeian tragedy toward a treatment of the sufferer that has greater
comic elements? Although the concerns and difficulties are still fundamentally serious, the comic elements in *Henderson*, in *Herzog*, even in
Seize the Day seem much more prominent than in *Dangling Man* or
The Victim.

BELLOW: Yes, because I got very tired of the solemnity of complaint, altogether impatient with complaint. Obliged to choose between complaint
and comedy, I choose comedy, as more energetic, wiser, and manlier.
This is really one reason why I dislike my own early novels. I find them
plaintive, sometimes querulous. *Herzog* makes comic use of complaint.

INTERVIEWER: When you say that you are obliged to choose between complaint and comedy, does it mean this is the only choice—that you are
limited to choosing between just these two alternatives?

BELLOW: I'm not inclined to predict what will happen. I may feel drawn
to comedy again, I may not. But modern literature was dominated by
a tone of elegy from the twenties to the fifties, the atmosphere of Eliot
in "The Waste Land" and that of Joyce in *A Portrait of the Artist as a
Young Man*. Sensibility absorbed this sadness, this view of the artist as
the only contemporary link with an age of gold, forced to watch the
sewage flowing in the Thames, every aspect of modern civilization
doing violence to his (artist-patrician) feelings. This went much farther
than it should have been allowed to go. It descended to absurdities, of
which I think we have had enough.

INTERVIEWER: I wonder if you could say something about how important
the environments are in your works. I take it that for the realist tradition the context in which the action occurs is of vital importance. You
set your novels in Chicago, New York, as far away as Africa. How
important are these settings for the fiction?

BELLOW: Well, you present me with a problem to which I think no one has

the answer. People write realistically but at the same time they want
to create environments which are somehow desirable, which are surrounded by atmospheres in which behavior becomes significant, which
display the charm of life. What is literature without these things?
Dickens's London is gloomy, but also cozy. And yet realism has always
offered to annihilate precisely such qualities. That is to say, if you want
to be ultimately realistic you bring artistic space itself in danger. In
Dickens, there is no void beyond the fog. The environment is human,
at all times. Do you follow me?

INTERVIEWER: I'm not sure I do.

BELLOW: The realistic tendency is to challenge the human significance of
things. The more realistic you are the more you threaten the grounds
of your own art. Realism has always both accepted and rejected the
circumstances of ordinary life. It accepted the task of writing about
ordinary life and tried to meet it in some extraordinary fashion. As
Flaubert did. The subject might be common, low, degrading, all this
was to be redeemed by art. I really do see those Chicago environments
as I represent them. They suggest their own style of presentation. I
elaborate it.

INTERVIEWER: Then you aren't especially disturbed by readers of *Henderson*, for example, who say that Africa really isn't like that? One sort
of realist would require a writer to spend several years on location before daring to place his characters there. You're not troubled by him,
I take it?

BELLOW: Perhaps you should say "factualist" rather than "realist." Years
ago, I studied African ethnography with the late Professor Herskovits.
Later he scolded me for writing a book like *Henderson*. He said the
subject was much too serious for such fooling. I felt that my fooling
was fairly serious. Literalism, factualism, will smother the imagination
altogether.

INTERVIEWER: You have on occasion divided recent American fiction into
what you call the "cleans" and the "dirties." The former, I gather, tend
to be conservative and easily optimistic, the latter the eternal nay-sayers,
rebels, iconoclasts. Do you feel this is still pretty much the picture of
American fiction today?

BELLOW: I feel that both choices are rudimentary and pitiful, and though
I know the uselessness of advocating any given path to other novelists,
I am still inclined to say, Leave both these extremes. They are useless,
childish. No wonder the really powerful men in our society, whether
politicians or scientists, hold writers and poets in contempt. They do it
because they get no evidence from modern literature that anybody is
thinking about any significant question. What does the radicalism of
radical writers nowadays amount to? Most of it is hand-me-down
bohemianism, sentimental populism, D. H. Lawrence-and-water, or imitation Sartre. For American writers radicalism is a question of honor.

They must be radicals for the sake of their dignity. They see it as their function, and a noble function, to say Nay, and to bite not only the hand that feeds them (and feeds them with comic abundance, I might add) but almost any other hand held out to them. Their radicalism, however, is contentless. A genuine radicalism, which truly challenges authority, we need desperately. But a radicalism of posture is easy and banal. Radical criticism requires knowledge, not posture, not slogans, not rant. People who maintain their dignity as artists, in a small way, by being mischievous on television, simply delight the networks and the public. True radicalism requires homework—thought. Of the cleans, on the other hand, there isn't much to say. They seem faded.

INTERVIEWER: Your context is essentially that of the modern city, isn't it? Is there a reason for this beyond the fact that you come out of an urban experience?

BELLOW: Well, I don't know how I could possibly separate my knowledge of life, such as it is, from the city. I could no more tell you how deeply it's gotten into my bones than the lady who paints radium dials in the clock factory can tell you.

INTERVIEWER: You've mentioned the distractive character of modern life. Would this be most intense in the city?

BELLOW: The volume of judgments one is called upon to make depends upon the receptivity of the observer, and if one is very receptive, one has a terrifying number of opinions to render—"What do you think about this, about that, about Viet Nam, about city planning, about expressways, or garbage disposal, or democracy, or Plato, or pop art, or welfare states, or literacy in a 'mass society'?" I wonder whether there will ever be enough tranquillity under modern circumstances to allow our contemporary Wordsworth to recollect anything. I feel that art has something to do with the achievement of stillness in the midst of chaos. A stillness which characterizes prayer, too, and the eye of the storm. I think that art has something to do with an arrest of attention in the midst of distraction.

INTERVIEWER: I believe you once said that it is the novel which must deal particularly with this kind of chaos, and that as a consequence certain forms appropriate to poetry or to music are not available to the novelist.

BELLOW: I'm no longer so sure of that. I think the novelist can avail himself of similar privileges. It's just that he can't act with the same purity or economy of means as the poet. He has to traverse a very muddy and noisy territory before he can arrive at a pure conclusion. He's more exposed to the details of life.

INTERVIEWER: Is there anything peculiar about the *kind* of distractions you see the novelist having to confront today? Is it just that there are more details, or is their quality different today from what it used to be?

BELLOW: The modern masterpiece of confusion is Joyce's *Ulysses*. There the mind is unable to resist experience. Experience in all its diversity, its pleasure and horror, passes through Bloom's head like an ocean through a sponge. The sponge can't resist; it has to accept whatever the waters bring. It also notes every microorganism that passes through it. This is what I mean. How much of this must the spirit suffer, in what detail is it obliged to receive this ocean with its human plankton? Sometimes it looks as if the power of the mind has been nullified by the volume of experiences. But of course this is assuming the degree of passivity that Joyce assumes in *Ulysses*. Stronger, more purposeful minds can demand order, impose order, select, disregard, but there is still the threat of disintegration under the particulars. A Faustian artist is unwilling to surrender to the mass of particulars.

INTERVIEWER: Some people have felt your protagonists are seeking the answer to a question that might be phrased, How is it possible today for a good man to live? I wonder if you feel there is any single recurring question like this in the novels?

BELLOW: I don't think that I've represented any really good men; no one is thoroughly admirable in any of my novels. Realism has restrained me too much for that. I should *like* to represent good men. I long to know who and what they are and what their condition might be. I often represent men who desire such qualities but seem unable to achieve them on any significant scale. I criticize this in myself. I find it a limitation.

INTERVIEWER: I'm sorry; what exactly is this limitation?

BELLOW: The fact that I have not discerned those qualities or that I have not shown them in action. Herzog wants very much to have effective virtues. But that's a source of comedy in the book. I think I am far more concerned with another matter, and I don't approach this as a problem with a ready answer. I see it rather as a piece of research, having to do with human characteristics or qualities which have no need of justification. It's an odd thing to do, it shouldn't be necessary to "justify" certain things. But there are many skeptical, rebellious, or simply nervous writers all around us, who, having existed a full twenty or thirty years in this universe, denounce or reject life because it fails to meet their standards as philosophical intellectuals. It seems to me that they can't know enough about it for confident denial. The mystery is too great. So when they knock at the door of mystery with the knuckles of cognition it is quite right that the door should open and some mysterious power should squirt them in the eye. I think a good deal of *Herzog* can be explained simply by the implicit assumption that existence, quite apart from any of our judgments, has value, that existence is worth-ful. Here it is possible, however, that the desire to go on with his creaturely career vulgarly betrays Herzog. He wants to live? What of it! The clay that frames him contains this common want. Simple *aviditas vitae*. Does a man deserve any credit for this?

INTERVIEWER: Would this help to explain, then, why many of the difficulties which Herzog's mind throws up for him throughout the novel don't ever seem to be *intellectually* resolved?

BELLOW: The book is not anti-intellectual, as some have said. It simply points to the comic impossibility of arriving at a synthesis that can satisfy modern demands. That is to say, full awareness of all major problems, together with the necessary knowledge of history, of science and philosophy. That's why Herzog paraphrases Thomas Marshall, Woodrow Wilson's Vice-President, who said what this country needs is a good five-cent cigar. (I think it was Bugs Baer who said it first.) Herzog's version: what this country needs is a good five-cent synthesis.

INTERVIEWER: Do you find many contemporary writers attempting to develop such syntheses or insisting that significant fiction provide them?

BELLOW: Well, I don't know that too many American novelists, young or old, are tormenting their minds with these problems. Europeans do. I don't know that they can ever reach satisfactory results on the grounds they have chosen. At any rate, they write few good novels. But that leads us into some very wide spaces.

INTERVIEWER: Do the ideas in *Herzog* have any other major roles to play? The "anti-intellectual" charge seems to come from people who don't feel the ideas are essential either in motivating the action, the decisions Herzog makes, or in helping him to come through at the end.

BELLOW: To begin with, I suppose I should say something about the difference in the role ideas play in American literature. European literature—I speak now of the Continent—is intellectual in a different sense from ours. The intellectual hero of a French or a German novel is likely to be a philosophical intellectual, an ideological intellectual. We here, intellectuals—or the educated public—know that in our liberal democracy ideas become effective within an entirely different tradition. The lines are less clearly drawn. We do not expect thought to have results, say, in the moral sphere, or in the political, in quite the way a Frenchman would. To be an intellectual in the United States sometimes means to be immured in a private life in which one thinks, but thinks with some humiliating sense of how little thought can accomplish. To call therefore for a dramatic resolution in terms of ideas in an American novel is to demand something for which there is scarcely any precedent. My novel deals with the humiliating sense that results from the American mixture of private concerns and intellectual interests. This is something which most readers of the book seem utterly to have missed. Some, fortunately, have caught it. But in part *Herzog* is intended to bring to an end, under blinding light, a certain course of development. Many people feel a "private life" to be an affliction. In some sense it is a genuine affliction; it cuts one off from a common life. To me, a significant theme of *Herzog* is the imprisonment of the individual in a shameful and impotent privacy. He feels humiliated by it; he struggles comically with it; and he comes to realize at last that what he considered his intellectual "privilege" has proved to be another form of bondage. Anyone who misses this misses the point of the book. So that to say that Herzog is not motivated in his acts by ideas is entirely false. Any *Bildungsroman* —and *Herzog* is, to use that heavy German term, a *Bildungsroman*—concludes with the first step. The first *real* step. Any man who has rid himself of superfluous ideas in order to take that first step has done something significant. When people complain of a lack of ideas in novels, they may mean that they do not find familiar ideas, fashionable ideas. Ideas outside the "canon" they don't recognize. So, if what they mean is ideas à la Sartre or ideas à la Camus, they are quite right: there are few such in *Herzog*. Perhaps they mean that the thoughts of a man fighting for sanity and life are not suitable for framing.

INTERVIEWER: Herzog rejects certain of these fashionable ideas, doesn't he —the ideas à la Sartre or à la Camus?

BELLOW: I think he tests them first upon his own sense of life and against his own desperate need for clarity. With him these thoughts are not a game. Though he may laugh as he thinks them, his survival depends upon them. I didn't have him engage in full combat with figures like Sartre. If he had chosen to debate with Sartre in typical Herzogian fashion he would perhaps have begun with Sartre's proposition that Jews exist only because of anti-Semitism, that the Jew has to choose between authentic and inauthentic existence, that authentic existence can never be detached from this anti-Semitism which determines it. Herzog might have remembered that for Sartre, the Jew exists because he is hated, not because he has a history, not because he has origins of his own—but simply because he is designated, created, in his Jewishness by an outrageous evil. Sartre offers a remedy for those Jews who are prepared to make the authentic choice: he extends to them the invitation to become Frenchmen. If this great prince of contemporary European philosophy offers Herzog ideas such as this to embrace (or dispute), who can blame him for his skepticism toward what is called, so respectfully, Thought, toward contemporary intellectual fare? Often Herzog deals with ideas in negative fashion. He needs to dismiss a great mass of irrelevancy and nonsense in order to survive. Perhaps this was what I meant earlier when I said that we were called upon to make innumerable judgments. We can be consumed simply by the necessity to discriminate between multitudes of propositions. We have to dismiss a great number of thoughts if we are to have any creaturely or human life at all. It seems at times that we are on trial seven days a week answering the questions, giving a clear account of ourselves. But when does one live? How does one live if it is necessary to render ceaseless judgments?

INTERVIEWER: Herzog's rejection of certain ideas has been widely recognized but—

BELLOW: —why he rejects them is not at all clear. Herzog's skepticism toward ideas is very deep. Though Jews are often accused of being "rootless" rationalists, a man like Herzog knows very well that habit, custom, tendency, temperament, inheritance, and the power to recognize real and human facts have equal weight with ideas.

INTERVIEWER: You've spoken also of the disabling effects of basing a novel on ideas. Does this mean structuring a novel according to a philosophical conception?

BELLOW: No, I have no objection to that, nor do I have any objection to basing novels on philosophical conceptions or anything else that works. But let us look at one of the dominant ideas of the century, accepted by many modern artists—the idea that humankind has reached a terminal point. We find this terminal assumption in writers like Joyce, Céline, Thomas Mann. In *Doktor Faustus* politics and art are joined in the destruction of civilization. Now here is an idea, found in some of the greatest novelists of the twentieth century. How good is this idea? Frightful things have happened, but is the apocalyptic interpretation true? The terminations did not fully terminate. Civilization is still here. The prophecies have not been borne out. Novelists are wrong to put an interpretation of history at the base of artistic creation—to speak "the last word." It is better that the novelist should trust his own sense of life. Less ambitious. More likely to tell the truth.

INTERVIEWER: Frequently in your fiction the hero strives to avoid being swallowed up by other people's ideas or versions of reality. On occasion you seem to present him with something like the whole range of contemporary alternatives—say, in *Augie March* or *Herzog*. Was this one of your intentions?

BELLOW: All these matters are really so complicated. Of course these books are somewhat concerned with free choice. I don't think that they pose the question successfully—the terms are not broad enough. I think I have let myself off easily. I seem to have asked in my books, How can one resist the controls of this vast society *without* turning into a nihilist, avoiding the absurdity of empty rebellion? I have asked, Are there other, more good-natured forms of resistance and free choice? And I suppose that, like most Americans, I have involuntarily favored the more comforting or melioristic side of the question. I don't mean that I ought to have been more "pessimistic," because I have found "pessimism" to be in most of its forms nearly as empty as "optimism." But I am obliged to admit that I have not followed these questions to the necessary depth. I can't blame myself for not having been a stern moralist; I can always use the excuse that I'm after all nothing but a writer of fiction. But I don't feel satisfied with what I have done to date, except in the comic form. There is, however, this to be added—that our French friends invariably see the answers to such questions, and all questions of truth, to be overwhelmingly formidable, uncongenial, hostile to us. It may be, however, that truth is not always so punitive. I've tried to suggest this in my books. There may be truths on the side of life. I am quite prepared to admit that being habitual liars and self-deluders, we have good cause to fear the truth, but I'm not at all ready to stop hoping. There may be some truths which are, after all, our friends in the universe.

William Burroughs

(1914–   )

William Burroughs came from a wealthy family in St. Louis, went to Harvard,
traveled in Europe, and then returned to the United States and worked at various
unusual jobs—unusual, that is, for a rich Harvard man: for example, as a detec-
tive, a bartender, an exterminator of roaches and rats. Out of boredom, as he
says, he became addicted to heroin, and his first book was Junkie: Confessions
of an Unredeemed Drug Addict, *which he published in 1953 under a pseudonym,*
Will Lee. *Six years later, with* Naked Lunch, *a raw and awkward but compelling*
novel, Burroughs announced himself as a serious writer; he was taken up as a
culture-hero by American intellectuals. He has written numerous other books,
in which he has made efforts of various kinds to break with given patterns of
literary perception and representation. In the Paris Review *interview that follows*
—it took place in 1965 in a luxury hotel in St. Louis—he makes some interesting
comments on drugs and writing. Most of the interview is concerned, however,
with Burroughs's attempts to open up his writing consciousness, to the end that
his eye would be able to take in everything out to the utmost periphery of vision,
and so that his mind could think not in words but in whole blocks of associa-
tions. A writer need not go all the way with Burroughs's cutups and manipula-
tions to be persuaded by his "principal message"—"For Godsake, keep your eyes
open"—and to be fascinated by some of his hints on how to see things in new
ways.

A PARIS REVIEW INTERVIEW
Interviewer: Conrad Knickerbocker

Firecrackers and whistles sounded the advent of the New Year of 1965
in Saint Louis, and stripteasers ran from the bars in Gaslight Square to
dance in the street when midnight came. William Seward Burroughs III,
who had watched television alone that night, was asleep in his room at
the Chase-Park Plaza Hotel, Saint Louis's most elegant. After an absence
of twenty years, he had returned to his birthplace from Tangier.

At noon the next day he was ready for the interview. He wore a gray
lightweight Brooks Brothers suit with vest, a blue-striped shirt from
Gibraltar cut in the English style, and a deep-blue tie with small white polka
dots. His manner was not so much pedagogic as didactic or forensic. He
might have been a senior partner in a private bank, charting the course
of huge but anonymous fortunes. A friend of the interviewer, spotting
him across the lobby, thought he was a British diplomat. At the age of

fifty, he is trim; he performs a complex abdominal exercise daily and walks a good deal. His face carries no excess flesh. His expression is taut, and his features are intense and chiseled. He did not smile during the interview and laughed only once, but he gives the impression of being capable of much dry laughter under other circumstances. His voice is sonorous, its tone reasonable and patient; his accent is mid-Atlantic, the kind of regionless inflection Americans acquire after many years abroad. He speaks elliptically, in short, clear bursts.

On the dresser of his room sat a European transistor radio, several science-fiction paperbacks, and *Romance* by Joseph Conrad, *The Day Lincoln Was Shot* by Jim Bishop, and *Ghosts in American Houses* by James Reynolds. A Zeiss Ikon camera in a scuffed leather case lay on one of the twin beds beside a copy of *Field & Stream.* On the other bed were a pair of long shears, clippings from newspaper society pages, photographs, and a scrapbook on which he had been working when the interviewer arrived. He had begun three scrapbooks several months earlier in Tangier. They consisted of typed material, photographs, and printed matter *en collage* in French ledger books. One was devoted to Gibraltar and the other two to general subjects. A Facit portable typewriter sat on the desk, and gradually one became aware that the room, although neat, contained a great deal of paper.

After a brief discussion of the use of the tape recorder to prepare cut-up interviews, he settled in a chair next to a window. He smoked incessantly, alternating between a box of English Ovals and a box of Benson & Hedges. As the interview progressed, the room filled with smoke. He opened the window. The temperature outside was seventy degrees, the warmest New Year's Day in Saint Louis history; a yellow jacket flew in and settled on the pane. The twelfth-story room overlooked the ample roofs of the houses on a series of private streets with gates at both ends, once the most substantial neighborhood in Saint Louis. In one of these homes, at 4664 Pershing Avenue, he had been born. The bright afternoon deepened. The faint cries of children rose up from the broad brick alleys in which he had played as a boy.

INTERVIEWER: You grew up here?

BURROUGHS: Yes. I went to John Burroughs School and the Taylor School, and was out West for a bit, and then went to Harvard.

INTERVIEWER: Any relation to the adding-machine firm?

BURROUGHS: My grandfather. You see, he didn't exactly invent the adding machine, but he invented the gimmick that made it work—namely, a cylinder full of oil and a perforated piston that will always move up and down at the same rate of speed. Very simple principle, like most inventions. And it gave me a little money, not much, but a little.

INTERVIEWER: What did you do at Harvard?

BURROUGHS: Studied English Lit. John Livingston Lowes. Whiting. I sat in on Kittredge's course. Those are the main people I recall. I lived in Adams House and then I got fed up with the food and I moved to Claverly Hall, where I lived the last two years. I didn't do any writing in college.

INTERVIEWER: When and why did you start to write?

BURROUGHS: I started to write about 1950; I was thirty-five at the time; there didn't seem to be any strong motivation. I simply was endeavoring to put down in a more-or-less straightforward journalistic style something about my experiences with addiction and addicts.

INTERVIEWER: Why did you feel compelled to record these experiences?

BURROUGHS: I didn't feel compelled. I had nothing else to do. Writing gave me something to do every day. I don't feel the results were at all spectacular. *Junkie* is not much of a book, actually. I knew very little about writing at that time.

INTERVIEWER: Where was this?

BURROUGHS: In Mexico City. I was living near Sears, Roebuck, right around the corner from the University of Mexico. I had been in the army four or five months and I was there on the G.I. Bill, studying native dialects. I went to Mexico partly because things were becoming so difficult with the drug situation in America. Getting drugs in Mexico was quite easy, so I didn't have to rush around, and there wasn't any pressure from the law.

INTERVIEWER: Why did you start taking drugs?

BURROUGHS: Well, I was just bored. I didn't seem to have much interest in becoming a successful advertising executive or whatever, or living the kind of life Harvard designs for you. After I became addicted in New York in 1944, things began to happen. I got in some trouble with the law, got married, moved to New Orleans and then went to Mexico.

INTERVIEWER: There seems to be a great deal of middle-class voyeurism in this country concerning addiction, and in the literary world, downright reverence for the addict. You apparently don't share these points of view.

BURROUGHS: No, most of it is nonsense. I think drugs are interesting principally as chemical means of altering metabolism and thereby altering what we call reality, which I would define as a more-or-less constant scanning pattern.

INTERVIEWER: What do you think of the hallucinogens and the new psychedelic drugs—LSD-25?

BURROUGHS: I think they're extremely dangerous, much more dangerous than heroin. They can produce overwhelming anxiety states. I've seen people try to throw themselves out of windows, whereas the heroin addict is mainly interested in staring at his own toe. Other than deprivation of the drug, the main threat to him is an overdose. I've tried most of the hallucinogens, without an anxiety reaction, fortunately. LSD-25 produced results for me similar to mescaline. Like all hallucinogens, LSD gave me an increased awareness, more a hallucinated viewpoint than any actual hallucination. You might look at a doorknob and it will appear to revolve, although you are conscious that this is the result of the drug. Also, Van Goghish colors, with all those swirls, and the crackle of the universe.

INTERVIEWER: Have you read Henri Michaux's book on mescaline?

BURROUGHS: His idea was to go into his room and close the door and hold in the experiences. I had my most interesting experiences with mescaline when I got outdoors and walked around—colors, sunsets, gardens. It produces a terrible hangover, though, nasty stuff. It makes one ill and interferes with coordination. I've had all the interesting effects I need, and I don't want any repetition of those extremely unpleasant physical reactions.

INTERVIEWER: The visions of drugs and the visions of art don't mix?

BURROUGHS: Never. The hallucinogens produce visionary states, sort of, but morphine and its derivatives decrease awareness of inner processes, thoughts and feelings. They are painkillers, pure and simple. They are absolutely contra-indicated for creative work, and I include in the lot alcohol, morphine, barbiturates, tranquilizers—the whole spectrum of sedative drugs. As for visions and heroin, I had a hallucinatory period at the very beginning of addiction, for instance, a sense of moving at high speed through space, but as soon as addiction was established, I had no visions—vision—at all and very few dreams.

INTERVIEWER: Why did you stop taking drugs?

BURROUGHS: I was living in Tangier in 1957, and I had spent a month in a tiny room in the Casbah staring at the toe of my foot. The room had filled up with empty Eukodol cartons; I suddenly realized I was not doing *anything*. I was dying. I was just apt to be finished. So I flew to London and turned myself over to Dr. John Yerbury Dent for treatment. I'd heard of his success with the apomorphine treatment. Apomorphine is simply morphine boiled in hydrochloric acid; it's nonaddicting. What the apomorphine did was to regulate my metabolism. It's a metabolic regulator. It cured me physiologically. I'd already taken the cure once at Lexington, and although I was off drugs when I got out, there was a physiological residue. Apomorphine eliminated that. I've been trying to get people in this country interested in it, but without much luck. The vast majority—social workers, doctors—have the cop's mentality toward addiction. A probation officer in California wrote me recently to inquire about the apomorphine treatment. I'll answer him at length. I always answer letters like that.

INTERVIEWER: Have you had any relapses?

BURROUGHS: Yes, a couple. Short. Both were straightened out with apomorphine and now heroin is no temptation for me. I'm just not interested. I've seen a lot of it around. I know people who are addicts. I don't have to use any will power. Dr. Dent always said there is no such thing as will power. You've got to reach a state of mind in which you don't want it or need it.

INTERVIEWER: You regard addiction as an illness, but also a central human fact, a drama?

BURROUGHS: Both, absolutely. It's as simple as the way in which anyone happens to become an alcoholic. They start drinking, that's all. They like it, and they drink, and then they become alcoholic. I was exposed to heroin in New York—that is, I was going around with people who were using it; I took it; the effects were pleasant. I went on using it and became addicted. Remember that if it can be readily obtained, you will have any number of addicts. The idea that addiction is somehow a psychological illness is, I think, totally ridiculous. It's as psychological as malaria. It's a matter of exposure. People, generally speaking, will take any intoxicant or any drug that gives them a pleasant effect if it is available to them. In Iran, for instance, opium was sold in shops until quite recently, and they had three million addicts in a population of twenty million. There are also all forms of spiritual addiction. Anything that can be done chemically can be done in other ways—that is, if we have sufficient knowledge of the processes involved. Many policemen and narcotics agents are precisely addicted to power, to exercising a certain nasty kind of power over people who are helpless. The nasty sort of power: white junk I call it—rightness; they're right, right, right—and if they lost that power, they would suffer excruciating withdrawal symptoms. The picture we get of the whole Russian bureaucracy, people who are exclusively preoccupied with power and advantage, this must be an addiction. Suppose they lose it? Well, it's been their whole life.

INTERVIEWER: Can you amplify your idea of junk as image?

BURROUGHS: It's only a theory and, I feel, an inadequate one. I don't think anyone really understands what a narcotic is or how it works, how it kills pain. My idea is sort of a stab in the dark. As I see it, what has been damaged in pain is, of course, the image, and morphine must in some sense replace this. We know it blankets the cells and that addicts are practically immune to certain viruses, to influenza and respiratory complaints. This is simple, because the influenza virus has to make a hole in the cell receptors. When those are covered, as they are in morphine addiction, the virus can't get in. As soon as morphine is withdrawn, addicts will immediately come down with colds and often with influenza.

INTERVIEWER: Certain schizophrenics also resist respiratory disease.

BURROUGHS: A long time ago I suggested there were similarities in terminal addiction and terminal schizophrenia. That was why I made the suggestion that they addict these people to heroin, then withdraw it and see if they could be motivated; in other words, find out whether they'd walk across the room and pick up a syringe. Needless to say, I didn't get very far, but I think it would be interesting.

INTERVIEWER: Narcotics, then, disturb normal perception—

BURROUGHS: —and set up instead a random craving for images. If drugs weren't forbidden in America, they would be the perfect middle-class vice. Addicts would do their work and come home to consume the huge dose of images awaiting them in the mass media. Junkies love to look at television. Billie Holiday said she knew she was going off drugs when she didn't like to watch TV. Or they'll sit and read a newspaper or magazine, and by God, read it all. I knew this old junkie in New York, and he'd go out and get a lot of newspapers and magazines and some candy bars and several packages of cigarettes and then he'd sit in his room and he'd read those newspapers and magazines right straight through. Indiscriminately. Every word.

INTERVIEWER: You seem primarily interested in bypassing the conscious, rational apparatus to which most writers direct their efforts.

BURROUGHS: I don't know about where fiction ordinarily directs itself, but I am quite deliberately addressing myself to the whole area of what we call dreams. Precisely what is a dream? A certain juxtaposition of word and image. I've recently done a lot of experiments with scrapbooks. I'll read in the newspaper something that reminds me of or has relation to something I've written. I'll cut out the picture or article and paste it in a scrapbook beside the words from my book. Or, I'll be walking down the street and I'll suddenly see a scene from my book and I'll photograph it and put it in a scrapbook. I'll show you some of those. I've found that when preparing a page, I'll almost invariably dream that night something relating to this juxtaposition of word and image. In other words, I've been interested in precisely how word and image get around on very, very complex association lines. I do a lot of exercises in what I call time travel, in taking coordinates, such as what I photographed on the train, what I was thinking about at the time, what I was reading and what I wrote; all of this to see how completely I can project myself back to that one point in time.

INTERVIEWER: In *Nova Express* you indicate that silence is a desirable state.

BURROUGHS: The *most* desirable state. In one sense a special use of words and pictures can conduce silence. The scrapbooks and time travel are exercises to expand consciousness, to teach me to think in association blocks rather than words. I've recently spent a little time studying hieroglyph systems, both the Egyptian and the Mayan. A whole block of associations—boonf!—like that! Words—at least the way we use them —can stand in the way of what I call nonbody experience. It's time we thought about leaving the body behind.

INTERVIEWER: Marshall McLuhan said that you believed heroin was needed to turn the human body into an environment that includes the universe. But from what you've told me, you're not at all interested in turning the body into an environment.

BURROUGHS: No, junk narrows consciousness. The only benefit to me as a writer (aside from putting me into contact with the whole carny world) came to me after I went off it. What I want to do is to learn to see more of what's out there, to look outside, to achieve as far as possible a complete awareness of surroundings. Beckett wants to go inward. First he was in a bottle and now he is in the mud. I am aimed in the other direction: outward.

INTERVIEWER: Have you been able to think for any length of time in images, with the inner voice silent?

BURROUGHS: I'm becoming more proficient at it, partly through my work with scrapbooks and translating the connections between words and images. Try this: Carefully memorize the meaning of a passage, then read it; you'll find you can actually read it without the words' making any sound whatever in the mind's ear. Extraordinary experience, and one that will carry over into dreams. When you start thinking in images, without words, you're well on the way.

INTERVIEWER: Why is the wordless state so desirable?

BURROUGHS: I think it's the evolutionary trend. I think that words are an around-the world, ox-cart way of doing things, awkward instruments, and they will be laid aside eventually, probably sooner than we think. This is something that will happen in the space age. Most serious writers refuse to make themselves available to the things that technology is doing. I've never been able to understand this sort of fear. Many of them are afraid of tape recorders and the idea of using any mechanical means for literary purposes seems to them some sort of a sacrilege. This is one objection to the cutups. There's been a lot of that, a sort of a superstitious reverence for the word. My God, they say, you can't cut up these words. Why *can't* I? I find it much easier to get interest in the cutups from people who are not writers—doctors, lawyers, or engineers, any open-minded, fairly intelligent person—than from those who are.

INTERVIEWER: How did you become interested in the cutup technique?

BURROUGHS: A friend, Brion Gysin, an American poet and painter, who has lived in Europe for thirty years, was, as far as I know, the first to create cutups. His cutup poem, "Minutes to Go," was broadcast by the BBC and later published in a pamphlet. I was in Paris in the summer of 1960; this was after the publication there of *Naked Lunch*. I became interested in the possibilities of this technique, and I began experimenting myself. Of course, when you think of it, "The Waste Land" was the first great cutup collage, and Tristan Tzara had done a bit along the same lines. Dos Passos used the same idea in "The Camera Eye" sequences in *U.S.A.* I felt I had been working toward the same goal; thus it was a major revelation to me when I actually saw it being done.

INTERVIEWER: What do cutups offer the reader that conventional narrative doesn't?

BURROUGHS: Any narrative passage or any passage, say, of poetic images is subject to any number of variations, all of which may be interesting and valid in their own right. A page of Rimbaud cut up and rearranged will give you quite new images. Rimbaud images—real Rimbaud images —but new ones.

INTERVIEWER: You deplore the accumulation of images and at the same time you seem to be looking for new ones.

BURROUGHS: Yes, it's part of the paradox of anyone who is working with word and image, and after all, that is what a writer is still doing. Painter too. Cutups establish new connections between images, and one's range of vision consequently expands.

INTERVIEWER: Instead of going to the trouble of working with scissors and all those pieces of paper, couldn't you obtain the same effect by simply free-associating at the typewriter?

BURROUGHS: One's mind can't cover it that way. Now, for example, if I wanted to make a cutup of this [*picking up a copy of the* Nation], there are many ways I could do it. I could read cross-column; I could say: "Today's men's nerves surround us. Each technological extension gone outside is electrical involves an act of collective environment. The human nervous environment system itself can be reprogrammed with all its private and social values because it is content. He programs logically as readily as any radio net is swallowed by the new environment. The sensory order." You find it often makes quite as much sense as the original. You learn to leave out words and to make connections. [*Gesturing*] Suppose I should cut this down the middle here, and put this up here. Your mind simply could not manage it. It's like trying to keep so many chess moves in mind, you just couldn't do it. The mental mechanisms of repression and selection are also operating against you.

INTERVIEWER: You believe that an audience can be eventually trained to respond to cutups?

BURROUGHS: Of course, because cutups make explicit a psychosensory process that is going on all the time anyway. Somebody is reading a newspaper, and his eye follows the column in the proper Aristotelian manner, one idea and sentence at a time. But subliminally he is reading the columns on either side and is aware of the person sitting next to him. That's a cutup. I was sitting in a lunchroom in New York having my doughnuts and coffee. I was thinking that one *does* feel a little boxed in New York, like living in a series of boxes. I looked out the window and there was a great big Yale truck. That's cutup—a juxtaposition of what's happening outside and what you're thinking of. I make this a practice when I walk down the street. I'll say, When I got to here I saw that sign, I was thinking this, and when I return to the house I'll type these up. Some of this material I use and some I don't. I have literally thousands of pages of notes here, raw, and I keep a diary as well. In a sense it's traveling in time.

Most people don't see what's going on around them. That's my principal message to writers: For Godsake, keep your *eyes* open. Notice what's going on around you. I mean, I walk down the street with friends. I ask, "Did you see him, that person who just walked by?" No, they didn't notice him. I had a very pleasant time on the train coming out here. I haven't traveled on trains in years. I found there were no drawing rooms. I got a bedroom so I could set up my typewriter and look out the window. I was taking photos, too. I also noticed all the signs and what I was thinking at the time, you see. And I got some extraordinary juxtapositions. For example, a friend of mine has a loft apartment in New York. He said "Every time we go out of the house and come back, if we leave the bathroom door open, there's a rat in the house." I look out the window, there's Able Pest Control.

INTERVIEWER: The one flaw in the cutup argument seems to lie in the linguistic base on which we operate, the straight declarative sentence. It's going to take a great deal to change that.

BURROUGHS: Yes, it is unfortunately one of the great errors of Western thought, the whole either-or proposition. You remember Korzybski and his idea of non-Aristotelian logic. Either-or thinking just is not accurate thinking. That's not the way things occur, and I feel the Aristotelian construct is one of the great shackles of Western civilization. Cutups are a movement toward breaking this down. I should imagine it would be much easier to find acceptance of the cutups from, possibly, the Chinese, because you see already there are many ways that they can read any given ideograph. It's already cut up.

INTERVIEWER: What will happen to the straight plot in fiction?

BURROUGHS: Plot has always had the definite function of stage direction, of getting the characters from here to there, and that will continue, but the new techniques, such as cutup, will involve much more of the total capacity of the observer. It enriches the whole aesthetic experience, extends it.

INTERVIEWER: *Nova Express* is a cutup of many writers?

BURROUGHS: Joyce is in there. Shakespeare, Rimbaud, some writers that people haven't heard about, someone named Jack Stern. There's Kerouac. I don't know, when you start making these foldins and cutups you lose track. Genet, of course, is someone I admire very much. But what he's doing is classical French prose. He's not a verbal innovator. Also Kafka, Eliot, and one of my favorites is Joseph Conrad. My story, "They Just Fade Away," is a foldin (instead of cutting, you fold) from *Lord Jim.* In fact, it's almost a retelling of the *Lord Jim* story. My Stein is the same Stein as in *Lord Jim.* Richard Hughes is another favorite of mine. And Graham Greene. For exercise, when I make a trip, such as from Tangier to Gibraltar, I will record this in three columns in a note book I always take with me. One column will contain simply an account of the trip, what happened: I arrived at the air terminal, what was said by the clerks, what I overheard on the plane, what hotel I checked into. The next column presents my memories: that is, what I was thinking of at the time, the memories that were activated by my encounters. And the third column, which I call my reading column, gives quotations from any book that I take with me. I have practically a whole novel alone on my trips to Gibraltar. Besides Graham Greene, I've used other books. I used *The Wonderful Country* by Tom Lea on one trip. Let's see . . . and Eliot's *The Cocktail Party; In Hazard* by Richard Hughes. For example, I'm reading *The Wonderful Country* and the hero is just crossing the frontier into Mexico. Well, just at this point I come to the Spanish frontier, so I note that down in the margin. Or I'm on a boat or a train and I'm reading *The Quiet American;* I look around and see if there's a quiet American aboard. Sure enough, there's a quiet sort of young American with a crew cut, drinking a bottle of beer. It's extraordinary, if you really keep your eyes open. I was reading Raymond Chandler, and one of his characters was an albino gunman. My God, if there wasn't an albino in the room. He wasn't a gunman.

Who else? Wait a minute, I'll just check my coordinate books to see if there's anyone I've forgotten—Conrad, Richard Hughes, science fiction, quite a bit of science fiction. Eric Frank Russell has written some very, very interesting books. Here's one, *The Star Virus;* I doubt if you've heard of it. He develops a concept here of what he calls Deadliners who have this strange sort of seedy look. I read this when I was in Gibraltar, and I began to find Deadliners all over the place. The story has a fish pond in it, and quite a flower garden. My father was always very interested in gardening.

INTERVIEWER: In view of all this, what will happen to fiction in the next twenty-five years?

BURROUGHS: In the first place, I think there's going to be more and more merging of art and science. Scientists are already studying the creative process, and I think the whole line between art and science will break down and that scientists, I hope, will become more creative and writers more scientific. And I see no reason why the artistic world can't absolutely merge with Madison Avenue. Pop art is a move in that direction. Why can't we have advertisements with beautiful words and beautiful images? Already some of the very beautiful color photography appears in whisky ads, I notice. Science will also discover for us how association blocks actually form.

INTERVIEWER: Do you think this will destroy the magic?

BURROUGHS: Not at all. I would say it would enhance it.

INTERVIEWER: Have you done anything with computers?

BURROUGHS: I've not done anything, but I've seen some of the computer poetry. I can take one of those computer poems and then try to find correlatives of it—that is, pictures to go with it; it's quite possible.

INTERVIEWER: Does the fact that it comes from a machine diminish its value to you?

BURROUGHS: I think that any artistic product must stand or fall on what's there.

INTERVIEWER: Therefore, you're not upset by the fact that a chimpanzee can do an abstract painting?

BURROUGHS: If he does a good one, no. People say to me, "Oh, this is all very good, but you got it by cutting up." I say that has nothing to do with it, how I got it. What is any writing but a cutup? Somebody has to program the machine; somebody has to *do* the cutting up. Remember that I first made selections. Out of hundreds of possible sentences that I might have used, I chose one.

INTERVIEWER: Incidentally, one image in *Nova Express* keeps coming back to me and I don't quite understand it: the gray room, "breaking through to the gray room."

BURROUGHS: I see that as very much like the photographic darkroom where the reality photographs are actually produced. Implicit in *Nova Express* is a theory that what we call reality is actually a movie. It's a film—what I call a biologic film. What has happened is that the underground and also the nova police have made a break-through past the guards and gotten into the darkroom where the films are processed, where they're in a position to expose negatives and prevent events from occurring. They're like police anywhere. All right, you've got a bad situation here in which the nova mob is about to blow up the planet. So the Heavy Metal Kid calls in the nova police. Once you get them in there, by God, they begin acting like any police. They're always an ambivalent agency. I recall once in South America that I complained to the police that a camera had been stolen and they ended up arresting me. I hadn't registered or something. In other words, once you get them on the scene they really start nosing around. Once the law starts asking questions, there's no end to it. For "nova police," read "technology," if you wish.

INTERVIEWER: Mary McCarthy has commented on the carnival origins of your characters in *Naked Lunch*. What are their other derivations?

BURROUGHS: The carny world was the one I exactly intended to create—a kind of Midwestern, small-town, cracker-barrel, pratfall type of folk-lore, very much my own background. That world was an integral part of America and existed nowhere else, at least not in the same form. My family was Southern on my mother's side. My grandfather was a circuit-riding Methodist minister with thirteen children. Most of them went up to New York and became quite successful in advertising and public relations. One of them, an uncle, was a master image-maker, Ivy Lee, Rockefeller's publicity manager.

INTERVIEWER: Is it true that you did a great deal of acting out to create your characters when you were finishing *Naked Lunch*?

BURROUGHS: Excuse me, there is no accurate description of the creation of a book, or an event. Read Durrell's "Alexandria" novels for four different ways of looking at the same thing. Gysin saw me pasting pictures on the wall of a Paris hotel room and using a tape recorder to act out several voices. Actually, it was written mainly in Tangier, after I had taken the cure with Dr. Dent in London in 1957. I came back to Tangier and I started working on a lot of notes that I had made over a period of years. Most of the book was written at that time. I went to Paris about 1959, and I had a great pile of manuscripts. Girodias was interested, and he asked if I could get the book ready in two weeks. This is the period that Brion is referring to when, from manuscripts collected over a period of years, I assembled what became the book from some thousand pages, something like that.

INTERVIEWER: But did you actually leap up and act out, say, Dr. Benway?

BURROUGHS: Yes, I have. Dr. Benway dates back to a story I wrote in 1938 with a friend of mine, Kells Elvins, who is now dead. That's about the only piece of writing I did prior to *Junkie*. And we did definitely act the thing out. We decided that was the way to write. Now here's this guy, what does he say, what does he do? Dr. Benway sort of emerged quite spontaneously while we were composing this piece. Something I've been meaning to do with my scrapbooks is to have files on every character, almost like police files: habits, idiosyncrasies, where born, pictures. That is, if I ever see anyone in a magazine or newspaper who looks like Dr. Benway (and several people have played Dr. Benway, sort of amateur actors), I take their photographs. Many of my characters first come through strongly to me as voices. That's why I use a tape recorder. They also carry over from one book to another.

INTERVIEWER: Do any have their origins in actual persons?

BURROUGHS: Hamburger Mary is one. There was a place in New York called Hamburger Mary's. I was in Hamburger Mary's when a friend gave me a batch of morphine syrettes. That was my first experience with morphine, and then I built up a whole picture of Hamburger Mary. She is also an actual person. I don't like to give her name for fear of being sued for libel, but she was a Scientologist who started out in a hamburger joint in Portland, Oregon, and now has eleven million dollars.

INTERVIEWER: What about the Heavy Metal Kid?

BURROUGHS: There again, quite complicated origins, partly based on my own experience. I felt that heavy metal was sort of the ultimate expression of addiction, that there's something actually metallic in addiction, that the final stage reached is not so much vegetable as mineral. It's increasingly inanimate, in any case. You see, as Dr. Benway said, I've now decided that junk is not green, but blue. Some of my characters come to me in dreams, Daddy Long Legs, for instance. Once, in a clinic, I had a dream in which I saw a man in this run-down clinic and his name in the dream was Daddy Long Legs. Many characters have come to me like that in a dream, and then I'll elaborate from there. I always write down all my dreams. That's why I've got that notebook beside the bed there.

INTERVIEWER: Earlier you mentioned that if junk had done nothing else, it at least put you in contact with the carny world.

BURROUGHS: Yes, the underworld, the old-time thieves, pickpockets, and people like that. They're a dying race; very few of those old-timers left. Yeah, well, they were show business.

INTERVIEWER: What's the difference between the modern junkie and the 1944 junkie?

BURROUGHS: For one thing, all these young addicts; that was quite unknown in 1944. Most of the ones I knew were middle-aged men or old. I knew some of the old-time pickpockets and sneak thieves and short-change artists. They had something called The Bill, a short-change deal. I've never been able to figure out how it works. One man I knew beat all the cashiers in Grand Central with this thing. It starts with a twenty-dollar bill. You give them a twenty-dollar bill and then when you get the change you say, "Well, wait a minute, I must have been dreaming, I've got the change after all." First thing you know, the cashier's short ten dollars. One day this short-change artist went to Grand Central, even though he knew it was burned down, but he wanted to change twenty dollars. Well, a guy got on the buzzer, and they arrested him. When they got up in court and tried to explain what had happened, none of them could do it. I keep stories like this in my files.

INTERVIEWER: In your apartment in Tangier?

BURROUGHS: No, all of it is right here in this room.

INTERVIEWER: In case Tangier is blown up, it's all safe?

BURROUGHS: Well, more than that. *I need it all.* I brought everything. That's why I have to travel by boat and by train, because, well, just to give you an idea, that's a photographic file. [*Thud*] Those are all photographs and photographs. When I sit down to write, I may suddenly think of something I wrote three years ago which should be in this file over here. It may not be. I'm always looking through these files. That's why I need a place where I can really spread them out, to see what's what. I'm looking for one particular paper, it often takes me a long time and sometimes I don't find it. Those dresser drawers are full of files. All those drawers in the closets are full of files. It's pretty well organized. Here's a file, THE 1920 MOVIE, which partly contains some motion picture ideas. Here's ALL THE SAD OLD SHOWMEN; has some business about bank robbers in it. Here's THE NOVA POLICE GAZETTE. This is ANALOG, which contains science-fiction material. This is THE CAPTAIN'S LOGBOOK. I've been interested in sea stories, but I know so little about the sea, I hesitate to do much. I collect sea disasters such as the *Mary Celeste*. Here's a file on Mr. Luce.

INTERVIEWER: Do you admire Mr. Luce?

BURROUGHS: I don't admire him at all. He has set up one of the greatest word-and-image banks in the world. I mean, there are thousands of photos, thousands of words about anything and everything, all in his files. All the best pictures go into the files. Of course, they're reduced to microphotos now. I've been interested in the Mayan system, which was a control calendar. You see, their calendar postulated really how everyone should feel at a given time, with lucky days, unlucky days, et cetera. And I feel that Luce's system is comparable to that. It is a control system. It has nothing to do with reporting. *Time-Life-Fortune* is some sort of a police organization.

INTERVIEWER: You've said your next book will be about the American West and a gunfighter.

BURROUGHS: Yes, I've thought about this for years and I have hundreds of pages of notes on the whole concept of the gunfighter. The gun duel was a sort of Zen contest, a real spiritual contest like Zen swordsmanship.

INTERVIEWER: Would this be cutup, or more a conventional narrative?

BURROUGHS: I'd use cutups extensively in the preparation, because they would give me all sorts of facets of character and place, but the final version would be straight narrative. I wouldn't want to get bogged down in too much factual detail, but I'd like to do research in New Mexico or Arizona, even though the actual towns out there have become synthetic tourist attractions. Occasionally I have the sensation that I'm repeating myself in my work, and I would like to do something different—almost a deliberate change of style. I'm not sure if it's possible, but I want to try. I've been thinking about the western for years. As a boy, I was sent to school in New Mexico, and during the war I was stationed in Coldspring, Texas, near Conroe. That's genuine backwoods country, and I picked up some real characters there. For instance, a fellow who actually lived in east Texas. He was always having trouble with his neighbors, who suspected him of rustling their cattle, I think with good reason. But he was competent with a gun and there wasn't anyone who would go up against him. He finally was killed. He got drunk and went to sleep under a tree by a campfire. The fire set fire to the tree, and it fell on him. I'm interested in extending newspaper and magazine formats to so-called literary materials. Here, this is one of my attempts. This is going to be published in a little magazine, *The Sparrow*.

INTERVIEWER [*reading*]: "The Coldspring News, All the News That Fits We Print, Sunday, September 17, 1899, William Burroughs, Editor." Here's Bradley Martin again.

BURROUGHS: Yes, he's the gunfighter. I'm not sure yet what's going to happen after Clem accuses him of rustling cattle. I guess Clem goes into Coldspring and there's gunplay between him and the gunfighter. He's going to kill Clem, obviously. Clem is practically a dead man. Clem is going to get "likkered up" and think he can tangle with Bradley Martin, and Bradley Martin is going to kill him, that's for sure.

INTERVIEWER: Will your other characters reappear? Dr. Benway?

BURROUGHS: He'd be the local doctor. That's what I'd like to do, you see, use all these characters in a straight western story. There would be Mr. Bradley Mr. Martin, whose name is Bradley Martin; there would be Dr. Benway; and we'd have the various traveling carny-and-medicine shows that come through with the Subliminal Kid and all of the con men. That was the heyday for those old joes.

INTERVIEWER: Do you think of the artist at all as being a con man?

BURROUGHS: In a sense. You see, a real con man is a creator. He creates a set. No, a con man is more a movie director than a writer. The Yellow Kid created a whole set, a whole cast of characters, a whole brokerage house, a whole bank. It was just like a movie studio.

INTERVIEWER: What about addicts?

BURROUGHS: Well, there will be a lot of morphine addiction. Remember that there were a great many addicts at that time. Jesse James was an addict. He started using morphine for a wound in his lung, and I don't know whether he was permanently addicted, but he tried to kill himself. He took sixteen grains of morphine and it didn't kill him, which indicates a terrific tolerance. So he must have been fairly heavily addicted. A dumb, brutal hick—that's what he was, like Dillinger. And there were so many genteel old ladies who didn't feel right unless they had their Dr. Jones mixture every day.

INTERVIEWER: What about the Green Boy, Izzy the Push, Green Tony, Sammy the Butcher, and Willie the Fink?

BURROUGHS: See, all of them could be western characters except Izzy the Push. The buildings weren't high enough in those days. Defenestration, incidentally, is a very interesting phenomenon. Some people who are prone to it will not live in high buildings. They get near a window, someone in the next room hears a cry, and they're gone. "Fell or jumped" is the phrase. I would add, "or was pushed."

INTERVIEWER: What other character types interest you?

BURROUGHS: Not the people in advertising and television, nor the American postman or middle-class housewife; not the young man setting forth. The whole world of high finance interests me, the men such as Rockefeller who were specialized types of organisms that could exist in a certain environment. He was really a money-making machine, but I doubt that he could have made a dime today because he required the old laissez-faire capitalism. He was a specialized monopolistic organism. My uncle Ivy created images for him. I fail to understand why people like J. Paul Getty have to come on with such a stuffy, uninteresting image. He decides to write his life history. I've never read anything so dull, so absolutely devoid of any spark. Well, after all, he was quite a playboy in his youth. There must have been something going on.

None of it's in the book. Here he is, the only man of enormous wealth who operates alone, but there's nobody to present the image. Well, yes, I wouldn't mind doing that sort of job myself. I'd like to take somebody like Getty and try to find an image for him that would be of some interest. If Getty wants to build an image, why doesn't he hire a first-rate writer to write his story? For that matter, advertising has a long way to go. I'd like to see a story by Norman Mailer or John O'Hara which just makes some mention of a product, say, Southern Comfort. I can see the O'Hara story. It would be about someone who went into a bar and asked for Southern Comfort; they didn't have it, and he gets into a long, stupid argument with the bartender. It shouldn't be obtrusive; the story must be interesting in itself so that people read this just as they read any story in *Playboy*, and Southern Comfort would be guaranteed that people will look at that advertisement for a certain number of minutes. You see what I mean? They'll read the story. Now, there are many other ideas; you could have serialized comic strips, serial stories. Well, all we have to do is have James Bond smoking a certain brand of cigarettes.

INTERVIEWER: Didn't you once work for an advertising agency?

BURROUGHS: Yes, after I got out of Harvard in 1936. I had done some graduate work in anthropology. I got a glimpse of academic life and I didn't like it at all. It looked like there was too much faculty intrigue, faculty teas, cultivating the head of the department, and so on and so forth. Then I spent a year as a copy writer in this small advertising agency, since defunct, in New York. We had a lot of rather weird accounts. There was some device called the Cascade for giving high colonics, and something called Endocreme. It was supposed to make women look younger, because it contained some female sex hormones. The Interstate Commerce Commission was never far behind. As you can see, I've recently thought a great deal about advertising. After all, they're doing the same sort of thing. They are concerned with the precise manipulation of word and image. Anyway, after the ad game I was in the army for a bit. Honorably discharged and then the usual strange wartime jobs—bartender, exterminator, reporter, and factory and office jobs. Then Mexico, a sinister place.

INTERVIEWER: Why sinister?

BURROUGHS: I was there during the Alemán regime. If you walked into a bar, there would be at least fifteen people in there who were carrying guns. Everybody was carrying guns. They got drunk and they were a menace to any living creature. I mean, sitting in a cocktail lounge, you always had to be ready to hit the deck. I had a friend who was shot, killed. But he asked for it. He was waving his little .25 automatic around in a bar and some Mexican blasted him with a .45. They listed the death as natural causes, because the killer was a political big shot. There was no scandal, but it was really as much as your life was worth to go into a cocktail lounge. And I had that terrible accident with Joan Vollmer, my wife. I had a revolver that I was planning to sell to a friend. I was checking it over and it went off—killed her. A rumor started that I was trying to shoot a glass of champagne from her head, William Tell style. Absurd and false. Then they had a big depistolization. Mexico City had one of the highest per-capita homicide rates in the world. Another thing, every time you turned around there was some Mexican cop with his hand out, finding some fault with your papers, or something, just anything he could latch onto. "Papers very bad, señor." It really was a bit much, the Alemán regime.

INTERVIEWER: From Mexico?

BURROUGHS: I went to Colombia, Peru, and Ecuador, just looking around. I was particularly interested in the Amazon region of Peru, where I took a drug called yage, *Bannisteria caapi*, a hallucinogen as powerful as mescaline, I believe. The whole trip gave me an awful lot of copy. A lot of these experiences went into *The Ticket That Exploded*, which is sort of midway between *Naked Lunch* and *The Soft Machine*. It's not a book I'm satisfied with in its present form. If it's published in the United States, I would have to rewrite it. *The Soft Machine*, which will come out here in due time, is an expansion of my South American experiences, with surreal extensions. When I rewrote it recently, I included about sixty-five pages of straight narrative concerning Dr. Benway, and the Sailor, and various characters from *Naked Lunch*. These people pop up everywhere.

INTERVIEWER: Then from South America you went to Europe. Is the geographic switch as important as it once was to American writing?

BURROUGHS: Well, if I hadn't covered a lot of ground, I wouldn't have encountered the extra dimensions of character and extremity that make the difference. But I think the day of the expatriate is definitely over. It's becoming more and more uncomfortable, more and more expensive, and less and less rewarding to live abroad, as far as I'm concerned. Now I'm particularly concerned with quiet writing conditions—being able to concentrate—and not so much interested in the place where I am. To me, Paris is now one of the most disagreeable cities in the world. I just hate it. The food is uneatable. It's either very expensive, or you just can't eat it. In order to get a good sandwich at three o'clock in the afternoon, I have to get into a taxi and go all the way over to the Right Bank. Here all I have to do is pick up the phone. They send me up a club sandwich and a glass of buttermilk, which is all I want for lunch anyway. The French have gotten so nasty and they're getting nastier and nastier. The Algerian war and then all those millions of people dumped back into France and all of them thoroughly dissatisfied. I don't know, I think the atmosphere there is unpleasant and not conducive to anything.

You can't get an apartment. You can't get a quiet place to work. Best you can do is a dinky hotel room somewhere. If I want to get something like this, it costs me thirty dollars a day. The main thing I've found after twenty years away from Saint Louis is that the standard of service is much better than New York. These are Claridge's or Ritz accommodations. If I could afford it, keep it, this would be an ideal place for me. There's not a sound in here. It's been very conducive to work. I've got a lot of room here to spread out all my papers in all these drawers and shelves. It's quiet. When I want something to eat, I pick up the phone. I can work right straight through. Get up in the morning, pick up the phone about two o'clock and have a sandwich, and work through till dinner time. Also, it's interesting to turn on the TV set every now and then.

INTERVIEWER: What do you find on it?

BURROUGHS: That's a *real* cutup. It flickers, just like the old movies used to. When talkies came in and they perfected the image, the movies became as dull as looking out the window. A bunch of Italians in Rabat have a television station and we could get the signal in Tangier. I just sat there openmouthed looking at it. What with blurring and contractions and visual static, some of their westerns became very, very odd. Gysin has been experimenting with the flicker principle in a gadget he calls a Dreamachine. There used to be one in the window of The English Bookshop on the Rue de Seine. Helena Rubenstein was so fascinated she bought a couple, and Harold Matson, the agent, thinks it's a million-dollar idea.

INTERVIEWER: Describe a typical day's work.

BURROUGHS: I get up about nine o'clock and order breakfast; I hate to go out for breakfast. I work usually until about two o'clock or two-thirty, when I like to have a sandwich and a glass of milk, which takes about ten minutes. I'll work through until six or seven o'clock. Then, if I'm seeing people or going out, I'll go out, have a few drinks, come back and maybe do a little reading and go to bed. I go to bed pretty early. I don't make myself work. It's just the thing I want to do. To be completely alone in a room, to know that there'll be no interruptions and I've got eight hours is just exactly what I want—yeah, just paradise.

INTERVIEWER: Do you compose on the typewriter?

BURROUGHS: I use the typewriter and I use scissors. I can sit down with scissors and old manuscripts and paste in photographs for hours; I have hundreds of photographs. I usually take a walk every day. Here in Saint Louis I've been trying to take 1920 photographs, alleys and whatnot. This [*pointing*] is a ghostly photograph of the house in which I grew up, seen back through forty-five years. Here's a photo of an old ashpit. It was great fun for children to get out there in the alley after Christmas and build a fire in the ashpit with all the excelsior and wrappings. Here, these are stories and pictures from the society columns.

I've been doing a cutup of society coverage. I had a lot of fun piling up these names; you get some improbable names in the society columns.

INTERVIEWER: You recently said you would like to settle in the Ozarks. Were you serious?

BURROUGHS: I would like to have a place there. It's a very beautiful area in the fall, and I'd like to spend periods of time, say every month or every two months, in complete solitude, just working, which requires an isolated situation. Of course, I'd have to buy a car, for one thing, and you run into considerable expense. I just have to think in terms of an apartment. I thought possibly an apartment here, but most likely I'll get one in New York. I'm not returning to Tangier. I just don't like it any more. It's become just a small town. There's no life there, and the place has no novelty for me at all. I was sitting there, and I thought, My God, I might as well be in Columbus, Ohio, as here, for all the interest that the town has for me. I was just sitting in my apartment working. I could have a better apartment and better working conditions somewhere else. After ten o'clock at night, there's no one on the streets. The old settlers like Paul Bowles and those people who have been there for years and years are sort of hanging on desperately asking, "Where could we go if we left Tangier?" I don't know, it just depresses me now. It's not even cheap there. If I travel anywhere, it will be to the Far East, but only for a visit. I've never been east of Athens.

INTERVIEWER: That reminds me, I meant to ask you what's behind your interest in the more exotic systems such as Zen, or Dr. Reich's orgone theories?

BURROUGHS: Well, these nonconventional theories frequently touch on something going on that Harvard and M.I.T. can't explain. I don't mean that I endorse them wholeheartedly, but I am interested in any attempt along those lines. I've used these orgone accumulators and I'm convinced that something occurs there, I don't know quite what. Of course, Reich himself went around the bend, no question of that.

INTERVIEWER: You mentioned Scientology earlier. Do you have a system for getting on, or are you looking for one?

BURROUGHS: I'm not very interested in such a crudely three-dimensional manipulative schema as L. Ron Hubbard's, although it's got its points. I've studied it and I've seen how it works. It's a series of manipulative gimmicks. They tell you to look around and see what you would have. The results are much more subtle and more successful than Dale Carnegie's. But as far as my living by a system, no. At the same time, I don't think anything happens in this universe except by some power— or individual—making it happen. Nothing happens of itself. I believe all events are produced by will.

INTERVIEWER: Then do you believe in the existence of God?

BURROUGHS: God? I wouldn't say. I think there are innumerable gods. What we on earth call God is a little tribal god who has made an awful mess. Certainly forces operating through human consciousness control events. A Luce writer may be an agent of God knows what power, a force with an insatiable appetite for word and image. What does this force propose to do with such a tremendous mound of image garbage? They've got a regular casting office. To interview Mary McCarthy, they'll send a shy Vassar girl who's just trying to get along. They had several carny people for me. "Shucks, Bill, you got a reefer?" *Reefer*, my God! "Certainly not," I told them. "I don't know what you're talking about." Then they go back and write a nasty article for the files.

INTERVIEWER: In some respects, *Nova Express* seems to be a prescription for social ailments. Do you see the need, for instance, of biologic courts in the future?

BURROUGHS: Certainly. Science eventually will be forced to establish courts of biologic mediation, because life forms are going to become more incompatible with the conditions of existence as man penetrates further into space. Mankind will have to undergo biologic alterations ultimately, if we are to survive at all. This will require biologic law to decide what changes to make. We will simply have to use our intelligence to plan mutations, rather than letting them occur at random. Because many such mutations—look at the sabertooth tiger—are bound to be very poor engineering designs. The future, decidedly, yes. I think there are innumerable possibilities, literally innumerable. The hope lies in the development of nonbody experience and eventually getting away from the body itself, away from three-dimensional coordinates and concomitant animal reactions of fear and flight, which lead inevitably to tribal feuds and dissension.

INTERVIEWER: Why did you choose an interplanetary war as the conflict in *Nova Express*, rather than discord between nations? You seem fascinated with the idea that a superterrestrial power is exercising an apparatus of control, such as the death dwarfs—

BURROUGHS: They're parasitic organisms occupying a human host, rather like a radio transmitter, which direct and control it. The people who work with encephalograms and brain waves point out that technically it will someday be possible to install at birth a radio antenna in the brain which will control thought, feeling, and sensory perceptions, actually not only control thought, but make certain thoughts impossible. The death dwarfs are weapons of the nova mob, which in turn is calling the shots in the Cold War. The nova mob is using that conflict in an attempt to blow up the planet, because when you get right down to it, what are America and Russia really arguing about? The Soviet Union and the United States will eventually consist of interchangeable social parts and neither nation is morally "right." The idea that anyone can run his own factory in America is ridiculous. The government and the unions—which both amount to the same thing: control systems—tell him who he can hire, how much he can pay them, and how he can sell his goods.

What difference does it make if the state owns the plant and retains him as manager? Regardless of how it's done, the same kind of people will be in charge. One's ally today is an enemy tomorrow. I have postulated this power—the nova mob—which forces us to play musical chairs.

INTERVIEWER: You see hope for the human race, but at the same time you are alarmed as the instruments of control become more sophisticated.

BURROUGHS: Well, whereas they become more sophisticated they also become more vulnerable. *Time-Life-Fortune* applies a more complex, effective control system than the Mayan calendar but it also is much more vulnerable because it is so vast and mechanized. Not even Henry Luce understands what's going on in the system now. Well, a machine can be redirected. One technical sergeant can fuck up the whole works. Nobody can control the whole operation. It's too complex. The captain comes in and says, "All right, boys, we're moving up." Now, who knows what buttons to push? Who knows how to get the cases of Spam up to where they're going, and how to fill out the forms? The sergeant does. The captain doesn't know. As long as there're sergeants around, the machine can be dismantled, and we may get out of all this alive yet.

INTERVIEWER: Sex seems equated with death frequently in your work.

BURROUGHS: That is an extension of the idea of sex as a biologic weapon. I feel that sex, like practically every other human manifestation, has been degraded for control purposes, or really for antihuman purposes. This whole puritanism. How are we ever going to find out anything about sex scientifically, when a priori the subject cannot even be investigated? It can't even be thought about or written about. That was one of the interesting things about Reich. He was one of the few people who ever tried to investigate sex—sexual phenomena, from a scientific point of view. There's this prurience and this fear of sex. We know nothing about sex. What is it? Why is it pleasurable? What is pleasure? Relief from tension? Well, possibly.

INTERVIEWER: Are you irreconcilably hostile to the twentieth century?

BURROUGHS: Not at all, although I can imagine myself as having been born under many different circumstances. For example, I had a dream recently in which I returned to the family home and I found a different father and a different house from any I'd ever seen before. Yet in a dream sense, the father and the house were quite familiar.

INTERVIEWER: Mary McCarthy has characterized you as a soured utopian. Is that accurate?

BURROUGHS: I do definitely mean what I say to be taken literally, yes, to make people aware of the true criminality of our times, to wise up the marks. All of my work is directed against those who are bent, through stupidity or design, on blowing up the planet or rendering it uninhabitable. Like the advertising people we talked about, I'm concerned with the precise manipulation of word and image to create an action, not to go out and buy a Coca-Cola, but to create an alteration in the reader's consciousness. You know, they ask me if I were on a desert island and knew nobody would ever see what I wrote, would I go on writing. My answer is most emphatically yes. I would go on writing for company. Because I'm creating an imaginary—it's always imaginary—world in which I would like to live.

PART SEVEN

The Writing Itself

In the end there is the work itself—the whole aim and point of
the craft. Exactly what is the actual experience of writing?
What are "the agonies of art," of which Flaubert writes? What
are the rewards, which surely must lie in the writing itself, and
nowhere else? To try to taste the experience as close to
first-hand as possible, we will follow seven quite different
accounts of the writing of a novel. Three of these accounts were
put down while the work was still in progress, and as it went
along; four, afterward, looking back on the struggle. The points
of emphasis in these pieces vary: in one it is the care devoted to
each sentence, each page; in another, the courage revision
requires; in a third, the process of preparation and gestation
before actual writing begins; in still another, the psychic energy
a writer must give to a work that takes months and years to
bring to an end.

Gustave Flaubert

(1821–1880)

Madame Bovary, *Percy Lubbock wrote in* The Craft of Fiction, *"remains perpetually the novel of all novels which the criticism of fiction cannot overlook." It is—perhaps even more so—the novel of all novels which any maker of fiction cannot get out of his mind once he has met, in it, its author's craftsmanship. It is preeminently the novelist's novel. The reason for this lies not simply in the work itself, but in a coming together of the book with the author's account of the care he took in writing it. In 1846, in the Paris studio of a breezy, violent, sensuous sculptor named James Pradier, who thought that every restless young creative man should have a mistress, Gustave Flaubert, a provincial would-be writer of twenty-four, met a beautiful woman in her mid-thirties named Louise Colet—a poet of sorts, the protégée of an elderly, powerful academic writer whose ardor for her was just then cooling. There began at once a passionate relationship. One peculiar aspect of this affair—Flaubert's stubborn preference for solitude in his own study at Croisset, near Rouen, to Louise Colet's company in her boudoir in Paris—led to long separations and a correspondence which itself took on an almost fictive quality. Flaubert's letters, while they spun out the strange story of the conflict between Flaubert's infatuation with Madame Colet and his love for his work—and there is never the slightest doubt which of the two will prevail—also defined and described Flaubert's ecstatically painstaking craft.*

LETTERS TO LOUISE COLET

Croisset, July 26, 1851

I write you because "my heart prompts me to speak kindly to you," dear friend. If I could make you happy I should joyfully do so; it would be only fair. I feel guilty at the thought of having made you suffer so; don't you understand that? However, neither I, nor you, but only the circumstances, can be held responsible for this—and for all the rest.

At Rouen the other day you must have found me very cold, though I assure you I was as warm as I found it possible to be. I made every effort to be kind. Tender, no; that would have been wretchedly hypocritical, and a kind of insult to the sincerity of your feelings.

Read, do not dream. Plunge into long studies; there is nothing continually good but the habit of stubborn work. It releases an opium which lulls the soul. . . .

Croisset, [September, 1851]

. . . I began my novel yesterday evening. Now I foresee terrifying difficulties of style. It is no small thing to be simple. I am afraid of turning into
a Paul de Kock or a kind of Chateaubriandized Balzac.

[Croisset, January 12 or 14, 1852]

I am hideously worried, mortally depressed. My accursed Bovary is
harrying me and driving me mad. Last Sunday Bouilhet criticized one of
my characters and the outline. I can do nothing about it: there is some
truth in what he says, but I feel that the opposite is true also. Ah, I am
tired and discouraged! You[1] call me Master. What a wretched Master!

No—it is possible that the whole thing hasn't had enough spadework,
for distinctions between thought and style are a sophism. Everything
depends on the conception. So much the worse! I am going to continue,
and as quickly as I can, in order to have a complete picture. There are
moments when all this makes me wish I were dead. Ah! No one will be
able to say that I haven't experienced the agonies of Art![2]

Friday night, [Croisset, January 16, 1852]

There are in me, literally speaking, two distinct persons: one who is
infatuated with bombasts, lyricism, eagle flights, sonorities of phrase and
the high points of ideas; and another who digs and burrows into the truth
as deeply as he can, who likes to treat a humble fact as respectfully as a
big one, who would like to make you feel almost *physically* the things he
reproduces; this latter person likes to laugh, and enjoys the animal sides
of man. . . .

What seems beautiful to me, what I should like to write, is a book
about nothing, a book dependent on nothing external, which would be
held together by the strength of its style, just as the earth, suspended in
the void, depends on nothing external for its support; a book which would
have almost no subject, or at least in which the subject would be almost
invisible, if such a thing is possible. The finest works are those that contain the least matter; the closer expression comes to thought, the closer
language comes to coinciding and merging with it, the finer the result. I
believe that the future of Art lies in this direction. I see it, as it has developed from its beginnings, growing progressively more ethereal, from the
Egyptian pylons to Gothic lancets, from the 20,000-line Hindu poems to
the effusions of Byron. Form, as it is mastered, becomes attenuated; it
becomes dissociated from any liturgy, rule, yardstick; the epic is discarded
in favor of the novel, verse in favor of prose; there is no longer any
orthodoxy, and form is as free as the will of its creator. This emancipation

[1] *In this letter the tu form of address [which Flaubert has foregone during a period of strained relations],
is resumed.*
[2] *Such, at least, would seem to be the least inadequate translation of Flaubert's famous phrase, "les
affres de l'Art."*

from matter can be observed everywhere: governments have gone through similar evolution, from the oriental despotisms to the socialisms of the future.

It is for this reason that there are no noble subjects or ignoble subjects; from the standpoint of pure Art one might almost establish the axiom that there is no such thing as subject, style in itself being an absolute manner of seeing things.

[Croisset,] Saturday night, February 1, 1852

Bad week. Work didn't go; I had reached a point where I didn't know what to say. It was all shadings and refinements; I was completely in the dark: it is very difficult to clarify by means of words what is still obscure in your thoughts. I made outlines, spoiled a lot of paper, floundered and fumbled. Now I shall perhaps find my way again. Oh, what a rascally thing style is! I think you have no idea of what kind of a book I am writing. In my other books[3] I was slovenly; in this one I am trying to be impeccable, and to follow a geometrically straight line. No lyricism, no comments, the author's personality absent. It will make sad reading; there will be atrociously wretched and sordid things. Bouilhet, who arrived last Sunday at three just after I had written you, thinks the tone is right and hopes the book will be good. May God grant it! But it promises to take up an enormous amount of time. I shall certainly not be through by the beginning of next winter. I am doing no more than five or six pages a week.

[Croisset,] February 8, [1852]

So you are decidedly enthusiastic about *Saint Antoine!* Well, that makes one, at least! That's something. Though I don't accept everything you say about it, I think my friends refused to see what there was in it. Their judgment was superficial; I don't say unfair, but superficial. . . .

Now I am in an entirely different world, a world of attentive observations of the most humdrum details. I am delving into the damp and moldy corners of the soul. It is a far cry from the mythological and theological fireworks of *Saint Antoine.* And, just as the subject is different, so I am writing in an entirely different manner. Nowhere in my book must the author express his emotions or his opinions.

I think that it will be less lofty than *Saint Antoine* as regards ideas (a fact that I consider of little importance), but perhaps it will be more intense and unusual, without being obviously so.

Wednesday, 1 A.M., [Croisset, March 3, 1852]

Thank you, thank you, my darling, for all the affection you send me. It makes me proud that you should feel happy about me; how I will embrace you next week!

---

[3]*Flaubert refers particularly to the first* Education sentimentale *and the first* Tentation de Saint Antoine.

I have just reread several children's books for my novel. I am half crazy tonight, after all the things I looked at today—from old keepsakes to tales of shipwrecks and buccaneers. I came upon old engravings that I had colored when I was seven or eight and that I hadn't seen since. There are rocks painted blue and trees painted green. At the sight of some of them (for instance a scene showing people stranded on ice floes) I re-experienced feelings of terror that I had as a child. I should like something that would put it out of my mind; I am almost afraid to go to bed. There is a story of Dutch sailors in ice-bound waters, with bears attacking them in their hut (this picture used to keep me awake), and one about Chinese pirates sacking a temple full of golden idols. My travels and my childhood memories color off from each other, fuse, whirl dazzlingly before my eyes, and rise up in a spiral. . . .

For two days now I have been trying to live the dreams of young girls, and for this purpose I have been navigating in milky oceans of books about castles and troubadours in white-plumed velvet caps. Remind me to speak to you about this. You can give me exact details that I need.

Saturday, 1 A.M., [*Croisset, March 20–21, 1852*]

The entire value of my book, if it has any, will consist of my having known how to walk straight ahead on a hair, balanced above the two abysses of lyricism and vulgarity (which I seek to fuse in analytical narrative). When I think of what it can be I am dazzled. But then, when I reflect that so much beauty has been entrusted to me, I am so terrified that I am seized with cramps and long to rush off and hide—anywhere. I have been working like a mule for fifteen long years. All my life I have lived with a maniacal stubbornness, keeping all my other passions locked up in cages and visiting them only now and then, for diversion. Oh, if ever I produce a good book I'll have worked for it! Would to God that Buffon's blasphemous words were true.[4] I should certainly be among the foremost.

Saturday, 12:30 A.M., [*Croisset, March 27, 1852*]

Tonight I finished scribbling the first draft of my young girl's dreams. I'll spend another fortnight sailing on these blue lakes, after which I'll go to a ball and then spend a rainy winter, which I'll end with a pregnancy. And about a third of my book will be done.

Saturday night, [*Croisset, April 24, 1852*]

If I haven't written sooner in reply to your sorrowful and discouraged-sounding letter, it is because I have been in a great fit of work. The day before yesterday I went to bed at five in the morning and yesterday at three. Since last Monday I have put everything else aside, and have done nothing all week but sweat over my *Bovary,* disgruntled at making such

[4]Le génie est une longue patience.

slow progress. I have now reached my ball, which I will begin Monday. I hope that may go better. Since you last saw me I have written 25 pages in all (25 pages in six weeks). They were tough. Tomorrow I shall read them to Bouilhet. As for myself, I have gone over them so much, recopied them, changed them, handled them, that for the time being I can't make head or tail of them. But I think they will stand up. You speak of your discouragements: if you could see mine! Sometimes I don't understand why my arms don't drop from my body with fatigue, why my brains don't melt away. I am leading a stern existence, stripped of all external pleasure, and am sustained only by a kind of permanent rage, which sometimes makes me weep tears of impotence but which never abates. I love my work with a love that is frenzied and perverted, as an ascetic loves the hair shirt that scratches his belly. Sometimes, when I am empty, when words don't come, when I find I haven't written a single sentence after scribbling whole pages, I collapse on my couch and lie there dazed, bogged in a swamp of despair, hating myself and blaming myself for this demented pride which makes me pant after a chimera. A quarter of an hour later everything changes; my heart is pounding with joy. Last Wednesday I had to get up and fetch my handkerchief; tears were streaming down my face. I had been moved by my own writing; the emotion I had conceived, the phrase that rendered it, and the satisfaction of having found the phrase— all were causing me to experience the most exquisite pleasure. At least I believe that all those elements were present in this emotion, which after all was predominantly a matter of nerves. There exist even higher emotions of this same kind: those which are devoid of the sensory element. These are superior, in moral beauty, to virtue—so independent are they of any personal factor, of any human implication. Occasionally (at great moments of illumination) I have had glimpses, in the glow of an enthusiasm that made me thrill from head to foot, of such a state of mind, superior to life itself, a state in which fame counts for nothing and even happiness is superfluous. If everything around us, instead of permanently conspiring to drown us in a slough of mud, contributed rather to keep our spirits healthy, who can tell whether we might not be able to do for aesthetics what stoicism did for morals. Greek art was not an art; it was the very constitution of an entire people, of an entire race, of the country itself. In Greece the profile of the mountains was different from elsewhere, and they were composed of marble, which was thus available to the sculptors, etc.

The time for Beauty is over. Mankind may return to it, but it has no use for it at present. The more Art develops, the more scientific it will be, just as science will become artistic. Separated in their early stages, the two will become one again when both reach their culmination. It is beyond the power of human thought today to foresee in what a dazzling intellectual light the works of the future will flower. Meanwhile we are in a shadowy corridor, groping in the dark. We are without a lever; the ground is slipping under our feet; we all lack a basis—literati and scribblers that we are. What's the good of all this? Is our chatter the answer to any need? Between the crowd and ourselves no bond exists. Alas for the crowd; alas for us, especially. But since there is a reason for everything, and since the fancy of one individual seems to me just as valid as the appetite of a million men and can occupy an equal place in the world, we must (regardless of material things and of mankind, which disavows us) live for our vocation, climb into our ivory tower, and dwell there along with our dreams. At times I have feelings of great despair and emptiness—doubts that taunt me at my moments of naïvest satisfaction. And yet I would not exchange all this for anything, because my conscience tells me that I am fulfilling my duty, obeying a decree of fate—that I am doing what is Good, that I am in the Right.

Tuesday, [*Croisset, July 6, 1852*]

Musset has never separated poetry from the sensations of which it is the consummate expression. Music, according to him, was made for serenades, painting for portraits, and poetry for consoling the heart. But if you put the sun inside your trousers, all you do is burn your trousers and wet the sun. That is what has happened to him. Nerves, magnetism: for him poetry is those things. Actually, it is something less turbulent. If sensitive nerves were the only requirement of a poet, I should be superior to Shakespeare and to Homer, whom I picture as a not very nervous individual. Such confusion is blasphemy. I know whereof I speak: I used to be able to hear what people were saying in low voices behind closed doors thirty paces away; all my viscera could be seen quivering under my skin; and sometimes I experienced in the space of a single second a million thoughts, images, associations of all kinds which exploded in my mind like a grand display of fireworks. But all this, closely related though it is to the emotions, is mere parlor talk.

Poetry is by no means an infirmity of the mind; whereas these nervous susceptibilities are. Extreme sensitivity is a weakness. Let me explain:

If my mind had been stronger, I shouldn't have fallen ill as a result of studying law and being bored. I'd have turned those circumstances to good account instead of being worsted by them. My unhappiness, instead of confining itself to my brain, affected the rest of my body and threw me into convulsions. It was a "deviation." One often sees children whom music hurts physically: they have great talent, retain melodies after but one hearing, become over-excited when they play the piano; their hearts pound, they grow thin and pale and fall ill, and their poor nerves writhe in pain at the sound of notes—like dogs. These are never the future Mozarts. Their vocation has been misplaced: the idea has passed into the flesh, and there it remains sterile and causes the flesh to perish; neither genius nor health results.

It is the same with art. Passion does not make poetry, and the more personal you are, the weaker. I have always sinned in that direction my-self, because I have always put myself into what I was doing. Instead of Saint Anthony, for example, *I* am in my book; and I, rather than the reader, underwent the temptation. *The less you feel a thing, the fitter you are to express it as it is* (as it *always* is, in itself, in its essence, freed of all ephemeral contingencies). But you must have the capacity to *make yourself feel it*. This capacity is what we call genius: the ability to *see*, to have your model constantly posing in front of you.

That is why I detest so-called poetic language. When there are no words, a glance is enough. Soulful effusions, lyricism, descriptions—I want all these embodied in Style. To put them elsewhere is to prostitute art and feeling itself.

Thursday, 4 A.M., [Croisset, July 22, 1852]

I am in the process of copying and correcting the entire first part of *Bovary.* My eyes are smarting. I should like to be able to read these 158 pages at a single glance and grasp them with all their details in a single thought. A week from Sunday I shall read the whole thing to Bouilhet, and a day or two later you will see me. What a bitch of a thing prose is! It is never finished; there is always something to be done over. Still, I think it is possible to give it the consistency of verse. A good prose sen-tence should be like a good line of poetry—*unchangeable*, just as rhythmic, just as sonorous. Such, at least, is my ambition (I am sure of one thing: no one has ever conceived a more perfect type of prose than I; but as to the execution, how weak, how weak, oh God!). Nor does it seem to me impossible to give psychological analysis[5] the swiftness, clarity, and impetus of a strictly dramatic narrative. That has never been attempted, and it would be beautiful. Have I succeeded a little in this? I have no idea. At this moment I have no definite opinion about my work.

Monday, 1 A.M., [Croisset, July 27, 1852]

Yes, it is a strange thing, the relation between one's writing and one's personality. Is there anyone more in love with antiquity than I, anyone more haunted by it, anyone who has made a greater effort to understand it? And yet in my books I am as far from antiquity as possible. From my appearance one would think me a writer of epic, drama, brutally factual narrative; whereas actually I feel at home only in analysis—in anatomy, if I may call it such. By natural disposition I love what is vague and misty; and it is only patience and study that have rid me of all the white fat that clogged my muscles. The books I most long to write are precisely those for which I am least endowed. *Bovary,* in this sense, is an unprecedented tour de force (a fact of which I alone shall ever be aware): its subject, characters, effects, etc.—all are alien to me. It should make it possible for

---

[5]*Flaubert's words are "l'analyse psychologique."*

me to take a great step forward later. Writing this book I am like a man playing the piano with leaden balls attached to his fingers. But once I have mastered my technique, and find a piece that's to my taste and that I can play at sight, the result will perhaps be good. In any case, I think I am doing the right thing. What one does is not for one's self, but for others. Art is not interested in the personality of the artist. So much the worse for him if he doesn't like red or green or yellow: all colors are beautiful, and his task is to use them. . . .

I have read the Gautier:[6] lamentable! Here and there a fine strophe, but not a single good poem. It is strained, contrived; he has pulled all the old strings. You feel that it's a mind that has taken aphrodisiacs. An inferior kind of erection—the man is weak. Ah, how old all these great men are! They drool: and for the state they're in they have only themselves to blame.

Sunday, 11 P.M., [Croisset, September 19, 1852]

What trouble my *Bovary* is giving me! Still, I am beginning to see my way a little. Never in my life have I written anything more difficult than what I am doing now—trivial dialogue. . . . I have to portray, simultaneously and in the same conversation, five or six characters who speak, several others who are spoken about, the scene, and the whole town, giving physical descriptions of people and objects; and in the midst of all that I have to show a man and a woman who are beginning (through a similarity in tastes) to fall in love with each other. If only I had space! But the whole thing has to be swift without being dry, and well worked out without taking up too much room; and many details which would be more striking here I have to keep in reserve for use elsewhere. I am going to put the whole thing down quickly, and then proceed by a series of increasingly drastic revisions; by going over and over it I can perhaps pull it together. The language itself is a great stumbling-block. My characters are completely commonplace, but they have to speak in a literary style, and politeness of language takes away so much picturesqueness from any speech!

Night of Friday–Saturday, 2 A.M., [Croisset, October 1–2, 1852]

The other day I learned that a young man I knew at school had been interned at Saint-Yon (the Rouen insane asylum). A year ago I read a book of stupid poems by him; but I was moved by the sincerity, enthusiasm, and faith expressed in the preface. I was told that like me he lived in the country, secluded and working as hard as he could. The bourgeois had the greatest contempt for him. He complained of being constantly slandered and insulted; he suffered the common ordeal of unrecognized geniuses. Eventually he lost his mind, and now he is raving and screaming and treated with cold baths. Who can assure me that I am not on the same

6*Théophile Gautier's volume of poems:* Emaux et Camées.

path? What is the line of demarcation between inspiration and madness, between stupidity and ecstasy? To be an artist is it not necessary to *see everything* differently from other men? Art is no mere game of the intellect; it is a special atmosphere that we breathe. But if in search of more and more potent air we descend ever deeper into art's subterranean recesses, who knows that we may not end by breathing deadly miasmas? It would make a nice book—the story of a man whose mind is sound (quite possibly my young friend is sane) locked up as insane and treated by stupid doctors.

Monday night, [*Croisset, November 22, 1852*]

I am going to read *Uncle Tom* in English. I admit that I am prejudiced against it. Literary merit alone doesn't account for that kind of success. A writer can go far if he combines a certain talent for dramatization and a facility for speaking everybody's language, with the art of exploiting the passions of the day, the concerns of the moment. Do you know what books sell best year after year? *Faublas* and *l'Amour conjugal,*[7] two inept productions. If Tacitus were to return to earth he would sell less well than M. Thiers. The public respects monuments, but has little love for them. They are given conventional admiration and no more. The bourgeoisie (which today comprises all of mankind including the "people") has the same attitude toward the classics as toward religion: it knows that they exist, would be sorry if they didn't, realizes that they serve some vague purpose, but makes no use of them and finds them very boring.

I have had the *Chartreuse de Parme* brought to me from the lending-library and shall read it carefully. I know *Le Rouge et le noir,* which I find badly written and incomprehensible as regards characters and intentions. I am quite aware that people of taste are not of my opinion; but people of taste are a queer caste: they have little saints of their own whom nobody knows. It was our friend Sainte-Beuve who launched this fashion. People swoon with admiration before parlor wits, before talents whose only recommendation is that they are obscure. As for Beyle, after reading *Le Rouge et le noir* I fail completely to understand Balzac's enthusiasm for such a writer. Speaking of reading, I read Rabelais and *Don Quixote* every Sunday with Bouilhet and never tire of them. What overwhelming books! The more one contemplates them the bigger they grow, like the pyramids, and in the end they almost frighten you. What is stupendous about *Don Quixote* is the absence of art, and that perpetual fusion of illusion and reality which makes the book so comic and so poetic. What dwarfs all others are beside it! How small one feels, oh Lord, how small one feels!

I am working quite well, I mean quite heartily; but it is difficult to give adequate expression to something one has never felt: one has to expend much care and rack one's brains devilishly in order not to go too far and

[7]Tableau de l'amour conjugal *by Dr. Nicolas Venette (1686) and* Amours du Chevalier Faublas *by J. B. Louvet de Couvray (one of the three parts of his novel* Les Aventures du Chevalier Faublas, *1787-89).*

yet go far enough. The psychological development of my characters is giving me a lot of trouble; and everything, in this novel, depends on it: for in my opinion ideas can be as entertaining as actions, but in order to be so they must flow one from the other like a series of cascades, carrying the reader along midst the throbbing of sentences and the seething of metaphors.

[Croisset,] *Saturday, 1 o'clock, December 11, 1852*
I begin by devouring you with kisses, for I am transported with joy. Your letter of this morning has lifted a terrible weight from my heart. It was time, too: yesterday I was unable to work all day; every time I moved (literally) my brain throbbed and pounded in my skull, and by eleven o'clock I had to go to bed. I had fever and felt prostrated. For three weeks I have been suffering horribly from worry, and have not stopped thinking of you for a second—but in a way that has been scarcely agreeable. . . . I should need a whole book to develop my feelings in a comprehensible manner. The idea of causing the birth of someone horrifies me. I should curse myself were I to become a father. I, have a son! Oh, no! No! No! I desire my flesh to perish, and have no wish to transmit to anyone the troubles and ignominies of existence. . . .

I also had a superstitious thought. Tomorrow I shall be thirty-one. I have just passed that fatal thirtieth year, the year that ranks a man. It is the age when a man takes his future shape, settles down, marries, chooses a trade. There are few people who do not become bourgeois at thirty. Paternity would have confined me within those ordinary ways of living. . . .

Why did you desire this bond between us? . . .

I breathe again! The day is fine, the sun is shining on the river, at this moment a brig is passing with all sails unfurled; my window is open, my fire blazing. Adieu! I love you more than ever, and I kiss you to suffocation in honor of my birthday.

Saturday night, 3 o'clock, [Croisset, January 15, 1853]
The beginning of the week was frightful, but things have been going better since Thursday. I still have six to eight pages to do before reaching a break, and then I'll come to see you. I think that will be in a fortnight. Bouilhet will probably come with me. His reason for not writing you more often is that he has nothing to report or has no time. Do you realize that the poor devil has to give eight hours of lessons a day? . . .

Last week I spent *five days writing one page,* and I dropped everything else for it—my Greek, my English; I gave myself up to it entirely. What worries me in my book is the element of *entertainment.* That side is weak; there is not enough action. I maintain, however, that *ideas* are action. It is more difficult to hold the reader's interest with them, I know, but this is a problem for style to solve. I now have fifty pages in a row without a single event. It is an uninterrupted portrayal of a bourgeois existence and of a love that remains inactive—a love all the more difficult to depict because it is timid and deep, but alas! lacking in inner turbulence, because my gentleman has a sober nature. I had something similar in the first part: the husband loves his wife in somewhat the same fashion as her lover. Here are two mediocrities in the same milieu, and I must differentiate between them. If I bring it off it will be a great achievement, I think, for it will be like painting in monotone without contrasts—not easy. But I fear that all these subtleties will be wearisome, and that the reader will long for more movement. But one must be loyal to one's conception. If I tried to insert action I should be following a rule and would spoil everything. One must sing with one's own voice: and mine will never be dramatic or attractive. Besides, I am convinced that everything is a question of style, or rather of form, of presentation. . . .

Sunday night, half-past one,
[Croisset, February 27–28, 1853]

You should write more coldly. We must be on our guard against that kind of over-heating called inspiration, which often consists more largely of nervous emotion than of muscular strength. At this very moment, for example, I am keyed up to a high pitch—my brow is burning, sentences keep rushing into my head; for the past two hours I have been wanting to write to you and haven't been able to wrench myself away from work for an instant. Instead of one idea I have six, and where the most simple type of exposition is called for I find myself writing similes and metaphors. I could keep going until tomorrow noon without fatigue. But I know these masked balls of the imagination! You emerge from them in a state of exhaustion and despair, having seen only falsity and uttered nothing but nonsense. Everything should be done coldly, with poise.

Sunday, 4 o'clock, Easter Day
[Croisset, March 27, 1853]

As for me, the more I realize the difficulties of writing, the more daring I become; this is what keeps me from pedantry, into which I should otherwise doubtless fall. I have plans for writing that will keep me busy till the end of my life, and though I sometimes have moments of bitterness that make me almost scream with rage (so acutely do I feel my own impotence and weakness) I have others when I can scarcely contain myself for joy. Something deep and extra-voluptuous gushes out of me, like an ejaculation of the soul. I feel transported, drunk with my own thought, as though a hot gust of perfume were being wafted to me through some inner conduit. I shall never go very far; I know my limitations. But the goal I have set for myself will be achieved by others: thanks to me someone more talented, more instinctive, will be set on the right path. It is perhaps absurd to want to give prose the rhythm of verse (keeping it distinctly prose, however) and to write of ordinary life as one writes history or epic (but without falsifying the subject). I often wonder about this. But on the other hand it is perhaps a great experiment, and very original too. I know where I fail. (Ah, if only I were fifteen!) No matter: I shall always be given some credit for my stubbornness. And then, who can tell? Some day I may find a good motif, an air completely suited to my voice, neither too high nor too low. In my case I shall have lived nobly and often delightfully.

There is a saying by La Bruyère that serves me as a guide: "A good author likes to think that he writes sensibly."[8] That is what I ask—to write sensibly; and it is asking a good deal. Still, one thing is depressing, and that is to see how easily the great men achieve their effects by means extraneous to Art. What is more badly put together than much of Rabelais, Cervantes, Molière, and Hugo? But such quick punches! Such power in a single word! We have to pile up a lot of little pebbles to build our pyramids; theirs, a hundred times greater, are made with a single block. But to seek to imitate the method of those geniuses would be fatal. They are great for the very reason that they have no method.

Thursday, half-past four, [*Croisset, March 31, 1853*]

Nothing great is ever done without fanaticism. Fanaticism is religion: and the eighteenth-century *philosophes* who decried the former actually overthrew the latter. Fanaticism is faith, the essence of faith, burning faith, active faith, the faith that works miracles. Religion is a relative conception, a thing invented by man—an idea, in sum; the other is a feeling. What has changed on earth is the dogmas, the *stories* of Vishnu, Ormuzd, Jupiter, Jesus Christ. But what has never changed is the amulets, the sacred springs, the votive offerings, etc., the brahmins, the santons, the hermits —in a word the belief in something superior to life and the need to put one's self under the protection of this force.

In Art too the creative impulse is essentially fanatical. Poetry is only a way of perceiving external objects, a special sense through which matter is strained and transfigured without being changed. Now, if you see the world solely through this lens, the color of the world will be the color of the lens and the words you use to express your feeling will thus be inevitably related to the facts that produce it. To be well done, a thing must accord with your constitution. A botanist's hands, eyes, and head must not be like those of an astronomer; and he must see the stars only in reference to plants. From this combination of innateness and education result sureness of touch, individual manner, taste, spontaneity—in short, illumination. How often have I heard people tell my father that he diagnosed illnesses without knowing how or why! The same feeling that made

[8]*La Bruyère's words:* "Un esprit médiocre croit écrire divinement, un bon esprit croit écrire raisonnablement." (Les Caractères. Des Ouvrages de l'esprit, *18.*)

him instinctively decide on the remedy must enable us to hit on the right word. One doesn't achieve this unless one has—first—been born to one's calling, and—second—practised it long and stubbornly.

We marvel at the men of the age of Louis XIV, and yet they were not men of great genius. Reading them we experience none of that awe which makes us feel that Homer, Rabelais, and above all Shakespeare are more than human; certainly not. But what conscientious workmen! How they strained to find the exact expression for their thought! Such labor! Such tireless revision! How they asked each other's advice! How well they knew Latin! How slowly they read! That is why we have their thought in its entirety; that is why their form is whole, crammed full of substance to the bursting-point. In this domain there are no degrees: one work well done is equal in value to any other. La Fontaine will live as long as Dante, and Boileau as long as Bossuet or even Hugo.

Wednesday night, midnight, [Croisset, April 6, 1853]
What is making me go so slowly is that nothing in this book is derived from myself; never has my personality been of less use to me. Later I may be able to produce things that are better (I certainly hope so); it is difficult for me to imagine that I will ever write anything more carefully calculated. Everything is deliberate. If it's a failure, it will at least have been good practice. What is natural for me is unnatural for others—I am at home in the realm of the extraordinary and the fantastic, in flights of metaphysics and mythology. *Saint Antoine* didn't demand a quarter of the mental tension that *Bovary* is causing me. It was an outlet for my feelings; I had only pleasure in writing it, and the eighteen months spent writing its five hundred pages were the most deeply voluptuous of my entire life. Think of me now: having constantly to be in the skins of people for whom I feel aversion. For six months I have been a platonic lover, and at this very moment the sound of church bells is causing me Catholic raptures and I feel like going to confession!

Tuesday night, an hour after midnight,
[Croisset, April 26–27, 1853]
In our day I believe that a thinker (and what is an artist if not a triple thinker?) should have neither religion, country, nor even any social conviction. Absolute doubt now seems to me so completely substantiated that it would be almost silly to seek to formulate it. Bouilhet told me the other day that he felt the need to proclaim himself publicly, in writing, setting down all his reasons, an apostate Christian and an apostate Frenchman, and then to leave Europe and if possible never hear of it again. Yes, it would be a relief to vomit out all the immense contempt that fills the heart to overflowing. What good cause is there these days to arouse one's interest, let alone one's enthusiasm?

Saturday night, 1 A.M., [*Croisset, June 25–26, 1853*]

At last I have finished the first section of my second part. I have now reached the point I should have reached before our last meeting at Mantes —you see how far behind I am. I shall spend another week reading it over and copying it, and a week from tomorrow shall spew it all out to Bouilhet. If it is all right it will be a great worry off my mind and a considerable accomplishment, I assure you, for I had very little to go on. But I think that this book will have a great defect: namely, a want of proportion between its various parts. I have so far 260 pages containing only preparations for action—more or less disguised expositions of character (some of them, it is true, more developed than others), of landscapes and of places. My conclusion, which will be the account of my little lady's death and funeral and of her husband's grief, will be sixty pages long at least. That leaves, for the body of the action itself, 120 to 160 pages at the most. Isn't this a real defect? What reassures me (though not completely) is that the book is a biography rather than a fully developed story. It is not essentially dramatic; and if the dramatic element is well submerged in the general tone of the book the lack of proportion in the development of the various parts may pass unnoticed. But then isn't life a little like this? An act of coition lasts a minute, and it has been anticipated for months on end. Our passions are like volcanoes; they are continually rumbling, but they erupt only from time to time.

Friday night, 1 A.M., [*Croisset, July 15, 1853*]

What artists we should be if we had never read, seen, or loved anything that was not beautiful; if from the outset some guardian angel of the purity of our pens had kept us from all contamination; if we had never known fools or read newspapers! The Greeks were like that. . . . But classic form is insufficient for our needs, and our voices are not made to sing such simple tunes. Let us be as dedicated to art as they were, if we can, but differently. The human mind has broadened since Homer. Sancho Panza's belly has burst the seams of Venus' girdle. Rather than persist in copying old modes we should exert ourselves to invent new ones. I think Leconte de Lisle is unaware of all this. He has no instinct for modern life; he lacks heart. By this I do not mean personal or even humanitarian feelings, no—but *heart,* almost in the medical sense of the word. His ink is pale; his muse suffers from lack of fresh air. Thoroughbred horses and thoroughbred styles have plenty of blood in their veins, and it can be seen pulsing everywhere beneath the skin and the words. Life! Life! . . . That is the only thing that counts! That is why I love lyricism so much. It seems to me the most natural form of poetry—poetry in all its nakedness and freedom. All the power of a work of art lies in this mystery, and it is this primordial quality, this *motus animi continuus* (vibration, continual movement of the mind—Cicero's definition of eloquence), which gives conciseness, distinctness, form, energy, rhythm, diversity. It doesn't require much brains to be a critic: you can judge the excellence of a book by the strength of its punches and the time it takes you to recover from them. And then the excesses of the great masters! They pursue an idea to its furthermost limits. In Molière's *Monsieur de Pourceaugnac* there is a question of giving a man an enema, and a whole troop of actors carrying syringes pour down the aisles of the theatre. Michelangelo's figures have cables rather than muscles; in Rubens' bacchanalian scenes men piss on the ground; and think of everything in Shakespeare, etc., etc., and the most recent representative of the family, old Hugo. What a beautiful thing *Notre-Dame* is! I lately reread three chapters in it, including the sack of the church by the vagabonds. That's the sort of thing that's strong! I think that the greatest characteristic of genius is, above all, *energy*. Hence, what I detest most of all in the arts, what sets me on edge, is the *ingenious*, the clever. This is not at all the same as bad taste, which is a good quality gone wrong. In order to have what is called bad taste, you must have a sense for poetry; whereas cleverness, on the contrary, is incompatible with genuine poetry. Who was cleverer than Voltaire, and who less a poet? In our darling France, the public will accept poetry only if it is disguised. If it is given to them raw they protest. They have to be treated like the horses of Abbas-Pasha, who are fed a tonic of meat balls covered with flour. That's what Art is: knowing how to make the covering! But have no fear: if you offer this kind of flour to lions, they will recognize the smell twenty paces away and spring at it. . . .

I have been in excellent form this week. I have written eight pages, all of which I think can stand pretty much as they are. Tonight I have just outlined the entire big scene of the Agricultural Show. It will be colossal—thirty pages at least. Against the background of this rustico-municipal celebration, with all its details (all my secondary characters will be shown in action), there will be continuous dialogue between a gentleman and the lady he is doing his best to seduce. Moreover, somewhere in the middle I have a solemn speech by a counselor of the prefecture, and at the end (this I have already finished) a newspaper article written by my pharmacist, who gives an account of the celebration in fine philosophical, poetical, progressive style. You see it is no small chore. I am sure of my local color and of many of my effects; but it's a hideous job to keep it from getting too long—especially since this sort of thing shouldn't be skimpy. Once this is behind me I shall soon reach my scene of the lovers in the autumn woods, with their horses cropping the leaves beside them; and then I think I'll have clear sailing—I'll have passed Charybdis, at least, even though Scylla still remains to be negotiated.

Sunday, 4 o'clock, [Trouville, August 14, 1853]
The day before yesterday, in the woods of Touques, in a charming spot beside a spring, I found old cigar butts and scraps of paté. People had been picnicking. I described such a scene in *Novembre*, eleven years ago;

it was entirely imagined, and the other day it came true. Everything one invents is true, you may be sure. Poetry is as precise as geometry. Induction is as accurate as deduction; and besides, after reaching a certain point one no longer makes any mistake about the things of the soul. My poor Bovary, without a doubt, is suffering and weeping at this very instant in twenty villages of France.

Friday night, 11 o'clock, [*Trouville, August 26, 1853*]

Try to write me a letter that will be waiting for me when I return to Croisset on Saturday, or rather Sunday morning. That will insure me a good home-coming. What a dose of work I'm going to give myself when I get back! This vacation hasn't been a waste of time; I feel refreshed. During the past two years I have scarcely given myself a breath of air: I needed one. I have drawn fresh strength from the sight of the sea, the meadows and the trees. We writers, always absorbed in Art, communicate with nature only by means of our imaginations. But sometimes it is good to look the moon or the sun in the face. As we stare stupidly at the trees, their sap flows into our hearts. Just as the tastiest mutton comes from sheep that graze on thyme, our minds become pungent from feasting on nature's riches. . . .

While I have been here I have taken stock of myself, and this is the conclusion I have come to at the end of these four idle weeks: adieu, adieu for ever to everything personal, intimate, relative! I have abandoned any idea of ever writing my memoirs. Nothing pertaining to myself interests me. Youthful attachments, beautiful though they may be in the perspective of memory, no longer seem attractive to me as subjects, even when I think of how they might lend themselves to stylistic treatment. Let all those things die, and may they never revive. What would be the good? A man is no more than a flea. Our joys, like our sorrows, must be sublimated in our works. The clouds are not recognizable as dewdrops drawn up by the sun. Evaporate, then, O earthly rain, tears of bygone days, and in the heavens form yourselves into gigantic scrolls all glowing with light! . . .

What seems to me the highest and the most difficult achievement of Art is not to make us laugh or cry, or to rouse our lust or our anger, but to do as nature does—that is, fill us with wonderment. The most beautiful works have indeed this quality. They are serene in aspect, incomprehensible. The means by which they act on us are various: they are as unmoving as cliffs, stormy as the ocean, leafy, green, and murmuring as forests, sad as the desert, blue as the sky. Homer, Rabelais, Michelangelo, Shakespeare, and Goethe seem to me *pitiless*. They are bottomless, infinite, multiple. Through small openings we glimpse abysses whose dark depths make us giddy. And yet over the whole there hovers an extraordinary gentleness. It is like the brilliance of light, the smile of the sun, and it is calm, calm, and strong. . . .

How insignificant a creation, for example, is Figaro, as against Sancho! How one pictures Sancho on his donkey, eating raw onions, urging the steed on, all the while talking with his master. How vividly we see the roads of Spain, though nowhere are they described. But Figaro—where is he? At the Comédie Française. Parlor literature.

Wednesday, 12:30 A.M., [*Croisset, September, 1853*]

I worked well today. In a week I shall be in the midst of my agricultural show, which I am now beginning to see clearly. I have a jumble of lowing cattle and chattering people, and above it all the dialogue of my two lovers—it will be good, I think. . . .

Here is winter arriving; the leaves are turning yellow, and already many have fallen. I have a fire now and work with my lamp lit and curtains drawn, as in December. Why do I like the first days of autumn more than those of spring? Certainly I have passed beyond my love for the pallid poetry of falling leaves and moonlit mists! But this golden color enchants me. There is a sad, intoxicating perfume everywhere. I keep thinking of great feudal hunts, of life as it was lived in the châteaux. There is the sound of stags belling beside a lake; the wind blows through the woods; flames leap high in the vast fireplaces. . . .

Friday night, 2 A.M., [*Croisset, December 23, 1853*]

I must love you to write you tonight, for I am *exhausted*. My head feels as though it were being squeezed in an iron vise. Since two o'clock yesterday afternoon (except for about twenty-five minutes for dinner), I have been writing *Bovary*. I am in the midst of love-making; I am sweating and my throat is tight. This has been one of the rare days of my life passed completely in illusion from beginning to end. At six o'clock this evening, as I was writing the word "hysterics," I was so swept away, was bellowing so loudly and feeling so deeply what my little Bovary was going through, that I was afraid of having hysterics myself. I got up from my table and opened the window to calm myself. My head was spinning. Now I have great pains in my knees, in my back, and in my head. I feel like a man who has ——ed too much (forgive me for the expression)—a kind of rapturous lassitude. And since I am in the midst of love it is only proper that I should not fall asleep before sending you a caress, a kiss, and whatever thoughts are left in me. Will what I write be good? I have no idea— I am hurrying a little, to be able to show Bouilhet a complete section when he comes to see me. What is certain is that my book has been going at a lively rate for the past week. May it continue so, for I am weary of my usual snail's pace. But I fear the awakening, the disillusion that may come from the recopied pages. No matter; it is a delicious thing to write, whether well or badly—to be no longer yourself but to move in an entire universe of your own creating. Today, for instance, man and woman, lover and beloved, I rode in a forest on an autumn afternoon under the yellow leaves, and I was also the horse, the leaves, the wind, the words my people spoke, even the red sun that made them half-shut their love-drowned eyes. Is this pride or piety? Is it a silly overflow of exaggerated self-satisfaction, or is it really a vague and noble religious instinct? But when I think of these marvelous pleasures I have enjoyed I am tempted to offer God a prayer of thanks—if only I knew he could hear me! Praised be the Lord for not creating me a cotton merchant, a vaudevillian, a wit, etc.! Let us sing to Apollo like the ancient bards, and breathe deeply of the cold air of Parnassus; let us strum our guitars and clash our cymbals, and whirl like dervishes in the eternal pageant of Forms and Ideas.

Monday night, 1 o'clock, [Croisset, January 2, 1854]
[Bouilhet] was satisfied with my love scene. However, before said passage I have a transition of eight lines which took me three days; it doesn't contain a superfluous word, yet I must do it over once again because it is too slow. It is a piece of direct discourse which has to be changed into indirect, and in which I haven't room to say everything that should be said. It all has to be swift and casual, since it must remain inconspicuous in the ensemble. After this I shall still have three or four other infinitesimal corrections, which will take me one more entire week. How slow I am! No matter; I am getting ahead. I have taken a great step forward, and feel an inner relief that gives me new vigor, even though tonight I literally sweated with effort. It is so difficult to undo what is done, and well done, in order to put something new in its place, and yet hide all traces of the patch. . . .

[Croisset, January 13, 1854]
As to when I shall be finished with *Bovary*, I have already set so many dates, and had to change them so often, that I refuse not only to speak about it any more, but even to think about it. I can only trust in God; it's beyond me. It will be finished when it is finished, even though I die of boredom and impatience—as I might very well do were it not for the fury that keeps me going. Till then I will visit you every two months, as I promised.

Now, poor dear Louise, shall I tell you what I think—or rather what you feel? I think that your love for me is wavering. Your dissatisfactions, your sufferings on my account, can have no other cause, for as I am now I have always been. But now you see me more clearly, and you judge me correctly, perhaps. I cannot tell. However, when we love completely we accept the loved one as he is, with his defects and his deformities; even festering sores seem adorable to us, we cherish a hunchback for his hump, and a foul breath fills us with delight. It is the same with moral qualities. Now you say I am twisted, infamous, selfish, etc. Do you know that I'm going to end by being unbearably proud as a result of being so constantly criticized? I do not think that there is a mortal on earth less approved of than I am, but I will not change. I will not reform. I have already scratched out, amended, suppressed, or gagged so many things in myself that I am tired of doing it. Everything has its limit, and I am a big enough boy now to consider my training completed. I have other things to think about. I was born with all the vices. I completely suppressed many of them, and have indulged the rest but slightly. God alone knows the martyrdom I suffered during that psychological breaking-in; but I have finished with it. That is the way of death, and I want to remain alive for three or four more books; therefore I am set, immovable. You say I am made of granite. Yes, my feelings are of granite. But if my heart is hard it is at least sturdy, and never gives way. Betrayals and unjust accusations will not change what is engraved on it. Everything will remain, and the thought of you, whatever you do or I do, will not be effaced.

Adieu, a long kiss . . .

Friday night, midnight, [*Croisset, April 7, 1854*]

I have just made a fresh copy of what I have written since New Year, or rather since the middle of February, for on my return from Paris I burned all my January work. It amounts to thirteen pages, no more, no less, thirteen pages in seven weeks. However, they are in shape, I think, and as perfect as I can make them. There are only two or three repetitions of the same word which must be removed, and two turns of phrase that are still too much alike. At last something is completed. It was a difficult transition: the reader had to be led gradually and imperceptibly from psychology to action. Now I am about to begin the dramatic, eventful part. Two or three more big pushes and the end will be in sight. By July or August I hope to tackle the denouement. What a struggle it has been! My God, what a struggle! Such drudgery! Such discouragement! I spent all last evening frantically poring over surgical texts. I am studying the theory of clubfeet. In three hours I devoured an entire volume on this interesting subject and took notes. I came upon some really fine sentences. "The maternal breast is an impenetrable and mysterious sanctuary, where . . . etc." An excellent treatise, incidentally. Why am I not young? How I should work! One ought to know everything, to write. All of us scribblers are monstrously ignorant. If only we weren't so lacking in stamina, what a rich field of ideas and similes we could tap! Books that have been the source of entire literatures, like Homer and Rabelais, contain the sum of all the knowledge of their times. They knew everything, those fellows, and we know nothing. Ronsard's poetics contains a curious precept: he advises the poet to become well versed in the arts and crafts—to frequent blacksmiths, goldsmiths, locksmiths, etc.—in order to enrich his stock of metaphors. And indeed that is the sort of thing that makes for rich and varied language. The sentences in a book must quiver like the leaves in a forest, all dissimilar in their similarity.

Saturday night, 1 o'clock, [*Croisset, April 22, 1854*]

I am still struggling with clubfeet. My dear brother failed to keep two appointments with me this week, and unless he comes tomorrow I shall be forced to make another trip to Rouen. No matter; my work progresses. I have had a good deal of trouble these last few days over a religious speech. From my point of view, what I have written is completely impious. How different it would have been in a different period! If I had been born a hundred years earlier how much rhetoric I'd have put into it! Instead, I have written a mere, almost literal description of what must have taken place. The leading characteristic of our century is its historical sense. This is why we have to confine ourselves to relating the facts—but *all* the facts, the *heart* of the facts. No one will ever say about me what is said about you in the sublime prospectus of the *Librairie Nouvelle*: "All her writings converge on this lofty goal" (the ideal of a better future). No, we must sing merely for the sake of singing. Why is the ocean never still? What is the *goal* of nature? Well, I think the goal of mankind exactly the same. Things exist because they exist, and you can't do anything about it, my good people. We are always turning in the same circle, always rolling the same stone. Weren't men freer and more intelligent in the time of Pericles than they are under Napoleon III? On what do you base your statement that I am losing "the understanding of certain feelings" that I do not experience? First of all, please note that I *do* experience them. My heart is "human," and if I do not want a child "of my own" it is because I feel that if I had one my heart would become too "paternal." I love my little niece as though she were my daughter, and my "active" concern for her is enough to prove that those are not mere words. But I should rather be skinned alive than "exploit" this in my writing. I refuse to consider Art a drain-pipe for passion, a kind of chamberpot, a slightly more elegant substitute for gossip and confidences. No, no! Genuine poetry is not the scum of the heart. Your daughter deserves better than to be portrayed in verse "under her blanket,"[9] called an angel, etc. . . . Some day much of contemporary literature will be regarded as puerile and a little silly, because of its sentimentality. Sentiment, sentiment everywhere! Such gushing and weeping! Never before have people been so softhearted. We must put blood into our language, not lymph, and when I say blood I mean heart's blood; it must pulsate, throb, excite. We must make the very trees fall in love, the very stones quiver with emotion. The story of a mere blade of grass can be made to express boundless love. The fable of the two pigeons has always moved me more than all of Lamartine, and it's all in the subject

[9]*Flaubert, always severe about Louise's poetry, had particularly disliked some lines in a poem called* A ma fille:

> De ton joli corps sous la couverture
> Plus souple apparaît le contour charmant;
> Telle au Parthénon quelque frise pure
> Nous montre une vierge au long vêtement.

He considered the first two lines "obscene." "And then," he wrote Louise, "what is the Parthenon doing there, so close to your daughter's blanket?"

matter. But if La Fontaine had expended his amative faculties in expounding his personal feelings, would he have retained enough of it to be able to depict the friendship of two birds? Let us be on our guard against frittering away our gold. . . .

How impatient you all are in Paris to become known, to rent your houses before the roofs are built! Where are those who follow the teaching of Horace—that a work should be kept hidden for nine years before it is shown?[10]

---

[10]*This is the latest available letter from Flaubert to Louise Colet, though the affair still had several tumultuous months to run. Louise is said to have precipitated its end herself by violating Flaubert's privacy—bursting in upon him, one day, in his study at Croisset. She was ejected from the house. Madame Flaubert, a witness of the scene, is said to have reproached her son for his mercilessness, declaring that she felt as though she had seen him "wound her own sex."*

Norman Mailer

(1923–   )

The lucky world does not want for data on the writer named Norman Mailer. He has freely given all of us, besides many other writings of explication, a 532-page book entitled Advertisements for Myself. *A powerfully gifted but immensely insecure writer, Mailer has chosen to carry on Ernest Hemingway's metaphor of the boxer: He is in the ring of literature, he welcomes bouts with all pretenders, he will be, he is, the champ. The protestations are childish, their monotone—apparently meant to be manly but finally whining—jars on the ear. Yet in his serious work Mailer has earned for himself a proper respect. He ironically achieves in them precisely what is lacking in those writings which come off his preening-mirror: a total honesty, an honesty charged with consequence such as no other American writer of his time has dared. Sometimes, as when he distills in* An American Dream *his own near-murderous assault on one of his wives, the honesty is dreadful. But wherever he probes more deeply the meaning of life in the latter half of the twentieth century for a man who is not satisfied with the way things are, he achieves powers of evocation, of clarification, of anger, of yearning, and of compassion, which give his prose a prophetic resonance. At his worst, he pouts and poses; at his best, he stands up and speaks sharply to mankind. What follows is an account of a painful task of revision.*

The Last Draft Of
THE DEER PARK

In his review of *The Deer Park*, Malcolm Cowley said it must have been a more difficult book to write than *The Naked and The Dead*. He was right. Most of the time, I worked on *The Deer Park* in a low mood; my liver, which had gone bad in the Philippines, exacted a hard price for forcing the effort against the tide of a long depression, and matters were not improved when nobody at Rinehart & Co. liked the first draft of the novel. The second draft, which to me was the finished book, also gave little enthusiasm to the editors, and open woe to Stanley Rinehart, the publisher. I was impatient to leave for Mexico, now that I was done, but before I could go, Rinehart asked for a week in which to decide whether he wanted to do the book. Since he had already given me a contract which allowed him no option not to accept the novel (a common arrangement for writers whose sales are more or less large) any decision to reject the manuscript would cost him a sizable advance. (I learned later he had been hoping his lawyers would find the book obscene, but they did not, at least not then in May 1954.) So he had really no choice but to agree to put the book out in February, and gloomily he consented. To cheer him a bit, I agreed to his request that he delay paying me my advance until publication, although the first half was due on delivery of the manuscript. I thought the favor might improve our relations.

Now, if a few of you are wondering why I did not take my book back and go to another publishing house, the answer is that I was tired, I was badly tired. Only a few weeks before, a doctor had given me tests for the liver, and it had shown itself to be sick and depleted. I was hoping that a few months in Mexico would give me a chance to fill up again.

But the next months were not cheerful. *The Deer Park* had been done as well as I could do it, yet I thought it was probably a minor work, and I did not know if I had any real interest in starting another book. I made efforts of course; I collected notes, began to piece together a few ideas for a novel given to bullfighting, and another about a concentration camp; I wrote "David Reisman Reconsidered" during this time, and "The Homosexual Villain"; read most of the work of the other writers of my generation (I think I was looking for a level against which to measure my third novel), went over the galleys when they came, changed a line or two, sent them back. Keeping half busy I mended a bit, but it was a time of dull drifting. When we came back to New York in October, *The Deer Park* was already in page proof. By November, the first advertisement was given to *Publishers' Weekly*. Then, with less than ninety days to publication, Stanley Rinehart told me I would have to take out a small piece of the book—six not very explicit lines about the sex of an old producer and a call girl. The moment one was ready to consider losing those six lines they moved into the moral center of the novel. It would be no tonic for my liver to cut them out. But I also knew Rinehart was serious, and since I was still tired, it seemed a little unreal to try to keep the passage. Like a miser I had been storing energy to start a new book; I wanted nothing to distract me now. I gave in on a word or two, agreed to rewrite a line, and went home from that particular conference not very impressed with myself. The next morning I called up the editor in chief, Ted Amussen, to tell him I had decided the original words had to be put back.

"Well, fine," he said, "fine. I don't know why you agreed to anything in the first place."

A day later, Stanley Rinehart halted publication, stopped all ads (he was too late to catch the first run of *Publishers' Weekly* which was already on its way to England with a full page for *The Deer Park*) and broke his contract to do the book. I was started on a trip to find a new publisher, and before I was done, the book had gone to Random House, Knopf, Simon and Schuster, Harper's, Scribner's, and unofficially to Harcourt, Brace. Some day it would be fine to give the details, but for now little more than a few lines of dialogue and an editorial report:

Bennett Cerf: This novel will set publishing back twenty years.
Alfred Knopf to an editor: Is this your idea of the kind of book which should bear a Borzoi imprint?

The lawyer for one publishing house complimented me on the six lines, word for word, which had excited Rinehart to break his contract. This lawyer said, "It's admirable the way you get around the problem here." Then he brought out more than a hundred objections to other parts of the book. One was the line, "She was lovely. Her back was adorable in its contours." I was told that this ought to go because "The principals are not married, and so your description puts a favorable interpretation upon a meretricious relationship."

Hiram Hayden had lunch with me some time after Random House saw the book. He told me he was responsible for their decision not to do it, and if I did not agree with his taste, I had to admire his honesty—it is rare for an editor to tell a writer the truth. Hayden went on to say that the book never came alive for him even though he had been ready to welcome it. "I can tell you that I picked the book up with anticipation. Of course I had heard from Bill, and Bill had told me that he didn't like it, but I never pay attention to what one writer says about the work of another. . . ." Bill was William Styron, and Hayden was his editor. I had asked Styron to call Hayden the night I found out Rinehart had broken his contract. One reason for asking the favor of Styron was that he sent me a long letter about the novel after I had shown it to him in manuscript. He had written, "I don't like The Deer Park, but I admire sheer hell out of it." So I thought to impose on him.

Other parts of the account are not less dreary. The only generosity I found was from the late Jack Goodman. He sent me a photostat of his editorial report to Simon and Schuster and, because it was sympathetic, his report became the objective estimate of the situation for me. I assumed that the book when it came out would meet the kind of trouble Goodman expected, and so when I went back later to work on the page proofs I was not free of a fear or two. But that can be talked about in its place. Here is the core of his report.

Mailer refuses to make any changes . . . [He] will consider suggestions, but reserves the right to make final decisions, so we must make our decision on what the book now is.

That's not easy. It is full of vitality and power, as readable a novel as I've ever encountered. Mailer emerges as a sort of post-Kinsey F. Scott Fitzgerald. His dialogue is uninhibited and the sexuality of the book is completely interwoven with its purpose, which is to describe a segment of society whose morality is nonexistent. Locale is evidently Palm Springs. Chief characters are Charles Eitel, movie director who first defies the House Un-American Committee, then becomes a friendly witness, his mistress, a great movie star who is his ex-wife, her lover who is the narrator, the head of a great movie company, his son-in-law, a strange, tortured panderer who is Eitel's conscience and, assorted demimondaines, homosexuals, actors.

My layman's opinion is that the novel will be banned in certain quarters and that it may very well be up for an obscenity charge, but this should of course be checked by our lawyers. If it were possible to recognize this at the start, to have a united front here and treat the whole issue positively and head-on, I would be for our publishing. But I am afraid such unanimity may be impossible of attainment and if so, we should reject, in spite of the fact that I am certain it will be one of the best-selling novels of the next couple of years. It is the work of a serious artist. . . .

The eighth house was G. P. Putnam's. I didn't want to give it to them, I was planning to go next to Viking, but Walter Minton kept saying, "Give us three days. We'll give you a decision in three days." So we sent it over to Putnam, and in three days they took it without conditions, and without a request for a single change. I had a victory, I had made my point, but in fact I was not very happy. I had grown so wild on my diet of polite letters from publishing houses who didn't want me, that I had been ready to collect rejections from twenty houses, publish *The Deer Park* at my own expense, and try to make a kind of publishing history. Instead I was thrown in with Walter Minton, who has since attracted some fame as the publisher of *Lolita*. He is the only publisher I ever met who would make a good general. Months after I came to Putnam, Minton told me, "I was ready to take *The Deer Park* without reading it. I knew your name would sell enough copies to pay your advance, and I figured one of these days you're going to write another book like *The Naked and The Dead*," which is the sort of sure hold of strategy you can have when you're not afraid of censorship.

Now I've tried to water this account with a minimum of tears, but taking *The Deer Park* into the nervous system of eight publishing houses was not so good for my own nervous system, nor was it good for getting to work on my new novel. In the ten weeks it took the book to travel the circuit from Rinehart to Putnam, I squandered the careful energy I had been hoarding for months; there was a hard comedy at how much of myself I would burn up in a few hours of hot telephone calls; I had never had any sense for practical affairs, but in those days, carrying *The Deer Park* from house to house, I stayed as close to it as a stage-struck mother pushing her child forward at every producer's office. I was amateur agent for it, messenger boy, editorial consultant, Machiavelli of the luncheon table, fool of the five o'clock drinks, I was learning the publishing business in a hurry, and I made a hundred mistakes and paid for each one by wasting a new bout of energy.

In a way there was sense to it. For the first time in years I was having the kind of experience which was likely to return some day as good work, and so I forced many little events past any practical return, even insulting a few publishers en route as if to discover the limits of each situation. I was trying to find a few new proportions to things, and I did learn a bit. But I'll never know what that novel about the concentration camp would have been like if I had gotten quietly to work when I came back to New York and *The Deer Park* had been published on time. It is possible I was not serious about the book, it is also possible I lost something good, but one way or the other, that novel disappeared in the excitement, as lost as "the little object" in *Barbary Shore*, and it has not stirred since.

The real confession is that I was making a few of my mental connections those days on marijuana. Like more than one or two of my generation, I had smoked it from time to time over the years, but it never had meant anything. In Mexico, however, down in my depression with a bad liver, pot gave me a sense of something new about the time I was convinced I had seen it all, and I liked it enough to take it now and again in New York.

Then *The Deer Park* began to go like a beggar from house to house and en route Stanley Rinehart made it clear he was going to try not to pay the advance. Until then I had had sympathy for him. I thought it had taken a kind of displaced courage to be able to drop the book the way he did. An expensive moral stand, and wasteful for me; but a moral stand. When it turned out that he did not like to bear the expense of being that moral, the experience turned ugly for me. It took many months and the service of my lawyer to get the money, but long before that, the situation had become real enough to drive a spike into my cast-iron mind. I realized in some bottom of myself that for years I had been the sort of comic figure I would have cooked to a turn in one of my books, a radical who had the nineteenth-century naïveté to believe that the people with whom he did business were 1) gentlemen, 2) fond of him, and 3) respectful of his ideas even if in disagreement with them. Now, I was in the act of learning that I was not adored so very much; that my ideas were seen as nasty; and that my fine America which I had been at pains to criticize for so many years was in fact a real country which did real things and ugly things to the characters of more people than just the characters of my books. If the years since the war had not been brave or noble in the history of the country, which I certainly thought and do think, why then did it come as surprise that people in publishing were not as good as they used to be, and that the day of Maxwell Perkins was a day which was gone, really gone, gone as Greta Garbo and Scott Fitzgerald? Not easy, one could argue, for an advertising man to admit that advertising is a dishonest occupation, and no easier was it for the working novelist to see that now were left only the cliques, fashions, vogues, snobs, snots, and fools, not to mention a dozen bureaucracies of criticism; that there was no room for the old literary idea of oneself as a major writer, a figure in the landscape. One had become a set of relations and equations, most flourishing when most incorporated, for then one's literary stock was ready for merger. The day was gone when people held on to your novels no matter what others might say. Instead one's good young readers waited now for the verdict of professional young men, academics who wolfed down a modern litera-

ture with an anxiety to find your classification, your identity, your similarity, your common theme, your corporate literary earnings, each reference to yourself as individual as a carloading of homogenized words. The
articles which would be written about you and a dozen others would be
done by minds which were expert on the aggregate and so had senses too
lumpy for the particular. There was a limit to how much appraisal could
be made of a work before the critic exposed his lack of the critical faculty,
and so it was naturally wiser for the mind of the expert to masticate the
themes of ten writers rather than approach the difficulties of any one.

I had begun to read my good American novels at the end of an era—
I could remember people who would talk wistfully about the excitement
with which they had gone to bookstores because it was publication day
for the second novel of Thomas Wolfe, and in college, at a Faculty tea, I
had listened for an hour to a professor's wife who was so blessed as to
have known John Dos Passos. My adolescent crush on the profession of
the writer had been more lasting than I could have guessed. I had even
been so simple as to think that the kind of people who went into publishing were still most concerned with the few writers who made the profession not empty of honor, and I had been taking myself seriously, I had
been thinking I was one of those writers.

Instead I caught it in the face and deserved it for not looking at the
evidence. I was out of fashion and that was the score; that was all the
score; the publishing habits of the past were going to be of no help for
my *Deer Park*. And so as the language of sentiment would have it, something broke in me, but I do not know if it was so much a loving heart, as
a cyst of the weak, the unreal, and the needy, and I was finally open to
my anger. I turned within my psyche I can almost believe, for I felt something shift to murder in me. I finally had the simple sense to understand
that if I wanted my work to travel further than others, the life of my talent
depended on fighting a little more, and looking for help a little less. But I
deny the sequence in putting it this way, for it took me years to come to
this fine point. All I felt then was that I was an outlaw, a psychic outlaw,
and I liked it, I liked it a good night better than trying to be a gentleman,
and with a set of emotions accelerating one on the other, I mined down
deep into the murderous message of marijuana, the smoke of the assassins,
and for the first time in my life I knew what it was to make your kicks.

I could write about that here, but it would be a mistake. Let the experience stay where it is, and on a given year it may be found again in a novel.
For now it is enough to say that marijuana opens the senses and weakens
the mind. In the end, you pay for what you get. If you get something big,
the cost will equal it. There is a moral economy to one's vice, but you learn
that last of all. I still had the thought it was possible to find something
which cost nothing. Thus, *The Deer Park* resting at Putnam, and new good
friends found in Harlem, I was off on that happy ride where you discover
a new duchy of jazz every night and the drought of the past is given a

rain of new sound. What has been dull and dead in your years is now tart to the taste, and there is sweet in the illusion of how fast you can change. To keep up with it all, I began to log a journal, a wild set of thoughts and outlines for huge projects—I wrote one hundred thousand words in eight weeks, more than once twenty pages a day in a style which came willy-nilly from the cramp of the past, a lockstep jargon of sociology and psychology that sours my teeth when I look at those pages today. Yet this journal has the start of more ideas than I will have again; ideas which came so fast and so rich that sometimes I think my brain was dulled by the heat of their passage. (With all proportions kept, one can say that cocaine may have worked a similar good and ill upon Freud.)

The journal wore down by February, about the time *The Deer Park* had once been scheduled to appear. By then I had decided to change a few things in the novel, nothing in the way of lawyer's deletions, just a few touches for style. They were not happy about this at Putnam. Minton argued that some interest in the book would be lost if the text were not identical to Rinehart's page proofs, and Ted Purdy, my editor, told me more than once that they liked the book "just the way it is." Besides, there was thought of bringing it out in June as a summer book.

Well, I wanted to take a look. After all, I had been learning new lessons. I began to go over the page proofs, and the book read as if it had been written by someone else. I was changed from the writer who had labored on that novel, enough to be able to see it without anger or vanity or the itch to justify myself. Now, after three years of living with the book, I could at last admit the style was wrong, that it had been wrong from the time I started, that I had been strangling the life of my novel in a poetic prose which was too self-consciously attractive and formal, false to the life of my characters, especially false to the life of my narrator who was the voice of my novel and so gave the story its air. He had been a lieutenant in the Air Force, he had been cool enough and hard enough to work his way up from an orphan asylum, and to allow him to write in a style which at its best sounded like Nick Carraway in *The Great Gatsby* must of course blur his character and leave the book unreal. Nick was legitimate, out of fair family, the Midwest and Princeton—he would write as he did, his style was himself. But the style of Sergius O'Shaugnessy, no matter how good it became (and the Rinehart *Deer Park* had its moments) was a style which came out of nothing so much as my determination to prove I could muster a fine style.

If I wanted to improve my novel, yet keep the style, I would have to make my narrator fit the prose, change his past, make him an onlooker, a rich pretty boy brought up let us say by two old-maid aunts, able to have an affair with a movie star only by luck and/or the needs of the plot, which would give me a book less distracting, well written but minor. If, however, I wanted to keep that first narrator, my orphan, flier, adventurer, *germ*—for three years he had been the frozen germ of some new theme—well, to keep him I would need to change the style from the inside of each sentence. I could keep the structure of my book, I thought—it had been put together for such a narrator—but the style could not escape. Probably I did not see it all so clearly as I now suggest. I believe I started with the conscious thought that I would tinker just a little, try to patch a compromise, but the navigator of my unconscious must already have made the choice, because it came as no real surprise that after a few days of changing a few words I moved more and more quickly toward the eye of the problem, and in two or three weeks I was tied to the work of doing a new *Deer Park*. The book was edited in a way no editor could ever have time or love to find; it was searched sentence by sentence, word for word, the style of the work lost its polish, became rough, and I can say real, because there was an abrupt and muscular body back of the voice now. It had been there all the time, trapped in the porcelain of a false style, but now as I chipped away, the work for a time became exhilarating in its clarity—I never enjoyed work so much—I felt as if finally I was learning how to write, learning the joints of language and the touch of a word, felt as if I came close to the meanings of sound and could say which of two close words was more female or more forward. I even had a glimpse of what Flaubert might have felt, for as I went on tuning the book, often five or six words would pile above one another in the margin at some small crisis of choice. (Since the Rinehart page proof was the usable copy, I had little space to write between the lines.) As I worked in this fine mood, I kept sending pages to the typist, yet so soon as I had exhausted the old galley pages, I could not keep away from the new typewritten copy—it would be close to say the book had come alive, and was invading my brain.

Soon the early pleasure of the work turned restless; the consequences of what I was doing were beginning to seep into my stamina. It was as if I were the captive of an illness whose first symptoms had been excitement, prodigies of quick work, and a confidence that one could go on forever, but that I was by now close to a second stage where what had been quick would be more like fever, a first wind of fatigue upon me, a knowledge that at the end of the drunken night a junkie cold was waiting. I was going to move at a pace deadly to myself, loading and overloading whatever little centers of the mind are forced to make the hard decisions. In ripping up the silk of the original syntax, I was tearing into any number of careful habits as well as whatever subtle fleshing of the nerves and the chemicals had gone to support them.

For six years I had been writing novels in the first person; it was the only way I could begin a book, even though the third person was more to my taste. Worse, I seemed unable to create a narrator in the first person who was not overdelicate, oversensitive, and painfully tender, which was an odd portrait to give, because I was not delicate, not physically; when it was a matter of strength I had as much as the next man. In those days I would spend time reminding myself that I had been a bit of an athlete (house football at Harvard, years of skiing) that I had not quit in combat, and once when a gang broke up a party in my loft, I had taken two cracks on the head with a hammer and had still been able to fight. Yet the first person seemed to paralyze me, as if I had a horror of creating a voice which could be in any way bigger than myself. So I had become mired in a false style for every narrator I tried. If now I had been in a fight, had found out that no matter how weak I could be in certain ways, I was also steady enough to hang on to six important lines, that may have given me new respect for myself, I don't know, but for the first time I was able to use the first person in a way where I could suggest some of the stubbornness and belligerence I also might have, I was able to color the empty reality of that first person with some real feeling of how I had always felt, which was to be outside, for Brooklyn where I grew up is not the center of anything. I was able, then, to create an adventurer whom I believed in, and as he came alive for me, the other parts of the book which had been stagnant for a year and more also came to life, and new things began to happen to Eitel my director and to Elena his mistress and their characters changed. It was a phenomenon. I learned how real a novel is. Before, the story of Eitel had been told by O'Shaugnessy of the weak voice; now by a confident young man: when the new narrator would remark that Eitel was his best friend and so he tried not to find Elena too attractive, the man and woman he was talking about were larger than they had once been. I was no longer telling of two nice people who fail at love because the world is too large and too cruel for them; the new O'Shaugnessy had moved me by degrees to the more painful story of two people who are strong as well as weak, corrupt as much as pure, and fail to grow despite their bravery in a poor world, because they are finally not brave enough, and so do more damage to one another than to the unjust world outside them. Which for me was exciting, for here and there *The Deer Park* now had the rare tenderness of tragedy. The most powerful leverage in fiction comes from point of view, and giving O'Shaugnessy courage gave passion to the others.

But the punishment was commencing for me. I was now creating a man who was braver and stronger than me, and the more my new style succeeded, the more was I writing an implicit portrait of myself as well. There is a shame about advertising yourself that way, a shame which became so strong that it was a psychological violation to go on. Yet I could not afford the time to digest the self-criticisms backing up in me, I was forced to drive myself, and so more and more I worked by tricks, taking marijuana the night before and then drugging myself into sleep with an overload of Seconal. In the morning I would be lithe with new perception, could read new words into the words I had already, and so could go on in the pace of my work, the most scrupulous part of my brain too sluggish to interfere. My powers of logic became weaker each day, but the book had its own logic, and so I did not need close reason. What I wanted and what the drugs gave me was the quick flesh of associations, and there I was often oversensitive, could discover new experience in the lines of my text like a hermit savoring the revelation of Scripture; I saw so much in some sentences that more than once I dropped into the pit of the amateur: since I was receiving such emotion from my words, I assumed everyone else would be stimulated as well, and on many a line I twisted the phrase in such a way that it could read well only when read slowly, about as slowly as it would take for an actor to read it aloud. Once you write that way, the quick reader (who is nearly all your audience) will stumble and fall against the vocal shifts of your prose. Then you had best have the cartel of a Hemingway, because in such a case it is critical whether the reader thinks it is your fault, or is so in awe of your reputation that he returns on the words, throttles his pace, and tries to discover why he is so stupid as not to swing on the off-bop of your style.

An example: in the Rinehart *Deer Park* I had this:

"They make Sugar sound so good in the newspapers," she declared one night to some people in a bar, "that I'll really try him. I really will, Sugar." And she gave me a sisterly kiss.

I happened to change that very little, I put in "said" instead of "declared" and later added "older sister," so that it now read:

And she gave me a sisterly kiss. Older sister.

Just two words, but I felt as if I had revealed some divine law of nature, had laid down an invaluable clue—the kiss of an older sister was a worldly universe away from the kiss of a younger sister—and I thought to give myself the Nobel Prize for having brought such illumination and *division* to the cliché of the sisterly kiss.

Well, as an addition it wasn't bad fun, and for two words it did a bit to give a sense of what was working back and forth between Sergius and Lulu, it was another small example of Sergius' hard eye for the world, and his cool sense of his place in it, and all this was to the good, or would have been for a reader who went slowly, and stopped, and thought. But if anyone was in a hurry, the little sentence "Older sister" was like a finger in the eye, it jabbed the unconscious, and gave an uncomfortable nip of rhythm to the mind.

I had five hundred changes of this kind. I started with the first paragraph of the book, on the third sentence which pokes the reader with its backed-up rhythm, "Some time ago," and I did that with intent, to slow my readers from the start, like a fighter who throws his right two seconds after the bell and so gives the other man no chance to decide on the pace.

There was a real question, however, whether I could slow the reader down, and so as I worked on further, at some point beginning to write paragraphs and pages to add to the new Putnam galleys, the attrition of the drugs and the possibility of failure began to depress me, and Benzedrine entered the balance, and I was on the way to wearing badly. Because, determined or no that they would read me slowly, praying my readers would read me slowly, there was no likelihood they would do anything of the sort if the reviews were bad. As I started to worry this it grew worse, because I knew in advance that three or four of my major reviews had to be bad—*Time* magazine for one, because Max Gissen was the book review editor, and I had insulted him in public once by suggesting that the kind of man who worked for a mind so exquisitely and subtly totalitarian as Henry Luce was not likely to have any ideas of his own. The New York Daily *Times* would be bad because Orville Prescott was well known for his distaste of books too forthrightly sexual; and *Saturday Review* would be bad. That is, they would probably be bad; the mentality of their reviewers would not be above the level of their dean of reviewers, Mr. Maxwell Geismar, and Geismar didn't seem to know that my second novel was titled *Barbary Shore* rather than *Barbary Coast*. I could spin this out, but what is more to the point is that I had begun to think of the reviews before finishing the book, and this doubtful occupation came out of the kind of inner knowledge I had of myself in those days. I knew what was good for my energy and what was poor, and so I knew that for the vitality of my work in the future, and yes even the quantity of my work, I needed a success and I needed it badly if I was to shed the fatigue I had been carrying since *Barbary Shore*. Some writers receive not enough attention for years, and so learn early to accommodate the habits of their work to little recognition. I think I could have done that when I was twenty-five. With *The Naked and The Dead* a new life had begun, however; as I have written earlier . . . , I had gone through the psychic labor of changing a good many modest habits in order to let me live a little more happily as a man with a name which could arouse quick reactions in strangers. If that started as an overlarge work, because I started as a decent but scared boy, well I had come to live with the new life, I had learned to like success—in fact I had probably come to depend on it, or at least my new habits did.

When *Barbary Shore* was ambushed in the alley, the damage to my nervous system was slow but thorough. My status dropped immediately— America is a quick country—but my ego did not permit me to understand that, and I went through tiring years of subtle social defeats because I did not know that I was no longer as large to others as I had been. I was always overmatching myself. To put it crudely, I would think I was dropping people when they were dropping me. And of course my unconscious knew better. There was all the waste of ferocious if unheard discussion between the armies of ego and id; I would get up in the morning with less snap in me than I had taken to sleep. Six or seven years of breathing that literary air taught me a writer stayed alive in the circuits of such hatred only if he were unappreciated enough to be adored by a clique, or was so overbought by the public that he excited some defenseless nerve in the

snob. I knew if *The Deer Park* was a powerful best seller (the magical figure had become one hundred thousand copies for me) that I would then
have won. I would be the first serious writer of my generation to have a
best seller twice, and so it would not matter what was said about the book.
Half of publishing might call it cheap, dirty, sensational, second-rate, and
so forth and so forth, but it would be weak rage and could not hurt, for
the literary world suffers a spot of the national taint—a serious writer is
certain to be considered major if he is also a best seller; in fact, most readers are never convinced of his value until his books do well. Steinbeck is
better known than Dos Passos, John O'Hara is taken seriously by people
who dismiss Farrell, and indeed it took three decades and a Nobel Prize
before Faulkner was placed on a level with Hemingway. For that reason,
it would have done no good if someone had told me at the time that the
financial success of a writer with major talent was probably due more to
what was meretricious in his work than what was central. The argument
would have meant nothing to me—all I knew was that seven publishing
houses had been willing to dismiss my future, and so if the book did
poorly, a good many people were going to congratulate themselves on
their foresight and be concerned with me even less. I could see that if I
wanted to keep on writing the kind of book I liked to write, I needed the
energy of new success, I needed blood. Through every bit of me, I knew
The Deer Park had damn well better make it or I was close to some serious
illness, a real apathy of the will.

Every now and again I would have the nightmare of wondering what
would happen if all the reviews were bad, as bad as *Barbary Shore*. I
would try to tell myself that could not happen, but I was not certain, and
I knew that if the book received a unanimously bad press and still showed
signs of selling well, it was likely to be brought up for prosecution as
obscene. As a delayed convulsion from the McCarthy years, the fear of
censorship was strong in publishing, in England it was critically bad, and
so I also knew that the book could lose such a suit—there might be no one
of reputation to say it was serious. If it were banned, it could sink from
sight. With the reserves I was throwing into the work, I no longer knew
if I was ready to take another beating—for the first time in my life I had
worn down to the edge, I could see through to the other side of my fear,
I knew a time could come when I would be no longer my own man, that I
might lose what I had liked to think was the incorruptible center of my
strength (which of course I had had money and freedom to cultivate).
Already the signs were there—I was beginning to avoid new lines in the
Putnam *Deer Park* which were legally doubtful, and once in a while, like
a gambler hedging a bet, I toned down individual sentences from the
Rinehart *Deer Park*, nothing much, always a matter of the new O'Shaugnessy character, a change from "at last I was able to penetrate into the
mysterious and magical belly of a movie star," to what was more in character for him: "I was led to discover the mysterious brain of a movie star."

Which "brain" in context was fun for it was accurate, and "discover" was a word of more life than the legality of "penetrate," but I could not be sure if I were chasing my new aesthetic or afraid of the cops. The problem was that *The Deer Park* had become more sexual in the new version, the characters had more force, the air had more heat, and I had gone through the kind of galloping self-analysis which makes one very sensitive to the sexual nuance of every gesture, word, and object—the book now seemed overcharged to me, even a terror of a novel, a cold chisel into all the dull mortar of our guilty society. In my mind it became a more dangerous book than it really was, and my drug-hipped paranoia saw long consequences in every easy line of dialogue. I kept the panic in its place, but by an effort of course, and once in a while I would weaken enough to take out a line because I could not see myself able to defend it happily in a court of law. But it was a mistake to nibble at the edges of censoring myself, for it gave no life to my old pride that I was the boldest writer to have come out of my flabby time, and I think it helped to kill the small chance of finding my way into what could have been a novel as important as *The Sun Also Rises.*

But let me spell it out a bit: originally *The Deer Park* had been about a movie director and a girl with whom he had a bad affair, and it was told by a sensitive but faceless young man. In changing the young man, I saved the book from being minor, but put a disproportion upon it because my narrator became too interesting, and not enough happened to him in the second half of the book, and so it was to be expected that readers would be disappointed by this part of the novel.

Before I was finished, I saw a way to write another book altogether. In what I had so far done, Sergius O'Shaugnessy was given an opportunity by a movie studio to sell the rights to his life and get a contract as an actor. After more than one complication, he finally refused the offer, lost the love of his movie star Lulu, and went off wandering by himself, off to become a writer. This episode had never been an important part of the book, but I could see that the new Sergius was capable of accepting the offer, and if he went to Hollywood and became a movie star himself, the possibilities were good, for in O'Shaughnessy I had a character who was ambitious, yet in his own way, moral, and with such a character one could travel deep into the paradoxes of the time.

Well, I was not in shape to consider that book. With each week of work, bombed and sapped and charged and stoned with lush, with pot, with benny, saggy, Miltown, coffee, and two packs a day, I was working live, and overalert, and tiring into what felt like death, afraid all the way because I had achieved the worst of vicious circles in myself, I had gotten too tired, I was more tired than I had ever been in combat, and so as the weeks went on, and publication was delayed from June to August and then to October, there was only a worn-out part of me to keep protesting into the pillows of one drug and the pinch of the other that I ought to have the guts to stop the machine, to call back the galleys, to cease—to rest, to give myself another two years and write a book which would go a little further to the end of my particular night.

But I had passed the point where I could stop. My anxiety had become too great. I did not know anything any more, I did not have that clear sense of the way things work which is what you need for the natural proportions of a long novel, and it is likely I would not have been writing a new book so much as arguing with the law. Of course another man might have had the stamina to write the new book and manage to be indifferent to everything else, but it was too much to ask of me. By then I was like a lover in a bad, but uncontrollable affair; my woman was publication, and it would have cost too much to give her up before we were done. My imagination had been committed—to stop would leave half the psyche in limbo.

Knowing, however, what I had failed to do, shame added momentum to the punishment of the drugs. By the last week or two, I had worn down so badly that with a dozen pieces still to be fixed, I was reduced to working hardly more than an hour a day. Like an old man, I would come up out of a Seconal stupor with four or five times the normal dose in my veins, and drop into a chair to sit for hours. It was July, the heat was grim in New York, the last of the book had to be in by August 1. Putnam had been more than accommodating, but the vehicle of publication was on its way, and the book could not be postponed beyond the middle of October or it would miss all chance for a large fall sale. I would sit in a chair and watch a baseball game on television, or get up and go out in the heat to a drug-store for sandwich and malted—it was my outing for the day: the walk would feel like a patrol in a tropical sun, and it was two blocks, no more. When I came back, I would lie down, my head would lose the outer wrappings of sedation, and with a crumb of Benzedrine, the first snake or two of thought would wind through my brain. I would go for some coffee—it was a trip to the kitchen, but when I came back I would have a scratch-board and pencil in hand. Watching some afternoon horror on television, the boredom of the performers coming through their tense hilarities with a bleakness to match my own, I would pick up the board, wait for the first sentence—like all working addicts I had come to an old man's fine sense of inner timing—and then slowly, but picking up speed, the actions of the drugs hovering into collaboration like two ships passing in view of one another, I would work for an hour, not well but not badly either. (Pages 195 to 200 of the Putnam edition were written this way.) Then my mind would wear out, and new work was done for the day. I would sit around, watch more television and try to rest my dulled mind, but by evening a riot of bad nerves was on me again, and at two in the morning I'd be having the manly debate of whether to try sleep with two double capsules, or settle again for my need of three.

Somehow I got the book done for the last deadline. Not perfectly—doing just the kind of editing and small rewriting I was doing, I could have used another two or three days, but I got it almost the way I wanted, and then I took my car up to the Cape and lay around in Provincetown with my wife, trying to mend, and indeed doing a fair job because I came off sleeping pills and the marijuana and came part of the way back into that world which has the proportions of the ego. I picked up on *The Magic Mountain*, took it slowly, and lowered *The Deer Park* down to modest size in my brain. Which events proved was just as well.

A few weeks later we came back to the city, and I took some mescaline. Maybe one dies a little with the poison of mescaline in the blood. At the end of a long and private trip which no quick remark should try to describe, the book of *The Deer Park* floated into mind, and I sat up, reached through a pleasure garden of velveted light to find the tree of a pencil and the bed of a notebook and brought them to union together. Then, out of some flesh in myself I had not yet known, with the words coming one by one, in separate steeps and falls, hip in their turnings, all cool with their flights, like the touch of being coming into other being, so the last six lines of my bloody book came to me, and I was done. And it was the only good writing I ever did directly from a drug, even if I paid for it with a hangover beyond measure.

That way the novel received its last sentence, and if I had waited one more day it would have been too late, for in the next twenty-four hours, the printers began their cutting and binding. The book was out of my hands.

Six weeks later, when *The Deer Park* came out, I was no longer feeling eighty years old, but a vigorous hysterical sixty-three, and I laughed like an old pirate at the indignation I had breezed into being with the equation of sex and time. The important reviews broke about seven good and eleven bad, and the out-of-town reports were almost three-to-one bad to good, but I was not unhappy because the good reviews were lively and the bad reviews were full of factual error, indeed so much so that it would be monotonous to give more than a good couple.

Hollis Alpert in the *Saturday Review* called the book "garish and gauche." In reference to Sergius O'Shaugnessy, Alpert wrote: "He has been offered $50,000 by Teppis to sell the rights to his rather dull life story...." As a matter of detail, the sum was $20,000, and it must have been mentioned a half dozen times in the pages of the book. Paul Pickrel in *Harper's* was blistering about how terrible was my style and then quoted the following sentence as an example of how I was often incomprehensible:

> (he) could talk opening about his personal life while remaining a dream of espionage in his business operations.

I happened to see Pickrel's review in *Harper's* galleys, and so was able to point out to them that Pickrel had misquoted the sentence. The fourth word was not "opening" but "openly." *Harper's* corrected his incorrect version, but of course left his remark about my style.

More interesting is the way reviews divided in the New York magazines and newspapers. *Time*, for example, was bad, *Newsweek* was good; *Harper's* was terrible but the *Atlantic* was adequate; the New York Daily *Times* was very bad, the Sunday *Times* was good; the Daily *Herald Tribune* gave a mark of zero, the Sunday *Herald Tribune* was better than good; *Commentary* was careful but complimentary, the *Reporter* was frantic; the *Saturday Review* was a scold and Brendan Gill writing for the *New Yorker* put together a series of slaps and superlatives which went partially like this:

> . . . a big, vigorous, rowdy, ill-shaped, and repellent book, so strong and so weak, so adroit and so fumbling, that only a writer of the greatest and most reckless talent could have flung it between covers.

It's one of the three or four lines I've thought perceptive in all the reviews of my books. That Malcolm Cowley used one of the same words in saying *The Deer Park* was "serious and reckless" is also, I think, interesting, for reckless the book was—and two critics, anyway, had the instinct to feel it.

One note appeared in many reviews. The strongest statement of it was by John Hutchens in The New York Daily *Herald Tribune*:

> . . . the original version reputedly was more or less rewritten and certain materials eliminated that were deemed too erotic for public consumption. And, with that, a book that might at least have made a certain reputation as a large shocker wound up as a cipher. . . .

I was bothered to the point of writing a letter to the twenty-odd newspapers which reflected this idea. What bothered me was that I could never really prove I had not "eliminated" the book. Over the years all too many readers would have some hazy impression that I had disemboweled large pieces of the best meat, perspiring in a coward's sweat, a publisher's directive in my ear. (For that matter, I still get an occasional letter which asks if it is possible to see the unbowdlerized *Deer Park*.) Part of the cost of touching the Rinehart galleys was to start those rumors, and in fact I was not altogether free of the accusation, as I have tried to show. Even the six lines which so displeased Rinehart had been altered a bit; I had shown them once to a friend whose opinion I respected, and he remarked that while it was impossible to accept the sort of order Rinehart had laid down, still a phrase like the "fount of power" had a Victorian heaviness about it. Well, that was true, it was out of character for O'Shaughnessy's new style and so I altered it to the "thumb of power" and then other changes became desirable, and the curious are invited to compare the two versions of this particular passage in this collection, but the mistake I made was to take a small aesthetic gain on those six lines and lose a larger clarity about a principle.

What more is there to say? The book moved fairly well, it climbed to seven and then to six on *The New York Times* bestseller list, stayed there for a week or two, and then slipped down. By Christmas, the tone of the *Park* and the Christmas spirit being not all that congenial, it was just about off the lists forever. It did well, however; it would have reached as high as three or two or even to number one if it had come out in June and then been measured against the low sales of summer, for it sold over fifty thousand copies after returns which surprised a good many in publishing, as well as disappointing a few, including myself. I discovered that I had been poised for an enormous sale or a failure—a middling success was cruel to take. Week after week I kept waiting for the book to erupt into some dramatic change of pace which would send it up in sales instead of down, but that never happened. I was left with a draw, not busted, not made, and since I was empty at the time, worn-out with work, waiting for the quick transfusions of a generous success, the steady sales of the book left me deeply depressed. Having reshaped my words with an intensity of feeling I had not known before, I could not understand why others were not overcome with my sense of life, of sex, and of sadness. Like a starved revolutionary in a garret, I had compounded out of need and fever and vision and fear nothing less than a madman's confidence in the identity of my being and the wants of all others, and it was a new dull load to lift and to bear, this knowledge that I had no magic so great as to hasten the time of the apocalypse, but that instead I would be open like all others to the attritions of half-success and small failure. Something God-like in my confidence began to leave, and I was reduced in dimension if now less a boy. I knew I had failed to bid on the biggest hand I ever held.

Now a few years have gone by, more years than I thought, and I have begun to work up another hand, a new book which will be the proper book of an outlaw, and so not publishable in any easy or legal way. Two excerpts from this novel come later in this collection, and therefore I'll say here only that O'Shaughnessy will be one of the three heroes, and that if I'm to go all the way this time, the odds are that my beat senses will have to do the work without the fires and the wastes of the minor drugs.

But that is for later, and the proper end to this account is the advertisement I took in *The Village Voice*. It was bought in November 1955, a month after publication, it was put together by me and paid for by me, and it was my way I now suppose of saying good-by to the pleasure of a quick triumph, of making my apologies for the bad flaws in the bravest effort I had yet pulled out of myself, and certainly for declaring to the world (in a small way, mean pity) that I no longer gave a sick dog's drop for the wisdom, the reliability, and the authority of the public's literary mind, those creeps and old ladies of vested reviewing.

Besides, I had the tender notion—believe it if you will—that the ad might after all do its work and excite some people to buy the book.

But here it is:

Thomas Mann

(1875–1955)

When Thomas Mann was twenty-five years old and already famous as the author of Buddenbrooks, *he jotted down three lines in a notebook outlining a possible novel on an artist who, like Faust, makes a deal with the devil. Forty-two years and many travails and writings later—after "Tonio Kröger," "Death in Venice,"* The Magic Mountain; *after the Nobel Prize; after self-chosen exile from Hitler's Germany and the adoption of United States citizenship; after the four volumes of* Joseph and His Brothers—*Mann returned to the Faust idea. He wrote the novel between his sixty-seventh and seventy-first years. Some time later he wrote an account of the writing of* Dr. Faustus. *A formidably systematic writer who, day in and day out for more than half a century, produced each morning one manuscript page of his imaginative work-in-progress, Mann also kept extensive journals, so* The Story of a Novel *is rich with fresh concrete details; the* Story *follows the making of the book, chapter by chapter, to the day of its completion. One notable fact about* Dr. Faustus *is that while Mann was writing the novel, in his seventieth year, he had a brush with the devil himself: he underwent dangerous chest surgery. He survived, as if for the sake of the novel (no pact appears to have been made), and went straight back to work. Mann had a scar "from chest to back," but it is impossible to find a seam in the massive novel. The excerpt from* The Story of a Novel *on the following pages tells of the period of gestation of what Mann himself called his "wildest" book.*

FROM
THE STORY OF A NOVEL

1

Diary entries for 1945 show me that on December 22 of that year the Los Angeles correspondent of *Time* called on me (it is an hour's drive from downtown Los Angeles to our country home). He came to challenge me concerning a prophecy I had made fifteen years before, the which was failing to be fulfilled. At the end of *Sketch of My Life*, written in 1930 and available also in English, I had, with half-sportive belief in certain symmetries and numerical correspondences in my life, ventured the guess that I would pass from this world in 1945, at the age of seventy, as had my mother. The foretold year, the man said, was virtually over, and I had not kept my word. What did I want to say to the public to excuse myself for still being alive?

My reply did not please my wife at all—the less so since her anxious heart had for a considerable time been concerned about my health. She tried to stop me, to protest, to unsay the things which I was permitting an interviewer to draw from me, and which I had previously kept even from her. The fulfillment of prophecies, I said, was a curious business. Often they did not come true literally, but suggestively. Fulfillment might be a bit wide of the mark, open to question and yet unmistakable. Certain factors might be substituted for other factors. To be sure, I conceded, in spite of my desire for matters to work out in an orderly fashion, I was not yet dead. But my visitor should know that in the year I had set for it, my life had—biologically speaking—reached a low such as I had never known before. I hoped that my vital forces would help me climb out of this abyss. But my present condition seemed to me fully to bear out my prophetic gifts, and I would be glad if he and his esteemed journal would also consider it good enough.

When I spoke in these terms, three months were yet to pass before the biological low to which I had referred reached its extremity: a serious physical crisis which forced upon me a surgical operation, for months prevented me from working, and tested my constitution in a way I had scarcely imagined possible. I mention this, however, because the experience caused me once more to note the curious divergence between biological and intellectual vitality. Periods of physical well-being and blooming health, when the body gives one no trouble at all and one's step is firm, are not at all necessarily periods of outstanding creativity. I wrote the best chapters of The Beloved Returns during a six-month bout with infectious sciatica. Never have I endured such wild pain—it cannot be described to those who have not had the disease. To escape these agonizing twinges, you vainly seek the right position day and night. There is no right position. After nights which may God keep me from ever having to live again, breakfast usually brought a certain respite to my burning, inflamed nerves; and then, sitting at my desk at one strange angle or another, I would perform the unio mystica with Goethe, the "star of sublime beauty." Still and all, sciatica is not a disease that reaches deep into the vitals. Despite all its torture, it is not an illness to be taken very seriously. On the other hand, the time of which I am speaking, and for which I had prophesied my death, was a period of real decline in all my vital forces, of unmistakable biological "reduction." Yet this was the very period in which a work germinated which, from the moment of its inception, has had an unusually far-reaching power.

There would be something doctrinaire about seeing a sinking of vitality as the cause and precondition for a creative effort that absorbs into itself the stuff of an entire life, that half unwittingly, half consciously synthesizes and unifies a man's entire life, and therefore embodies the vital charge which the physical self is no longer capable of. It would be easier to turn the explanation around and to blame my illness on the work.

For indeed, like no other of my books, this one consumed and took heavy toll of my innermost forces. Well-meaning intimates did take the relationship in that light, and when they saw me looking so rundown were apt to comment: "It is the book." And did I not say yes? There is a noble saying: that he who gives his life shall save it—a saying as applicable to the realm of art and literature as to religion. It is never from lack of vitality that such an offering of one's life is made, and surely no such lack is shown when—strange case indeed!—at seventy a man writes his "wildest" book. Nor was there any sign of that in the agility with which I rose up from the operation, marked with a scar from chest to back, and to the amusement of the doctors rushed home to finish that book. . . .

But I want to tell the story of *Faustus*, embedded as it is in the pressure and tumult of outward events. I want to try to reconstruct that story on the basis of my brief daily notes, for myself and for my friends.

2

In November 1942 a journey to the East delayed the completion of *Joseph the Provider*, which I had sought to bring to a conclusion during the preceding weeks, amid the thunder of the battles for burning Stalingrad. On this journey I took with me the manuscript of a lecture on the nearly finished tetralogy. The expedition led through Chicago to Washington and New York and was rich in encounters, public meetings, and appearances. Among other things, I once again saw Princeton and the friends belonging to that period of my life when I lived there: Frank Aydelotte, Einstein, Christian Gauss, Helen Lowe-Porter, Hans Rastede of the Lawrenceville School and his circle, Erich von Kahler, Hermann Broch, and others. The days in Chicago had been overshadowed by news of the war in North Africa, perturbing accounts of the march of German troops through unoccupied France, Pétain's protest, the transhipment of the Hitler Corps to Tunis, the Italian occupation of Corsica, the recapture of Tobruk. We read of feverish defensive measures by the Germans at all probable invasion points, of signs that the French fleet was preparing to go over to the side of the Allies.

The sight of Washington on a war footing was new and remarkable to me. A guest once more of Eugene Meyer and his beautiful wife in their palatial home on Crescent Place, I gazed in astonishment at the heavily militarized district around the Lincoln Memorial, with its barracks, office buildings, and bridges, and at the trains laden with war materials that incessantly rolled into the city. It was oppressively hot, a belated Indian summer. At a dinner in my hosts' house, at which the Brazilian and Czech ambassadors were present with their wives, the discussion turned to American collaboration with Darlan and the problem of "expediency." Opinions were divided. I did not conceal my distaste for it. After dinner we heard the radio address of Wendell Willkie, who had just returned from his One-World tour. Communiqués on the important naval victory off the Solomons cheered the gathering.

To my delight, the lecture arranged at the Library of Congress brought me together once more with Archibald MacLeish, then still Librarian of Congress, and his wife. And I regarded it as a special honor that Vice President Wallace, introduced by MacLeish, in his turn said an introductory word for me. After such a prelude, the reading itself met with a more than friendly response. My text was colored somewhat by current events, and the loudspeaker transmitted my words to a second closely packed hall.

The evening was concluded with a reception, abounding in personalities, at the Meyers' house. . . .

In hours free of social obligations I tried to push forward on the current chapter of *Joseph the Provider*—already one of the last, the chapter on the blessing of the sons. But what strikes me and impresses me as something mysterious is the kind of reading that I did on this trip during train journeys, evening hours, and brief rests. Contrary to my usual habit on lecture tours, it bore no relation to my present occupation, nor to the next work I had in view. Instead, I read the memoirs of Igor Stravinsky—studied "with the pencil," that is to say, making underlinings for rereading. I also read two books long familiar to me: *Nietzsches Zusammenbruch* (*Nietzsche's Collapse*) by Erich Friedrich Podach, and Lou Andreas-Salomé's recollections of Nietzsche, which I likewise went through making pencil marks. "Fateful mysticism, unpardonable, often arousing pity. The 'unfortunate'!" That is the diary jotting apropos this reading. Music, then, and Nietzsche. I would not be able to explain why my thoughts and interests were turning in this particular direction at that time.

In our New York hotel one day the agent Armin Robinson called upon us to present, most temptingly, a plan for a book to be published not only in English but also in four or five other languages; it was to bear the title *The Ten Commandments*. The project was to have a moral and polemic slant. Ten world-famous writers were to contribute to it, each treating one of the commandments and telling the tale of some criminal breach of the moral law. They were offering me a fee of one thousand dollars for a short essay introducing the whole thing. Traveling, one is more receptive to such commissions than at home. I agreed, and two days later in the office of a lawyer—where I met Sigrid Undset, who had likewise agreed to participate—I signed a contract full of pitfalls and barbed hooks. I had scarcely read the document, and in it I handed over to the entrepreneur the eternal rights to a work which did not yet exist, of whose development I had no conception, and which I was destined to take far more seriously than the occasion demanded. If it is foolish to buy "a pig in a poke," it is even more foolish to sell one in that manner.

The shocking war news that the commanders and crew of the French fleet had sunk their ships outside Toulon came in the midst of our days filled with going to concerts and to the theater, with invitations and meetings with friends; days in which many bits of occasional writing had also to be dashed off. The usually quiet pages of my notebook, which I still had from Switzerland, were now sprinkled with names. The Walters and Werfels, Max Reinhardt, the actor Karlweis, Martin Gumpert, the publisher Landshoff, Fritz von Unruh figured in it; also charming old Annette Kolb, Erich von Kahler, Molly Shenstone, our British friend from Princeton, and American colleagues of the younger generation, such as Glenway Wescott, Charles Neider, and Christopher Lazare. In addition there were our children. We spent Thanksgiving Day with South American guests at Alfred Knopf's country house in Purchase.

With the German-speaking group, we had various readings from works in progress; Kahler read some extremely impressive selections from his intellectual history of the human race, which was to be published under the title of *Man the Measure*. I myself once more trotted out the grateful annunciation chapter from *Joseph the Provider*, also the cup and recognition scenes, and received the praise and encouragement which is both the reward and the aim of such readings of relatively "surefire" passages from the work one is struggling with. What has been carefully forged in the course of long mornings is poured out over the listeners in a rapid hour of reading; the illusion of improvisation, of polished extemporization, intensifies the impression, and when others are stirred to marvel, we for our part believe that everything is fine.

3

We returned home before the middle of December, passing on the way through San Francisco, where we visited two of the children, our youngest son, the musician, and his pretty Swiss wife, and where once more I was charmed by the sky-blue eyes of my favorite grandson, little Frido, an utterly enchanting child. I immediately resumed work on the blessing chapter. After concluding this, all I had left was to describe Jacob's death and burial, and "The Great Progress" from Egypt to Canaan. The year 1943 was only a few days old when I set down the last lines of the fourth Joseph novel and therewith brought the whole work to its end. It was a curious day for me, that fourth of January, but certainly not one marked by high spirits. This great narrative work which had accompanied me through all these years of exile, insuring me the unity of my life, was done, was finished with, and I was unburdened—a state of doubtful weightlessness for one who since his early days, since the days of *Buddenbrooks*, has lived under multifarious burdens that had to be carried long distances, and who scarcely knows how to live without them.

Antonio Borgese and his wife, our Elisabeth, were with us, and that same evening I read the two final chapters to the family circle. The impression was comforting. We drank champagne. Bruno Frank, informed of the event of the day, telephoned to congratulate me, his voice vibrant with feeling. Why I should have been "suffering, sorrowful, deeply perturbed and weary" during the next few days is something known only to God, to whose knowledge—even about Himself—we must consign so much. Perhaps the prevailing torrid winds, like a Swiss *föhn*, contributed to my state; also the news of the idiotic cruelty of the Nazis, who in spite of Swedish intervention were going to deport the eighty-three-year-old widow of Max Liebermann to Poland. She took poison instead. . . . At the same time Russian corps were advancing upon Rostov; the expulsion of the Germans from the Caucasus was nearly completed; and in a strong, confident speech to the new Congress, Roosevelt announced the invasion of Europe.

I set to work giving titles to the chapters of the fourth volume and dividing it into seven principal parts, or "books." Meanwhile I read such things as Goethe's essay, *Israel in the Desert*, Freud's *Moses*, Erich Auerbach's *Wüste und Gelobtes Land* (*Desert and Promised Land*), and also dipped into the Pentateuch. I had long been asking myself why I should contribute only an essayistic foreword to the book of stories by distinguished writers —why not rather an "organ prelude," as Werfel later put it? Why not a tale of the issuance of the Commandments, a Sinai novella? That seemed very natural to me as a postlude to the Joseph story; I was still warm from the epic. Notes and preparations for this work required only a few days. One morning I delivered my radio broadcast on the tenth year of Nazi rule, and the next morning I began writing the Moses story. I was already in the eleventh chapter when on February 11—it happened also to be our wedding anniversary—there drew round for the tenth time the day we had left Munich with scanty baggage, without suspecting that we would not return.

In not quite two months—a short span for me, with my way of working—I wrote the story down almost without corrections. In contrast to the quasi-scientific circumstantiality of the *Joseph*, this one was swiftly paced from the start. During the writing, or perhaps even before, I had given it the title of *Das Gesetz* (*The Law*),[1] by which I was referring not only to the Decalogue but also to the moral law in general, man's civilization. It was a subject I was serious about, for all that I treated the legendary material jestingly and made use of Voltairean mockery for the characterization—again in contrast to the *Joseph* stories. Probably under the unconscious influence of Heine's portrait of Moses, I did not give my hero the features of Michelangelo's Moses but of Michelangelo himself, in order to depict him as an artist toiling laboriously over refractory human raw material and suffering dispiriting defeats. The curse at the end, against the present-day wretches to whom power was given to profane his work, the Tables of the Law, came from my heart and at least at the end leaves no doubt of the militant intent of this otherwise somewhat frivolous little thing.

[1]*Published as* The Tables of the Law.

The morning after completing this story I cleared away all the mythological and Oriental material that had accumulated in the course of the *Joseph*—pictures, excerpts, drafts. The stuff was all packed away. The books I had read for the purpose remained on their shelves, a little library in itself. And only one day later—March 15, to be exact—my evening notes contained the curt jotting: "Dr. Faust." This is its first mention, and in only the briefest of references: "Looking through old papers for material on 'Dr. Faust.' " What papers? I can hardly say. But the notation, which occurs again the following day, is connected with letters to Professor Gustav Arlt of the University of California in Los Angeles and to MacLeish in Washington, asking for an extended loan of the Faust chapbook and—the letters of Hugo Wolf. The combination suggests that I had long been pursuing a rather definite outline of an idea which on the other hand was also extremely nebulous. Apparently the theme was to be some demonic intoxication and its liberating but catastrophic effects—the chief character to be an artist of a still unspecified sort, but evidently a complicated creature. "Going through old notes in the morning," I have down for the 27th. "Dug up the three-line outline of the Dr. Faust of 1901. Association with the Tonio Kröger period, the Munich days, the never-realized plans for *The Lovers* and *Maya*. 'Old Love, old friendship rise along with these.' Shame and strong sentimentality at remembrance of these youthful sorrows. . . ."

Forty-two years had passed since I had set down something about an artist's pact with the devil as a possible subject for a piece of writing, and the seeking and finding of these notes was accompanied by a degree of emotion, not to say inner tumult, which made one thing very clear to me: that the meager and vague nucleus had been surrounded from the beginning by a belt of personal concern, a density of biographical feeling, which from the first destined the long short story for a novel—though this was far from my mind. It was all this inner stirring which caused me to expand my usually laconic diary notes into monologues: "Only now do I realize what it means to be without the *Joseph* work, the task which always stood beside me, before me, all through this decade. Only now that *The Law* postlude is finished do I become conscious of the novelty and peril of the situation. It was comfortable, working away on what I had already dredged up. Do I still have strength for new conceptions? Have I not used up my subject matter? And if not—will I still be able to summon up the desire for work? Gloomy weather: rainy, cold. With a headache, I drew up outline and notes for the novella. To Los Angeles for the concert; in Steinberg's box with his ladies. Horowitz played the B flat major Piano Concerto of Brahms, the orchestra did the *Don Juan* overture and Tschaikovsky's *Pathétique*. 'In compliance with many requests,' the phrase would once have been. Yet it is his melancholy best, the highest he could rise to, and there is always something beautiful and moving in seeing a limited talent reaching, by who knows what set of circumstances, the peak of its abilities. I remembered, too, how Stravinsky, years ago in Zürich, confessed to me that he admired Tschaikovsky (I had asked him about it). With the conductor in the green room. . . . Read with amusement stories in the *Gesta Romanorum*, likewise *Nietzsche und die Frauen (Nietzsche's Women)* by [Hellmut Walter] Brann, and Stevenson's masterpiece, *Dr. Jekyll and Mr. Hyde*, with my thoughts fixed on the Faust subject—which, however, is far from taking shape. Although the pathological aspect could be shifted into the realm of fable, could be linked with mythology, the whole thing has something forbidding about it; the difficulties seem insuperable, and it is possible that I shrink from the undertaking because I have always regarded it as my last."

Reading that over, I know that the supposition was right. Right about the lineage of the barely definable idea, whose long roots reach far down into my life—and right that in my life plan, which was always a plan of work, I had from the start kept the treatment of this idea for the end. To myself I had called this work, which might some day have to be done, my "Parsifal." Strange though it seem that a work of old age should be placed on the agenda in youth—it was so. It is likely that there is a connection between this and my conscious interest, expressed in many a critical essay, in the late works of artists—*Parsifal* itself, the second part of *Faust*, the last works of Ibsen, the prose of Adalbert Stifter and Theodor Fontane in the latter years of their lives.

The question was whether the hour had come for this task so long ago though so dimly sighted. Clearly, I felt certain instinctive scruples, reinforced by the premonition that there was something uncanny about this subject and that it would cost heart's blood, a great deal of it, to whip it into shape. Added to this was a vague notion of how radical its demands would be, how everything in it would have to be carried to extremes. This whole thing could be comprised in the cry: "Let me try something else first!" The something else, which had the merit of putting off the other project for a good long time, was to pick up and complete the fragmentary novel I had laid aside before the First World War, the *Confessions of Felix Krull, Confidence Man*.

"K." (that is my wife) "speaks of finishing the *Krull*, which friends have often petitioned for. The idea is not altogether alien to me, but I had considered the book, which springs from a period when the artist-bourgeois problem was my most dominant concern, superannuated and outmoded by the *Joseph*. Nevertheless, reading and listening to music last night, I was curiously stirred by the thought of resuming it, chiefly from the point of view of life's unity. After thirty-two years there would be something intriguing about taking up again where I left off before *Death in Venice*, for whose sake I interrupted the *Krull*. It would mean that all my major and incidental works had been an interpolation, occupying a whole generation, into the undertaking that the thirty-six-year-old had been engaged on. Also, the advantage of building on an old foundation."

What all this came to was: "Let me try something else first." And yet the thorn was in my flesh, the thorn of curiosity about the new and dangerous task. There were diversions during the next few days. I had to write some occasional pieces: a broadcast to Germany, an Open Letter to Alexei Tolstoi as a contribution to a Russian-American exchange. Then came shock at the sudden death of Heinrich Zimmer, the brilliant Indologist and husband of Christiane Hofmannsthal; I had drawn the material for *The Transposed Heads* from his great book on Indian mythology. From New York came news of a countermovement, led by Sforza, Maritain, and others, to Coudenhove's capitalists' club—his reactionary Pan-Europe. This occupied me, made it necessary that I state my position. The War in North Africa, where Montgomery had brought Rommel to a standstill, held me in suspense. But the books I had asked for had arrived: the Faust chapbook and the collected letters of Hugo Wolf in many volumes, placed at my disposal by the Library of Congress. And for all my sputterings on the "advantages" of resuming the *Krull*, all my diary notes of the end of March and the beginning of April reveal that I was mulling over the Faust theme.

"Extracts from the Faust chapbook. Evening, reading in it. Second air raid on Berlin in 48 hours. . . . Excerpts from Hugo Wolf's letters. Thoughts, dreams, notes. Evening, Wolf's letters to Grohe. The lack of judgment, the dreadful facetiousness, the enthusiasm for his bad opera libretti, the stupid remarks on Dostoevsky. Euphoric anticipations of madness which then, as in Nietzsche, expresses itself in megalomaniac ideas but has nothing of greatness about it. Sad illusions about the operas. Not a sensible word. . . . The letters again. What form could it all take? The basic presentation is questionable. Even time and place. . . . Notes on the Faust theme. After dinner, dipping into Paul Bekker's *Musikgeschichte* [*History of Music*], which he gave me in 1927 with the inscription 'For the train.' More reading of it when I had the chance in the evening. . . . Massive and systematic bombings of Hitler's continent. Advances of the Russians in the Crimea. Signs of imminent invasion of Europe. . . . At Bruno and Liesl Frank's in Beverly Hills for dinner. He read his Nazi story on the Fourth Commandment. Excellently done. Some words in confidence about the plan for Faust. . . ."

What was that—was I already announcing this plan of mine to old friends, unclear though I was in my own mind concerning form, plot, manner of presentation, even time and place? How exactly had I put it? In any case, this was the first time that I opened my mouth about it, except for consultations with my wife, who favored the new plan rather than the resumption of the old one. Incidentally, I was not feeling well. A throat and bronchial catarrh was giving me trouble in spite of the clear, warm weather, and I found myself "very dull in spirit," unsure of myself and pessimistic about my future creativity. And yet I had only recently done things like *Tamar, Annunciation,* and the second half of the Moses! . . .

"Dipping into books on Nietzsche. Moved by a letter of Rohde concerning him. At night, *Murr the Tomcat* by E. T. A. Hoffmann. In Bekker's history of music, on playfulness in the art of Haydn, gaiety in the sense of being beyond jest and earnestness, the surmounting of reality."

One day, in spite of everything, I set about untying the bundles of material on the *Confidence Man* and rereading the preliminary studies—with a result that was passing strange. It was "insight into the inner kinship of the Faust subject with this one (the motif of loneliness, in the one case mystic and tragic, in the other humorous and roguish); nevertheless my feeling is that the Faust, if I am capable of shaping it, is more appropriate for me today, more topical, more urgent. . . ." The balance had been swung. The *Joseph* business was not to be followed by a preliminary "something else" in the form of my novel about a rogue. The radically serious, menacing subject, around which the lightning of grave sacrifice seemed to flash, had proved the stronger in its demands and in its promise. Heaven grant that it would prove possible to let it partake a little of artistic playfulness and jest, irony, travesty, higher humor! My notes of the next several weeks no longer deal with anything else. I was burying myself in this new field, recollecting and summoning up material, accumulating sidelights, in order to create a body for the hovering shadow.

"On German urban life in Luther's region. Also, medical and theological reading. Gropings, attempts, and a tentative feeling of greater security in the atmosphere of the subject. Walked the mountain road with K. All day reading Luther's letters. Took up *Ulrich von Hutten* by D. F. Strauss. Decided to study books on music. Finished Bekker's history with greatest attentiveness. Nothing yet has been done about staffing the book with characters, filling it out with meaningful subsidiary figures. In *The Magic Mountain* these were provided by the personnel of the sanatorium, in *Joseph* by the Bible; there it was a question of realizing the potentialties of the Biblical figures. In *Krull* the world could permissibly have been phantasmagorical. It may be so here, too, to a certain extent; but here much full-bodied reality is needed, and for that there is a deficiency of concrete observation. . . . The characters will have to be supplied out of the past, out of memory, pictures, intuition. But the entourage must first be invented and fixed. . . ."

I wrote to Professor Paul Tillich of the Union Theological Seminary to ask about the procedures of studying for the ministry. Curiously enough, there came almost simultaneously a letter from Bermann Fischer transmitting a Swedish proposal that I write a book on Germany, its past and future. "If one could only do everything. But the demands of the era, which employs the voices of people for its purposes—at bottom we meet them, but differently from the way asked." Still and all, a letter from the Office of War Information was also received at this time, thanking me "for the article on Germany's future, which has met with much approval in Sweden." I no longer have any idea what article it referred to.

"Made extracts of Lamentation of Faust and mockery of the 'spirit' (intended as a symphony). Notes, excerpts, meditations, and calculations on time sequence. Luther's letters. Dürer pictures. Ernest Newman's *Hugo Wolf*, in English. Thoughts on the way the subject was identified with things German, with German solitude in the world in general. Symbolic values here . . . Reading of the *Witches' Hammer*. Details of youth in Munich. Figure of Rud. Schwerdtfeger, violinist in the Zapfenstösser orchestra (!) . . . Drawing up a list of characters for the novel, and their names. *Pascal and the Medieval Definition of God* by Nitze. . . ."

Amid such surveys and studies the month of May 1943 began, a month in which the tenderest, most delicate impressions and feelings were coupled with a striving, testing, inventing which had already become the dominant factor in my life and which arrogated for its own purposes all that reality brought my way. The children from San Francisco came for a longish visit, "with the two boys, who look fine and strong. Moved, as always, by Frido's beautiful eyes. Went walking with him before dinner. He ate with us. . . . Much jesting with the little fellow, who is just beginning to talk." Tuesday, May 4: "In the afternoon, on the promenade with little Fridolin. When the walk is over, he says 'Nuff.' This for Nepomuk Schneidewein. Evening, reading the *Malleau Maleficarum*. . . . Frido is very attached to me. . . . After the walk, lunch with him in the Miramar; the child was very well behaved."

A letter to Bruno Walter in New York was written about this time, "not without connection with the subject"—that is to say, with the sketch of the novel, and incidentally full of stories and anecdotes about the charming child. In reply, Walter expressed warm interest in the plan for a "musician novel," saying that few were so called to it as I. He also made what I referred to—I know not with what feelings—as "a remarkable suggestion"; namely, that Frido should play a part in the book—he could imagine the episode, he said, as an *allegretto moderato*. This dear friend and splendid musician had no notion of the cold breath of inhumanity that blows through the book at the end. He could not know that I would be constrained to tell the story of the child of God in quite another spirit from that of *allegretto moderato*.

A sizable pile of notes had accumulated, testifying to the complexity of the plan. I found I had some two hundred half-quarto sheets: a wild medley of disordered, boxed-in notes from many fields—linguistic, geographic, politico-social, theological, medical, biological, historical, and musical. I was still continuing to gather and hoard everything useful to my purpose, but I find it good to see that, in spite of such preoccupation and obsession, my mind was still open to impressions from outside the magic circle, from the world that did not pertain to the novel. "Read an excellent article in the *Nation*, a piece by Henry James on Dickens," I set down one day. "Written in 1864 at the age of twenty-two. Amazing! Is there anything like it in Germany? The critical writings of the West are far superior. . . . Extensive reading in Niebuhr's book, *The Nature and Destiny of Man* . . . Till after midnight reading in its entirety Stifter's wonderful *Rock Crystal*." But then, too: "The coal miner strike, serious crisis. Government takeover of the mines. Troops to protect those willing to work—which will be few. . . . Read some curious things on the inglorious defeat of the Germans in Africa. Nothing of Nazi fanaticism's 'to the last drop of blood . . .' Talking in the evening with Bruno Frank about the new strike wave here and the administration's responsibility for it. Concern about the American home front . . . Heaviest bombing of Dortmund, with more than a thousand planes. All Europe in invasion fever. Preparations of the French underground organization. Announcement of general strike. The garrison in Norway is instructed to fight 'to the last man'—which never happens. In Africa 200,000 prisoners were taken. Superiority of matériel in quantity and quality explains the victory. . . . Expectation of the invasion of Italy. Undertakings against Sardinia and Sicily are in the offing. . . . In the evening read *Love's Labour's Lost*."

The Shakespeare play is pertinent. It falls within the magic circle—while around it sounds the uproar of the world. "Supper with the Werfels and Franks. Conversation on Nietzsche and the pity he arouses—for his and for more general desperation. Meetings with Schönberg and Stravinsky planned. . . . Calculations of time and age relationships in the novel, vital statistics and names. . . . On Riemenschneider and his time. Purchases. Volbach's *Instrumentenkunde* [a handbook on musical instruments]. Notes concerning Leverkühn as musician. His given name to be Anselm, Andreas, or Adrian. Notes on Fascist ideology of the period. Gathering at the Werfels with the Schönbergs. Pumped S. a great deal on music and the life of a composer. To my deep pleasure, he himself insists we must all get together more often. . . . The Alfred Neumanns with us for supper. While the ladies were preparing the meal (we are without a maid), I expounded the plan of the novel to N., who was stirred to amazement."

I shall never forget that. This faithful friend, for whom I had always had such high regard, listened with exclamations of the keenest interest. His attitude confirmed me in all I had felt about the book—all the pleasure and pain which emanated from the idea as I outlined it to him, my words coming to me swiftly and easily. What most impressed him, I think, was the central idea: the flight from the difficulties of the cultural crisis into the pact with the devil, the craving of a proud mind, threatened by sterility, for an unblocking of inhibitions at any cost, and the parallel between pernicious euphoria ending in collapse with the nationalistic frenzy of Fascism. I heard later that on the drive home he spoke to his wife the whole way of what I had confided to him.

On May 23, 1943, a Sunday morning little more than two months after I had fetched out that old notebook, and also the date on which I had my narrator, Serenus Zeitblom, set to work, I began writing *Doctor Faustus*.

Virginia Woolf

(1882–1941)

Virginia Woolf had a fragile sensibility held together—but also threatened—by a powerful creative drive. Formidably educated—she was the daughter of Sir Leslie Stephen, author of fifteen books of history, criticism, and biography, and by her own fifteenth year she was reading not only Dickens and George Eliot but also such authors as Carlyle, Macaulay, Pepys, and Froude—she was from childhood through her twenty-second year the terror-frozen object of incestuous advances by a half-brother fourteen years older than she. Much of her later writing life was a battle against male exploitation of women. She was able, at twenty-nine, to bring herself to marry Leonard Woolf, himself a sensitive, rather passive man who fed and supported her mind but made small demands on her body. The Woolfs founded and controlled the Hogarth Press, through which most of her books were published. She was one of the originators of the stream-of-consciousness method, exemplified in Mrs. Dalloway *and* To the Lighthouse. *The following passage is from* A Writer's Diary, *a volume culled from her journals by her widower after her death; it leads us through her writing of* The Waves, *which for some time she thought of calling* The Moths. *Moths and waves and the fin of the shark obsessed her. In "The Death of the Moth" she describes a day-moth trying in vain to get out through a window pane to the light outside. It fell exhausted on its back. Its legs struggled. "Nothing, I knew, had any chance against death. Nevertheless after a pause of exhaustion the legs fluttered again. It was superb this last protest. . . . When there was nobody to care or to know, this gigantic effort on the part of an insignificant little moth, against a power of such magnitude, moved one strangely. . . ."*

FROM

A WRITER'S DIARY

1929

Friday, January 4th

Now is life very solid or very shifting? I am haunted by the two contradictions. This has gone on for ever; will last for ever; goes down to the bottom of the world—this moment I stand on. Also it is transitory, flying, diaphanous. I shall pass like a cloud on the waves. Perhaps it may be that though we change, one flying after another, so quick, so quick, yet we are somehow successive and continuous we human beings, and show the light through. But what is the light? I am impressed by the transitoriness of human life to such an extent that I am often saying a farewell—after dining with Roger[1] for instance; or reckoning how many more times I shall see Nessa.[2]

Thursday, March 28th

It is a disgrace indeed; no diary has been left so late in the year. The truth was that we went to Berlin on 16th January, and then I was in bed for three weeks afterwards and then could not write, perhaps for another three, and have spent my energy since in one of my excited outbursts of composition—writing what I made up in bed, a final version of *Women and Fiction*.

And as usual I am bored by narrative. I want only to say how I met Nessa in Tottenham Court Road this afternoon, both of us sunk fathoms deep in that wash of reflection in which we both swim about. She will be gone on Wednesday for 4 months. It is queer how instead of drawing apart, life draws us together. But I was thinking a thousand things as I carried my teapot, gramophone records and stockings under my arm. It is one of those days that I called "potent" when we lived in Richmond.

Perhaps I ought not to go on repeating what I have always said about the spring. One ought perhaps to be forever finding new things to say, since life draws on. One ought to invent a fine narrative style. Certainly there are many new ideas always forming in my head. For one, that I am going to enter a nunnery these next months; and let myself down into my mind; Bloomsbury being done with. I am going to face certain things. It is going to be a time of adventure and attack, rather lonely and painful I think. But solitude will be good for a new book. Of course, I shall make friends. I shall be external outwardly. I shall buy some good clothes and go out into new houses. All the time I shall attack this angular shape in my mind. I think *The Moths* (if that is what I shall call it) will be very sharply cornered. I am not satisfied though with the frame. There is this sudden fertility which may be mere fluency. In old days books were so many sentences absolutely struck with an axe out of crystal: and now my mind is so impatient, so quick, in some ways so desperate.

Sunday, May 12th

Here, having just finished what I call the final revision of *Women and Fiction*[3] so that L. can read it after tea, I stop; surfeited. And the pump, which I was so sanguine as to think ceased, begins again. About *Women and Fiction* I am not sure—a brilliant essay?—I daresay: it has much work in it, many opinions boiled down into a kind of jelly, which I have stained red as far as I can. But I am eager to be off—to write without any boundary

---

[1]*Roger Fry. (Ed. note.)*
[2]*Vanessa Bell, sister of Virginia Woolf and mother of Quentin Bell, author, many years later, of* Virginia Woolf: A Biography *(New York: Harcourt Brace Jovanovich, 1972). (Ed.)*
[3]*A Room of One's Own.*

coming slick in one's eyes: here my public has been too close; facts; getting them malleable, easily yielding to each other.

Tuesday, May 28th

Now about this book, *The Moths*. How am I to begin it? And what is it to be? I feel no great impulse; no fever; only a great pressure of difficulty. Why write it then? Why write at all? Every morning I write a little sketch, to amuse myself. I am not saying, I might say, that these sketches have any relevance. I am not trying to tell a story. Yet perhaps it might be done in that way. A mind thinking. They might be islands of light—islands in the stream that I am trying to convey; life itself going on. The current of the moths flying strongly this way. A lamp and a flower pot in the centre. The flower can always be changing. But there must be more unity between each scene than I can find at present. Autobiography it might be called. How am I to make one lap, or act, between the coming of the moths, more intense than another; if there are only scenes? One must get the sense that this is the beginning; this the middle; that the climax—when she opens the window and the moth comes in. I shall have the two different currents— the moths flying along; the flower upright in the centre; a perpetual crumbling and renewing of the plant. In its leaves she might see things happen. But who is she? I am very anxious that she should have no name. I don't want a Lavinia or a Penelope: I want "she." But that becomes arty, Liberty greenery yallery somehow: symbolic in loose robes. Of course I can make her think backwards and forwards; I can tell stories. But that's not it. Also I shall do away with exact place and time. Anything may be out of the window—a ship—a desert—London.

Sunday, June 23rd

It was very hot that day, driving to Worthing to see Leonard's mother, my throat hurt me. Next morning I had a headache—so we stayed on at Rodmell[4] till today. At Rodmell I read through *The Common Reader*; and this is very important—I must learn to write more succinctly. Especially in the general idea essays like the last, "How it strikes a Contemporary," I am horrified by my own looseness. This is partly that I don't think things out first; partly that I stretch my style to take in crumbs of meaning. But the result is a wobble and diffusity and breathlessness which I detest. One must correct *A Room of One's Own* very carefully before printing. And so I pitched into my great lake of melancholy. Lord how deep it is! What a born melancholic I am! The only way I keep afloat is by working. A note for the summer—I must take more work than I can possibly get done.— No, I don't know what it comes from. Directly I stop working I feel that I am sinking down, down. And as usual I feel that if I sink further I shall reach the truth. That is the only mitigation; a kind of nobility. Solemnity. I shall make myself face the fact that there is nothing—nothing for any of

---

[4]*At Monks House, Rodmell, near Lewes, which the Woolfs had bought in 1919. (Ed.)*

us. Work, reading, writing are all disguises; and relations with people. Yes, even having children would be useless.

However, I now begin to see *The Moths* rather too clearly, or at least strenuously, for my comfort. I think it will begin like this: dawn; the shells on a beach; I don't know—voices of cock and nightingale; and then all the children at a long table—lessons. The beginning. Well, all sorts of characters are to be there. Then the person who is at the table can call out anyone of them at any moment; and build up by that person the mood, tell a story; for instance about dogs or nurses; or some adventure of a child's kind; all to be very Arabian Nights; and so on: this shall be childhood; but it must not be *my* childhood; and boats on the pond; the sense of children; unreality; things oddly proportioned. Then another person or figure must be selected. The unreal world must be round all this—the phantom waves. The Moth must come in; the beautiful single moth. Could one not get the waves to be heard all through? Or the farmyard noises? Some odd irrelevant noises. She might have a book—one book to read in—another to write in—old letters. Early morning light—but this need not be insisted on; because there must be great freedom from "reality." Yet everything must have relevance.

Well all this is of course the "real" life; and nothingness only comes in the absence of this. I have proved this quite certainly in the past half hour. Everything becomes green and vivified in me when I begin to think of *The Moths*. Also, I think, one is much better able to enter into others'—

Monday, August 19th

I suppose dinner interrupted. And I opened this book in another train of mind—to record the blessed fact that for good or bad I have just set the last correction to *Women and Fiction,* or *A Room of One's Own.* I shall never read it again I suppose. Good or bad? Has an uneasy life in it I think: you feel the creature arching its back and galloping on, though as usual much is watery and flimsy and pitched in too high a voice.

Monday, September 10th

Leonard is having a picnic at Charleston and I am here—"tired." But why am I tired? Well I am never alone. This is the beginning of my complaint. I am not physically tired so much as psychologically. I have strained and wrung at journalism and proof correction; and underneath has been forming my Moth book. Yes, but it forms very slowly; and what I want is not to write it, but to think it for two or three weeks say—to get into the same current of thought and let that submerge everything. Writing perhaps a few phrases here at my window in the morning. (And they've gone to some lovely place—Hurstmonceux perhaps, in this strange misty evening;—and yet when the time came to go, all I wanted was to walk off into the hills by myself. I am now feeling a little lonely and deserted and defrauded, inevitably.) And every time I get into my current of thought I am jerked out of it. We have the Keynes; then Vita came; then Angelica and Eve;[5] then we went to Worthington, then my head begins throbbing—so here I am, not writing—that does not matter, but not thinking, feeling or seeing—and seizing an afternoon alone as a treasure— Leonard appeared at the glass door at this moment; and they didn't go to Hurstmonceux or anywhere; and Sprott was there and a miner, so I missed nothing—one's first egotistical pleasure.

Really these premonitions of a book—states of soul in creating—are very queer and little apprehended . . .

And then I am 47: yes; and my infirmities will of course increase. To begin with my eyes. Last year, I think, I could read without spectacles; would pick up a paper and read it in a tube; gradually I found I needed spectacles in bed; and now I can't read a line (unless held at a very odd angle) without them. My new spectacles are much stronger than the old and when I take them off I am blinded for a moment. What other infirmities? I can hear, I think, perfectly: I think I could walk as well as ever. But then will there not be the change of life? And may that not be a difficult and even dangerous time? Obviously one can get over it by facing it with common sense—that it is a natural process; that one can lie out here and read; that one's faculties will be the same afterwards; that one has nothing to worry about in one sense—I've written some interesting books, can make money, can afford a holiday—Oh no; one has nothing to bother about; and these curious intervals in life—I've had many—are the most fruitful artistically—one becomes fertilised—think of my madness at Hogarth—and all the little illnesses—that before I wrote the *Lighthouse* for instance. Six weeks in bed now would make a masterpiece of *Moths*. But that won't be the name. Moths, I suddenly remember, don't fly by day. And there can't be a lighted candle. Altogether, the shape of the book wants considering—and with time I could do it. Here I broke off.

Wednesday, September 25th

Yesterday morning I made another start on *The Moths*, but that won't be its title; and several problems cry out at once to be solved. Who thinks it? And am I outside the thinker? One wants some device which is not a trick.

Friday, October 11th

And I snatch at the idea of writing here in order not to write *Waves* or *Moths* or whatever it is to be called. One thinks one has learnt to write quickly; and one hasn't. And what is odd, I'm not writing with gusto or pleasure: because of the concentration. I am not reeling it off; but sticking it down. Also, never, in my life, did I attack such a vague yet elaborate design; whenever I make a mark I have to think of its relation to a dozen others. And though I could go on ahead easily enough, I am always stopping to consider the whole effect. In particular is there some radical fault in my scheme? I am not quite satisfied with this method of picking out things in the room and being reminded by them of other things. Yet I can't at the moment divine anything which keeps so close to the original design and admits of movement. Hence, perhaps, these October days are to me a little strained and surrounded with silence. What I mean by this last word I don't quite know, since I have never stopped "seeing" people—Nessa and Roger, the Jeffers, Charles Buxton, and should have seen Lord David[6] and am to see the Eliots—oh and there was Vita too. No, it's not physical silence; it's some inner loneliness—interesting to analyse if one could. To give an example—I was walking up Bedford Place is it—the straight street with all the boarding houses this afternoon—and I said to myself spontaneously, something like this. How I suffer. And no one knows how I suffer, walking up this street, engaged with my anguish, as I was after Thoby[7] died—alone; fighting something alone. But then I had the devil to fight, and now nothing. And when I come indoors it is all so silent—I am not carrying a great rush of wheels in my head—yet I am writing—oh and we are very successful—and there is—what I most love—change ahead. Yes, that last evening at Rodmell when Leonard came down against his will to fetch me, the Keynes came over. And Maynard is giving up the *Nation*, and so is Hubert[8] and so no doubt shall we. And it is autumn; and the lights are going up; and Nessa is in Fitzroy Street—in a great misty room with flaring gas and unsorted plates and glasses on the floor—and the Press is booming—and this celebrity business is quite chronic—and I am richer than I have ever been—and bought a pair of earrings today—and for all this, there is vacancy and silence somewhere in the machine. On the whole, I do not much mind; because what I like is to flash and dash from side to side, goaded on by what I call reality. If I never felt these extraordinarily pervasive strains—of unrest or rest or happiness or discomfort—I should float down into acquiescence. Here is something to fight; and when I wake early I say to myself Fight, fight. If I could catch the feeling, I would; the feeling of the singing of the real world, as one is driven by loneliness and silence from the habitable world; the sense that comes to me of being bound on an adventure; of being strangely free now, with money and so on, to do anything. I go to take theatre tickets (The Matriarch) and see a list of cheap excursions hanging there, and at once think that I will go to Stratford on Avon Mob Fair tomorrow—why not?—or to Ireland or to Edinburgh for a weekend. I daresay I shan't. But anything is possible. And this curious steed, life, is genuine. Does any of this convey what I want to say? But I have not really laid hands on the emptiness after all. It's odd, now I come to think of it—I miss Clive.[9]

[6]*David Cecil. (Ed.)*
[7]*J. T. Stephen, brother of V. W. He died in 1906.*
[8]*Hubert Henderson, editor.*
[9]*Clive Bell, husband of Vanessa. (Ed.)*

Wednesday, October 23rd

As it is true—I write only for an hour, then rush back feeling I cannot keep my brain on that spin any more—then typewrite, and am done by 12. I will here sum up my impressions before publishing *A Room of One's Own*. It is a little ominous that Morgan[10] won't review it. It makes me suspect that there is a shrill feminine tone in it which my intimate friends will dislike. I forecast, then, that I shall get no criticism, except of the evasive jocular kind, from Lytton,[11] Roger and Morgan; that the press will be kind and talk of its charm and sprightliness; also I shall be attacked for a feminist and hinted at for a Sapphist; Sybil[12] will ask me to luncheon; I shall get a good many letters from young women. I am afraid it will not be taken seriously. Mrs. Woolf is so accomplished a writer that all she says makes easy reading . . . this very feminine logic . . . a book to be put in the hands of girls. I doubt that I mind very much. The Moths; but I think it is to be waves, is trudging along; and I have that to refer to, if I am damped by the other. It is a trifle, I shall say; so it is; but I wrote it with ardour and conviction.

He wrote yesterday, 3 Dec. and said he very much liked it.

We dined last night with the Webbs[13] and I had Eddy[14] and Dotty[15] to tea. As for these mature dinner parties one has some friendly easy talk with one man—Hugh Macmillan[16]—about the Buchans and his own career; the Webbs are friendly but can't be influenced about Kenya; we sit in two lodging house rooms (the dining room had a brass bedstead behind a screen) eat hunks of red beef; and are offered whisky. It is the same enlightened, impersonal, perfectly aware of itself atmosphere. "My little boy shall have his toys"—but don't let that go any further—"that's what my wife says about my being in the Cabinet." No they have no illusions. And I compared them with L. and myself, and felt, (I daresay for this reason) the pathos, the symbolical quality of the childless couple; standing for something, united.

Saturday, November 2nd

Oh but I have done quite well so far with *Room of One's Own*; and it sells, I think; and I get unexpected letters. But I am more concerned with my *Waves*. I've just typed out my morning's work; and can't feel altogether sure. There is *something* there (as I felt about *Mrs. Dalloway*) but I can't get at it, squarely; nothing like the speed and certainty of the *Lighthouse: Orlando* mere child's play. Is there some falsity of method, somewhere? Something tricky?—so that the interesting things aren't firmly based? I am in an odd state; feel a cleavage; here's my interesting thing;

---

[10]*E. M. Forster. (Ed.)*
[11]*Lytton Strachey. (Ed.)*
[12]*Lady Colfax. (Ed.)*
[13]*Beatrice and Sidney Webb. (Ed.)*
[14]*E. Sackville-West.*
[15]*Dorothy Wellesley, later Duchess of Wellington. (Ed.)*
[16]*Afterwards Lord Macmillan.*

and there's no quite solid table on which to put it. It might come in a flash, on re-reading—some solvent. I am convinced that I am right to seek for a station whence I can set my people against time and the sea—but Lord, the difficulty of digging oneself in there, with conviction. Yesterday I had conviction; it has gone today.

Saturday, November 30th

I fill in this page, nefariously; at the end of a morning's work. I have begun the second part of *Waves*—I don't know. I don't know. I feel that I am only accumulating notes for a book—whether I shall ever face the labour of writing it, God knows. From some higher station I may be able to pull it together—at Rodmell, in my new room. Reading the *Lighthouse* does not make it easier to write . . .

Sunday, December 8th

I read and read and finished I daresay 3 foot thick of MS. read carefully too; much of it on the border, and so needing thought. Now, with this load despatched, I am free to begin reading Elizabethans—the little unknown writers, whom I, so ignorant am I, have never heard of, Pullenham, Webb, Harvey. This thought fills me with joy—no overstatement. To begin reading with a pen in my hand, discovering, pouncing, thinking of phrases, when the ground is new, remains one of my great excitements. Oh but L. will sort apples and the little noise upsets me; I can't think what I was going to say.

So I stopped writing, by which no great harm was done, and made out a list of Elizabethan poets. And I have, with great happiness, refused to write Rhoda Broughton, Ouida for de la Mare. That vein, popular as it is, witness Jane and Geraldine, is soon worked out in me. I want to write criticism. Yes, and one might make out an obscure figure or two. It was the Elizabethan prose writers I loved first and most wildly, stirred by Hakluyt, which father lugged home for me—I think of it with some sentiment—father tramping over the Library with his little girl sitting at H.P.G.[17] in mind. He must have been 65; I 15 or 16 then; and why I don't know but I became enraptured, though not exactly interested, but the sight of the large yellow page entranced me. I used to read it and dream of those obscure adventurers and no doubt practised their style in my copybook. I was then writing a long picturesque essay upon the Christian religion, I think; called Religio Laici, I believe, proving that man has need of a God; but the God was described in process of change; and I also wrote a history of Women; and a history of my own family—all very longwinded and Elizabethan in style.

RODMELL—*Boxing Day*

I find it almost incredibly soothing—a fortnight alone—almost impossible to let oneself have it. Relentlessly we have crushed visitors. We will

---

[17]*Hyde Park Gate, where the Stephen family lived when V. W. was a child.*

be alone this once, we say; and really, it seems possible. Then Annie is to me very sympathetic. My bread bakes well. All is rather rapt, simple, quick, effective—except for my blundering on at *The Waves*. I write two pages of arrant nonsense, after straining; I write variations of every sentence; compromises; bad shots; possibilities; till my writing book is like a lunatic's dream. Then I trust to some inspiration on re-reading; and pencil them into some sense. Still I am not satisfied. I think there is something lacking. I sacrifice nothing to seemliness. I press to my centre. I don't care if it all is scratched out. And there is something there. I incline now to try violent shots—at London—at talk—shouldering my way ruthlessly—and then, if nothing comes of it—anyhow I have examined the possibilities. But I wish I enjoyed it more. I don't have it in my head all day like the *Lighthouse* and *Orlando*.

1930

Sunday, January 12th

Sunday it is. And I have just exclaimed: "And now I can think of nothing else." Thanks to my pertinacity and industry, I can now hardly stop making up *The Waves*. The sense of this came acutely about a week ago on beginning to write the *Phantom Party:* now I feel that I can rush on, after 6 months' hacking, and finish: but without the least certainty how it's to achieve any form. Much will have to be discarded: what is essential is to write fast and not break the mood—no holiday, no interval if possible, till it is done. Then rest. Then re-write.

Sunday, January 26th

I am 48: we have been at Rodmell—a wet, windy day again; but on my birthday we walked among the downs, like the folded wings of grey birds; and saw first one fox, very long with his brush stretched; then a second; which had been barking, for the sun was hot over us; it leapt lightly over a fence and entered the furze—a very rare sight. How many foxes are there in England? At night I read Lord Chaplin's life. I cannot yet write naturally in my new room, because the table is not the right height and I must stoop to warm my hands. Everything must be absolutely what I am used to.

I forgot to say that when we made up our 6 months accounts, we found I had made about £3,020 last year—the salary of a civil servant: a surprise to me, who was content with £200 for so many years. But I shall drop very heavily I think. *The Waves* won't sell more than 2,000 copies. I am stuck fast in that book—I mean, glued to it, like a fly on gummed paper. Sometimes I am out of touch; but go on; then again feel that I have at last, by violent measures—like breaking through gorse—set my hands on something central.

It has sold about 6,500 today, Oct. 30th, 1931—after 3 weeks. But will stop now, I suppose.

Perhaps I can now say something quite straight out; and at length; and need not be always casting a line to make my book the right shape. But how to pull it together, how to comport it—press it into one—I do not know; nor can I guess the end—it might be a gigantic conversation. The interludes are very difficult, yet I think essential; so as to bridge and also to give a background—the sea; insensitive nature—I don't know. But I think, when I feel this sudden directness, that it must be right: anyhow no other form of fiction suggests itself except as a repetition at the moment.

Sunday, February 16th

To lie on the sofa for a week. I am sitting up today in the usual state of unequal animation. Below normal, with spasmodic desire to write, then to doze. It is a fine cold day and if my energy and sense of duty persist, I shall drive up to Hampstead. But I doubt that I can write to any purpose. A cloud swims in my head. One is too conscious of the body and jolted out of the rut of life to get back to fiction. Once or twice I have felt that odd whirr of wings in the head, which comes when I am ill so often—last year for example at this time I lay in bed constructing *A Room of One's Own* (which sold 10,000 two days ago). If I could stay in bed another fortnight (but there is no chance of that) I believe I should see the whole of *The Waves*. Or of course I might go off on something different. As it is I half incline to insist upon a dash to Cassis; but perhaps this needs more determination than I possess; and we shall dwindle on here. Pinker is walking about the room looking for the bright patch—a sign of spring. I believe these illnesses are in my case—how shall I express it?—partly mystical. Something happens in my mind. It refuses to go on registering impressions. It shuts itself up. It becomes chrysalis. I lie quite torpid, often with acute physical pain—as last year; only discomfort this. Then suddenly something springs. Two nights ago Vita was here; and when she went I began to feel the quality of the evening—how it was spring coming: a silver light; mixing with the early lamps; the cabs all rushing through the streets; I had a tremendous sense of life beginning; mixed with that emotion which is the essence of my feeling, but escapes description (I keep on making up the Hampton Court scene in *The Waves*—Lord how I wonder if I shall pull this book off! It is a litter of fragments so far). Well, as I was saying, between these long pauses, for I am swimming in the head and write rather to stabilise myself than to make a correct statement—I felt the spring beginning; and Vita's life so full and flush; and all the doors opening; and this is I believe the moth shaking its wings in me. I then begin to make up my story whatever it is; ideas rush in me; often though this is before I can control my mind or pen. It is no use trying to write at this stage. And I doubt if I can fill this white monster. I would like to lie down and sleep, but feel ashamed. Leonard brushed off his influenza in one day and went about his business feeling ill. Here am I still loafing, undressed, with Elly[18] coming tomorrow. But as I was saying, my

[18]*Elly Rendel, V. W.'s doctor.*

mind works in idleness. To do nothing is often my most profitable way. I am reading Byron: Maurois: which sends me to *Childe Harold:* makes me speculate. How odd a mixture: the weakest sentimental Mrs. Hemans combined with trenchant bare vigour. How did they combine? And sometimes the descriptions in *C.H.* are "beautiful"; like a great poet. There are the three elements in Byron:

1. The romantic dark haired lady singing drawing room melodies to the guitar.

> "Tambourgi! Tambourgi! thy 'larum afar
> Gives hope to the valiant and promise of war;"

> "Oh! who is more brave than a dark Suliote,
> In his snowy camese and his shaggy capote"

—something manufactured; a pose; silliness.

2. Then there is the vigorous rhetorical, like his prose, and good as prose.

> "Hereditary Bondsmen! know ye not
> Who would be free themselves must strike the blow?
> By their right arms the conquest must be wrought?
> Will Gaul or Muscovite redress ye? No!"

3. Then what rings to me truer, and is almost poetry.

(All in Canto
II of *C.H.*)

> "Dear Nature is the kindest mother still!
> Though always changing, in her aspect mild;
> From her bare bosom let me take my fill,
> Her never-weaned, though not her favoured child.

> To me by day or night she ever smiled,
> Though I have marked her when none other hath,
> And sought her more and more and loved her best in wrath."

4. And then there is of course the pure satiric, as in the description of a London Sunday; and

5. Finally (but this makes more than three) the inevitable half assumed half genuine tragic note, which comes as a refrain, about death and the loss of friends.

> All thou could have of mine, stern Death! thou hast;
> The parent, Friend, and now the more than Friend:
> Ne'er yet for me thine arrows flew so fast,
> And grief with grief continuing still to blend,
> Hath snatched the little joy that life had yet to lend.

These I think make him up; and make much that is spurious, vapid, yet very changeable, and then rich and with greater range than the other poets, could he have got the whole into order. A novelist, he might have been. It is odd however to read in his letters his prose and apparently genuine feeling about Athens; and to compare it with the convention he adopted in verse. (There is some sneer about the Acropolis.) But then the sneer may have been a pose too. The truth may be that if you are charged at such high voltage you can't fit any of the ordinary human feelings; must pose; must rhapsodise; don't fit in. He wrote in the Fun Album that his age was 100. And this is true, measuring life by feeling.

Monday, February 17th

And this temperature is up: but it has now gone down; and now

Thursday, February 20th

I must canter my wits if I can. Perhaps some character sketches.

Monday, March 17th

The test of a book (to a writer) is if it makes a space in which, quite naturally, you can say what you want to say. As this morning I could say what Rhoda said. This proves that the book itself is alive: because it has not crushed the thing I wanted to say, but allowed me to slip it in, without any compression or alteration.

Friday, March 28th

Yes, but this book is a very queer business. I had a day of intoxication when I said "Children are nothing to this": when I sat surveying the whole book complete and quarrelled with L. (about Ethel Smyth) and walked it off, felt the pressure of the form—the splendour, the greatness—as perhaps I have never felt them. But I shan't race it off in intoxication. I keep pegging away; and find it the most complex and difficult of all my books. How to end, save by a tremendous discussion, in which every life shall have its voice—a mosaic—I do not know. The difficulty is that it is all at high pressure. I have not yet mastered the speaking voice. Yet I think something is there; and I propose to go on pegging it down, arduously, and then rewrite, reading much of it aloud, like poetry. It will bear expansion. It is compressed I think. It is—whatever I make of it—a large and potential theme—which *Orlando* was not perhaps. At any rate, I have taken my fence.

Wednesday, April 9th

What I now think (about *The Waves*) is that I can give in a very few strokes the essentials of a person's character. It should be done boldly, almost as caricature. I have yesterday entered what may be the last lap. Like every piece of the book it goes by fits and starts. I never get away with it; but am tugged back. I hope this makes for solidity; and must look to my sentences. The abandonment of *Orlando* and *Lighthouse* is much checked by the extreme difficulty of the form—as it was in *Jacob's Room*.

I think this is the furthest development so far; but of course it may miss fire somewhere. I think I have kept stoically to the original conception. What I fear is that the re-writing will have to be so drastic that I may entirely muddle it somehow. It is bound to be very imperfect. But I think it possible that I have got my statues against the sky.

Sunday, April 13th

I read Shakespeare *directly* I have finished writing. When my mind is agape and red-hot. Then it is astonishing. I never yet knew how amazing his stretch and speed and word coining power is, until I felt it utterly outpace and outrace my own, seeming to start equal and then I see him draw ahead and do things I could not in my wildest tumult and utmost press of mind imagine. Even the less known plays are written at a speed that is quicker than anybody else's quickest; and the words drop so fast one can't pick them up. Look at this. "Upon a gather'd lily almost wither'd." (That is a pure accident. I happen to light on it.) Evidently the pliancy of his mind was so complete that he could furbish out any train of thought; and, relaxing, let fall a shower of such unregarded flowers. Why then should anyone else attempt to write? This is not "writing" at all. Indeed, I could say that Shakespeare surpasses literature altogether, if I knew what I meant.

Wednesday, April 23rd

This is a very important morning in the history of *The Waves*, because I think I have turned the corner and see the last lap straight ahead. I think I have got Bernard into the final stride. He will go straight on now, and then stand at the door: and then there will be a last picture of the waves. We are at Rodmell and I daresay I shall stay on a day or two (if I dare) so as not to break the current and finish it. O Lord and then a rest; and then an article; and then back again to this hideous shaping and moulding. There may be some joys in it all the same.

Tuesday, April 29th

And I have just finished, with this very nib-ful of ink, the last sentence of *The Waves*. I think I should record this for my own information. Yes, it was the greatest stretch of mind I ever knew; certainly the last pages; I don't think they flop as much as usual. And I think I have kept starkly and ascetically to the plan. So much I will say in self-congratulation. But I have never written a book so full of holes and patches; that will need rebuilding, yes, not only re-modelling. I suspect the structure is wrong. Never mind. I might have done something easy and fluent; and this is a reach after that vision I had, the unhappy summer—or three weeks—at Rodmell, after finishing the *Lighthouse*. (And that reminds me—I must hastily provide my mind with something else, or it will again become pecking and wretched—something imaginative, if possible, and light; for

I shall tire of Hazlitt and criticism after the first divine relief; and I feel pleasantly aware of various adumbrations in the back of my head; a life of Duncan; no, something about canvases glowing in a studio; but that can wait.)

P.M.   And I think to myself as I walk down Southampton Row, "And I have given you a new book."

Thursday, May 1st

And I have completely ruined my morning. Yes that is literally true. They sent a book from *The Times,* as if advised by Heaven of my liberty; and feeling my liberty wild upon me, I rushed to the cable and told Van Doren I would write on Scott. And now having read Scott, or the editor whom Hugh[19] provides, I won't and can't; and have got into a fret trying to read it, and writing to Richmond to say I can't: have wasted the brilliant first of May which makes my skylight blue and gold; have only a rubbish heap in my head; can't read and can't write and can't think. The truth is, of course, I want to be back at *The Waves.* Yes that is the truth. Unlike all my other books in every way, it is unlike them in this, that I begin to re-write it, or conceive it again with ardour, directly I have done. I begin to see what I had in my mind; and want to begin cutting out masses of irrelevance and clearing, sharpening and making the good phrases shine. One wave after another. No room. And so on. But then we are going touring Devon and Cornwall on Sunday, which means a week off; and then I shall perhaps make my critical brain do a month's work for exercise. What could it be set to? Or a story?—no, not another story now . . .

Wednesday, August 20th

The Waves is I think resolving itself (I am at page 100) into a series of dramatic soliloquies. The thing is to keep them running homogeneously in and out, in the rhythm of the waves. Can they be read consecutively? I know nothing about that. I think this is the greatest opportunity I have yet been able to give myself; therefore I suppose the most complete failure. Yet I respect myself for writing this book—yes—even though it exhibits my congenital faults.

Monday, September 8th

I will signalise my return to life—that is writing—by beginning a new book, and it happens to be Thoby's birthday, I remark. He would have been, I think, 50 today. After coming out here I had the usual—oh how usual—headache; and lay, like a fibre of tired muscle on my bed in the sitting room, till yesterday. Now up again and on again; with one new picture in my mind; my defiance of death in the garden.

But the sentence with which this book was to open ran "Nobody has

---

[19]*Hugh Walpole. (Ed.)*

ever worked so hard as I do"—exclaimed in driving a paper fastener through the 14 pages of my Hazlitt just now. Time was when I dashed off these things all in the day's work. Now, partly because I must do them for America and make arrangements far ahead, I spend I daresay a ridiculous amount of time, more of trouble, on them. I began reading Hazlitt in January I think. And I am not sure that I have speared that little eel in the middle—that marrow—which is one's object in criticism. A very difficult business no doubt to find it, in all these essays; so many; so short; and on all subjects. Never mind; it shall go today; and my appetite for criticism is, oddly, whettened. I have some gift that way, were it not for the grind and the screw and the torture.

Tuesday, December 2nd

No, I cannot write that very difficult passage in *The Waves* this morning (how their lives hang lit up against the Palace) all because of Arnold Bennett and Ethel's[20] party. I can hardly get one word after another. There I was for 2 hours so it seemed, alone with B., in Ethel's little back room. And this meeting I am convinced was engineered by B. to "get on good terms with Mrs. Woolf"—when Heaven knows I don't care a rap if I'm on terms with B. or not. B. I say, because he can't say B. He ceases; shuts his eyes; leans back; one waits. "Begin," he at last articulates quietly, without any fluster. But the method lengthens out intolerably a rather uninspired discourse. It's fun. I like the old creature. I do my best, as a writer, to detect signs of genius in his smoky brown eye: I see certain sensuality, power, I suppose; but O as he cackled out "What a blundering fool I am—what a baby—compared with Desmond MacCarthy—how clumsy—how could I attack professors?" This innocence is engaging; but would be more so if I felt him, as he infers, a "creative artist." He said that George Moore in *The Mummer's Wife* had shown him *The Five Towns*: taught him what to see there: has a profound admiration for G. M.; but despises him for boasting of his sexual triumphs. "He told me that a young girl had come to see him. And he asked her, as she sat on the sofa, to undress. And he said she took off all her clothes and let him look at her. . . . Now that I don't believe . . . But he is a prodigious writer—he lives for words. Now he's ill. Now he's an awful bore—he tells the same stories over and over. And soon people will say of me 'He's dead.' " I rashly said: "Of your books?" "No, of me," he replied, attaching, I suppose, a longer life than I do to his books.

"It's the only life," he said (this incessant scribbling, one word after another, one thousand words daily). "I don't want anything else. I think of nothing but writing. Some people are bored." "You have all the clothes

Soon after this A.B. went to France, drank a glass of water and died of typhoid. (March 30th. His funeral today.)

---

[20]*Ethel Sands.*

you want, I suppose," I said. "And bath. And beds. And a yacht." "Oh yes, my clothes couldn't be better cut."

And at last I drew Lord David in. And we taunted the old creature with thinking us refined. He said the gates of Hatfield were shut—"shut away from life." "But open on Thursdays," said Lord D. "I don't want to go on Thursdays," said B. "And you drop your aitches on purpose," I said, "thinking that you possess more 'life' than we do." "I sometimes tease," said B., "but I don't think I possess more life than you do. Now I must go home. I have to write one thousand words tomorrow morning." And this left only the scrag end of the evening; and this left me in a state where I can hardly drive my pen across the page.

Reflection: It is presumably a bad thing to look through articles, reviews, etc. to find one's own name. Yet I often do.

Thursday, December 4th

One word of slight snub in the *Lit. Sup.* today makes me determine, first, to alter the whole of *The Waves;* second, to put my back up against the public—one word of slight snub.

Friday, December 12th

This, I think, is the last day's breathing space I allow myself before I tackle the last lap of *The Waves.* I have had a week off—that is to say I have written three little sketches; and dawdled and spent a morning shopping and a morning, this morning, arranging my new table and doing odds and ends—but I think I have got my breath again and must be off for three or perhaps four weeks more. Then, as I think, I shall make one consecutive writing of *The Waves* etc.—the interludes—so as to work it into one—and then, oh dear, some must be written again; and then, corrections; and then send to Mabel; and then correct the type; and then give to Leonard. Leonard perhaps shall get it some time late in March. Then put away; then print, perhaps in June.

Monday, December 22nd

It occurred to me last night while listening to a Beethoven quartet that I would merge all the interjected passages into Bernard's final speech and end with the words O solitude: thus making him absorb all those scenes and having no further break. This is also to show that the theme effort, effort, dominates: not the waves: and personality: and defiance: but I am not sure of the effect artistically; because the proportions may need the intervention of the waves finally so as to make a conclusion.

RODMELL. *Saturday, December 27th*

But what's the use of talking about Bernard's final speech? We came down on Tuesday and next day my cold was the usual influenza and I am in bed with the usual temperature and can't use my wits or, as is visible, form my letters. I daresay two days will see me normal; but then the sponge behind my forehead will be dry and pale—and so my precious fortnight of exaltation and concentration is snatched; and I shall go back to the racket and Nelly without a thing done. I clear myself by thinking that I may evolve some thoughts. Meanwhile it rains; Annie's child is ill; the dogs next door yap and yap; all the colours are rather dim and the pulse of life dulled. I moon torpidly through book after book: Defoe's *Tour*; Rowan's autobiography; Benson's Memoirs; Jeans: in the familiar way. The parson—Skinner—who shot himself emerges like a bloody sun in a fog: a book worth, perhaps, looking at again in a clearer mood. He shot himself in the beechwoods above his house; he spent a life digging up stones and reducing all places to Camelodunum; quarrelled; bickered; yet loved his sons; yet turned them out of doors—a clear hard picture of one type of human life—the exasperated, unhappy, struggling, intolerably afflicted. Oh and I've read Q. V.'s[21] letters; and wonder what would happen had Ellen Terry been born Queen. Complete disaster to the Empire? Q. V. entirely unaesthetic; a kind of Prussian competence and belief in herself her only prominences; material; brutal to Gladstone; like a mistress with a dishonest footman. Knew her own mind. But the mind radically commonplace, only its inherited force and cumulative sense of power making it remarkable.

Diary of a Somerset rector.

Tuesday, December 30th

What it wants is presumably unity; but it is I think rather good (I am talking to myself over the fire about *The Waves*). Suppose I could run all the scenes together more?—by rhythms chiefly. So as to avoid those cuts; so as to make the blood run like a torrent from end to end—I don't want the waste that the breaks give; I want to avoid chapters; that indeed is my achievement, if any, here: a saturated unchopped completeness; changes of scene, of mind, of person, done without spilling a drop. Now if it could be worked over with heat and currency, that's all it wants. And I am getting my blood up (temp. 99). But all the same I went into Lewes and the Keynes came to tea; and having got astride my saddle the whole world falls into shape; it is this writing that gives me my proportions.

1931

Wednesday, January 7th

My head is not in the first spring of energy: this fortnight has brought me no views of the lapping downs—no fields and hedges—too many firelit houses and lit up pages and pen and ink—curse my influenza. It is very quiet here—not a sound but the hiss of the gas. Oh but the cold was too

[21]*Queen Victoria.*

great at Rodmell. I was frozen like a small sparrow. And I did write a few
staggering sentences. Few books have interested me more to write than
The Waves. Why even now, at the end, I'm turning up a stone or two: no
glibness, no assurance; you see, I could perhaps do B.'s soliloquy in such
a way as to break up, dig deep, make prose move—yes I swear—as prose
has never moved before; from the chuckle, the babble to the rhapsody.
Something new goes into my pot every morning—something that's never
been got at before. The high wind can't blow, because I'm chopping and
tacking all the time. And I've stored a few ideas for articles: one on Gosse—
the critic, as talker: the armchair critic; one on Letters—one on Queens.

Now this is true: *The Waves* is written at such high pressure that I can't
take it up and read it through between tea and dinner; I can only write it
for about one hour, from 10 to 11:30. And the typing is almost the hardest
part of the work. Heaven help me if all my little 80,000 word books are
going in future to cost me two years! But I shall fling off, like a cutter
leaning on its side, on some swifter, slighter adventure—another *Orlando*
perhaps.

Tuesday, January 20th

I have this moment, while having my bath, conceived an entire new
book[22]—a sequel to *A Room of One's Own*—about the sexual life of
women: to be called Professions for Women perhaps Lord
how exciting! This sprang out of my paper to be read on
Wednesday to Pippa's society. Now for *The Waves*. Thank
God—but I'm very much excited.

(This is
Here and Now,
I think.
May '34.)

Friday, January 23rd

Too much excited, alas, to get on with *The Waves*. One goes on making
up "The Open Door," or whatever it is to be called. The didactive demon-
strative style conflicts with the dramatic: I find it hard to get back inside
Bernard again.

Monday, January 26th

Heaven be praised, I can truthfully say on this first day of being 49
that I have shaken off the obsession of *Opening the Door*, and have returned to *Waves:* and have this instant seen the entire book whole, and
now I can finish it—say in under 3 weeks. That takes me to February 16th;
then I propose, after doing Gosse, or an article perhaps, to dash off the
rough sketch of *Open Door*, to be finished by April 1st. (Easter is April
3rd.) We shall then, I hope, have an Italian journey; return say May 1st
and finish *Waves*, so that the MS. can go to be printed in June and appear
in September. These are possible dates anyhow. Yesterday at Rodmell we
saw a magpie and heard the first spring birds: sharp egotistical, like man.
A hot sun; walked over Caburn; home by Horley and saw three men dash

[22]*Eventually* Three Guineas.

from a blue car and race without hats across a field. We saw a silver and blue aeroplane in the middle of a field, apparently unhurt, among trees and cows. This morning the paper says three men were killed—the aeroplane dashing to the earth. But we went on, reminding me of that epitaph in the Greek anthology: when I sank, the other ships sailed on.

Monday, February 2nd

I think I am about to finish *The Waves*. I think I might finish it on Saturday.

This is merely an author's note: never have I screwed my brain so tight over a book. The proof is that I am almost incapable of other reading or writing. I can only flop wide once the morning is over. Oh Lord the relief when this week is over and I have at any rate the feeling that I have wound up and done with that long labour: ended that vision. I think I have just done what I meant; of course I have altered the scheme considerably; but my feeling is that I have insisted upon saying, by hook or by crook, certain things I meant to say. I imagine that the hookedness may be so great that it will be a failure from a reader's point of view. Well, never mind: it is a brave attempt. I think, something struggled for. Oh and then the delight of skirmishing free again—the delight of being idle and not much minding what happens; and then I shall be able to read again, with all my mind—a thing I haven't done these four months I daresay. This will have taken me 18 months to write: and we can't publish it till the autumn I suppose.

Wednesday, February 4th

A day ruined, for us both. L. has to go every morning at 10:15 to the Courts, where his jury is still called, but respited always till 10:15 the next day; and this morning, which should have dealt a formidable blow at *The Waves*—B. is within two days I think of saying O Death—was ruined by Elly, who was to have come at 9:30 sharp but did not come till 11. And it is now 12:30 and we sat talking about the period and professional women, after the usual rites with the stethoscope, seeking vainly the cause of my temperature. If we like to spend 7 guineas we might catch a bug—but we don't like. And so I am to eat Bemax and—the usual routine.

How strange and wilful these last exacerbations of *The Waves* are! I was to have finished it at Christmas.

Today Ethel[23] comes. On Monday I went to hear her rehearse. A vast Portland Place house with the cold wedding cake Adams plaster: shabby red carpets; flat surfaces washed with dull greens. The rehearsal was in a long room with a bow window looking on, in fact in, to other houses— iron staircases, chimneys, roofs—a barren brick outlook. There was a roaring fire in the Adams grate. Lady L. a now shapeless sausage, and Mrs.

[23]*Ethel Smyth.*

Hunter,[24] a swathed satin sausage, sat side by side on a sofa. Ethel stood at the piano in the window, in her battered felt, in her jersey and short skirt conducting with a pencil. There was a drop at the end of her nose. Miss Suddaby was singing the Soul, and I observed that she went through precisely the same attitudes of ecstasy and inspiration in the room as in a hall: there were two young or youngish men. Ethel's *pince nez* rode nearer and nearer the tip of her nose. She sang now and then; and once, taking the bass, made a cat squalling sound—but everything she does with such forthrightness, directness, that there is nothing ridiculous. She loses self-consciousness completely. She seems all vitalised; all energised. She knocks her hat from side to side. Strides rhythmically down the room to signify to Elizabeth that this is the Greek melody; strides back. Now the furniture moving begins, she said, referring to some supernatural gambols connected with the prisoner's escape, or defiance or death. I suspect the music is too literary—too stressed—too didactic for my taste. But I am always impressed by the fact that it is music—I mean that she has spun these coherent chords, harmonies, melodies out of her so practical vigorous student mind. What if she should be a great composer? This fantastic idea is to her the merest commonplace: it is the fabric of her being. As she conducts, she hears music like Beethoven's. As she strides and turns and wheels about to us perched mute on chairs she thinks this is about the most important event now taking place in London. And perhaps it is. Well —I watched the curiously sensitive, perceptive Jewish face of old Lady L. trembling like a butterfly's antennae to the sound. How sensitive to music old Jewesses are—how pliable, how supple. Mrs. Hunter sat like a wax figure, composed, upholstered, transfixed, with her gold chain purse.

Saturday, February 7th

Here in the few minutes that remain, I must record, heaven be praised, the end of *The Waves*. I wrote the words O Death fifteen minutes ago, having reeled across the last ten pages with some moments of such intensity and intoxication that I seemed only to stumble after my own voice, or almost, after some sort of speaker (as when I was mad) I was almost afraid, remembering the voices that used to fly ahead. Anyhow, it is done; and I have been sitting these 15 minutes in a state of glory, and calm, and some tears, thinking of Thoby and if I could write Julian Thoby Stephen 1881–1906 on the first page. I suppose not. How physical the sense of triumph and relief is! Whether good or bad, it's done; and, as I certainly felt at the end, not merely finished, but rounded off, completed, the thing stated—how hastily, how fragmentarily I know; but I mean that I have netted that fin in the waste of water which appeared to me over the marshes out of my window at Rodmell when I was coming to an end of *To the Lighthouse*.

[24]*Ethel Smyth's sister.*

What interests me in the last stage was the freedom and boldness with which my imagination picked up, used and tossed aside all the images, symbols which I had prepared. I am sure that this is the right way of using them—not in set pieces, as I had tried at first, coherently, but simply as images, never making them work out; only suggest. Thus I hope to have kept the sound of the sea and the birds, dawn and garden subconsciously present, doing their work under ground.

Saturday, March 28th

Arnold Bennett died last night; which leaves me sadder than I should have supposed. A lovable genuine man; impeded, somehow a little awkward in life; well meaning; ponderous; kindly; coarse; knowing he was coarse; dimly floundering and feeling for something else; glutted with success; wounded in his feelings; avid; thicklipped; prosaic intolerably; rather dignified; set upon writing; yet always taken in; deluded by splendour and success; but naive; an old bore; an egotist; much at the mercy of life for all his competence; a shopkeeper's view of literature; yet with the rudiments, covered over with fat and prosperity and the desire for hideous Empire furniture, of sensibility. Some real understanding power, as well as a gigantic absorbing power. These are the sort of things that I think by fits and starts this morning, as I sit journalising; I remember his determination to write 1,000 words daily; and how he trotted off to do it that night, and feel some sorrow that now he will never sit down and begin methodically covering his regulation number of pages in his workmanlike beautiful but dull hand. Queer how one regrets the dispersal of anybody who seemed—as I say—genuine: who had direct contact with life—for he abused me; and I yet rather wished him to go on abusing me; and me abusing him. An element in life—even in mine that was so remote—taken away. This is what one minds.[25]

Saturday, April 11th

Oh I am so tired of correcting my own writing—these 8 articles—I have however learnt I think to dash: not to finick. I mean the writing is free enough; it's the repulsiveness of correcting that nauseates me. And the cramming in and the cutting out. And articles and more articles are asked for. Forever I could write articles.

But I have no pen—well, it will just make a mark. And not much to say, or rather too much and not the mood.

Wednesday, May 13th

Unless I write a few sentences here from time to time I shall, as they say, forget the use of my pen. I am now engaged in typing out from start

[25]*There is an entry in Arnold Bennett's diary for 1930 in which he records that he went to a dinner party at which V. W. was another guest, and adds: "Virginia is all right; other guests held their breath to listen to us."*

to finish the 332 pages of that very condensed book *The Waves*. I do 7 or 8 daily; by which means I hope to have the whole complete by June 16th or thereabouts. This requires some resolution; but I can see no other way to make all the corrections and keep the lilt and join up and expand and do all the other final processes. It is like sweeping over an entire canvas with a wet brush.

Saturday, May 30th

No, I have just said, it being 12:45, I cannot write any more, and indeed

p. 162.
therefore
halfway in
26 days.
Shall finish
by 1st July
with luck.

I cannot: I am copying the death chapter; have re-written it twice. I shall go at it again and finish it, I hope, this afternoon. But how it rolls into a tight ball the muscles in my brain! This is the most concentrated work I have ever done —and oh the relief when it is finished. But also the most interesting.

Tuesday, June 23rd

And yesterday, 22nd June, when, I think, the days begin to draw in, I finished my re-typing of *The Waves*. Not that it is finished—oh dear no. For then I must correct the re-re-typing. This work I began on May 5th, and no one can say that I have been hasty or careless this time; though I doubt not the lapses and slovenliness are innumerable.

Tuesday, July 7th

O to seek relief from this incessant correction (I am doing the interludes) and write a few words carelessly. Still better, to write nothing; to tramp over the downs, blown like thistle, as irresponsible. And to get away from this hard knot in which my brain has been so tight spun—I mean *The Waves*. Such are my sentiments at half past twelve on Tuesday July 7th—a fine day I think—and everything, so the tag runs in my head, handsome about us.

Tuesday, July 14th

It is now twelve o'clock on the morning of July 14th—and Bob[26] has come in to ask me to sign a paper to get Palmer a pension. Bob says . . . mostly about his new house, washing basins, can he use a candle still to go to bed with; Bessy is moving in today; he is off to Italy for a month; will I send a copy of my new book to Count Moira, all Italians are Counts, once he showed four Counts round Cambridge; Palmer . . . and so on: shuffling from foot to foot, taking his hat off and putting it on again, moving to the door and returning.

I had meant to say that I have just finished correcting the Hampton

[26]*R. C. Trevelyan.*

Court scene. (This is the final correction, please God!)

But my *Waves* account runs, I think, as follows:—

I began it, seriously, about September 10th 1929.

I finished the first version on April 10th 1930.

I began the second version on May 1st 1930.

I finished the second version on February 7th 1931.

I began to correct the second version on May 1st 1931, finished 22nd June 1931.

I began to correct the typescript on 25th June 1931.

Shall finish (I hope) 18th July 1931.

Then remain only the proofs.

Friday, July 17th

Yes, this morning I think I may say I have finished. That is to say I have once more, for the 18th time, copied out the opening sentences. L. will read it tomorrow; and I shall open this book to record his verdict. My own opinion—oh dear—it's a difficult book.

Which I then lost. I don't know that I've ever felt so strained. And I'm nervous, I confess, about L. For one thing he will be honest, more than usually. And it may be a failure. And I can't do any more. And I'm inclined to think it good but incoherent, inspissate; one jerk succeeding another. Anyhow it is laboured, compact. Anyhow I had a shot at my vision—if it's not a catch, it's a cast in the right direction. But I'm nervous. It may be small and finicky in general effect. Lord knows. As I say, repeating it to enforce the rather unpleasant little lift in my heart, I shall be nervous to hear what L. says when he comes out, say tomorrow night or Sunday morning, to my garden room, carrying the MS. and sits himself down and begins "Well!"

Sunday, July 19th

"It is a masterpiece," said L., coming out to my lodge this morning. "And the best of your books." This note I make; adding that he also thinks the first 100 pages extremely difficult and is doubtful how far any common reader will follow. But Lord! what a relief! I stumped off in the rain to make a little round to Rat Farm in jubilation and am almost resigned to the fact that a goat farm, with a house to be built, is now in process on the slope near Northease.

Monday, August 10th

I have now—10:45—read the first chapter of *The Waves*, and made no changes, save 2 words and 3 commas. Yes, anyhow this is exact and to the point. I like it. And see that for once my proofs will be despatched with a few pencil strokes. Now my brood mounts: I think "I am taking my fences . . . We have asked Raymond. I am forging through the sea, in spite of headache, in spite of bitterness. I may also get a———."[27] I will now write a little at *Flush*.

Saturday, August 15th

I am in rather a flutter—proof reading. I can only read a few pages at a time. So it was when I wrote it and Heaven knows what virtue it has, this ecstatic book.

Sunday, August 16th

I should really apologise to this book for using it as I am doing to write off my aimlessness; that is I am doing my proofs—the last chapter this morning—and find that I must stop after half an hour and let my mind spread, after these moments of concentration. I cannot write my life of *Flush*, because the rhythm is wrong. I think *The Waves* is anyhow tense and packed; since it screws my brain up like this. And what will the reviewers say? And my friends? They can't, of course, find anything very new to say.

Monday, August 17th

Well now, it being just after 12:30, I have put the last corrections in *The Waves*; done my proofs; and they shall go tomorrow—never, never to be looked at again by me, I imagine.

Tuesday, September 22nd

And Miss Holtby says "It is a poem, more completely than any of your other books, of course. It is most rarely subtle. It has seen more deeply into the human heart, perhaps, than even *To the Lighthouse* . . ." and though I copy the sentence, because it is in the chart of my temperature, Lord, as I say, that temperature which was deathly low this time last week and then fever high, doesn't rise: is normal. I suppose I'm safe; I think people can only repeat. And I've forgotten so much. What I want is to be told that this is solid and means something. What it means I myself shan't know till I write another book. And I'm the hare, a long way ahead of the hounds my critics.

52 TAVISTOCK SQUARE. *Monday, October 5th*

A note to say I am all trembling with pleasure—can't go on with my Letter—because Harold Nicolson has rung up to say *The Waves* is a masterpiece. Ah Hah—so it wasn't all wasted then. I mean this vision I had here has some force upon other minds. Now for a cigarette and then a return to sober composition.

Well, to continue this egotistic diary: I am not terribly excited; no; at arms length more than usual; all this talk, because if the *W.* is anything it is an adventure which I go on alone; and the dear old *Lit. Sup*: who

[27]*The word is illegible.*

twinkles and beams and patronises—a long, and for *The Times*, kind and outspoken review—don't stir me very much. Nor Harold in *Action* either. Yes; to some extent; I should have been unhappy had they blamed, but Lord, how far away I become from all this; and we're jaded too, with people, with doing up parcels. I wonder if it is good to feel this remoteness —that is, that *The Waves* is not what they say. Odd, that they (*The Times*) should praise my characters when I meant to have none. But I'm jaded; I want my marsh, my down, a quiet waking in my airy bedroom. Broadcasting tonight; to Rodmell tomorrow. Next week I shall have to stand the racket.

Friday, October 9th

Really, this unintelligible book is being better "received" than any of them. A note in *The Times* proper—the first time this has been allowed me. And it sells—how unexpected, how odd that people can read that difficult grinding stuff!

Saturday, October 17th

More notes on *The Waves*. The sales, these past three days, have fallen to 50 or so: after the great flare up when we sold 500 in one day, the brushwood has died down, as I foretold. (Not that I thought we should sell more than 3,000.) What has happened is that the library readers can't get through it and are sending their copies back. So I prophesy, it will now dribble along till we have sold 6,000 and then almost die, yet not quite. For it has been received, as I may say, quoting the stock phrases without vanity, with applause. All the provinces read enthusiastically. I am rather, in a sense, as the M.'s would say, touched. The unknown provincial reviewers say with almost one accord, here is Mrs. Woolf doing her best work; it can't be popular; but we respect her for so doing; and find *The Waves* positively exciting. I am in danger, indeed, of becoming our leading novelist, and not with the highbrows only.

Monday, November 16th

Here I will give myself the pleasure—shall I?—of copying a sentence or two from Morgan's unsolicited letter on *The Waves:*—

"I expect I shall write to you again when I have re-read *The Waves*. I have been looking in it and talking about it at Cambridge. It's difficult to express oneself about a work which one feels to be so very important, but I've the sort of excitement over it which comes from believing that one's encountered a classic."

I daresay that gives me more substantial pleasure than any letter I've had about any book. Yes, I think it does, coming from Morgan. For one thing it gives me reason to think I shall be right to go on along this very lonely path. I mean in the City today I was thinking of another book—about shopkeepers, and publicans, with low life scenes: and I ratified this sketch by Morgan's judgment. Dadie agrees too. Oh yes, between 50 and 60 I think I shall write out some very singular books, if I live. I mean I think I am about to embody at last the exact shapes my brain holds. What a long toil to reach this beginning—if *The Waves* is my first work in my own style! To be noted, as curiosities of my literary history: I sedulously avoid meeting Roger and Lytton whom I suspect do not like *The Waves.*

I am working very hard—in my way, to furbish up two long Elizabethan articles to front a new *Common Reader:* then I must go through the whole long list of those articles. I feel too, at the back of my brain, that I can devise a new critical method; something far less stiff and formal than these *Times* articles. But I must keep to the old style in this volume. And how, I wonder, could I do it? There must be some simpler, subtler, closer means of writing about books, as about people, could I hit upon it. (*The Waves* has sold more than 7,000.)

Thomas Wolfe

(1900–1938)

"I don't know how I became a writer," Thomas Wolfe wrote in a part of this Story not quoted here, "but I think it was because of a certain force in me that had to write and that finally burst through and found a channel." This outpouring liquid force he described elsewhere as "burning lava from a volcano." Wolfe was a phenomenon—a giant of frame and energy. One sees him writing for days on end, standing up, using the top of an icebox for a desk; filling scores and scores of accountant's ledgers; cramming big wooden packing cases with his manuscripts. He suffered from a logorrhea of writing; he could not stop his hand. When he published this account of how he wrote Of Time and the River, *and in it told how his editor at Scribner's, Maxwell Perkins, had announced to him the point at which the novel was finished and then had helped him piece its unruly huge parts together, one critic, in an essay entitled, "Genius Is Not Enough," raised the question whether Wolfe could have functioned at all as a writer without Perkins. This cruel piece stirred doubts which eventually drove Wolfe to break with Perkins as an editor, in order to prove that he could write on his own. All his writing life, in fact, was a struggle in more senses than the editorial one. The metaphor of the volcano was apt. Wolfe saw himself as "life's monstrous outcast"; someone once spoke of him as a misfit somehow crossed with Everyman. Always as he wrote he had a powerful urge to tell* everything *about America. After his death, Perkins wrote that "he was wrestling, as no artist in Europe would have to, with the material of literature—a great country not yet revealed to its own people."*

FROM
THE STORY OF A NOVEL

. . . Now I was faced with another fundamental problem which every young writer must meet squarely if he is to continue. How is a man to get his writing done? How long should he work at writing? and how often? What kind of method, if any, must he find in following his work? I suddenly found myself face to face with the grim necessity of constant, daily work. And as simple as this discovery may seem to everyone, I was not prepared for it. A young writer without a public does not feel the sense of necessity, the pressure of time, as does a writer who has been published and who must now begin to think of time schedules, publishing seasons, the completion of his next book. I realized suddenly with a sense of

definite shock that I had let six months go by since the publication of my
first book and that, save for a great many notes and fragments, I had done
nothing. Meanwhile, the book [*Look Homeward, Angel*] continued to
sell slowly but steadily, and in February 1930, about five months after its
publication, I found it possible to resign from the faculty of New York
University and devote my full time to the preparation of a second book.
That spring I was also fortunate enough to be awarded the Guggenheim
Fellowship which would enable me to live and work abroad for a year.
And accordingly, at the beginning of May, I went abroad again.

I was in Paris for a couple of months, until the middle of July, and
although I now compelled myself to work for four or five hours a day,
my effort at composition was still confused and broken, and there was
nothing yet that had the structural form and unity of a book. The life of
the great city fascinated me as it had always done, but also aroused all
the old feelings of naked homelessness, rootlessness, and loneliness which
I have always felt there. . . . During that summer in Paris, I think I felt
this great homesickness more than ever before, and I really believe that
from this emotion, this constant and almost intolerable effort of memory
and desire, the material and the structure of the books I now began to
write were derived.

The quality of my memory is characterized, I believe, in a more than
ordinary degree by the intensity of its sense impressions, its power to
evoke and bring back the odors, sounds, colors, shapes, and feel of things
with concrete vividness. Now my memory was at work night and day, in
a way that I could at first neither check nor control and that swarmed
unbidden in a stream of blazing pageantry across my mind, with the million forms and substances of the life that I had left, which was my own,
America. I would be sitting, for example, on the terrace of a café watching
the flash and play of life before me on the Avenue de l'Opéra and suddenly I would remember the iron railing that goes along the boardwalk
at Atlantic City. I could see it instantly just the way it was, the heavy iron
pipes; its raw, galvanized look; the way the joints were fitted together.
It was all so vivid and concrete that I could feel my hand upon it and
know the exact dimensions, its size and weight and shape. And suddenly
I would realize that I had never seen any railing that looked like this in
Europe. And this utterly familiar, common thing would suddenly be revealed to me with all the wonder with which we discover a thing which
we have seen all our life and yet have never known before.

Or again, it would be an American street with all its jumble of a thousand
ugly architectures. It would be Montague Street or Fulton Street in Brooklyn, or Eleventh Street in New York, or other streets where I had lived;
and suddenly I would see the gaunt and savage webbing of the elevated
structure along Fulton Street, and how the light swarmed through in
dusty, broken bars, and I could remember the old, familiar rusty color,

that incomparable rusty color that gets into so many things here in America. And this also would be like something I had seen a million times and lived with all my life.

I would sit there, looking out upon the Avenue de l'Opéra and my life would ache with the whole memory of it; the desire to see it again; somehow to find a word for it; a language that would tell its shape, its color, the way we have all known and felt and seen it. . . . It was as if I had discovered a whole new universe of chemical elements and had begun to see certain relations between some of them but had by no means begun to organize the whole series into a harmonious and coherent union. From this time on, I think my efforts might be described as the effort to complete that organization, to discover that articulation for which I strove, to bring about that final coherent union. . . .

I cannot really say the book was written. It was something that took hold of me and possessed me, and before I was done with it—that is, before I finally emerged with the first completed part—it seemed to me that it had done for me. It was exactly as if a great black storm cloud had opened up and, mid flashes of lightning, was pouring from its depth a torrential and ungovernable flood. Upon that flood everything was swept and borne along as by a great river. And I was borne along with it. . . .

I spent the winter of that year in England from October until March, and here perhaps because of the homely familiarity of the English life, the sense of order and repose which such a life can give one, my work moved forward still another step from this flood tide chaos of creation. For the first time the work began to take on the lineaments of design. These lineaments were still confused and broken, sometimes utterly lost, but now I really did get the sense at last that I was working on a great block of marble, shaping a figure which no one but its maker could as yet define, but which was emerging more and more into the sinewy lines of composition.

From the beginning—and this was one fact that in all my times of hopelessness returned to fortify my faith in my conviction—the idea, the central legend that I wished my book to express had not changed. And this central idea was this: the deepest search in life, it seemed to me, the thing that in one way or another was central to all living was man's search to find a father, not merely the father of his flesh, not merely the lost father of his youth, but the image of a strength and wisdom external to his need and superior to his hunger, to which the belief and power of his own life could be united. . . .

So far as I can describe with any accuracy, the progress of that winter's work in England was not along the lines of planned design, but along this line that I have mentioned—writing some of the sections which I knew would have to be in the book. Meanwhile what was really going on in my whole creative consciousness, during all this time, although I did not realize it at the moment, was this: What I was really doing, what I had been doing all the time since my discovery of my America in Paris the summer before, was to explore day by day and month by month with a fanatical intensity, the whole material domain of my resources as a man and as a writer. This exploration went on for a period which I can estimate conservatively as two years and a half. . . .

In a way, during that period of my life, I think I was like the Ancient Mariner who told the Wedding Guest that his frame was wrenched by the woeful agony which forced him to begin his tale before it left him free. In my own experience, my wedding guests were the great ledgers in which I wrote, and the tale which I told to them would have seemed, I am afraid, completely incoherent, as meaningless as Chinese characters, had any reader seen them. I could by no means hope to give a comprehensive idea of the whole extent of this labor because three years of work and perhaps a million and a half words went into these books. It included everything from gigantic and staggering lists of the towns, cities, counties, states, and countries I had been in, to minutely thorough, desperately evocative descriptions of the undercarriage, the springs, wheels, flanges, axle rods, color, weight, and quality of the day coach of an American railway train. There were lists of the rooms and houses in which I had lived or in which I had slept for at least a night, together with the most accurate and evocative descriptions of those rooms that I could write—their size, their shape, the color and design of the wallpaper, the way a towel hung down, the way a chair creaked, a streak of water rust upon the ceiling. . . .

In addition, one might come upon other sections under some such cryptic heading as "Where now?" Under such a heading as this, there would be brief notations of those thousands of things which all of us have seen for just a flash, a moment in our lives, which seem to be of no consequence whatever at the moment that we see them, and which live in our minds and hearts forever, which are somehow pregnant with all the joy and sorrow of the human destiny, and which we know, somehow, are therefore more important than many things of more apparent consequence. "Where now?" Some quiet steps that came and passed along a leafy night-time street in summer in a little town down South long years ago; a woman's voice, her sudden burst of low and tender laughter; then the voices and the footsteps going, silence, the leafy rustle of the trees. "Where now?" Two trains that met and paused at a little station at some little town at some unknown moment upon the huge body of the continent; a girl who looked and smiled from the window of the other train; another passing in a motor car on the streets of Norfolk; the winter boarders in a little boarding house down South twenty years ago; Miss Florrie Mangle, the trained nurse; Miss Jessie Rimmer, the cashier at Reed's drug store; Dr. Richards, the clairvoyant; the pretty girl who cracked the whip and thrust her head into the lion's mouth with Johnny J. Jones Carnival and Combined Shows. . . .

It may be objected, it has been objected already by certain critics, that in such research as I have here attempted to describe there is a quality of intemperate excess, an almost insane hunger to devour the entire body of human experience, to attempt to include more, experience more, than the measure of one life can hold, or than the limits of a single work of art can well define. I readily admit the validity of this criticism. I think I realize as well as anyone the fatal dangers that are consequent to such a ravenous desire, the damage it may wreak upon one's life and on one's work. But having had this thing within me, it was in no way possible for me to reason it out of me, no matter how cogently my reason worked against it. The only way I could meet it was to meet it squarely not with reason, but with life. . . .

When I returned to America in the spring of 1931, although I had three or four hundred thousand words of material, I had nothing that could be published as a novel. Almost a year and a half had elapsed since the publication of my first book and already people had begun to ask that question which is so well meant, but which as year followed year was to become more intolerable to my ears than the most deliberate mockery: "Have you finished your next book yet?" "When is it going to be published?"

At this time I was sure that a few months of steady work would bring the book to completion. I found a place, a little basement flat in the Assyrian quarter in South Brooklyn, and there I went about my task.

The spring passed into the summer; the summer, into autumn. I was working hard, day after day, and still nothing that had the unity and design of a single work appeared. October came and with it a second full year since the publication of my first book. And now, for the first time, I was irrevocably committed so far as the publication of my book was concerned. I began to feel the sensation of pressure, and of naked desperation which was to become almost maddeningly intolerable in the next three years. For the first time I began to realize that my project was much larger than I thought it would be. . . .

All of this time I was being baffled by a certain time element in the book, by a time relation which could not be escaped, and for which I was now desperately seeking some structural channel. There were three time elements inherent in the material. The first and most obvious was an element of actual present time, an element which carried the narrative forward, which represented characters and events as living in the present and moving forward into an immediate future. The second time element was of past time, one which represented these same characters as acting and as being acted upon by all the accumulated impact of man's experience so that each moment of their life was conditioned not only by what they experienced in that moment, but by all that they had experienced up to that moment. In addition to these two time elements, there was a third which I conceived as being time immutable, the time of rivers, mountains, oceans, and the earth; a kind of eternal and unchanging universe of time against which would be projected the transience of man's life, the bitter briefness of his day. It was the tremendous problem of these three time elements that almost defeated me and that cost me countless hours of anguish in the years that were to follow.

As I began to realize the true nature of the task I had set for myself, the image of the river began to haunt my mind. I actually felt that I had a great river thrusting for release inside of me and that I had to find a channel into which its floodlike power could pour. I knew I had to find it or I would be destroyed in the flood of my own creation, and I am sure that every artist who ever lived has had the same experience. . . .

I would work furiously day after day until my creative energies were utterly exhausted. . . . I reached that state of naked need and utter isolation which every artist has got to meet and conquer if he is to survive at all. Before this I had been sustained by that delightful illusion of success which we all have when we dream about the books we are going to write instead of actually doing them. Now I was face to face with it, and suddenly I realized that I had committed my life and my integrity so irrevocably to this struggle that I must conquer now or be destroyed. I was alone with my own work, and now I knew that I had to be alone with it, that no one could help me with it now no matter how anyone might wish to help. For the first time I realized another naked fact which every artist must know, and that is that in a man's work there are contained not only the seeds of life, but the seeds of death, and that that power of creation which sustains us will also destroy us like a leprosy if we let it rot stillborn in our vitals. I had to get it out of me somehow. I saw that now. And now for the first time a terrible doubt began to creep into my mind that I might not live long enough to get it out of me, that I had created a labor so large and so impossible that the energy of a dozen lifetimes would not suffice for its accomplishment.

During this time, however, I was sustained by one piece of inestimable good fortune. I had for a friend a man of immense and patient wisdom and a gentle but unyielding fortitude. I think that if I was not destroyed at this time by the sense of hopelessness which these gigantic labors had awakened in me, it was largely because of the courage and patience of this man. I did not give in because he would not let me give in, and I think it is also true that at this particular time he had the advantage of being in the position of a skilled observer at a battle. I was myself engaged in that battle, covered by its dust and sweat and exhausted by its struggle, and I understood far less clearly than my friend the nature and the progress of the struggle in which I was engaged. At this time there was little that this man could do except observe, and in one way or another keep me at my task, and in many quiet and marvelous ways he succeeded in doing this. . . .

My friend, the editor, has likened his own function at this painful time to that of a man who is trying to hang on to the fin of a plunging whale, but hang on he did, and it is to his tenacity that I owe my final release. Meanwhile, my creative power was functioning at the highest intensity it had ever known. I wrote at times without belief that I would ever finish, with nothing in me but black despair, and yet I wrote and wrote and could not give up writing. . . .

People have sometimes asked me what happened to my life during these years. They have asked me how I ever found time to know anything that was going on in the world about me when my life was so completely absorbed by this world of writing. Well, it may seem to be an extraordinary fact, but the truth is that never in my whole life have I lived so fully, have I shared so richly in the common life of man as I did during these three years when I was struggling with the giant problem of my own work.

For one thing, my whole sensory and creative equipment, my powers of feeling and reflection—even the sense of hearing, and above all, my powers of memory, had reached the greatest degree of sharpness that they had ever known. At the end of the day of savage labor, my mind was still blazing with its effort, could by no opiate of reading, poetry, music, alcohol, or any other pleasure, be put at rest. I was unable to sleep, unable to subdue the tumult of these creative energies, and as a result of this condition, for three years I prowled the streets, explored the swarming web of the million-footed city and came to know it as I had never done before. It was a black time in the history of the nation, a black time in my own life and, I suppose, it is but natural that my own memory of it now should be a pretty grim and painful one. . . .

Such was the state my life had come to in the early winter of 1933, and even at that moment, although I could not see it, the end of my huge labor was in sight. In the middle of December of that year the great editor, of whom I have spoken, and who, during all this tormented period, had kept a quiet watch upon me, called me to his home and calmly informed me that my book was finished. I could only look at him with stunned surprise, and finally I only could tell him out of the depth of my own hopelessness that he was mistaken, that the book was not finished, that it could never be completed, that I could write no more. He answered with the same quiet finality that the book was finished whether I knew it or not, and then he told me to go to my room and spend the next week in collecting in its proper order the manuscript which had accumulated during the last two years.

I followed his instructions, still without hope and without belief. I worked for six days sitting in the middle of the floor surrounded by mountainous stacks of typed manuscript on every side. At the end of a week I had the first part of it together, and just two days before Christmas, 1933, I delivered to him the manuscript of "The October Fair," and a few days later, the manuscript of "The Hills Beyond Pentland." The manuscript of

"The Fair" was, at that time, something over 1,000,000 words in length. He had seen most of it in its dismembered fragments during the three preceding years, but now, for the first time, he was seeing them in their sequential order, and once again his marvelous intuition was right; he had told me the truth when he said that I had finished the book.

It was not finished in any way that was publishable or readable. It was really not a book so much as it was the skeleton of a book, but for the first time in four years the skeleton was all there. An enormous labor of revision, weaving together, shaping, and, above all, cutting, remained, but I had the book now so that nothing, not even the despair of my own spirit, could take it from me. He told me so, and suddenly I saw that he was right.

I was like a man who is drowning and who suddenly, at the last gasp of his dying effort, feels earth beneath his feet again. . . .

It was evident that many problems were before us, but now we had the thing, and we welcomed the labor before us with happy confidence. In the first place there was the problem of the book's gigantic length. Even in this skeletonized form the manuscript of "The October Fair" was over a million words in length, which is about twelve times the length of the average novel or twice the length of "War and Peace." It was manifest, therefore, that it would not only be utterly impossible to publish such a manuscript in a single volume, but that even if it were published in several volumes, the tremendous length of such a manuscript would practically annihilate its chances of ever finding a public which would read it.

This problem now faced us, and the editor grappled with it immediately. As his examination of the manuscript of "The October Fair" proceeded, he found that the book did describe two complete and separate cycles. The first of these was a movement which described the period of wandering and hunger in a man's youth. The second cycle described the period of greater certitude, and was dominated by the unity of a single passion. It was obvious, therefore, that what we had in the two cyclic movements of this book was really the material of two completely different chronicles, and although the second of the two was by far the more finished, the first cycle, of course, was the one which logically we ought to complete and publish first, and we decided on this course.

We took the first part. I immediately prepared a minutely thorough synopsis which described not only the course of the book from the first to the last, but which also included an analysis of those chapters which had been completed in their entirety, of those which were completed only in part, and of those which had not been written at all, and with this synopsis before us, we set to work immediately to prepare the book for press. This work occupied me throughout the whole of the year 1934. The book was completed at the beginning of 1935, and was published in March of that year under the title of *Of Time and the River*.

In the first place, the manuscript, even in its unfinished form, called for the most radical cutting, and because of the way in which the book had been written, as well as the fatigue which I now felt, I was not well prepared to do by myself the task that lay ahead of us.

Cutting had always been the most difficult and distasteful part of writing to me; my tendency had always been to write rather than to cut. Moreover, whatever critical faculty I may have had concerning my own work had been seriously impaired, for the time being at least, by the frenzied labor of the past four years. When a man's work has poured from him for almost five years like burning lava from a volcano; when all of it, however superfluous, has been given fire and passion by the white heat of his own creative energy, it is very difficult suddenly to become coldly surgical, ruthlessly detached.

To give a few concrete illustrations of the difficulties that now confronted us: The opening section of the book describes the journey of a train across the State of Virginia at night. Its function in the book is simply to introduce some of the chief characters, to indicate a central situation, to give something of the background from which the book proceeds, and perhaps through the movement of the train across the stillness of the earth to establish a certain beat, evoke a certain emotion which is inherent to the nature of the book. Such a section, therefore, undoubtedly serves an important function, but in proportion to the whole purport of the book, its function is a secondary one and must be related to the whole book in a proportionate way.

Now in the original version, the manuscript which described the journey of the train across Virginia at night was considerably longer than the average novel. What was needed was just an introductory chapter or two, and what I had written was over 100,000 words in length, and this same difficulty, this lack of proportion, was also evident in other parts of the manuscript.

What I had written about the great train was really good. But what I had to face, the very bitter lesson that everyone who wants to write has got to learn, was that a thing may in itself be the finest piece of writing one has ever done, and yet have absolutely no place in the manuscript one hopes to publish. This is a hard thing, but it must be faced, and so we faced it.

My spirit quivered at the bloody execution. My soul recoiled before the carnage of so many lovely things cut out upon which my heart was set. But it had to be done, and we did it. . . .

And so it went all up and down the line. Chapters 50,000 words long were reduced to ten or fifteen thousand words, and having faced this inevitable necessity, I finally acquired a kind of ruthlessness of my own, and once or twice, myself, did more cutting than my editor was willing to allow. . . .

Meanwhile I was proceeding at full speed with the work of completing my design, finishing the unfinished parts and filling in the transition links which were essential.

This in itself was an enormous job and kept me writing all day long as hard as I could go for a full year. Here again the nature of my chief fault was manifest. I wrote too much again. I not only wrote what was essential, but time and time again my enthusiasm for a good scene, one of those enchanting vistas which can open up so magically to a man in the full flow of his creation would overpower me, and I would write thousands of words upon a scene which contributed nothing of vital importance to a book whose greatest need already was ruthless condensation.

During the course of this year, I must have written well over a half million words of additional manuscript, of which, of course, only a small part was finally used. . . .

The end came suddenly—the end of those five years of torment and incessant productivity. In October I took a trip to Chicago, a two weeks' vacation, my first in over a year. When I returned I found that my editor had quietly and decisively sent the manuscript to the press, the printers were already at work on it, the proof was beginning to come in. I had not foreseen it; I was desperate, bewildered. "You can't do it," I told him, "the book is not yet finished. I must have six months more on it."

To this he answered that the book was not only finished, but that if I took six months more on it, I would then demand another six months and six months more beyond that, and that I might very well become so obsessed with this one work that I would never get it published. He went on to say, and I think with complete justice, that such a course was wrong for me. I was not, he said, a Flaubert kind of writer. I was not a perfectionist. I had twenty, thirty, almost any number of books in me, and the important thing was to get them produced and not to spend the rest of my life in perfecting one book. . . .

He told me finally that I would go on and do better work, that I would learn to work without so much confusion, waste, and useless torment, that my future books would more and more achieve the unity, sureness, and finality that every artist wants his work to have, but that I had to learn in the way I had learned, groping, struggling, finding my own way for myself, that this was the only way to learn.

In January 1935, I finished the last of my revisions on the proof; the first printed copies came from the press in February. The book was released for final publication early in March. I was not here when it came out. I had taken a ship for Europe the week before, and as the ship got farther and farther from the American shores, my spirits sank lower and lower, reaching, I think, the lowest state of hopeless depression they had ever known. This, I believe, was largely a physical reaction, the inevitable effect of relaxation upon a human organism which had for five years been strained to its utmost limit. My life seemed to me to be like a great spring which had been taut for years and which was now slowly uncoiling from its tension. I had the most extraordinary sense of desolation I had ever known when I thought about my book. I had never realized until now how close I had been to it, how much a part of me it had become, and now that it had been taken away from me, my life felt utterly futile, hollow as a shell. . . .

Now I had an overwhelming sense of shame greater than any I have felt before. I felt as if I had ruinously exposed myself as a pitiable fool who had no talent and who once and for all had completely vindicated the prophecies of the critics who had felt the first book was just a flash in the pan. It was in this frame of mind that I arrived in Paris on March 8, the day the book was to be published in America. I had come away to forget about it, and yet I thought about it all the time. I walked the streets from dawn to dark, from night to morning, at least a dozen times in two short weeks I heard the celebration of mass at Sacré Coeur, and then would walk the streets again and come back to my hotel at ten o'clock and lie upon the bed, and still I could not sleep.

After several days of this, I steeled myself to go to the office of the travel agency where a message might be waiting for me. I found a cablegram there. It was from my publisher, and it said simply: "Magnificent reviews somewhat critical in ways expected, full of greatest praise."

John Fowles

(1926–   )

For a number of years before writing The French Lieutenant's Woman, *John Fowles had lived in a house looking down over the harbor of Lyme Regis, in Dorset, on the rim of the Hardy country. While writing* The Collector *and* The Magus, *Fowles had become more and more fascinated by Hardy and other Victorian novelists, and finally, drawn into the undertaking by the hypnopompic vision of a woman on the Lyme breakwater that he describes in these notes, he decided to try his hand at a novel a Victorian novelist might have written—but couldn't have, at that, because it would be a twentieth-century novel, too. In the thirteenth chapter of his book Fowles draws back, something like an intervening Victorian author but also as one who works "in the age of Robbe-Grillet and Roland Barthes," and he writes, "I do not know. This story I am telling is all imagination. These characters I create never existed outside my own mind . . ." For several pages, risking a break in the illusions he has painstakingly built, he writes about what a novelist tries to do and how he goes about it; and he isolates the single common motive for writing that animates all novelists: "We wish to create worlds as real as, but other than, the world that is."*

NOTES ON AN UNFINISHED NOVEL

The novel I am writing at the moment (provisionally entitled *The French Lieutenant's Woman*) is set about a hundred years back. I don't think of it as a historical novel, a genre in which I have very little interest. It started four or five months ago as a visual image. A women stands at the end of a deserted quay and stares out to sea. That was all. This image rose in my mind one morning when I was still in bed half asleep. It corresponded to no actual incident in my life (or in art) that I can recall, though I have for many years collected obscure books and forgotten prints, all sorts of flotsam and jetsam from the last two or three centuries, relics of past lives—and I suppose this leaves me with a sort of dense hinterland from which such images percolate down to the coast of consciousness.

These mythopoeic "stills" (they seem almost always static) float into my mind very often. I ignore them, since that is the best way of finding whether they really are the door into a new world.

So I ignored this image; but it recurred. Imperceptibly it stopped coming to me. I began deliberately to recall it and to try to analyze and hypothesize why it held some sort of imminent power. It was obviously mysterious. It was vaguely romantic. It also seemed, perhaps because of the latter quality, not to belong to today. The woman obstinately refused to stare out of the window of an airport lounge; it had to be this ancient quay—as I happen to live near one, so near that I can see it from the bottom of my garden, it soon became a specific ancient quay. The woman had no face, no particular degree of sexuality. But she was Victorian; and since I always saw her in the same static long shot, with her back turned, she represented a reproach on the Victorian Age. An outcast. I didn't know her crime, but I wished to protect her. That is, I began to fall in love with her. Or with her stance. I didn't know which.

This—not literally—pregnant female image came at a time (the autumn of 1966) when I was already halfway through another novel and had, still have, three or four others planned to follow it. It was an interference, but of such power that it soon came to make the previously planned work seem the intrusive element in my life. This accidentality of inspiration has to be allowed for in writing; both in the work one is on (unplanned development of character, unintended incidents, and so on) and in one's works as a whole. Follow the accident, fear the fixed plan—that is the rule.

Narcissism, or pygmalionism, is the essential vice a writer must have. Characters (and even situations) are like children or lovers, they need constant caressing, concern, listening to, watching, admiring. All these occupations become tiring for the active partner—the writer—and only something akin to love can provide the energy. I've heard people say "I want to write a book." But wanting to write a book, however ardently, is not enough. Even to say "I want to be possessed by my own creations" is not enough; all natural or born writers are possessed, and in the old magical sense, by their own imaginations long before they even begin to think of writing.

This fluke genesis must break all the rules of creative writing; must sound at best childlike, at worst childish. I suppose the orthodox method is to work out what one wants to say and what one has experience of, and then to correlate the two. I have tried that method and started out with an analytically arrived-at theme and a set of characters all neatly standing for something; but the manuscripts have all petered out miserably. *The Magus* (written before *The Collector*, which also originated in a single image) sprang from a very trivial visit to a villa on a Greek island; nothing in the least unusual happened. But in my unconscious I kept arriving at the place again and again; something wanted to happen there, something that had not happened to me at the time. Why it should have been at *that* villa, *that* one visit, among so many thousands of other possible launching-pads, I do not know. Only a month ago someone showed me some recent photographs of the villa, which is now deserted; and it was just a deserted villa. Its mysterious significance to me fifteen years ago remains mysterious.

Once the seed germinates, reason and knowledge, culture and all the rest, have to start to grow it. You cannot create a world by hot instinct; but only by cold experience. That is one good reason why so many novelists produce nothing until, or do all their best work after, the age of forty.

I find it very difficult to write if I don't know I shall have several days absolutely clear. All visits, all intrusions, all daily duties become irksome. This is during the first draft. I wrote the first draft of *The Collector* in under a month; sometimes ten thousand words a day. Of course a lot of it was poorly written and had to be endlessly amended and revised. First-draft and revision writing are so different they hardly seem to belong to the same activity. I never do any "research" until the first draft is finished; all that matters to begin with is the flow, the story, the narrating. Research material then is like swimming in a strait-jacket.

During the revision period I try to keep some sort of discipline. I make myself revise whether I feel like it or not; in some ways, the more disinclined and dyspeptic one feels, the better—one is harsher with oneself. All the best cutting is done when one is sick of the writing.

But all this advice from senior writers to establish a discipline always, to get down a thousand words a day whatever one's mood, I find an absurdly puritanical and impractical approach. Writing is like eating or making love; a natural process, not an artificial one. Write, if you must, because you feel like writing; never because you feel you ought to write.

I write memoranda to myself about the book I'm on. On this one: *You are not trying to write something one of the Victorian novelists forgot to write; but perhaps something one of them failed to write. And· Remember the etymology of the word. A novel is something new. It must have relevance to the writer's now—so don't ever pretend you live in 1867; or make sure the reader knows it's a pretence.*

In the matter of clothes, social manners, historical background, and the rest, writing about 1867 is merely a question of research. But I soon get into trouble over dialogue, because the genuine dialogue of 1867 (insofar as it can be heard in books of the time) is far too close to our own to sound convincingly old. It very often fails to agree with our psychological picture of the Victorians—it is not stiff enough, not euphemistic enough, and so on; and here at once I have to start cheating and pick out the more formal and archaic (even for 1867) elements of spoken speech. It is this kind of "cheating," which is intrinsic to the novel, that takes the time.

Even in modern-novel dialogue the most real is not the most conformable to actual current speech. One has only to read a transcribed tape of actual conversation to realize that it is, in the literary context, not very real. Novel dialogue is a form of shorthand, an *impression* of what people actually say; and besides that it has to perform other functions—to keep the narrative moving (which real conversation rarely does), to reveal character (real conversation often hides it), and so on.

This is the greatest technical problem I have; it is hard enough with modern characters, and doubly so with historical ones.

Memorandum: *If you want to be true to life, start lying about the reality of it.*

And: *One cannot describe reality; only give metaphors that indicate it. All human modes of description (photographic, mathematical and the rest, as well as literary) are metaphorical. Even the most precise scientific description of an object or movement is a tissue of metaphors.*

Alain Robbe-Grillet's polemical essay *Pour un nouveau roman* (1963) is indispensable reading for the profession, even where it produces no more than total disagreement. His key question: *Why bother to write in a form whose great masters cannot be surpassed?* The fallacy of one of his conclusions—we must discover a new form to write in if the novel is to survive—is obvious. It reduces the purpose of the novel to the discovery of new forms: whereas its other purposes—to entertain, to satirize, to describe new sensibilities, to record life, to improve life, and so on—are clearly just as viable and important. But his obsessive pleading for new form places a kind of stress on every passage one writes today. To what extent am I being a coward by writing inside the old tradition? To what extent am I being panicked into avant-gardism? Writing about 1867 doesn't lessen the stress; it increases it, since so much of the subject matter must of its historical nature be "traditional."

There are apparent parallels in other arts: Stravinsky's eighteenth century rehandlings, Picasso's and Francis Bacon's use of Velasquez. But in this context words are not nearly so tractable as musical notes or brush-strokes. One can parody a rococo musical ornament, a baroque face. Very early on I tried, in a test chapter, to put modern dialogue into Victorian mouths. But the effect was absurd, since the real historical nature of the characters is hopelessly distorted; the only people to get away with this (Julius Caesar speaking with a Brooklyn accent, and so on) are the professional funny men. One is led inevitably, by such a technique, into a comic novel.

My two previous novels were both based on more or less disguised existentialist premises. I want this one to be no exception; and so I am trying to show an existentialist awareness before it was chronologically possible. Kierkegaard was, of course, totally unknown to the British and American Victorians; but it has always seemed to me that the Victorian Age, especially from 1850 on, was highly existentialist in many of its personal dilemmas. One can almost invert the reality and say that Camus and Sartre have been trying to lead us, in their fashion, to a Victorian seriousness of purpose and moral sensitivity.

Nor is this the only similarity between the 1960's and 1860's. The great nightmare of the respectable Victorian mind was the only too real one created by the geologist Lyell and the biologist Darwin. Until then man had lived like a child in a small room. They gave him—and never was a present less welcome—infinite space and time, and a hideously mechanistic explanation of human reality into the bargain. Just as we "live with the bomb" the Victorians lived with the theory of evolution. They were hurled into space. They felt themselves infinitely isolated. By the 1860's the great iron structures of their philosophies, religions, and social stratifications were already beginning to look dangerously corroded to the more perspicacious.

Just such a man, an existentialist before his time, walks down the quay and sees that mysterious back, feminine, silent, also existentialist, turned to the horizon.

Magnificent though the Victorian novelists were, they almost all (an exception, of course, is the later Hardy) failed miserably in one aspect; nowhere in "respectable" Victorian literature (and most of the pornography was based on the brothel—or eighteenth-century accounts) does one see a man and a woman described together in bed. We do not know how they made love, what they said to each other in their most intimate moments, what they felt then.

Writing as I have been today—about two Victorians making love—with no guides except my imagination and vague deductions from the spirit of the age and so on—is really science fiction. A journey is a journey, backwards or forwards.

The most difficult task for a writer is to get the right "voice" for his material; by voice I mean the overall impression one has of the creator behind what he creates. Now I've always liked the ironic voice that the line of great nineteenth-century novelists, from Austen through to Conrad, all used so naturally. We tend today to remember the failures of that tone—the satirical overkill in Dickens, the facetiousness of Thackeray, the strained sarcasm of Mark Twain, the priggishness in George Eliot—rather than its virtues. The reason is clear enough: irony needs the assumption of superiority in the ironist. Such an assumption must be anathema to a democratic, egalitarian century like our own. We suspect people who pretend to be omniscient; and that is why so many of us twentieth-century novelists feel driven into first-person narration.

I have heard writers claim that this first-person technique is a last bastion of the novel against the cinema, a form, where the camera dictates an inevitable third-person point of view of what happens, however much we may identify with one character. But the matter of whether a contemporary novelist uses "he" or "I" is largely irrelevant. The great majority of modern third-person narration is "I" narration very thinly disguised. The real "I" of the Victorian writers—the writer himself—is as rigorously repressed

there (out of fear of seeming pretentious, etc.) as it is, for obvious seman-
tic and grammatical reasons, when the narration is in literal first-person
form.

But in this new book, I shall try to resurrect this technique. It seems in
any case natural to look back at the England of a hundred years ago with
a somewhat ironical eye—and "I"—although it is my strong belief that history is horizontal in terms of the ratio between understanding and *available*
knowledge and (far more important) horizontal in terms of the happiness
the individual gets from being alive. In short, there is a danger in being
ironic about the apparent follies and miseries of any past age. So I have
written myself another memorandum: *You are not the "I" who breaks
into the illusion, but the "I" who is a part of it.*

In other words, the "I" who will make first-person commentaries here
and there in my story, and who will finally even enter it, will not be my
real "I" in 1967; but much more just another character, though in a different category from the purely fictional ones.

An illustration. Here is the beginning of a minor novel (*Lovel the
Widower,* 1861) by Thackeray:

> Who shall be the hero of this tale? Not I who write it. I am but the Chorus
> of the Play. I make remarks on the conduct of the characters: I narrate their
> simple story.

Today I think we should assume (not knowing who the writer was) that
the "I" here is the writer's "I." For three or four pages more we might
still just believe this; but then suddenly Thackeray introduces his epony-
mous hero as "my friend Lovel" and we see we've been misled. "I" is
simply another character. But then a few pages on the "I" cuts in again in
the description of a character.

> She never could speak. Her voice was as hoarse as a fishwoman's. Can that
> immense stout old box-keeper at the —— theatre . . . be the once brilliant Emily
> Montanville? I am told there are *no* lady box-keepers in the English theatres.
> This, I submit, is a proof of my consummate care and artifice in rescuing from
> a prurient curiosity the individual personages from whom the characters of the
> present story are taken. Montanville is *not* a box-opener. She *may,* under another
> name, keep a trinket-shop in the Burlington Arcade, for what you know: but
> this secret no torture shall induce me to divulge. Life has its rises and down-
> falls, and you have had yours, you hobbling old creature. Montanville, indeed!
> Go thy ways! Here is a shilling for thee. (Thank you, sir.) Take away that con-
> founded footstool, and never let us see thee more!

We can just still suppose that the "I" is another character here; but the
strong suspicion is that it is Thackeray himself. There is the characteristic
teasing of the reader, the shock new angle of the present tense, the com-
pensatory self-mocking in the already revealed "secret no torture shall

induce me to divulge." But clearly he doesn't mean us to be sure; it is not the whole Thackeray.

Lovel rates poorly by Thackeray's own standards elsewhere; it is nevertheless a brilliant technical exercise in the use of "voice." I cannot believe that it is a dead technique. Nothing can get us off the charge of omniscience —and certainly not the *nouveau roman* theory. Even that theory's most brilliant practical demonstrations—say Robbe-Grillet's own *La Jalousie*— fail to answer the accusation. Robbe-Grillet may have removed the writer Robbe-Grillet totally from the text; but he has never denied he wrote it. If the writer really believes in the statement "I know nothing about my characters except what can be tape-recorded and photographed (and then 'mixed' and 'cut')," the logical step is to take up tape-recording and photography—not writing. But if he still writes, and writes well, as Robbe-Grillet does, then he is self-betrayed: he belongs to Cosa Nostra, and is transparently far more deeply implicated than he will admit.

September 2nd, 1967. Now I am about two thirds of the way through. Always a bad stage, when one begins to doubt major things like basic motivations, dramatic design, the whole bloody enterprise; in the beginning one tends to get dazzled by each page, by one's fertility, those nice Muses always at one's shoulder . . . but then the inherent faults in the plot and characters begin to emerge. One starts to doubt the wisdom of the way the latter make things go; at the stage in an *affaire*, when one begins to thank God that marriage never raised its ugly head. But here one is condemned to a marriage of sorts—I have the woman on the quay (whose name is Sarah) for better or for worse, so to speak; and all seems worse.

I have to break off for a fortnight to go down to Majorca, where they're filming *The Magus*. I have written the script, but like most scripts it's really a team effort. The two producers have had their say, and the director; and a number of non-human factors, such as the budget, the nature of the locations, and the casting of the main roles, have had theirs. Most of the time I feel like a skeleton at the feast; this isn't what I had imagined, either in the book or in the script.

Yet it is interesting to watch, on a big film production, how buttressed each key man is by the other key men; to see how often one will turn to the other and say "Will it work?" I compare this with the loneliness of the long-distance writer; and I come back with a sort of relief, a re-affirmation in my faith in the novel. For all its faults, it is a statement by one person. In my novels I am the producer, director, and all the actors; I photograph it. This may seem a megalomania beside which the more celebrated cases from Hollywood pale to nothingness. There *is* a vanity about it, a wish to play the godgame, which all the random and author-removing devices of avant-garde technique cannot hide. But there must be a virtue, in an age that is out to exterminate both the individual and the enduring, in the individual's attempt to endure by his own efforts alone.

The truth is, the novel is a free form. Unlike the play or the filmscript, it has no limits other than those of the language. It is like a poem; it can be what it wants. This is its downfall and its glory; and explains why both forms have been so often used to establish freedom in other fields, social and political.

A charge all of us who sell film rights have to answer is that we wrote our books with this end in view. What has to be distinguished here is the legitimate and the illegitimate influence of the cinema on the novel. I saw my first film when I was six; I suppose I've seen on average—and discounting television—a film a week ever since: let's say some two and a half thousand films up to now. How can so frequently repeated an experience not have indelibly stamped itself on the *mode* of imagination? At one time I analyzed my dreams in detail; again and again I recalled purely cinematic effects . . . panning shots, close shots, tracking, jump cuts, and the rest. In short, this mode of imagining is far too deep in me to eradicate— not only in me, in all my generation.

This doesn't mean we have surrendered to the cinema. I don't share the general pessimism about the so-called decline of the novel and its present status as a minority cult. Except for a brief period in the nineteenth century, when a literate majority and a lack of other means of entertainment coincided, it has always been a minority cult.

One has in fact only to do a filmscript to realize how inalienably in possession of a still vast domain the novel is; how countless the forms of human experience only to be described in and by it. There is too an essential difference in the quality of image evoked by the two media. The cinematic visual image is virtually the same for all who see it; it stamps out personal imagination, the response from individual *visual* memory. A sentence or paragraph in a novel will evoke a different image in each reader. This necessary co-operation between writer and reader, the one to suggest, the other to make concrete, is a privilege of *verbal* form; and the cinema can never usurp it.

Nor is that all. Here (the opening four paragraphs of a novel) is a flagrant bit of writing for the cinema. The man has obviously spent too much time on filmscripts, and can now think only of his movie sale.

The temperature is in the 90's and the boulevard is absolutely empty.
Lower down, the inky water of a canal reaches in a straight line. Midway between two locks is a barge full of timber. On the bank, two rows of barrels.
Beyond the canal, between houses separated by workyards, a huge cloudless tropical sky. Under the throbbing sun white façades, slate roofs and granite quays hurt the eyes. An obscure distant murmur rises in the hot air. All seems drugged by the Sunday peace and the sadness of summer days.
Two men appear.

It first appeared on March 25, 1881. The writer's name is Flaubert. All I have done is to transpose his past historic into the present.

I woke in the small hours, and the book tormented me. All its failings rose up in the darkness. I saw the novel I dropped in order to write *The French Lieutenant's Woman* was much better. This one was not my sort of book; but an aberration, a folly, a delusion. Sentences from vitriolic reviews floated through my mind . . . "a clumsy pastiche of Hardy," "pretentious imitation of an inimitable genre," "pointless exploration of an already overexplored age . . . ," and so on and so on.

Now it is day, I am back on it again, and it denies what I felt in the night. But the horror of such realizations is that someone, some reader or reviewer, *will* realize them. The nightmare of the writer is that all his worst private fears and self-criticisms will be made public.

The shadow of Thomas Hardy, the heart of whose "country" I can see in the distance from my workroom window, I cannot avoid. Since he and Peacock are my two favourite male novelists of the nineteenth century I don't mind the shadow. It seems best to use it; and by a curious coincidence, which I didn't realize when I placed my own story in that year, 1867 was the crucial year in Hardy's own mysterious personal life. It is somehow encouraging that while my fictitious characters weave their own story in their 1867, only thirty miles away in the real 1867 the pale young architect was entering his own fatal life-incident.

My female characters tend to dominate the male. I see man as a kind of artifice, and woman as a kind of reality. The one is cold idea, the other is warm fact. Daedalus faces Venus, and Venus must win. If the technical problems hadn't been so great, I should have liked to make Conchis in *The Magus* a woman. The character of Mrs. de Seitas at the end of the book was simply an aspect of his character; as was Lily. Now Sarah exerts this power. She doesn't realize how. Nor do I yet.

I was stuck this morning to find a good answer from Sarah at the climax of a scene. Characters sometimes reject all the possibilities one offers. They say in effect: *I would never say or do a thing like that.* But they don't say what they would say; and one has to proceed negatively, by a very tedious coaxing kind of trial and error. After an hour over this one wretched sentence, I realized that she had in fact been telling me what to do: silence from her was better than any line she might have said.

By the time I left Oxford I found myself much more at home in French than in English literature. There seems to me to be a vital distinction between the French and Anglo-Saxon cultures in this field. Since 1650 French writers have assumed an international audience; and the Anglo-Saxons a national one. This may be no more than a general tendency; the literatures of the two cultures offer hundreds of exceptions, even among the best-known books. Nevertheless I have always found this French assumption that the proper audience of a book is one without frontiers more attractive than the extreme opposite view, which is still widely held in both Britain and America, that the proper job of a writer is to write of and for his own country and countrymen.

I am aware of this when I write, and especially when I revise. English references that will mean nothing to a foreigner I usually cut out, or avoid in the first place. In the present book I have the ubiquity in the West of the Victorian ethos: that helps greatly.

Various things have long made me feel an exile in England. Some years ago I came across a sentence in an obscure French novel: *Ideas are the only motherland.* Ever since I have kept it as the most succinct summary I know of what I believe. Perhaps "believe" is the wrong verb—if you are without national feeling, if you find many of your fellow countrymen and most of their beliefs and their institutions foolish and antiquated, you can hardly *believe* in anything, but only accept the loneliness that results.

So I live completely away from other English writers and the literary life of London. What I have to think of as my "public" self is willy-nilly absorbed into or rejected by (mostly the latter, in my case) the national literary "world." Even to me it seems, that public self, very remote and often distastefully alien and spurious; just one more thing that I feel my real self in exile from.

My real self is here and now, writing. Whenever I think of this (the writing, not the written) experience, images to do with exploring, single-handed voyages, lone mountain ascents always spring unwanted to my mind. They sound romantic, but they're not meant to. It's the damned solitude, the fear of failure (by which I do *not* mean bad reviews), the tedium of the novel form, the often nauseating feeling that one is prey to an unhealthy obsession. . . .

When I go out and meet other people, become mixed in their lives and social routines, my own solitude, routinelessness, and freedom (which is a subtle imprisonment) from economic "worries" often make me feel like a visitor from outer space. I like earthmen, but I'm not quite sure what they're at. I mean we regulate things better at home. But there it is—I've been posted here. And there's no transport back.

Something like this lies behind all I write.

This total difference between the written and the writing world is what non-writers never realize about us. They see us as we were; we live with what we are. It is not subjects that matter to writers; but the experience of handling them. In those romantic terms, a difficult pitch scaled, a storm survived, the untrodden moon beneath one's feet. Such pleasures are unholy; and the world in general does right to regard us with malice and suspicion.

I loathe the day a manuscript is sent to the publisher, because on that day the people one has loved die; they become what they are—petrified, fossil organisms for others to study and collect. I get asked what I meant by this and by that. But what I wrote is what I meant. If it wasn't clear in the book, it shouldn't be clear now.

I find Americans especially, the kind people who write and ask questions, have a strangely pragmatic view of what books are. Perhaps because of the miserable heresy that creative writing can be taught ("creative" is here a euphemism for "imitative") they seem to believe that a writer always knows exactly what he's doing. Obscure books, for them, are a kind of crossword puzzle. Somewhere, they feel, in some number of a paper they missed, all the answers have been given to all the clues.

They believe, in short, that a book is like a machine; that if you have the knack, you can take it to bits.

Ordinary readers can hardly be blamed for thinking like this. Both academic criticism and weekly reviewing have in the last forty years grown dangerously scientific, or pseudoscientific, in their general tenor. Analysis and categorization are indispensable scientific tools *in the scientific field;* but the novel, like the poem, is only partly a scientific field. No one wants a return to the kind of bellelettrist and onanistic accounts of new books that were fashionable in the early years of the century; but we could do with something better than what we have got.

I am an interested party? I confess it. Ever since I began writing *The French Lieutenant's Woman* I've been reading obituaries of the novel; a particularly gloomy one came from Gore Vidal in the December 1967 issue of *Encounter*. And I have been watching novel-reviewing in England become this last year increasingly impatient and dismissive. Any moment now I expect one of our fashionable newspapers to decide to drop their *New Novels* column for good and give the released space over to television or pop music. Of course I am interested—but, like Mr. Vidal, I can hardly be personally resentful. If the novel is dead, the corpse still remains oddly fertile. We are told no one reads novels any more; so the authors of *Julian* and *The Collector* must be grateful to the two million ghosts or more who have bought copies of their respective books. But I don't want to be sarcastic. More is at issue here than self-interest.

One has the choice of two views: either that the novel, along with printed-word culture in general, is moribund or that there is something sadly shallow and blinded in our age. I know which view I hold; and the people who astound me are the ones who are sure that the first view is true. If you want omniscience, you have it there; and it ought to worry you, you the reader who is neither critic nor writer, that this omniscient contempt for print is found so widely among people who make a living out of literary dissection. Surgery is what we want, not dissection. It is not only the extirpation of the mind that kills the body; the heart will do the trick just as well.

October 27th, 1967. I finished the first draft, which was begun on January 25th. It is about 140,000 words long, and exactly as I imagined it: perfect, flawless, a lovely novel. But that, alas, is indeed only how I imagine it. When I re-read it I see 140,000 things need to be changed; then it will, perhaps, be less imperfect. But I haven't the energy; the dreaded research now, the interminable sentence-picking. I want to get on with another book. I had a strange image last night . . .

SELECTED BIBLIOGRAPHY

ANDERSON, SHERWOOD (1876–1941), "A Writer's Conception of Realism," in *The Achievement of Sherwood Anderson*, edited by Ray L. White. Chapel Hill: The University of North Carolina Press, 1966.

BALDWIN, JAMES (1924–   ), *Notes of a Native Son*. Boston: Beacon Press, 1962.

BELLOW, SAUL (1915–   ), "Distractions of a Fiction Writer" in *The Living Novel: A Symposium*, edited by Granville Hicks. New York: Macmillan, 1957. "Skepticism and the Depth of Life" in *The Arts and the Public*, edited by James E. Miller Jr. and Paul D. Herring. Chicago: University of Chicago Press, 1967.

BENNETT, ARNOLD (1867–1931), *The Author's Craft*. London and New York: Hodder and Stoughton, 1914.

BESANT, SIR WALTER (1836–1901), *The Art of Fiction*. Boston: Cupples and Hurd, 1887.

BUTLER, SAMUEL (1835–1902), *Notebooks*, edited by Geoffrey Keynes and Brian Hill; entry entitled "Genius" and numerous entries on writing. London: Cape, 1951.

CARY, JOYCE (1888–1957), *Art and Reality*. Cambridge, England: Cambridge University Press, 1958.

CHEKHOV, ANTON (1860–1904), *The Selected Letters of Anton Chekhov*, edited by Lillian Hellman. New York: Farrar, Straus and Company, 1955. *Letters of Anton Chekhov*, edited, with commentary, by Simon Karlinsky. New York: Harper and Row, 1973. *Letters of Anton Chekhov*, edited by Avrahm Yarmolinsky. New York: Viking, 1973.

CLEMENS, SAMUEL L. (1835–1910), *The Autobiography of Mark Twain*, arranged and edited, with an introduction and notes, by Charles Neider. New York: Harper and Brothers, 1959.

COCTEAU, JEAN (1889–1963), *The Journals of Jean Cocteau*, edited and translated, with an introduction, by Wallace Fowlie. New York: Criterion Books, 1956.

COLERIDGE, SAMUEL TAYLOR (1772–1834), *Biographia Literaria: or Biographical Sketches of My Literary Life and Opinions*; see especially Chapter XI, "An Affectionate Exhortation to Those Who in Early Life Feel Themselves Disposed to Become Authors." In *The Complete Works of Samuel Taylor Coleridge*, edited by W. G. T. Shedd. New York: Harper and Brothers, 1884.

CONRAD, JOSEPH (1847–1924), *A Personal Record: Some Reminiscences*. New York: Doubleday Page and Company, 1923. See also Prefaces in *The Works of Joseph Conrad*. London: J. M. Dent, 1923–1929.

DOSTOEVSKI, FEODOR MIKHAILOVICH (1821–1881), *The Diary of a Writer*, translated and annotated by Boris Brasol. New York: Charles Scribner's Sons, 1949. *The Notebooks for Crime and Punishment*, edited and translated by Edward Wasiolek; *The Notebooks for The Brothers Karamazov*, edited and translated by Edward Wasiolek; *The Notebooks for The Idiot*, edited, with an introduction, by Edward Wasiolek, translated by Katharine Strelsky; and *The Notebooks for The Possessed*, edited, with an introduction, by Edward Wasiolek, translated by Victor Terras. Chicago: University of Chicago Press, 1967, 1971, 1967, 1968.

ELLISON, RALPH (1915–   ), *Shadow and Act*. New York: Random House, 1964. "A Very Stern Discipline," an interview with Steve Cannon, Lennox Raphael, and James Thompson. *Harper's Magazine*, 234, 1402 (March 1967). "Indivisible Man," by Ellison and James Alan McPherson. *The Atlantic*, 226, 6 (December 1970).

FARRELL, JAMES T. (1904–   ), Introduction to *Studs Lonigan*. New York: The Modern Library, 1938. "Reflections at Fifty," "How *The Face of Time* Was Written," and "My Beginnings as a Writer" in *Reflections at Fifty*. New York: Vanguard Press, 1954.

FAULKNER, WILLIAM (1897–1962), Introduction to *The Sound and the Fury*, for an unpublished limited edition. *The New York Times Book Review*, November 5, 1972.

FITZGERALD, F. SCOTT (1896–1940), *Last Tycoon*, with notes for the novel, edited by Edmund Wilson. New York: Charles Scribner's Sons, 1941. *The Crack-Up*, with other uncollected pieces, notebooks, and unpublished letters, edited by Edmund Wilson. New York: New Directions, 1945.

GALSWORTHY, JOHN (1867–1933), *The Creation of Character in Literature*. Oxford: The Clarenden Press, 1931.

GIDE, ANDRÉ (1869–1936), *The Counterfeiters, with Journal of "The Counterfeiters,"* the novel translated by Dorothy Bussy, the journal translated and annotated by Justin O'Brien. New York: Alfred A. Knopf, 1951.

GORKY, MAXIM (1868–1936), *Autobiography*, translated by Isidor Schneider. New York: Citadel Press, 1949.

HEMINGWAY, ERNEST (1898–1961), *A Moveable Feast*. New York: Charles Scribner's Sons, 1964.

JAMES, HENRY (1843–1916), Prefaces in *The Novels and Tales of Henry James*, especially the Prefaces to *The Ambassadors* and *The Spoils of Poynton*. See also *The Notebooks of Henry James*, edited by F. O. Mathiessen and Kenneth B. Murdoch. New York: Oxford University Press, 1947.

LARDNER, RING W. (1885–1933), "How to Write Short Stories," in *How to Write Short Stories (With Samples)*. New York: Charles Scribner's Sons, 1924.

LAWRENCE, D. H. (1885–1930), "Why the Novel Is Important" in *Phoenix: the Posthumous Papers of D. H. Lawrence*, edited, with an introduction, by Edward D. McDonald. New York: Viking Press, 1964. "The Novel" and "Autobiographical Sketch" (the second of two in the volume) in *Phoenix II: Uncollected, Unpublished, and Other Prose Works by D. H. Lawrence*, edited, with an introduction and notes, by Warren Roberts and Harry T. Moore. London: Heinemann, 1968.

MAUGHAM, W. SOMERSET (1874–1965), "How I Write Short Stories" in *East and West*. New York: Doubleday and Company, 1934.

MERRILL, JAMES (1926–   ), *The (Diblos) Notebook*. New York: Atheneum, 1965.

MILLER, HENRY (1891–   ), "Reflections on Writing," in *The Wisdom of the Heart*. Norfolk, Connecticut: New Directions, 1941.

NIETSZCHE, FRIEDRICH WILHELM (1844–1900), *Ecce Homo*, translated by Clifton Fadiman. New York: The Modern Library, 1927.

THE PARIS REVIEW, *Writers at Work: The Paris Review Interviews, First Series*, edited, with an introduction, by Malcolm Cowley; *Second Series*, edited by George Plimpton, with an introduction by Van Wyck Brooks; *Third Series*, edited by George Plimpton, with an introduction by Alfred Kazin. New York: Viking Press, 1958, 1963, 1967.

SPENDER, STEPHEN (1909–   ), "The Making of a Poem" in *The Making of a Poem*. New York: Norton, 1962.

STEIN, GERTRUDE (1874–1946), *The Autobiography of Alice B. Toklas*. New York: Random House, 1933.

STEINBECK, JOHN (1902–1968), *Journal of a Novel: The East of Eden Letters*. New York: Viking Press, 1969.

STEVENSON, ROBERT LOUIS (1850–1894), *Essays of Travel and In the Art of Writing*. New York: Charles Scribner's Sons, 1908. See also "A Humble Remonstrance" in *Selected Writings of Robert Louis Stevenson*, edited, with an introduction, by Saxe Cummins. New York: The Modern Library, 1950.

TATE, ALLEN (1899–   ), "Narcissus as Narcissus" in *Reason and Madness*. New York: G. P. Putnam's Sons, 1941.

TURGENEV, IVAN SERGEEVICH (1818–1883), *Turgenev's Literary Reminiscences*, translated by David Magarshack. New York: Farrar, Straus, and Cudahy, 1958.

WHARTON, EDITH (1862–1937), *The Writing of Fiction*. London: Charles Scribner's Sons, 1925.

WHITE, E. B. (1899–   ), "An Approach to Style" in *Elements of Style*, by William Strunk and E. B. White. New York: Macmillan, 1972.

ABOUT THE AUTHOR

John Hersey was born in Tientsin, China, in 1914, and lived there until 1925, when his family returned to the United States. He was graduated from Yale in 1936 and attended Clare College, Cambridge University for a year. He was private secretary to Sinclair Lewis during a subsequent summer and then worked as a journalist and war correspondent. His first novel, *A Bell for Adano*, won the Pulitzer Prize in 1945, and the next year he wrote *Hiroshima*, an account of the first atomic bombing. Since 1947 he has devoted his time mainly to fiction and has published *The Wall* (1950), *The Marmot Drive* (1953), *A Single Pebble* (1956), *The War Lover* (1959), *The Child Buyer* (1960), *Here to Stay* (1963), *White Lotus* (1965), *Too Far to Walk* (1966), and *Under the Eye of the Storm* (1967). *The Algiers Motel Incident*, about the Detroit riot of 1967, was published the next year, and *Letter to the Alumni* in 1970. From 1965 to 1970 he was Master of Pierson College at Yale, and he spent the following year as Writer-in-Residence at the American Academy in Rome, where he wrote *The Conspiracy* (1972). Since then he has taught at Yale and lives in New Haven, Connecticut.

A NOTE ON THE TYPE

The text of this book was set in Palatino, a type face designed by the noted German typographer Hermann Zapf. Named after Giovanbattista Palatino, a writing master of Renaissance Italy, Palatino was the first of Zapf's type faces to be introduced to America. The first designs for the face were made in 1948, and the fonts for the complete face were issued between 1950 and 1952. Like all Zapf-designed type faces, Palatino is beautifully balanced and exceedingly readable.

Composed by Cherry Hill Composition, Pennsauken, New Jersey
Printed and bound by Halliday Lithograph Corp., West Hanover, Mass.